Out.

D0944887

OXFORD READINGS IN FEMINISM

FEMINISM AND HISTORY

OXFORD READINGS IN FEMINISM

Feminism and History

Edited by
Joan Wallach Scott

Oxford · New York
OXFORD UNIVERSITY PRESS
1996

Oxford University Press, Walton Street, Oxford OX2 6DP

Oxford New York
Athens Auckland Bangkok Bombay
Calcutta Cape Town Dar es Salaam Delhi
Florence Hong Kong Istanbul Karachi
Kuala Lumpur Madras Madrid Melbourne
Mexico City Nairobi Paris Singapore
Taipei Tokyo Toronto
and associated companies in
Berlin Ibadan

Oxford is a trade mark of Oxford University Press

Published in the United States
by Oxford University Press Inc., New York

Introduction and selection © Oxford University Press 1996

British Library Cataloguing in Publication Data
Data available

Library of Congress Cataloging in Publication Data
Data available
ISBN 0–19–875168–0
ISBN 0–19–875169–9 (Pbk.)

10 9 8 7 6 5 4 3 2 1

Typeset by Hope Services (Abingdon) Ltd.
Printed in Great Britain on acid-free paper by
Bookcraft (Bath) Ltd, Midsomer Norton, Avon

Contents

Notes on Contributors

ELSA BARKLEY BROWN teaches in the Department of History and Center for Afro-American and African Studies, University of Michigan. Her articles have appeared in *Signs, SAGE, History Workshop,* and *Feminist Studies.* She was the recipient of the 1989 Lutetia Woods Brown Article Publication Prize and of the University of Kentucky's first Martin Luther King, Jr., Prize for the best scholarly article in African-American history.

TANI BARLOW is a historian of modern China teaching in the Women Studies Program at the University of Washington. She has translated (with Gary Bjorge) *I Myself Am a Woman: Selected Works of Ding Ling.* She is co-editor (with Angela Zito) of *Body, Subject, and Power in China*; and editor of *Gender Politics in Modern China.*

GISELA BOCK is professor of history at the University of Bielefeld (Germany). She has published books and articles, in a number of languages, on political thought and women's history in early modern Italy, the American labour movement, the history of women's domestic labour, National Socialist racism and sexism, women's place in the rise of the welfare state, and on theory and methodology of gender history.

CÉCILE DAUPHIN, *et al.* The contributors to this jointly-authored article all participated in an ongoing interdisciplinary seminar concerning the problematics of 'masculine/feminine', held at the Centre de Recherches Historiques (CRH) of the Centre Nationale de la Recherche Scientifique (CNRS) in Paris. Their names and affiliations at the time of publication are listed below: Cécile Dauphin (CRH-CNRS); Arlette Farge (CRH-CNRS); Geneviève Fraise (Philosophy-CNRS); Christiane Klapisch-Zuber (CRH-École des Hautes Études en Science Sociale (EHESS); Rose-Marie Lagrave (Sociology-EHESS); Michelle Perrot (History-University of Paris VII); Pierrette Pézsert (CRH-EHESS); Yannick Ripa (History-INRP); Pauline Schmitt-Pantel (History-University of Paris VII); Danièle Voldman (Institut d'Histoire du Temps Present-CNRS).

NATALIE ZEMON DAVIS is the Henry Charles Lea Professor of History at Princeton University. Her most recent book is *Women on the Margins: Three Seventeenth-Century Lives* (1995).

BONNIE THORNTON DILL is Professor of Women's Studies at the University of Maryland at College Park. She is author of *Across the Boundaries of Race and Class* and co-editor with Maxine Baca Zinn of *Women of Color in U.S. Society.* She was founding director of the Center for Research on Women at the University of Memphis and she is currently working on a study of low-income single mothers in rural communities.

Evelyn Brooks Higginbotham is Professor of Afro-American Studies (Arts and Sciences) and African American Religious History (Divinity) at Harvard University. She is the author of the prize-winning book *Righteous Discontent: The Women's Movement in the Black Baptist Church, 1880–1920* (1993).

Dolores Janiewski is a Senior Lecturer in US History at Victoria University in Wellington, New Zealand. Her next monograph is a study of gender, race, citizenship, and criminality in the American South from 1866 to 1932, entitled *Passion, Power, and Punishment.* Her current research involves a comparative study of race, gender, and colonialism in Samoa, Hawaii, and three Native American societies.

Marilyn Lake was the founding Director of the Program in Women's Studies at La Trobe University, Australia, where she currently holds a Personal Chair in the School of History. Her most recent books include the feminist history of Australia, *Creating a Nation* (1994) with Patricia Grimshaw, Marian Quartly, and Ann McGrath, and *Gender and War* (1995) co-edited with Joy Damousi. She is currently writing a history of feminism in Australia, with special interest in feminist conceptions of citizenship.

Anne Phillips is now Professor of Politics at London Guildhall University. Her interest in feminist economics resulted in the publication of *Hidden Hands: Women and Economic Policies* (1983), but her subsequent work has been in the field of political theory. Her most recent publications are *Engendering Democracy* (1991), *Democracy and Difference* (1993), and *The Politics of Presence* (1995).

Denise Riley teaches at Goldsmiths' College, London University. Her prose books include *War in the Nursery: Theories of the Child and Mother* (1983), and *'Am I That Name?' Feminism and the Category of 'Women' in History* (1988). She edited *Poets on Writing: Britain 1970–1991.* Her most recent collection of poetry is *Mop Mop Georgette* (1993).

Lyndal Roper is an Australian who teaches history at Royal Holloway, University of London. She is the author of *The Holy Household: Women and Morals in Reformation Germany* (1989) and of *Oedipus and the Devil: Witchcraft, sexuality and religion in early modern Europe* (1994). She is currently working on a larger study of witchcraft and fantasy.

Gayle Rubin is an anthropologist who is currently teaching at the University of California, Santa Cruz. A collection of her essays will soon be published by the University of California Press. She is now working on a book based on ethnographic and historical research on the gay male leather community in San Francisco.

Joan Wallach Scott is Professor of Social Science at the Institute for Advanced Study. Her most recent work includes *Gender and the Politics of*

History (1988) and *Only Paradoxes to Offer: French Feminists and the Rights of Man* (1996).

MRINALINI SINHA is the author of *Colonial Masculinity: The 'Manly Englishman' and the 'Effeminate Bengali' in the Late Nineteenth Century* (Manchester University Press, 1995). She currently teaches British and Indian history at Boston College.

BONNIE G. SMITH teaches at Rutgers University. She is the author of *Ladies of the Leisure Class: The Bourgeoises of Northern France in the Nineteenth Century, Changing Lives: Women in European History Since 1715, Confessions of a Concierge*, and other books and articles in modern European, women's, and gender history.

CARROLL SMITH-ROSENBERG is Professor of Humanities in the Department of History, University of Pennsylvania.

ANN SNITOW has been a feminist activist since 1969, when she was a founding member of New York Radical Feminists. She was co-editor, with Christine Stansell and Sharon Thompson, of *Powers of Desire: The Politics of Sexuality*. A professor of literature and a member of the Committee on Gender Studies and Feminist Theory at the New School for Social Research, her most recent writing and political work is about the changing situation of women in Eastern and Central Europe.

ANN LAURA STOLER is Professor of Anthropology, History, and Women's Studies at the University of Michigan. She is author of *Capitalism and Confrontation in Sumatra's Plantation Belt* (1985), *Race and the Education of Desire: Foucault's History of Sexuality and the Colonial Order of Things* (1995), and co-editor with Frederick Cooper of *Tensions of Empire: Colonial Cultures in a Bourgeois World* (1996).

BARBARA TAYLOR is a historian working on early feminism. Her first book, *Eve and the New Jerusalem*, was on Owenite Socialist feminism, and she is currently completing a study of Mary Wollstonecraft's thought. She is an editor of *History Workshop Journal*, and a Senior Lecturer in the Department of Cultural Studies, University of West London.

VICTORIA THOMPSON is an Assistant Professor of History at Xavier University in Cincinnati. She is currently working on a book manuscript, 'Gender, Class, and the Marketplace: Women's Work and the Transformation of Paris, 1825–1870'.

Introduction

Joan Wallach Scott

FEMINISM AND HISTORY

There is a long history of feminists who write the history of women in order to make an argument for the equal treatment of women and men. Typically, this approach has involved substituting positive examples of women's capabilities in place of negative characterizations. Countering stereotypes has built a tension into the writing of women's history. On the one hand, an essentializing tendency assumes (with feminism's opponents) that there are fixed characteristics belonging to women. (The disagreement is over what they are.) On the other hand, an historicizing approach stresses differences among women and even within the concept of 'women'.

For centuries, those advocating the elevation of women's status have culled the past for examples of exemplary figures: artists, writers, politicians, religious devotees, scientists, educators. Depending on the period and the purpose, they assembled stories to counter the presumptions about female incapacity contained in the prescriptive literature or legal codes of their day. When the argument was about education, feminists came up with stunning cases of brilliant women to demonstrate that learning did not distort femininity or, more radically, that sex had nothing to do with the operations of the mind. As feminists mobilized to demand citizenship in the wake of the democratic revolutions of the eighteenth century, they pointed to the political capacities of queens and of ordinary women such as Joan of Arc to legitimize their claims that political rights ought not to be denied them because of their sex. A wonderful example comes from a speech delivered in 1793 to the Parisian Society of Revolutionary Republican Women by 'La femme Monic', a haberdasher:

I am grateful to Mary Louise Roberts and Debra Keates for their careful critical readings.

1

From the famous Deborah, who succeeded Moses and Joshua, to the two Frei sisters, who fought so valiantly in our republican armies, not a single century has passed which has not produced a woman warrior. See how Thomyris, queen of the Scythians, battles and conquers the great Cyrus; the Marullus girl chases the Turks from [Stylimène] . . . Joan of Arc, who forced the English to flee before her, shamed them into raising the siege of Orléans . . . Without my having to cite for you the individual names of these courageous female warriors . . . I will remind you of the virile and warriorlike vigour of that colony of Amazons whose existence has been cast into doubt because of people's jealousy of women. . . . What do all these examples prove, if not that women can form battalions, command armies, battle, and conquer as well as men? If any doubt remained, I would cite Panthee, Ingonded, Clotilde, Isabelle, Margueritte, etc., etc. But I will not stop here, and I will say to these men who think they are our masters: Who delivered Judea and Syria from the tyranny of Holofernes? Judith. To whom did Rome owe her liberty and the Republic? To two women. Who were those who gave the final lesson in courage to the Spartans? Mothers and wives . . . If women are suited for combat, they are no less suited for government. How many of them have governed with glory! My only problem is how to select examples. Theodelinda, queen of Lombardy, brought down Agilulf and extinguished the wars of religion which were blazing in her territories. Everyone knows that Semiramis was a dove in the cabinet and an eagle in the field. Isabelle of Spain governed with glory. Here again is a woman who supported the discovery of the New World. In our times Catherine of Russia achieved what Peter only outlined . . .

The examples go on and on as Monic seeks to prove conclusively that women 'deserve to govern', that they do so better than men, and that in a republic they ought not to be excluded from government and administration.[1]

I cite this speech not only because its excess so clearly illustrates my point, but also because it has a double resonance. It is evidence of the way feminists in the past have turned to history to legitimate their demands, and it is evidence that is available to us as a result of the efforts of recent feminist historians (in this case, Darline Levy, Harriet Applewhite, and Mary Johnson, who combed the archives for documents about women in Paris during the tumultuous years of the French Revolution). Inspired by the feminist movement of the 1960s, these historians set out to establish not only women's presence, but their active participation in the events that were seen to constitute history. If women's subordination—past and present—was secured at least in part by their invisibility, then emancipation might be advanced by making them visible in narratives of social struggle and political achievement.

The titles of some of the major books of that period—*Becoming Visible, Hidden From History*—reveal this preoccupation with making women evident to readers of historical accounts. By recovering stories of women's activism, feminists provided not just new information about women's behaviour, but new knowledge—another way of understanding, of seeing, women, and another way of seeing and understanding what counted as history. For if women were present and active, then history was neither the story of 'man's' heroism nor the means by which exclusive masculine agency (rational, self-determining, self-representing) was affirmed. As a corrective to the phallocentric themes of most historical accounts, women were portrayed as makers of history. But the metaphor of visibility carried contradictory messages. Equating visibility with transparency made the feminist historian's task simply the recovery of previously ignored facts. When the questions of why these facts had been ignored and how they were now to be understood were raised, history became more than a search for facts. Since new visions of history depended on the perspectives and questions of the historian, making women visible was not simply a matter of unearthing new facts; it was a matter of advancing new interpretations which not only offered new readings of politics, but of the changing significance of families and sexuality.

The feminist recovery of women for history has been a far-reaching, complex, and contradictory project. It is beset by a version of the 'sameness versus difference' conundrum that feminists have long faced as they argued for equality with men. Feminist historians have made the identity of 'women' coherent and singular at the same time that they have provided empirical evidence for irreducible differences among women. Feminist historians have offered examples from many centuries and countries to counter contemporary claims that women are, by physical constitution and psychological temperament, weaker, more passive, more concerned with children, less productive as workers, less rational, and more emotional than men. This approach simultaneously establishes women as historical subjects operating in time and makes the idea of 'women' singular and timeless: those women in the past (or in other cultures) whose actions set precedents for our own are taken in some fundamental way to be just like us. (They have to be like us if the comparisons and precedents are to be meaningful.)

Even as it created this sense of identity over time, however, the work of historical recovery turned up women whose difference from 'us' needed to be acknowledged and explained. Could a shared identity of 'women' exist at all if the conditions of life and the meanings of actions were fundamentally different from our own? The eloquent writings of seventeenth-century aristocratic Frenchwomen might be used to prove that women as a group did not lack creative talent, but they also raised the issue of how these particular women came to write as they did. The facts of the hard working lives of early English factory women may have demonstrated an innate capacity for women to work, but they also provoked questions about how such work was tolerated in societies that equated domesticity with femininity. And how to interpret eroticized expressions of passion for one another by early nineteenth-century North American women living according to the rules of heterosexual social organization? The specificity and diversity of historical evidence cannot easily be read as a simple manifestation of the innate capacity of women.

This is perhaps another way of saying that conflicting understandings of the uses of the past have been intrinsic to the project of feminist history. The desire to legitimize feminist claims about women in order to consolidate an effective feminist political movement treats 'women' uniformly and so ahistorically. But the creation of women as subjects of history places them temporally in the contexts of their action, and explains the possibilities for such action in terms of those contexts. Thus history contains examples of fundamental differences, in experience and self-understanding, among women, potentially undermining the political task of creating an enduring common identity.

The unresolved question of whether 'women' is a singular or radically diverse category, whether 'women' is a social category that pre-exists or is produced by history, is at the heart of both feminist history and the history of feminism. This ought not to be surprising when we consider that the two are interrelated projects. Feminism as a politics appeals to the 'women' in whose name it acts as if they were a permanent and clearly distinguishable social group in order to mobilize them into a coherent political movement; the history of feminism thus has been the history of the project of reducing diversities (of class, race, sexuality, ethnicity, politics, religion, and socio-economic status) among females to a common identity of women (usually in opposition to patriarchy, a system of male domination). To the extent that feminist history serves the political ends of feminism, it participates in producing this essentialized common identity of women.

At the same time, however, and as part of the aim of recovering women's past, feminist history analyses the conditions which have or have not produced a shared identity of women by examining the different contexts in which women have lived, the different ways in which they have experienced their lives, the different influences of their acquiescence or resistance to the rules societies have elaborated for their behaviour. The results of this analysis point to fundamental differences in the identities attributed to and avowed by women. These identities change over time, vary in different societies, and even change for the same women depending on the contexts they are in. Except for the fact of the similarity of their sexual organs, it is hard to find a common identity (based either on an objective oppression or subjective perception) between aristocratic *salonières* in the seventeenth century and nineteenth-century middle-class housewives, or between those religious women of the Middle Ages who sought transcendence of their bodies in the service of Christ and twentieth-century sex workers whose bodies serve as a source of income.

Feminist history has provided both a subject (women) and a lineage (a long line of foremothers) for contemporary feminist political movements as well as ways of analysing the emergence of such subjects and movements in the past. It has posited 'women' as a social category that pre-exists history and, at the same time, demonstrated that the very existence of the social category of women varied according to history. I would say that, difficult as it is to live with tension, this is one of those useful and productive tensions worth living with. Feminism has provided focus, commitment, and critical stimulus for those of us who have undertaken to write history from its perspective, while history has provided an important and sobering corrective to the essentialist tendencies of feminist politics.

DIFFERENCE AS AN ANALYTIC CATEGORY FOR FEMINISM

Feminism's search for a common ground for 'women' repressed differences but it did not eliminate them. We can read the history of feminist movements in terms of a tension between unity and difference. In the United States, feminists divided over questions of slavery and race. Not everyone accepted Soujourner Truth's argument in 1851 that she, too, was a woman—having borne and nursed thirteen children. In fact, claims for women's rights often came from feminists who did not include African-Americans when they spoke of 'women' in universalist terms. Early in the twentieth century a meeting of French feminists divided over the question of class. When the majority defeated a resolution calling for a day off for domestic servants (some delegates argued that girls with free time might become prostitutes), socialists among them denounced feminism as a cloak for middle-class women's interests. Some argued that there could never be solidarity among women across class lines. Defending feminism as a movement for all women (and 'women' as a homogeneous category), Hubertine Auclert replied, 'there cannot be a bourgeois feminism and a socialist feminism because there are not two female sexes'.[2]

Auclert's comment seeks to deny the problem of (class) difference that it also recognizes. The feminist movements of the late twentieth century have not been able to or willing to deny differences in the same way. Indeed, it could be said that difference is at the very heart of the practice and theory of contemporary feminism; national and international debates among feminists have been understood in terms of differences among women. In the United States in the late 1970s 'women of colour' took this name as a way of exposing the implicit whiteness of feminism. They argued that race could not be set apart in considerations of women's experience and that, therefore, the differences among white and non-white women might be irreducible—their needs and interests so different as to preclude the formation of a common programme. The African-American poet Audre Lorde (in an argument that recalls the French debates about class) put it this way at an international feminist conference in New York in 1979:

If white American feminist theory need not deal with the differences between us, and the resulting difference in our oppressions, then how do you deal with the fact that the women who clean your houses and tend your children while you attend conferences on feminist theory are, for the most part, poor women and women of color? What is the theory behind racist feminism?[3]

The issue of sexuality has posed formidable questions of difference as well, leading to serious fractures in feminist solidarity and to the appearance of 'radical' feminism—a term used to refer to those who deem heterosexuality the source of women's oppression. The French philosopher Monique Wittig argued in this connection that lesbians were not 'women' since they were outside the symbolic economy of heterosexual relationships. Could there then be a common feminist ground for lesbians and 'women'? Who were the 'women' to be mobilized for feminist campaigns?

Over the past twenty years successive United Nations conferences on women and population (in Copenhagen, Nairobi, Mexico City, and Cairo) have revealed as many differences as similarities among women in the First and Third Worlds, West and East, North and South, whether the topic is family planning and infant mortality, development and economic opportunity, or legal status and political participation. Differences within the established categories of difference, such as race and ethnicity, have also troubled deliberations; not all black women or Islamic women or Jewish women share the same conceptions of femininity or social role or politics. In post-communist societies, as in post-colonial societies, politics, ethnicity, and religion lead women to identify their needs, desires, and interests so differently that it has been hard to articulate a readily shared agenda. The recent history of feminism shows not the impossibility of establishing such an agenda, but the fact that it does not emerge automatically when women get together. Rather, the platforms and policy recommendations offered in the name of 'women' were produced by intense negotiations. It is this political process that identifies 'women'; they do not exist as identical natural beings outside of it.

As differences among feminist activists have become increasingly visible and contested, feminist historians (many of them activists as well) have sought to understand difference by giving it a history. Much of the effort has involved descriptions of differences among women; gender identity is compounded and internally differentiated by social and sometimes political identities. The categories are offered as self-evident facts; there are working-class women, African-American women, Muslim women, bourgeois women, peasant women, lesbian women, Jewish lesbian women, socialist women, Nazi women—the list goes on and on, peopling women's history with the complexity and diversity that characterizes standard histories focused on men. But the descriptive labels which separate these different women often also essentialize them. In place of a singular 'women's' history, we now have fixed categories of working-class or African-American or Islamic women. Writing their history without asking where the identities come from, when they arise, and what ends they serve, gives these groups a certain eternal being.

But, just as metaphors of visibility assumed *and* contradicted the transparency of the social category 'women', so histories of different groups of women implicitly raise questions about the relational and contingent nature of difference. The category 'working-class women', for example, refers descriptively in many studies to wage-earning persons with female bodies. But when, in some historical contexts, 'working-class women' has meant only white wage-earning women, it has not been enough to add 'white' to the descriptive label. Some kind of analysis is needed of a complicated and highly specific relationship of power. What is the process by which race or class becomes salient for making social distinctions in certain periods and not in others? What is the relationship between gender and these other categories? Does race take priority over class and class over gender, or are there inseparable connections among them? Under what conditions? In what circumstances? These questions call for an analysis of how, specifically, differences such as those of class, race, and gender are constructed. In the late twentieth century, difference has become an important analytic category for feminism.

Describing difference establishes social distinctions as social facts; analysing the history by which those differences have been produced disrupts their fixity as enduring facts and recasts them (and the social hierarchies they organize) as the effects of contingent and contested processes of change. Difference and the different identities it establishes (for and among women) are understood relative to specific contexts—to history.

Describing differences among women establishes the fact of separate identities, but also raises the issue of the relational nature of difference. When we ask how nineteenth-century white women dealt with black women, or English women with Indian women, we imply that those identities had something to do with one another, that they were not only interconnected socially, but definitionally. Part of being white, in other words, meant not being black; Englishness was established in contrast to Indianness. Identity did not inhere in one's body or nationality, but was produced discursively by contrasts with others. And these contrasts, whether of race or class or gender, have had a history. Historian Thomas Holt has written, for example, of the ways in which 'black' and 'white' identities were conceived by African-Jamaican rebels during the Morant Bay uprising of 1865.

Contrary to the dominant discursive system, which identified blacks as those who worked and whites as those who ruled, the Morant Bay rebels appear generally to have recognized as white those directly implicated in the system of their oppression (planters, magistrates, and their supporters) and as black those who were the victims of that system. In more liminal but protected statuses were those less directly implicated in the system, like white medical doctors, and those almost entirely outside it, like the physically black Maroons who by treaty had secured a separate existence from 'the blacks'. Of course, this is not to say that their own discursive system for recognizing the enemy bore any better resemblance to reality than did the dominant white discourse. The Maroons were soon organized by 'the whites' into a fierce counterinsurgency force to crush the rebellion of 'the blacks'.[4]

In the same way that historical explorations of women's past experience produce *and* undermine the singular category of 'women', histories of different groups have both consolidated contemporary categories of identity (those of 'class', 'race', and 'sexuality', to take just a few examples) *and* made them relative to specific moments and circumstances of history at the same time.

HISTORICIZING DIFFERENCE

Although the historicizing of difference is implicit in much recent feminist history, it is not the focus of everyone's work. Indeed, there has been controversy among feminist historians about whether or not this effort is even appropriate. The controversy is symptomatic of the tensions within feminist history, between the political imperative to essentialize 'women' and the relativizing effects of history. Some historians have argued that attention to the construction of categories of difference distracts them from the activities of real women; others have suggested that 'relativism' undermines the possibilities for political action; still others maintain that differences (between women and men and among women) are self-evident facts that need only be reported and are unnecessarily complicated by abstract theoretical analysis. In part the controversy reflects different philosophies of history: those with a more or less positivist outlook who want to report what really happened (in the case of feminists, to correct the biases that masculinist views have imposed on our knowledge of the past) are in conflict with those who insist that history cannot recover an unmediated past, but rather actively produces visions of the past. For them it follows that historians must focus on the interpretation of the past. These days, this interpretation often uses 'difference' as an analytic category to explore the ways in which identities have been produced.

This book is a collection of articles written by feminist historians (and in a few cases, scholars from allied disciplines of sociology, anthropology, and literature) interested in analysing the production of identities historically. Rather than illustrate the full range of approaches to women's history (a difficult task in any case and one that other collections of articles have already accomplished), I have chosen articles that make the case for the usefulness to feminism of historicizing categories of social differentiation.

The approach to this historicizing is by no means uniform. There have been a number of diverse influences on it: Marxism, cultural and symbolic anthropology, psychoanalysis, linguistics, literary criticism, deconstruction. The work of Michel Foucault on discourse and power generally, but specifically on the history of sexuality, opened up a new field of inquiry for those interested in sexual difference. Sex was no longer a timeless biological drive, sexuality no longer a fixed set of attributes; instead, according to Foucault, sex and sexuality were the effects of changing concepts of human behaviour which could be studied in the pronouncements of doctors and jurists as well as in the activities of men and women. Not only were there different forms of sexuality to be documented, but similar kinds of behaviour had vastly different meanings. Those who performed sodomitical acts in the Middle Ages, for example, might have been punished for immorality, but they would not have been identified as gay or lesbian (until well into the nineteenth century) and it is anachronistic to so identify them in our histories. For that matter the terms which constituted normative heterosexuality changed dramatically over time as well.

Attention to changing identities over time has not been the exclusive preoccupation of feminist historians. They have shared in a project with those writing labour history, post-colonial history, and the history of race and race relations. E. P. Thompson tracked the historical and relational definitions of class in his monumental *Making of the English Working Class* in 1963: 'Class is defined by men as they live their own history, and, in the end, this is its only definition.'[5] Edward Said and the Indian Subaltern Studies historians argued that Western perspectives were inadequate for recounting the histories of colonial subjects. Western histories were part of the process by which imperialism was established, they argued, not objective accounts of the pre-colonial and colonial past. The terms and categories of Western histories were dethroned as instruments, becoming instead objects, of analysis. Working on African-American history in the United States, Barbara Fields concluded that race was not 'an observable fact', but rather 'a notion that is profoundly and in its very essence ideological'.

Race is a product of history . . . not of nature. As an element of ideology, it is best understood in connection with other elements of ideology and not as a phenomenon *sui generis*. Only when set next to contemporary ideas having nothing to do with race can ideas about race be placed in the context of the ideological ensemble of which they form a part.[6]

To understand race required, Fields maintained, the critical appraisal of the history of ideology. By ideology, she meant the terms which people took for granted as they organized and interpreted themselves, their relationships, and their worlds. Ideology, in this use of it, means neither a superstructural reflection nor a mystification of reality, but the organizing principle of social identity. Others prefer to use discourse to refer to the processes by which the facts of social difference are produced. Whatever the term, the goal is the same: to understand how social relationships are conceptualized and organized.

The essays in this volume address the question of identity as a problem of discourse or ideology in historical context. They do so in different ways, with different purposes, and with different combinations of analysis and empirical evidence. Some are more programmatic in emphasis, others make their arguments through specific case-studies. Some seek to denaturalize categories which have come to appear natural because they refer to biology: these are the categories of 'women', 'gender', 'race', and sexuality. They do this by demonstrating not only that ideas about women and femininity have changed over time, but that they have varied in the same periods among groups differentiated by race, class, and nationality. The readings in Parts I and V particularly, point out from many different vantages that sexual difference and differences of sexuality cannot be understood apart from their histories.

The articles in Parts I, II, III, and IV challenge the notion that categories that signify difference ('women', 'gender', 'race', and 'class') are in any way homogeneous or consistent or singular in their operations. They stress not only the diversity of groups and individuals covered by the term 'women', but the shifting meanings of the term itself. ' "Women" is historically, discursively constructed, and always relative to other categories which themselves change', writes Denise Riley. Her emphasis on the interaction of categories is taken up by a number of other authors. They demonstrate over and over again that categories of identity interact complexly (race and gender draw boundaries of class, definitions of class are gendered) and differently (Nazi doctrines of racial purity produced different meanings for motherhood than did nineteenth-century middle-class ideals of domesticity). They describe identities as shifting, articulated in specific contexts to organize social relationships (as Tani Barlow demonstrates for the case of China), to assert power (as in the example of imperial policy in colonial Asia), or to enact new ideas of social order (as in the example of homosexuality in nine-teenth-century France). And they see difference not as simple diver-sity, but as hierarchy operating to serve certain interests (male workers, employers, politicians, imperial administrators) at the expense of others.

If lines of difference implement relationships of power, they also create identities which can be strategically deployed for resistance and change. The essays in Part VI explore the ways in which women have invoked identities of race, nationality, class, and gender to form feminist movements or to inject feminist claims into other political movements or, in the instance cited by Elsa Barkley-Brown, to develop a movement (and a political identity) which did not treat race and gender as separable problems. But they also show how difficult it could be to stabilize the identity invoked. Ann Snitow writes of a recurring 'tension—between needing to act as women and needing an identity not overdetermined by our gen-der—[which] is as old as Western feminism'. And she describes the impossibility in the American feminist movement of resolving the question of whether feminists want to be 'women' as society defines them or to be freed of that identity altogether.

It is probably inevitable that analyses which use history to make their case ask questions about the writing of history itself. Feminists have long criticized traditional accounts of the past for excluding women; they have provided supplements to existing histories, and replacements as well. They have offered critical analyses of the rea-sons for women's exclusion. They have argued that attention to women would not only provide new information, but expose the limits of histories written only from the perspective of men. And they have documented (as Bonnie Smith does) the subtle and not so subtle obstacles which prevented women from writing history. Feminists like Smith have shown the ways in which the practices and reigning definitions of history were deeply gendered and they have argued that the inclusion of women (as subjects and as histo-rians) will change the way in which history is conceived. The French historians who wrote the final piece in this volume insist that empirical research alone—by and about women—will not solve the problem of exclusion entirely. Rather, they argue that the questions posed and the analytic approaches taken are crucial to the results feminists hope to obtain. 'How does the difference between the sexes function in the face of historical cataclysm or significant event?' they ask. And by implication, we could add, 'How do these cataclysms and events bring about new definitions of the relations between the sexes?' To their suggestion that contradiction and paradox be the focus of feminist historical analysis, we might add that the scope of such research ought not to be confined solely to gender. To the extent that gender enables and depends on other differences for its enunciation, we understand its operations more fully in this broader frame.

When feminist historians analyse social differentiation as the contingent, variable product of particular histories (as they do in this volume) they provide an alternative to categorical histories that take difference as fixed, stable, and eternal. In this they open possibilities for reinterpreting not only the history of women, but for understanding feminism in a new light. Not as a clearly definable entity, but as a site where differences conflict and coalesce, where common interests are articulated and contested, where identities achieve temporary stability—where politics and history are made.

Notes

1. Cited in Darline Levy, Harriet Applewhite, and Mary Johnson, *Women in Revolutionary Paris, 1789–1795* (Urbana: University of Illinois Press, 1979), 167–9.
2. Steven C. Hause with Anne R. Kenney, *Women's Suffrage and Social Politics in the French Third Republic* (Princeton: Princeton University Press, 1984), 70.
3. Audre Lorde, *Sister Outsider* (Trumansburg, NY: The Crossing Press, 1984), 112.
4. Thomas C. Holt, 'Experience and the Politics of Intellectual Inquiry', in James Chandler, Arnold I. Davidson, and Harry Harootunian (eds.), *Questions of Evidence: Proof, Practice, and Persuasion across the Disciplines* (University of Chicago Press, 1994), 392–3.
5. E. P. Thompson, *The Making of the English Working Class* (New York: Vintage Books, 1966), 11.
6. Barbara J. Fields, 'Ideology and Race in American History', in J. Morgan Kousser and James M. McPherson (eds.), *Region, Race and Reconstruction* (New York: Oxford University Press, 1982), 143–77, quotes, 150.

Part I. Women

1 Does A Sex Have a History?

Denise Riley

> *Desdemona*: Am I that name, Iago?
> *Iago*:   What name, fair lady?
> *Desdemona*: Such as she says my lord did say I was.
>
> Shakespeare, *Othello*, IV. ii.

The black abolitionist and freed slave, Sojourner Truth, spoke out at the Akron convention in 1851, and named her own toughness in a famous peroration against the notion of woman's disqualifying frailty. She rested her case on her refrain 'Ain't I a woman?' It's my hope to persuade readers that a new Sojourner Truth might well—except for the catastrophic loss of grace in the wording—issue another plea: 'Ain't I a fluctuating identity?' For both a concentration on and a refusal of the identity of 'women' are essential to feminism. This its history makes plain.

The volatility of 'woman' has indeed been debated from the perspective of psychoanalytic theory; her fictive status has been proposed by some Lacanian work,[1] while it has been argued that, on the other hand, sexual identities are ultimately firmly secured by psychoanalysis.[2] From the side of deconstruction, Derrida among others has advanced what he calls the 'undecidability' of woman.[3] I want to sidestep these debates to move to the ground of historical construction, including the history of feminism itself, and suggest that not only 'woman' but also 'women' is troublesome—and that this extension of our suspicions is in the interest of feminism. That we can't bracket off either Woman, whose capital letter has long alerted us to her dangers, or the more modest lower-case 'woman', while leaving unexamined the ordinary, innocent-sounding 'women'.

This 'women' is not only an inert and sensible collective; the

Chapter 1 in *Am I That Name?* by Denise Riley. Reprinted by permission of Macmillan Ltd. and the University of Minnesota Press.

dominion of fictions has a wider sway than that. The extent of its reign can be partly revealed by looking at the crystallizations of 'women' as a category. To put it schematically: 'women' is historically, discursively constructed, and always relatively to other categories which themselves change; 'women' is a volatile collectivity in which female persons can be very differently positioned, so that the apparent continuity of the subject of 'women' isn't to be relied on; 'women' is both synchronically and diachronically erratic as a collectivity, while for the individual, 'being a woman' is also inconstant, and can't provide an ontological foundation. Yet it must be emphasized that these instabilities of the category are the *sine qua non* of feminism, which would otherwise be lost for an object, despoiled of a fight, and, in short, without much life.

But why should it be claimed that the constancy of 'women' can be undermined in the interests of feminism? If Woman is in blatant disgrace, and woman is transparently suspicious, why lose sleep over a straightforward descriptive noun, 'women'? Moreover, how could feminism gain if its founding category is also to be dragged into the shadows properly cast by Woman? And while, given the untidiness of word use, there will inevitably be some slippery margins between 'woman' and 'women', this surely ought not to worry any level-headed speaker? If the seductive fraud of 'woman' is exposed, and the neutral collectivity is carefully substituted, then the ground is prepared for political fights to continue, armed with clarity. Not woman, but women—then we can get on with it.

It is true that socialist feminism has always tended to claim that women are socially produced in the sense of being 'conditioned' and that femininity is an effect. But 'conditioning' has its limits as an explanation, and the 'society' which enacts this process is a treacherously vague entity. Some variants of American and European cultural and radical feminism do retain a faith in the integrity of 'women' as a category. Some proffer versions of a female nature or independent system of values, which, ironically, a rather older feminism has always sought to shred to bits,[4] while many factions flourish in the shade cast by these powerful contemporary naturalisms about 'women'. Could it be argued that the only way of avoiding these constant historical loops which depart or return from the conviction of women's natural dispositions, to pacifism for example, would be to make a grander gesture—to stand back and announce that there *aren't any* 'women'? And then, hard on that defiant and initially absurd-sounding assertion, to be scrupulously careful to elaborate it—to plead that it means that all definitions of gender must be looked at with an eagle eye, wherever they emanate from and whoever pronounces them, and that such a scrutiny is a thoroughly feminist undertaking. The will to support this is not blandly social-democratic, for in no way does it aim to vault over the stubborn harshness of lived gender while it queries sexual categorization. Nor does it aim at a glorious indifference to politics by placing itself under the banner of some renewed claim to androgyny, or to a more modern aspiration to a 'post-gendered subjectivity'. But, while it refuses to break with feminism by naming itself as a neutral deconstruction, at the same time it refuses to iden- tify feminism with the camp of the lovers of 'real women'.

Here someone might retort that there are real, concrete women. That what Foucault did for the concept of 'the homosexual' as an invented classification just cannot be done for women, who indu- bitably existed long before the nineteenth century unfolded its tedious mania for fresh categorizations. That historical construc- tionism has run mad if it can believe otherwise. How can it be over- looked that women are a natural as well as a characterized category, and that their distinctive needs and sufferings are all too real? And how could a politics of women, feminism, exist in the company of such an apparent theoreticist disdain for reality, which it has mis- takenly conflated with ideology as if the two were one?

A brief response would be that unmet needs and sufferings do not spring from a social reality of oppression, which has to be posed against what is said and written about women—but that they spring from the ways in which women are positioned, often harshly or stu- pidly, *as* 'women'. This positioning occurs both in language, forms of description, and what gets carried out, so that it is misleading to set up a combat for superiority between the two. Nor, on the other hand, is any complete identification between them assumed.

It is true that appeals to 'women's' needs or capacities do not, on their own, guarantee their ultimately conservative effects any more than their progressivism; a social policy with innovative implica- tions may be couched in a deeply familial language, as with state welfare provision at some periods. In general, which female persons under what circumstances will be heralded as 'women' often needs some effort of translation to follow; becoming or avoiding being named as a sexed creature is a restless business.

Feminism has intermittently been as vexed with the urgency of disengaging from the category 'women' as it has with laying claim to it; twentieth-century European feminism has been constitution- ally torn between fighting against over-feminization and against under-feminization, especially where social policies have been at stake. Certainly the actions and the wants of women often need to be fished out of obscurity, rescued from the blanket dominance of 'man', or 'to be made visible'. But that is not all. There are always too many invocations of 'women', too much visibility, too many appellations which were better dissolved again—or are in need of some accurate and delimiting handling. So the precise specifying of 'women' for feminism might well mean occasionally forgetting them—or remembering them more accurately by refusing to enter into the terms of some public invocation. At times feminism might have nothing to say on the subject of 'women'—when their excessive identification would swallow any opposition, engulfing it hopelessly.

This isn't to imply that every address to 'women' is bad, or that feminism has some special access to a correct and tolerable level of feminization. Both these points could generate much debate. What's suggested here is that the volatility of 'women' is so marked that it makes feminist alliances with other tendencies as difficult as they are inescapable. A political interest may descend to illuminate 'women' from almost anywhere in the rhetorical firmament, like lightning. This may happen against an older, slower backdrop of altering understandings as to what sexual characterizations are, and a politician's fitful concentration on 'women' may be merely superimposed on more massive alternations of thought. To understand all the resonances of 'women', feminist tactics would need to possess not only a great elasticity for dealing with its contemporary deployments, but an awareness of the long shapings of sexed classifications in their post-1790s upheavals.

This means that we needn't be tormented by a choice between a political realism which will brook no nonsense about the uncertainties of 'women', or deconstructionist moves which have no political allegiances. No one needs to believe in the solidity of 'women'; doubts on that score do not have to be confined to the giddy detachment of the academy, to the semiotics seminar rooms where politics do not tread. There are alternatives to those schools of thought which in saying that 'woman' is fictional are silent about 'women', and those which, from an opposite perspective, proclaim that the reality of women is yet to come, but that this time, it's we, women, who will define her. Instead of veering between deconstruction and transcendence, we could try another train of speculations: that 'women' is indeed an unstable category, that this instability has a historical foundation, and that feminism is the site of the systematic fighting-out of that instability—which need not worry us.

It might be feared that to acknowledge any semantic shakiness inherent in 'women' would plunge one into a vague whirlpool of 'postgendered' being, abandoning the cutting edges of feminism for an ostensibly new but actually well-worked indifference to the real masteries of gender, and that the known dominants would only be strengthened in the process. This could follow, but need not. The move from questioning the presumed ahistoricity of sexed identities does not have to result in celebrating the carnival of diffuse and contingent sexualities. Yet this question isn't being proposed as if, on the other hand, it had the power to melt away sexual antagonism by bestowing a history upon it.

What then is the point of querying the constancy of 'men' or 'women'? Foucault has written, 'The purpose of history, guided by genealogy, is not to discover the roots of our identity but to commit itself to its dissipation.'[5] This is terrific—but, someone continues to ask, whatever does feminism want with dissipated identities? Isn't it trying to consolidate a progressive new identity of women who are constantly mis-defined, half-visible in their real differences? Yet the history of feminism has also been a struggle against over-zealous identifications; and feminism must negotiate the quicksands of 'women' which will not allow it to settle on either identities or counter-identities, but which condemn it to an incessant striving for a brief foothold. The usefulness of Foucault's remark here is, I think, that it acts as a pointer to history. It's not that our identity is to be dissipated into airy indeterminacy, extinction; instead it is to be referred to the more substantial realms of discursive historical formation. Certainly the indeterminacy of sexual positionings can be demonstrated in other ways, most obviously perhaps by comparative anthropology with its berdache, androgynous and unsettling shamanistic figures. But such work is often relegated to exoticism, while psychoanalytic investigations reside in the confined heats of clinical studies. It is the misleading familiarity of 'history' which can break open the daily naturalism of what surrounds us.

There are differing temporalities of 'women', and these substitute the possibility of being 'at times a woman' for eternal difference on the one hand, or undifferentiation on the other. This escapes that unappetizing choice between 'real women' who are always solidly in the designation, regardless, or post-women, no-longer-women, who have seen it all, are tired of it, and prefer evanescence. These altering periodicities are not only played out moment by moment for the individual person, but they are also historical, for the characterizations of 'women' are established in a myriad mobile formations.

Feminism has recognized this temporality in its preoccupation with the odd phenomenology of possessing a sex, with finding some unabashed way of recognizing aloud that which is privately obvious—that any attention to the life of a woman, if traced out carefully, must admit the degree to which the effects of lived gender are at least sometimes unpredictable, and fleeting. The question of how far anyone can take on the identity of being a woman in a thoroughgoing manner recalls the fictive status accorded to sexual identities by some psychoanalytic thought. Can anyone fully inhabit a gender without a degree of horror? How could someone 'be a woman' through and through, make a final home in that classification without suffering claustrophobia? To lead a life soaked in the passionate consciousness of one's gender at every single moment, to will to be a sex with a vengeance—these are impossibilities, and far from the aims of feminism.

But if being a woman is more accurately conceived as a state which fluctuates for the individual, depending on what she and/or others consider to characterize it, then there are always different densities of sexed being in operation, and the historical aspects are in play here. So a full answer to the question, 'At this instant, am I a woman as distinct from a human being?', could bring into play three interrelated reflections. First, the female speaker's rejections of, adoptions of, or hesitations as to the rightness of the self description at that moment; second, the state of current understandings of 'women', embedded in a vast web of description covering public policies, rhetorics, feminisms, forms of sexualization or contempt; third, behind these, larger and slower subsidings of gendered categories, which in part will include the sedimented forms of previous characterizations, which once would have undergone their own rapid fluctuations.

Why is this suggestion about the consolidations of a classification any different from a history of ideas about women? Only because in it nothing is assumed about an underlying continuity of real women, above whose constant bodies changing aerial descriptions dance. If it's taken for granted that the category of women simply refers, over time, to a rather different content, a sort of Women Through the Ages approach, then the full historicity of what is at stake becomes lost. We would miss seeing the alterations in what 'women' are posed against, as well as established by—Nature, Class, Reason, Humanity and other concepts—which by no means form a passive backdrop to changing conceptions of gender. That air of a wearingly continuous opposition of 'men' and 'women', each always identically understood, is in part an effect of other petrifications.

To speculate about the history of sexual consolidations does not spring from a longing for a lost innocence, as if 'once', as John Donne wrote,[6]

> Difference of sex no more wee knew
> Than our Guardian Angells doe

Nor is it a claim made in the hope of an Edenic future; to suggest that the polarity of the engaged and struggling couple, men and women, isn't timeless, is not a gesture towards reconciliation, as if once the two were less mercilessly distinguished, and may be so again if we could stop insisting on divisive difference, and only love each other calmly enough. My supposition here—and despite my disclaimer, it may be fired by a conciliatory impulse—is rather that the arrangement of people under the banners of 'men' or 'women' are enmeshed with the histories of other concepts too, including those of 'the social' and 'the body'. And that this has profound repercussions for feminism.

It follows that both theories about the timelessness of the binary opposition of sexual antagonism and about the history of ideas of women could be modified by looking instead at the course of alignments into gendered categories. Some might object that the way to deal with the monotonous male/female opposition would be to substitute democratic differences for the one difference, and to let that be an end to it. But this route, while certainly economical, would also obliterate the feverish powers exercised by the air of eternal polarity, and their overwhelming effects. Nor does that pluralizing move into 'differences' say anything about their origins and precipitations.

I've written about the chances for a history of alternations in the collectivity of 'women'. Why not 'men' too? It's true that the completion of the project outlined here would demand that, and would not be satisfied by studies of the emergence of patriarchs, eunuchs, or the cult of machismo, for example; more radical work could be done on the whole category of 'men' and its relations with Humanity. But nothing will be ventured here, because the genesis of these speculations is a concern with 'women' as a condition of and a trial to feminist history and politics. Nor will the term 'sexual difference' appear as an analytic instrument, since my point is neither to validate it nor to completely refuse it, but to look instead at how changing massifications of 'men' and 'women' have thrown up such terms within the armoury of contemporary feminist thought.

How might this be done? How could the peculiar temporality of 'women' be demonstrated? Most obviously, perhaps, by the changing relations of 'woman' and her variants to the concept of a general humanity. The emergence of new entities after the Enlightenment and their implicatedness with the collectivity of women—like the idea of 'the social'. The history of an increasing sexualization, in which female persons become held to be virtually saturated with their sex which then invades their rational and spiritual faculties; this reached a pitch in eighteenth-century Europe. Behind this, the whole history of the idea of the person and the individual, including the extents to which the soul, the mind, and the body have been distinguished and rethought, and how the changing forms of their sexualization have operated. For the nineteenth century, arguments as to how the concept of class was developed in a profoundly gendered manner, and how it in turn shaped modern notions of 'women'.[7] These suggestions could proliferate endlessly; in these pages I have only offered sketches of a couple of them.

What does it mean to say that the modern collectivity of women was established in the midst of other formations? Feminism's impulse is often, not surprisingly, to make a celebratory identification with a rush of Women onto the historical stage. But such 'emergences' have particular passages into life; they are the tips of an iceberg. The more engaging question for feminism is then what lies beneath. To decipher any collision which tosses up some novelty, you must know the nature of the various pasts that have led up to it, and allow to these their full density of otherness. Indeed there are no moments at which gender is utterly unvoiced. But the ways in which 'women' will have been articulated in advance of some prominent 'emergence' of the collectivity will differ, so what needs to be sensed is upon what previous layers the newer and more formalized outcropping has grown.

The grouping of 'women' as newly conceived political subjects is marked in the long suffrage debates and campaigns, which illustrate their volatile alignments of sexed meaning. Demands for the franchise often fluctuated between engagement with and disengagement from the broad category of Humanity—first as an abstraction to be exposed in its masculine bias and permeated, and then to be denounced for its continual and resolute adherence, after women had been enfranchised, to the same bias. An ostensibly unsexed Humanity, broken through political pressures of suffragist and antisuffragist forces into blocs of humans and women, men and women, closed and resealed at different points in different nations. In the history of European socialism, 'men' have often argued their way to universal manhood suffrage through a discourse of universal rights. But for women to ascend to being numbered among Humanity, a severe philosophical struggle to penetrate this category has not eliminated the tactical need to periodically break again into a separately gendered designation. The changing fate of the ideal of a non-sexed Humanity bears witness to its ambiguity.

Yet surely—it could be argued—some definitive upsurge of combative will among women must occur for the suffrage to be demanded in the first place? Must there not, then, be some unambiguously progressive identity of 'women' which the earliest pursuers of political rights had at their disposal? For, in order to contemplate joining yourself to unenfranchised men in their passion for emancipation, you would first have to take on that identity of being a woman among others *and* of being, as such, a suitable candidate too. But there is a difficulty; a dozen qualifications hedge around that simple 'woman', as to whether she is married or not, a property-owner or not, and so forth. 'Women' *en masse* rarely present themselves, unqualified, before the thrones of power; their estates divide them as inequalities within their supposed unity.

Nevertheless, to point to sociological faults in the smoothness of 'women' does not answer the argument that there must be a progressive identity of women. How is it that they ever come to rank themselves together? What are the conditions for any joint consciousness of women, which is more than the mutual amity or commiseration of friends or relations? Perhaps it could be argued that in order for 'women' to speak as such, some formal consolidation of 'men against women' is the gloomy prerequisite. That it is sexual antagonism which shapes sexual solidarity; and that assaults and counter-assaults, with all their irritations, are what make for a rough kind of feminism.

Here there is plenty of ground. We could think of those fourteenth- and fifteenth-century treatises which began to work out a formal alignment of sex against sex. These included a genre of women's defences against their vilification. So Christine de Pisan wrote 'for

25

women' in the *querelle des femmes*. The stage was set between a sexual cynicism which took marriage to be an outdated institution— Jean de Meung's stance in his popular *Roman de la Rose*—and a contrasted idealism which demanded that men profess loyalty to women, and adhere to marriage as a mark of respect for the female sex—Christine de Pisan's position in the *Débat sur le Roman de la Rose*, of about 1400 to 1402. This contest was waged again in her *Livre de la Cité des Dames* in 1405. As the narrator, she is visited by an allegorical triad; Reason, Rectitude and Justice. It is Reason who announces to her that her love of study has made her a fit choice of champion for her sex, as well as an apt architect to design an ideal city to be a sanctum for women of good repute. This city needs to be built, because men will vilify women. Their repeated slanders stem not only from their contempt for Eve, and her contribution to the Fall, but also from their secret convictions as to the superior capacities of all women. Christine de Pisan's earlier *Épistre au Dieu d'Amours* is also couched in this protective vein.

To suffer slights in patience is the strategy recommended by this literature, which itself conspicuously does the opposite. Here submission can be a weapon, a brandished virtue secured against great odds. The more rigorous the trial, the higher the merits of the tenaciously submissive woman. Her *Épistre de la prison de vie humaine*, composed between 1416 and 1418, dedicated to Marie de Berry, was designed as a formal comfort to women for the deaths at Agincourt of their brothers, fathers, and husbands; now these were liberated from life's long pains. But this resignation in the face of death did not eclipse sexual triumph. Christine de Pisan's last surviving work, the *Ditié de Jehann d'Arc*, was published in 1429, but written before Joan's execution; this was a song to celebrate her life as 'an honour for the female sex'.

Both the *querelles* and these other writings defend 'women' as unjustly slandered, champion heroines, and marry defiance with the advocacy of resignation, with the faith that early sufferings, if patiently endured, might be put to good account in the hereafter. Do these ingredients make a fifteenth-century feminism the start of a long chain ending in the demand for emancipation? Certainly there are some constant features of this literature which are echoed through the seventeenth-century writings. It argues in the name of 'women', and in that it is unlike the earlier complicated typologies of the sexes of the works of the women mystics. The fourteenth- and fifteenth-century polemic proposes that noble women should withdraw to a place apart, a tower, a city, there to pursue their devotions untroubled by the scorn of men in the order of the world. In this, it is not far from some seventeenth-century suggestions, like those made by Mary Astell, that 'women' have no choice but to form an order apart if they want to win spiritual clarity.

Between the fifteenth- and the seventeenth-century composi-tions, what remains constant is the formal defences of the sex, the many reiterations of 'Women are not, as you men so ignorantly and harshly claim, like that—but as we tell you now, we are really like this, and better than you.' This highly stylized counter-antagonism draws in 'all women' under its banner against 'all men'. Even though its references are to women of a high social standing and grace, nevertheless it is the collectivity which is being claimed and redeemed by debate. At times this literature abandons its claims to stoicism, fights clear of its surface resignation, and launches into unbridled counter-aggression. Thus 'Jane Anger', who in 1589 pub-lished a broadside, *Jane Anger her Protection for Women, to defend them against the Scandalous Reports of a late Surfeiting Love*. The writer, whether truly female or *agent provocateur*, burns on the page with wild rhetoric, the cry of sex against the attacking other sex, the medieval defences wound to the highest pitch:

Their slanderous tongues are so short, and all the time wherein they have lavished out their words freely has been so long, that they know we cannot catch hold of them to pull them out. And they think we will not write to reprove their lying lips, which conceits have already made them cocks.[8]

The retort to the surfeited lover's charges is to invert them, to mass all women against all men:

We are the grief of man, in that we take all the grief from man: we languish when they laugh, we sit sighing when they sit singing, and sit sobbing when they lie slugging and sleeping. *Mulier est hominis confusio* because her kind heart cannot so sharply reprove their frantic fits as these mad frenzies deserve.[9]

It is a litany of pure sexual outrage:

If our frowns be so terrible and our anger so deadly, men are too foolish in offering occasions of hatred, which shunned, a terrible death is pre-vented. There is a continual deadly hatred between the wild boar and tame hounds. I would there were the like between women and men, unless they amend their manners, for so strength should predominate, where now flattery and dissimulation have the upper hand. The lion rages when he is hungry, but man rails when he is glutted. The tiger is robbed of her young ones when she is ranging abroad, but men rob women of their honour undeservedly under their noses. The viper storms when his tail is trodden on, and may we not fret when all our body is a footstool to their vile lust?[10]

This furious lyricism is a late and high pitch of the long literature which heralded 'women' *en bloc* to redeem their reputations. Is this in any sense a precondition of feminism; a pre-feminism which is established, indeed raging, in Europe for centuries before the Enlightenment? Certainly seventeenth-century women writers were acutely conscious of the need to establish their claims to enter full humanity, and to do so by demonstrating their intellectual capacities. If women's right to any early democracy had to be earned, then their virtues did indeed have to be enunciated and defended; while traces of seemingly sex-specific vices were to be explained as effects of a thoughtless conditioning, an impoverished education—the path chosen by Poulain de la Barre in his *De l'Egalité des Deux Sexes* of 1673. When Mary Wollstonecraft argued that 'the sexual should not destroy the human character'[11] in her *A Vindication of the Rights of Woman*, this encapsulated the seventeenth-century feminist analysis that women must somehow disengage from their growing endemic sexualization.

It is this which makes it difficult to interpret the defences and proclamations of 'women' against 'men' as pre-feminism. To read the work of 'Jane Anger' and others as preconditions for eighteenth-century feminism elides too much, for it suggests that there is some clear continuity between defensive celebrations of 'women' and the beginning of the 1790s claims to rights for women, and their advancement as potential political subjects. But the more that the category of woman is asserted, whether as glowingly moral and unjustly accused, or as a sexual species fully apart, the more its apparent remoteness from 'humanity' is underwritten. It is a cruel irony, which returns at several watersheds in the history of feminism, that the need to insist on the moral rehabilitation of 'women' should have the effect of emphasizing their distinctiveness, despite the fact that it may aim at preparing the way into the category of humanity. The transition, if indeed there is one, from passing consolidations of 'women' as candidates for virtue, to 'women' as candidates for the vote, is intricate and obscure.

When the name of feminism is plunged into disgrace—for example, in Britain immediately after the end of the First World War—then the mantle of a progressive democracy falls upon Humanity; though the resurgences of feminism in the 1920s tore this apart. But before even a limited suffrage is granted, it may have to be sought for a sex in the name of a sex-blind humanism, as an ethical demand. This may work for men, but not for women. Most interesting here are the intricate debates in Britain between socialist and feminist proponents of a universal adult suffrage, and feminists who supported a limited female suffrage instead as the best route to eventual democracy; these are discussed in detail below. But what has Humanity been conjugated against? Must it be endlessly undemocratic because 'gender-blind'—or 'race-blind'? Its democratic possibilities would depend on, for example, how thoroughly, at the time of any one articulation of the idea, the sex of the person was held to infuse and characterize her whole being, how much she was gender embodied. The question of race would demand analogous moves to establish the extent of the empire of racially suffused being over the general existence of the person. A history of several categories, then, would be demanded in order to glimpse the history of one.

If it is fair to speculate that 'women' as a category does undergo a broadly increasing degree of sexualization between the late seventeenth and the nineteenth centuries, what would constitute the evidence? To put clear dates to the long march of the empires of gender over the entirety of the person would be difficult indeed. My suggestion isn't so much that after the seventeenth century a change in ideas about women and their nature develops; rather that 'women' itself comes to carry an altered weight, and that a re-ordered idea of Nature has different intimacy of association with 'woman' who is accordingly refashioned. It is not only that concepts are forced into new proximities with one another—but they are so differently shot through with altering positions of gender that what has occurred is something more fundamental than a merely sequential innovation—that is, a reconceptualization along sexed lines, in which the understandings of gender both re-order and are themselves re-ordered.

The nineteenth-century collective 'women' is evidently voiced in new ways by the developing human sciences of sociology, demography, economics, neurology, psychiatry, and psychology, at the same time as a newly established realm of the social becomes both the exercising ground and the spasmodic vexation for feminism. The resulting modern 'women' is arguably the result of long processes of closure which have been hammered out, by infinite mutual references, from all sides of these classifying studies; closures which were then both underwritten and cross-examined by nineteenth- and twentieth-century feminisms, as they took up, or respecified, or dismissed these productions of 'women'.

'Women' became a modern social category when their place as newly re-mapped entities was distributed among the other collectivities established by these nineteenth-century sciences. 'Men' did not undergo any parallel re-alignments. But 'society' relied on 'man' too, but now as the opposite which secured its own balance. The couplet of man and society, and the ensuing riddle of their relationship, became the life-blood of anthropology, sociology, and social psychology—the endless problem of how the individual stood *vis-à-vis* the world. This was utterly different from the ways in which the concept of the social realm both encapsulated and illuminated 'women'. When this effectively feminized social was then set over and against 'man', then the alignments of the sexes in the social realm were conceptualized askew. It was not so much that women were omitted, as that they were too thoroughly included in an asymmetrical manner. They were not the submerged opposite of man, and as such only in need of being fished up; they formed, rather, a kind of continuum of sociality against which the political was set.

'Man in society' did not undergo the same kind of immersion as did woman. He *faced* society, rather; a society already permeated by the feminine. This philosophical confrontation was the puzzle for those nineteenth-century socialist philosophies which contemplated historic and economic man. An intractable problem for Marxist philosophy was how to engage with the question of individualization; how was the individual himself historically formed? Marx tried, in 1857, to effect a new historicization of 'man' across differing modes of production, because he wanted to save man as the political animal from mutation into a timeless extra-economic figure, the Robinson Crusoe advanced by some political economies.[12] But the stumbling-block for Marx's aim was its assumption of some prior, already fully constituted 'man' who was then dragged through the transformations of history; this 'man' was already locked into his distinctiveness from the social, so he was already a characterized and compromised creation.

As with man, so here—for once—with woman. No philosophical anthropology of woman can unfurl those mysteries it tries to solve, because that which is to be explicated, woman, stands innocently in advance of the task of 'discovering her'. To historicize woman across the means of production is also not enough. Nevertheless, another reference to Marx may be pressed into the service of sexual consolidations, and into the critique of the idea that sexual polarities are constant—his comment on the concept of Labour:

The most general abstractions arise only in the midst of the richest possible concrete development, where one thing appears as common to many, to all . . . Labour shows strikingly how even the most abstract categories, despite their validity—precisely because of their abstractness—for all epochs are nevertheless, in the specific character of this abstraction, themselves likewise a product of historical relations, and possess their full validity only for and within those relations.[13]

The ideas of temporality which are suggested here need not, of course, be restricted to 'women'. The impermanence of collective identities in general is a pressing problem for any emancipating movement which launches itself on the appeal to solidarity, to the common cause of a new group being, or an ignored group identity. This will afflict racial, national, occupational, class, religious, and other consolidations. While you might choose to take on being a disabled person or a lesbian, for instance, as a political position, you might not elect to make a politics out of other designations. As you do not live your life fully defined as a shop assistant, nor do you as a Greek Cypriot, for example, and you can always refute such identifications in the name of another description which, because it is more individuated, may ring more truthfully to you. Or, most commonly, you will skate across the several identities which will take your weight, relying on the most useful for your purposes of the moment; like Hanif Kureishi's suave character in the film *My Beautiful Laundrette*, who says impatiently, 'I'm a professional businessman, not a professional Pakistani'.

The troubles of 'women', then, aren't unique. But aren't they arguably peculiar in that 'women', half the human population, do suffer from an extraordinary weight of characterization? 'Mothers' also demonstrate this acutely, and interact with 'women' in the course of social policy invocations especially; in Britain after 1945 for instance, women were described as either over-feminized mothers, or as under-feminized workers, but the category of the working mother was not acknowledged.[14] So the general feminine description can be split in such ways, and its elements played off against each other. But the overall effect is only to intensify the excessively described and attributed being of 'women'.

Feminism of late has emphasized that indeed 'women' are far from being racially or culturally homogeneous, and it may be thought that this corrective provides the proper answer to the hesitations I've advanced here about 'women'. But this is not the same preoccupation. Indeed there is a world of helpful difference between making claims in the name of an annoyingly generalized 'women' and doing so in the name of, say, 'elderly Cantonese women living in Soho'. Any study of sexual consolidations, of the differing metaphorical weightings of 'women', would have to be alerted to the refinements of age, trade, ethnicity, and exile, but it would not be satisfied by them. However, the specifications of difference are elaborated, they still come to rest on 'women', and it is the isolation of this last which is in question.

It's not that a new slogan for feminism is being proposed here—of feminism without 'women'. Rather, the suggestion is that 'women' is a simultaneous foundation of and an irritant to feminism, and that this is constitutionally so. It is true that the trade-off for the myriad namings of 'women' by politics, sociologies, policies, and psychologies is that at this cost 'women' do, sometimes, become a force to be reckoned with. But the caveat remains: the risky elements to the processes of alignment in sexed ranks are never far away, and the very collectivity which distinguishes you may also be wielded, even unintentionally, against you. Not just against you as an individual, that is, but against you as a social being with needs and attributions. The dangerous intimacy between subjectification and subjection needs careful calibration. There is, as we have repeatedly learned, no fluent trajectory from feminism to a truly sexually democratic humanism; there is no easy passage from 'women' to 'humanity'. The study of the historical development and precipitations of these sexed abstractions will help to make sense of why not. That is how Desdemona's anguished question, 'Am I that name?', may be transposed into a more hopeful light.

Notes

1. See Jacqueline Rose, 'Introduction—II', in J. Mitchell and J. Rose (eds.), *Feminine Sexuality, Jacques Lacan and the École Freudienne* (London: Macmillan, 1982).
2. See Stephen Heath, 'Male Feminism', *Dalhousie Review*, 64/2 (1986).
3. Jacques Derrida, *Spurs: Nietzsche's Styles* (Chicago: University of Chicago Press, 1978), 51, 55.
4. See arguments in Lynne Segal, *Is the Future Female? Troubled Thoughts on Contemporary Feminism* (London: Virago, 1987).
5. Michel Foucault, 'Nietzsche, Genealogy, History', in Donald F. Bouchard and Sherry Simon (eds. and trans.), *Language, Counter-Memory, Practice: Selected Essays and Interviews* (Ithaca, NY: Cornell University Press, 1977), 162.

6. John Donne, 'The Relique', *Poems* (London, 1633).
7. See Joan Scott, ' "L'Ouvrière! Mot Impie, Sordide ...": Women Workers in the Discourse of French Political Economy (1840–1860)', in P. Joyce (ed.), *The Historical Meanings of Work* (Cambridge University Press, 1987).
8. Jane Anger, 'Jane Anger her Protection for Women ...' (London, 1589), in Joan Goulianos (ed.), *By a Woman Writt: Literature from Six Centuries By and About Women* (Baltimore: Penguin, 1974), 25.
9. Ibid. 27.
10. Ibid. 28.
11. Mary Wollstonecraft, *A Vindication of the Rights of Woman, 1792* (Harmondsworth: Penguin, 1982), 142.
12. Karl Marx, *Grundrisse* (Harmondsworth: Penguin, 1973), 83, 496.
13. Ibid. 104, 105.
14. Denise Riley, *War in the Nursery: Theories of the Child and Mother* (London: Virago, 1983), 150–5, 195.

2 The Dialectics of Black Womanhood

Bonnie Thornton Dill

A new scholarship about black women, strengthened by the grow-ing acceptance of black and women's studies as distinct areas of aca-demic inquiry and by the need to refute myths and stereotypes about black women and black family life which helped shape social policies of the mid-1960s, is examining aspects of black family life that have been overlooked or distorted. Several studies have argued that a historical tradition of work forms an essential component in the lives of Afro-American women.[1] Beginning from that premiss, this paper seeks to demonstrate that the emphasis on women's work role in Afro-American culture has generated alternative notions of womanhood contradictory to those that have been traditional in modern American society.[2]

These new models project images of female sexual and intellec-tual equality, economic autonomy, and legal as well as personal par-ity with men. While they represent a new direction in the social ideology, they reflect an aspect of life that has been dominant for generations among many Afro-American women. Dialectical analysis enables us to clarify and illuminate this contradiction, and could provide theoretical direction to the new scholarship. But understanding the dialectics of black womanhood first requires rethinking several areas of scholarship about black women and their families.

This is a revision of a paper presented at the Seventieth Annual Meeting of the American Sociological Association, 25–9 Aug. 1975, San Francisco. I would like to thank Elizabeth Higginbotham and Carroll Seron for their helpful comments and criticism. Reprinted by permission of the University of Chicago Press from *Signs*, 4/3 (Spring 1979), 543–55.

BLACK WOMEN IN BLACK FAMILY LITERATURE

Four major problems pervade the literature on Afro-American families. The first of these derives from the use of inadequate historical data and/or the misinterpretation of that data. The second entails erroneous or partially conceived assumptions about the relationship of blacks to white society. The third problem is a direct result of the second and arises because of the differences between the values of the researcher and those of the subject. Fourth is the general confusion of class and culture.

Problem One: Issues in Black Family History

The dominant influence on the study of the black family and the role of black women was Frazier's *The Negro Family in the United States*.[3] While his major contribution was to provide a historical and sociological analysis of black family life in a period when psychological and biological theories of racial inferiority abounded, his historical methodology had serious shortcomings.

According to Gutman, Frazier did not explain the conditions he studied but 'read that condition back into the past and linked it directly to the nineteenth-century slave experience'.[4] He concluded that female-headed families, which he termed the 'matriarchate', had developed during the slave period and gained prominence after emancipation among those blacks who were economically unstable or otherwise removed from the direct influence of Euro-American culture. In his view, poverty and limited assimilation into the dominant culture inhibited their adopting the normative family patterns of the society. Since these conditions were characteristic of most black families, he concluded that female-headed households were prototypical of black family life. Using a linear model of historical change, Frazier argued that the subsequent crises of reconstruction and urbanization served only to intensify this type of family disorganization.

The overriding image of black women that emerged from his work is that of a strong and independent person who placed little value on marriage, engaged without conscience in free sexual activity, and had no notion of male supremacy. As a grandmother, she is depicted as the 'oldest head' in a maternal family organization, ideotypically defined as a three-generation household. Thus, while Frazier identified some of the historical conditions which encouraged the development of self-reliance and autonomy in black women, the limitations of his historical interpretation resulted in his evaluating these qualities negatively, suggesting that they were contributory factors in the disorganization of Afro-American family life.

Probably the most debated of recent studies which drew heavily on Frazier's history is 'The Moynihan Report'.[5] Moynihan accepted, without examination, Frazier's linear model of the historical development of the black family and used it as an explanation for contemporary data. The effect of his work, focusing on marital dissolution, illegitimacy rates, female-headed families, and welfare dependency, was to 'prove' that Frazier's interpretation was still relevant. However, Frazier's analysis of black family history is being refuted, not only because of its methodological weakness but also because of its findings.

Gutman's recent study of black families suggests the breadth and detail required for a more accurate understanding of the history of black families, particularly with regard to its structure and normative patterns.[6] He contends that the female-headed household, while a recurrent pattern, was atypical in the period before 1925 and generally exaggerated in studies of black family life. His findings indicate that: (1) there is little evidence of a matriarchal form of household; (2) the typical household everywhere was a simple nuclear household headed by a male; (3) there is no significant difference in the household structure of field hands as opposed to artisans and house servants (this finding addresses itself directly to the issue of assimilation); (4) some of the physical movement associated with emancipation involved the reconstruction of broken slave households; and (5) sustained marriage among slaves, common everywhere, meant that the role models of marriage and family existed *within* the slave world and were constantly available to younger slaves.[7]

Gutman's work is important in developing a dialectical analysis of black women and their families because he has begun the process of examining the detailed components of family structure at specific historical moments. This permits us to begin an analysis of why and how the family and women's roles therein have changed over time. Of particular interest is the fact that he explains this trend in terms of distinct Afro-American cultural norms which emphasized marriage while refraining from stigmatizing women who gave birth out of wedlock. Since the establishment of paternity has had so profound an influence on the social position of Euro-

American women, Gutman's documentation of the existence of norms which differed radically from those of the dominant culture supports the potential of Afro-American culture to generate alternative notions of womanhood and poses this contradiction as an important problem for further study.

Problem Two: Black Families in a White World

Fundamental to the proposal of a dialectical framework to analyse the condition of black women in the family is a conviction that the relationship of blacks to white society is dialectical in nature. This contention, while not new, has yet to be systematically applied to the study of black families. Frazier, influenced by the theories of Robert Park, determined that incomplete assimilation and isolation of blacks from white society explained their divergent family forms. The matriarchate was the result of the failure to assimilate, while patriarchal forms developed among those who had not been isolated from Euro-American norms and values.

A different theoretical position about the relationship of blacks to white society has been proposed by Billingsley.[8] He adopted Parson's social systems model and argued that the black family must be viewed as a separate but interrelated social system within the nexus of the larger society. The functionality of black families depends on the smooth interrelationship of these systems. Applying Billingsley's model, one could analyse black women in their complex of social roles: first in terms of their roles within the family—mother, daughter, or sister; second, within the community—church member, PTA president, etc.; and third within the wider society—secretary, housekeeper, teacher, or welfare recipient.

While this model recognizes the existence of a distinct Afro-American culture, its focus on the lives of black women as a set of interacting roles provides only a limited understanding of the dynamic and contradictory nature of their experience. Emphasis on functionality and dysfunctionality of their roles predisposes us to view black women more in relationship to the dominant culture than within Afro-American culture itself.

Valentine has suggested the concept of 'biculturation' to describe the relationship of blacks to white society.[9] This concept assumes that blacks have been simultaneously socialized into two different cultural systems: white Euro-American and black Afro-American. However much of the learning about Euro-American culture remains latent because discrimination prohibits blacks from achieving many mainstream values. While this concept may be particularly useful in explaining role conflict where role expectations derived from Afro-American culture contradict those derived from Euro-American culture, its major weakness is failure to account for the interrelatedness of these two cultural streams or to explain the basis of their unequal interaction.

Ladner's study of adolescent black girls, rather than emphasizing the shared and interacting norms which link Afro- and Euro-American traditions, illuminated the conflicts and dualities which the young women in her sample coped with as maturing adolescents.[10] She argued that the attitudes, behaviours, and interpersonal relationships of these women were adaptations to a variety of factors, including the harsh realities of their environment, Afro-American cultural images of black womanhood, and the sometimes conflicting values and norms of the wider society. This is exemplified in her discussion of attitudes toward premarital sex:

> Often in the absence of material resources, . . . sex becomes the resource that is exchanged. . . . It is here that sexual involvement transcends any conventional analysis because the standards that the individuals apply to their actions are created out of their own situations. Although many girls found it to be a means of expression in a variety of ways, they were still influenced by the conventional code of morality. Some of them were more influenced by the conventional codes of morality than others and experienced conflict and sometimes trauma over whether or not they should defy these codes. The sharp conflict . . . had a profound effect upon their lives.[11]

At the same time, she describes the reciprocal effects of distinctive aspects of black life upon the wider society.

Ladner's work comes closest to the perspective which we are proposing in this paper. By self-consciously applying the dialectical mode of analysis to the experiences of black women, we may make explicit the complex interaction of political, social, and economic forces in shaping the broad historical trends that characterize black women as a group as well as the particular lives of individual women. In this way, we move beyond the deficit models of Frazier and Moynihan and even beyond the models of Billingsley and Valentine. These models illuminate the complexities of black and white social roles but have limitations in accounting for the impact of racial oppression on the economic, political, or social life of black Americans and in explaining the historical or geographic variations in the black experience. The dialectic permits us to focus on the dynamic and contradictory aspects of black American life and to account for the simultaneity of conflict and interdependence which characterize black–white relations in American society.

Problem Three: Value Discrepancies between Researcher and Subject

The third problem is a direct result of the second and arises because of the differences between the values of the researcher and those of the subject. The values about family life underlying the work of Frazier and Moynihan are those that form the foundation of the bourgeois family: monogamy, nuclearity, and patriarchy. Female independence of male authority and economic control is viewed as destructive of this family form. This analysis denied the existence of a distinct Afro-American culture and ignored the meaning that these behaviours might have for the people being studied. To a large extent, the matriarchy thesis was based on the combination of erroneous historical interpretation with the actualities of black female labour-force participation.

As Aldridge, Jackson, Lewis and others have pointed out, black females have historically had high participation rates in the labour force—higher than their white counterparts, even with children (see Tables 2.1 and 2.2, and Fig. 2.1). Moynihan combined these high levels of labour-force participation with notions of female dominance in husband–wife families and with the large (relative to white families) percentage of female-headed families in the black

Table 2.1. Labour-force participation rates of women by race and year

Selected years	All women	Black	White
1900	20.4	41.2	—
1910	25.2	58.2	—
1920	23.3	43.7	—
1930	24.3	—	—
1940	25.4	37.3	—
1950	29.0	46.9	32.6
1960	34.5	48.2	36.5
1970	—	49.5	42.6
1974	—	49.1	45.2

Sources: Joe Feagin, 'Black Women in the American Work-Force', in Charles Willie (ed.), *The Family Life of Black People* (Columbus, Ohio: Merrill, 1970), 23–4; Valerie K. Oppenheimer, *The Female Labor-Force in the United States*, Population Series Monographs no. 5 (Berkeley: University of California, 1970); US Commerce Department, *Negro Population 1790–1915* (Washington, DC: Government Printing Office, 1918).

Table 2.2. Percentage of Mothers in Labour-Force by Age of Children, Colour, and Marital Status (March 1967)

Age of children (years)	Race of mother		Differential
	Non-white	White	
Under 6*	44	27	+17
6–17	58	48	+10
Under 18	50	37	+13

*Percentage participation of black and white mothers for 1973 are 54 and 31, respectively, a differential of +23.

Source: Adapted from Joe Feagin, 'Black Women in the American Work-Force', in Charles Willie (ed.), *The Family Life of Black People* (Columbus, Ohio: Merrill, 1970, 23–4).

community to conclude that matriarchy was characteristic of black family life.

As a result, in much of the social science literature on black families, black women became scapegoats, responsible for the psychological emasculation of black men and for the failure of the black community to gain parity with the white community.

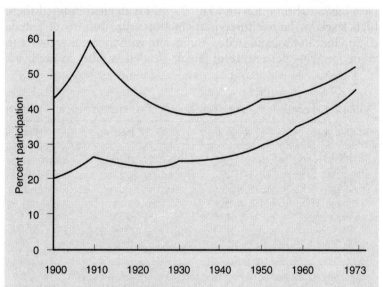

Fig. 2.1. Trends in labour-force participation for all women and black women, 1900–1973. (The sharp increase in 1910 has been accounted for by differing instructions to the census takers for that year.)

Ryan has labelled this type of reasoning 'blaming the victim'. It is an ideology which, he says, '. . . attributes defect and inadequacy to the malignant nature of poverty, injustice, slum life, and racial difficulties. The stigma that marks the victim . . . is an acquired stigma, a stigma of social, rather than genetic, origin. But the stigma . . . is still located *within* the victim, inside his skin. . . . It is a brilliant ideology for justifying a perverse form of social action designed to change, not society, as one might expect, but rather society's victims.'[12] In general, the justification of the matriarchy thesis has been based on the combination of erroneous historical interpretation with the actualities of black female participation in the labour-force. Ten Houten states: 'In modern urban society the subdominance of the black husband to the wife is attributed to employment behaviours.'[13]

It is a cruel irony that the black woman's role as a worker has been used to represent dominance over and emasculation of black men. This predisposition ignores both historical and socio-economic realities. Black women were brought to this country for two economic reasons: to work and to produce workers. Although they were valued for their reproductive function, as were white women settlers, it was only of equal importance with their labour.

There was no concern about the legitimacy of their children because there was nothing for them to inherit. The protective barriers which gradually forced white women out of production and changed their relationship to labour and society did not exist for most black women. Davis, in an analysis of the historical significance of black women's relationship to labour, emphasizes this point.

It is true that she was a victim of the myth that only the woman, with the diminished capacity for mental and physical labour, should do degrading household work. Yet, the alleged benefits of the ideology of femininity did not accrue to her. She was not sheltered or protected; she would not remain oblivious to the desperate struggle for existence unfolding outside the 'home'. She was also there in the fields, alongside the man, toiling under the lash. . . . This was one of the supreme ironies of slavery: In order to approach its strategic goal—to extract the greatest possible surplus from the labour of slaves—the black woman had to be released from the chains of the myth of femininity. . . . The black woman shared the deformed equality of equal oppression with the black man.[14]

Too often, social science researchers have sought to describe black women and their families as if they were a monolithic whole, without regard for differences in social class. At the other extreme is the contention that social-class differences obliterate distinctions of race. In other words, social science has generally supported the idea that Afro-American culture is synonymous with lower-class culture and that it disappears as black Americans gain middle-class status.

To illuminate the complexities of the interaction of class and culture, Billingsley adopts Milton Gordon's concept of 'ethnic subsociety'. According to Gordon,

the ethnic group is the locus of a sense of *historical identification*, while the eth-class (the intersection of ethnicity and social class) is the locus of a sense of *participational identification*. With a person of the same social class but of a different ethnic group, one shares behavioral similarities but not a sense of peoplehood. With those of the same ethnic group but of a different social class, one shares the sense of peoplehood but not behavioral similarities. The only group which meets both these criteria are people of the same ethnic group *and* social class.[15]

The concept of 'eth-class' is useful in that it communicates a sense of the ways in which ethnic differences interact with social class. However, it has serious limitations because it ignores the elements of domination and oppression which are at the root of black–white relations in the United States and which account for the high concentration of blacks in the lower class.

Blauner argues that black culture is not merely a phenomenon of lower-class life but a product of the experience of discrimination which cuts across all social classes.[16] More important, he links racial oppression to economic exploitation and the structure of classes within a capitalist economy. Thus his analysis goes beyond a merely descriptive portrayal of the interaction of the two variables, class and race, and focuses on the dynamic and contradictory influence that each has on the other. Thus while he sees race as a form of stratification which has economic, political, and ideological dimensions, he argues that it is a basic rather than epiphenomenal aspect of American industrial capitalism. He concludes, 'In American society, races and classes interpenetrate one another. Race affects class formation and class influences racial dynamics in ways that have not yet been adequately investigated.'[17]

IMPLICATIONS FOR THE STUDY OF BLACK WOMEN AND THEIR JOBS

It is the contention of this paper, therefore, that the study of black women and their families requires serious revision. First, it must be placed within a historical framework which is carefully researched, documented, and reinterpreted. Gutman, Pleck, Lammermeier, and others have only recently begun to provide this data.[18] Serious historical research promises to provide new information regarding the structure and organization of black families at different historical periods and in different regions of the United States. Information about values, attitudes, and the vicissitudes of daily life will remain, however, to be pieced together from oral history and other descriptive reports.

Second, black women must be studied within a dynamic and contradictory framework to understand the complexities of their relations to all aspects of society. Thus, an examination of the impact of work on the family life of women whose occupational categories result in class differences would be expected to yield important distinctions. At the same time, however, the experience of slavery, whether house servant or field hand, and the continued economic precariousness of most black families which has resulted in high rates of female labour-force participation, would be expected to have a particular impact on the growth and development of women in Afro-American culture.

Third, we must continue to research and provide good descriptive studies of the lives of black women and their families across the social class spectrum. Studies such as Stack's offer considerable insight into the ways in which economic oppression impacts on daily life, family patterns, and women's self-concepts.[19] Her work and Ladner's are examples of studies which provide the data necessary for concept development and theory-building in this area.[20] They reveal the ways in which black women conceptualize work, its meaning in their lives, and its importance in the development of their models of womanhood.

CONCLUSION: TOWARD A NEW MODEL

We began developing a historical framework for the study of black women by focusing on the contradiction cited at the outset: the historical role as a labourer in a society where ideals of femininity emphasized domesticity. A dominant image of black women as 'beasts of burden'[21] stands in direct contrast to American ideals of womanhood: fragile, white, and not too bright. The impact of this contradiction is profound. It has already been alluded to in discussions of the values pervading much of the pejorative literature on black women. It can also be expected to have affected self-images as well as their interpretations and expectations of various role-relationships.

In concluding, however, it is important to explore the implications of this historical tradition for contemporary models of black womanhood. Ladner suggests several in her study of adolescent black girls. These revolve around the girls' images of womanhood, goals for themselves, and their relationships to their families and to boys. In developing their ideals of womanhood, Ladner reports that 'the strongest conception of womanhood that exists among all pre-adult females is that of how the woman has to take a strong family role'.[22] The pervasiveness of this image of an economically independent, resourceful, and hardworking woman was resented by some, adopted by others, and accepted with resignation by still others. Nevertheless, its overriding importance remained even though Ladner observed other models which existed alongside it. One of these other models, which appears to me as a variation, is that of an upwardly mobile middle-class woman. Ladner points out that education was most frequently seen as the means to this end. The choice of this model had a serious impact on the entire life of girls who chose it, particularly as it affected their relationship with boys. These girls most often avoided serious involvement with boys, particularly premarital sex and the risk of pregnancy which represented a definite end to their aspirations. Success in attaining their middle-class goals was not only measured in terms of the training or job acquired but also 'by the extent to which one can not only care for himself, but help others in the family'.[23]

Girls who rejected the dominant model often adopted a model which Ladner calls a 'carefree, laissez-faire, egalitarian model of womanhood'. Different though this model was, it too encompasses a sense of self-reliance, strength, and autonomy. This image, as described by Ladner, was primarily directed toward relationships with boys. Inherent in it was an attitude of equality between men and women, a rejection of the sexual double standard, and a general belief that a woman can do whatever a man does. This practical attitude toward male–female relations was not without conflict, particularly as it was confronted by the ideals of the wider society. Neither, however, were the other models. They, too, support an image of womanhood which, until recently, has been out of step with the values of white society.

The image of independent, self-reliant, strong, and autonomous women which pervades the models of the young black women in Ladner's study has been reinforced by the work experience and social conditions of black women throughout history. The image, therefore, represents both the oppressive experiences of work and the liberating attitudes of personal autonomy and sexual equality. It may explain the findings of the *1970 Virginia Slims American Women's Opinion Poll* that 'an essentially urban coalition of black women and the young and the educated of both races are ready to follow the examples of blacks and the young and challenge the status quo in American society'.[24] This finding is particularly interesting in light of the goals of the women's liberation movement and the relationship of black women to this movement. It has been acknowledged that black women have not identified strongly with what many have seen as a movement of middle-class white women.[25] I would suggest that the image of women—as more than housewives and as sexual equals—toward which white women strive is, in large part, synonymous with the dominant image and much of the experience of black women. Ladner says it well in the closing statement of one of the chapters of *Tomorrow's Tomorrow*: 'Black womanhood has always been the very essence of what American womanhood is attempting to become on some levels.'[26] And again in her final chapter:

. . . much of the current focus on being liberated from the constraints and protectiveness of the society which is proposed by Women's Liberation groups has never been applied to Black women, and in this sense, we have always been 'free', and able to develop as individuals even under the most harsh circumstances. This freedom, as well as the tremendous hardships from which Black women suffered, allowed for the development of a female personality that is rarely described in scholarly journals for its obstinate strength and ability to survive. Neither is its peculiar humanistic character and quiet courage viewed as the epitome of what the American model of femininity should be.[27]

Thus the contradiction between the subjection of women from West Africa to the harsh deprivations of slavery, farm, factory, and domestic work and the sense of autonomy and self-reliance which developed, points in the direction of a new avenue for studying black American women. And it is the potential synthesis of these contradictions which embraces the future problems and possibilities of a new definition of femininity for *all* American women.

Notes

1. See Delores Aldridge, 'Black Women in the Economic Marketplace: A Battle Unfinished', *Journal of Social and Behavioral Scientists*, 21 (Winter 1975): 48–61; Jacqueline Jackson, 'Family Organization and Ideology', in Kent Miller and Ralph Dreger (eds.), *Comparative Studies of Blacks and Whites in the United States* (New York: Seminar Press, 1973); and Diane K. Lewis, 'A Response to Inequality: Black Women, Racism, and Sexism', *Signs*, 3 (Winter 1977): 339–61.
2. Natalie J. Sokoloff, 'The Economic Position of Women in the Family', in Peter J. Stein, Judith Richman, and Natalie Hannon (eds.), *The Family* (Reading, Mass.: Addison-Wesley Publishing Co., 1977).
3. E. Franklin Frazier, *The Negro Family in the United States* (Chicago: University of Chicago Press, 1966).
4. Herbert Gutman, 'Persistent Myths about the Afro-American Family', *Journal of Interdisciplinary History*, 6/2 (Autumn 1975).
5. US Department of Labor, Office of Policy Planning and Research, *The Negro Family: The Case for National Action* (Washington, DC: Government Printing Office, March 1965).
6. Herbert Gutman, *The Black Family in Slavery and Freedom* (New York: Pantheon Books, 1976).
7. These findings were quoted in Clarence Turner, 'Some Theoretical and Conceptual Considerations for Black Family Studies', *Blacklines*, 2 (Winter 1972): 16. The assumption that slavery was a closed system (item no. 5) without any influences from outside the plantation or from traditional African life has been hotly debated. Two people who have presented findings to the contrary are Melville Herskovitz (*The Myth of the Negro Past* (Boston: Beacon Press, 1941)) and John Blassingame (*The Slave Community* (New York: Oxford University Press, 1972)). In general, revisionist history seeks to examine the existence and influence of African survivals in Afro-American culture.
8. Andrew Billingsley, *Black Families in White America* (Englewood Cliffs, NJ: Prentice-Hall, 1968).
9. Charles Valentine, 'Deficit, Difference and Bicultural Models of Afro-American Behavior', *Harvard Educational Review*, 41/2 (May 1971).
10. Joyce A. Ladner, *Tomorrow's Tomorrow* (Garden City, NY: Doubleday, 1971).
11. Ibid. 212–13.
12. William Ryan, *Blaming the Victim* (New York: Vintage, 1971), 7–8.
13. Warren Ten Houten, 'The Black Family: Myth and Reality', in Arlene Skolnick and Jerome Skolnick (eds.), *The Family in Transition* (Boston: Little, Brown, 1971), 420.

14. Angela Davis, 'Reflections on the Black Woman's Role in the Community of Slaves', *Black Scholar*, 3 (Dec. 1971): 7.
15. Quoted in Billingsley, p. 10.
16. Robert Blauner, *Racial Oppression in America* (New York: Harper & Row, 1972), ch. 4.
17. Blauner, 28–9.
18. Particular attention is called to the work of Elizabeth Pleck, 'The Two Parent Household: Black Family Structure in Late Nineteenth-Century Boston', *Journal of Social History*, 6 (Fall 1972); Paul Lammermeier, 'The Urban Black Family of the Nineteenth Century: A Study of Black Family Structure in the Ohio Valley, 1850–1880', *Journal of Marriage and the Family*, 35 (Aug. 1973); and the developing activity in oral history of the Kinte Foundation.
19. Carol Stack, *All Our Kin* (New York: Harper & Row, 1974).
20. See forthcoming Ph.D. diss. by Bonnie Dill (New York University), which explores the meanings of work and its perceived impact on the family lives of black female household workers; and Elizabeth Higginbotham (Brandeis University), which examines the interrelationship of education, career, and family among college-educated black women. Both studies focus on the women's self-presentations, their goals and strategies for survival, upward mobility, and its relationship to their family lives. An article by Robert D. Abrahams ('Negotiating Respect: Patterns of Presentation among Black Women', *Journal of American Folklore*, 88 [Jan.–Mar. 1975]: 58–80) utilizes the data in novels and several sociological studies in an attempt to develop a systematic analysis of the manner in which black women attain respect. It is a preliminary step in the direction of concept development using descriptive data.
21. This conceptualization is drawn from the writings of Jeanne L. Noble. It was presented in a draft of an article being prepared for the *World Encyclopedia of Black Peoples* which the author generously shared with me.
22. Ladner, p. 127.
23. Ibid., p. 121.
24. Louis Harris and Associates, *The Virginia Slims American Women's Opinion Poll* (1970), 78.
25. For discussions of black women's responses to the women's liberation movement see Robert Staples, *The Black Woman in America* (Chicago: Nelson-Hall, 1973); Inez Reid, *'Together' Black Women* (New York: Emerson Hall, 1972); selections in Toni Cade (ed.), *The Black Woman: An Anthology* (New York: New American Library, 1970); Linda LaRue, 'The Black Woman and Women's Liberation', *Black Scholar*, 1 (May 1970); and Lewis (n. 1 above) for a discussion of the structural factors affecting the variety of responses that have been noted among black women.
26. Ladner, p. 239.
27. Ibid., p. 280.

Theorizing Woman: *Funü, Guojia, Jiating* (Chinese Women, Chinese State, Chinese Family)*

Tani Barlow

What narratives produce the signifiers of the subject for other traditions?

Gayatri Spivak[1]

It would make no sense . . . to define gender as the cultural interpretation of sex, if sex itself is a gendered category. *Gender ought not to be conceived merely as the cultural inscription of meaning on a pregiven sex . . . [but as] the very apparatus of production whereby the sexes themselves are established.*

Judith Butler[2]

This essay critically rethinks some assumptions made in previous anglophone histories of Chinese women. Primarily, I see historical context as literally producing not reflecting realities. That is why I parse historical texts rather than deploy abstract, ahistorical, prediscursive 'woman'.[3] The essay also suggests an outline for a genealogy of concrete female subject positions in sinophone texts over the last two centuries. I desire a feminist politics rooted in difference without identity, what Chandra Mohanty calls a 'non-imperialist feminism . . . a real space for the articulation, interpretation, theorization, and reflection about the historical specificity of the construction of women'.[4]

The essay's historical lesson is that *funü*, the pre-eminent Chinese, female, subject position between about 1940 and 1985,

Reprinted from *Genders* 10 by permission of the author and the University of Texas Press.

I am enormously grateful to the following pioneer scholars: Marilyn B. Young, Margery Wolf, Phyllis Andors, Kay Anne Johnson, Wolfgang Kubin, Charlotte Beahan, and Roxanne Witke.

*Chinese is not inflected. All nouns are both singular and plural and are read according to the sense of the English syntax.

was in fact a catechrisis, that is, an imaginary master word with very real political effects and power. I document my point by investigating the history of contests over signifiers of the subject 'modern Chinese woman'. I suggest that between the mid-Qing dynasty and the 1920s cultural revolution, the dominant formula *funü* signified kinswomen within a discursive economy that circulated power via a specialized, patrilineal, canonical rhetoric. In the 'semifeudal, semicolonial' 1920s, when post-Confucian cultural revolutionaries rewrote the past as dead Tradition/*quantong*, intellectuals and activists made Woman/*nuxing*—a neologism that Chinese intellectuals produced as a consequence of their encounter with global colonial discourse in the semi-colony world of the treaty ports—into a privileged site of struggle. Eventually, the Chinese Communist Party inherited the organized women's movement. An alternative, massified, politicized subject known within the CCP *nomenklatura* as *funü* superseded *nuxing*/Woman, which was then redesignated as 'Westernized', 'bourgeois', erotic. Under the triumphant Maoist state's centralizing discourses, *funü*/woman got situated first in *guojia*/state and then, through the magic of metonymy, within the modern *jiating*/family. Modern People's Republic of China *funü*/women thus provided one site for state socialist transformation.

Staging my argument in this way accomplishes several objectives. First, history emerges from this productive textuality to make genealogical claims about the past and its persistence. But although it is true that the Chinese monarchy had long been concerned with hegemonizing female subject positions,[5] the key words of the socialist imaginary's rhetoric— *guojia*/nation-state,[6] *jiating*/family, and female subject/*nuxing*—show the marks of intense struggle in modern rhetoric: they do not directly partake of older, dynastic social formations. Second, this argument locates *funü*/women synchronically in discursive constellation with other modern state categories, like 'worker/*gongren*' and 'youth/*qingnian*' and 'proletariat/*wuchanjieji*'. *Funü*, that is, forms a part of the 'system of designations by ... which', until the repudiation of Maoism, party 'political authorities regulate[d] all important social relationships'.[7] Third, the project explains gendered subject positionalities in social-political rather than psychodynamic terms. The Women's Federation, Fulian, has sustained *funü* as a political category since the 1940s and ensured that gender inscription remained a province of the state—at least until very recently.

PRODUCING VIRTUOUS MOTHERS AND GOOD WIVES

In late-imperial Chinese discourses, *funü* signified female family members. In his *Jiaonu yigui* or 'Inherited Guide for Educating Women', the eighteenth-century scholar Chen Hongmou neatly illustrated what I mean:[8]

When *fu*1 [persons, sages, women of rank] are in the *jia* [lineage unit] they are *nu* [female, woman, daughter]; when they marry they are *fu*4 [wives] and when they bear children they are *mu* [mothers]. [If you start with] a *xiannu* [virtuous unmarried daughter/female] then you will end up with a *xianfu* [virtuous wife]; if you have virtuous wives, you will end up with *xianmu* [virtuous mothers]. Virtuous mothers insure virtuous descendants. Civilizing begins in the women's quarters. Everyone in the *jia* benefits from female chastity. That is why educating women is so important.[9]

Chen's statement usefully demonstrates why later cultural radicals found colonialist categories worth borrowing and even, perhaps, why the Maoist state's recuperation of *funü* had such nativist overtones.

My first point involves categories. The citation presents a *fu*1 who marries a husband, has children, is her father's daughter ('she' appears in quotation marks since Chinese pronouns are not gendered). Chen says that the *fu*1 is a person of rank within the differential patrilineal sublineage group, the *jia*. The point, however, is that the text's very specificity concerning *fu*1 forecloses a general category of generic woman, a category that would incorporate *fu*1, *nu*, *fu*4, *funü*, *xiannu*, plus all poor women of no rank and *nu*2/slaves. In other words, I could render the passage into English as follows: 'before [women] are married they are *nu*/female/daughters, when they get married they are *fu*/wives, and when they give birth to children, then they are *mu*/mothers.' But as soon as I did so I would substantiate a category—Woman—*that does not appear in the syntax of the sentence.*

What does this imply? The subjects Chen's passage situates and addresses are primarily wives and daughters or *fu*4*nü*. (They are 'women', of course, but, as I will demonstrate momentarily, by virtue of protocols specific to their subject positions and not necessarily or even in the first case by reference to a physiological ground.) *Funü* is a frame of differential *jia*-relation, while Woman is a transcendental signifier. There exists no moment in Chen's text where 'woman' operates as a framing category outside of *jia* or the relationality implied in *funü*. Another way to phrase this point is that Chen Hongmou assumes no foundational status for Woman. Rather than frame kin-specific situations as instances of 'things women do', Chen explains that acting within specified ethical-practical boundaries produces a recognizably female person.

So *funü* female kin was the (con)text that produced subject positions like *xianmu*/virtuous mother as always already gendered.[10] But what made it work? How did this discursive context magically deploy positionalities of kin like *xianmu* and make them stick? To develop a response I turn to Elizabeth Cowie, who argued a decade ago that rather than theorizing women as prediscursively '*situated in the family*' we ought to grasp that 'it is in the family—as the effect of kinship structures—that women as women are produced'.[11] Cowie sought to understand 'kinship' not as a system of exchange but as a production line for subjectivities. I agree: relational nomenclature produce subject positions. Cowie also sought to expose the ways Victorian anthropological discourses had essentialized Man and Woman into binaried, exclusionary, sexist reductions from the start. Reading Chen with Cowie in mind, I can argue that the exchange of actual women in patrilineal, patrilocal Chinese kin fields produced not the sign Woman, but a profusion of signs with one thing in common: though they all accommodated 'real' women, none could be reduced to a prediscursive *hegemonic sign*.

Yin/yang logic structured disciplinary gendering in Chen Hongmou's world just as it structured religious, generational, and many associated juridical relations.[12] To cast my point negatively, Chen Hongmou's texts do not refer to women's bodies, nor to their body parts, as proofs of their social existence. Rather, his text argues that appropriately disciplined behaviours for *funü* constrained within the capacious relations of *yin/yang* logic (remaining within, filial caretaking, service to parents, moral instruction of children, individual normative practice) all contribute to the coherence of human culture.[13]

When I refer to these processes as social-cosmological activities enacted on the never stable or fully boundaried primary site of the *jia*, I am rendering into my own language the point the late sixteenth-century physician, Li Shichen, made in his *Materia Medica*. 'Normally *qian* and *kun* make fathers and mothers; but there are five kinds of nonmales/*feinan* who cannot become fathers and five kinds of nonfemales/*feinu* who cannot become mothers'.[14] Now *qian* and *kun* are the first and last hexagrams of the *I Ching* or *Book of Changes*, since the Song dynasty the foundational text of hegemonic Confucian studies. *Qian* and *kun* refer to forces operating in *tiandi*, the realms extrinsic to human culture, as well as the realm of *wen*, of human social life. The forces *yin* and *yang* are many things: logical relationships (up/down, in/out, husband/wife), practical forces, 'designations for the polar aspects of effects', and, in a social sense, powers inscribing hierarchy (i.e. *yang* subordinates *yin* because it encloses the lesser force within itself), but *yin/yang* is neither as totalistic nor as ontologically binaried a construct as current cliché would have it. What Li says is that the dynamic forces of *yin/yang* do 'produce'—not only women and men (themselves subject positions but in another discourse) so much as subject positions named mother and father, husband and wife, brother and sister, and so on.

The anomaly confronting the physician in the cases Li cites rests on the general instability of bodies in most Confucian discourse. Here the non-man and the non-woman, whose defective bodies forestall production, as well as the castrated, impotent, vaginally impenetrable, and bodies known to change from female to male and from male to female, *all* present to the physician unstable surfaces that resist customary 'gendering'. In Li Shichen and Chen Hongmou's time, Simone de Beauvoir's odd notion that 'women are not born Women but become Women' makes sense. Why? Because the surface onto which eighteenth-century Chinese subjectivities were inscribed (i.e. Li Shichen's fecund body) were more flexible than the (gendering) subject positions that producing sons and daughters enabled women to occupy and possess.[15]

What appear in Chen's texts are not the 'sexes' but a profusion of relational, bound, unequal dyads, each signifying difference and positioning difference analogically. A *nu* is a daughter, unequally related to parents and parents-in-law. A *xiaozi* or filial son is differentially unequal to mother and father, *yin* to their *yang*. A *fu* is a wife, tied in a secondary relation to her husband. A *xianfu* is a wife who, grasping the powers visited upon the secondary *yin* term, masters her domain through familiarity with protocol.[16] Obviously (invoking Cowie's point), subjects got produced within the *jia* (more properly *jia*-ist or familist *discourses*). Chen Hongmou's definition of *nu*, *fu*4, and *mu* makes it clear that while (good) women in the *jia* did effect social relations outside the family, no position existed for female persons (or for male persons, for that matter) outside of the *jia* boundaries. The *fu*1 exists within the kin world of reciprocal inequality, by virtue of her father's high standing.

Chen Hongmou advocated educating women to produce more *xiannu* and enhance the *jia*. Learning to act virtuously is coterminous with acting 'like a woman', in Chen Hongmou's view, and 'acting like a woman' required the maintenance of difference.[17] [Just as] the *yin* and the *yang* are different qualities/*shuxing*, so males and females/*nan nu* should act differently', as Chen's text puts it.[18] In the view of Lu Jingxi, Chen Hongmou's own cited authority, 'there is a difference between the *li*/ritual of men and women/*nan nu*. If you do not maintain the distinction, then you will cause gossip'.[19] Protocols consisted primarily of *li*—behaviours, scripted actions, and normatized manners—that shaped appropriate, proper, good behaviour. Social norms and gendered experience were inextricable.[20] In the cadence of the texts: when the daughters act on the *li* of daughterhood, married women act on the *li* of wives, and so on, then the distinction between men and women is accomplished and gendering is effected.

Protocols took virtually everything into consideration. 'As a kinswoman/*nuzi* you must establish yourself in life/*lishen*', for instance. 'In behaviour don't turn your head from side to side; if you wish to speak do so without moving your lips; if you wish to sit, do so without moving your knees, and if you stand do not wiggle your skirt. If you are happy do not giggle, if you are unhappy, do not yell aloud. Within and without/*nei/wai* [the *jia*] women and men (*nan/nu*) should be separate.' Chen Hongmou cited reams of text from ancient times describing in minute detail the *lishu* (body etiquette) he felt would allow people in the present, through their physical actions, to resurrect the splendid world of the Confucian past.

Protocol effected 'gender' rationally by linking good behaviour to correct enactment of texts that inscribed kin difference. 'The father-in-law/*ahweng* and mother-in-law/*agu* are the heads of the husband's family', a typical specimen reads. 'You are their daughter-in-law when you marry your husband, so you must support them as you supported your own parents' (i.e. specified practices enumerated in concrete detail: serve parents only when properly dressed, listen attentively while remaining in a standing posture, prepare their wash water and towels in the morning, premasticate their food, prepare their bedding, and avoid disorder, criticizing, or neglecting their comfort).[21] Such protocols were neither mere code, nor maps or roles. They instructed in the fashion of advice literature and they provided continuously reinforced subject positions because they linked the archaic past, where culture heroes had initially written them down, to contemporary texts. Protocol formed a bulwark of order against the undoing of difference and positioned subjects in social narrative.[22]

PRODUCING *NUXING*/WOMAN

Western imperialism forced into crisis the text protocols Chen Hongmou and those like him had (re)produced. The Manchu dynasty's long, slow implosion and the imperialists' relentless penetration of the heartland via 'treaty ports' transformed the political elite's social configuration and powers. Where previously the monarchy's texts enabled Confucian officials to regulate the meaningful world, gargantuan pressures dispersed the older stacked powers; they collapsed in 1905 when the Qing throne abolished the civil-service examination system. Eager to replace Chen Hongmou, who hegemonized the Confucian production of gendering, a modern, post-Confucian, professionalized intellectual emerged, who oversaw the appropriation of foreign signs into the new, domestic, urban, mass-market, print economy, an 'intellectual' who signalled a shift from the widely diffused textuality of the old society to the scriptural economy of realist representation in a peripheralized world economy.[23]

In the early twentieth century a new social formation arose calling itself *zhishi jieji* or intellectual class, later to become *qiming xuezhe* ('enlightened scholars'), and finally, under the same forces that produced *funü*/women as a political category, *zhishifenzi* or Chinese intellectual under Maoist inscription. *Zhishifenzi* were the 'Western'-educated offshoot of the tiny, very significant new commercial bourgeoisie, who monopolized the appropriation of Western ideas, forms, signs, and discourses. In their hands, peripheralization of signs proceeded as new missionary-educated and college-graduated professionals imported, translated, republished, and commented on texts from foreign languages. Historically, this group constituted itself as a colonized elite, meaning two things: that the imperialist semicolonization of China forced into existence 'new intellectuals', and that these elements did not just 'import' neologisms from Japan and the European West, they redrew the discursive boundaries of elite social existence. In this way *zhishifenzi* occupied (thereby further valorizing) a new, modernist, social field of *shehui* or 'society'. Situated inside the treaty ports in a crude material sense—the palladian English banks and French boulevards, the German beer, American YMCAs, and Japanese factories—terms like *shehui* acquired concrete referents. The powerful older terms *guan*/official, *gong*/common, and *si*/singular from Chen Hongmou's time increasingly gave up ground. Once-robust conventions were gradually reduced into something intellectuals of the 1920s would call 'tradition/*chuantong*' and regarded with either painful nostalgia or contempt and fear.[24]

A longer project would require far more comment on colonialist discourses among the treaty port *zhishifenzi*. Here let it suffice that the discourses of 'semicolonialism' had an effect on older Chinese gendering practices. A rash of masculinist interest in the universal sign of woman had surfaced as early as the 1830s, when there occurred what Mary Rankin calls an efflorescence of 'pro-feminine' male writing. Male reformers in the 1860s spoke admiringly of 'enlightened' relations between women and men in Western countries. Anti-footbinding and pro-female academy arguments held key positions, in the late 1890s and the first decade of the twentieth century, in the work of major male new-style intellectuals.[25]

Indeed, masculinist redeployment of *nu* initiated, according to Charlotte Beahan, an unprecedented female journalism within the slackening Old-World discourses between 1890 and 1910.[26] Calling themselves 'sisters/*jiemei*', female writers reversed the strategy Chen Hongmou had adopted when he argued for female literacy on the grounds that ethical women in families produced strong states. 'Why isn't China strong?' one asked. 'Because there are no persons of talent. Why are there no persons of talent? Because women do not prosper.'[27] Late-Confucian women sought liberty on 'nationalist' grounds. The sisters' publications contributed to what rapidly emerged as 'myths of the nation'.[28] That is to say, writers positioned themselves as citizens of the Chinese nation, as advocates of national emancipation from Western imperialism and Manchu occupation, and as different from men of their own 'Han Chinese' nationalist group. On those unimpeachable grounds they sought to mobilize China's 'beloved but weak two hundred million women . . . the direct slaves of slaves'.[29]

The expression 'slaves of slaves' as a term for Chinese women signified a noteworthy change in the theorization of *nu*. 'Slave' referred to male Han Chinese 'enslaved' to the Manchu monarchy and thus signalled democratic patriotism. Women, as the 'slaves of slaves', reached into domestic units to recategorize all Chinese women in a patriotic unity against the myriad imperialists seeking to 'divide China up as though it were a melon', as people put it then. The kin-inflected category of *funü* began the referential shift. Writers offered Chinese *nuren* (female person) as one specific instance of a universal category consisting of all women, and they did so under a patriotic inscription. An example of the mechanics of the referential shift comes from Zhen Ziyang's *Nuzi xin duben* (New Study Book for Women), a collection of stories about virtuous women linked generically to narratives in the Chen Hongmou book I cited earlier. The older text had celebrated 'just mothers', 'ethical stepmothers', and other situated kinswomen who had managed the *jia* sphere well, thereby effecting, through their adept use of protocol under difficult circumstances, the space beyond their own *jia*, that is, the *gong* or general world. The modern text, in contrast, provided not one, but two sets of ethical narratives about good women, set off from each other in two separate 'books'.[30]

Book 1 retold stories familiar to readers even before Chen Hongmou's time, like the story of Mencius's mother, who sacrificed to provide her son an appropriate ethical environment; Yue Fei's wife Liang, who personally fought the Nuzhen barbarians on behalf of the Song dynasty; and Hua Mulan of the Liang dynasty, who masqueraded as a filial son and fought as her father's proxy for twelve years. It also included examples of women who had, in the hoary past, transgressed unfairly gendered boundaries or had been unjustly ignored in masculinist histories. Huang Zongjia, for instance, 'was born a girl but did not want to be a woman [*nuzi*]' so she masqueraded as a man, served as an official; Suo Maoyi taught the master calligrapher Wang Xizi his calligraphy style; and so on.

Book 2 assembled a set of parallel stories about famous women of the West who matched or exceeded Hua Mulan's filial devotion, because they served not father, husband, or patriline but the nation. 'Sha Latuo' or Charlotte Corday, according to the Chinese version of her story, studied at a nunnery for six years, became engrossed in a particular book (I cannot figure out who 'Puluhua' might have been in a European language) about national heroes. The book's inspiration sent Sha Latuo to Paris, where she surprised the tyrant Mala (Marat) while he was with his concubine. In prison for his murder, she sent her father a filial letter declaring that tyrannicide was not a crime, and met her death with 'Puluhua's' book clutched in her hands. Another narrative venerated Madame Roland, who studied 'the Confucianism of her country' but who preferred the example of the Greeks and Romans. After marrying Roland for his politics, she inspired her timid husband to resist Robespierre's 'People's Party/*mindang*'. When Robespierre executed Madame Roland her husband committed suicide and their servants, overcome, also petitioned execution; their requests were carried out.[31]

The juxtaposition of 'Chinese' and 'Other' stories engendered meaning in two significant ways. First, obviously the reworked 'Chinese' stories and the 'Western' parallels jointly showed female heroes shifting their loyalties from husband or father to 'nation', without directly requiring that they abandon the prior object. A certain 'Frances' (Frances Willard, perhaps) appears to have been selected because, following her father's death, she remained unmarried and devoted herself to the improvement of North America through a renovation of the family, the nation, and finally the entire world. Nation rose up to peripheralize Father, never precluding his importance at the personal level.[32]

Second, the bilateral mutual exchange of 'Western' signs and 'Chinese' narrative had the effect of producing a category of universal womanhood. 'Chinese' narratives changed in a generic sense, that is, when the subjects of their interest became 'Western' women. When Zhen located Chinese female heroes in the company of European women-of-the-state like Joan of Arc, Charlotte Corday, and Madame Roland, the effect was to legitimate and universalize *nuzi* within a statist, universal (i.e. Europeanized) world history. Zhen sought to conjoin bourgeois state revolts like the Glorious Revolution, the French and Italian Revolutions, to the expected Chinese Revolution (the Xinhai Revolution occurred a decade later in 1911). Giving such remarkable prominence to Western women in their national revolutions, moreover, granted universality to heroic female actions of whatever kind, at whatever time. Remarkably, the 'Chinese' section of the text went so far as to legitimate Wu Zetian of the Tang dynasty, previously reviled as a female usurper and defiler of her husband's throne. Changes in pro-feminine discourses did condition the form that *nuxing* eventually took. Before the 1920s, however, female heroes continued to rest securely in the inherited binarism familiar from Confucian contexts of hero and the throne. The term *nuxing* (literally, female sex) erupted into circulation during the 1920s when treaty-port intellectuals overthrew the literary language of the Confucius canon. Critics replaced the *wen*/culture of the old world with *wenxue*/literature, inscribed in a hybrid (part colloquial Chinese, part 'European' syntax garnered reading Western fiction in Chinese translation) literary language. *Wenxue* consisted of an appropriated realist representationalism, and thus supported the production of modernist subjectivities. The field of *wenxue* unfolded in the 1920s as a general terrain of combat for intellectuals. The May Fourth Movement of 1919 established *wenxue* as a field of realist referentiality: the second most significant major figure of that new textuality, after the 'hyper-trophied self' of the writer himself, was *nuxing*.[33]

Women did not deploy *nuxing*. Like the recuperation of *nu* as a trope of nationalist universality in masculinist discourse, *nuxing* constituted a discursive sign and a subject position in the larger frames of anti-Confucian discourse. When intellectuals overthrew the Confucius canon they sought the total transformation of 'Chinese culture'. The same modernist revolution that invoked new, modern signs—'society/*shehui*', 'culture/*wenhua*', 'intellectuals/*zhishifenzi*', 'individualism/*geren zhuyi*', and innumerable other Westernized Chinese words—gave *nuxing* or 'Woman' wide discursive powers. *Nuxing* played a particularly significant role in two separate textual streams: literary representation and the body of writing known as Chinese feminism. Historically, women writers did not predominate in either one.[34]

'Historical languages constitute classes', Talal Asad has argued, 'they do not merely justify groups already in place according to universal economic structures.'[35] So *nuxing* coalesced as a category when, as part of the project of social class formation, Chinese moderns disavowed the older literary language of power. After the May Fourth Movement, Chinese writers wrote in a newly modernized, Westernized, semi-colloquial language in which *nuxing* played the part of a subject of representation and an autonomous agent. *Nuxing* operated as one half of the Western, exclusionary, male/female binary. Within the *zhishifenzi* as a class, the sign of the sex binary had enormous utility. *Nuxing* and its correlate *nanxing*, or male sex, acted as a magnet, attracting around its universal, sexological, scientistic core a psychologized personal identity that allowed its possessor to act as the fulcrum for upending Confucianism and all received categories. Chinese translations of European fiction and social theory also relocated agency in the individual at the level of sex-opposition and sex-attraction. In particular, colloquial fiction established sex as the core of an oppositional personal identity and woman as a sexological category.[36]

The career of *nuxing* firmly established a foundational womanhood beyond kin categories. It did so on the ground of European humanism. That is, when it introduced the category of 'woman' as a universal category of *nuxing*, Chinese feminist writing flooded texts with representations of women as the 'playthings of men', 'parasites', 'slaves'; as dependencies of men or simply as degraded to the point of non-existence. Feminist texts accorded a foundational status to physiology and, deploying the Victorian ideology of Europe in the last century, they grounded sexual identity in sexual physiology. Indeed, the most shocking of all of Chinese feminism's arguments substituted sexual desire for reproductive service to *jia* as the foundation of human identity. The secret attraction of European texts was their emphasis on what Foucault termed 'sexuality' as historical artefact. Yet when the leading male feminist Yeh Shengtao spoke of women, even while he granted foundational status to male/female, it was often in terms of Chinese women's lack of personality or human essence.[37] In other words, when Chinese translators invoked the sex binary of a Darwin or an Ellis, they valorized notions of female passivity, biological inferiority, intellectual inability, sexuality, and social absence through reference to the location of these 'truths' in European social scientism and social theory. Thus, Chinese women became Women/*nuxing* only when they become the other of Man in the Victorian binary.[38] Woman was foundational only in so far as she constituted a replication of Man, his other.

Ching-ku Chan's recent exploration of *nuxing* in the literature of major male May Fourth realist writers makes this point at the level of literary texts. When the intellectual or *zhishifenzi* turned to European-style realism, Chan argues, 'the classical mimetic function of realism' required that the writer represent himself through his own representations of the Other, and the Other of male realist choice was Woman. *Nuxing* was first and foremost a trope in the discourses of masculinist Western-inspired realist fiction. As Chan puts it, 'textually speaking', *nuxing* appeared in realist texts, 'but as an innocent scapegoat, paying for the crimes that society has committed'. Indeed, Woman appeared within a cruel equation: 'The root of *your* [female] suffering is to be found in *my* [male writer's] inability to right the wrongs that society has done *me*.'[39]

Chan's point can also be made in a slightly different way. When the modernist female writer Ding Ling began producing texts in the late 1920s she too had to struggle with the self/other dynamic coded into the sex binary Man/Woman. Ding Ling's texts sought to take Woman as a subject position and social psychology. Yet the texts she produced during that period of her career invoke a *nuxing* who either must die, commit suicide, or lose herself in sexual excess and mental disorder. No positivity, no universal Woman independent of Man could exist under the terms of the sex binary. In the end Ding Ling, who continued to write but not as a Woman, simply abandoned psychological realism.[40]

The social history of the trope *nuxing* requires more space than I am allotted here. Once it entered elite *zhishifenzi* discourses, *nuxing* as a representation took on a life of its own. Her image appeared in popular movies, in pulp fiction, in photographs and fashions, schools, and parks. These indigenous representations of *nuxing* constructed a universal category of Woman in the image of an object of consumption, to paraphrase Annette Kuhn, and *nuxing* 'enter[ed] cultural and economic circulation on [its] own accord'.[41] It ceased to be a 'Western' sign, and became a sign of modernity in bourgeois New China. Once recontextualized, the sign Woman/ *nuxing*, had a career and a politics of its own.

PRODUCING *FUNÜ*/WOMEN

The sex binary Man/Woman and the sign Woman/*nuxing* never went uncontested. Carolyn Brown has vividly shown Lu Xun criticizing the initial formulation, arguing that the physical body of modern Chinese women 'had become the repository of a meaning—the signified, that it did not rightfully bear'.[42] Social critique from Chinese Communist Party theorist Xiang Jingyu, who employed *funü*/women as a Marxist trope, contested the pervasive irrationalization of *nuxing*.[43] Xiang lost no time classifying *nuxing* as a product of bourgeois preoccupations, and her comments in the early 1920s set the tone of Communist theorizing for decades. Regardless, Xiang Jingyu's early Communist *funü* entered discourse the same way as sex-opposed *nuxing* had, through *zhishifenzi* appropriation. In the process of transmitting social theory, Communists re-translated out of the European revolutionary heritage the Woman of their political theory as *funü*. The bourgeois social sciences, political rights theory, and nineteenth-century patriarchal-theory left-wing *zhishifenzi*/intellectuals found valuable also shared elements of the sex essentialism manifest in realist fiction. But appropriators shaped their critique to emphasize social production, thus weighing historical and institutional teleology over organic, biogenetic time. Moreover, the *funü*/woman of early Chinese Marxist categories could never exist as more than half of her potential within the all-encompassing revolutionary equation of theory/praxis. So unlike *nuxing*, Marxist *funü* found its referential framework in revolutionary practice and in the historical woman that future world historical teleology would produce.

The Chinese translation of Bebel's *Women and Socialism* established *funü* in its political usage. Its chiliastic tone and the systematic use of *funü* as the figure par excellence of general social revolution relied on a conjuncture of woman and society that attracted Chinese Marxists from the start. Joining it later in CCP theory were Engels's *Origin of the Family, Private Property, and the State*, Lenin's 'Soviet Political Power and Women's Status', 'International Women's Day', and 'On the Freedom to Love', and Stalin's 'International Women's Day'.[44] *Nuxing* had taken over the foundational sex binary Man/Woman from Victorian literary texts and feminist theory in translation. The Communist inscription of *funü* engaged other colonialist discourses, the Euro-Marxist machinery of production/reproduction, teleology, stage theory, state/society binarism and, of course, the discourse's universal, international referentiality.

A social history of Chinese Marxist discourses on *funü* substantiates how thoroughly the history of 'women' in China had by the early 1950s become, for all intents and purposes, a subsidiary to the history of the European working class. Du Zhunhui's 1949 *Funü wenti jianghua* (Lectures on the Woman Problem), exemplified how, when Europe gets placed at the hegemonic centre of 'universal' theories of capital, Chinese history is inevitably reduced to being a subsidiary, local growth, possessing historical significance only as a semicolony of Europe, following a two-thousand-year dark night of 'feudalism'. Significantly, Du's sophisticated historical critique berates the Chinese women's movement's 'failures' measured against the 'universal' European women's movement.[45]

State-building supplanted bourgeois consolidation in both the 'white' as well as the Communist camps, as the Japanese advanced in the late 1930s. Socialist *funü* obviated *nuxing* once the right allowed the discourses of national salvation (*jiuguo*) to fall into the left's special province. The reactionary right rescinded its pallid remaining feminist-rights arguments and dissolved the women's movement into a 'feminine mystique'. Socialist mobilization politics targeted *funü* as a tactical object, eventually a triangulating category mediating modern state and the modern Chinese family. But in the provinces during the late 1920s and 1930s an increasingly Maoist CCP grafted elements appropriated from local categories to its international Marxist teleology of women in social production/reproduction.

'Keep in mind', said a 1932 activists' organizing manual for party cadre doing women's work under the auspices of the Jiangxi Soviet, 'what world revolutionary leader Lenin said [to the effect that] "socialism cannot succeed without the participation of women." At the same time we must keep in mind *that the liberation of Chinese women and the victory of soviet state power are inseparable.*'[46] The Communist party's fugitive state projects ('fugitive' in the sense that during these years the CCP decamped from its various territories) made the *funü* of Chinese Marxism into a category of political praxis. In so doing it reversed and cancelled the earlier relationship of theory and practice.

Thus, the 'universal' woman of Euro-Marxism, an agent in the 'universal' history of capital, not only relinquished her theoretical centrality to the women of practical village mobilizations, but Chinese Communist practices cancelled out the existence of that older European woman and she simply vanished. The peripheralized sign of woman realized its own independent local politics, to put it another way. Context revised text. The Jiangxi Soviet (1930–4), for instance, identified 'woman' as a political subject who was over 14 years of age; had been emancipated from the *tongyangxi*, prostitution, and female slave systems; had recourse from family violence; whose physical body did not bear the marks of 'feudalism' (no ear-rings or footbinding); and named herself as a *funü* in liberating political praxis.[47]

This subject existed inside a structured sphere of politics beyond the rural calendar of fieldwork and beyond village social relations. She laboured according to schedule,[48] and according to protective laws.[49] A rudimentary bureaucracy concerned itself with her welfare,[50] and insured her freedom of marriage.[51] Political networks, such as the Working Women's Congress,[52] operated to rationalize her political outlook.[53] The symbolic centre of this Woman as a subject was undoubtedly the effort to propagandize 'Women's Day'.[54]

Discourse of woman under the fugitive state had a proto-mass-line role that allowed activists, party Central Committee, and local women to speak in different voices and that opened a large range of positions to local people.[55] These included *qingfu*/young women, *ludai de tongyangxi*/oppressed wives by virtue of infant-bride sale, *da pinku laodong funü*/the large suffering masses of labouring women, *nongcun zhong di laodong funü*/labouring women of the rural villages, *nugong nongfu*/women workers and peasants. Even the heterogeneous *funü* of this period, however, was always already a subject-effect of state discourses and a by-product of its legal, ideological, and organizational apparatus. It is just that before 1949 the 'line' did not attempt political closure. *Funü* appeared in it as a range of subject positions inside the Soviet state, beyond the reach of family and feudalism. As one document put it, village women do not understand the agitation for liberation and need to have explained to them the link between victory in class struggle and the liberation of women. They must be taught that their self-interest is connected to the state not the family.[56]

Thus the ideological ideal was a healthy semiliterate woman of 18 to 35 who could 'destroy her familist outlook and serve [the state even when called upon to make] government transfers'.[57] She was expected to act out of self-interest/*benshen liyi* for personal rights/*quanli*,[58] 'representing' herself through grass-roots mass organizational work.[59] The *funü* encountered in these texts, appeared never to have understood what was meant by 'women's self-interest' until propagandists explained the stakes in concrete detail.[60] The natural interests women theoretically possessed, in other words, had first to be inscribed via the actions of recruiting, educating, nurturing, and mobilizing. *Funü*'s proper field was 'the organizational sphere of the party/*dang di zuzhi fanwei*',[61] where she sustained herself in the political space of the CCP through election/*xuanzhi*, mobilization/*dongyuan*, and various organizational/*zuzhi* practices.[62] Maoism in the late 1930s and 1940s constantly reformulated *funü*, always retaining the statist slant.[63] The formula that emerged in the early 1940s, consequently, involved a synecdochic process of exchange between two, interpenetrated, objects of political discourse: the state/*guojia* and the family/*jiating*. Rather than posit independent *funü* as an agent of politics outside domestic closure, as the brief earlier experiments had done, the later Soviets' praxis emphasized production of *funü* through political processes that retained women and men in a sphere of politicized domestic relations.

After 1943 the party's line turned to the transformation of the family itself. By 1947 Maoist state policy had shifted—in contradistinction to Marxist theory and socialist practices elsewhere—toward a reinvented family, which appears in these texts as *jiating*. The homily of the Zhu Fusheng family conference, for instance, treats the 'history' of domestic politics as a party historiographer might chronicle a Central Committee meeting. The women of the Zhu family, though oppressed, did not have the 'habit of democracy, and did not know how to speak, ask questions, or actually say a thing'. After Zhu Fusheng explained democratic procedure to them they collectively transformed themselves from an autocracy/ *jiazhang zhuanzhi* into a 'democratic family/*minzhu jiating*'. In the subsequent months family members instituted political-democratic policies such as self-criticism/*ziwo piping*, domestic production of thread and cloth, and planning, all domestic production activities the CCP promoted at the time. The homily of the Zhu family nicely exhibits how statist political practices interpenetrated family relations, lodging *funü* through democratic rhetoric in a renovated statist *jiating* or nucleating family.[64]

The recuperation required that the politicized new family reconstitute itself in the language of politics. Leading party officials promoted domestic political construction, as Xhou Enlai did, for instance, when he argued that women did not need emancipation from family, that men needed to take family responsibilities as seriously as women.[65] As Patricia Stranahan has argued, it was precisely this reorientation of woman policy that provided the stable base peasant women eagerly accepted; the resulting line both reflected 'peasant realism' and achieved revolutionary transformation through social production.[66] The resulting collaboration of village women and Central Committee, was, I want to stress, neither 'traditional' nor universally 'Marxist'. It was syncretic and as 'modern' as any alternative.[67]

The newly minted Maoist metonymic interpenetration of state/family made the body of women a field of the state at the same time that it opened the state to inflection by kin categories.[68] The entry point was reproductive science. Woman-work/*ganbu*, armed with medical knowledge, brought to political activity the power/knowledge of sanitation, physiology, and scientific midwifery. Texts drilled village women in reproductive physiology ('it's just like your farm animals') and dispensed information on bodily functions like menstrual cycle and hygiene ('don't borrow pads, don't drink cold water, stay away from the dirty menstrual blood that carries disease, don't have intercourse during your period, visit the doctor for irregularities, etc.'). Scientific midwifery connected reproduction to politics.[69]

The dawning of the golden era of Chinese Communist familism in the 1950s found the modern Chinese *jiating* sandwiched between a pre-1949 peasant-inflected formation and idealized revolutionary images flooding in from the more advanced socialist USSR. By that time the *jiating* had become the nineteenth-century Europeanized family of *zhishifenzi* idealization: mommy, daddy, and me.[70] So *jiating* grounded social production in a context heavily marked with traces of older formations, just as the nation did. The modern socialist *jiating* and Maoist *guojia* coexisted in synecdochic unity, as concept metaphors of each other. That, at least, is how I interpret mobilizations like the 1957 campaign 'Industrious and Frugal in Establishing the Nation, Industrious and Frugal in Managing the Family', where state and family are virtually synonymous; what operates in one sphere translates directly into the other.[71] 'The material and cultural life of our state's [guo] masses of people has improved substantially in the last few years. But the lives of many families [jiating] are still not comfortable', the text reads. To raise the jiating's level the masses must 'industriously develop our state's industry and agriculture'. The work of housewives (jiating zhufu) must mirror the work going on outside the jiating, in the guojia. 'Every housewife could be industrious and frugal in managing the family affairs, if she institutionalizes a rational planning schedule. . . . Industriousness and frugality in the family labour strengthens industriousness and frugality in the nation.'[72]

WOMEN'S FEDERATION AND *FUNÜ* AS A STATE CATEGORY

William Parish and Martin Whyte once commented that after socialist Liberation in 1949 the Chinese state took no clear measures to transform family structure, and that Fulian, the state's Women's Federation, was an 'amorphous' government bureaucracy, the only mass organization that people belonged to by virtue of physiology.[73] This does not explain the very real powers of the Women's Federation. The importance of Fulian lay in its power to subordinate and dominate all inscriptions of womanhood in official discourse. It is not that Fulian actually represented the 'interests' of women, but rather that one could not until recently be 'represented' *as a woman* without the agency and mediation of Fulian. That fact is a measure of its success and its importance.[74]

In late 1948 the government commissioned its leading female officials, dignitaries, and luminaries in the Liberated Areas with the task of planning the All-China Democratic Women's Association's (later simply Women's Association) first meeting as soon as Beijing fell.[75] With formal gravity the Planning Committees and Standing Committee began directing the installation of new bureaucratic frameworks charged with deciding national policy and convening the association's first representative congress.[76]

In these initiating moments Fulian consolidated its power as a national, state organ for responsibly representing 'new China's women'. With mechanical deliberation the bylaws connect representation of 'female masses' to the international socialist women's movement, through the accumulating processes of representation.[77] 'What is most deserving of pride', one document read, 'is that the representatives/*daibiao* from the liberated areas are all picked by election from the local area women's congresses. . . . We have been commissioned by the female masses. We must loyally represent their opinions.'[78] And the proviso: 'Representation/ *daibiao* means representing the masses, [it does] not [mean] controlling/*guan* the masses.'[79]

This bureaucratization and Fulian's transformation from active production of *funü* to formally representing them in Beijing relied on past struggle. But it emanated a new sort of definitional power. Representative bodies like congresses and the federation itself did 'represent the masses' but they also consolidated and mediated internal differences/*tuanjiele gezhong butong de funü*, homogenizing, so to speak, through political democracy. The inception of Fulian initiated for '*funü*' unprecedented participation in the rituals of state formation and promised bureaucratic power: but only so long as it, Fulian, the government, retained the power to determine what, in fact, constituted a *funü*.[80]

Deng Yingchao, speaking to this issue, laid out the official view when she argued that Woman in the discourses of the state had achieved 'political, economic, cultural, and social elevation and elevation of herself in the family'.[81] Fulian's charge involved consolidating and expanding the political sphere carved out earlier under the fugitive state: a process, the document argued, that ensured achieved equal status for women by transforming them from consumers into producers.[82] By its third congress Fulian spoke in even broader, less autonomous terms, the gray, ponderous language of the state:

The All-China Women's Federation is, under the leadership of the Chinese Communist party, an organization for the basic organization of every strata of labouring women. [It] has achieved enormous work success since the second National Congress. . . . [But now it] must improve and strengthen its mass viewpoint, and its mass-line work methods . . . be concerned with and reflect the real interests and demands of women, struggle energetically against discrimination and harming of women [etc.] . . . so that Fulian and the mass of women have an even more intimate relationship.[83]

The founding of the Fulian, however, was *not* specific to women.[84] The same ritual unfolded in the mass groups that 'reflected and represented' youth, trade unions, and other politically delineated constituencies. The Fulian organization (and its replicants) took part in a reinscription of the national itself, and thus, it represented at a subordinated level the processes of state-building commencing at levels superior to itself. The socialist state consolidated gender difference on the material grounds of scientific physiology. Part of this scientism, clearly reflected in Fulian documents, is the notion that people are in literal fact material because their organic reproductive capacity makes them like animals.[85] Thus gendering under Maoist inscription located itself as a process of reproductive differentiation within 'scientific socialism'. The fusion of peasant realism and socialist scientism gave rise to texts like 'People and Wealth Flourish/*Ren yu cai wang*', which 'encourage the people of the liberated areas not merely to work hard to get enough to wear and eat, but also to have more children, who, once they are born must be supported/*yanghuo*'. Lyrically conflating 'production' and 'reproduction' the state vowed to train midwives, investigate infant mortality, propagandize for scientific sanitation, oppose feudal superstition, and publish popular chapbooks on infant care, all predicated on popularizing a modern understanding of reproductive physiology and sanitary childbirth practices.

Much work among women aimed at producing people who would collaborate in the biopolitical agenda of the state. Before the twentieth century, birth and death had possessed no direct link to the throne, or to state political economy. Life and death commenced in the spatial boundaries of *jia* or sect and took form as matters of pollution, rupture, reconsolidation.[86] Although late-imperial domestic and popular medical practices regarding menstruation, conception, parturition, suckling, and so on were sophisticated, they participated in the same neo-Confucian epistemic order as gendering—reference to the state through dyadic obligation to Father, Husband, and Monarch. The socialist state, on the other hand, made popular and clear the direct linkage of state's practice and modern obstetric medicine. *Study Guide for the New Woman* straightforwardly declaimed that 'the 27 lessons in this book ... are for the exclusive use of village women in their study/*xuexi*, literacy classes, and political lessons [which the CCP attempted to organize at the village level whenever possible]. It is appropriate as a refresher for teachers and active elements [representing the CCP's agenda at the village level] studying self-discipline'. The book concluded each of its lessons (see 'The *lijiao*/ritual etiquette of the feudal society is the source of women's suffering', for instance) with an attached series of study questions like 'How does the old power of feudalism in your village oppress women?'

Study/*xuexi*, or learning the correct 'line', transmitted physiology as the foundation of gender difference. It inscribed this difference as scientific fact, and understood the base line of reproductive physiology as the basis for the production of male and female. Thus, as has been the case elsewhere, the CCP's statist discourse inserted anatomical difference into a discourse on life and death. It also assumed a binary base (the 'physiology of the human female' versus the 'physiology of the human male') for the reproductive biology that physiology took as its 'scientific' foundation. But the inscription of gender difference at the level of reproductive physiology elided something very interesting. It required material (re)production as site of difference, but it did not reduce personality to physiological terms. In Fulian writing there is a tendency to inscribe difference at the level of physiology while still curtailing attribution of difference at the level of personality. This latter, the realm of feeling and identity, remained, until recently, bound to conventions identified under Maoism in terms of social class, not sex or 'gender'.

It is easier to see the statist construction of *funü* under Maoism in the wake of post-Mao critique. Particularly since 1985 in literary and social science theory, questions of sex and female subjectivity have become explosive.[87] The post-Mao state's efforts to re-establish mass organizations like Fulian brought on an overt conflict between the national subject *funü* and a defiantly sexualized, retheorized *nuxing*. The resurgence of subversive *nuxing* helps clarify the contradictory formation of *nuxing/funü* from a final angle.[88] Under the previous statist protocol, *funü* allowed for the social production of Woman in politics but disallowed any psychology of gender difference. The even older, initial May Fourth literary inscription of *nuxing* made Woman the 'other' of Man, but proved insufficiently stable to resist statist inscriptions of *funü*. The recuperation of *nuxing*'s heterosexist male/female binary does enable difference as 'femininity' and thus provides potential for resistance. Post-Mao *nuxing*, however, renders itself powerless in the face of clearly prejudicial 'scientific' claims to female inferiority.

It is not surprising at all that the most intriguing new, post-Mao critique is not *nuxing* theory but women's studies/*funüxue*. Leading figures in this movement include Deng Weizhi, Li Min, Wang Fukang, and Li Xiaojiang. They and others work as women's advocates in the government, often within the Women's Federation.

Contemporary women's studies scholarship is Marxist, historical, and seeks to resuscitate the Chinese women's movement in extrastatist terms, from a China-centred frame of proletarian revolution to an international frame of human liberation. The subject of women's studies discourse is neither *funü* nor *nuxing* but *nuren* (which I have glossed as woman in social science representation or, *nuren* as a category/*fanchou*).

Tracing a genealogy for the inscription of 'modern Chinese woman' thus has allowed ways of thinking Mohanty's 'historical specificity in the construction of women'. I engaged Gayatri Spivak's question—what narratives produced signifiers for women in another tradition—and can now conclude with Judith Butler's insight that gender is not a relation but an apparatus of production that establishes the 'sexes' as themselves.

Notes

1. Gayatri Spivak, 'The Political Economy of Women', in Elizabeth Weed (ed.), *Coming to Terms: Feminism, Theory, Politics* (New York: Routledge, 1989), 227. An earlier version of this paper appeared in *Genders*, 10 (Spring 1991). Thanks to Mayfair Meihui Yang, Wendy Larson, Charlotte Furth, Renli Wang, Susan Porter Benson, Marilyn B. Young, Judith Farquhar, Inderpal Grewal, and Donald M. Lowe.

2. Judith Butler, *Gender Trouble: Feminism and the Subversion of Identity* (New York: Routledge, 1990), 7, 111.

3. One should, given requisite space, begin with a long discourse on the genealogy of Victorian Woman. (See Denise Riley, *'Am I That Name?': Feminism and the Category of 'Women'* (Minneapolis: University of Minnesota Press, 1988)). But I will not do it here, to some degree for the reason Mary E. John has stated in her 'Postcolonial Feminists in the Western Intellectual Field: Anthropologists *and* Native Informants', *Inscriptions*, 5 (1989).

4. I am indebted to Chandra Mohanty, 'Under Western Eyes: Feminist Scholarship and Colonial Discourses', in *boundary 2*, 12:3; 13:1 (Spring/Fall 1984), and her 'Feminist Encounters: Locating the Politics of Experience', *Copyright*, 1 (Fall 1987): 30–44. The quotation is alas, from neither. The notion of differences without identity is from Donald M. Lowe, *History of Bourgeois Perception* (Chicago: University of Chicago Press, 1982).

5. See Mark Elvin, 'Female Virtue and the State in China', *Past and Present*, 104 (Aug. 1984): 114–52.

6. The word translates as 'state' or as 'nation' depending on context and speaker.

7. Jean-François Billeter, 'The System of Class Status', in S. R. Schram, *The System of State Power in China* (Hong Kong: Chinese University Press, 1985), 138.

8. Chen Hongmou, *Wuzhong yigui* [Five Posthumous Regulations], 'Jiaonu yigui' [Posthumous regulation on educating women]. *Sibubeiyao* edn., iii (n.p., Zhonghua shujyu, n.d.). Henceforth cited as ZNYG.

9. Ibid., Introduction, 1b–2a.

10. Chen Hongmou did not have to provide his readers with charts of differential gendered positions since these constituted local common sense. For a discussion of the textual foundations of the cult of the gendered position and relation see Hsu Dao-lin, 'The Myth of the "Five Human Relations" of Confucious', *Monumenta Serica*, 29 (1970–1).

11. Elizabeth Cowie, 'Woman as Sign', *m/f* 1 (1978): 61–2.

12. Both Judith Butler and Teresa de Lauretis point out that gender for post-Cartesian Western subjects originates on the privileged site of heterosexuality. Indeed, the insight has become a commonplace of much feminist theory. Women become women within the compass of masculine, heterosexual desire. My point in focusing on the *jia* as the privileged site under Confucianism is to suggest: (1) heterosexuality, sexuality as an institution *à la* Foucault, and sexual identity as a European invention have no particular historicity here, and (2) the sexed body of 'Western' gender processes does not serve as the place for gender inscription.

13. Many people have made the point that civilization/*wen* serves as the base of human existence in late dynastic episteme, but none so eloquently as Angela Zito, 'Grand Sacrifice as Text/Performance in Eighteenth Century China' (unpub. Ph.D. diss., Chicago, 1989).

14. The statement is emended and re-romanized from Charlotte Furth's 'Androgynous Males and Deficient Females: Biology and Gender Boundaries in Sixteenth and Seventeenth Century China', in *Late Imperial China*, 9 (Dec. 1988): 1–31.

15. The instance cited could be joined by many more. Gendering proceeded in late-imperial China not at the level of one but in multiple discourses beyond my present scope, many, like *Yi* commentary, not directly addressing immediate persons at all, others placing 'men' in 'female' positions, yet others appropriating 'female' for subversive purpose. Its processes changed under different social and discursive circumstances, and it produced bodily effects—the bound foot, for instance, forever after its infliction marking its possessor's body as feminine. But at no time was gender 'a property of bodies or something originally existent in human beings'; it was always already 'the set of effects produced in bodies, behaviours, and social relations' through deployment of 'complex political technologies'. The first part of the citation is Teresa de Lauretis, 'The Technology of Gender', in *The Technology of Gender* (Bloomington: Indiana University Press, 1987), 3. The second part is Michel Foucault, as cited in de Lauretis, same page.

16. See Manfred Porkert, *The Theoretical Foundations of Chinese Medicine: Systems of Correspondence* (Cambridge, 1985), 22–3, to the effect that while *yang* initiates, *yin* constructs or completes action. The power of the weaker in the dyad 'perfects' or shapes action.

17. Gender is accomplished not so much through female virtues *per se* as through the behaviours of persons in specific subject positions of kin relation. This sense is made explicit in Joseph Lau's discussion of *dayi*/public virtue but is not joined to a general discussion of *ren*/benevolence in 'self'. Tu Weiming provides an important discussion of *ren* in 'The Creative Tension between *Jen* and *Li*', in Tu Weiming, *Humanity and Self-Cultivation in Confucian Thought* (New York: Asian Humanities Press, 1979). But Tu does not talk about women possessing *ren*/benevolence as Joseph Lau does. (For non-Sinologists: *ren* and *jen* are the same word in different systems of romanization.)

18. Chen, *ZNYG*, 15. Emphasis on learning how to act is commonly found in Confucian popular writing on personal behaviour. The locus classicus is the *Lunyu* or Analects in which Confucius responded when asked about government, 'There is government/*zbeng* when the monarch is a monarch, and the minister is minister; when the father is father, and the son is son.' One is not (only) born a son, one becomes a son; one is not born a wife, yet becomes one.
19. Ibid. 15.
20. Thanks to Jing Wang for reminding me of this fact. I am not unaware of the literary tradition that made 'woman' the sign and cause of political instability. I simply think that the genealogy I draw here represents the naturalized base that supports the other, more pointedly misogynist tropes.
21. Chen, 'Song Shanggong *Nulunyu*', in *ZNYG*, 6b.
22. In a larger sense, protocols are similar to what Spivak calls 'regulative psychobiographies' ('The Political Economy of Women', 227). Having reached a similar conclusion independently, I agree with Spivak that the history of women must rely on the excavation of the narratives that have effected our construction, though I regret her choice of the term 'psychobiography', which to me conjures up memories of the 'psychohistory' movement of the 1970s.
23. For discussion of these politics see Roxanne Witke's venerable and still-unsurpassed dissertation, 'The Transformation of Attitudes of Women During the May Fourth Era' (unpubl. Ph.D. diss., University of California, Berkeley, 1970).
24. See my '*Zhishifenzi* [Chinese intellectuals] and Power', *Dialectical Anthropology* (Winter 1990). I argue that peripheralizing signs involved *zhishifenzi* in the appropriation and redeployment of 'modernity' within a representational, nationalist, anti-imperialist economy of representation.
25. See Mary Backus Rankin, 'The Emergence of Women at the End of the Ch'ing', in Margery Wolf and Roxanne Witke (eds.), *Women in Chinese Society* (Stanford: Stanford University Press, 1975); Witke, 'Transformation of Attitudes'; and Li Yunging and Zhang Yufa, *Jindai Zhungguo nuquan yundong shiliao* [Documents on the Feminist Movement in Modern China], i and ii (Taipei: Biographical Literature Publishing Company, 1975).
26. See Charlotte Beahan, 'Feminism and Nationalism in the Chinese Women's Press, 1902–1911', in *Modern China* 1:4 (October 1975); and 'Mothers of Citizens: Feminism and Nationalism in the late Ch'ing' (unpub. paper).
27. *Nuxuebao* [Women's Study Journal], cited in Beahan, 'Feminism and Nationalism', 383.
28. Timothy Brennan, 'The National Longing for Form', in Homi K. Bhabha (ed.), *Nation and Narrative* (London: Routledge, 1990), 44.
29. Beahan, 'Feminism and Nationalism', 384.
30. Zhen Ziyang, *Nuzi xin duben* [New Study Book for Women] (n.p.: 1907, 6th edn.).
31. Ibid. 2, ch. 10, 'Lolan furen' [Madame Roland], 7b–9a.
32. Ibid. ch. 13, 'Fulanzhisi', 10a–12a.
33. I am indebted to Theodore Huters for this phrase. The production of subjectivities in modern literary texts is developed very nicely in Wendy Larson, *Literary Authority and the Chinese Writer: A Study of Early Twentieth Century Chinese Writers* (Durham, NC: Duke University Press, 1991).
34. Tani E. Barlow, *Imagining Woman: Ding Ling and the Gendering of Chinese Modernity* (forthcoming, Duke University Press).

35. Talal Asad, 'Are There Histories of People Without Europe: A Review Article', *Comparative Study of Society and History*, 29 (July 1987), 606.
36. Mei Sheng, *Zhongguo funü wenti taolunji* [General discussion of the Chinese women's question] (Shanghai: Wenhua Books, 1929). The compendium of key articles allows the reader a marvellous overview of the debate on feminism.
37. Barlow, *Imagining*.
38. Ibid. ch. 2, 'Chinese Feminism'.
39. Ching-ku Stephen Chan, 'The Language of Despair: Ideological Representations of the "New Women" [*xin nuxing*] by May Fourth Writers', in Tani E. Barlow (ed.), *Gender Politics in Modern China: Feminism and Literature* (Durham, NC: Duke University Press, forthcoming).
40. Tani E. Barlow, 'Feminism and Literary Technique in Ding Ling's Early Work', in *Women Writers of Twentieth-Century China* (Eugene: Asian Studies Publications, University of Oregon, 1982).
41. Annette Kuhn, *The Power of the Image* (London: Routledge and Kegan Paul, 1985), 19, cited in Linda Hutcheon, *The Politics of Postmodernism* (London: Routledge, 1989), 22.
42. Carolyn T. Brown, 'Woman as a Trope: Gender and Power in Lu Xun's "Soap"', in Barlow, (ed.), *Gender Politics in Modern China*.
43. See Suzanne Leith, 'Chinese Women in the Early Communist Movement', who summarizes three articles: *Zhungguo zhishi funü di sanpai* [Three groups of educated women], *Zhungguo zuijin funü yungdong* [The contemporary Chinese women's movement], and *Shanghai nuquan yundong zhihou ying shudi sanjian* [Three things the Shanghai women's rights movement should concentrate on]. In Marilyn Young (ed.), *Women in China* (Ann Arbor: Michigan Papers in Chinese Studies, 1973), 50–1, 61.
44. The references are in order of citation: Beibeier [Bebel], *Funü yu shehui* [Woman and Society], Shen Ruixian, trans. (Shanghai: Kaiming Books, 1949); *Makesi, Liening, Engesi, Sidalin lun funü jiefang* [Marx, Lenin, Engels, and Stalin on Women's Liberation]; ed. Chinese Democratic Women's Association (Hong Kong: New People's Press, 1949), 1–38; *Makesi, Engesi, Liening, Sidalin lun Funü Jiefang* [Marx, Engels, Lenin, Stalin on Women's Liberation]; ed. Fulian (Beijing: Renmin Press, 1949). This collection has a slightly different composition. See p. 39 for Stalin's 'International Women's Day'.
45. Du Zhunhui, *Funü wenti jianghua* (Lectures on the Woman Problem] (Hong Kong: New China Books, 1949). The argument is a straight Marxist narrative that classifies China as an interminably feudal country. Du's strength is her insistence that '*funü*' is a social category.
46. Jiangxi Women's Association (ed.), *Jiangxi suchu funnu yundong shiliao xuanpian* [Selected materials for the Jiangxi Soviet women's movement], 1932.3.2/2, 53–4. It is absolutely true if you read the statement literally.
47. Ibid. 21.
48. Ibid. 1931.11, items 1–7, 38.
49. Ibid. 1931.12, 231. Considering the situation, this seems totally inappropriate.
50. Ibid. 1932.2.1, 46.
51. See ibid. 1932.2, 52, for the statement that 'marriage is a relationship of two persons, male and female'.
52. Ibid. 1932.2.1, 43.
53. Ibid. 1932.1.2, 44–5. This is a splendid document detailing instructions

governing women's organizations. It clarifies how model organizers in the women's work movement establish proper form, possess pre-established work plans, fix topics for each meeting (for instance, 'opposing feudal bonds', or 'enlisting men, comforting troops, doing mass work, getting literature', etc.).

54. See ibid. 1932.3.2, 53, and many other subsequent documents. Women's Day and propaganda of the marriage law are the two major work areas for *ganbu* (cadres) undertaking women's work. 1933.2.7 uses it to demonstrate why Woman is connected to state and suggests that workers use magazines, newspapers, and storytellers to spread the word. The effort is also reflected in regional document 1933.2.10, 77.

55. The provisional nature of the laws and the multiplicity of voices are clear in 1932.6.20, 60–5, which talks about the resistance to certain laws, and the resistance to others. Its self-critical tone is significant.

56. Ibid., stipulation 5 in part 2.

57. Ibid. 1933.8.31, 104.

58. Ibid. 'Provisional Central Government's Announcement Instructions to the People's Committees as regards Protecting Women's Rights and Establishing Women's Life Improvement Committees, Organizations, and Work'.

59. Ibid. 1933.3.14, 87. The document gives instructions on the mechanics of representation. For example, set a time for a conference, locate the labouring women's Congress inside the system of other mass organizations, recruit according to certain forms, get 10 to 20 women, establish a representative, elect a presidium, etc., capped by a party member, and so on. See p. 88 for a good discussion of how representation works.

60. 1933.6.25, 95, suggests that quite strongly.

61. Ibid. 90.

62. Ibid. 1933.3.28, 89.

63. See Patricia Stranahan, *Yan'an Women and the Chinese Communist Party* (Berkeley: Center for Chinese Studies Press, 1983) and 'Labor Heroines of Yan'an', *Modern China*, 7/1 (Jan. 1981).

64. Lu Fu (pseud.), *Xinfunü duben* [New Woman's Study Book] (Hong Kong: Xinminshu Press, 1949), 60–1.

65. Zhou Enlai, 'Lun xianqi liang mu yu muzhi' [On virtuous wife, good mother, and the mother's responsibility], *Jiefang Ribao* [Liberation Daily], 20 Nov. 1942. Zhou argued that not just mothers but fathers, too, had a substantial political obligation to be the best parents possible. This was the founding statement from on high; ever after, kin-style protocols made their presence known within liberated constructs.

66. See Stranahan, *Yan'an Women and the Chinese Communist Party*, 63–86. This is the single best empirical documentary study available in English. Stranahan argues that, in fact, given the context, CCP post-1942 policy on women's affairs was remarkably fair and probably productive both in party terms and in the view of the women policy that was effected. See also Phyllis Andors, *The Unfinished Liberation of Chinese Women, 1949–1980* (Bloomington: Indiana University Press, 1983) and 'Studying Chinese Women', *Bulletin of Concerned Asian Scholars* (Oct.–Dec. 1975).

67. See the case histories and subject biographies in the Fulian (ed.), *Zhongguo jiefangchu nongcun funü fanshen yundong sumiao* [A rough sketch of the fanshen movement among rural women in the liberated regions of China] (n.p.: Xinhua Books, 1949).

68. Fulian (ed.), *Zhongguo jiefanchu funnu canzhan yundong* [Political participation movement of the women of the Chinese liberated areas] (Hong Kong: New Peoples Press (date not available)), 7–11.
69. See Lu Fu, *Xinfunü duben* [New Woman's Study Book], 74–80, particularly the chapter 'Women yao yanjiu xin fajiesheng' [We want to study new methods for assisting in childbirth], 78–80.
70. This at least is how I interpret the writing on love and family construction that appeared in the 1950s. See, for example, Dan Fu, *Mantan liangxing guanxi zhong de daode wenti* [Conversation about moral questions concerning relations between the sexes] (Shanghai: Xuexi Shenghuo Press, 1956). Also see Li Di, *Zhufu shouji* [Handbook for housewives] (Beijing: Tongsu weni Press, 1955).
71. Fulian (ed.), *Zhongguofunü disansi quanguo daibiao dahui zongyao wenxuan* [Selected key documents of the Third National Congress of Chinese Women] (Beijing: Zhongguo Funü Zazhi Press, 1958), 27.
72. Ibid. 2.
73. William Parish and Martin Whyte, *Village and Family in Contemporary China* (Chicago: University of Chicago Press, 1978), 39.
74. For information on founding and early propaganda/literary outreach, see Elizabeth Croll, *Feminism and Socialism in China* (London: Routledge and Kegan Paul, 1978); E. Croll, *The Women's Movement in China: A Selection of Readings, 1949–1973* (London: Anglo-Chinese Educational Institute, Modern China Series, no. 6 (1974)); Vibeke Hemmel and Pia Sindbjergh, *Women in Rural China: Policy Towards Women Before and After the Cultural Revolution* (Curzon: Scandinavian Institute of Asian Studies, no. 7 (1984)).
75. These luminaries and dignitaries were, in descending order, Cai Chang, Deng Yingchao, Zhang Chinqiu, Li Dechuan, Chen Shaomei, Kang Keqing, DIng Ling, and Ho Xiangning. Fulian (ed.), *Quanguo funü diyici quanguo daibiao dahui* [First Congress of the All-China Women's Association] (Hong Kong: Xinmin Press, 1949), 102–8. The only real surprise here is Ding Ling, who, it will be recalled, had been purged from her women's work following the publication of her 'Thoughts on March 8' essay in 1942. To my knowledge there is no history of the Women's Association presently available.
76. Ibid. 5.
77. Ibid., *Zhonghua quanguominzhu funü lianhohui zhangcheng* [Regulations of the All-China Democratic Women's Association] and its various articles of incorporation, provisions, and systems, 94–100.
78. Ibid. 20–1.
79. Ibid. 'Linqiu funü daihiaohui jieshao' [An Introduction to the Linqiu County Women's Association], 73.
80. Ibid. 73–4.
81. Ibid. 28.
82. Ibid. 31. I quote this slogan because it is so outrageous. How Chinese women became 'consumers' in the rhetorics of state discourse before there was anything to consume is suggestive, to say the least.
83. Fulian (ed.), *Selected Key Documents of the Third National Congress*, 3.
84. Nor, of course, was inscription as *funü* exclusionary, since a woman could at the same time be inscribed as 'youth', as 'worker', and as 'daughter of a revolutionary martyr'.
85. See David Kwok's underused and very keen book, *Scientism in Chinese Thought* (Berkeley: University of California Press, 1965).

86. See Emily Martin [Ahern], 'The Power and Pollution of Chinese Women', in Wolf and Witke, (eds.), *Women*.

87. For instances of literary representations see Wang Zheng, 'Three Interviews', *Modern Chinese Literature* 4:1 and 2 (1988 (1990)) for Dai Qing's and Wang Anyi's discussions about sexuality in their work. The concluding arguments are taken from my article 'Politics and Protocols of *funü*: (un)Making the National Woman', forthcoming in Gail Hershatter *et al.* (eds.), *Engendering China* (Harvard University Press, 1993).

88. For a succinct formulation of this contradictory relation of feminism/Asian women, see Aihwa Ong, 'Colonialism and Modernity: Feminist Re-Presentations of Women in Non-Western Societies', *Inscriptions*, 3/4 (1988). Lydia Liu suggests that this disdain may have more to do with popular loathing of Fulian than real antagonism toward 'feminism'.

Part II. **Gender**

'Women's History' in Transition: The European Case

Natalie Zemon Davis

The genre of women's history is no newcomer on the scene. In one form it goes back to Plutarch, who composed little biographies of virtuous women, intended to show that the female sex could and should profit by education. Taken up again by Boccaccio in the fourteenth century, the collective memorials of 'Women Worthies' continued in an unbroken line—from the *City of Ladies* of Christine de Pisan through Madame Briquet's 1804 *Dictionary . . . of French Women . . . known for their Writings*; from the seventeenth-century *Gynaikeion* of Thomas Heywood to the eighteenth-century *British Ladies . . . Celebrated for their Writings* of George Ballard. Sometimes the subjects had talents in many fields; other times they were all religious, as in Osbern Bokenham's medieval *Legends of Hooly Wommen*; or all literary; or all political, as in the *Lives of the Queens of England* by the Victorian Strickland sisters.[1] Some studies were seriously researched; others mixed the mythical with the real. But all of them had a polemical purpose: to disclose the range of female capacity, to provide exemplars, to argue from what some women had done to what women could do, if given the chance and the education. Indeed, a certain part of women's history today is still in the tradition of Women Worthies.

Now, however useful and hopeful was this body of literature, it had its limitations. Establishing the record of female activity in the past, it nevertheless wrenched it from its historical context. Treating women in isolation from men, it ordinarily said little about the significance of sex roles in social life and historical change. And written with special goals for a special audience, it had little effect on the main body of historical writing or periodization.

The second early form of women's history was the biography of

The research for this paper was aided by a Humanities Research Fellowship given by the University of California, Berkeley. Reprinted with permission from *Feminist Studies*, 3:3/4 (Spring/Summer 1976), 83–103.

the individual woman—the religious or political luminary. The nun Baudonivia wrote about her queen, the Merovingian Radegundis; the royal herald William Camden wrote about his queen, Elizabeth I; in the seventeenth century a French religious of the Visitation composed the life of her foundress Saint Jeanne de Chantal. On occasion, the religious biographies fanned out into institutional histories of a whole house or order, as with Hroswitha's history of the Abbey of Gandesheim and Chaugy's *Lives* of the nuns of the Visitation, thus providing the first European accounts of female collective experience and association.[2] The study of individual lives was the more frequent form, however, and it had the advantage over that of the Women Worthies in being able to embed a woman more carefully in her culture and society. For instance, Marie Thiroux d'Arconville's three-volume *Life of Marie de Médicis*, published in 1774, was based on extensive work in Parlementary registers and manuscripts in the Bibliothèque royale, as well as in printed sources. She even noted non-political changes in custom, such as the queen's being delivered by a midwife rather than by the male *accoucheur* who served aristocratic women at that time.[3]

On the other hand, the biographical form did not of itself prompt speculation on sex roles, except in so far as it accepted woman as a significant public actor. For Thiroux d'Arconville, *Marie de Médicis* was a device for talking about the history of France in the early seventeenth century. Gender was at issue for the female historian only in summing up the queen's political style: 'This Princess had all the faults of her sex and none of the qualities fit to further her ambition. . . . How dangerous and imprudent it is to want to rule others when one is incapable of governing oneself'.[4] The biography has, of course, continued to be a major mode for presenting women in history. Extended finally to a wide range of public figures, such studies are still sometimes inattentive to how sex roles may shape a career (for example, J. B. Nettl's otherwise admirable life of Rosa Luxemburg), while others (for example, recent work on Jeanne d'Albret and Mary Wollstonecraft) now make it a major question.[5]

If certain ways of conceiving women's history are very old, transitions in that subject have also occurred well before our time. I am thinking of the work of late eighteenth- and nineteenth-century writers in expanding the boundaries of social history so as to include subjects in which the activities of women, or of women and men together, could not fail to be considered explicitly: studies of the labouring poor, of the past and present of prostitution, and of private law; and collections by antiquarians and folklore societies of old customs and rites in regard to marriage and other stages of life.[6]

More important, however, was the gradual realization that the institution of the family and the relations between the sexes should not be perceived as essentially unchanging features of the European past. Rather they had varied appreciably, along with political, economic, or cultural changes. The reasons for this new perception are several, and we cannot dwell on them here,[7] but it took hold among both supporters and opponents of the patriarchal family. Thus at the end of the eighteenth century the somewhat sentimental Scottish physician William Alexander wrote a work entitled *The History of Women from the Earliest Antiquity to the Present Time*; and at the end of the nineteenth century the suffragette Georgiana Hill published her *Women in English Life from Medieval to Modern Times*. The philologist and folklorist Karl Weinhold, in the course of the Revolutions of 1848, composed his *German Women in the Middle Ages* and saw the 'womanly heart' and the family as the hope of the German future. The patriarchal Charles de Ribbe, in the France of the Third Republic, wrote his nostalgic but quite well documented *Families and Society . . . before the Revolution*.[8] J. J. Bachofen and Friedrich Engels developed their diverse theories of the stages of human history, in which the relations between the sexes and/or sexual traits are central to the characterization of each period.[9] And finally, in the last decades of the century and in the years up to and just after World War I, a set of serious monographs appeared in Germany, Italy, France, and England, in which the status, activities, and consciousness of women are examined—and not always just of upper-class women—for a manageable period, such as the Middle Ages or the Renaissance.[10]

I can find no better way to introduce and assess our own current 'transition in women's history' than to examine two of the best products of that earlier achievement. One of them is *Working Life of Women in the Seventeenth Century* (1919) by the Fabian socialist Alice Clark, research student at the London School of Economics. Writing under the inspiration of Olive Schreiner's *Women and Labour* (1911), Clark had help from a cluster of female scholars— the economic historian Lillian Knowles, the medievalist Eileen Power, and M. Dorothy George—and money from Mrs George Bernard Shaw.[11] The other work is *La femme et le féminisme en France avant la Révolution* (1923) by the French Jew Léon Abensour, who intended, as he said, 'to take female activity of the eighteenth century away from the level of anecdote and scandal and place it in the mainstream of history'. This was not such an easy task. Professor of history and geography at the Lycée Voltaire in Paris, Abensour received encouragement from his literary friends, but evidently had no connection with the men who were to found the *Annales* a few years later. Though Henri Berr had accepted an article on early feminist thought in France for his *Revue de synthèse historique* in 1906, nothing substantial on women appeared again till 1929. Lucien Febvre's interest in the history of women seems to have been aroused only in the 1940s.[12]

What then did Clark and Abensour do and how would we do it differently? In the first place, they went to the sources—not just to the printed courtesy books, the pamphlets on the female sex, the agricultural manuals and the letters and memoirs of aristocratic women, but also to archival materials: local judicial, financial, and administrative records and, for the English historian, local account-books as well.[13] However much the written records of pre-industrial Europe may underrepresent the female (along with the peasant, the poor, the illiterate, and the young of both sexes), Clark and Abensour were rightly dazzled by the wealth of the material they found on women of all classes; and they had not even yet turned to the marriage contracts, wills, parish and hospital records which nourish so much of the research of social historians today.

Second, Clark and Abensour did not refer generally to 'women' when a process or event they were describing involved only one social group. Clark spelled out the differences among her working women, from midwives and merchants through agricultural labourers, while Abensour gave separate consideration to the women of the courtly and provincial nobility, of the 'bourgeoisie' and of artisanal and peasant families.

Third, neither historian assumed that laws regarding marriage, guild regulations, informal prescriptions, rules of social intercourse, and other 'images' of women necessarily showed what female behaviour was really like. Indeed, a major argument of Abensour was that the legal tutelage of propertied women to their husbands in the eighteenth century and their legal exclusion from most forms of politics were in fact undermined by the considerable informal power that aristocratic women possessed in private life and in political discussion and patronage.

Next, both historians had some kind of theory to account for the changing relations of women to power, work, and property. Clark's view was by far the more interesting. A woman's independence, she thought, was a function of the full realization of her productive powers, biological, educational, and economic. In the centuries before industrial capitalism and the commercialization of agriculture on a large scale, such independence was enjoyed by all but a handful of impoverished wage earners at the bottom of society and of parasites at the top. Most women were contributing essential support to their families, providing them with food and clothing and producing and/or selling goods for local markets. The widely accepted belief in the subjection of the wife to the husband did not lead to serious oppression, so Clark argued, as long as the wife's work was respected and she and her husband made up a community in which work and wages were shared. Then, with capitalism, the wives of prosperous merchants and farmers withdrew from productive activity and became dependent on their husbands. With capitalism, Clark went on, the small female farmer lost her cow and vegetable garden; manufacture was removed from her household to the factory; the family income was replaced by the individual wage; and the skilled and decently paying employments went to men. Married women of the lower classes either could find no work or had to take it at extremely low wages. Their ability to bring children into the world diminished with their economic productivity.

Now surely there is much to criticize in Clark's theory. For instance, as I put together my own research with that of E. Le Roy Ladurie, Pierre Goubert, and Olwen Hufton, female wage-earners emerge as a much larger sector of the pre-industrial economy than Clark imagined, part of the female labour force making up, together with unskilled males, a kind of preproletariat.[14] Further, as Joan Scott and Louise Tilly are showing, concern for family and the sharing of wages persisted well beyond the initial stages of industrialization. Nevertheless, Clark's view continues to be helpful in understanding the withdrawal of middle-class women from work outside the home and the eventual constriction of opportunities for women in industry. It was also a surprising anticipation of recent studies of the impact of so-called modernization on the economic position of women in black Africa.[15]

And finally, in my observations on Clark and Abensour, they respected their subjects, treating them neither as passive victims of historical injustice nor as constant heroines struggling to change society. It is true that Clark sometimes wrings her hands about Capitalism as the ruin of the working woman, as if she were Pamela Andrewes expecting the worst; and Abensour sometimes talks of 'the magnificent display of feminine energies for the service of fatherland and the freeing of women',[16] as if he were given a 14th of July oration. But ordinarily, their women are resourceful human beings, some failing, some fighting, most of them coping as best they could to survive with their families whatever the odds.

These are solid achievements in these books of fifty years ago. We are all disappointed that some of our present-day production in women's history still does not match them in methodology and analysis. Nevertheless, the last fifteen years have seen improvement in the study of sex roles. Let me consider a few of the ways we would want to rewrite Clark and Abensour. Neither of them devoted any attention to the demographic questions about which the French and English schools of population study have now told us so much—about life expectancy, age at marriage, rates of fertility, intervals between births, patterns of geographical mobility, and the like. Clark would indeed have had to modify her argument about the productive power of seventeenth-century working women, for it rested on the explicit assumption that their rate of fertility was *the same* as that of aristocratic women.[17]

In fact, in most regions of Western Europe in the seventeenth century, upper-class women differed from women of the lower orders both in regard to their 'natural' fertility and in regard to limitation of fertility. Few women anywhere could rival Lady Ann Fanshawe's record of eighteen pregnancies in twenty-one years, but on the whole women from aristocratic and wealthy families did give birth more frequently than women of artisanal and peasant families. Poor women married later and died earlier than rich ones; later marriage by itself need not cut down female fertility (as recent studies have shown), but poor mothers were less likely to live out their child-bearing years. Furthermore, aristocratic and wealthy women conceived more often because they put their babies to wet-nurse. In contrast, until the eighteenth century women from artisanal families usually nursed their own babies (it was the orphans and foundlings among the city poor who were wet-nursed), while mothers in the countryside always preferred to nurse their own children and sometimes other people's besides. Perhaps too, a less adequate food supply and greater vulnerability to disease increased the incidence of amenorrhea and natural abortion among poorer women.[18]

At any rate, by the end of the seventeenth century, married women in peerage families in France and among the urban elite in Geneva were taking steps with their husbands—not by resuming breast-feeding, but by some adjustment in the frequency or in the practice of intercourse—to limit their fertility once they had, say, enough living male children to count on an heir. Women in poorer families, where conceptions were less frequent and where more children died early, had such a choice to make less often. Increasingly in the eighteenth century, the unwanted child of an indigent married couple might be left at the foundling hospital.[19]

Both Clark and Abensour talked about the family and marriage, of course, but primarily in terms of the legal position of the woman and her property, the doctrine of subjection, and the work arrangements of the spouses. While valuable research continues on these questions, some historians have gone on to consider the functions and size of dowry, patterns of inheritance, the relations of families to their kin, the strength of family sentiment, and the varied relations between the generations.[20] To take but one example, the results of research on household size have exploded the old generalization about the historical transition in Europe from what was called 'the extended family' to 'the nuclear family'—a generalization which has left its mark on thinking about female labour and associational life. It is now clear that the nuclear family, augmented by servants (even quite modest rural families would have a teenaged girl living in, perhaps a relative, perhaps not), was the prevalent form of household in Western Europe from at least the late Middle Ages on; but that it readily expanded on occasion to include other kin. When economic, fiscal, or personal considerations required it, grandparents or a widowed grandparent, parents, and young children might live together—or parents and their married children—for a few years of the life cycle. When the labour supply was short, as in the Languedoc in the fifteenth century, brothers might live together with their families to work the land.[21] Whether any individual family 'breathed' in this fashion depended on several things, such as the longevity of grandparents and spouses, the remarriage of widows or widowers, and the occupations and geographical mobility of children. All of these patterns need to be examined for their implications for women, for ties among mothers, daughters, and siblings, and for the mobility and dependency of women.

This brings me to a third way in which our study of women's history differs from that of Clark and Abensour: we want to reckon more than they did. To their impressionistic sampling of, say, wages or numbers of parish schools, we are finally adding statistics not only on demography, but on the sex variable in migration,[22] in crime,[23] and in literacy,[24] to mention only a few. Some of these studies move beyond figures to remarkable analysis, as in Nicole

Castan's examination of 500 cases appealed to the Parlement of Toulouse in the late seventeenth and early eighteenth centuries; there she shows how a narrowly defined concept of feminine honour gave licence to the woman of the lower orders to insult, speak out, threaten, strike back, dissemble and do other acts which would imperil her husband's 'dignity' if he performed them.[25] Much still remains to be done, however, in areas which can combine qualitative and qualitative work. There exist, for example, no published long-term series of female wages (in cash or in food and cash) from the late Middle Ages to the nineteenth century, though scattered European evidence suggests that the ratio of female to male wages varied in interesting ways from period to period and from place to place, and not merely in response to market conditions.[26]

In the fourth place, these older works on women offered little or nothing about their sexual or erotic activity. Abensour was perhaps trying to break with the old tradition of scandalous anecdote. Clark, in a book on the working life of women, did not say a word about prostitution, her omission perhaps explained by the particularly moralistic character of her feminism. At any rate, these matters engage us a great deal nowadays, for what they can tell us both about intimate relations between and within the sexes and about patterns of culture and social organization more generally. For the medieval and early modern periods, most of the novel and reliable research that has been published is still limited to *attitudes*: attitudes toward sexual intercourse, contraception, and fornication in the canon law, in Puritan sermons, in literary works, utopias, and the like.[27] On attitudes toward homosexuality and lesbianism and on the laws regarding adultery, we still need a set of well-documented monographs. The same is true for the history of prostitution, where new research is now being done by Jacques Rossiaud, who has found interesting evidence of collective rape and intercourse with prostitutes as alternate forms of sexual initiation for young males in south-eastern French cities in the late Middle Ages; by Marie Benabou, who is completing a *thèse* on *Libertinage, prostitution et police des moeurs* in Paris in the eighteenth century; and by Judith Walkowitz, who is depicting prostitution as a stage of life for single working women living in lodging-houses in nineteenth-century England.[28]

As for other sexual behaviour, some helpful studies have been made for nineteenth- and twentieth-century Germany, England, and France, though it is not yet clear whether the trend (aside from the poor joyless middle class) was toward greater expression or greater repression. A fresh investigation of sexual behaviour in the medieval and early modern period has just begun, with some interesting figures on consensual unions in the fourteenth and late eighteenth centuries and on illegitimacy from the late sixteenth century on.[29] Much can be uncovered, however—as is shown in a recent publication by Jean-Louis Flandrin—in a systematic search of medical literature, the judicial records of various religious and secular courts, notarized arbitration contracts between unmarried sexual partners for the support of the pregnant mother, and the abundant materials on folk customs, sanctions and ritual.[30]

The evidence so far suggests that Edward Shorter is wrong in maintaining that most European women did not have orgasms until industrialization revved up their engines. How can we imagine masses of frigid women and indifferent men in the earlier period, when we can document from the thirteenth through the eighteenth centuries a widespread belief that both females and males had to have orgasms in order for the woman to conceive?[31] When medical doctors and village midwives thought men and women needed a certain amount of sexual intercourse for good health? ('It rejoices the heart, makes breathing freer, chases melancholy, assuages sadness . . . and brings sleep to those who have long lain awake', prescribed one seventeenth-century physician.)[32] When the vernacular vocabularies of Europe to the eighteenth century were so rich and comic in terms for coition and sexual play, and peasant proverbs turned so easily to imaginative sexual metaphor to make their point?[33]

What may distinguish the sexual experience of the earlier period from that of the nineteenth and twentieth centuries is something analogous to the contrast between medieval Catholicism and Calvinism. In the earlier period there is a blurring of the boundary between the sexual and the non-sexual, a partial suffusion of everyday life with sexual feeling. At the same time, within a context of irregularity in women's periods and uncertainty about conception and survival, sexual action is articulated into myriad steps, to be taken one by one, and constrained to flow, like ritual, only at certain times of the woman's month, or of the agricultural season or the sacred calendar. Like religion, sex can be enjoyed that way. The modern organization of sex hardens the boundary between the sexual and the non-sexual. And within a context of more regular expectations about the conditions of life and its creation, it simplifies the steps toward the genital goal and allows sexual action to flow more evenly during the year, timed more by the choices of the partners to turn themselves on or off.[34] These would, at any rate, be fruitful hypotheses for research.

Finally, in contrasting the work of Clark and Abensour of five decades ago with what I take to be our best present course, I think our goals are or should be more general and more sweeping than theirs. They wrote mostly about women; so too do we, to rectify the deep and longlasting bias of the historical record. They wanted to make the relations between the sexes more just; so, too, do many of us, though it is no more true today than in the nineteenth century that all practitioners of women's history have the same political hopes. But it seems to me that we should be interested in the history of both women and men, that we should not be working only on the subjected sex any more than an historian of class can focus exclusively on peasants. Our goal is to understand the significance of the *sexes*, of gender groups in the historical past. Our goal is to discover the range in sex roles and in sexual symbolism in different societies and periods, to find out what meaning they had and how they functioned to maintain the social order or to promote its change. Our goal is to explain why sex roles were sometimes tightly prescribed and sometimes fluid, sometimes markedly asymmetrical and sometimes more even.

Unlike the compilation of Women Worthies, this is a relatively new goal for historians. Thus it should make some changes in the practice of the field at large. Just as the extension of motivational psychology to the female case should lead to some kind of reassessment of the significance of the achievement motive in everyone;[35] just as the extension of economic analysis to 'women's work' should call forth a redefinition of 'labour-force' and market measures of value, so too the study of sex roles should modify some of the historian's rules. It should become second nature for the historian, whatever her or his speciality, to consider the consequences of gender as readily, say, as those of class. (I hope five years from now historians will not use the term 'Renaissance individualism' to describe social, economic, or political activities that were undertaken—and thought at the time to be undertaken—by males acting on behalf of their families or households.)[36] The study of sex roles should stretch the interdisciplinary training of its practitioners, to the general benefit of the profession. It should also make available to the profession at large new bodies of source material. I wonder how many historians of agriculture know, for instance, that as late as the nineteenth century in France menstruating women had to be kept away from the wine harvest and wine-pressing, lest they turn the wine sour, or that they were paraded through the fields when there was a plague of insects because of their power to destroy grasshoppers and locusts.[37]

Especially important, the study of the sexes should help promote a rethinking of some of the central issues faced by historians—power, social structure, property, symbols, and periodization.

The nature of power: as with work on the lower classes, slave populations and peasants, work on relations between the sexes makes the location of power a trickier business than when one is looking at governments, parties, factions, and clientage systems. Power can lodge in dangerous nooks and crannies, as our menstruating pest-killers suggest. It can be informal, unpredictable, unaccountable, frittered away, or saved for important occasions. It needs to be examined in its full complexity.

The nature of social structure: all the recent debates on the criteria for social stratification and on societies of orders as opposed to societies of classes have been concerned to locate males as heads of families on some kind of one- or two-dimensional chart. The contribution of women to that position, when it is considered at all, is usually confined to the advantages or disadvantages that dowry and family alliances may bring. But anyone concentrating on women is likely before long to ask to what extent, even in societies which seem to assign all prestige to male occupations, certain attributes of the females in a family (their literacy, their occupations, their standing among women, and the like) may be affecting the family's economic and social position. Furthermore, anyone concentrating on women is likely to wonder whether a multidimensional charting of social structure—one that would give expression, say, to the relations male/female and clergy/lay—would not be preferable to the simpler models we are using.[38]

Third, the study of gender groups extends notions of property and exchange to a new good—sex—ordinarily property and exchange in women. How and why these function in the European case is still far from clear. Is the control of access to women a matter of trying to guarantee legitimate heirs and lines of descent? Or is copulation truly the core of personal honour? Or is it a matter of exchanging women between families (as Lévi-Strauss claims) so as to procreate and produce social solidarity without incest? Or rather (as I think) are sexual property and exchange available for multiple purposes, including economic ones, and to both sexes, their use depending on the historical context? Answers to this hard question will come only from many well-designed projects on topics ranging from bride price and dowry to marriage pools and the double standard. In the meanwhile to whet your appetite, I recommend Bridget O'Laughlin's recent African case-study of bride-wealth, 'Why Mbum Women Do Not Eat Chicken'.[39]

O'Laughlin's chicken turns out to be metaphoric for women, and this takes me to another area in which the study of gender groups can promote new reflection: the social and cultural function of symbols. Since the contrast female/male is universal in our species, sexual symbols and symbolic behaviour based on sex are always easily available for making statements about nature and human experience. The question is what do they mean? Some scholars seem to think that they literally reflect and prescribe the position and behaviour of the sexes. An abundance of female goddesses in a society means women have the power there; a woman-conceiving-a-baby as a symbol of passivity means that women in that society are in fact passive, erotically and otherwise. But this relation between symbol and behaviour is usually much too simple. Anthropologists find that societies with many female goddesses may have women contributing heavily to agriculture or have matrilineal descent systems, but they do not have all-female or matriarchal rule. Brothers or certain other males continue to have some authority. Societies with symbols of female passivity, such as early modern Europe, may also be well supplied with symbols of female activity and violence.[40]

Thus the connection between sexual symbols and the actual behaviour of females and males, though surely real, is complex. What seems most likely is that they are used to describe or evaluate situations or kinds of experience, but a situation described, say, by a male symbol may still involve participants of both sexes. For instance, Eric Wolf in an analysis of the symbol of the Virgin Mary in the Middle Ages suggests that it expresses the private realm of kin and friends as opposed to the masculine public and political sphere. The anthropologists Michelle Rosaldo and Louise Lamphere have generalized this, arguing that the opposition female/male:domestic/public is found in all societies. Sherry Ortner has offered a related, but somewhat different polarity in her study 'Is Female to Male as Nature Is to Culture?'[41] Their essays are teeming with ideas (Ortner has particularly helpful remarks on female marginality) and should be widely read, though I will go on to express the reservations of a European historian about them.

First, my answer to 'Is Female to Male as Nature Is to Culture?' is no, not always, despite the female's connection with childbearing.

For example, some strains in the chivalric tradition and even more in nineteenth-century thought conceive of male sexuality as close to nature and female sentiment as civilizing. If Ceres is the goddess of agriculture, the Muses are all female. The Old Testament has many images of sacred marriage between the bride Israel and Yahweh, so that the analogy female to male becomes social to supernatural.[42]

But a more important reservation about these polarities is that they are based on categories which are themselves historically bound. 'Culture' is not even a clear-cut concept in Europe till the nineteenth century. 'Nature' has very different boundaries in European thought over two thousand years and its relation to 'culture' is perplexed. Similarly 'domestic' and 'public' are categories that slip and side over time, both for peasants and for philosophers; nor do they exhaust the terms in which European societies would divide the realms of activity. For Aristotle, the economy was a domestic art; for Adam Smith it was not. In certain centuries of the Middle Ages, the concept of 'public' was much eroded or might apply to religious as well as political activity.[43]

Thus I think we would do better to use these polarities only when our historical evidence supports them, and not assume that they always represent the fundamental meanings that society sees in the sexes. I must say that if I were to look for universal poles in sexual symbolism, I'd try something like right/left and high/low. But better yet, I would follow O'Laughlin and her chickens, that is, accept the symbols and symbolic behaviour as the texts supply them, and then explore their meaning within the context of a given period. What is striking about sexual symbolism is not its poverty, but its richness, especially when one extends the investigation to include the ambiguous cases like transvestites and hermaphrodites and the cases of reversal as in carnivals and ritual. I would expect to find that some of these symbols could be used not merely to keep women down and men up, women in and men outside, but could be twisted around so as to threaten the lines between these places and justify behaviour of a very disorderly sort.[44]

A final way in which the study of the sexes can help transform historical reflection is in periodization. The sociologists Janet Zollinger Giele and Randall Collins have offered imaginative schemes for stages in the history of the sexes, each one coinciding in Europe roughly with our existing divisions of ancient, medieval, early modern, and modern.[45] Both schemes see things as getting better for women, Giele using an evolutionary model in which as society and symbols become more differentiated, women have more choices independent of their sex; Collins using a Weberian model in which (after an initial decline in the position of women from tribal societies), the development of government, market economy, and romantic love strengthen the female hand against perenially stronger male force and unrepressed lust. Their valuable essays should be read and discussed. I want to add here only a few critical suggestions about the path we should follow in this general enterprise.

First, it is essential that we distinguish speculation from generalization, that we know when we are working from inadequate evidence. Giele and Collins, for instance, both assumed as part of their argument for improvement that Lawrence Stone's description of the aristocratic household and family at the end of the Middle Ages held for the rest of society, though this was not in fact the case.[46] Perhaps at this stage of our work, efforts at grand periodization should be phrased more often as alternate hypotheses, with proposed designs for research.

Secondly, I think we should be slow to assume that the existing temporal and typological divisions in European history, used by Giele and Collins, will always be the significant ones for classifying the history of the sexes. It may sometimes be more important to use periods set off by major demographic changes or by major changes in sexual practice. Important landmarks might be the decline in female infanticide in the eleventh century, hypothesized by Le Roy Ladurie and Emily Coleman;[47] or the Gregorian war against a married clergy in the eleventh and twelfth centuries; or the elimination of a celibate clergy in parts of Europe in the sixteenth century and the simultaneous stiffening everywhere of laws against homosexuality and prostitution. Cross-cultural studies should give us much help here.

Lastly, I think we want to realize how difficult it is to decide what constituted a favourable context in the past for the improvement of the relations between the sexes. It is hardly even clear that the improvement has been unremitting. In any case, Giele's theory rests on the assumption that social and symbolic differentiation is always a good thing for the freedom of the female sex. Sometimes indeed it is. Ellen McDonald Gumperz' description of how strong caste lines in India loosened sexual restrictions on upper caste women is a relevant example.[48] But we can all imagine situations—like revolutions, for instance—when de-differentiation, when a simplification of choices, may have creative results for a time. What was most transformational about early Protestantism for both women and men was a simplification of social hierarchy and ritual, a de-differentiation between the laity and the clergy and between the religious and the worldly life.[49] We might go on to ask with Alice Clark and Michelle Rosaldo whether a de-differentiation between the worlds of childrearing, production, and political power, a simplification of the places where our life goes on, might not at *this* moment in history be a useful step toward more autonomy for both sexes.

In the field of women's history, at any rate, it is evident that the walled City of Ladies must give way to the open forum, perhaps the battlefield, for the serious study of the sexes. From Women Worthies to a worthier craft.

Notes

1. Philip A. Stadter, *Plutarch's Historical Methods: An Analysis of the 'Mulierum Virtutes'* (Cambridge, Mass.: Harvard University Press, 1965). Giovanni Boccaccio, *De Claris Mulieribus* (c.1359) [Concerning Famous Women], trans. G. A. Guarino (New Brunswick, NJ: Rutgers University Press, 1963). Giovanni Filippo Foresti, Bergomensis, *De plurimis claris sceletisque mulieribus* (Ferrara: L. de Rubeis, 1497), with 172 woodcuts. Francesco Agostino della Chiesa, *Theatro delle donne letterate* (Mondovi: G. Gistandi, 1620). Christine de Pisan, *La cité des dames* (c.1405), printed as *La Trésor de la cité des dames* in Paris in 1497, 1503, and 1536 and in an English translation by Bryan Anslay, *The Cyte of Ladyes* (London: H. Pepwell, 1521). Antoine Dufour, *Les vies des femmes célèbres* (MS, 1504), published with an introduction by G. Jeanneau (Geneva: Librairie Droz, S.A., 1970). Pierre de Bourdeille, seigneur de Brantôme (1537–1614), *Les Dames*, first published in Leyden in 1665–6 in three volumes (the first part, *Vies des dames illustres* was on contemporary queens of England and France; the other two parts, *Vies des dames gallantes*, were on the sexual doings of contemporary ladies). Abbé Joseph de La Porte and Jean-François de La Croix, *Histoire littéraire des femmes françaises* (Paris: Lacombe, 1769). Marguerite U. F. Bernier Briquet, *Dictionnaire historique, littéraire et bibliographique des françaises et des étrangères naturalisées en France connues par leurs écrits* ... (Paris: Treuttel and Würtz, 1804). Polycarp Friedrich Schacher, *Dissertatio historica-critica de Feminis ex arte medica claris* (Leipzig, 1738). Osbern Bokenham (early fifteenth century), *Legends of Hooly Wommen*, ed. from MS. Arundel 327 by M. S. Serjeantson, *Early English Text Society*, no. 206 (1930). Thomas Heywood, *Gynaikeion, or Nine Books of Various History, concerning Women* (London: Adam Islip, 1624). John Shirley, *The Illustrious History of Women* (London: J. Harris, 1686). George Ballard, *Memoirs of several Ladies of Great Britain who have been celebrated for their writings or skill in the Learned Languages, Arts and Sciences* (Oxford, 1752). Agnes and Elizabeth Strickland, *Lives of the Queens of England from the Norman Conquest ... Now first published from official records ...* (London, 1840–8, 1851–2, and later edns.).
2. Baudonivia, nun of Poitiers (fl. 600), 'De Vita Sanctae Radegundis Libri Duo',

Monumenta Germanicae Historica, Scriptores rerum merovingicarum, 7 vols. (Hanover, 1885–1919), ii. 358–95. Hroswitha (fl. 965), 'Primordia Coenobii Gendeshemensis', in *Hrotsvithae Opera*, P. de Winterfeld (ed.) (*Scriptores Rerum Germanicarum in usum scholarum*, 48; Berlin, 1902), 229–46. Bertha, nun of Willich (eleventh century), 'Vita Adelheidis Abbatissae Vilicensis', in *Monumenta Germanicae Historica, Scriptores*, 32 vols. (Hanover, 1826–1937), xv. 754–63. (I am grateful to John Coughlan for bibliographical assistance on the work of these nuns.)

3. William Camden, *Annales. The True and Royall History . . . of Elizabeth Queen of England* (London, 1625). Camden initially wrote the *Annales in Latin*. Madame de La Fayette, *Vie de la Princesse d'Angleterre* (a life of Henriette d'Angleterre), first published posthumously in Amsterdam in 1720 and now re-edited by M. T. Hipp (Geneva: Librairie Droz, 1967). Francoise Madeleine de Chaugy, *Les Vies de VIII vénérables veuves, religieuses de l'ordre de la Visitation Sainte-Marie* (Annecy: J. Clerc, 1659). (Marie Geneviève Charlotte Thiroux d'Arconville (1720–1805)), *Vie de Marie de Médicis, princesse de Toscane, Reine de France et de Navarre*, 3 vols. (Paris: Ruault, 1774), i. preface and p. 51.

4. Thiroux d'Arconville, *Vie*, iii. 515. Interestingly enough, the Radical Whig historian Catharine Sawbridge Macauley also used traditional images of masculine and feminine in her assessment of Elizabeth I, whose fame she thought 'unmerited'. The queen's vices could not exist in someone who had a good heart, nor her weaknesses in someone with a good head, 'but to the unaccountable caprice of party zeal she owes the reputation of qualities that would do honour to a masculine mind' (*The History of England from the Accession of James I to that of the Brunswick Line* (London: J. Nourse, 1763), 2).

5. J. B. Nettl, *Rosa Luxemburg*, 2 vols. (London: Oxford University Press, 1966). Nettl, of course, does speak briefly about Luxemburg's lack of interest in the movement for women's rights (pp. 136, 672) and of her relations with Clara Zetkin (pp. 193–4) and other women, but he does not consider directly how her experience as a woman might have influenced her political consciousness and activity. Nancy L. Roelker, *Queen of Navarre: Jeanne d'Albret, 1528–1572* (Cambridge, Mass.: Harvard University Press, 1968). Margaret George, *One Woman's 'Situation'. A Study of Mary Wollstonecraft* (Urbana, Ill.: University of Illinois Press, 1970). Eleanor Flexner, *Mary Wollstonecraft: A Biography* (New York: Coward, McCann and Geoghegan, 1972). Claire Tomalin, *The Life and Death of Mary Wollstonecraft* (London: Wiedenfeld and Nicholson, 1974).

6. For example [Louis-Sebastien Mercier], *Tableau de Paris*, 12 vols. (Amsterdam, 1782–8). Frederick Morton Eden, *The State of the Poor or, An History of the labouring classes from the conquest to the present period* (London: J. Davis, 1797). Friedrich Engels, *The Condition of the Working Class in England in 1844* (first published in German in 1845). Henry Mayhew, *London Labour and the London Poor* (London: Griffin and Co., 1861–4). A. J. B. Parent-Duchatelet, *De la prostitution dans la ville de Paris* (Paris: Baillière, 1836) with an important historical section. Paul La Croix, *Histoire de la prostitution chez tous les peuples du monde* (Paris: Seré, 1851–3). A. P. E. Rabutaux, *De la prostitution en Europe depuis l'antiquité jusqu'à la fin du 16ᵉ siécle* (Paris: Seré, 1851). Henri Klimrath, *Travaux sur l'histoire du droit français* (Paris: Joubert, 1843), with material on family, marriage, divorce, inheritance,

and the like. Henry Bourne, *Antiquitates Vulgares; or the Antiquities of the Common People* (Newcastle: J. White, 1725). John Brand, *Observations on Popular Antiquities* (Newcastle and London: J. Johnson, 1777). Joseph Strutt, *Glig-gamena angel-deud: Or the Sports and pastimes of the people of England* (1st edn., London, 1801). Jacques-Antoine Du Laure, *Des divinités generatirices, ou du Culte du phallus chez les anciens et les modernes* (Paris: Dentu, 1805). *Mémoires de l'académie celtique ou Recherches sur les antiquités celtiques, gauloises et françaises, publiés pr l'Académie Celtique, I–VI* (1807–12).

7. I have given some preliminary consideration to this subject in 'Women on Top', *Society and Culture in Early Modern France: Eight Essays* (Stanford, Calif.: Stanford University Press, 1975), 143–4.

8. William Alexander the Younger, *The History of Women from the Earliest Antiquity to the Present Time*, 2 vols. (London: W. Strahan and T. Cadell, 1799). Georgiana Hill, *Women in English Life from Medieval to Modern Times* (London: R. Bentley and Son, 1896). Christoph Meiners, *Geschichte des weiblichen Geschlechts*, 4 vols. (Hanover: Helwingsche hufbuchhandlung, 1788–1800). Kark Weinhold, *Die deutschen Frauen in dem Mittelalter* (Vienna: Carl Gerold, 1851); copy at the University of California, Berkeley, is signed from the author 'to his dear parents'. Alexander Joseph Pierre, Vicomte de Ségur, *Les femmes, leur condition et leur influence dans l'ordre social chez différens peuples anciens et modernes*, 3 vols. (Paris: Treuttel and Würtz, 1803). Charles de Ribbe, *La Famille et al société en France avant la Révolution d'après des documents originaux* (Paris: J. Albanel, 1873).

9. J. J. Bachofen, *Das mutterrecht. Eine untersuchung über die gynaikokratie der Alten Welt nach ihrer religiösen und rechtlichen natur* (Stuttgart: Krais and Hoffman, 1861). Friedrich Engels, *Der ursprung der Familie, des Privateigenthums und des Staats* (Zürich, 1884).

10. Weinhold's *Die deutschen Frauen in dem Mittelalter* came out in a new edition in 1897, now enlarged to two volumes, and at least three other books on allied subjects appeared in the decades just before or just after that date: Gustav Reinsch, *Stellung und leben der deutschen frau im mittelalter* (Berlin: C. Hubel, 1882); Wilhelm Behagel, *Die gewerbliche stellung der frau in mittelalterlichen Köln* (Berlin and Leipzig: W. Rothschild, 1910); Karl Bücher, *Die Frauenfrage im Mittelalter* (Tübingen: H. Laupp'sche Buchhandlung, 1910). Isadero del Lungo, *La Donna fiorentine del buon tempo antico* (Florence: R. Bemporad e figlio, 1905). René-Alphonse-Marie de Maulde la Clavière, *Vers le bonheur! Les femmes de la Renaissance* (Paris: Perrin, 1898), trans. into English and published in London in 1900. In 1899, Henri Hauser devoted a chapter to 'Le travail des femmes' in the first edition of his *Ouvriers du temps passé* (Paris: Librairie Félix Alcan). G. Fagniez, *La femme et la société française dans la première moitié du 17ᵉ siècle* (Paris: J. Gamber, 1929); chs. 1–4 had already appeared in the *Revue des deux mondes* as early as 1909–12.

11. Alice Clark, *Working Life of Women in the Seventeenth Century* (London: Routledge and Sons, 1919), preface. M. Dorothy George, *London Life in the Eighteenth Century* (London: Paul, Trench Trubnek and Co., 1925), preface. Rebecca Scott, author of a recent M. Phil. thesis at the London School of Economics, on 'Women in the Stuart Economy', has kindly passed on to me some details about Alice Clark. Clark enrolled in the LSE as an adult student from Somerset in 1912, intending to study geography and methods of teaching. Named Shaw Scholar the following year, she soon began to concentrate

on history, working with Dorothy Knowles in 1917–18 and taking a course in social psychology with Graham Wallas the following year. Lucy Kerman, in an unpublished seminar paper at the University of California, Berkeley, on 'Capitalism and Women's Economic Position', has shown striking similarities between Clark's theories and those of a Fabian Tract of 1914, written by 'M. A.' and published as part of the Fabian Women's Group Series.

12. Gyges (pseud.), *Les juifs dans la France d'aujourd'hui* (Paris: Documents et témoignages, 1965), 161. Born in 1889, Abensour had written his first book on feminism in his early twenties, *Le féminisme sous le règne de Louis-Philippe et en 1848* (2nd edn., Paris, 1913), with a preface by the poet Jules Bois. *Les Vaillantes: Héroines, martyres et remplaçantes* came out during the war (1917), with a preface by the literary and musical L. Barthou; and *Histoire générale du féminisme des origines à nos jours* followed in 1921. My own copy of *La femme et le féminisme en France avant la Révolution* (Paris: Editions Ernest Leron, 1923) has an inscription from Abensour to 'mon cher et vieil ami Jules Gobe, mon compagnon d'exploits historiques et Sorboniques, en toute affection et à sa charmante femme, avec mes respectueuses hommages'. In 1906, Georges Ascoli's long 'Essai sur l'histoire des idées féministes en France due XVIe siècle à la Révolution', appeared in the *Revue de synthèse historique*. Subsequently, we see only book reviews of biographies of females, a worried review article by S. Jankelevitch in 1910, and a moderately interesting article by R. Bouvier in 1929, 'Les femmes et la science' (47: 99–110). The *Annales*, which began publishing the same year, had its first article on the family in 1936, 'La famille dans l'ancienne Provence' by R. Aubenas, a professor of law. Lucien Febvre's first important work related to women was his study of Marguerite de Navarre, *Autour de l'Heptameron, amour sacré, amour profane* (Paris: Gallimard, 1944).

13. Though Abensour used some manuscripts at the Archives Nationales, he worked primarily from the *Inventaires-sommaires des archives départmentales* for all departments, which often have extensive summaries from the originals (*Le femme et le féminisme*, p. 464). Though this would hardly be adequate for present research, his chapter on 'La femme du peuple'—with material on female work, rural and urban, on female criminality and associational life, and on the role of women in uprisings—shows the directions in which he was sent by even this partial contact with archives.

14. Emmanuel Le Roy Ladurie, *Les paysans de Languedoc*, 2 vols. (Paris: S.E.V.P.E.N., 1966), 271–80 and Annexe 8, p. 758. Pierre Goubert, *Beauvais et le Beauvaisis de 1600 à 1730*, 2 vols. (Paris: S.E.V.P.E.N., 1960), 139–40, 296–7. Olwen H. Hufton, 'Women and the Family Economy in Eighteenth-Century France', *French Historical Studies*, 9 (1975), 1–22 and ead., *The Poor of Eighteenth-Century France* (Oxford: Clarendon Press, 1974), *passim*. N. Z. Davis, 'City Women and Religious Change', in *Society and Culture*, 70–1, 291.

15. Joan W. Scott and Louise A. Tilly, 'Women's Work and the Family in Nineteenth-Century Europe', *Comparative Studies in Society and History*, 17 (Jan. 1975), 36–64; Louise A. Tilly and Joan W. Scott, with the assistance of R. Burr Litchfield, 'Married Women and Work in Nineteenth-Century France and England', paper presented at the Second Berkshire Conference on the History of Women, Radcliffe College, 25–7 Oct. 1974. Louise Tilly, 'Women at Work in Milan, Italy, 1880–World War I', paper presented at the annual meeting of the American Historical Association, New Orleans, 28 Dec. 1972.

Sidney Mintz, 'Men, Women and Trade', *Comparative Studies in Society and History*, 13 (1971), 247–69. Ester Boserup, *Women's Role in Economic Development* (London: Allen and Unwin, 1970).

16. Abensour, *La femme et le féminisme*, 462.

17. Clark, *Working Life*, 305–6.

18. Anne Harrison Fanshawe (1625–80), *Memoirs of Lady Fanshawe*, ed. B. Marshall (London and New York: J. Lane, 1905). She lists eighteen pregnancies between February 1644 and 1655, of which four terminated in miscarriage. When her husband died in 1666, she had five surviving children aged thirteen and under, four girls and a boy. Ursula Cowgill, 'The People of York: 1538–1812', *Scientific American*, 223 (Jan. 1970), 108. E. Wrigley, *Population and History* (London: Weidenfeld and Nicolson, 1969). Pierre Goubert, *Beauvais et Beauvaisis*, 30–82; idem, 'Historical Demography and the Reinterpretation of Early Modern French History: A Research Review', *Journal of Interdisciplinary History*, 1 (1970), 37–48 (includes data on variations in fertility, including an almost yearly fertility in eighteenth-century Brittany); idem, 'Les fondements démographiques', in F. Braudel and E. Labrousse (eds.), *Histoire économique et sociale de la France* (Paris: Presses universitaires de France, 1970), ii. 9–87; especially 33–4. Thomas Hollingsworth, *The Demography of the British Peerage*, supplement to *Population Studies*, 18/2 (Nov. 1964). Claude Lévy and Louis Henry, 'Ducs et pairs sous l'Ancien Régime', *Population*, 15 (1960), 807–30. Louis Henry, 'Fécondité des mariages dans le quart sud-ouest de la France de 1720 à 1829', *Annales. Economies. Sociétés. Civilisations* [henceforth *Annales. ESC*], 27 (1972), 612–40, 977–1023. Ansley J. Coale, 'The Decline of Fertility in Europe from the French Revolution to World War II', in S. J. Behrman *et al.* (eds.), *Fertility and Family Planning: A World View* (Ann Arbor, Mich.: University of Michigan Press, 1969), 3–24. Daniel Scott Smith, 'A Homeostatic Demographic Regime: Patterns in West European Family Reconstitution Studies', paper presented to the Conference on Behavioral Models in Historical Demography, University of Pennsylvania, 24–6 Oct., 1974 (an excellent review of the literature). Maurice Garden, *Lyon et les lyonnais au XVIIIe siècle* (Paris: Société d'edition 'Les Belles-Lettres', 1970), 95–140: high mortality and high fertility among artisanal families in eighteenth-century Lyon. He finds butchers' families where annual births are the norm and where presumably babies were sent out to wet-nurse. This is in contrast to sixteenth-century Lyon, all of whose extant parish records I have examined, where the birth interval for stable artisanal families in the first years of marriage is rarely under two years. E. Le Roy Ladurie, 'L'aménorrhée de famine, 17e à 20e siècle', *Annales. ESC*, 24 (1969). 1589–1601. Rose E. Frisch, 'Demographic Implications of the Biological Determinants of Female Fecundity', a paper presented to the annual meeting of the Population Association of America, Apr. 1974.

19. In addition to the sources above, many of which discuss the question of limitation of fertility, see Louis Henry, *Anciennes familles genevoises: Etude démographique, XVIe–XXe siècle* (Paris: Presses universitaires françaises, 1956). J. Dupaquier and M. Lachiver, 'Les débuts de la contraception en France ou les deux malthusianismes', *Annales. ESC*, 24 (1969), 1391–406. E. Wrigley, 'Family Limitation in Pre-Industrial England', *Economic History Review*, 2nd ser., 19 (1966), 82–109. The English aristocracy seem to have adopted fertility

control later than the families of the French peers. Hufton, *The Poor*, 329 ff. on 'The Unwanted Legitimate Child'.

20. For instance, H. J. Habakkuk, 'Marriage Settlements in the Eighteenth Century', *Transactions of the Royal Historical Society* (1950), 15–30; Lawrence Stone, *The Crisis of the Aristocracy* (Oxford: Clarendon Press, 1965), ch. 11: 'Marriage and the Family'; Stanley Chojnacki, 'Dowries and Kinsmen in Early Renaissance Venice', *Journal of Interdisciplinary History* 5 (1975), 571–600. Jean Yver, *Egalité entre héritiers et exclusion des enfants dotés: Essai de géographie coutumière* (Paris: Editions Sirey, 1966); this work is discussed by E. Le Roy Ladurie in 'Structure familiale et coutumes d'héritage en France au XVIᶜ siècle: Systeme de la coutume', *Annales. ESC*, 27 (1972), 825–46. G. Duby, 'Lignage, noblesse et chevalerie au XIIᶜ siècle dans la region mâconnaise', *Annales. ESC*, 27 (1972), 803–24; Ralph Giesey, 'National Stability and Hereditary Transmission of Political and Economic Power', paper presented to the Fourteenth International Congress of Historical Sciences, San Francisco, 22–9 Aug. 1975. Philippe Ariès, *L'Enfant et la vie familiale sous l'ancien régime* (2nd edn., Paris: Librairie Plon, 1973). Diane Owen Hughes, 'Urban Growth and Family Structure in Medieval Genoa', *Past and Present*, 66 (1975), 3–28. Yves Castan, *Honnêteté et relations sociales en Languedoc 1715–1780* (Paris: Librairie Plon, 1974). N. Z. Davis, 'The Reasons of Misrule: Youth Groups and Charivaris in Sixteenth-Century France', *Past and Present*, 50 (Feb. 1971), 41–75, repr. as chap. 4 in *Society and Culture*. John R. Gillis, *Youth and History: Tradition and Change in European Age Relations, 1770–Present* (New York: Academic Press, 1974).

21. Peter Laslett (ed.), with the assistance of Richard Wall, *Household and Family in Past Time* (Cambridge, Mass.: Cambridge University Press, 1972). A. Collomp, 'Famille nucléaire et famille élargie en Huate Provence au XVIIIᶜ siècle', *Annales. ESC*, 72 (1972), 969–75. E. Le Roy Ladurie, *Les paysans de Languedoc*, 160–8 on the *frérèche*. Idem, 'Le domus à Montaillou et en Haute Ariège au XIVᶜ siècle', in D. Fabre and J. Lacroix (eds.), *Communautés du sud* (Paris: Union générale d'Éditions, 1975), esp. pp. 198–213. Lutz K. Berkner, 'The Stem Family and the Developmental Cycle of the Peasant Household: An Eighteenth-Century Austrian Example', *American Historical Review*, 77 (1972), 398–418; idem, 'Recent Research in the History of the Family in Western Europe', *Journal of Marriage and the Family*, 35 (Aug. 1973), 395–405. Idem, 'The Use and Misuses of Census Data for the Historical Analysis of Family Structure', *Journal of Interdisciplinary History*, 5 (1975), 721–38. Robert Wheaton, 'Bordeaux before the Fronde: A Study of Family, Class and Social Structure' (doctoral diss., Harvard University, 1973); idem, 'Family and Kinship in Western Europe: The Problem of the Joint Family Household', *Journal of Interdisciplinary History*, 5 (1975), 601–28.

22. Migration data in N. Z. Davis, 'City Women and Religious Change', in *Society and Culture*, 69, 291. Richard Gascon, 'Immigration et croissance urbaine au XVIᶜ siècle: l'exemple de Lyon', *Annales. ESC*, 25 (1970), 994. David Herlihy, 'The Tuscan Town in the Quattrocento: A Demographic Profile', *Medievalia et Humanistica*, N.S. 1 (1970), 99–100. Marcel Lachiver, *La population de Meulan du 17ᶜ au 19ᶜ siècle* (Paris: S.E.V.P.E.N., 1969). Peter Clark, 'The Migrant in Kentish Towns, 1580–1640', in Peter Clark and Paul Slade (eds.), *Crisis and Order in English Towns, 1500–1700* (Toronto: University of Toronto Press, 1972), 117–63. Maurice Garden, *Lyon et les lyonnais*, 67–81, 643–7). A.

Chatelain, 'Migrations et domesticité féminine urbaine en France, 18ᶜ–20ᶜ siècle', *Revue d'histoire économique et sociale*, 47 (1969), 506–28. Etienne Van de Walle, *The Female Population of France in the Nineteenth Century: A reconstruction of 82 départements* (Princeton, NJ: Princeton University Press, 1974), 79–98.

23. J. C. Gegot, 'Etude par sondage de la criminalité dans le bailliage de Falaise (XVIIᶜ–XVIIIᶜ siècle)', *Annales de Normandie* (1966), 103–49, esp. 126. P. Petrovitch, 'Recherches sur la criminalité à Paris dans la seconde moitié du XVIIIᶜ siècle', in A. Abbiateci *et al. Crimes et criminalité en France 17ᶜ–18ᶜ siècles* (Cahiers des annales, 33, Paris: Librairie Armand Colin, 1971), 187–261. Arlette Farge, *Le vol d'aliments à Paris au XVIIIᶜ siècle* (Paris: Plon, 1974). Barbara Hanawalt, 'The Peasant Family and crime in England', *Journal of British Studies*, 13 (1974), 1–18; eadem, 'Th Female Felon in Fourteenth-Century England', *Viator*, 5 (1974): 253–68. Martha Ellis Francois, 'Women against the Law in Elizabethan Essex', paper presented at the Second Berkshire Conference on the History of Women. Carol Z. Wiener, 'Sex-Roles and Crime in Late Elizabethan Hertfordshire', *Journal of Social History*, 8 (Summer 1975), 38–60. John Beattie, 'The Criminality of Women in Eighteenth-Century England', *Journal of Social History*, 8 (Summer 1975), 80–116. E. William Monter, 'Patterns of Witchcraft in the Jura', *Journal of Social History*, 5 (1971), 1–25. H. C. Erik Mideifort, *Witch-Hunting in Southwestern Germany, 1562–1684* (Stanford, Calif.: Stanford University Press, 1972), 178–90. Alan Macfarlane, *Witchcraft in Tudor and Stuart England: A Regional and Comparative Study* (London: Routledge and Kegan Paul, 1970), esp. 147–207.

24. Carol Cipolla, *Literacy and Development in the West* (New York: Pelican Books, 1969), 45–67, 85–6. N. Z. Davis *Society and Culture*, 72–3, 209–10. Jan de Vries, *The Dutch Rural Economy in the Golden Age, 1500–1700* (New Haven: Yale University Press, 1974), citing the work in Dutch of S. Hart on seventeenth-century Amsterdam. Pierre Deyon, *Amiens, capitale provinciale* (Paris: Mouton, 1967), 342–3. M. Fleury and P. Valmary, 'Les progrès de l'instruction élémentaire de Louis XIV à Napoléon III', *Population*, 12 (1957), 71–90. Garden, *Lyon et les Lyonnais*, 350–3. Roger Girod, 'Le recul de l'analphabétisme dans le région de Genéve à la fin du XVIIIᶜ siècle et au début du XIXᶜ siècle', *Mélanges d'histoire économique et sociale en hommage au professeur Antony Babel* (Geneva, 1963). Michael Sanderson, 'Literacy and Social Mobility in the Industrial Revolution in England', *Past and Present*, 56 (1972), 75–103.

25. Nicole Castan, 'La criminalité familiale dans le ressort du Parlement de Toulouse, 1690–1703', in *Crimes et criminalité*, 91–107.

26. See, for instance, Philippe Wolff, *Commerces et marchands de Toulouse (vers 1350–vers 1450)* (Paris: Librairie Plon, 1954), 441–5. Le Roy Ladurie, *Les paysans de Languedoc*, 276–9, Annexe 32, p. 859. Pierre Goubert, *Beauvais et le Beauvaisis*, 139–40, 296–7, 550–75 *passim*. G. E. and K. R. Fussell, *The English Countrywoman: A Farmhouse Social History, A.D. 1500–1900* (London, 1953; New York: Benjamin Blon, 1971, repr. edn.), 95. F. M. Eden, *The State of the Poor*, 733. On the division of food within the working-class family in the nineteenth century, see Laura Oren, 'The Welfare of Women in Laboring Families: England, 1860–1950', *Feminist Studies*, 1, no. 3/4 (Winter–Spring 1973), 107–25, repr. in Mary Hartman and Lois W. Banner (eds.), *Clio's*

Consciousness Raised: New Perspectives on the History of Women, Harper and Row, 1974), 226–44.

27. For instance, John Noonan, Jr., *Contraception: A History of its Treatment by the Catholic Theologians and Canonists* (Cambridge, Mass.: Harvard University Press, 1966). J. L. Flandrin 'Contraception, marriage et relations amoureuses dans l'Occident chrétien', *Annales. ESC*, 24 (1969), 1370–90; idem, 'Mariage tardif et vie sexuelle: Discussion et hypothèse de recherche', *Annales. ESC*, 27 (1972), 1351–78. André Burguière, 'De Malthus à Max Weber: Le mariage tardif et l'esprit d'entreprise', *Annales. ESC*, 27 (1972), 1128–38. Keith Thomas, 'The Double Standard', *Journal of the History of Ideas*, 20 (1959), 195–216. Robert V. Schnucker, 'La position puritaine à l'égard de l'adultère', *Annales. ESC*, 27 (1972), 1379–88; idem, 'Elizabethan Birth Control and Puritan Attitudes', *Journal of Interdisciplinary History*, 5 (1975), 655–67. Nicholas James Perella, *The Kiss Sacred and Profane: An Interpretative History of Kiss Symbolism and Related Religio-Erotic Themes* (Berkeley and Los Angeles: University of California Press, 1969). Among very recent pieces on the nineteenth century: William Langer, 'The Origins of the Birth Control Movement in England in the Early Nineteenth Century', *Journal of Interdisciplinary History*, 5 (1975), 669–86. Angus McLaren, 'Some Secular Attitudes toward Sexual Behavior in France: 1760–1860', *French Historical Studies*, 8 (1974), 604–25.

28. On homosexuality, there is some useful historical material in Derrick S. Bailey, *Homosexuality and the Western Christian Tradition* (London and New York: Longmans, Green, 1955); Gordon Rattray Taylor, 'Historical and Mythological Aspects of Homosexuality', in Judd Marmor (ed.), *Sexual Inversion: The Multiple Roots of Homosexuality* (New York: Basic Books, 1965); Philip E. Slater, *The Glory of Hera* (Bolton: Beacon Press, 1968); Arno Karlen, *Sexuality and Homosexuality: A New View* (New York: W. W. Norton & Co., 1971); Dolores Klaich, *Woman plus Woman: Attitudes Toward Lesbianism* (New York: Simon and Schuster, 1974). Caroline Bingham, 'Seventeenth-Century Attitudes Toward Deviant Sex', *Journal of Interdisciplinary History*, 1 (1971), 447–67. E. W. Monter, 'La sodomie à l'époque moderne en Suisse romande', *Annales. ESC*, 29 (1974), 1023–35. The Arno Press has begun a new series of books on *Homosexuality: Lesbians and Gay Men in Society, History and Literature*. On prostitution, see Jacques Solé, 'Passion charnelle et société urbaine d'Ancien Régime: Amour vénal, amour libre et amour fou à Grenoble au milieu de règne de Louis XIV', *Villes de l'Europe méditerranéenne et de l'Europe occidentale du Moyen Age* (Actes du colloque de Nice, 27–8 Mar. 1967); *Annales de la Faculté des Lettres et Sciences Humaines de Nice*, 9–10 (1969), 211–32; Richard C. Cobb, *The Police and the People: French Popular Protest, 1789–1820* (Oxford: Clarendon Press, 1970), 234–9. Brian Pullan, *Rich and Poor in Renaissance Venice* (Cambridge, Mass.: Harvard University Press, 1971), 376–94. Judith R. Walkowitz and Daniel J. Walkowitz, ' "We Are Not Beasts of the Field": Prostitution and the Poor in Plymouth and Southampton Under the Contagious Diseases Act', *Feminist Studies*, 1, no. 3/4 (Winter–Spring 1973), 73–106, repr. in *Clio's Consciousness Raised*, 192–225; Judith R. Walkowitz, 'The Making of an Outcast Group: Prostitutes and Working Women in Nineteenth-Century Plymouth and Southampton', forthcoming in a new collection of essays on Victorian women, edited by Martha Vicinus and published by Indiana University Press. Richard J. Evans,

'Prostitution, State and Society in Imperial Germany', forthcoming in *Past and Present*. Jacques Rossiaud, 'Prostitution, jeunesse et société dans les villes du sud-est à la fin du Moyen Age', forthcoming in *Annales. ESC*. Marie Benabou (Centre National de Recherche Scientifique) is completing a *thèse* on 'Libertinage, prostitution et police des mœurs dans le Paris du XVIIIe siècle'.

29. R. P. Neuman, 'Industrialization and Sexual Behavior: Some Aspects of Working-Class Life in Imperial Germany', in Robert J. Bezucha (ed.), *Modern European and Social History* (Lexington, Mass.: D. C. Heath and Co., 1972), 270–300; Edward Shorter, 'Différence de classe et sentiment depuis 1750: L'exemple de France', *Annales. ESC*, 29 (1974), 1034–57. Michael M. Sheehan, 'The Formation and Stability of Marriage in Fourteenth-Century England: Evidence of an Ely Register', *Mediaeval Studies*, 33 (1971), 228–63; Edward Shorter, 'Sexual Change and Illegitimacy: The European Experience', in *Modern European Social History*, 231–69; Jacques Depauw, 'Amour illégitime et société à Nantes au XVIIIe siècle', *Annales. ESC*, 27 (1972), 1155–82; David Levine and Keith Wrightson, 'The Social Context of Illegitimacy in Early Modern England', forthcoming in the *Journal of Interdisciplinary History*.

30. J. F. Flandrin, *Les amours paysannes (XVIe–XIXe siècle)* (Paris: Editions Gallimard/Julliard, 1975). The notarized arbitration contract, made between an unwed mother or pregnant woman and the father of the child, adds a new set of documents to the varied court records, visitation accounts, and hospital records used by M. Flandrin and the articles cited in n. 29. Examples from Lyon in 1556 show something of the relationship between a baker's daughter and a dyer's journeyman, both living in Lyon, and a carter's daughter and a canvas merchant, the latter living in Villefranche in the Beaujolais. Archives départementales du Rhone, 3E348, ff. 44–6^v, 135^r–138^v, 143^v–144^v.

31. Edward Shorter, 'Female Emancipation, Birth Control and Fertility', *American Historical Review*, 78 (1973), 605–40, esp. 626. John Benton, 'Clio and Venus: An Historical View of Medieval Love', in F. X. Newman (ed.), *The Meaning of Courtly Love* (Albancy, NY: SUNY Press, 1968), 32, and n. 41–2. Michel Millot and Jean L'Ange, *The School of Venus*, trans. Donald Thomas (first pub. in French, 1655; New York: New American Library, 1971), 157 ('it is well known to doctors and proved by experience that two orgasms coming together are the thing which causes conception and pregnancy'). Noonan, *Contraception*, 405–6 (quoting the theologian Alphonse Liguori, 1750, on the female orgasm—'According to all, it contributes greatly to the perfection of offspring ... it is necessary, or at least helpful, to generation'). Interestingly enough several students at Toronto and Berkeley, especially of recent Mediterranean background, have reported to me that their parents taught them that the female orgasm was necessary for pregnancy. A letter from a married woman to a medical advice column in the *San Francisco Chronicle* during October 1975, asked if this were true or not. (Some contemporary research argues that uterine contractions do facilitate the rapid movement of the sperm through the female duct to the ovum. R. Berde, *Recent Progress in Oxytocin Research* (Springfield, Ill.: Thomas, 1959) and A. V. Nalbandov, *Reproductive Physiology* (2nd edn., San Francisco: W. H. Freeman, 1964), cited by Alice Rossi, 'The Missing Body in Sociology: Closing the Gap between Physiology and Sociology', Presidential Address, Eastern Sociological Society, Philadelphia, Pennsylvania, 6 Apr. 1974.)

32. Village midwives held the belief, found also in Greek and Renaissance medical literature, that hysteria was caused by the wandering of the womb due to insufficient sexual intercourse (see Ilza Veigh, *Hysteria: The History of a Disease* (Chicago: University of Chicago Press, 1965)). Collection of midwives' secrets always included a remedy for 'a fit of the mother' as the uterus was called, that of Trotula of Salerno, for example, being to anoint 'the womb' inside and out and to put cupping glasses on the pubic hair and groin of the woman (Trotula of Salerno, *The Diseases of Women*, trans. Elizabeth Mason-Hohl (Los Angeles: Wand-Ritchie Press, 1940), 10–11). In the eighteenth century, physician Jean Astruc still found matrimony the 'sovereign remedy' for female hysteria (Jean Astruc, *A Treatise on all the Diseases Incident to Women . . . Translated from a Manuscript Copy of the Author's Lectures read at Paris 1740* (London: M. Cooper, 1743), 290). Quotation in text from Philibert Guybert, *Toutes les œuvres charitables de Philibert Guybert Escuyer, Docteur Regent en la Faculté de Medecine à Paris* (Lyon, 1654). Like other physicans, Guybert believed that there was a natural buildup of sexual fluids in both male and female, which required a moderate evacuation in sexual intercourse (505–8).

33. See, for instance, Eric Partridge, *Shakespeare's Bawdy: A literary and Psychological Essay and a Comprehensive Glossary* (rev. edn., London: Routledge and Paul, 1955), and Mihail Bakhtin, *Rabelais and His World*, trans. Helene Iswolsky (Cambridge, Mass.: MIT Press, 1968). A popular proverb to signify a 'truly unfortunate man': 'Il est plus malheureux qu'une femme qui n'a point de con' (quoted by Jacques Duval, *Des Hermaphrodits, accouchemens des femmes et traitement qui est requis pour les relever en santé* (Rouen: David Geoffroy, 1612), 278).

34. Among discussions on seasonality in sexual intercourse, see Giovanni Boccaccio, *The Decameron*, 'Second Day, The Tenth Story'; Jean Benedicti, *La Somme des Pechez, et le Remede d'iceux* (Paris: Denis Binet, 1595), 154–6; Cowgill, 'People of York', 104–10; Smith 'Homeostatic Demographic Regime', 29–32.

35. Matina Horner, 'Toward an Understanding of Achievement-Related Conflicts in Women', *Journal of Social Issues*, 28 (1972), 157–75.

36. A good example of the new approach is Ralph Giesey, 'National Stability and Hereditary Transmission of Political and Economic Power', paper presented to the Fourteenth International Congress of Historical Sciences, San Francisco, 22–9 Aug. 1975. Giesey points out that the 'possessive individualism' of seventeenth-century English thought should better be understood as 'family possessiveness'.

37. Arnold Van Gennep, *Manuel de folklore français* (Paris: A. and J. Pichard, 1946–72), i. 2155, 2622. Another menstrual taboo, current in sixteenth-century France: pregnant mares will abort if touched by a menstruating girl or woman, especially if it is the female's first period (Jean Massé, *L'art veterinaire ou grande marechalerie* (Paris: Charles Periér, 1563), f. 164ᵛ). Aletta Biersack of the University of Michigan passes on from her conversation with a female German immigrant that as late as World War II in Germany, menstruating women were not supposed to can food lest they defile it.

38. See Roland Mousnier, *Les institutions de la France sous la monarchie absolue* (Paris: Presses universitaires de France, 1974) and Lawrence Stone, 'Social Mobility in England, 1500–1700', *Past and Present*, 33 (1966), 16–55. Each provides a very useful and nuanced way of talking about social structure in

the early modern period, but charts males only. For examples outside the historical profession of efforts to use both male and female to measure status and to consider a multi-dimensional model for social structure, see Peter Rossi *et al.*, 'Measuring Household Social Standing', *Social Science Research*, 3 (1974), 169–90; George DeVos, 'Social Stratification and Ethnic Pluralism', *Race*, 13 (July 1971–April 1972), 435–60; idem, 'Conflict, Dominance, and Exploitation', in Nevitt Sanford and Craig Comstock (eds.), *Sanctions for Evil* (San Francisco: Jossey-Bass, Inc., 1971), 155–73.

39. Among relevant studies, see Keith Thomas, 'The Double Standard'; Claude Lévi-Strauss, 'The Family', in H. L. Shapiro (ed.), *Man, Culture and Society* (New York: Oxford University Press, 1956); Pierre Bourdieu, 'Les stratégies matrimoniales dans le système de reproduction', *Annales. ESC*, 27 (1972), 1105–27; Jack Goody and S. J. Tambiah, *Bridewealth and Dowry* (Cambridge Papers in Social Anthropology, 7; Cambridge: Cambridge University Press, 1973). Bridget O'Laughlin, 'Mediation of Contradiction: Why Mbum Women Do Not Eat Chicken', in Michelle Zimbalist Rosaldo and Louise Lamphere (eds.), *Woman, Culture and Society* (Stanford, Calif.: Stanford University Press, 1974), 301–18.

40. Kathleen Gough, *The Origin of the Family* (Toronto: Hogtown Press, 1973). David M. Schneider and Kathleen Gough (eds.), *Matrilineal Kinship* (Berkeley and Los Angeles: University of California Press, 1962), esp. 1–29. Peggy Sanday, 'Female Status in the Public Domain', in Rosaldo and Lamphere (eds.), *Woman*, 189–206. Melveena McKendrick, *Woman and Society in the Spanish Drama of the Golden Age: A Study of the 'Mujer Varonil'* (Cambridge: Cambridge University Press, 1974); Walter Kendrick, 'Earth of Flesh, Flesh of Earth: Mother Earth, in the "Faerie Queene"', *Renaissance Quarterly*, 26 (1974), 533–48; N. Z. Davis, 'Women on Top', in *Society and Culture*, ch. 5.

41. Eric Wolf, 'Society and Symbols in Latin Europe and in the Islamic Near East: Some Comparisons', *Anthropological Quarterly*, 42 (1968), 287–301 (I am grateful to Aletta Biersack for calling this article to my attention). Essays by Rosaldo and Lamphere (eds.), in *Woman*, 1–16, and by Sherry B. Ortner in *Feminist Studies*, 1/2 (1973), 5–32, repr. in *Woman*, 67–88.

42. Mary Wakeman, Mary Callaway *et al.*, 'Images of Women in the Bible', *Women's Caucus Religious Studies Newsletter*, 2/3 (Fall 1974).

43. Lionel Gossman, *Medievalism and the Ideologies of the Englightenment: The World and Work of La Curne de Sainte-Palaye* (Baltimore: Johns Hopkins Press, 1968), 176, 353; Clifford Geertz, *The Interpretation of Cultures: Selected Essays* (New York: Basic Books, 1973), chs. 2–3. Brian Tierney, *Medieval Poor Law: A Sketch of Canonical Theory and Its Application in England* (Berkeley and Los Angeles: University of California Press, 1959), ch. 2, esp. p. 43. Discussion of the changing of the boundary between private and public in the nineteenth century, and the different character of male space, female space, and mixed space in Maurice Agulhon, 'Les Chambrées en Basse-Provence: Histoire et ethnologie', *Revue historique*, 498 (1971), 337–68, and in Erna Olafson Hellerstein, 'French Women and the Orderly Household, 1830–1870', paper presented to the Western Society for French History, Denver, Colorado, 5 Dec. 1975.

44. Davis, 'Women on Top', in *Society and Culture*, ch. 5.

45. Janet Zollinger Giele, 'Centuries of womanhood: An evolutionary Perspective on the Feminine Role', *Women's Studies*, 1 (1972), 97–110. Randall Collins, 'A Conflict Theory of Sexual Stratification', *Social Problems*, 19 (1971), 2–21 (I am grateful to Thomas Reicher for calling this article to my attention.)

46. See the recent interesting essay by Lawrence Stone on 'The Rise of the Nuclear Family in Early Modern England', in which among other things, he takes into account some of the differences in family development in different classes (in Charles E. Rosenberg (ed.), *The Family in History* (Philadelphia: University of Pennsylvania Press, 1975), 13–57).

47. Emily R. Coleman, 'Infanticide dans le Haut Moyen Age', *Annales. ESC*, 29 (1974), 315–35 and n. 64, in which Professor Coleman acknowledges the suggestion of Le Roy Ladurie on this matter.

48. Ellen E. McDonald [Gumperz], 'Educated Women: The Last Minority', *Columbia University Forum*, 10/2 (Summer 1967), 30–5.

49. N. Z. Davis, 'City Women and Religious Change', in *Society and Culture*, ch. 3. See also the discussion of de-differentiation and the role of the female in creating permeable boundaries in Elizabeth Douvan, 'Directions and Needs of Research on Women', forthcoming in *New Research on Women*, 2, published by the Center for the Continuing Education of Women, University of Michigan, Ann Arbor.

5 The Traffic in Women: Notes on the 'Political Economy' of Sex

Gayle Rubin

The literature on women—both feminist and anti-feminist—is a long rumination on the question of the nature and genesis of women's oppression and social subordination. The question is not a trivial one, since the answers given it determine our visions of the future, and our evaluation of whether or not it is realistic to hope for a sexually egalitarian society. More importantly, the analysis of the causes of women's oppression forms the basis for any assessment of just what would have to be changed in order to achieve a society without gender hierarchy. Thus, if innate male aggression and dominance are at the root of female oppression, then the feminist programme would logically require either the extermination of the offending sex, or else a eugenics project to modify its character. If sexism is a by-product of capitalism's relentless appetite for profit, then sexism would wither away in the advent of a successful socialist revolution. If the world historical defeat of women occurred at the hands of an armed patriarchal revolt, then it is time for Amazon guerrillas to start training in the Adirondacks.

It lies outside the scope of this paper to conduct a sustained critique of some of the currently popular explanations of the genesis of sexual inequality—theories such as the popular evolution exemplified by *The Imperial Animal*, the alleged overthrow of prehistoric

 Acknowledgments are an inadequate expression of how much this paper, like most, is the product of many minds. They are also necessary to free others of the responsibility for what is ultimately a personal vision of a collective conversation. I want to free and thank the following persons: Tom Anderson and Arlene Gorelick, with whom I co-authored the paper from which this one evolved; Rayna Reiter, Larry Shields, Ray Kelly, Peggy White, Norma Diamond, Randy Reiter, Frederick Wyatt, Anne Locksley, Juliet Mitchell, and Susan Harding, for countless conversations and ideas; Marshall Sahlins, for the revelation of anthropology; Lynn Eden, for sardonic editing; the members of Women's Studies 340/004, for my initiation into teaching; Sally Brenner, for heroic typing; Susan Lowes, for incredible patience; and Emma Goldman, for the title.

matriarchies, or the attempt to extract all of the phenomena of social subordination from the first volume of *Capital*. Instead, I want to sketch some elements of an alternate explanation of the problem.

Marx once asked:

What is a Negro slave? A man of the black race. The one explanation is as good as the other. A Negro is a Negro. He only becomes a slave in certain relations. A cotton spinning jenny is a machine for spinning cotton. It becomes *capital* only in certain relations. Torn from these relationships it is no more capital than gold in itself is money or sugar is the price of sugar (Marx, 1971*b*: 28).

One might paraphrase: What is a domesticated woman? A female of the species. The one explanation is as good as the other. A woman is a woman. She only becomes a domestic, a wife, a chattel, a playboy bunny, a prostitute, or a human dictaphone in certain relations. Torn from these relationships, she is no more the helpmate of man than gold in itself is money . . . etc. What then are these relationships by which a female becomes an oppressed woman? The place to begin to unravel the system of relationships by which women become the prey of men is in the overlapping works of Claude Lévi-Strauss and Sigmund Freud. The domestication of women, under other names, is discussed at length in both of their *œuvres*. In reading through these works, one begins to have a sense of a systematic social apparatus which takes up females as raw materials and fashions domesticated women as products. Neither Freud nor Lévi-Strauss sees his work in this light, and certainly neither turns a critical glance upon the processes he describes. Their analyses and descriptions must be read, therefore, in something like the way in which Marx read the classical political economists who preceded him (on this, see Althusser and Balibar, 1970: 11–69). Freud and Lévi-Strauss are in some sense analogous to Ricardo and Smith: They see neither the implications of what they are saying, nor the implicit critique which their work can generate when subjected to a feminist eye. Nevertheless, they provide conceptual tools with which one can build descriptions of the part of social life which is the locus of the oppression of women, of sexual minorities, and of certain aspects of human personality within individuals. I call that part of social life the 'sex/gender system', for lack of a more elegant term. As a preliminary definition, a 'sex/gender system' is the set of arrangements by which a society transforms biological sexuality into products of human activity, and in which these transformed sexual needs are satisfied.

The purpose of this essay is to arrive at a more fully developed definition of the sex/gender system, by way of a somewhat idiosyncratic and exegetical reading of Lévi-Strauss and Freud. I use the word 'exegetical' deliberately. The dictionary defines 'exegesis' as a 'critical explanation or analysis; especially, interpretation of the Scriptures'. At times, my reading of Lévi-Strauss and Freud is freely interpretative, moving from the explicit content of a text to its presuppositions and implications. My reading of certain psychoanalytic texts is filtered through a lens provided by Jacques Lacan, whose own interpretation of the Freudian scripture has been heavily influenced by Lévi-Strauss.[1]

I will return later to a refinement of the definition of a sex/gender system. First, however, I will try to demonstrate the need for such a concept by discussing the failure of classical Marxism to fully express or conceptualize sex oppression. This failure results from the fact that Marxism, as a theory of social life, is relatively unconcerned with sex. In Marx's map of the social world, human beings are workers, peasants, or capitalists; that they are also men and women is not seen as very significant. By contrast, in the maps of social reality drawn by Freud and Lévi-Strauss, there is a deep recognition of the place of sexuality in society, and of the profound differences between the social experience of men and women.

MARX

There is no theory which accounts for the oppression of women— in its endless variety and monotonous similarity, cross-culturally and throughout history—with anything like the explanatory power of the Marxist theory of class oppression. Therefore, it is not surprising that there have been numerous attempts to apply Marxist analysis to the question of women. There are many ways of doing this. It has been argued that women are a reserve labour force for capitalism, that women's generally lower wages provide extra surplus to a capitalist employer, that women serve the ends of capitalist consumerism in their roles as administrators of family consumption, and so forth.

However, a number of articles have tried to do something much more ambitious—to locate the oppression of women in the heart of the capitalist dynamic by pointing to the relationship between housework and the reproduction of labour (see Benston, 1969;

Dalla Costa, 1972; Larguia and Dumoulin, 1972; Gerstein, 1973; Vogel, 1973; Secombe, 1974; Gardiner, 1974; Rowntree, M. and J., 1970). To do this is to place women squarely in the definition of capitalism, the process in which capital is produced by the extraction of surplus value from labour by capital.

Briefly, Marx argued that capitalism is distinguished from all other modes of production by its unique aim: the creation and expansion of capital. Whereas other modes of production might find their purpose in making useful things to satisfy human needs, or in producing a surplus for a ruling nobility, or in producing to insure sufficient sacrifice for the edification of the gods, capitalism produces capital. Capitalism is a set of social relations—forms of property, and so forth—in which production takes the form of turning money, things, and people into capital. And capital is a quantity of goods or money which, when exchanged for labour, reproduces and augments itself by extracting unpaid labour, or surplus value, from labour and into itself.

The result of the capitalist production process is neither a mere product (use-value) nor a *commodity*, that is, a use-value which has exchange value. Its result, its product, is the creation of *surplus-value* for capital, and consequently the actual *transformation* of money or commodity into capital. . . . (Marx, 1969: 399; italics in the original)

The exchange between capital and labour which produces surplus value, and hence capital, is highly specific. The worker gets a wage; the capitalist gets the things the worker has made during his or her time of employment. If the total value of the things the worker has made exceeds the value of his or her wage, the aim of capitalism has been achieved. The capitalist gets back the cost of the wage, plus an increment—surplus value. This can occur because the wage is determined not by the value of what the labourer makes, but by the value of what it takes to keep him or her going—to reproduce him or her from day to day, and to reproduce the entire work-force from one generation to the next. Thus, surplus value is the difference between what the labouring class produces as a whole, and the amount of that total which is recycled into maintaining the labouring class.

The capital given in exchange for labour power is converted into necessaries, by the consumption of which the muscles, nerves, bones, and brains of existing labourers are reproduced, and new labourers are begotten . . . the individual consumption of the labourer, whether it proceed within the workshop or outside it, whether it be part of the process of production or not, forms therefore a factor of the production and reproduction of capital; just as cleaning machinery does. . . . (Marx, 1972: 572)

Given the individual, the production of labour-power consists in his reproduction of himself or his maintenance. For his maintenance he requires a given quantity of the means of subsistence. . . . Labour-power sets itself in action only by working. But thereby a definite quantity of human muscle, brain, nerve, etc., is wasted, and these require to be restored. . . . (Ibid. 171)

The amount of the difference between the reproduction of labour power and its products depends, therefore, on the determination of what it takes to reproduce that labour power. Marx tends to make that determination on the basis of the quantity of commodities—food, clothing, housing, fuel—which would be necessary to maintain the health, life, and strength of a worker. But these commodities must be consumed before they can be sustenance, and they are not immediately in consumable form when they are purchased by the wage. Additional labour must be performed upon these things before they can be turned into people. Food must be cooked, clothes cleaned, beds made, wood chopped, etc. Housework is therefore a key element in the process of the reproduction of the labourer from whom surplus value is taken. Since it is usually women who do housework, it has been observed that it is through the reproduction of labour power that women are articulated into the surplus value nexus which is the *sine qua non* of capitalism.[2] It can be further argued that since no wage is paid for housework, the labour of women in the home contributes to the ultimate quantity of surplus value realized by the capitalist. But to explain women's usefulness to capitalism is one thing. To argue that this usefulness explains the genesis of the oppression of women is quite another. It is precisely at this point that the analysis of capitalism ceases to explain very much about women and the oppression of women.

Women are oppressed in societies which can by no stretch of the imagination be described as capitalist. In the Amazon valley and the New Guinea highlands, women are frequently kept in their place by gang rape when the ordinary mechanisms of masculine intimidation prove insufficient. 'We tame our women with the banana', said one Mundurucu man (Murphy, 1959: 195). The ethnographic record is littered with practices whose effect is to keep women 'in their place'—men's cults, secret initiations, arcane male knowledge, etc. And pre-capitalist, feudal Europe was hardly a society in which there was no sexism. Capitalism has taken over, and rewired, notions of male and female which predate it by centuries. No analysis of the reproduction of labour power under capitalism can explain foot-binding, chastity belts,or any of the incredible array of Byzantine, fetishized indignities, let alone the more ordinary ones, which have been inflicted upon women in various times and places. The analysis of the reproduction of labour power does not even explain why it is usually women who do domestic work in the home, rather than men.

In this light it is interesting to return to Marx's discussion of the reproduction of labour. What is necessary to reproduce the worker is determined in part by the biological needs of the human organism, in part by the physical conditions of the place in which it lives, and in part by cultural tradition. Marx observed that beer is necessary for the reproduction of the English working class, and wine necessary for the French.

> ... the number and extent of his [the worker's] so-called necessary wants, as also the modes of satisfying them, are themselves the product of historical development, and depend therefore to a great extent on the degree of civilization of a country, more particularly on the conditions under which, and consequently on the habits and degree of comfort in which, the class of free labourers has been formed. *In contradistinction therefore to the case of other commodities, there enters into the determination of the value of labour-power a historical and moral element.* ... (Marx, 1972: 171, my italics)

It is precisely this 'historical and moral element' which determines that a 'wife' is among the necessities of a worker, that women rather than men do housework, and that capitalism is heir to a long tradition in which women do not inherit, in which women do not lead, and in which women do not talk to God. It is this 'historical and moral element' which presented capitalism with a cultural heritage of forms of masculinity and femininity. It is within this 'historical and moral element' that the entire domain of sex, sexuality, and sex oppression is subsumed. And the briefness of Marx's comment only serves to emphasize the vast area of social life which it covers and leaves unexamined. Only by subjecting this 'historical and moral element' to analysis can the structure of sex oppression be delineated.

ENGELS

In *The Origin of the Family, Private Property, and the State*, Engels sees sex oppression as part of capitalism's heritage from prior social forms. Moreover, Engels integrates sex and sexuality into his theory of society. *Origin* is a frustrating book. Like the nineteenth-century tomes on the history of marriage and the family which it echoes, the state of the evidence in *Origin* renders it quaint to a reader familiar with more recent developments in anthropology. Nevertheless, it is a book whose considerable insight should not be overshadowed by its limitations. The idea that the 'relations of sexuality' can and should be distinguished from the 'relations of production' is not the least of Engels' intuitions:

According to the materialistic conception, the determining factor in history is, in the final instance, the production and reproduction of immediate life. *This again, is of a twofold character: on the one hand, the production of the means of existence, of food, clothing, and shelter and the tools necessary for that production; on the other side, the production of human beings themselves,* the propagation of the species. The social organization under which the people of a particular historical epoch and a particular country live is determined by both kinds of production: by the stage of development of labour on the one hand, and of the family on the other . . . (Engels, 1972: 71–2; my italics)

This passage indicates an important recognition—that a human group must do more than apply its activity to reshaping the natural world in order to clothe, feed, and warm itself. We usually call the system by which elements of the natural world are transformed into objects of human consumption the 'economy'. But the needs which are satisfied by economic activity even in the richest, Marxian sense, do not exhaust fundamental human requirements. A human group must also reproduce itself from generation to generation. The needs of sexuality and procreation must be satisfied as much as the need to eat, and one of the most obvious deductions which can be made from the data of anthropology is that these needs are hardly ever satisfied in any 'natural' form, any more than are the needs for food. Hunger is hunger, but what counts as food is culturally determined and obtained. Every society has some form of organized economic activity. Sex is sex, but what counts as sex is equally culturally determined and obtained. Every society also has a sex/gender system—a set of arrangements by which the biological raw material of human sex and procreation is shaped by human, social intervention and satisfied in a conventional manner, no matter how bizarre some of the conventions may be.[3]

The realm of human sex, gender, and procreation has been subjected to, and changed by, relentless social activity for millennia. Sex as we know it—gender identity, sexual desire and fantasy, concepts of childhood—is itself a social product. We need to understand the relations of its production, and forget, for a while, about food, clothing, automobiles, and transistor radios. In most Marxist tradition, and even in Engels's book, the concept of the 'second aspect of material life' has tended to fade into the background or to be incorporated into the usual notions of 'material life'. Engels's suggestion has never been followed up and subjected to the refinement which it needs. But he does indicate the existence and importance of the domain of social life which I want to call the sex/gender system.

Other names have been proposed for the sex/gender system. The most common alternatives are 'mode of reproduction' and 'patriarchy'. It may be foolish to quibble about terms, but both of these can lead to confusion. All three proposals have been made in order to introduce a distinction between 'economic' systems and 'sexual' systems, and to indicate that sexual systems have a certain autonomy and cannot always be explained in terms of economic forces. 'Mode of reproduction', for instance, has been proposed in opposition to the more familiar 'mode of production'. But this terminology links the 'economy' to production, and the sexual system to 'reproduction'. It reduces the richness of either system, since 'productions' and 'reproductions' take place in both. Every mode of production involves reproduction—of tools, labour, and social relations. We cannot relegate all of the multi-faceted aspects of social reproduction to the sex system. Replacement of machinery is an example of reproduction in the economy. On the other hand, we cannot limit the sex system to 'reproduction' in either the social or biological sense of the term. A sex/gender system is not simply the reproductive moment of a 'mode of production'. The formation of gender identity is an example of production in the realm of the sexual system. And a sex/gender system involves more than the 'relations of procreation', reproduction in the biological sense.

The term 'patriarchy' was introduced to distinguish the forces maintaining sexism from other social forces, such as capitalism. But the use of 'patriarchy' obscures other distinctions. Its use is analogous to using capitalism to refer to all modes of production, whereas the usefulness of the term 'capitalism' lies precisely in that it distinguishes between the different systems by which societies are provisioned and organized. Any society will have some system of 'political economy'. Such a system may be egalitarian or socialist. It may be class-stratified, in which case the oppressed class may consist of serfs, peasants, or slaves. The oppressed class may consist of wage-labourers, in which case the system is properly labelled 'capitalist'. The power of the term lies in its implication that, in fact, there are alternatives to capitalism.

Similarly, any society will have some systematic ways to deal with sex, gender, and babies. Such a system may be sexually egalitarian, at least in theory, or it may be 'gender stratified', as seems to be the case for most or all of the known examples. But it is important—even in the face of a depressing history—to maintain a distinction between the human capacity and necessity to create a sexual world, and the empirically oppressive ways in which sexual worlds have been organized. Patriarchy subsumes both meanings into the same term. 'Sex/gender system', on the other hand, is a neutral term which refers to the domain and indicated that oppression is not inevitable in that domain, but is the product of the specific social relations which organize it.

Finally, there are gender-stratified systems which are not adequately described as patriarchal. Many New Guinea societies (Enga, Maring, Bena Bena, Huli, Melpa, Kuma, Gahuku-Gama, Fore, Marind Anim, *ad nauseam*; see Berndt, 1962; Langness, 1967; Rappaport, 1975; Read, 1952; Meggitt, 1970; Glasse, 1971; Strathern, 1972; Reay, 1959; Van Baal, 1966; Lindenbaum, 1973) are viciously oppressive to women. But the power of males in these groups is not founded on their roles as fathers or patriarchs, but on their collective adult maleness, embodied in secret cults, men's houses, warfare, exchange networks, ritual knowledge, and various initiation procedures. Patriarchy is a specific form of male dominance, and the use of the term ought to be confined to the Old Testament-type pastoral nomads from whom the term comes, or groups like them. Abraham was a Patriarch—one old man whose absolute power over wives, children, herds, and dependants was an aspect of the institution of fatherhood, as defined in the social group in which he lived.

Whichever term we use, what is important is to develop concepts to describe adequately the social organization of sexuality and the reproduction of the conventions of sex and gender. We need to pursue the project Engels abandoned when he located the subordination of women in a development within the mode of production.[4] To do this, we can imitate Engels in his method rather than in his results. Engels approached the task of analysing the 'second aspect of material life' by way of an examination of a theory of kinship systems. Kinship systems are and do many things. But they are made up of, and reproduce, concrete forms of socially organized sexuality. Kinship systems are observable and empirical forms of sex/gender systems.

KINSHIP (ON THE PART PLAYED BY SEXUALITY IN THE TRANSITION FROM APE TO 'MAN')

To an anthropologist, a kinship system is not a list of biological relatives. It is a system of categories and statuses which often contradict actual genetic relationships. There are dozens of examples in which socially defined kinship statuses take precedence over biology. The Nuer custom of 'woman marriage' is a case in point. The Nuer define the status of fatherhood as belonging to the person in whose name cattle bridewealth is given for the mother. Thus, a woman can be married to another woman, and be husband to the wife and father of her children, despite the fact that she is not the inseminator (Evans–Pritchard, 1951: 107–9).

In pre-state societies, kinship is the idiom of social interaction, organizing economic, political, and ceremonial, as well as sexual, activity. One's duties, responsibilities, and privileges *vis-à-vis* others are defined in terms of mutual kinship or lack thereof. The exchange of goods and services, production and distribution, hostility and solidarity, ritual and ceremony, all take place within the organizational structure of kinship. The ubiquity and adaptive effectiveness of kinship has led many anthropologists to consider its invention, along with the invention of language, to have been the developments which decisively marked the discontinuity between semi-human hominids and human beings (Sahlins, 1960; Livingstone, 1969; Lévi-Strauss, 1969).

While the idea of the importance of kinship enjoys the status of a first principle in anthropology, the internal workings of kinship systems have long been a focus for intense controversy. Kinship systems vary wildly from one culture to the next. They contain all sorts of bewildering rules which govern whom one may or may not marry. Their internal complexity is dazzling. Kinship systems have for decades provoked the anthropological imagination into trying to explain incest taboos, cross-cousin marriage, terms of descent, relationships of avoidance or forced intimacy, clans and sections, taboos on names—the diverse array of items found in descriptions of actual kinship systems. In the nineteenth century, several thinkers attempted to write comprehensive accounts of the nature and history of human sexual systems (see Fee, 1973). One of these was *Ancient Society*, by Lewis Henry Morgan. It was this book which inspired Engels to write *The Origin of the Family, Private Property, and the State*. Engels's theory is based upon Morgan's account of kinship and marriage.

In taking up Engels's project of extracting a theory of sex oppression from the study of kinship, we have the advantage of the maturation of ethnology since the nineteenth century. We also have the advantage of a peculiar and particularly appropriate book, Lévi-Strauss's *The Elementary Structures of Kinship*. This is the boldest twentieth-century version of the nineteenth-century project to understand human marriage. It is a book in which kinship is explicitly conceived of as an imposition of cultural organization upon the facts of biological procreation. It is permeated with an awareness of the importance of sexuality in human society. It is a description of society which does not assume an abstract, genderless human subject. On the contrary, the human subject in Lévi-Strauss's work is always either male or female, and the divergent social destinies of the two sexes can therefore be traced. Since Lévi-Strauss sees the essence of kinship systems to lie in an exchange of women between men, he constructs an implicit theory of sex oppression. Aptly, the book is dedicated to the memory of Lewis Henry Morgan.

'VILE AND PRECIOUS MERCHANDISE' (MONIQUE WITTIG)

The Elementary Structures of Kinship is a grand statement on the origin and nature of human society. It is a treatise on the kinship systems of approximately one-third of the ethnographic globe. Most fundamentally, it is an attempt to discern the structural principles of kinship. Lévi-Strauss argues that the application of these principles (summarized in the last chapter of *Elementary Structures*) to kinship data reveals an intelligible logic to the taboos and marriage rules which have perplexed and mystified Western anthropologists. He constructs a chess game of such complexity that it cannot be recapitulated here. But two of his chess pieces are particularly relevant to women—the 'gift' and the incest taboo, whose dual articulation adds up to his concept of the exchange of women.

The Elementary Structures is in part a radical gloss on another famous theory of primitive social organization, Mauss's *Essay on the Gift* (see also Sahlins, 1972: ch. 4). It was Mauss who first theorized as to the significance of one of the most striking features of primitive societies: the extent to which giving, receiving, and reciprocating gifts dominates social intercourse. In such societies, all sorts of things circulate in exchange—food, spells, rituals, words, names, ornaments, tools, and powers.

Your own mother, your own sister, your own pigs, your own yams that you have piled up, you may not eat. Other people's mothers, other people's sisters, other people's pigs, other people's yams that they have piled up, you may eat. (Arapesh, cited in Lévi-Strauss, 1969: 27)

In a typical gift transaction, neither party gains anything. In the Trobriand Islands, each household maintains a garden of yams and each household eats yams. But the yams a household grows and the yams it eats are not the same. At harvest time, a man sends the yams he has cultivated to the household of his sister; the household in which he lives is provisioned by his wife's brother (Malinowski, 1929). Since such a procedure appears to be a useless one from the point of view of accumulation or trade, its logic has been sought elsewhere. Mauss proposed that the significance of gift-giving is that it expresses, affirms, or creates a social link between the partners of an exchange. Gift-giving confers upon its participants a special relationship of trust, solidarity, and mutual aid. One can solicit a friendly relationship in the offer of a gift; acceptance implies a willingness to return a gift and a confirmation of the relationship. Gift-exchange may also be the idiom of competition and rivalry. There are many examples in which one person humiliates another by giving more than can be reciprocated. Some political systems, such as the Big Man systems of highland New Guinea, are based on exchange which is unequal on the material plane. An aspiring Big Man wants to give away more goods than can be reciprocated. He gets his return in political prestige.

Although both Mauss and Lévi-Strauss emphasize the solitary aspects of gift exchange, the other purposes served by gift-giving only strengthen the point that it is an ubiquitous means of social commerce. Mauss proposed that gifts were the threads of social discourse, the means by which such societies were held together in the absence of specialized governmental institutions. 'The gift is the primitive way of achieving the peace that in civil society is secured by the state. . . . Composing society, the gift was the liberation of culture' (Sahlins, 1972: 169, 175).

Lévi-Strauss adds to the theory of primitive reciprocity the idea that marriages are a most basic form of gift exchange, in which it is women who are the most precious of gifts. He argues that the incest taboo should best be understood as a mechanism to insure that such exchanges take place between families and between groups. Since the existence of incest taboos is universal, but the content of their prohibitions variable, they cannot be explained as having the aim of preventing the occurrence of genetically close matings.

Rather, the incest taboo imposes the social aim of exogamy and alliance upon the biological events of sex and procreation. The incest taboo divides the universe of sexual choice into categories of permitted and prohibited sexual partners. Specifically, by forbidding unions within a group it enjoins marital exchange between groups.

> The prohibition on the sexual use of a daughter or a sister compels them to be given in marriage to another man, and at the same time it establishes a right to the daughter or sister of this other man. . . . The woman whom one does not take is, for that very reason, offered up. (Lévi-Strauss, 1969: 51)

> The prohibition of incest is less a rule prohibiting marriage with the mother, sister, or daughter, than a rule obliging the mother, sister, or daughter to be given to others. It is the supreme rule of the gift. . . . (Ibid. 481)

The result of a gift of women is more profound than the result of other gift transactions, because the relationship thus established is not just one of reciprocity, but one of kinship. The exchange partners have become affines, and their descendants will be related by blood: 'Two people may meet in friendship and exchange gifts and yet quarrel and fight in later times, but intermarriage connects them in a permanent manner' (Best, cited in Lévi-Strauss, 1969: 481). As is the case with other gift-giving, marriages are not always so simply activities to make peace. Marriages may be highly competitive, and there are plenty of affines who fight each other. Nevertheless, in a general sense the argument is that the taboo on incest results in a wide network of relations, a set of people, whose connections with one another are a kinship structure. All other levels, amounts, and directions of exchange—including hostile ones—are ordered by this structure. The marriage ceremonies recorded in the ethnographic literature are moments in a ceaseless and ordered procession in which women, children, shells, words, cattle names, fish, ancestors, whale's teeth, pigs, yams, spells, dances, mats, etc., pass from hand to hand, leaving as their tracks the ties that bind. Kinship is organization, and organization gives power. But who is organized?

But it is women who are being transacted, then it is the men who give and taken them who are linked, the woman being a conduit of a relationship rather than a partner to it.[5] The exchange of women does not necessarily imply that women are objectified, in the modern sense, since objects in the primitive world are imbued with highly personal qualities. But it does imply a distinction between gift and giver. If women are the gifts, then it is men who are the exchange partners. And it is the partners, not the presents, upon whom reciprocal exchange confers its quasi-mystical power of social linkage. The relations of such a system are such that women are in no position to realize the benefits of their own circulation. As long as the relations specify that men exchange women, it is men who are the beneficiaries of the product of such exchanges—social organization.

The total relationship of exchange which constitutes marriage is not established between a man and a woman, but between two groups of men, and the woman figures only as one of the objects in the exchange, not as one of the partners. . . . This remains true even when the girl's feelings are taken into consideration, as, moreover, is usually the case. In acquiescing to the proposed union, she precipitates or allows the exchange to take place, she cannot alter its nature. . . . (Lévi-Strauss, 1969: 115)[6]

To enter into a gift exchange as a partner, one must have something to give. If women are for men to dispose of, they are in no position to give themselves away.

'What woman', mused a young Northern Melpa man, 'is ever strong enough to get up and say, "Let us make *moka*, let us find wives and pigs, let us give our daughters to men, let us wage war, let us kill our enemies!" No indeed not! . . . they are little rubbish things who stay at home simply, don't you see?' (Strathern, 1972: 161)

What women indeed! The Melpa women of whom the young man spoke can't get wives, they *are* wives, and what they get are husbands, an entirely different matter. The Melpa women can't give their daughters to men, because they do not have the same rights in their daughters that their male kin have, rights of bestowal (although *not* of ownership).

The 'exchange of women' is a seductive and powerful concept. It is attractive in that it places the oppression of women within social systems, rather than in biology. Moreover, it suggests that we look for the ultimate locus of women's oppression within the traffic in women, rather than within the traffic in merchandise. It is certainly not difficult to find ethnographic and historical examples of trafficking in women. Women are given in marriage, taken in battle, exchanged for favours, sent as tribute, traded, bought, and sold. Far from being confined to the 'primitive' world, these practices seem only to become more pronounced and commercialized in more 'civilized' societies. Men are of course also trafficked—but as slaves, hustlers, athletic stars, serfs, or as some other catastrophic social status, rather than as men. Women are transacted as slaves, serfs, and prostitutes, but also simply as women. And if men have been sexual subjects—exchangers—and women sexual semi-objects—gifts—for much of human history, then many customs, clichés, and personality traits seem to make a great deal of sense (among others, the curious custom by which a father gives away the bride).

The 'exchange of women' is also a problematic concept. Since Lévi-Strauss argues that the incest taboo and the results of its application constitute the origin of culture, it can be deduced that the world historical defeat of women occurred with the origin of culture, and is a prerequisite of culture. If his analysis is adopted in its pure form, the feminist programme must include a task even more onerous than the extermination of men; it must attempt to get rid of culture and substitute some entirely new phenomena on the face of the earth. However, it would be a dubious proposition at best to argue that if there were no exchange of women there would be no culture, if for no other reason than that culture is, by definition, inventive. It is even debatable that 'exchange of women' adequately describes all of the empirical evidence of kinship systems. Some cultures, such as the Lele and the Luma, exchange women explicitly and overtly. In other cultures, the exchange of women can be inferred. In some—particularly those hunters and gatherers excluded from Lévi-Strauss's sample—the efficacy of the concept becomes altogether questionable. What are we to make of a concept which seems so useful and yet so difficult?

The 'exchange of women' is neither a definition of culture nor a system in and of itself. The concept is an acute, but condensed, apprehension of certain aspects of the social relations of sex and gender. A kinship system is an imposition of social ends upon a part of the natural world. It is therefore 'production' in the most general sense of the term: a moulding, a transformation of objects (in this case, people) to and by a subjective purpose (for this sense of production, see Marx, 1971a: 80–99). It has its own relations of production, distribution, and exchange, which include certain 'property' forms in people. These forms are not exclusive, private property rights, but rather different sorts of rights that various people have in other people. Marriage transactions—the gifts and material which circulate in the ceremonies marking a marriage—are a rich source of data for determining exactly who has which rights in whom. It is not difficult to deduce from such transactions that in most cases women's rights are considerably more residual than those of men.

Kinship systems do not merely exchange women. They exchange sexual access, genealogical statuses, lineage names and ancestors, rights and *people*—men, women, and children—in concrete systems of social relationships. These relationships always include certain rights for men, others for women. 'Exchange of women' is a shorthand for expressing that the social relations of a kinship system specify that men have certain rights in their female kin, and that women do not have the same rights either to themselves or to their male kin. In this sense, the exchange of women is a profound perception of a system in which women do not have full rights to themselves. The exchange of women becomes an obfuscation if it is seen as a cultural necessity, and when it is used as the single tool with which an analysis of a particular kinship system is approached.

If Lévi-Strauss is correct in seeing the exchange of women as a fundamental principle of kinship, the subordination of women can be seen as a product of the relationships by which sex and gender are organized and produced. The economic oppression of women is derivative and secondary. But there is an 'economics' of sex and gender, and what we need is a political economy of sexual systems. We need to study each society to determine the exact mechanisms by which particular conventions of sexuality are produced and maintained. The 'exchange of women' is an initial step toward building an arsenal of concepts with which sexual systems can be described.

DEEPER INTO THE LABYRINTH

More concepts can be derived from an essay by Lévi-Strauss, 'The Family', in which he introduces other considerations into his analysis of kinship. In *The Elementary Structures of Kinship*, he describes rules and systems of sexual combination. In 'The Family', he raises the issue of the preconditions necessary for marriage systems to operate. He asks what sort of 'people' are required by kinship systems, by way of an analysis of the sexual division of labour.

Although every society has some sort of division of tasks by sex, the assignment of any particular task to one sex or the other varies enormously. In some groups, agriculture is the work of women, in others, the work of men. Women carry the heavy burdens in some societies, men in others. There are even examples of female hunters and warriors, and of men performing child-care tasks. Lévi-Strauss concludes from a survey of the division of labour by sex that it is not a biological specialization, but must have some other purpose. This purpose, he argues, is to insure the union of men and women by making the smallest viable economic unit contain at least one man and one woman.

The very fact that it [the sexual division of labour] varies endlessly according to the society selected for consideration shows that . . . it is the mere fact of its existence which is mysteriously required, the form under which it comes to exist being utterly irrelevant, at least from the point of view of any natural necessity . . . the sexual division of labour is nothing else than a device to institute a reciprocal state of dependency between the sexes. (Lévi-Strauss, 1971: 347–8)

The division of labour by sex can therefore be seen as a 'taboo': a taboo against the sameness of men and women, a taboo dividing the sexes into two mutually exclusive categories, a taboo which exacerbates the biological differences between the sexes and thereby *creates* gender. The division of labour can also be seen as a taboo against sexual arrangements other than those containing at least one man and one woman, thereby enjoining heterosexual marriage.

The argument in 'The Family' displays a radical questioning of all human sexual arrangements, in which no aspect of sexuality is taken for granted as 'natural' (Hertz, 1960, constructs a similar argument for a thoroughly cultural explanation of the denigration of left-handedness). Rather, all manifest forms of sex and gender are seen as being constituted by the imperatives of social systems. From such a perspective, even *The Elementary Structures of Kinship* can be seen to assume certain preconditions. In purely logical terms, a rule forbidding some marriages and commanding others presupposes a rule enjoining marriage. And marriage presupposes individuals who are disposed to marry.

It is of interest to carry this kind of deductive enterprise even further than Lévi-Strauss does, and to explicate the logical structure which underlies his entire analysis of kinship. At the most general level, the social organization of sex rests upon gender, obligatory heterosexuality, and the constraint of female sexuality.

Gender is a socially imposed division of the sexes. It is a product of the social relations of sexuality. Kinship systems rest upon marriage. They therefore transform males and females into 'men' and 'women', each as incomplete half which can only find wholeness when united with the other. Men and women are, of course, different. But they are not as different as day and night, earth and sky, yin and yang, life and death. In fact, from the standpoint of nature, men

and women are closer to each other than either is to anything else—
for instance, mountains, kangaroos, or coconut palms. The idea
that men and women are more different from one another than
either is from anything else must come from somewhere other than
nature. Furthermore, although there is an average difference
between males and females on a variety of traits, the range of variation of those traits shows considerable overlap. There will always
be some women who are taller than some men, for instance, even
though men are on the average taller than women. But the idea that
men and women are two mutually exclusive categories must arise
out of something other than a nonexistent 'natural' opposition.[7]
Far from being an expression of natural differences, exclusive gender identity is the suppression of natural similarities. It requires
repression: in men, of whatever is the local version of 'feminine'
traits; in women, of the local definition of 'masculine' traits. The
division of the sexes has the effect of repressing some of the personality characteristics of virtually everyone, men and women. The
same social system which oppresses women in its relations of
exchange, oppresses everyone in its insistence upon a rigid division
of personality.

Furthermore, individuals are engendered in order that marriage
be guaranteed. Lévi-Strauss comes dangerously close to saying that
heterosexuality is an instituted process. If biological and hormonal
imperatives were as overwhelming as popular mythology would
have them, it would hardly be necessary to insure heterosexual
unions by means of economic interdependency. Moreover, the
incest taboo presupposes a prior, less articulate taboo on homosexuality. A prohibition against *some* heterosexual unions assumes a
taboo against *non*-heterosexual unions. Gender is not only an identification with one sex; it also entails that sexual desire be directed
toward the other sex. The sexual division of labour is implicated in
both aspects of gender—male and female—it creates them, and it
creates them heterosexual. The suppression of the homosexual
component of human sexuality, and by corollary, the oppression of
homosexuals, is therefore a product of the same system whose rules
and relations oppress women.

In fact, the situation is not so simple, as is obvious when we move
from the level of generalities to the analysis of specific sexual systems. Kinship systems do not merely encourage heterosexuality to
the detriment of homosexuality. In the first place, specific forms of
heterosexuality may be required. For instance, some marriage systems have a rule of obligatory cross-cousin marriage. A person in

such a system is not only heterosexual, but 'cross-cousin-sexual'. If the rule of marriage further specifies matrilateral cross-cousin marriage, then a man will be 'mother's-brother's-daughter-sexual' and a woman will be 'father's-sister's-son-sexual'.

On the other hand, the very complexities of a kinship system may result in particular forms of institutionalized homosexuality. In many New Guinea groups, men and women are considered to be so inimical to one another that the period spent by a male child *in utero* negates his maleness. Since male life-force is thought to reside in semen, the boy can overcome the malevolent effects of his fetal history by obtaining and consuming semen. He does so through a homosexual partnership with an older male kinsman (Kelly, 1974; see also Van Baal, 1966; Williams, 1936).

In kinship systems where bridewealth determines the statuses of husband and wife, the simple prerequisites of marriage and gender may be overridden. Among the Azande, women are monopolized by older men. A young man of means may, however, take a boy as wife while he waits to come of age. He simply pays a bridewealth (in spears) for the boy, who is thereby turned into a wife (Evans-Pritchard, 1970). In Dahomey, a woman could turn herself into a husband if she possessed the necessary bridewealth (Herskovitz, 1937).

The institutionalized 'transvesticism' of the Mohave permitted a person to change from one sex to the other. An anatomical man could become a woman by means of a special ceremony, and an anatomical woman could in the same way become a man. The transvestite then took a wife or husband of her/his own anatomical sex and opposite social sex. These marriages, which we would label homosexual, were heterosexual ones by Mohave standards, unions of opposite socially defined sexes. By comparison with our society, this whole arrangement permitted a great deal of freedom. However, a person was not permitted to be some of both genders—he/she could be either male or female, but not a little of each (Devereaux, 1937; see also McMurtrie, 1914; Soneschein, 1966).

In all of the above examples, the rules of gender division and obligatory heterosexuality are present even in their transformations. These two rules apply equally to the constraint of both male and female behaviour and personality. Kinship systems dictate some sculpting of the sexuality of both sexes. But it can be deduced from *The Elementary Structures of Kinship* that more constraint is applied to females when they are pressed into the service of kinship than to males. If women are exchanged, in whatever sense we take the term, marital debts are reckoned in female flesh. A woman must become the sexual partner of some man to whom she is owed as return on a previous marriage. If a girl is promised in infancy, her refusal to participate as an adult would disrupt the flow of debts and promises. It would be in the interests of the smooth and continuous operation of such a system if the woman in question did not have too many ideas of her own about whom she might want to sleep with. From the standpoint of the system, the preferred female sexuality would be one which responded to the desire of others, rather than one which actively desired and sought a response.

This generality, like the ones about gender and heterosexuality, is also subject to considerable variation and free play in actual systems. The Lele and the Kuma provide two of the clearest ethnographic examples of the exchange of women. Men in both cultures are perpetually engaged in schemes which necessitate that they have full control over the sexual destinies of their female kinswomen. Much of the drama in both societies consists in female attempts to evade the sexual control of their kinsmen. Nevertheless, female resistance in both cases is severely circumscribed (Douglas, 1963; Reay, 1959).

One last generality could be predicted as a consequence of the exchange of women under a system in which rights to women are held by men. What would happen if our hypothetical woman not only refused the man to whom she was promised, but asked for a woman instead? If a single refusal were disruptive, a double refusal would be insurrectionary. If each woman is promised to some man, neither has a right to dispose of herself. If two women managed to extricate themselves from the debt nexus, two other women would have to be found to replace them. As long as men have rights in women which women do not have in themselves, it would be sensible to expect that homosexuality in women would be subject to more suppression than in men.

In summary, some basic generalities about the organization of human sexuality can be derived from an exegesis of Lévi-Strauss's theories of kinship. These are the incest taboo, obligatory heterosexuality, and an asymmetric division of the sexes. The asymmetry of gender—the difference between exchanger and exchanged—entails the constraint of female sexuality. Concrete kinship systems will have more specific conventions, and these conventions vary a great deal. While particular socio-sexual systems vary, each one is specific, and individuals within it will have to conform to a finite set of possibilities. Each new generation must learn and become its sexual destiny, each person must be encoded with its appropriate status within the system. It would be extraordinary for one of us to calmly assume that we would conventionally marry a mother's brother's daughter, or a father's sister's son. Yet there are groups in which such a marital future is taken for granted.

Anthropology, and descriptions of kinship systems, do not explain the mechanisms by which children are engraved with the conventions of sex and gender. Psychoanalysis, on the other hand, is a theory about the reproduction of kinship. Psychoanalysis describes the residue left within individuals by their confrontation with the rules and regulations of sexuality of the societies to which they are born.

PSYCHOANALYSIS AND ITS DISCONTENTS

The battle between psychoanalysis and the women's and gay movements has become legendary. In part, this confrontation between sexual revolutionaries and the clinical establishment has been due to the evolution of psychoanalysis in the United States, where clinical tradition has fetishized anatomy. The child is thought to travel through its organismic stages until it reaches its anatomical destiny and the missionary position. Clinical practice has often seen its mission as the repair of individuals who somehow have become derailed *en route* to their 'biological' aim. Transforming moral law into scientific law, clinical practice has acted to enforce sexual convention upon unruly participants. In this sense, psychoanalysis has often become more than a theory of the mechanisms of the reproduction of sexual arrangements; it has been one of those mechanisms. Since the aim of the feminist and gay revolts is to dismantle the apparatus of sexual enforcement, a critique of psychoanalysis has been in order.

But the rejection of Freud by the women's and gay movements has deeper roots in the rejection by psychoanalysis of its own insights. Nowhere are the effects on women of male-dominated social systems better documented than within the clinical literature. According to the Freudian orthodoxy, the attainment of 'normal' femininity extracts severe costs from women. The theory of gender acquisition could have been the basis of a critique of sex roles. Instead, the radical implications of Freud's theory have been radically repressed. This tendency is evident even in the original formulations of the theory, but it has been exacerbated over time until the potential for a critical psychoanalytic theory of gender is visible only in the symptomatology of its denial—an intricate rationalization of sex roles as they are. It is not the purpose of this paper to conduct a psychoanalysis of the psychoanalytic unconscious; but I do hope to demonstrate that it exists. Moreover, the salvage of psychoanalysis from its own motivated repression is not for the sake of Freud's good name. Psychoanalysis contains a unique set of concepts for understanding men, women, and sexuality. It is a theory of sexuality in human society. Most importantly, psychoanalysis provides a description of the mechanisms by which the sexes are divided and deformed, of how bisexual, androgynous infants are transformed into boys and girls.[8] Psychoanalysis is a feminist theory *manqué*.

THE OEDIPUS HEX

Until the late 1920s, the psychoanalytic movement did not have a distinctive theory of feminine development. Instead, variants of an 'Electra' complex in women had been proposed, in which female experience was thought to be a mirror image of the Oedipal complex described for males. The boy loved his mother, but gave her up out of fear of the father's threat of castration. The girl, it was thought, loved her father, and gave him up out of fear of maternal vengeance. This formulation assumed that both children were subject to a biological imperative toward heterosexuality. It also assumed that the children were already, before the Oedipal phase, 'little' men and women.

Freud had voiced reservations about jumping to conclusions about women on the basis of data gathered from men. But his objections remained general until the discovery of the pre-Oedipal phase in women. The concept of the pre-Oedipal phase enabled both Freud and Jeanne Lampl de Groot to articulate the classic psychoanalytic theory of femininity.[9] The idea of the pre-Oedipal phase in women produced a dislocation of the biologically derived presuppositions which underlay notions of an 'Electra' complex. In the pre-Oedipal phase, children of both sexes were psychically indistinguishable, which meant that their differentiation into masculine and feminine children had to be explained, rather than assumed. Pre-Oedipal children were described as bisexual. Both sexes exhibited the full range of libidinal attitudes, active and passive. And for children of both sexes, the mother was the object of desire.

In particular, the characteristics of the pre-Oedipal female challenged the ideas of a primordial heterosexuality and gender identity. Since the girl's libidinal activity was directed toward the mother, her adult heterosexuality had to be explained:

It would be a solution of ideal simplicity if we could suppose that from a particular age onwards the elementary influence of the mutual attraction between the sexes makes itself felt and impels the small woman towards men. ... But we are not going to find things so easy; we scarcely know whether we are to believe seriously in the power of which poets talk so much and with such enthusiasm but which cannot be further dissected analytically. (Freud, 1965: 119)

Moreover, the girl did not manifest a 'feminine' libidinal attitude. Since her desire for the mother was active and aggressive, her ultimate accession to 'femininity' had also to be explained:

In conformity with its peculiar nature, psychoanalysis does not try to describe what a woman is . . . but sets about enquiring how she comes into being, how a woman develops out of a child with a bisexual disposition. (Ibid. 116)

In short, feminine development could not longer be taken for granted as a reflex of biology. Rather, it had become immensely problematic. It is in explaining the acquisition of 'femininity' that Freud employs the concepts of penis envy and castration which have infuriated feminists since he first introduced them. The girl turns from the mother and represses the 'masculine' elements of her libido as a result of her recognition that she is castrated. She compares her tiny clitoris to the larger penis, and in the face of its evident superior ability to satisfy the mother, falls prey to penis envy and a sense of inferiority. She gives up her struggle for the mother and assumes a passive feminine position *vis-à-vis* the father. Freud's account can be read as claiming that femininity is a consequence of the anatomical differences between the sexes. He has therefore been accused of biological determinism. Nevertheless, even in his most anatomically stated versions of the female castration complex, the 'inferiority' of the women's genitals is a product of the situational context: the girl feels less 'equipped' to possess and satisfy the mother. If the pre-Oedipal lesbian were not confronted by the heterosexuality of the mother, she might draw different conclusions about the relative status of her genitals.

Freud was never as much of a biological determinist as some

127

would have him. He repeatedly stressed that all adult sexuality resulted from psychic, not biologic, development. But his writing is often ambiguous, and his wording leaves plenty of room for the biological interpretations which have been so popular in American psychoanalysis. In France, on the other hand, the trend in psycho-analytic theory has been to de-biologize Freud, and to conceive of psychoanalysis as a theory of information rather than organs. Jacques Lacan, the instigator of this line of thinking, insists that Freud never meant to say anything about anatomy, and that Freud's theory was instead about language and the cultural meanings imposed upon anatomy. The debate over the 'real' Freud is extremely interesting, but it is not my purpose here to contribute to it. Rather, I want to rephrase the classic theory of femininity in Lacan's terminology, after introducing some of the pieces on Lacan's conceptual chessboard.

KINSHIP, LACAN, AND THE PHALLUS

Lacan suggests that psychoanalysis is the study of the traces left in the psyches of individuals as a result of their conscription into systems of kinship.

Isn't it striking that Lévi-Strauss, in suggesting that implication of the structures of language with that part of the social laws which regulate marriage ties and kinship, is already conquering the very terrain in which Freud situates the unconscious? (Lacan, 1968: 48)

For where on earth would one situate the determinations of the unconsciousness if it is not in those nominal cadres in which marriage ties and kinship are always grounded. . . . And how would one apprehend the analytical conflicts and their Oedipean prototype outside the engagements which have fixed, long before the subject came into the world, not only his destiny, but his identity itself? (Ibid. 126)

This is precisely where the Oedipus complex . . . may be said, in this connection, to mark the limits which our discipline assigns to subjectivity: that is to say, what the subject can know of his unconscious participation in the movement of the complex structures of marriage ties, by verifying the symbolic effects in his individual existence of the tangential movement towards incest. . . . (Ibid. 40)

Kinship is the culturalization of biological sexuality on the societal level; psychoanalysis describes the transformation of the biological sexuality of individuals as they are enculturated.

Kinship terminology contains information about the system. Kin terms demarcate statuses, and indicate some of the attributes of those statuses. For instance, in the Trobriand Islands a man calls the women of his clan by the term for 'sister'. He calls the women of clans into which he can marry by a term indicting their marriage-ability. When the young Trobriand male learns these terms, he learns which women he can safely desire. In Lacan's scheme, the Oedipal crisis occurs when a child learns of the sexual rules embedded in the terms for family and relatives. The crisis begins when the child comprehends the system and his or her place in it; the crisis is resolved when the child accepts that place and accedes to it. Even if the child refuses its place, he or she cannot escape knowledge of it. Before the Oedipal phase, the sexuality of the child is labile and relatively unstructured. Each child contains all of the sexual possibilities available to human expression. But in any given society, only some of these possibilities will be expressed, while others will be constrained. When the child leaves the Oedipal phase, its libido and gender identity have been organized in conformity with the rules of the culture which is domesticating it.

The Oedipal complex is an apparatus for the production of sexual personality. It is a truism to say that societies will inculcate in their young the character traits appropriate to carrying on the business of society. For instance, E. P. Thompson (1963) speaks of the transformation of the personality structure of the English working class, as artisans were changed into good industrial workers. Just as the social forms of labour demand certain kinds of personality, the social forms of sex and gender demand certain kinds of people. In the most general terms, the Oedipal complex is a machine which fashions the appropriate forms of sexual individuals (see also the discussion of different forms of 'historical individuality' in Althusser and Balibar, 1970: 112, 251–3).

In the Lacanian theory of psychoanalysis, it is the kin terms that indicate a structure of relationships which will determine the role of any individual or object within the Oedipal drama. For instance, Lacan makes a distinction between the 'function of the father' and a particular father who embodies this function. In the same way, he makes a radical distinction between the penis and the 'phallus', between organ and information. The phallus is a set of meanings conferred upon the penis. The differentiation between phallus and penis in contemporary French psychoanalytic terminology emphasizes the idea that the penis could not and does not play the role attributed to it in the classical terminology of the castration complex.[10]

In Freud's terminology, the Oedipal complex presents two alternatives to a child: to have a penis or to be castrated. In contrast, the Lacanian theory of the castration complex leaves behind all reference to anatomical reality:

The theory of the castration complex amounts to having the male organ play a dominant role—this time as a symbol—to *the extent that its absence or presence transforms an anatomical difference into a major classification of humans, and to the extent that, for each subject, this presence or absence is not taken for granted, is not reduced purely and simply to a given, but is the problematical result of an intra- and intersubjective process* (the subject's assumption of his own sex). (Laplanche and Pontalis, in Mehlman, 1972: 198–9; my italics)

The alternative presented to the child may be rephrased as an alternative between having, or not having, the phallus. Castration is not having the (symbolic) phallus. Castration is not a real 'lack', but a meaning conferred upon the genitals of a woman:

Castration may derive support from . . . the apprehension in the Real of the absence of the penis in women—but even this supposes a symbolization of the object, since the Real is full, and 'lacks' nothing. In so far as one finds castration in the genesis of neurosis, it is never real but symbolic. . . . (Lacan, 1968: 271)

The phallus is, as it were, a distinctive feature differentiating 'castrated' and 'non-castrated'. The presence or absence of the phallus carries the differences between two sexual statuses, 'man' and 'woman' (see Jakobson and Halle, 1971, on distinctive females). Since these are not equal, the phallus also carries a meaning of the dominance of men over women, and it may be inferred that 'penis envy' is a recognition thereof. Moreover, as long as men have rights in women which women do not have in themselves, the phallus also carries the meaning of the difference between 'exchanger' and 'exchanged', gift and giver. Ultimately, neither the classical Freudian nor the rephrased Lacanian theories of the Oedipal process make sense unless at least this much of the paleolithic relations of sexuality are still with us. We still live in a 'phallic' culture.

Lacan also speaks of the phallus as a symbolic object which is exchanged within and between families (see also Wilden, 1968: 303–5). It is interesting to think about this observation in terms of primitive marriage transactions and exchange networks. In those transactions, the exchange of women is usually one of many cycles of exchange. Usually, there are other objects circulating as well as women. Women move in one direction, cattle, shells, or mats in the other. In one sense, the Oedipal complex is an expression of the circulation of the phallus in intrafamily exchange, an inversion of the circulation of women in interfamily exchange. In the cycle of exchange manifested by the Oedipal complex, the phallus passes through the medium of women from one man to another—from father to son, from mother's brother to sister's son, and so forth. In this family *Kula* ring, women go one way, the phallus the other. It is where we aren't. In this sense, the phallus is more than a feature which distinguishes the sexes: it is the embodiment of the male status, to which men accede, and in which certain rights inhere—among them, the right to a woman. It is an expression of the transmission of male dominance. It passes through women and settles upon men.[11] The tracks which it leaves include gender identity, the division of the sexes. But it leaves more than this. It leaves 'penis envy', which acquires a rich meaning of the disquietude of women in a phallic culture.

OEDIPUS REVISITED

We return now to the two pre-Oedipal androgynes, sitting on the border between biology and culture. Lévi-Strauss places the incest taboo on that border, arguing that its initiation of the exchange of women constitutes the origin of society. In this sense, the incest taboo and the exchange of women are the content of the original social contract (see Sahlins, 1972: ch. 4). For individuals, the Oedipal crisis occurs at the same divide, when the incest taboo initiates the exchange of the phallus.

The Oedipal crisis is precipitated by certain items of information. The children discover the differences between the sexes, and that each child must become one or the other gender. They also discover the incest taboo, and that some sexuality is prohibited—in this case, the mother is unavailable to either child because she 'belongs' to the father. Lastly, they discover that the two genders do not have the same sexual 'rights' or futures.

In the normal course of events, the boy renounces his mother for fear that otherwise his father would castrate him (refuse to give him the phallus and make him a girl). But by this act of renunciation, the boy affirms the relationships which have given mother to father and which will give him, if he becomes a man, a woman of his own. In exchange for the boy's affirmation of his father's right to his

131

mother, the father affirms the phallus in his son (does not castrate him). The boy exchanges his mother for the phallus, the symbolic token which can later be exchanged for a woman. The only thing required of him is a little patience. He retains his initial libidinal organization and the sex of his original love object. The social contract to which he has agreed will eventually recognize his own rights and provide him with a woman of his own.

What happens to the girl is more complex. She, like the boy, discovers the taboo against incest and the division of the sexes. She also discovers some unpleasant information about the gender to which she is being assigned. For the boy, the taboo on incest is a taboo on certain women. For the girl, it is a taboo on all women. Since she is in a homosexual position *vis-à-vis* the mother, the rule of heterosexuality which dominates the scenario makes her position excruciatingly untenable. The mother, and all women by extension, can only be properly beloved by someone 'with a penis' (phallus). Since the girl has no 'phallus', she has no 'right' to love her mother or another woman, since she is herself destined to some man. She does not have the symbolic token which can be exchanged for a woman.

If Freud's wording of this moment of the female Oedipal crisis is ambiguous, Lampl de Groot's formulation makes the context which confers meaning upon the genitals explicit:

> ... *if the little girl comes to the conclusion that such an organ is really indispensable to the possession of the mother, she experiences* in addition to the narcissistic insults common to both sexes still another blow, namely *a feeling of inferiority about her genitals.* (Lampl de Groot, 1933: 497; my italics)

The girl concludes that the 'penis' is indispensable for the possession of the mother because only those who possess the phallus have a 'right' to a woman, and the token of exchange. She does not come to her conclusion because of the natural superiority of the penis either in and of itself, or as an instrument for making love. The hierarchical arrangement of the male and female genitals is a result of the definitions of the situation—the rule of obligatory heterosexuality and the relegation of women (those without the phallus, castrated) to men (those with the phallus).

The girl then begins to turn away from the mother, and to the father.

To the girl, it [castration] is an accomplished fact, which is irrevocable, but the recognition of which compels her finally to renounce her first love object and to taste to the full the bitterness of its loss ... the father is chosen as a love-object, the enemy becomes the beloved. . . . (Lampl de Groot, 1948: 213)

This recognition of 'castration' forces the girl to redefine her relationship to herself, her mother, and her father.

She turns from the mother because she does not have the phallus to give her. She turns from the mother also in anger and disappointment, because the mother did not give her a 'penis' (phallus). But the mother, a woman in a phallic culture, does not have the phallus to give away (having gone through the Oedipal crisis herself a generation earlier). The girl then turns to the father because only he can 'give her the phallus', and it is only through him that she can enter into the symbolic exchange system in which the phallus circulates. But the father does not give her the phallus in the same way that he gives it to the boy. The phallus is affirmed in the boy, who then has it to give away. The girl never gets the phallus. It passes through her, and in its passage is transformed into a child. When she 'recognizes her castration', she accedes to the place of a woman in a phallic exchange network. She can 'get' the phallus—in intercourse, or as a child—but only as a gift from a man. She never gets to give it away.

When she turns to the father, she also represses the 'active' portions of her libido:

The turning away from her mother is an extremely important step in the course of a little girl's development. It is more than a mere change of object . . . hand in hand with it there is to be observed a marked lowering of the active sexual impulses and a rise of the passive ones. . . . The transition to the father object is accomplished with the help of the passive trends in so far as they have escaped the catastrophe. The path to the development of femininity now lies open to the girl. (Freud, 1961b: 239)

The ascendance of passivity in the girl is due to her recognition of the futility of realizing her active desire, and of the unequal terms of the struggle. Freud locates active desire in the clitoris and passive desire in the vagina, and thus describes the repression of active desire as the repression of clitoral eroticism in favour of passive vaginal eroticism. In this scheme, cultural stereotypes have been mapped onto the genitals. Since the work of Masters and Johnson, it is evident that this genital division is a false one. Any organ—penis, clitoris, vagina—can be the locus of either active or passive eroticism. What is important in Freud's scheme, however, is not the geography of desire, but its self-confidence. It is not an organ which is repressed, but a segment of erotic possibility. Freud notes that 'more constraint has been applied to the libido when it is pressed into the service of the feminine function . . .' (Freud, 1965: 131). The girl has been robbed.

If the Oedipal phase proceeds normally and the girl 'accepts her castration', her libidinal structure and object choice are now congruent with the female gender role. She has become a little woman—feminine, passive, heterosexual. Actually, Freud suggests that there are three alternate routes out of the Oedipal catastrophe. The girl may simply freak out, repress sexuality altogether, and become asexual. She may protest, cling to her narcissism and desire, and become either 'masculine' or homosexual. Or she may accept the situation, sign the social contract, and attain 'normality'.

Karen Horney is critical of the entire Freud/Lampl de Groot scheme. But in the course of her critique she articulates its implications:

. . . when she [the girl] first turns to a man (the father), it is in the main only by way of the narrow bridge of resentment . . . we should feel it a contradiction if the relation of woman to man did not retain throughout life some tinge of this enforced substitute for that which was really desired. . . . The same character of something remote from instinct, secondary and substitutive, would, even in normal women, adhere to the wish for motherhood. . . . The special point about Freud's viewpoint is rather that it sees the wish for motherhood not as an innate formation, but as something that can be reduced psychologically to its ontogenetic elements and draws its energy originally from homosexual or phallic instinctual elements. . . . It would follow, finally, that women's whole reaction to life would be based on a strong subterranean resentment. (Horney, 1973: 148–9)

Horney considers these implications to be so far-fetched that they challenge the validity of Freud's entire scheme. But it is certainly plausible to argue instead that the creation of 'femininity' in women in the course of socialization is an act of psychic brutality, and that it leaves in women an immense resentment of the suppression to which they were subjected. It is also possible to argue that women have few means for realizing and expressing their residual anger. One can read Freud's essays on femininity as descriptions of how a group is prepared psychologically, at a tender age, to live with its oppression.

There is an additional element in the classic discussions of the attainment of womanhood. The girl first turns to the father because she must, because she is 'castrated' (a woman, helpless, etc.). She then discovers that 'castration' is a prerequisite to the father's love, that she must be a woman for him to love her. She therefore begins to desire 'castration', and what had previously been a disaster becomes a wish.

Analytic experience leaves no room for doubt that the little girl's first libidinal relation to her father is masochistic, and the masochistic wish in its earliest distinctively feminine phase is: 'I want to be castrated by my father.' (Deutsch, 1948a: 228)

Deutsch argues that such masochism may conflict with the ego, causing some women to flee the entire situation in defence of their self-regard. Those women to whom the choice is 'between finding bliss in suffering or peace in renunciation' (ibid. 231) will have difficulty in attaining a healthy attitude to intercourse and motherhood. Why Deutsch appears to consider such women to be special cases, rather than the norm, is not clear from her discussion.

The psychoanalytic theory of femininity is one that sees female development based largely on pain and humiliation, and it takes some fancy footwork to explain why anyone ought to enjoy being a woman. At this point in the classic discussions biology makes a triumphant return. The fancy footwork consists in arguing that finding joy in pain is adaptive to the role of women in reproduction, since childbirth and defloration are 'painful'. Would it not make more sense to question the entire procedure? If women, in finding their place in a sexual system, are robbed of libido and forced into a masochistic eroticism, why did the analysts not argue for novel arrangements, instead of rationalizing the old ones?

Freud's theory of femininity has been subjected to feminist critique since it was first published. To the extent that it is a rationalization of female subordination, this critique has been justified. To the extent that it is a description of a process which subordinates women, this critique is a mistake. As a description of how phallic culture domesticates women, and the effects in women of their domestication, psychoanalytic theory has no parallel (see also Mitchell, 1971 and 1974; Lasch, 1974). And since psychoanalysis is a theory of gender, dismissing it would be suicidal for a political movement dedicated to eradicating gender hierarchy (or gender itself). We cannot dismantle something that we underestimate or do not understand. The oppression of women is deep; equal pay, equal work, and all of the female politicians in the world will not extirpate the roots of sexism. Lévi-Strauss and Freud elucidate what would otherwise be poorly perceived parts of the deep structures of sex oppression. They serve as reminders of the intractability and magnitude of what we fight, and their analyses provide preliminary charts of the social machinery we must rearrange.

WOMEN UNITE TO OFF THE OEDIPAL RESIDUE OF CULTURE

The precision of the fit between Freud and Lévi-Strauss is striking. Kinship systems require a division of the sexes. The Oedipal phase divides the sexes. Kinship systems include sets of rules governing sexuality. The Oedipal crisis is the assimilation of these rules and taboos. Compulsory heterosexuality is the product of kinship. The Oedipal phase constitutes heterosexual desire. Kinship rests on a radical difference between the rights of men and women. The Oedipal complex confers male rights upon the boy, and forces the girl to accommodate herself to her lesser rights.

This fit between Lévi-Strauss and Freud is by implication an argument that our sex/gender system is still organized by the principles outlines by Lévi-Strauss, despite the entirely non-modern character of his data base. The more recent data on which Freud bases his theories testifies to the endurance of these sexual structures. If my reading of Freud and Lévi-Strauss is accurate, it suggests that the feminist movement must attempt to resolve the Oedipal crisis of culture by reorganizing the domain of sex and gender in such a way that each individual's Oedipal experience would be less destructive. The dimensions of such a task are difficult to imagine, but at least certain conditions would have to be met.

Several elements of the Oedipal crisis would have to be altered in order that the phase not have such disastrous effects on the young female ego. The Oedipal phase institutes a contradiction in the girl by placing irreconcilable demands upon her. On the one hand, the girl's love for the mother is induced by the mother's job of child care. The girl is then forced to abandon this love because of the female sex role—to belong to a man. If the sexual division of labour were such that adults of both sexes cared for children equally, primary object choice would be bisexual. If heterosexuality were not obligatory, this early love would not have to be suppressed, and the penis would not be overvalued. If the sexual property system were reorganized in such a way that men did not have overriding rights in women (if there was no exchange of women) and if there were no gender, the entire Oedipal drama would be a relic. In short, feminism must call for a revolution in kinship.

The organization of sex and gender once had functions other than itself—it organized society. Now, it only organizes and reproduces itself. The kinds of relationships of sexuality established in the dim human past still dominate our sexual lives, our ideas about men and women, and the ways we raise our children. But they lack the functional load they once carried. One of the most conspicuous features of kinship is that it has been systematically stripped of its functions—political, economic, educational, and organizational. it has been reduced to its barest bones—*sex and gender.*

Human sexual life will always be subject to convention and human intervention. It will never be completely 'natural', if only because our species is social, cultural, and articulate. The wild profusion of infantile sexuality will always be tamed. The confrontation between immature and helpless infants and the developed social life of their elders will probably always leave some residue of disturbance. But the mechanisms and aims of this process need not be largely independent of conscious choice. Cultural evolution provides us with the opportunity to seize control of the means of sexuality, reproduction, and socialization, and to make conscious decisions to liberate human sexual life from the archaic relationships which deform it. Ultimately, a thoroughgoing feminist revolution would liberate more than women. It would liberate forms of sexual expression, and it would liberate human personality from the straight-jacket of gender.

'DADDY, DADDY, YOU BASTARD, I'M THROUGH.' (SYLVIA PLATH)

In the course of this essay I have tried to construct a theory of women's oppression by borrowing concepts from anthropology and psychoanalysis. But Lévi-Strauss and Freud write within an intellectual tradition produced by a culture in which women are oppressed. The danger in my enterprise is that the sexism in the tradition of which they are a part tends to be dragged in with each borrowing. 'We cannot utter a single destructive proposition which has not already slipped into the form, the logic, and the implicit postulations of precisely what it seeks to contest' (Derrida, 1972: 250). And what slips in is formidable. Both psychoanalysis and structural anthropology are, in one sense, the most sophisticated ideologies of sexism around.[12]

For instance, Lévi-Strauss sees women as being like words, which are misused when they are not 'communicated' and exchanged. On the last page of a very long book, he observes that this creates something of a contradiction in women, since women are at the same time 'speakers' and 'spoken'. His only comment on this contradiction is this:

> But woman could never become just a sign and nothing more, since even in a man's world she is still a person, and since in so far as she is defined as a sign she must be recognized as a generator of signs. In the matrimonial dialogue of men, woman is never purely what is spoken about; for if women in general represent a certain category of signs, destined to a certain kind of communication, each woman preserves a particular value arising from her talent, before and after marriage, for taking her part in a duet. In contrast to words, which have wholly become signs, woman has remained at once a sign and a value. *This explains why the relations between the sexes have preserved that affective richness, ardour and mystery which doubtless originally permeated the entire universe of human communications.* (Lévi-Strauss, 1969: 496; my italics)

This is an extraordinary statement. Why is he not, at this point, denouncing what kinship systems do to women, instead of presenting one of the greatest rip-offs of all time as the root of romance?

A similar insensitivity is revealed within psychoanalysis by the inconsistency with which it assimilates the critical implications of its own theory. For instance, Freud did not hesitate to recognize that his findings posed a challenge to conventional morality:

> We cannot avoid observing with critical eyes, and we have found that it is impossible to give our support to conventional sexual morality or to approve highly of the means by which society attempts to arrange the practical problems of sexuality in life. *We can demonstrate with ease that what the world calls its code of morals demands more sacrifices than it is worth*, and that its behaviour is neither dictated by honesty nor instituted with wisdom. (Freud, 1943: 376–7; my emphasis)

Nevertheless, when psychoanalysis demonstrates with equal facility that the ordinary components of feminine personality are masochism, self-hatred, and passivity,[13] a similar judgement is *not* made. Instead, a double standard of interpretation is employed. Masochism is bad for men, essential to women. Adequate narcissism is necessary for men, impossible for women. Passivity is tragic in man, while lack of passivity is tragic in a woman.

It is this double standard which enables clinicians to try to accommodate women to a role whose destructiveness is so lucidly detailed in their own theories. It is the same inconsistent attitude which permits therapists to consider lesbianism as a problem to be cured, rather than as the resistance to a bad situation that their own theory suggests.[14]

There are points within the analytic discussions of femininity where one might say, 'This is oppression of women', or 'We can demonstrate with ease that what the world calls femininity demands more sacrifices than it is worth'. It is precisely at such points that the implications of the theory are ignored, and are replaced with formulations whose purpose is to keep those implications firmly lodged in the theoretical unconscious. It is at these points that all sorts of mysterious chemical substances, joys in pain, and biological aims are substituted for a critical assessment of the costs of femininity. These substitutions are the symptoms of theoretical repression, in that they are not consistent with the usual canons of psychoanalytic argument. The extent to which these rationalizations of femininity go against the grain of psychoanalytic logic is strong evidence for the extent of the need to suppress the radical and feminist implications of the theory of femininity (Deutsch's discussions are excellent examples of this process of substitution and repression).

The argument which must be woven in order to assimilate Lévi-Strauss and Freud into feminist theory is somewhat tortuous. I have engaged it for several reasons. First, while neither Lévi-Strauss nor Freud questions the undoubted sexism endemic to the systems they describe, the questions which ought to be posed are blindingly obvious. Second, their work enables us to isolate sex and gender from 'mode of production', and to counter a certain tendency to explain sex oppression as a reflex of economic forces. Their work provides a framework in which the full weight of sexuality and marriage can be incorporated into an analysis of sex oppression. It suggests a conception of the women's movement as analogous to, rather than isomorphic with, the working-class movement, each addressing a different source of human discontent. In Marx's vision, the working-class movement would do more than throw off the burden of its own exploitation. It also had the potential to change society, to liberate humanity, to create a classless society. Perhaps the women's movement has the task of effecting the same kind of social change for a system of which Marx had only an imperfect apperception. Something of this sort is implicit in Wittig

(1973)—the dictatorship of the Amazon *guérillères* is a temporary means for achieving a genderless society.

The sex/gender system is not immutably oppressive and has lost much of its traditional function. Nevertheless, it will not wither away in the absence of opposition. It still carries the social burden of sex and gender, of socializing the young, and of providing ultimate propositions about the nature of human beings themselves. And it serves economic and political ends other than those it was originally designed to further (cf. Scott, 1965). The sex/gender system must be reorganized through political action.

Finally, the exegesis of Lévi-Strauss and Freud suggests a certain vision of feminist politics and the feminist utopia. It suggests that we should not aim for the elimination of men, but for the elimination of the social system which creates sexism and gender. I personally find a vision of an Amazon matriarchate, in which men are reduced to servitude or oblivion (depending on the possibilities for parthenogenetic reproduction), distasteful and inadequate. Such a vision maintains gender and the division of the sexes. It is a vision which simply inverts the arguments of those who base their case for inevitable male dominance on ineradicable and *significant* biological differences between the sexes. But we are not only oppressed *as* women, we are oppressed by having to *be* women, or men as the case may be. I personally feel that the feminist movement must dream of even more than the elimination of the oppression of women. It must dream of the elimination of obligatory sexualities and sex roles. The dream I find most compelling is one of an androgynous and genderless (though not sexless) society, in which one's sexual anatomy is irrelevant to who one is, what one does, and with whom one makes love.

THE POLITICAL ECONOMY OF SEX

It would be nice to be able to conclude here with the implications for feminism and gay liberation of the overlap between Freud and Lévi-Strauss. But I must suggest, tentatively, a next step on the agenda: a Marxism analysis of sex/gender systems. Sex/gender systems are not ahistorical emanations of the human mind; they are products of historical human activity.

We need, for instance, an analysis of the evolution of sexual exchange along the lines of Marx's discussion in *Capital* of the evolution of money and commodities. There is an economics and a politics to sex/gender systems which is obscured by the concept of 'exchange of women'. For instance, a system in which women are exchangeable only for one another has different effects on women than one in which there is a commodity equivalent for women.

That marriage in simple societies involves an 'exchange' is a somewhat vague notion that has often confused the analysis of social systems. The extreme case is the exchange of 'sisters', formerly practised in parts of Australia and Africa. Here the term has the precise dictionary meaning of 'to be received as an equivalent for', 'to give and receive reciprocally'. From quite a different standpoint the virtually universal incest prohibition means that marriage systems necessarily involve 'exchanging' siblings for spouses, giving rise to a reciprocity that is purely notational. But in most societies marriage is mediated by a set of intermediary transactions. If we see these transactions as simply implying immediate or long-term reciprocity, then the analysis is likely to be blurred. . . . The analysis is further limited if one regards the passage of property simply as a symbol of the transfer of rights, for then the nature of the objects handed over . . . is of little importance. . . . Neither of these approaches is wrong; both are inadequate. (Goody, 1973: 2)

There are systems in which there is no equivalent for a woman. To get a wife, a man must have a daughter, a sister, or other female kinswoman in whom he has a right of bestowal. He must have control over some female flesh. The Lele and Kuna are cases in point. Lele men scheme constantly in order to stake claims in some as yet unborn girl, and scheme further to make good their claims (Douglas, 1963). A Kuma girl's marriage is determined by an intricate web of debts, and she has little say in choosing her husband. A girl is usually married against her will, and her groom shoots an arrow into her thigh to symbolically prevent her from running away. The young wives almost always do run away, only to be returned to their new husbands by an elaborate conspiracy enacted by their kin and affines (Reay, 1959).

In other societies, there is an equivalent for women. A woman can be converted into bridewealth, and bridewealth can be in turn converted into a woman. The dynamics of such systems vary accordingly, as does the specific kind of pressure exerted upon women. The marriage of a Melpa woman is not a return for a previous debt. Each transaction is self-contained, in that the payment of a bridewealth in pigs and shells will cancel the debt. The Melpa woman therefore has more latitude in choosing her husband than does her Kuma counterpart. On the other hand, her destiny is

141

linked to bridewealth. If her husband's kin are slow to pay, her kin may encourage her to leave him. On the other hand, if her consanguineal kin are satisfied with the balance of payments, they may refuse to back her in the event that she wants to leave her husband. Moreover, her male kinsmen use the bridewealth for their own purposes, in *moka* exchange and for their own marriages. If a woman leaves her husband, some or all of the bridewealth will have to be returned. If, as is usually the case, the pigs and shells have been distributed or promised, her kin will be reluctant to back her in the event of marital discord. And each time a woman divorces and remarries, her value in bridewealth tends to depreciate. On the whole, her male consanguines will lose in the event of a divorce, unless the groom has been delinquent in his payments. While the Melpa woman is freer as a new bride than a Kuma woman, the bridewealth system makes divorce difficult or impossible (Strathern, 1972).

In some societies, like the Nuer, bridewealth can only be converted into brides. In others, bridewealth can be converted into something else like political prestige. In this case, a woman's marriage is implicated in a political system. In the Big Man systems of Highland New Guinea, the material which circulates for women also circulates in the exchanges on which political power is based. Within the political system, men are in constant need of valuables to disburse, and they are dependent upon input. They depend not only upon their immediate partners, but upon the partners of their partners, to several degrees of remove. If a man has to return some bridewealth he may not be able to give it to someone who planned to give it to someone else who intended to use it to give a feast upon which his status depends. Big Men are therefore concerned with the domestic affairs of others, whose relationship with them may be extremely indirect. There are cases in which headmen intervene in marital disputes involving indirect trading partners in order that *moka* exchanges not be disrupted (Bulmer, 1969: 11). The weight of this entire system may come to rest upon one woman kept in a miserable marriage.

In short, there are other questions to ask of a marriage system than whether or not it exchanges women. Is the woman traded for a woman, or is there an equivalent? Is this equivalent only for women, or can it be turned into something else? If it can be turned into something else, is it turned into political power or wealth? On the other hand, can bridewealth be obtained only in marital exchange, or can it be obtained from elsewhere? Can women be accumulated through amassing wealth? Can wealth be accumulated by disposing of women? Is a marriage system part of a system of stratification?[15]

These last questions point to another task for a political economy of sex. Kinship and marriage are always parts of total social systems, and are always tied into economic and political arrangements.

Lévi-Strauss . . . rightly argues that the structural implications of a marriage can only be understood if we think of it as one item in a whole series of transactions between kin groups. So far, so good. But in none of the examples which he provides in his book does he carry this principle far enough. The reciprocities of kinship obligation are not merely symbols of alliance, they are also economic transactions, political transactions, charters to rights of domicile and land use. No useful picture of 'how a kinship system works' can be provided unless these several aspects or implications of the kinship organization are considered simultaneously. (Leach, 1971: 90)

Among the Kachin, the relationship of a tenant to a landlord is also a relationship between a son-in-law and a father-in-law. 'The procedure for acquiring land rights of any kind is in almost all cases tantamount to marrying a woman from the lineage of the lord' (ibid. 88). In the Kachin system, bridewealth moves from commoners to aristocrats, women moving in the opposite direction.

From an economic aspect the effect of matrilateral cross-cousin marriage is that, on balance, the headman's lineage constantly pays wealth to the chief's lineage in the form of bridewealth. The payment can also, from an analytical point of view, be regarded as a rent paid to the senior landlord by the tenant. The most important part of this payment is in the form of consumer goods—namely cattle. The chief converts this perishable wealth into imperishable prestige through the medium of spectacular feasting. The ultimate consumers of the goods are in this way the original producers, namely, the commoners who attend the feast. (Ibid. 89)

In another example, it is traditional in the Trobriands for a man to send a harvest gift—*urigubu*—of yams to his sister's household. for the commoners, this amounts to a simple circulation of yams. But the chief is polygamous, and marries a woman from each subdistrict within his domain. Each of these subdistricts therefore sends *urigubu* to the chief, providing him with a bulging storehouse out of which he finances feasts, craft production, and *kula* expeditions. This 'fund of power' underwrites the political system and forms the basis for chiefly power (Malinowski, 1970).

In some systems, position in a political hierarchy and position in a marriage system are intimately linked. In traditional Tonga,

143

women married up in rank. Thus, low-ranking lineages would send women to higher-ranking lineages. Women of the highest lineage were married into the 'house of Fiji', a lineage defined as outside the political system. If the highest ranking chief gave his sister to a lineage other than one which had no part in the ranking system, he would no longer be the highest ranking chief. Rather, the lineage of his sister's son would outrank his own. In times of political rearrangement, the demotion of the previous high-ranking lineage was formalized when it gave a wife to a lineage which it had formerly outranked. In traditional Hawaii, the situation was the reverse. Women married down, and the dominant lineage gave wives to junior lines. A paramount would either marry a sister or obtain a wife from Tonga. When a junior lineage usurped rank, it formalized its position by giving a wife to its former senior line.

There is even some tantalizing data suggesting that marriage systems may be implicated in the evolution of social strata, and perhaps in the development of early states. The first round of the political consolidation which resulted in the formation of a state in Madagascar occurred when one chief obtained title to several autonomous districts through the vagaries of marriage and inheritance (Henry Wright, personal communication). In Samoa, legends place the origin of the paramount title—the *Tafa'ifa*—as a result of intermarriage between ranking members of four major lineages. My thoughts are too speculative, my data too sketchy, to say much on this subject. But a search ought to be undertaken for data which might demonstrate how marriage systems intersect with large-scale political processes like state-making. Marriage systems might be implicated in a number of ways: in the accumulation of wealth and the maintenance of differential access to political and economic resources; in the building of alliances; in the consolidation of high-ranking persons into a single closed strata of endogamous kin.

These examples—like the Kachin and the Trobriand ones—indicate that sexual systems cannot, in the final analysis, be understood in complete isolation. A full-bodied analysis of women in a single society, or throughout history, must take *everything* into account: the evolution of commodity forms in women, systems of land tenure, political arrangements, subsistence technology, etc. Equally important, economic and political analyses are incomplete if they do not consider women, marriage, and sexuality. Traditional concerns of anthropology and social science—such as the evolution of social stratification and the origin of the state—must be reworked to include the implications of matrilateral cross-cousin marriage, surplus extracted in the form of daughters, the conversion of female labour into male wealth, the conversion of female lives into marriage alliances, the contribution of marriage to political power, and the transformations which all of these varied aspects of society have undergone in the course of time.

This sort of endeavour is, in the final analysis, exactly what Engels tried to do in his effort to weave a coherent analysis of so many of the diverse aspects of social life. He tried to relate men and women, town and country, kinship and state, forms of property, systems of land tenure, convertibility of wealth, forms of exchange, the technology of food production, and forms of trade, to name a few, into a systematic historical account. Eventually, someone will have to write a new version of *The Origin of the Family, Private Property, and the State*, recognizing the mutual interdependence of sexuality, economics, and politics without underestimating the full significance of each in human society.

References

Althusser, Louis (1969), 'Freud and Lacan', *New Left Review*, 55: 48–65.

—— and Balibar, Étienne (1970), *Reading Capital* (London: New Left Books).

Benston, Margaret (1969), 'The Political Economy of Women's Liberation', *Monthly Review*, 21/4: 13–27.

Berndt, Ronald (1962), *Excess and Restraint* (Chicago: University of Chicago Press).

Bulmer, Ralph (1969), 'Political Aspects of the Moka Ceremonial Exchange System Among the Kyaka People of the Western Highlands of New Guinea', *Oceania*, 31/1: 1–13.

Chasseguet-Smirgel, J. (1970), *Female Sexuality* (Ann Arbor: University of Michigan Press).

Dalla Costa, Mariarosa, and James, Selma (1972), *The Power of Women and the Subversion of the Community* (Bristol: Falling Wall Press).

Derrida, Jacques (1972), 'Structure, Sign, and Play in the Discourse of the Human Sciences', in R. Macksey and E. Donato (eds.), *The Structuralist Controversy*, (Baltimore: Johns Hopkins Press).

Deutsch, Helene (1948a), 'The Significance of Masochism in the Mental Life of Women', in R. Fleiss (ed.), *The Psychoanalytic Reader* (New York: International Universities Press).

—— (1948b), 'On Female Homosexuality', in R. Fleiss (ed.), *The Psychoanalytic Reader* (New York: International Universities Press).

Devereaux, George (1937), 'Institutionalized Homosexuality Among the Mohave Indians', *Human Biology*, 9: 498–529.

Douglas, Mary (1963), *The Lele of Kasai* (London: Oxford University Press).

Engels, Frederick (1972), *The Origin of the Family, Private Property, and the State*, ed. Eleanor Leacock (New York: International Publishers).

Evans-Pritchard, E. E. (1951), *Kinship and Marriage Among the Nuer* (London: Oxford University Press).

—— (1970), 'Sexual Inversion Among the Azande', *American Anthropologist*, 72: 1428–34.

Fee, Elizabeth (1973), 'The Sexual Politics of Victorian Social Anthropology', *Feminist Studies* (Winter/Spring): 23–9.

Ford, Clellan, and Beach, Frank (1972), *Patterns of Sexual Behavior* (New York: Harper).

Foucault, Michel (1970), *The Order of Things* (New York: Pantheon).

Freud, Sigmund (1943), *A General Introduction to Psychoanalysis* (Garden City, NY: Garden City Publishing Company).

—— (1961a), 'Some Psychical Consequences of the Anatomical Distinction Between the Sexes', in *The Complete Works of Sigmund Freud*, xix, ed. J. Strachey (London: Hogarth).

—— (1961b), 'Female Sexuality', in *The Complete Works of Sigmund Freud*, xix, ed. J. Strachey (London: Hogarth).

—— (1965), 'Femininity', in *New Introductory Lectures in Psychoanalysis*, ed. J. Strachey (New York: W. W. Norton).

Gardiner, Jean (1974), 'Political Economy of Female Labor in Capitalist Society', unpublished manuscript.

Gerstein, Ira (1973), 'Domestic Work and Capitalism', *Radical America* 7/4 and 5: 101–28.

Glasse, R. M. (1971), 'The Mask of Venery', paper read at the 70th Annual Meeting of the American Anthropological Association, New York City, Dec. 1971.

Goodale, Jane, and Chowning, Ann (1971), 'The Contaminating Woman', paper read at the 70th Annual Meeting of the American Anthropological Association, New York City, Dec. 1971.

Goody, Jack, and Tambiah, S. J. (1973), *Bridewealth and Dowry* (Cambridge: Cambridge University Press).

Gough, Ian (1972), 'Marx and Productive Labour', *New Left Review*, 76: 47–72.

Gough, Kathleen (1959), 'The Nayars and the Definition of Marriage', *Journal of the Royal Anthropological Institute*, 89: 23–4.

Hefner, Robert (1974), 'The *Tel Quel* Ideology: Material Practice Upon Material Practice', *Substance*, 8: 127–38.

Herskovitz, Melville (1937), 'A Note on "Woman Marriage" in Dahomey', *Africa*, 10/3: 335–41.

Hertz, Robert (1960), *Death and the Right Hand* (Glencoe, Ill.: Free Press).

Horney, Karen (1973), 'The Denial of the Vagina', in Karen Horney, *Feminine Psychology*, ed. Harold Kelman (New York: W. W. Norton).

Jakobson, Roman, and Halle, Morris (1971), *Fundamentals of Language* (The Hague: Mouton).

Jones, Ernest (1933), 'The Phallic Phase', *International Journal of Psychoanalysis*, 14: 1–33.

Kelly, Raymond (1974), 'Witchcraft and Sexual Relations: An Exploration of the Social and Semantic Implications of the Structure of Belief', paper read at the 73rd Annual Meeting of the American Anthropological Association, Mexico City.

Lacan, Jaques (1968), 'The Function of Language in Psychoanalysis', in Anthony Wilden (ed.), *The Language of Self*.

Lampl de Groot, Jeanne (1933), 'Problems of Femininity', *Psychoanalytic Quarterly*, 2: 489–518.

—— (1948), 'The Evolution of the Oedipus Complex in Women', in R. Fleiss (ed.), *The Psychoanalytic Reader* (New York: International Universities Press).

Langness, L. L. (1967), 'Sexual Antagonism in the New Guinea Highlands: A Bena Bena Example', *Oceania*, 37/3: 161–77.

Larguia, Isabel, and Dumoulin, John (1972), 'Towards a Science of Women's Liberation', *NACLA Newsletter*, 6/10: 3–20.

Lasch, Christopher (1974), 'Freud and Women', *New York Review of Books*, 21/15: 12–17.

Leach, Edmund (1971), *Rethinking Anthropology* (New York: Humanities Press).

Lévi-Strauss, Claude (1969), *The Elementary Structures of Kinship* (Boston: Beacon Press).

—— (1971), 'The Family', in H. Shapiro (ed.), *Man, Culture and Society* (London: Oxford University Press).

Lindenbaum, Shirley (1973), 'A Wife is the Hand of Man', paper read at the 72nd Annual Meeting of the American Anthropological Association.

Livingstone, Frank (1969), 'Genetics, Ecology, and the Origins of Incest and Exogamy', *Current Anthropology*, 10/1: 45–9.

Malinowski, Bronislaw (1929), *The Sexual Life of Savages* (London: Routledge & Kegan Paul).

—— (1970), 'The Primitive Economics of the Trobriand Islanders', in T. Harding, and B. Wallace (eds.), *Cultures of the Pacific* (New York: Free Press).

Marx, Karl (1969), *Theories of Surplus Value, Part I* (Moscow: Progress Publishers).

—— (1971*a*), *Pre-Capitalist Economic Formations* (New York: International Publishers).

—— (1971*b*), *Wage-Labor and Capital* (New York: International Publishers).

—— (1972), *Capital*, i (New York: International Publishers).

McMurtie, Douglas (1914), 'A Legend of Lesbian Love Among North American Indians', *Urologic and Cutaneous Review* (Apr.), 192–3.

Meggitt, M. J. (1964), 'Male–Female Relationships in the Highlands of Australian New Guinea', *American Anthropologist* 66/4, 2: 204–24.

Mehlman, Jeffrey (1972), *French Freud: Structural Studies in Psychoanalysis* (New Haven: Yale French Studies, No. 48).

Mitchell, Juliet (1971), *Women's Estate* (New York: Vintage).

—— (1974), *Psychoanalysis and Feminism* (New York: Pantheon).

Murphy, Robert (1959), 'Social Structure and the Sex Antagonism', *South-Western Journal of Anthropology*, 15/1: 81–96.

Rappaport, Roy, and Buchbinder, Georgeda (forthcoming), 'Fertility and Death Among the Maring', in Paula Brown and G. Buchbinder (eds.), *Sex Roles in the New Guinea Highlands* (Cambridge, Mass.: Harvard University Press).

Read, Kenneth (1952), 'The Nama Cult of the Central Highlands, New Guinea', *Oceania*, 23/1: 1–25.

Reay, Marie (1959), *The Kuma* (London: Cambridge University Press).

Rowntree, M., and J. (1970), 'More on the Political Economy of Women's Liberation', *Monthly Review*, 21/8: 26–32.

Sahlins, Marshall (1960), 'The Origin of Society', *Scientific American*, 203/3: 76–86.

—— (1972), *Stone Age Economics* (Chicago: Aldine-Atherton).

Schneider, David, and Gough, Kathleen (eds.) (1961), *Matrilineal Kinship* (Berkley: University of California Press).

Secombe, Wally (1973), 'Housework Under Capitalism', *New Left Review*, 83: 3–24.

Sonenschein, David (1966), 'Homosexuality as a Subject of Anthropological Investigation', *Anthropological Quarterly*, 2: 73–82.

Strathern, Marilyn (1972), *Women in Between* (New York: Seminar).

Thompson, E. P. (1963), *The Making of the English Working Class* (New York: Vintage).

Thurnwald, Richard (1916), 'Banaro Society', *Memoirs of the American Anthropological Association*, 3/4: 251–391.

Van Baal, J. (1966), *Dema* (The Hague: Nijhoff).

Vogel, Lise (1973), 'The Earthly Family', *Radical America* 7/4 and 5: 9–50.

Williams, F. E. (1936), *Papuans of the Trans-Fly* (Oxford: Clarendon Press).

Wittig, Monique (1973), *Les Guérillères* (New York: Avon).

Wolff, Charlotte (1971), *Love Between Women* (London: Duckworth).

Yalmon, Nur (1963), 'On the Purity of Women in the Castes of Ceylon and Malabar', *Journal of the Royal Anthropological Institute*, 93/1: 25–58.

Notes

1. Moving between Marxism, structuralism, and psychoanalysis produces a certain clash of epistemologies. In particular, structuralism is a can from which worms crawl out all over the epistemological map. Rather than trying to cope

with this problem, I have more or less ignored the fact that Lacan and Lévi-Strauss are among the foremost living ancestors of the contemporary French intellectual revolution (see Foucault, 1970). It would be fun, interesting, and, if this were France, essential, to start my argument from the centre of the structuralist maze and work my way out from there, along the lines of a 'dialectical theory of signifying practices' (see Hefner, 1974).

2. A lot of the debate on women and housework has centred around the question of whether or not housework is 'productive' labour. Strictly speaking, housework is not ordinarily 'productive' in the technical sense of the term (I. Gough, 1972: Marx, 1969: 387–413). But this distinction is irrelevant to the main line of the argument. Housework may not be 'productive', in the sense of directly producing surplus value and capital, and yet be a crucial element in the production of surplus value and capital.

3. That some of the conventions are pretty bizarre, from our point of view, only demonstrates the point that sexuality is expressed through the intervention of culture (see Ford and Beach, 1972). Some examples may be chosen from among the exotica in which anthropologists delight. Among the Banaro, marriage involves several socially sanctioned sexual partnerships. When a woman is married, she is initiated into intercourse by the sib-friend of her groom's father. After bearing a child by this man, she begins to have intercourse with her husband. She also has an institutionalized partnership with the sib-friend of her husband. A man's partners include his wife, the wife of his sib-friend, and the wife of his sib-friend's son (Thurnwald, 1916). Multiple intercourse is a more pronounced custom among the Marind Anim. At the time of marriage, the bride has intercourse with all of the members of the groom's clan, the groom coming last. Every major festival is accompanied by a practice known as *otiv-bombari*, in which semen is collected for ritual purposes. A few women have intercourse with many men, and the resulting semen is collected in coconut-shell buckets. A Marind male is subjected to multiple homosexual intercourse during initiation (Van Baal, 1966). Among the Etoro, heterosexual intercourse is taboo for between 205 and 260 days a year (Kelly, 1974). In much of New Guinea, men fear copulation and think that it will kill them if they engage in it without magical precautions (Glasse, 1971; Meggitt, 1964). Usually, such ideas of feminine pollution express the subordination of women. But symbolic systems contain internal contradictions, whose logical extensions sometimes lead to inversions of the propositions on which a system is based. In New Britain, men's fear of sex is so extreme that rape appears to be feared by men rather than women. Women run after the men, who flee from them, women are the sexual aggressors, and it is bridegrooms who are reluctant (Goodale and Chowning, 1971). Other interesting sexual variations can be found in Yalmon (1963) and K. Gough (1959).

4. Engels thought that men acquired wealth in the form of herds and, wanting to pass this wealth to their own children, overthrew 'mother right' in favour of patrilineal inheritance. 'The overthrow of mother right was the *world historical defeat of the female sex.* The man took command in the home also; the woman was degraded and reduced to servitude; she became the slave of his lust and a mere instrument for the production of children' (Engels, 1972: 120–1; italics in original). As has been often pointed out, women do not necessarily have significant social authority in societies practicing matrilineal inheritance (Schneider and Gough, 1961).

GAYLE RUBIN

5. 'What, would you like to marry your sister? What is the matter with you? Don't you want a brother-in-law? Don't you realize that if you marry another man's sister and another man marries your sister, you will have at least two brothers-in-law, while if you marry your own sister you will have none? With whom will you hunt, with whom will you garden, whom will you go visit?' (Arapesh, cited in Lévi-Strauss, 1969: 485).

6. This analysis of society as based on bonds between men by means of women makes the separatist responses of the women's movement thoroughly intelligible. Separatism can be seen as a mutation in social structure, as an attempt to form social groups based on unmediated bonds between women. It can also be seen as a radical denial of men's 'rights' in women, and as a claim by women of rights in themselves.

7. 'The woman shall not wear that which pertaineth unto a man, neither shall a man put on a woman's garment: for all that do so *are* abomination unto the LORD thy God' (Deuteronomy 22: 5; emphasis not mine).

8. 'In studying women we cannot neglect the methods of a science of the mind, a theory that attempts to explain how women become women and men, men. The borderline between the biological and the social which finds expression in the family is the land psychoanalysis sets out to chart, the land where sexual distinction originates.' (Mitchell, 1971: 167).

   'What is the *object* of psychoanalysis? . . . but the "*effects*", prolonged into the surviving adult, of the extraordinary adventure which from birth the liquidation of the Oedipal phase transforms a small animal conceived by a man and a woman into a small human child . . . the "effects" still present in the survivors of the forced "humanization" of the small human animal into a *man* or a *woman*. . . .' (Althusser, 1969: 57, 59; italics in original)

9. The psychoanalytic theories of femininity were articulated in the context of a debate which took place largely in the *International Journal of Psychoanalysis* and *The Psychoanalytic Quarterly* in the late 1920s and early 1930s. Articles representing the range of discussion include: Freud, 1961a, 1961b, 1965; Lampl de Groot, 1933, 1948; Deutsch, 1948a, 1948b; Horney, 1973; Jones, 1933. Some of my dates are of reprints; for the original chronology, see Chasseguet-Smirgel (1970: Introduction). The debate was complex, and I have simplified it. Freud, Lampl de Groot, and Deutsch argued that femininity developed out of a bisexual, 'phallic' girl-child; Horney and Jones argued for an innate femininity. The debate was not without its ironies. Horney defended women against penis envy by postulating that women are born and not made; Deutsch, who considered women to be made and not born, developed a theory of feminine masochism whose best rival is *Story of O*. I have attributed the core of the 'Freudian' version of female development equally to Freud and to Lampl de Groot. In reading through the articles, it has seemed to me that the theory is as much (or more) hers as it is his.

10. I have taken my position on Freud somewhere between the French structuralist interpretations and American biologistic ones, because I think that Freud's wording is similarly somewhere in the middle. He does talk abut penises, about the 'inferiority' of the clitoris, about the psychic consequences of anatomy. The Lacanians, on the other hand, argue from Freud's text that he is unintelligible if his words are taken literally, and that a thoroughly non-anatomical theory can be deduced as Freud's intention (see Althusser, 1969). I think that they are right; the penis is walking around too much for its role

to be taken literally. The detachability of the penis, and its transformation in fantasy (e.g. penis = faeces = child = gift), argue strongly for a symbolic interpretation. Nevertheless, I don't think that Freud was as consistent as either I or Lacan would like him to have been, and some gesture must be made to what he said, even as we play with what he must have meant.

11. The pre-Oedipal mother is the 'phallic mother', e.g. she is believed to possess the phallus. The Oedipal-inducing information is that the mother does not possess the phallus. In other words, the crisis is precipitated by the 'castration' of the mother, by the recognition that the phallus only passes through her, but does not settle on her. The 'phallus' must pass through her, since the relationship of a male to every other male is defined through a woman. A man is linked to a son by a mother, to his nephew by virtue of a sister, etc. Every relationship between male kin is defined by the woman between them. If power is a male prerogative, and must be passed on, it must go through the women-in-between. Marshall Sahlins (personal communication) once suggested that the reason women are so often defined as stupid, polluting, disorderly, silly, profane, or whatever, is that such categorizations define women as 'incapable' of possessing the power which must be transferred through them.

12. Parts of Wittig's *Les Guérillères* (1973) appear to be tirades against Lévi-Strauss and Lacan. For instance:

> Has he not indeed written, power and the possession of women, leisure and the enjoyment of women? He writes that you are currency, an item of exchange. He writes, barter, barter, possession and acquisition of women and merchandise. Better for you to see your guts in the sun and utter the death rattle than to live a life that anyone can appropriate. What belongs to you on this earth? Only death. No power on earth can take that away from you. And—consider explain tell yourself—if happiness consists in the possession of something, then hold fast to this sovereign happiness—to die. (Wittig, 1973: 115–16; see also 106–7; 113–14; 134)

The awareness of French feminists of Lévi-Strauss and Lacan is most clearly evident in a group called 'Psychoanalyse et Politique' which defined its task as a feminist use and critique of Lacanian psychoanalysis.

13. 'Every woman adores a fascist'—Sylvia Plath.

14. One clinician, Charlotte Wolff (1971) has taken the psychoanalytic theory of womanhood to its logical extreme and proposed that lesbianism is a healthy response to female socialization.

> Women who do not rebel against the status of object have declared themselves defeated as persons in their own right. (Wolff, 1971: 65)

> The lesbian girl is the one who, by all means at her disposal, will try to find a place of safety inside and outside the family, through her fight for equality with the male. She will not, like other women, play up to him: indeed, she despises the very idea of it. (Ibid. 59)

> The lesbian was and is unquestionably in the avant-garde of the fight for equality of the sexes, and for the psychical liberation of women. (Ibid. 66)

It is revealing to compare Wolff's discussion with the articles on lesbianism in Marmor, 1965.

15. Another line of inquiry would compare bridewealth systems to dowry systems Many of these questions are treated in Goody and Tambiah, 1973.

6 Gender: A Useful Category of Historical Analysis

Joan Wallach Scott

> Gender. *n.* a grammatical term only. To talk of persons or
> creatures of the masculine or feminine gender, meaning of the
> male or female sex, is either a jocularity (permissible or not
> according to context) or a blunder.
>
> H. W. Fowler, Dictionary of Modern English Usage

Those who would codify the meanings of words fight a losing
battle, for words, like the ideas and things they are meant to signify,
have a history. Neither Oxford dons nor the Académie française has
been entirely able to stem the tide, to capture and fix meanings free
of the play of human invention and imagination. Mary Wortley
Montagu added bite to her witty denunciation 'of the fair sex' ('my
only consolation for being of that gender has been the assurance of
never being married to any one among them') by deliberately mis-
using the grammatical reference.[1] Through the ages, people have
made figurative allusions by employing grammatical terms to evoke
traits of character or sexuality. For example, the usage offered by the
Dictionnaire de la langue française in 1876 was: 'On ne sait de quel
genre il est, s'il est mâle ou femelle, se dit d'un homme très-caché,
dont on ne connait pas les sentiments.'[2] And Gladstone made this
distinction in 1878: 'Athene has nothing of sex except the gender,
nothing of the woman except the form.'[3] Most recently—too

© 1988 Columbia University Press. This essay was first prepared for delivery at the
meetings of the American Historical Association in December 1985. It was subsequently published in its current form in the *American Historical Review*, 91/5 (Dec.
1986), and is my *Gender and the Politics of History*, and is reprinted with permission. Discussions with Denise Riley, Janice Doane, Yasmine Ergas, Anne Norton,
and Harriet Whitehead helped formulate my ideas on the various subjects touched
in the course of this paper. The final version profited from comments by Ira
Katznelson, Charles Tilly, Louise Tilly, Elisabetta Galeotti, Rayna Rapp, Christine
Stansell, and Joan Vincent. I am also grateful for the unusually careful editing done
at the *AHR* by Allyn Roberts and David Ransell.

recently to find its way into dictionaries or the *Encyclopedia of the Social Sciences*—feminists have in a more literal and serious vein begun to use 'gender' as a way of referring to the social organization of the relationship between the sexes. The connection to grammar is both explicit and full of unexamined possibilities. Explicit because the grammatical usage involves formal rules that follow from the masculine or feminine designation; full of unexamined possibilities because in many Indo-European languages there is a third category—unsexed or neuter. In grammar, gender is understood to be a way of classifying phenomena, a socially agreed-upon system of distinctions rather than an objective description of inherent traits. In addition, classifications suggest a relationship among categories that makes distinctions or separate groupings possible.

In its most recent usage, 'gender' seems to have first appeared among American feminists who wanted to insist on the fundamentally social quality of distinctions based on sex. The word denoted a rejection of the biological determinism implicit in the use of such terms as 'sex' or 'sexual difference'. 'Gender' also stressed the relational aspect of normative definitions of femininity. Those who worried that women's studies scholarship focused too narrowly and separately on women used the term 'gender' to introduce a relational notion into our analytic vocabulary. According to this view, women and men were defined in terms of one another, and no understanding of either could be achieved by entirely separate study. Thus Natalie Davis suggested in 1975:

It seems to me that we should be interested in the history of both women and men, that we should not be working only on the subjected sex any more than a historian of class can focus entirely on peasants. Our goal is to understand the significance of the *sexes*, of gender groups in the historical past. Our goal is to discover the range in sex roles and in sexual symbolism in different societies and periods, to find out what meaning they had and how they functioned to maintain the social order or to promote its change.[4]

In addition, and perhaps most important, 'gender' was a term offered by those who claimed that women's scholarship would fundamentally transform disciplinary paradigms. Feminist scholars pointed out early on that the study of women would not only add new subject matter but would also force a critical re-examination of the premisses and standards of existing scholarly work. 'We are learning', wrote three feminist historians, 'that the writing of women into history necessarily involves redefining and enlarging traditional notions of historical significance, to encompass personal, subjective experience as well as public and political activities.

It is not too much to suggest that however hesitant the actual beginnings, such a methodology implies not only a new history of women, but also a new history.'⁵ The way in which this new history would both include and account for women's experience rested on the extent to which gender could be developed as a category of analysis. Here the analogies to class and race were explicit; indeed, the most politically inclusive of scholars of women's studies regularly invoked all three categories as crucial to the writing of a new history.⁶ An interest in class, race, and gender signalled, first, a scholar's commitment to a history that included stories of the oppressed and an analysis of the meaning and nature of their oppression and, second, scholarly understanding that inequalities of power are organized along at least three axes.

The litany of class, race, and gender suggests a parity for each term, but, in fact, that is not at all the case. While 'class' most often rests on Marx's elaborate (and since elaborated) theory of economic determination and historical change, 'race' and 'gender' carry no such associations. No unanimity exists among those who employ concepts of class. Some scholars employ Weberian notions, others use class as a temporary heuristic device. Still, when we invoke class, we are working with or against a set of definitions that, in the case of Marxism, involve an idea of economic causality and a vision of the path along which history has moved dialectically. There is no such clarity or coherence for either race or gender. In the case of gender, the usage has involved a range of theoretical positions as well as simple descriptive references to the relationships between the sexes.

Feminist historians, trained as most historians are to be more comfortable with description than theory, have none the less increasingly looked for usable theoretical formulations. They have done so for at least two reasons. First, the proliferation of case studies in women's history seems to call for some synthesizing perspective that can explain continuities and discontinuities and account for persisting inequalities as well as radically different social experiences. Second, the discrepancy between the high quality of recent work in women's history and its continuing marginal status in the field as a whole (as measured by textbooks, syllabi, and monographic work) points up the limits of descriptive approaches that do not address dominant disciplinary concepts, or at least that do not address these concepts in terms that can shake their power and perhaps transform them. It has not been enough for historians of women to prove either that women had a history or that women participated in the major political upheavals of Western civilization. In the case of women's history, the response of most non-feminist historians has been acknowledgment and then separation or dismissal ('women had a history separate from men's, therefore let feminists do women's history which need not concern us'; or 'women's history is about sex and the family and should be done separately from political and economic history'). In the case of women's participation, the response has been minimal interest at best ('my understanding of the French Revolution is not changed by knowing that women participated in it'). The challenge posed by these responses is, in the end, a theoretical one. It requires analysis not only of the relationship between male and female experience in the past but also of the connection between past history and current historical practice. How does gender work in human social relationships? How does gender give meaning to the organization and perception of historical knowledge? The answers depend on gender as an analytic category.

For the most part, the attempts of historians to theorize about gender have remained within traditional social scientific frameworks, using long-standing formulations that provide universal causal explanations. These theories have been limited at best because they tend to contain reductive or overly simple generalizations that undercut not only history's disciplinary sense of the complexity of social causation but also feminist commitments to analyses that will lead to change. A review of these theories will expose their limits and make it possible to propose an alternative approach.

The approaches used by most historians fall into two distinct categories. The first is essentially descriptive; that is, it refers to the existence of phenomena or realities without interpreting, explaining, or attributing causality. The second usage is causal; it theorizes about the nature of phenomena or realities, seeking an understanding of how and why these take the form they do.

In its simplest recent usage, 'gender' is a synonym for 'women'. Any number of books and articles whose subject is women's history have, in the past few years, substituted 'gender' for 'women' in their titles. In some cases, this usage, though vaguely referring to certain analytic concepts, is actually about the political acceptability of the field. In these instances, the use of 'gender' is meant to denote the scholarly seriousness of a work, for 'gender' has a more neutral and objective sound than does 'women'. 'Gender' seems to fit within the scientific terminology of social science and thus dissociates itself from the (supposedly strident) politics of feminism. In this usage, 'gender' does not carry with it a necessary statement about inequality or power nor does it name the aggrieved (and hitherto invisible) party. Whereas the term 'women's history' proclaims its politics by asserting (contrary to customary practice) that women are valid historical subjects, 'gender' includes, but does not name women, and so seems to pose no critical threat. This use of 'gender' is one facet of what might be called the quest of feminist scholarship for academic legitimacy in the 1980s.

But only one facet. 'Gender' as a substitute for 'women' is also used to suggest that information about women is necessarily information about men, that one implies the study of the other. This usage insists that the world of women is part of the world of men, created in and by it. This usage rejects the interpretive utility of the idea of separate spheres, maintaining that to study women in isolation perpetuates the fiction that one sphere, the experience of one sex, has little or nothing to do with the other. In addition, gender is also used to designate social relations between the sexes. Its use explicitly rejects biological explanations, such as those that find a common denominator for diverse forms of female subordination in the facts that women have the capacity to give birth and men have greater muscular strength. Instead, gender becomes a way of denoting 'cultural constructions'—the entirely social creation of ideas about appropriate roles for women and men. It is a way of referring to the exclusively social origins of the subjective identities of men and women. Gender is, in this definition, a social category imposed on a sexed body.[7] Gender seems to have become a particularly useful word as studies of sex and sexuality have proliferated, for it offers a way of differentiating sexual practice from the social roles assigned to women and men. Although scholars acknowledge the connection between sex and (what the sociologists of the family called) 'sex roles', these scholars do not assume a simple or direct linkage. The use of gender emphasizes an entire system of relationships that may include sex, but is not directly determined by sex nor directly determining of sexuality.

These descriptive usages of gender have been employed by historians most often to map out a new terrain. As social historians turned to new objects of study, gender was relevant for such topics as women, children, families, and gender ideologies. This usage of gender, in other words, refers only to those areas—both structural and ideological—involving relations between the sexes. Because, on the face of it, war, diplomacy, and high politics have not been explicitly about those relationships, gender seems not to apply and so continues to be irrelevant to the thinking of historians concerned with issues of politics and power. The effect is to endorse a certain functionalist view ultimately rooted in biology and to perpetuate the idea of separate spheres (sex or politics, family or nation, women or men) in the writing of history. Although gender in this usage asserts that relationships between the sexes are social, it says nothing about why these relationships are constructed as they are, how they work, or how they change. In its descriptive usage, then, gender is a concept associated with the study of things related to women. Gender is a new topic, a new department of historical investigation, but it does not have the analytic power to address (and change) existing historical paradigms.

Some historians were, of course, aware of this problem, hence the efforts to employ theories that might explain the concept of gender and account for historical change. Indeed, the challenge was to reconcile theory, which was framed in general or universal terms, and history, which was committed to the study of contextual specificity and fundamental change. The result has been extremely eclectic: partial borrowings that vitiate the analytic power of a particular theory or worse, employ its precepts without awareness of their implications; or accounts of change that, because they embed universal theories, only illustrate unchanging themes; or wonderfully imaginative studies in which theory is none the less so hidden that these studies cannot serve as models for other investigations. Because the theories on which historians have drawn are often not spelled out in all their implications, it seems worthwhile to spend some time doing that. Only through such an exercise can we evaluate the usefulness of these theories and begin to articulate a more powerful theoretical approach.

Feminist historians have employed a variety of approaches to the analysis of gender, but the approaches come down to a choice among three theoretical positions.[8] The first, an entirely feminist effort, attempts to explain the origins of patriarchy. The second locates itself within a Marxian tradition and seeks there an accommodation with feminist critiques. The third, fundamentally divided between French post-structuralist and Anglo-American object-relations theorists, draws on these different schools of psychoanalysis to explain the production and reproduction of the subject's gendered identity.

Theorists of patriarchy have directed their attention to the subordination of women and found their explanation for it in the male 'need' to dominate the female. In Mary O'Brien's ingenious adaptation of Hegel, she defined male domination as the effect of men's desire to transcend their alienation from the means of the reproduction of the species. The principle of generational continuity restores the primacy of paternity and obscures the real labour and the social reality of women's work in childbirth. The source of women's liberation lies in 'an adequate understanding of the process of reproduction', an appreciation of the contradiction between the nature of women's reproductive labour and (male) ideological mystifications of it.[9] For Shulamith Firestone, reproduction was also the 'bitter trap' for women. In her more materialist analysis, however, liberation would come with transformations in reproductive technology, which might in some not too distant future eliminate the need for women's bodies as the agents of species reproduction.[10]

If reproduction was the key to patriarchy for some, sexuality itself was the answer for others. Catherine MacKinnon's bold formulations were at once her own and characteristic of a certain approach: 'Sexuality is to feminism what work is to marxism: that which is most one's own, yet most taken away.' 'Sexual objectification is the primary process of the subjection of women. It unites act with word, construction with expression, perception with enforcement, myth with reality. Man fucks woman; subject verb object.'[11] Continuing her analogy to Marx, MacKinnon offered, in the place of dialectical materialism, consciousness-raising as feminism's method of analysis. By expressing the shared experience of objectification, she argued, women come to understand their common identity and so are moved to political action. Although sexual relations are defined in MacKinnon's analysis as social, there is nothing except the inherent inequality of the sexual relation itself to explain why the system of power operates as it does. The source of unequal relations between the sexes is, in the end, unequal relations between the sexes. Although the inequality of which sexuality is the source is said to be embodied in a 'whole system of social relationships', how this system works is not explained.[12]

Theorists of patriarchy have addressed the inequality of males and females in important ways, but, for historians, their theories pose problems. First, while they offer an analysis internal to the gender system itself, they also assert the primacy of that system in all social organization. But theories of patriarchy do not show what gender inequality has to do with other inequalities. Second, whether domination comes in the form of the male appropriation of the female's reproductive labour or in the sexual objectification of women by men, the analysis rests on physical difference. Any physical difference takes on a universal and unchanging aspect, even if theorists of patriarchy take into account the existence of changing forms and systems of gender inequality.[13] A theory that rests on the single variable of physical difference poses problems for historians: it assumes a consistent or inherent meaning for the human body—outside social or cultural construction—and thus the ahistoricity of gender itself. History becomes, in a sense, epiphenomenal, providing endless variations on the unchanging theme of a fixed gender inequality.

Marxist feminists have a more historical approach, guided as they are by a theory of history. But, whatever the variations and adaptations have been, the self-imposed requirement that there be a 'material' explanation for gender has limited or at least slowed the development of new lines of analysis. Whether a so-called dual-systems solution is preferred (one that posits the separate but interacting realms of capitalism and patriarchy) or an analysis based more firmly in orthodox Marxist discussions of modes of production is developed, the explanation for the origins of and changes in gender systems is found outside the sexual division of labour. Families, households, and sexuality are all, finally, products of changing modes of production. That is how Engels concluded his explorations of the *Origins of the Family*;[14] that is where economist Heidi Hartmann's analysis ultimately rests. Hartmann insists on the importance of taking into account patriarchy and capitalism as separate but interacting systems. Yet, as her argument unfolds, economic causality takes precedence, and patriarchy always develops and changes as a function of relations of production.[15]

Early discussions among Marxist feminists circled around the same set of problems: a rejection of the essentialism of those who would argue that the 'exigencies of biological reproduction' determine the sexual division of labour under capitalism; the futility of inserting 'modes of reproduction' into discussions of modes of production (it remains an oppositional category and does not assume equal status with modes of production); the recognition that economic systems do not directly determine gender relationships, indeed, that the subordination of women pre-dates capitalism and continues under socialism; the search none the less for a materialist explanation that excludes natural physical differences.[16] An important attempt to break out of this circle of problems came from Joan

Kelly in her essay 'The Doubled Vision of Feminist Theory', where she argued that economic and gender systems interact to produce social and historical experiences; that neither system was casual, but both 'operate simultaneously to reproduce the socioeconomic and male-dominant structures of . . . [a] particular social order'. Kelly's suggestion that gender systems have an independent existence provided a crucial conceptual opening, but her commitment to remain within a Marxist framework led her to emphasize the causal role of economic factors even in the determination of the gender system. 'The relation of the sexes operates in accordance with, and through, socioeconomic structures, as well as sex/gender ones.'[17] Kelly introduced the idea of a 'sexually based social reality', but she tended to emphasize the social rather than the sexual nature of that reality, and, most often, 'social', in her usage, was conceived in terms of economic relations of production.

The most far-reaching exploration of sexuality by American Marxist feminists is in *Powers of Desire*, a volume of essays published in 1983.[18] Influenced by increasing attention to sexuality among political activists and scholars, by French philosopher Michel Foucault's insistence that sexuality is produced in historical contexts, and by the conviction that the current 'sexual revolution' requires serious analysis, the authors make 'sexual politics' the focus of their inquiry. In so doing, they open the question of causality and offer a variety of solutions to it; indeed, the real excitement of this volume is its lack of analytic unanimity, its sense of analytic tension. If individual authors tend to stress the causality of social (by which is often meant 'economic') contexts, they none the less include suggestions about the importance of studying 'the psychic structuring of gender identity'. If 'gender ideology' is sometimes said to 'reflect' economic and social structures, there is also a crucial recognition of the need to understand the complex 'link between society and enduring psychic structure'.[19] On the one hand, the editors endorse Jessica Benjamin's point that politics must include attention to 'the erotic, fantastic components of human life', but, on the other hand, no essays besides Benjamin's deal fully or seriously with the theoretical issues she raises.[20] Instead, a tacit assumption runs through the volume that Marxism can be expanded to include discussions of ideology, culture, and psychology and that this expansion will happen through the kind of concrete examination of evidence undertaken in most of the articles. The advantage of such an approach lies in its avoidance of sharp differences of position, the disadvantage in its leaving in place an already fully articulated theory that leads back from relations of the sexes to relations of production.

A comparison of American Marxist-feminist efforts, exploratory and relatively wide-ranging, to those of their British counterparts, tied more closely to the politics of a strong and viable Marxist tradition, reveals that the British have had greater difficulty in challenging the constraints of strictly determinist explanations. This difficulty can be seen most dramatically in the debates in the *New Left Review* between Michèle Barrett and her critics, who charge her with abandoning a materialist analysis of the sexual division of labour under capitalism.[21] It can be seen as well in the replacement of an initial feminist attempt to reconcile psychoanalysis and Marxism with a choice of one or another of these theoretical positions by scholars who earlier insisted that some fusion of the two was possible.[22] The difficulty for both British and American feminists working within Marxism is apparent in the work I have mentioned here. The problem they face is the opposite of the one posed by patriarchal theory. For within Marxism, the concept of gender has long been treated as the by-product of changing economic structures; gender has had no independent analytic status of its own.

A review of psychoanalytic theory requires a specification of schools, since the various approaches have tended to be classified by the national origins of the founders and the majority of the practitioners. There is the Anglo-American school, working within the terms of theories of object-relations. In the United States, Nancy Chodorow is the name most readily associated with this approach. In addition, the work of Carol Gilligan has had a far-reaching impact on American scholarship, including history. Gilligan's work draws on Chodorow's, although it is concerned less with the construction of the subject than with moral development and behaviour. In contrast to the Anglo-American school, the French school is based on structuralist and post-structuralist readings of Freud in terms of theories of language (for feminists, the key figure is Jacques Lacan).

Both schools are concerned with the processes by which the subject's identity is created; both focus on the early stages of child development for clues to the formation of gender identity. Object-relations theorists stress the influence of actual experience (the child sees, hears, relates to those who care for it, particularly, of course, to its parents), while the post-structuralists emphasize the centrality of language in communicating, interpreting, and representing gender. (By 'language', post-structuralists do not mean words but systems of meaning—symbolic orders—that precede the actual mastery of speech, reading, and writing.) Another difference between the two schools of thought focuses on the unconscious, which for Chodorow is ultimately subject to conscious understanding and for Lacan is not. For Lacanians, the unconscious is a critical factor in the construction of the subject; it is the location, moreover, of sexual division and, for that reason, of continuing instability for the gendered subject.

In recent years, feminist historians have been drawn to these theories either because they serve to endorse specific findings with general observations or because they seem to offer an important theoretical formulation about gender. Increasingly, those historians working with a concept of 'women's culture' cite Chodorow's or Gilligan's work as both proof of and explanation for their interpretations; those wrestling with feminist theory look to Lacan. In the end, neither of these theories seems to me entirely workable for historians; a closer look at each may help explain why.

My reservation about object-relations theory concerns its literalism, its reliance on relatively small structures of interaction to produce gender identity and to generate change. Both the family division of labour and the actual assignment of tasks to each parent play a crucial role in Chodorow's theory. The outcome of prevailing Western systems is a clear division between male and female: 'The basic feminine sense of self is connected to the world, the basic masculine sense of self is separate.'[23] According to Chodorow, if fathers were more involved in parenting and present more often in domestic situations, the outcome of the oedipal drama might be different.[24]

This interpretation limits the concept of gender to family and household experience and, for the historian, leaves no way to connect the concept (or the individual) to other social systems of economy, politics, or power. Of course, it is implicit that social arrangements requiring fathers to work and mothers to perform most child-rearing tasks structure family organization. Where such arrangements come from and why they are articulated in terms of a sexual division of labour is not clear. Neither is the issue of inequality, as opposed to that of asymmetry, addressed. How can we account within this theory for persistent associations of masculinity with power, for the higher value placed on manhood than on womanhood, for the way children seem to learn these associations and evaluations even when they live outside nuclear households or in households where parenting is equally divided between husband

and wife? I do not think we can without some attention to signifying systems, that is, to the ways societies represent gender, use it to articulate the rules of social relationships, or construct the meaning of experience. Without meaning, there is no experience; without processes of signification, there is no meaning.

Language is the centre of Lacanian theory; it is the key to the child's induction into the symbolic order. Through language, gendered identity is constructed. According to Lacan, the phallus is the central signifier of sexual difference. But the meaning of the phallus must be read metaphorically. For the child, the oedipal drama sets forth the terms of cultural interaction, since the threat of castration embodies the power, the rules of (the Father's) law. The child's relationship to the law depends on sexual difference, on its imaginative (or fantastic) identification with masculinity or femininity. The imposition, in other words, of the rules of social interaction is inherently and specifically gendered, for the female necessarily has a different relationship to the phallus than the male does. But gender identification, although it always appears coherent and fixed, is in fact, highly unstable. As meaning systems, subjective identities are processes of differentiation and distinction, requiring the suppression of ambiguities and opposite elements in order to ensure (create the illusion of) coherence and common understanding. The principle of masculinity rests on the necessary repression of feminine aspects—of the subject's potential for bisexuality—and introduces conflict into the opposition of masculine and feminine. Repressed desires are present in the unconscious and are constantly a threat to the stability of gender identification, denying its unity, subverting its need for security. In addition, conscious ideas of masculine or feminine are not fixed, since they vary according to contextual usage. Conflict always exists, then, between the subject's need for the appearance of wholeness and the imprecision of terminology, its relative meaning, its dependence on repression.[25] This kind of interpretation makes the categories of 'man' and 'woman' problematic by suggesting that masculine and feminine are not inherent characteristics but subjective (or fictional) constructs. This interpretation also implies that the subject is in a constant process of construction, and it offers a systematic way of interpreting conscious and unconscious desire by pointing to language as the appropriate place for analysis. As such, I find it instructive.

I am troubled, none the less, by the exclusive fixation on questions of the individual subject and by the tendency to reify subjectively originating antagonism between males and females as the central fact of gender. In addition, although there is openness in the concept of how 'the subject' is constructed, the theory tends to universalize the categories and relationship of male and female. The outcome for historians is a reductive reading of evidence from the past. Even though this theory takes social relationships into account by linking castration to prohibition and law, it does not permit the introduction of a notion of historical specificity and variability. The phallus is the only signifier; the process of constructing the gendered subject is, in the end, predictable because always the same. If, as film theorist Teresa de Lauretis suggests, we need to think in terms of the construction of subjectivity in social and historical contexts, there is no way to specify those contexts within the terms offered by Lacan. Indeed, even in de Lauretis's attempt, social reality (that is, 'material, economic and interpersonal [relations] which are in fact social, and in a larger perspective historical') seems to lie outside, apart from the subject.[26] A way to conceive of 'social reality' in terms of gender is lacking.

The problem of sexual antagonism in this theory has two aspects. First, it projects a certain timeless quality, even when it is historicized as well as it has been by Sally Alexander. Alexander's reading of Lacan led her to conclude that 'antagonism between the sexes is an unavoidable aspect of the acquisition of sexual identity. . . . If antagonism is always latent, it is possible that history offers no final resolution, only the constant reshaping, reorganizing of the symbolization of difference, and the sexual division of labour.'[27] It may be my hopeless utopianism that gives me pause before this formulation, or it may be that I have not yet shed the episteme of what Foucault called the Classical Age. Whatever the explanation, Alexander's formulation contributes to the fixing of the binary opposition of male and female as the only possible relationship and as a permanent aspect of the human condition. It perpetuates rather than questions what Denise Riley refers to as 'the dreadful air of constancy of sexual polarity'. She writes: 'The historically constructed nature of the opposition [between male and female] produces as one of its effects just that air of an invariant and monotonous men/women opposition.'[28]

It is precisely that opposition, in all its tedium and monotony, that (to return to the Anglo-American side) Carol Gilligan's work has promoted. Gilligan explains the divergent paths of moral development followed by boys and girls in terms of differences of 'experience' (lived reality). It is not surprising that historians of women have picked up her ideas and used them to explain the 'different voices' their work has enabled them to hear. The problems with these borrowings are manifold, and they are logically connected.[29] The first is a slippage that often happens in the attribution of causality: the argument moves from a statement such as 'women's experience leads them to make moral choices contingent on contexts and relationships' to 'women think and choose this way because they are women'. Implied in this line of reasoning is the ahistorical, if not essentialist, notion of woman. Gilligan and others have extrapolated her description, based on a small sample of late twentieth-century American schoolchildren, into a statement about all women. This extrapolation is evident especially, but not exclusively, in the discussions by some historians of 'women's culture' that take evidence from early saints to modern militant labour activists and reduce it to proof of Gilligan's hypothesis about a universal female preference for relatedness.[30] This use of Gilligan's ideas provides sharp contrast to the more complicated and historicized conceptions of 'women's culture' evident in the *Feminist Studies* 1980 symposium.[31] Indeed, a comparison of that set of articles with Gilligan's formulations reveals the extent to which her notion is ahistorical, defining woman/man as a universal, self-reproducing binary opposition—fixed always in the same way. By insisting on fixed differences (in Gilligan's case, by simplifying data with more mixed results about sex and moral reasoning to underscore sexual difference), feminists contribute to the kind of thinking they want to oppose. Although they insist on the revaluation of the category 'female' (Gilligan suggests that women's moral choices may be more humane than men's), they do not examine the binary opposition itself.

We need a refusal of the fixed and permanent quality of the binary opposition, a genuine historicization and deconstruction of the terms of sexual difference. We must become more self-conscious about distinguishing between our analytic vocabulary and the material we want to analyze. We must find ways (however imperfect) continually to subject our categories to criticism, our analyses to self-criticism. If we employ Jacques Derrida's definition of deconstruction, this criticism means analysing in context the way any binary opposition operates, reversing and displacing its hierarchical construction, rather than accepting it as real or self-evident or in the nature of things.[32] In a sense, of course, feminists have been doing this for years. The history of feminist thought is a history of the refusal of the hierarchical construction of the relationship between male and female in its specific contexts and an attempt to reverse or displace its operations. Feminist historians are now in a position to theorize their practice and to develop gender as an analytic category.

Concern with gender as an analytic category has emerged only in the late twentieth century. It is absent from the major bodies of social theory articulated from the eighteenth to the early twentieth century. To be sure, some of those theories built their logic on analogies to the opposition of male and female, others acknowledged a 'woman question', still others addressed the formation of subjective sexual identity, but gender as a way of talking about systems of social or sexual relations did not appear. This neglect may in part explain the difficulty that contemporary feminists have had incorporating the term 'gender' into existing bodies of theory and convincing adherents of one or another theoretical school that gender belongs in their vocabulary. The term 'gender' is part of the attempt by contemporary feminists to stake claim to a certain definitional ground, to insist on the inadequacy of existing bodies of theory for explaining persistent inequalities between women and men. It seems to me significant that the use of the world 'gender' has emerged at a moment of great epistemological turmoil that takes the form, in some cases, of a shift from scientific to literary paradigms among social scientists (from an emphasis on cause to one on meaning, blurring genres of inquiry, in anthropologist Clifford Geertz's phrase)[33] and, in other cases, the form of debates about theory between those who assert the transparency of facts and those who insist that all reality is construed or constructed, between those who defend and those who question the idea that 'man' is the rational master of his own destiny. In the space opened by this debate and on the side of the critique of science developed by the humanities, and of empiricism and humanism by post-structuralists, feminists have begun to find not only a theoretical voice of their own but scholarly and political allies as well. It is within this space that we must articulate gender as an analytic category.

What should be done by historians who, after all, have seen their discipline dismissed by some recent theorists as a relic of humanist thought? I do not think we should quit the archives or abandon the study of the past, but we do have to change some of the ways we've gone about working, some of the questions we have asked. We need to scrutinize our methods of analysis, clarify our operative assumptions, and explain how we think change occurs. Instead of a search

for single origins, we have to conceive of processes so interconnected that they cannot be disentangled. Of course, we identify
problems to study, and these constitute beginnings or points of
entry into complex processes. But it is the processes we must continually keep in mind. We must ask more often how things happened in order to find out why they happened; in anthropologist
Michelle Rosaldo's formulation, we must pursue not universal, general causality but meaningful explanation: 'It now appears to me
that women's place in human social life is not in any direct sense a
product of the things she does, but of the meaning her activities
acquire through concrete social interaction.'[34] To pursue meaning,
we need to deal with the individual subject as well as social organization and to articulate the nature of their interrelationships, for
both are crucial to understanding how gender works, how change
occurs. Finally, we need to replace the notion that social power is
unified, coherent, and centralized with something like Michel
Foucault's concept of power as dispersed constellations of unequal
relationships, discursively constituted in social 'fields of force'.[35]
Within these processes and structures, there is room for a concept
of human agency as the attempt (at least partially rational) to construct an identity, a life, a set of relationships, a society within certain limits and with language—conceptual language that at once
sets boundaries and contains the possibility for negation, resistance, reinterpretation, the play of metaphoric invention and imagination.

My definition of gender has two parts and several subsets. They
are interrelated but must be analytically distinct. The core of the
definition rests on an integral connection between two propositions: gender is a constitutive element of social relationships based
on perceived differences between the sexes, and gender is a primary
way of signifying relationships of power. Changes in the organization of social relationships always correspond to changes in representations of power, but the direction of change is not necessarily
one way. As a constitutive element of social relationships based on
perceived differences between the sexes, gender involves four interrelated elements: first, culturally available symbols that evoke multiple (and often contradictory) representations—Eve and Mary as
symbols of woman, for example, in the Western Christian tradition—but also, myths of light and dark, purification and pollution,
innocence and corruption. For historians, the interesting questions
are: Which symbolic representations are invoked, how, and in what
contexts? Second, normative concepts that set forth interpretations

167

of the meanings of the symbols, that attempt to limit and contain their metaphoric possibilities. These concepts are expressed in religious, educational, scientific, legal, and political doctrines and typically take the form of a fixed binary opposition, categorically and unequivocally asserting the meaning of male and female, masculine and feminine. In fact, these normative statements depend on the refusal or repression of alternative possibilities, and sometimes overt contests about them take place (at what moments and under what circumstances ought to be a concern of historians). The position that emerges as dominant, however, is stated as the only possible one. Subsequent history is written as if these normative positions were the product of social consensus rather than of conflict. An example of this kind of history is the treatment of the Victorian ideology of domesticity as if it were created whole and only afterwards reacted to instead of being the constant subject of great differences of opinion. Another kind of example comes from contemporary fundamentalist religious groups that have forcibly linked their practice to a restoration of women's supposedly more authentic 'traditional' role, when, in fact, there is little historical precedent for the unquestioned performance of such a role. The point of new historical investigation is to disrupt the notion of fixity, to discover the nature of the debate or repression that leads to the appearance of timeless permanence in binary gender representation. This kind of analysis must include a notion of politics and reference to social institutions and organizations—the third aspect of gender relationships.

Some scholars, notably anthropologists, have restricted the use of gender to the kinship system (focusing on household and family as the basis for social organization). We need a broader view that includes not only kinship but also (especially for complex modern societies) the labour market (a sex-segregated labour market is a part of the process of gender construction), education (all-male, single-sex, or coeducational institutions are part of the same process), and the polity (universal male suffrage is part of the process of gender construction). It makes little sense to force these institutions back to functional utility in the kinship system, or to argue that contemporary relationships between men and women are artefacts of older kinship systems based on the exchange of women.[36] Gender is constructed through kinship, but not exclusively; it is constructed as well in the economy and the polity, which, in our society at least, now operate largely independently of kinship.

The fourth aspect of gender is subjective identity. I agree with anthropologist Gayle Rubin's formulation that psychoanalysis offers an important theory about the reproduction of gender, a description of the 'transformation of the biological sexuality of individuals as they are enculturated'.[37] But the universal claim of psychoanalysis gives me pause. Even though Lacanian theory may be helpful for thinking about the construction of gendered identity, historians need to work in a more historical way. If gender identity is based only and universally on fear of castration, the point of historical inquiry is denied. Moreover, real men and women do not always or literally fulfill the terms either of their society's prescriptions or of our analytic categories. Historians need instead to examine the ways in which gendered identities are substantively constructed and relate their findings to a range of activities, social organizations, and historically specific cultural representations. The best efforts in this area so far have been, not surprisingly, biographies: Biddy Martin's interpretation of Lou Andreas Salomé, Kathryn Sklar's depiction of Catharine Beecher, Jacqueline Hall's life of Jessie Daniel Ames, and Mary Hill's discussion of Charlotte Perkins Gilman.[38] But collective treatments are also possible, as Mrinalina Sinha and Lou Ratté have shown in their respective studies of the terms of construction of gender identity for British colonial administrators in India and for British-educated Indians who emerged as anti-imperialist, nationalist leaders.[39]

The first part of my definition of gender consists, then, of all four of these elements, and no one of them operates without the others. Yet they do not operate simultaneously, with one simply reflecting the others. A question for historical research is, in fact, what the relationships among the four aspects are. The sketch I have offered of the process of constructing gender relationships could be used to discuss class, race, ethnicity, or, for that matter, any social process. My point was to clarify and specify how one needs to think about the effect of gender in social and institutional relationships, because this thinking is often not done precisely or systematically. The theorizing of gender, however, is developed in my second proposition: gender is a primary way of signifying relationships of power. It might be better to say, gender is a primary field within which or by means of which power is articulated. Gender is not the only field, but it seems to have been a persistent and recurrent way of enabling the signification of power in the West, in the Judaeo-Christian as well as the Islamic tradition. As such, this part of the definition might seem to belong in the normative section of the argument, yet it does not, for concepts of power, thought they may build on

gender, are not always literally about gender itself. French sociologist Pierre Bourdieu has written about how the 'di-vision du
monde', based on references to 'biological differences and notably
those that refer to the division of the labour of procreation and
reproduction', operates as 'the best founded of collective illusions'.
Established as an objective set of references, concepts of gender
structure perception and the concrete and symbolic organization of
all social life.[40] To the extent that these references establish distrib-
utions of power (differential control over or access to material and
symbolic resources), gender becomes implicated in the conception
and construction of power itself. The French anthropologist
Maurice Godelier has put it this way: 'It is not sexuality which
haunts society, but society which haunts the body's sexuality. Sex-
related differences between bodies are continually summoned as
testimony to social relations and phenomena that have nothing to
do with sexuality. Not only as testimony to, but also testimony for—
in other words, as legitimation'.[41]

The legitimizing function of gender works in many ways.
Bourdieu, for example, showed how, in certain cultures, agricultural exploitation was organized according to concepts of time
and season that rested on specific definitions of the opposition
between masculine and feminine. Gayatri Spivak has done a
pointed analysis of the uses of gender and colonialism in certain
texts of British and American women writers.[42] Natalie Davis has
shown how concepts of masculine and feminine related to understandings and criticisms of the rules of social order in early modern France.[43] Historian Caroline Bynum has thrown new light on
medieval spirituality through her attention to the relationships
between concepts of masculine and feminine and religious behaviour. Her work gives us important insight into the ways in which
these concepts informed the politics of monastic institutions as
well as of individual believers.[44] Art historians have opened a new
territory by reading social implications from literal depictions of
women and men.[45] These interpretations are based on the idea
that conceptual languages employ differentiation to establish
meaning and that sexual difference is a primary way of signifying
differentiation.[46]Gender, then, provides a way to decode meaning
and to understand the complex connections among various forms
of human interaction. When historians look for the ways in which
the concept of gender legitimizes and constructs social relationships, they develop insight into the reciprocal nature of gender
and society and into the particular and contextually specific ways

in which politics constructs gender and gender constructs politics.

Politics is only one of the areas in which gender can be used for historical analysis. I have chosen the following examples relating to politics and power in their most traditionally construed sense, that is, as they pertain to government and the nation-state, for two reasons. First, the territory is virtually uncharted, since gender has been seen as antithetical to the real business of politics. Second, political history—still the dominant mode of historical inquiry—has been the stronghold of resistance to the inclusion of material or even questions about women and gender.

Gender has been employed literally or analogically in political theory to justify or criticize the reign of monarchs and to express the relationship between ruler and ruled. One might have expected that the debates of contemporaries over the reigns of Elizabeth I in England and Catherine de Medici in France would dwell on the issue of women's suitability for political rule, but, in the period when kinship and kingship were integrally related, discussions about male kings were equally preoccupied with masculinity and femininity.[47] Analogies to the marital relationship provide structure for the arguments of Jean Bodin, Robert Filmer, and John Locke. Edmund Burke's attack on the French Revolution is built around a contrast between ugly, murderous *sansculotte* hags ('the furies of hell, in the abused shape of the vilest of women') and the soft femininity of Marie Antoinette, who escaped the crowd to 'seek refuge at the feet of a king and husband' and whose beauty once inspired national pride. (It was in reference to the appropriate role for the feminine in the political order that Burke wrote, 'To make us love our country, our country ought to be lovely.')[48] But the analogy is not always to marriage or even to heterosexuality. In medieval Islamic political theory, the symbols of political power alluded most often to sex between man and boy, suggesting not only forms of acceptable sexuality akin to those that Foucault's last work described in classical Greece but also the irrelevance of women to any notion of politics and public life.[49]

Lest this last comment suggest that political theory simply reflects social organization, it seems important to note that changes in gender relationships can be set off by views of the needs of state. A striking example is Louis de Bonald's argument in 1816 about why the divorce legislation of the French Revolution had to be repealed:

Just as political democracy, 'allows the people, the weak part of political society, to rise against the established power,' so divorce, 'veritable domestic democracy,' allows the wife, 'the weak part, to rebel against marital authority. . . . in order to keep the state out of the hands of the people, it is necessary to keep the family out of the hands of wives and children.'[50]

Bonald begins with an analogy and then establishes a direct correspondence between divorce and democracy. Harking back to much earlier arguments about the well-ordered family as the foundation of the well-ordered state, the legislation that implemented this view redefined the limits of the marital relationship. Similarly, in our own time, conservative political ideologues would like to pass a series of laws about the organization and behaviour of the family that would alter current practices. The connection between authoritarian regimes and the control of women has been noted but not thoroughly studied. Whether at a crucial moment for Jacobin hegemony in the French Revolution, at the point of Stalin's bid for controlling authority, the implementation of Nazi policy in Germany, or with the triumph in Iran of the Ayatollah Khomeini, emergent rulers have legitimized domination, strength, central authority, and ruling power as masculine (enemies, outsiders, subversives, weakness as feminine) and made that code literal in laws (forbidding women's political participation, outlawing abortion, prohibiting wage-earning by mothers, imposing female dress codes) that put women in their place.[51] These actions and their timing make little sense in themselves; in most instances, the state had nothing immediate or material to gain from the control of women. The actions can only be made sense of as part of an analysis of the construction and consolidation of power. An assertion of control or strength was given form as a policy about women. In these examples, sexual difference was conceived in terms of the domination or control of women. These examples provide some insight into the kinds of power relationships being constructed in modern history, but this particular type of relationship is not a universal political theme. In different ways, for example, the democratic regimes of the twentieth century have also constructed their political ideologies with gendered concepts and translated them into policy; the welfare state, for example, demonstrated its protective paternalism in laws directed at women and children.[52] Historically, some socialist and anarchist movements have refused metaphors of domination entirely, imaginatively presenting their critiques of particular regimes or social organizations in terms of transformations of gender identities. Utopian socialists in France and England in the 1830s and 1840s conceived their dreams for a harmonious future in terms of the complementary natures of individuals, as exemplified in the union of man and woman, 'the social individual'.[53] European anarchists were long known not only for refusing the conventions of bourgeois marriage but for their visions of a world in which sexual difference did not imply hierarchy.

These examples are of explicit connections between gender and power, but they are only a part of my definition of gender as a primary way of signifying relationships of power. Attention to gender is often not explicit, but it is none the less a crucial part of the organization of equality or inequality. Hierarchical structures rely on generalized understandings of the so-called natural relationships between male and female. The concept of class in the nineteenth century relied on gender for its articulation. While middle-class reformers in France, for example, depicted workers in terms coded as feminine (subordinated, weak, sexually exploited like prostitutes), labour and socialist leaders replied by insisting on the masculine position of the working class (producers, strong, protectors of their women and children). The terms of this discourse were not explicitly about gender, but they were strengthened by references to it. The gendered 'coding' of certain terms established and 'naturalized' their meanings. In the process, historically specific, normative definitions of gender (which were taken as given) were reproduced and embedded in the culture of the French working class.[54]

The subject of war, diplomacy, and high politics frequently comes up when traditional political historians question the utility of gender in their work. But here, too, we need to look beyond the actors and the literal import of their words. Power relations among nations and the status of colonial subjects have been made comprehensible (and thus legitimate) in terms of relations between male and female. The legitimizing of war—of expending young lives to protect the state—has variously taken the forms of explicit appeals to manhood (to the need to defend otherwise vulnerable women and children), of implicit reliance on belief in the duty of sons to serve their leaders or their (father the) king, and of associations between masculinity and national strength.[55] High politics itself is a gendered concept, for it establishes its crucial importance and public power, the reasons for and the fact of its highest authority, precisely in its exclusion of women from its work. Gender is one of the recurrent references by which political power has been conceived, legitimated, and criticized. It refers to but also establishes the meaning of the male/female opposition. To vindicate political power, the reference must seem sure and fixed, outside human construction, part of the natural or divine order. In that way, the binary opposition and the social process of gender relationships both become part of the meaning of power itself; to question or alter any aspect threatens the entire system.

If significations of gender and power construct one another, how do things change? The answer in a general sense is that change may be initiated in many places. Massive political upheavals that throw old orders into chaos and bring new ones into being may revise the terms (and so the organization) of gender in the search for new forms of legitimation. But they may not; old notions of gender have also served to validate new regimes.[56] Demographic crises, occasioned by food shortages, plagues, or wars, may have called into question normative visions of heterosexual marriage (as happened in some circles, in some countries in the 1920s), but they have also spawned pronatalist policies that insist on the exclusive importance of women's maternal and reproductive functions.[57] Shifting patterns of employment may lead to altered marital strategies and to different possibilities for the construction of subjectivity, but they can also be experienced as new arenas of activity for dutiful daughters and wives.[58] The emergence of new kinds of cultural symbols may make possible the reinterpreting or, indeed, rewriting of the oedipal story, but it can also serve to reinscribe that terrible drama in even more telling terms. Political processes will determine which outcome prevails—political in the sense that different actors and different meanings are contending with one another for control. The nature of that process, of the actors and their actions, can only be determined specifically, in the context of time and place. We can write the history of that process only if we recognize that 'man' and 'woman' are at once empty and overflowing categories. Empty because they have no ultimate, transcendent meaning. Overflowing because even when they appear to be fixed, they still contain within them alternative, denied, or suppressed definitions.

Political history has, in a sense, been enacted on the field of gender. It is a field that seems fixed yet whose meaning is contested and in flux. If we treat the opposition between male and female as problematic rather than known, as something contextually defined, repeatedly constructed, then we must constantly ask not only what is at stake in proclamations or debates that invoke gender to explain or justify their positions but also how implicit understandings of gender are being invoked and reinscribed. What is the relationship between laws about women and the power of the state? Why (and since when) have women been invisible as historical subjects, when we know they participated in the great and small events of human history? Has gender legitimized the emergence of professional careers?[59] Is (to quote the title of a recent article by French feminist Luce Irigaray) the subject of science sexed?[60] What is the relationship between state politics and the discovery of the crime of homosexuality?[61] How have social institutions incorporated gender into their assumptions and organizations? Have there ever been genuinely egalitarian concepts of gender in terms of which political systems were projected, if not built?

Investigation of these issues will yield a history that will provide new perspectives on old questions (about how, for example, political rule is imposed, or what the impact of war on society is), redefine the old questions in new terms (introducing considerations of family and sexuality, for example, in the study of economics or war), make women visible as active participants, and create analytic distance between the seemingly fixed language of the past and our own terminology. In addition, this new history will leave open possibilities for thinking about current feminist political strategies and the (utopian) future, for it suggests that gender must be redefined and restructured in conjunction with a vision of political and social equality that includes not only sex but class and race.

Notes

1. *The Compact Edition of the Oxford English Dictionary* (Oxford: Oxford University Press, 1971), i. 1126.
2. E. Littré, *Dictionnaire de la langue française* (Paris, 1876).
3. Raymond Williams, *Keywords* (New York: Oxford University Press, 1983), 285.
4. Natalie Zemon Davis, 'Women's History in Transition: The European Case', *Feminist Studies*, 3 (1975–6), 90.
5. Ann D. Gordon, Mari Jo Buhle, and Nancy Shrom Dye, 'The Problem of Women's History', in Berenice Carroll (ed.), *Liberating Women's History* (Urbana: University of Illinois Press), 89.
6. The best and most subtle example is from Joan Kelly, 'The Doubled Vision of Feminist Theory', in her *Women, History and Theory* (Chicago: University of Chicago Press, 1984), 51–64, esp. p. 61.
7. For an argument against the use of gender to emphasize the social aspect of sexual difference, see Moira Gatens, 'A Critique of the Sex/Gender Distinction', in J. Allen and P. Patton (eds.), *Beyond Marxism?* (Leichhardt, NSW: Intervention Publications, 1985), 143–60. I agree with her argument that the sex/gender distinction grants autonomous or transparent determination to the body, ignoring the fact that what we know about the body is culturally produced knowledge.

8. For a different characterization of feminist analysis, see Linda J. Nicholson, *Gender and History: The Limits of Social Theory in the Age of the Family* (New York: Columbia University Press, 1986).
9. Mary O'Brien, *The Politics of Reproduction* (London: Routledge and Kegan Paul, 1981), 8–15, 46.
10. Shulamith Firestone, *The Dialectic of Sex* (New York: Bantam Books, 1970). The phrase 'bitter trap' is O'Brien's (*Politics of Reproduction*, p. 8).
11. Catherine McKinnon, 'Feminism, Marxism, Method, and the State: An Agenda for Theory', *Signs*, 7 (1982), 515, 541.
12. Ibid. 541, 543.
13. For an interesting discussion of the strengths and limits of the term 'patriarchy', see the exchange among historians Sheila Rowbotham, Sally Alexander, and Barbara Taylor in Raphael Samuel (ed.), *People's History and Socialist Theory* (London: Routledge and Kegan Paul, 1981), 363–73.
14. Friedrich Engels, *The Origins of the Family, Private Property, and the State* (1884; repr., New York: International Publishers, 1972).
15. Heidi Hartmann, 'Capitalism, Patriarchy, and Job Segregation by Sex', *Signs*, 1 (1976), 168. See also 'The Unhappy Marriage of Marxism and Feminism: Towards a More Progressive Union', *Capital and Class*, 8 (1979), 1–33; 'The Family as the Locus of Gender, Class, and Political Struggle: The Example of Housework', *Signs*, 6 (1981), 366–94.
16. Discussions of Marxist feminism include Zillah Eisenstein, *Capitalist Patriarchy and the Case for Socialist Feminism* (New York: Longman, 1981); A. Kuhn, 'Structures of Patriarchy and Capital in the Family', in A. Kuhn and A. Wolpe (eds.), *Feminism and Materialism: Women and Modes of Production* (London: Routledge and Kegan Paul, 1978); Rosalind Coward, *Patriarchal Precedents* (London: Routledge and Kegan Paul, 1983); Hilda Scott, *Does Socialism Liberate Women? Experiences from Eastern Europe* (Boston: Beacon Press, 1974); Jane Humphries, 'Working Class Family, Women's Liberation and Class Struggle: The Case of Nineteenth-Century British History', *Review of Radical Political Economics*, 9 (1977), 25–41; Jane Humphries, 'Class Struggle and the Persistence of the Working Class Family', *Cambridge Journal of Economics*, 1 (1971), 241–58; and see the debate on Humphries's work in *Review of Radical Political Economics*, 12 (1980), 76–94.
17. Kelly, 'Doubled Vision of Feminist Theory', 61.
18. Ann Snitow, Christine Stansell, and Sharon Thompson (eds.), *Powers of Desire: The Politics of Sexuality* (New York: Monthly Review Press, 1983).
19. Ellen Ross and Rayna Rapp, 'Sex and Society: A Research Note from Social History and Anthropology', in *Powers of Desire*, 53.
20. 'Introduction', *Powers and Desire*, 12; and Jessica Benjamin, 'Master and Slave: The Fantasy of Erotic Domination', *Powers of Desire*, 297.
21. Johanna Brenner and Maria Ramas, 'Rethinking Women's Oppression', *New Left Review* (1984) 144: 33–71; Michèle Barrett, 'Rethinking Women's Oppression: A Reply to Brenner and Ramas', *New Left Review*, 146 (1984), 123–8; Angela Weir and Elizabeth Wilson, 'The British Women's Movement', *New Left Review*, 148 (1984), 74–103; Michèle Barrett, 'A Response to Weir and Wilson', *New Left Review*, 150 (1985), 143–7; Jane Lewis, 'The Debate on Sex and Class', *New Left Review*, 149 (1985), 108–20. See also Hugh Armstrong and Pat Armstrong, 'Beyond Sexless Class and Classless Sex: Towards Feminist Marxism', *Studies in Political Economy*, 10 (1983), 7–44; Hugh

Armstrong and Pat Armstrong, 'Comments: More on Marxist Feminism', *Studies in Political Economy*, 15 (1984), 179–84; and Jane Jenson, 'Gender and Reproduction: Or, Babies and the State', unpub. paper, June 1985, 1–7.

22. For early theoretical formulations, see *Papers on Patriarchy: Conference, London 76* (London: n.p., 1976). I am grateful to Jane Caplan for telling me of the existence of this publication and for her willingness to share with me her copy and her ideas about it. For the psychoanalytic position, see Sally Alexander, 'Women, Class and Sexual Difference', *History Workshop*, 17 (1984), 125–35. In seminars at Princeton University in early 1986, Juliet Mitchell seemed to be returning to an emphasis on the priority of materialist analyses of gender. For an attempt to get beyond the theoretical impasse of Marxist feminism, see Coward, *Patriarchal Precedents*. See also the brilliant American effort in this direction by anthropologist Gayle Rubin, 'The Traffic in Women: Notes on the Political Economy of Sex', ch. 5 this vol., p. 105.

23. Nancy Chodorow, *The Reproduction of Mothering: Psychoanalysis and the Sociology of Gender* (Berkeley: University of California Press, 1978), 169.

24. 'My account suggests that these gender-related issues may be influenced during the period of the oedipus complex, but they are not its only focus or outcome. The negotiation of these issues occurs in the context of broader object-relational and ego processes. These broader processes have equal influence on psychic structure formation, and psychic life and relational modes in men and women. They account for differing modes of identification and orientation to heterosexual objects, for the more asymmetrical oedipal issues psychoanalysts describe. These outcomes, like more traditional oedipal outcomes, arise from the asymmetrical organization of parenting, with the mother's role as primary parent and the father's typically greater remoteness and his investment in socialization especially in areas concerned with gender-typing.' (Nancy Chodorow, *The Reproduction of Mothering*, 166.) It is important to note that there are differences in interpretation and approach between Chodorow and British object-relations theorists who follow the work of D. W. Winicott and Melanie Klein. Chodorow's approach is best characterized as a more sociological or sociologized theory, but it is the dominant lens through which object-relations theory has been viewed by American feminists. On the history of British object-relations theory in social policy, see Denise Riley, *War in the Nursery* (London: Virago, 1984).

25. Juliet Mitchell and Jacqueline Rose (eds.), *Jacques Lacan and the Ecole Freudienne* (New York: Norton, 1983); Alexander, 'Women, Class and Sexual Difference'.

26. Teresa de Lauretis, *Alice Doesn't: Feminism, Semiotics, Cinema* (Bloomington: Indiana University Press, 1984), 159.

27. Alexander, 'Women, Class and Sexual Difference', 135.

28. E. M. Denise Riley, 'Summary of Preamble to Interwar Feminist History Work', unpub. paper, presented to the Pembroke Center Seminar, May 1985, p. 11. The argument is fully elaborated in Riley's brilliant book, '*Am I That Name?': Feminism and the Category of 'Women' in History* (London: Macmillan, 1988).

29. Carol Gilligan, *In a Different Voice: Psychological Theory and Women's Development* (Cambridge, Mass.: Harvard University Press, 1982).

30. Useful critiques of Gilligan's book are: J. Auerbach *et al.*, 'Commentary on Gilligan's In a Different Voice', *Feminist Studies*, 11 (1985), 149–62, and

'Women and Morality', a special issue of *Social Research* 50 (1983). My comments on the tendency of historians to cite Gilligan come from reading unpublished manuscripts and grant proposals, and it seems unfair to cite those here. I have kept track of the references for over five years, and they are many and increasing.

31. *Feminist Studies*, 6 (1980), 26–64.
32. For a succinct and accessible discussion of Derrida, see Jonathan Culler, *On Deconstruction: Theory and Criticism after Structuralism* (Ithaca, NY: Cornell University Press, 1982), esp. 156–79. See also Jacques Derrida, *Of Grammatology*, trans. Gayatri Chakravotry Spivak (Baltimore: Johns Hopkins University Press, 1974); Jacques Derrida, *Spurs* (Chicago: University of Chicago Press, 1979); and a transcription of Pembroke Center Seminar, 1983, in *Subjects/Objects* (Fall 1984).
33. Clifford Geertz, 'Blurred Genres', *American Scholar*, 49 (1980), 165–79.
34. Michelle Zimbalist Rosaldo, 'The Uses and Abuses of Anthropology: Reflections on Feminism and Cross-Cultural Understanding', *Signs* 5 (1980), 400.
35. Michel Foucault, *The History of Sexuality*, i. *An Introduction* (New York: Vintage, 1980); Michel Foucault, *Power/Knowledge: Selected Interviews and Other Writings, 1972–1977* (New York: Pantheon, 1980).
36. For this argument, see Rubin, 'The Traffic in Women', ch. 5 this vol.
37. Ibid.
38. Biddy Martin, 'Feminism, Criticism and Foucault', *New German Critique*, 27 (1982), 3–30; Kathryn Kish Sklar, *Catharine Beecher: A Study in American Domesticity* (New Haven: Yale University Press, 1973); Mary A. Hill, *Charlotte Perkins Gilman: The Making of a Radical Feminist, 1860–1896* (Philadelphia: Temple University Press, 1980); Jacqueline Dowd Hall, *Revolt Against Chivalry: Jesse Daniel Ames and the Women's Campaign Against Lynching* (New York: Columbia University Press, 1974).
39. Lou Ratté, 'Gender Ambivalence in the Indian Nationalist Movement', unpub. paper, Pembroke Center Seminar, Spring 1983; and Mrinalina Sinha, 'Manliness: A Victorian Ideal and the British Imperial Elite in India', unpub. paper, Department of History, State University of New York, Stony Brook, 1984, and Sinha, 'The Age of Consent Act: The Ideal of Masculinity and Colonial Ideology in Late 19th Century Bengal', *Proceedings*, Eighth International Symposium on Asian Studies, 1986, 1199–214.
40. Pierre Bourdieu, *Le Sens Pratique* (Paris: Les Editions de Minuit, 1980), 246–7, 333–461, esp. 366.
41. Maurice Godelier, 'The Origins of Male Domination', *New Left Review*, 127 (1981), 17.
42. Gayatri Chakravorty Spivak, 'Three Women's Texts and a Critique of Imperialism', *Critical Inquiry*, 12 (1985), 243–6. See also Kate Millett, *Sexual Politics* (New York: Avon, 1969). An examination of how feminine references work in major texts of Western philosophy is carried out by Luce Irigaray in *Speculum of the Other Woman* trans. Gillian C. Gill (Ithaca, NY: Cornell University Press, 1985).
43. Natalie Zemon Davis, 'Women on Top', in her *Society and Culture in Early Modern France* (Stanford: Stanford University Press, 1975), 124–51.
44. Caroline Walker Bynum, *Jesus as Mother: Studies in the Spirituality of the High Middle Ages* (Berkeley: University of California Press, 1982); Caroline Walker

Bynum, 'Fast, Feast, and Flesh: The Religious Significance of Food to Medieval Women', *Representations*, 11 (1985), 1–25; Caroline Walker Bynum, 'Introduction', *Religion and Gender: Essays on the Complexity of Symbols* (Boston: Beacon Press, 1987).

45. See, for example, T. J. Clark, *The Painting of Modern Life* (New York: Knopf, 1985).

46. The difference between structuralist and post-structuralist theorists on this question rests on how open or closed they view the categories of difference. To the extent that post-structuralists do not fix a universal meaning for the categories or the relationship between them, their approach seems conducive to the kind of historical analysis I am advocating.

47. Rachel Weil, 'The Crown Has Fallen to the Distaff: Gender and Politics in the Age of Catherine de Medici', *Critical Matrix*, Princeton Working Papers in Women's Studies, no. 1 (1985). See also Louis Montrose, Shaping Fantasies: Figurations of Gender and Power in Elizabethan Culture', *Representations*, 1 (1983), 61–94; and Lynn Hunt, 'Hercules and the Radical Image in the French Revolution', *Representations*, 1 (1983), 95–117.

48. Edmund Burke, *Reflections on the French Revolution* (1892; repr., New York, 1909), 208–9, 214. See Jean Bodin, *Six Books of the Commonwealth* (1606; repr., New York: Barnes and Noble, 1967); Robert Filmer, *Patriarchia and Other Political Works* (Oxford; Blackwell, 1949); and John Locke, *Two Treatises of Government* (1690; repr., Cambridge: Cambridge University Press, 1970). See also Elizabeth Fox-Genovese, 'Property and Patriarchy in Classical Bourgeois Political Theory', *Radical History Review*, 4 (1977), 36–59; and Mary Lyndon Shanley, 'Marriage Contract and Social Contract in Seventeenth-Century English Political Thought', *Western Political Quarterly*, 3 (1979), 79–91.

49. I am grateful to Bernard Lewis for the reference to Islam. Michel Foucault, *Historie de la Sexualité*, ii. *L'Usage des plaisirs* (Paris: Gallimard, 1984). On women in classical Athens, see Marilyn Arthur, ' "Liberated Woman": The Classical Era', in Renate Bridenthal and Claudia Koonz (eds.), *Becoming Visible: Women in European History* (Boston: Houghton Mifflin, 1977), 75–8.

50. Cited in Roderick Phillips, 'Women and Family Breakdown in Eighteenth-Century France: Rouen 1780–1800', *Social History*, 2 (1976), 217.

51. On the French Revolution, see Darline Gay Levy, Harriet Applewhite, and Mary Durham Johnson (eds.), *Women in Revolutionary Paris, 1789–1795* (Urbana: University of Illinois Press, 1979), 209–20; on Soviet legislation, see the documents in Rudolph Schlesinger, *Changing Attitudes in Soviet Russia: Documents and Readings*, i. *The Family in the USSR* (London: Routledge and Kegan Paul, 1949), 62–71, 251–4; on Nazi policy, see Tim Mason, 'Women in Nazi Germany', *History Workshop*, 1 (1976), 74–113, and Tim Mason, 'Women in Germany, 1925–40: Family, Welfare and Work', *History Workshop*, 2 (1976), 5–32.

52. Elizabeth Wilson, *Women and the Welfare State* (London: Tavistock, 1977); Jane Jenson, 'Gender and Reproduction'; Jane Lewis, *The Politics of Motherhood: Child and Maternal Welfare in England, 1900–1939* (London: Croom Helm, 1980); Mary Lynn McDougall, 'Protecting Infants: The French Campaign for Maternity Leaves, 1890s–1913', *French Historical Studies*, 13 (1983), 79–105.

53. On English Utopians, see Barbara Taylor, *Eve and the New Jerusalem* (New York: Pantheon, 1983).

54. Louis Deviance, 'Femme, famille, travail et morale sexuelle dans l'idéologie de 1848', in *Mythes et représentations de la femme au XIXᵉ siècle* (Paris: Champion, 1977); Jacques Rancière and Pierre Vauday, 'En allant à l'éxpo: L'ouvrier, sa femme et les machines', *Les révoltes logiques*, 1 (1975), 5–22.

55. Gasyatri Chakravorty Spivak, ' "Draupadi" by Mahasveta Devi', *Critical Inquiry*, 8 (1981), 381–401; Homi Bhabha, 'Of Mimicry and Man: The Ambivalence of Colonial Discourse', *October*, 28 (1984), 125–33; Karin Hausen, 'The German Nation's Obligations to the Heroes' Widows of World War I', in Margaret R. Higonnet *et al.*, *Behind the Lines: Gender and the Two World Wars* (New Haven: Yale University Press, 1987), 126–40. See also Ken Inglis, 'The Representation of Gender on Australian War Memorials', *Daedalus*, 116 (1987), 35–59.

56. On the French Revolution, see Levy *et al.*, *Women in Revolutionary Paris*. On the American Revolution, see Mary Beth Norton, *Liberty's Daughters: The Revolutionary Experience of American Women* (Boston: Little, Brown, 1980); Linda Kerber, *Women of the Republic* (Chapel Hill: University of North Carolina Press, 1980); Joan Hoff-Wilson, 'The Illusion of Change: Women and the American Revolution', in Alfred Young (ed.), *The American Revolution: Explorations in the History of American Radicalism* (DeKalb: Northern Illinois University Press, 1976), 383–446. On the French Third Republic, see Steven Hause, *Women's Suffrage and Social Politics in the French Third Republic* (Princeton: Princeton University Press, 1984). An extremely interesting treatment of a recent case is Maxine Molyneux, 'Mobilization without Emancipation? Women's Interests, the State and Revolution in Nicaragua', *Feminist Studies*, 11 (1985), 227–54.

57. On pronatalism, see Riley, *War in the Nursery*, and Jenson, 'Gender and Reproduction'. On the 1920s, see the essays in *Stratégies des Femmes* (Paris: Editions Tierce, 1984).

58. For various interpretations of the impact of new work on women, see Louise A. Tilly and Joan W. Scott, *Women, Work and Family* (New York: Holt, Rinehart and Winston, 1978; Methuen, 1987); Thomas Dublin, *Women at Work: The Transformation of Work and Community in Lowell, Massachusetts, 1826–1860* (New York: Columbia University Press, 1979); and Edward Shorter, *The Making of the Modern Family* (New York: Basic Books, 1975).

59. See, for example, Margaret Rossiter, *Women Scientists in America: Struggles and Strategies to 1914* (Baltimore: Johns Hopkins University Press, 1982).

60. Luce Irigaray, 'Is the Subject of Science Sexed?', *Cultural Critique*, 1 (1985), 73–88.

61. Louis Crompton, *Byron and Greek Love: Homophobia in Nineteenth-Century England* (Berkeley: University of California Press, 1985). This question is touched on also in Jeffrey Weeks, *Sex, Politics and Society: The Regulation of Sexuality Since 1800* (London: Leyman, 1981).

Part III. **Race**

African-American Women's History and the Metalanguage of Race

Evelyn Brooks Higginbotham

Theoretical discussion in African-American women's history begs for greater voice. I say this as a black woman who is cognizant of the strengths and limitations of current feminist theory. Feminist scholars have moved rapidly forward in addressing theories of subjectivity, questions of difference, the construction of social relations as relations of power, the conceptual implications of binary oppositions such as male versus female or equality versus difference—all issues defined with relevance to gender and with potential for intellectual and social transformations.[1] Notwithstanding a few notable exceptions, this new wave of feminist theorists finds little to say about race. The general trend has been to mention black and Third World feminists who first called attention to the glaring fallacies in essentialist analysis and to claims of a homogeneous 'womanhood', 'woman's culture', and 'patriarchal oppression of women'.[2] Beyond this recognition, however, white feminist scholars pay hardly more than lip service to race as they continue to analyse their own experience in ever more sophisticated forms.

This narrowness of vision is particularly ironic in that these very issues of equality and difference, the constructive strategies of power, and subjectivity and consciousness have stood at the core of black scholarship for some half-century or more. Historian W. E. B. Du Bois, sociologist Oliver Cox, and scientist Charles R. Drew are only some of the more significant pre-1950s contributors to the discussion of race as a social category and to the refutation of essentialist biological and genetic explanations.[3] These issues continue to be salient in our own time, when racism in America grows with both verve and subtlety and when 'enlightened' women's historians

A number of people read earlier versions of this article. I am especially grateful to the insights, suggestions, and probing questions of Sharon Harley, Paul Hanson, Darlene Clark-Hine, and Carroll Smith-Rosenberg. Reprinted by permission of the University of Chicago Press from *Signs*, 17/2 (Winter 1992), 251–74.

witness, as has been the case in recent years, recurrent racial tensions at our own professional and scholarly gatherings.

Feminist scholars, especially those of African-American women's history, must accept the challenge to bring race more prominently into their analyses of power. The explication of race entails three interrelated strategies, separated here merely for the sake of analysis. First of all, we must define the construction and 'technologies' of race as well as those of gender and sexuality.[4] Second, we must expose the role of race as a metalanguage by calling attention to its powerful, all-encompassing effect on the construction and representation of other social and power relations, namely, gender, class, and sexuality. Third, we must recognize race as providing sites of dialogic exchange and contestation, since race has constituted a discursive tool for both oppression and liberation. As Michael Omi and Howard Winant argue, 'the effort must be made to understand race as an unstable and "decentred" complex of social meanings constantly being transformed by political struggle'.[5] Such a three-pronged approach to the history of African-American women will require borrowing and blending work by black intellectuals, white feminist scholars, and other theorists such as white male philosophers and linguists. Indeed, the very process of borrowing and blending speaks to the tradition of syncretism that has characterized the Afro-American experience.

DEFINING RACE

When the US Supreme Court had before it the task of defining obscenity, Justice Potter Stewart claimed that, while he could not intelligibly define it, 'I know it when I see it'.[6] When we talk about the concept of race, most people believe that they know it when they see it but arrive at nothing short of confusion when pressed to define it. Chromosome research reveals the fallacy of race as an accurate measure of genotypic or phenotypic difference between human beings. Cross-cultural and historical studies of miscegenation law reveal shifting, arbitrary, and contradictory definitions of race. Literary critics, as in the collection of essays 'Race,' Writing, and Difference, edited by Henry Louis Gates, compellingly present race as the 'ultimate trope of difference'—as artificially and arbitrarily contrived to produce and maintain relations of power and subordination. Likewise, historian Barbara Fields argues that race is neither natural nor transhistorical, but must rather be analysed with an eye to its functioning and maintenance within specific contexts.[7]

Like gender and class, then, race must be seen as a social construction predicated upon the recognition of difference and signifying the simultaneous distinguishing and positioning of groups vis-à-vis one another. More than this, race is a highly contested representation of relations of power between social categories by which individuals are identified and identify themselves. The recognition of racial distinctions emanates from and adapts to multiple uses of power in society. Perceived as 'natural' and 'appropriate', such racial categories are strategically necessary for the functioning of power in countless institutional and ideological forms, both explicit and subtle. As Michel Foucault has written, societies engage in 'a perpetual process of strategic elaboration' or a constant shifting and reforming of the apparatus of power in response to their particular cultural or economic needs.[8]

Furthermore, in societies where racial demarcation is endemic to their sociocultural fabric and heritage—to their laws and economy, to their institutionalized structures and discourses, and to their epistemologies and everyday customs—gender identity is inextricably linked to and even determined by racial identity. In the Jim Crow South prior to the 1960s and in South Africa until very recently, for instance, little black girls learned at an early age to place themselves in the bathroom for 'black women', not in that for 'white ladies'. As such a distinction suggests, in these societies the representation of both gender and class is coloured by race. Their social construction becomes racialized as their concrete implications and normative meanings are continuously shaped by what Louis Althusser terms 'ideological state apparatuses'—the school, family, welfare agency, hospital, television and cinema, the press.[9]

For example, the metaphoric and metonymic identification of welfare with the black population by the American public has resulted in tremendous generalization about the supposed unwillingness of many blacks to work. Welfare immediately conjures up images of black female-headed families, despite the fact that the aggregate number of poor persons who receive benefits in the form of aid to dependent children or medicare is predominantly white. Likewise, the drug problem too often is depicted in the mass media as a pathology of black lower-class life, set in motion by drug dealers, youthful drug runners, and addicted victims of the ghetto. The drug problem is less often portrayed as an underground economy that mirrors and reproduces the exploitative relations of the dominant economy. The 'supply-side' executives who make the 'big' money are neither black nor residents of urban ghettos.

Race might also be viewed as myth, 'not at all an abstract, purified essence' (to cite Roland Barthes on myth) but, rather, 'a formless, unstable, nebulous condensation, whose unity and coherence are above all due to its function'.[10] As a fluid set of overlapping discourses, race is perceived as arbitrary and illusionary, on the one hand, while natural and fixed on the other. To argue that race is myth and that it is an ideological rather than a biological fact does not deny that ideology has real effects on people's lives. Race serves as a 'global sign', a 'metalanguage', since it speaks about and lends meaning to a host of terms and expressions, to myriad aspects of life that would otherwise fall outside the referential domain of race.[11] By continually expressing overt and covert analogic relationships, race impregnates the simplest meanings we take for granted. It makes hair 'good' or 'bad', speech patterns 'correct' or 'incorrect'. It is, in fact, the apparent overdeterminancy of race in Western culture, and particularly in the United States, that has permitted it to function as a metalanguage in its discursive representation and construction of social relations. Race not only tends to subsume other sets of social relations, namely, gender and class, but it blurs and disguises, suppresses and negates its own complex interplay with the very social relations it envelops. It precludes unity within the same gender group but often appears to solidify people of opposing economic classes. Whether race is textually omitted or textually privileged, its totalizing effect in obscuring class and gender remains.

This may well explain why women's studies for so long rested upon the unstated premiss of racial (i.e. white) homogeneity and with this presumption proceeded to universalize 'woman's' culture and oppression, while failing to see white women's own investment and complicity in the oppression of other groups of men and women. Elizabeth Spelman takes to task this idea of 'homogeneous womanhood' in her exploration of race and gender in *Inessential Woman*. Examining thinkers such as Aristotle, Simone de Beauvoir, and Nancy Chodorow, among others, Spelman observes a double standard on the part of many feminists who fail to separate their whiteness from their womanness. White feminists, she argues, typically discern two separate identities for black women, the racial and the gender, and conclude that the gender identity of black women is the same as their own: 'In other words, the womanness underneath the black woman's skin is white woman's and deep down inside the Latina woman is an Anglo woman waiting to burst through'.[12]

Afro-American history, on the other hand, has accentuated race by calling explicit attention to the cultural as well as socio-economic implications of American racism but has failed to examine the differential class and gender positions men and women occupy in black communities—thus uncritically rendering a monolithic 'black community', 'black experience', and 'voice of the Negro'. Notwithstanding that this discursive monolith most often resonates with a male voice and as the experience of men, such a rendering precludes gender subordination by black men by virtue of their own blackness and social subordination. Even black women's history, which has consciously sought to identify the importance of gender relations and the interworkings of race, class, and gender, none the less reflects the totalizing impulse of race in such concepts as 'black womanhood' or the 'black woman cross-culturally'—concepts that mask real differences of class, status and colour, regional culture, and a host of other configurations of difference.

RACIAL CONSTRUCTIONS OF GENDER

To understand race as a metalanguage, we must recognize its historical and material grounding—what Russian linguist and critic M. M. Bakhtin referred to as 'the power of the word to mean'.[13] This power evolves from concrete situational and ideological contexts, that is, from a position of enunciation that reflects not only time and place but values as well. The concept of race, in its verbal and extraverbal dimension, and even more specifically, in its role in the representation as well as self-representation of individuals in American society (what psychoanalytic theorists call 'subjectifica-tion'), is constituted in language in which (as Bakhtin points out) there have never been ' "neutral" words and forms—words and forms that can belong to "no one"; language has been completely taken over, shot through with intentions and accents'.[14]

The social context for the construction of race as a tool for black oppression is historically rooted in the context of slavery. Barbara Fields reminds us: 'The idea one people has of another, even when the difference between them is embodied in the most striking physical characteristics, is always mediated by the social context within which the two come in contact'.[15] Race came to life primarily as the signifier of the master/slave relation and thus emerged superimposed upon class and property relations. Defined by law as 'animate chattel', slaves constituted property as well as a social class and were exploited under a system that sanctioned white ownership of black bodies and black labour.[16] Studies of black women in slavery, however, make poignantly clear the role of race not only in shaping the class relations of the South's 'peculiar institution', but also in constructing gender's 'power to mean'. Sojourner Truth's famous and haunting question, 'Ar'nt I a Woman?' laid bare the racialized configuration of gender under a system of class rule that compelled and expropriated women's physical labour and denied them legal right to their own bodies and sexuality, much less to the bodies to which they gave birth. While law and public opinion idealized motherhood and enforced the protection of white women's bodies, the opposite held true for black women's. Sojourner Truth's personal testimony demonstrated gender's racial meaning. She had 'ploughed, and planted, and gathered into barns', and no male slave had outdone her. She had given birth to thirteen children, all of whom were sold away from her. When she cried out in grief from the depths of her motherhood, 'none but Jesus heard'.[17]

Wasn't Sojourner Truth a woman? The courts answered this question for slavewomen by ruling them outside the statutory rubric 'woman'.[18] In discussing the case of *State of Missouri v. Celia*, A. Leon Higginbotham, Jr., elucidates the racial signification of gender. Celia was fourteen years old when purchased by a successful farmer, Robert Newsome. During the five years of his ownership, Newsome habitually forced her into sexual intercourse. At age nineteen she had borne a child by him and was expecting another. In June 1855, while pregnant and ill, Celia defended herself against attempted rape by her master. Her testimony reveals that she warned him she would hurt him if he continued to abuse her while sick. When her threats would not deter his advances, she hit him over the head with a stick, immediately killing him. In an act presaging Richard Wright's *Native Son*, she then burned his body in the fireplace and the next morning spread his ashes on the pathway. Celia was apprehended and tried for first-degree murder. Her counsel sought to lower the charge of first degree to murder in self-defence, arguing that Celia had a right to resist her master's sexual advances, especially because of the imminent danger to her health. A slave master's economic and property rights, the defence contended, did not include rape. The defence rested its case on Missouri statutes that protected women from attempts to ravish, rape, or defile. The language of these particular statutes explicitly used the term 'any woman', while other unrelated Missouri statutes explicitly used terms such as 'white female' and 'slave' or negro' in their criminal codes. The question centred on her womanhood. The court found Celia guilty: 'If Newsome was in the habit of having intercourse with the defendant who was his slave, . . . it is murder in the first degree.' Celia was sentenced to death, having been denied an appeal, and was hanged in December 1855 after the birth of her child.[19]

Since racially based justifications of slavery stood at the core of Southern law, race relations, and social etiquette in general, then proof of 'womanhood' did not rest on a common female essence, shared culture, or mere physical appearance. (Sojourner Truth, on one occasion, was forced to bare her breasts to a doubting audience in order to vindicate her womanhood.) This is not to deny gender's role within the social and power relations of race. Black women experienced the vicissitudes of slavery through gendered lives and thus differently from slave men. They bore and nursed children and performed domestic duties—all on top of doing fieldwork. Unlike slave men, slave women fell victim to rape precisely because of their gender. Yet gender itself was both constructed and fragmented by race. Gender, so coloured by race, remained from birth until death inextricably linked to one's personal identity and social status. For black and white women, gendered identity was reconstructed and represented in very different, indeed antagonistic, racialized contexts.

RACIAL CONSTRUCTIONS OF CLASS

Henry Louis Gates argue that 'race has become a trope of ultimate, irreducible difference between cultures, linguistic groups, or adherents of specific belief systems which—more often than not—also have fundamentally opposed economic interest.'[20] It is interesting that the power of race as a metalanguage that transcends and masks real differences lies in the remarkable and long-standing success with which it unites whites of disparate economic positions against blacks. Until the Civil Rights era of the 1960s, race effectively served as a metaphor for class, albeit a metaphor rife with complications.

For example, not all Southern whites were slave owners. Nor did they share the same economic and political interests. Up-country yeomen protested the predominance of planters' interests over their own in state legislatures, and white artisans decried competition from the use of slave labour.[21] Yet, while Southern whites hardly constituted a homogeneous class, they united for radically different reasons around the banner of white supremacy, waged civil war, and for generations bemoaned the Lost Cause.

The metalanguage of race also transcended the voices of class and ethnic conflict among Northern whites in the great upheavals of labour during the late nineteenth and early twentieth centuries. Amid their opposition, capital and labour agreed sufficiently to exclude blacks from union membership and from more than a marginal place within the emerging industrial work-force.[22] Job ceilings and hiring practices limited the overwhelming majority of black men and women to dead-end, low-paying employment—employment whites disdained or were in the process of abandoning.[23] The actual class positions of blacks did not matter, nor did the acknowledgment of differential statuses (such as by income, type of employment, morals and manners, education, or colour) by blacks themselves. An entire system of cultural preconceptions disregarded these complexities and tensions by grouping all blacks into a normative well of inferiority and subserviency.[24]

The interplay of the race–class conflation with gender evoked very different social perceptions of black and white women's work roles. This is exhibited by the concern about 'female loaferism', which arose in the years immediately following Emancipation. Jacqueline Jones vividly exposes the ridicule and hostility meted out to black families who attempted to remove their wives and mothers from the work-force to attend to their own households. In contrast to the domestic ideal for white women of all classes, the larger society deemed it 'unnatural', in fact an 'evil', for black married women 'to play the lady' while their husbands supported them. In the immediate post-war South, the role of menial worker outside their homes was demanded of black women, even at the cost of physical coercion.[25]

Dolores Janiewski calls attention to the racialized meaning of class in her study of women's employment in a North Carolina tobacco factory during the twentieth century. She shows that race fractured the division of labour by gender. Southern etiquette demanded protection of white women's 'racial honour' and required that they work under conditions described as 'suitable for ladies' in contradistinction to the drudgery and dirty working conditions considered acceptable for black women. Janiewski notes that at least one employer felt no inhibition against publicly admitting his 'brute treatment' of black female employees.[26]

The most effective tool in the discursive welding of race and class proved to be segregation in its myriad institutional and customary forms. Jim Crow railroad cars, for instance, became strategic sites of contestation over the conflated meaning of class and race: blacks who could afford 'first-class' accommodations vehemently protested the racial basis for being denied access to them. This is dramatically evident in the case of Arthur Mitchell, Democratic congressman to the US House of Representatives from Illinois during the 1930s. Mitchell was evicted from first-class railroad accommodations while travelling through Hot Springs, Arkansas. Despite his protests, he was forced to join his social 'inferiors' in a Jim Crow coach with no flush toilet, washbasin, running water, or soap. The transcript of the trial reveals the following testimony:

When I offered my ticket, the train conductor took my ticket and tore off a piece of it, but told me at that time that I couldn't ride in that car. We had quite a little controversy about it, and when he said I couldn't ride there I thought it might do some good for me to tell him who I was. I said . . .: 'I am Mr Mitchell, serving in the Congress of the United States.' He said it didn't make a damn bit of difference who I was, that as long as I was a nigger I couldn't ride in that car.[27]

Neither the imprimatur of the US House of Representatives nor the ability to purchase a first-class ticket afforded Mitchell the more privileged accommodations. The collective image of race represented Mitchell, the individual, just as he singularly represented the entire black race. Despite the complicating factor of his representing the federal government itself, Mitchell, like his socially constructed race, was unambiguously assigned to the second-class car, ergo lower-class space.

A long tradition of black protest focused on such treatment of women. During the late nineteenth century, segregated railroad trains were emblematic of racial configurations of both class and gender; the first-class railroad car also was called the 'ladies car'. Indeed, segregation's meaning for gender was exemplified in the trope of 'lady'. Ladies were not merely women; they represented a class, a differentiated status within the generic category of 'women'. Nor did society confer such status on all white women. White prostitutes, along with many working-class white women, fell outside its rubric. But no black woman, regardless of income, education, refinement, or character, enjoyed the status of lady. John R. Lynch, black congressman from Mississippi during Reconstruction, denounced the practice of forcing black women of means and refinement out of first-class accommodations and into smoking cars. He characterized the latter accommodations as 'filthy . . . with drunkards, gamblers, and criminals'. Arguing in support of the Civil Rights Bill of 1875, Lynch used the trope of 'lady' in calling attention to race's inscription upon class distinctions:

Under our present system of race distinctions a *white woman* of a questionable social standing, yea, I may say, of an admitted immoral character, can go to any public place or upon any public conveyance and be the recipient of the same treatment, the same courtesy, and the same respect that it usually accorded to the most refined and virtuous; but let an intelligent, modest, refined *colored lady* present herself and ask that the same privileges be accorded to her that have just been accorded to her social inferior of the white race, and in nine cases out of ten, except in certain portions of the country, she will not only be refused, but insulted for making the request. (Emphasis added)[28]

Early court cases involving discrimination in public transportation reveal that railroad companies seldom if ever looked upon black women as 'ladies'. The case of Catherine Brown, a black woman, was the first racial public transportation case to come before the US Supreme Court. In February 1868, Brown was denied passage in the 'ladies car' on a train travelling from Alexandria, Virginia, to Washington, DC. Brown disregarded the demand that she sit in the 'colored car' instead. Her persistence in entering the ladies car was met with violence and verbal insults.[29] The resultant court case, decided in her favour in 1873, indicated not an end to such practices but merely the federal government's shortlived support of black civil rights during the era of radical Reconstruction. The outcome of Brown's case proved to be an exception to those that would follow.

Within a decade, Ida B. Wells sued the Chesapeake, Ohio, and Southwestern Railroad for physically ejecting her out of the 'ladies' car. When the conductor grabbed her arm, she bit him and held firmly to her seat. It took two men finally to dislodge her. They dragged her into the smoking car and (as she recalled in her autobiography) 'the white ladies and gentlemen in the car even stood on the seats so that they could get a good view and continued applauding the conductor for his brave stand'. Although her lawsuit was successful at the lower court level, the state Supreme Court of Tennessee reversed the earlier decision, sustaining both the discrimination and the bodily harm against her.[30] The racist decision, like others of the courts, led to *Plessy v. Ferguson* in 1896 and the euphemistic doctrine of 'separate but equal'.

RACIAL CONSTRUCTIONS OF SEXUALITY

The exclusion of black women from the dominant society's definition of 'lady' said as much about sexuality as it did about class. The metalanguage of race signifies, too, the imbrication of race within the representation of sexuality. Historians of women and of science, largely influenced by Michel Foucault, now attest to the variable quality of changing conceptions of sexuality over time—conceptions informed as much by race and class as by gender.[31] Sexuality has come to be defined not in terms of biological essentials or as a universal truth detached and transcendent from other aspects of human life and society. Rather, it is an evolving conception applied to the body but given meaning and identity by economic, cultural, and historical context.[32]

In the centuries between the Renaissance and the Victorian era, Western culture, constructed and represented changing and conflicting images of woman's sexuality, which shifted diametrically from images of lasciviousness to moral purity. Yet Western conceptions of black women's sexuality resisted change during this same time.[33] Winthrop Jordan's now classic study of racial attitudes toward blacks between the sixteenth and nineteenth centuries argues that black women's bodies epitomized centuries-long European perceptions of Africans as primitive, animal-like, and savage. In America, no less distinguished and learned a figure than Thomas Jefferson conjectured that black women mated with orangutans.[34] While such thinking rationalized slavery and the sexual exploitation of slave women by white masters, it also perpetuated an enormous division between black people and white people on the 'scale of humanity': carnality as opposed to intellect and/or spirit; savagery as opposed to civilization; deviance as opposed to normality; promiscuity as opposed to purity; passion as opposed to passionlessness. The black woman came to symbolize, according to Sander Gilman, an 'icon for black sexuality in general'.[35] This discursive gap between the races was if anything greater between white and black women than between white and black men.

Violence figured pre-eminently in racialized constructions of sexuality. From the days of slavery, the social construction and representation of black sexuality reinforced violence, rhetorical and real, against black women and men.[36] That the rape of black women could continue to go on with impunity long after slavery's demise underscores the pervasive belief in black female promiscuity. This belief found expression in the statement of one Southern white woman in 1904: 'I cannot imagine such a creation as a virtuous black woman.'[37]

The lynching of black men, with its often attendant castration, reeked of sexualized representations of race.[38] The work of black feminists of the late nineteenth century makes clear that lynching, while often rationalized by whites as a punishment for the rape of white women, more often was perpetrated to maintain racial etiquette and the socio-economic and political hegemony of whites. Ida Wells-Barnett, Anna J. Cooper, Mary Church Terrell, and Pauline Hopkins exposed and contrasted the spectre of the white woman's rape in the case of lynching and the sanctioned rape of black women by white men. Hazel Carby, in discussing these black feminist writers, established their understanding of the intersection of strategies of power with lynching and rape:

Their legacy to us is theories that expose the colonization of the black female body by white male power and the destruction of black males who attempted to exercise any oppositional patriarchal control. When accused of threatening the white female body, the repository of heirs to property and power, the black male, and his economic, political, and social advancement, is lynched out of existence. Cooper, Wells, and Hopkins assert the necessity of seeing the relation between histories: the rape of black women in the nineties is directly linked to the rape of the female slave. Their analyses are dynamic and not limited to a parochial understanding of 'women's issues'; they have firmly established the dialectical relation between economic/political power and economic/sexual power in the battle for control of women's bodies.[39]

Through a variety of mediums—theatre, art, the press, and literature—discourses of racism developed and reified stereotypes of sexuality. Such representations grew out of and facilitated the larger subjugation and control of the black population. The categorization of class and racial groups according to culturally constituted sexual identities facilitated blacks' subordination within a stratified society and rendered them powerless against the intrusion of the state into their innermost private lives. This intrusion went hand in hand with the role of the state in legislating and enforcing racial segregation, disfranchisement, and economic discrimination.

James Jones's *Bad Blood: The Tuskegee Syphilis Experiment* provides us with a profoundly disturbing example of such intrusion into blacks' private lives. Jones recounts how a federal agency, the Public Health Service, embarked in 1932 upon decades of tests on black men with syphilis, denying them access to its cure in order to assess the disease's debilitating effects on the body.[40] The federal agency felt at liberty to make the study because of its unquestioning acceptance of stereotypes that conflated race, gender, and class. By defining this health problem in racial terms, 'objective scientific researchers' could be absolved of all responsibility. Some even posited that blacks had 'earned their illness as just recompense for wicked life-styles'.[41]

The Public Health Service's willingness to prolong syphilis despite the discovery of penicillin discloses not only the federal government's lack of concern for the health of the men in its study, but its even lesser concern for black women in relationships with these men. Black women failed to receive so much as a pretence of protection, so widely accepted was the belief that the spread of the disease was inevitable because black women were promiscuous by nature. This emphasis on black immorality precluded any sensitivity to congenital syphilis; thus innocent black babies born with the disease went unnoticed and equally unprotected. Certainly the officials of the Public Health Service realized that blacks lived amid staggering poverty, amid a socio-economic environment conducive to disease. Yet these public servants encoded hegemonic articulations of race into the language of medicine and scientific theory. Their perceptions of sexually transmitted disease, like those of the larger society, were affected by race.[42] Jones concludes:

The effect of these views was to isolate blacks even further within American society—to remove them from the world of health and to lock them within a prison of sickness. Whether by accident or design, physicians had come dangerously close to depicting the syphilitic black as the representative black. As sickness replaced health as the normal condition of the race, something was lost from the sense of horror and urgency with which physicians had defined disease. The result was a powerful rationale for inactivity in the face of disease, which by their own estimates, physicians believed to be epidemic.[43]

In response to assaults upon black sexuality, according to Darlene Clark Hine, there arose among black women a politics of silence, a 'culture of dissemblance'. In order to 'protect the sanctity of inner aspects of their lives', black women, especially those of the middle class, reconstructed and represented their sexuality through its absence—through silence, secrecy, and invisibility. In so doing, they sought to combat the pervasive negative images and stereotypes. Black clubwomen's adherence to Victorian ideology, as well as their self-representation as 'super moral', according to Hine, was perceived as crucial not only to the protection and upward mobility of black women but also the attainment of respect, justice, and opportunity for all black Americans.[44]

RACE AS A DOUBLE-VOICED DISCOURSE

As this culture of dissemblance illustrates, black people endeavoured not only to silence and conceal but also to dismantle and deconstruct the dominant society's deployment of race. Racial meanings were never internalized by blacks and whites in an identical way. The language of race has historically been what Bakhtin calls a double-voiced discourse—serving the voice of black oppression and the voice of black liberation. Bakhtin observes: 'The word in language is half someone else's. It becomes 'one's own' only when the speaker populates it with his [or her] own intention, his [or her] own accent, when he [or she] appropriates the word, adapting it to his [or her] own semantic and expressive intention.'[45] Blacks took 'race' and empowered its language with their own meaning and intent, just as the slaves and freedpeople had appropriated white surnames, even those of their masters, and made them their own.[46]

For African-Americans, race signified a cultural identity that defined and connected them as a people, even as a nation. To be called a 'race leader', 'race man', or 'race woman' by the black community was not a sign of insult or disapproval, nor did such titles refer to any and every black person. Quite to the contrary, they were conferred in Carter G. Woodson, W. E. B. Du Bois, Ida Wells-Barnett, Mary McLeod Bethune, and the other men and women who devoted their lives to the advancement of their people. When the National Association of Colored Women referred to its activities as 'race work', it expressed both allegiance and commitment to the concerns of black people. Through a range of shifting, even contradictory meanings and accentuations expressed at the level of individual and group consciousness, blacks fashioned race into a cultural identity that resisted white hegemonic discourses.

The 'two-ness' of being both American and Negro, which Du Bois so eloquently captured in 1903, resonates across time. If blacks as individuals referred to a divided subjectivity—'two warring ideals in one dark body'—they also spoke of a collective identity in the colonial terms of a 'nation within a nation'.[47] The many and varied voices of black nationalism have resounded again and again from the earliest days of the American republic. Black nationalism found advocates in Paul Cuffee, John Ruswurm, and Martin Delany in the nineteenth century, and Marcus Garvey, Malcolm X, and Stokely Carmichael in the twentieth.[48] We know far too little about women's perceptions of nationalism, but Pauline Hopkins's serialized novel *Of One Blood* (1903) counterposes black and Anglo-Saxon races: 'The dawn of the Twentieth century finds the Black race fighting for existence in every quarter of the globe. From over the sea Africa stretches her hands to the American Negro and cries aloud for sympathy in her hour of trial. . . . In America, caste prejudice has received fresh impetus as the "Southern brother" of the Anglo-Saxon family has arisen from the ashes of secession, and like the prodigal of old, has been gorged with fatted calf and "fixin's".'[49]

Likewise Hannah Nelson, an elementary school graduate employed most of her life in domestic service, told anthropologist John Langston Gwaltney in the 1970s: 'We are a nation. The best of us have said it and everybody feels it. I know that will probably bother your white readers, but it is none the less true that black people think of themselves as an entity.'[50] Thus, when historian Barbara Fields observes that 'Afro-Americans invented themselves, not as a race, but as a nation,' she alludes to race as a double-voiced discourse.[51] For blacks, race signified cultural identity and heritage, not biological inferiority. However, Fields's discussion understates the power of race to mean nation—specifically, race as the sign of perceived kinship ties between blacks in Africa and throughout the diaspora. In the crucible of the Middle Passage and American slavery, the multiple linguistic, tribal, and ethnic divisions among Africans came to be forged into a single, common ancestry. While not adhering to 'scientific' explanations of superior and inferior races, African-Americans inscribed the black nation with racially laden meanings of blood ties that bespoke a lineage and culture more imagined than real.

Such imaginings were not unique to African-Americans.[52] As nation states emerged in Europe during the fifteenth and sixteenth centuries, the concept of 'race' came increasingly to articulate a nationalist ideology. Racial representations of nation included, on the one hand, 'cosmopolitan' views that characterized each national grouping as contributing its own 'special gift' to the complementarity of humankind, and, on the other hand, views of hierarchical difference that justified the existence of nation states and the historical dominance of certain groupings over others. Hence, Thomas Arnold could speak of the Anglo-Saxon's lineage in an 1841 lecture at Oxford: 'Our English race is the German race; for though our Norman forefathers had learnt to speak a stranger's language, yet in blood, as we know, they were the Saxons' brethren: both alike belonged to the Teutonic or German stock.'[53] Such cultural conceptions surely informed nineteenth-century African-American perceptions of the black nation as a site of group uniqueness.

Throughout the nineteenth century, blacks and whites alike subscribed to what George Fredrickson terms 'romantic racialism'.[54] Blacks constructed and valorized a self-representation essentially antithetical to that of whites. In his article 'The Conservation of Races', published in 1897, Harvard-trained W. E. B. Du Bois disclosed his admiration for what he believed to be the 'spiritual, psychical' uniqueness of his people—their 'special gift' to humanity.[55] Twentieth-century essentialist concepts such as 'negritude', 'soul', and most recently 'Afrocentricity' express in new and altered form the continued desire to capture transcendent threads of racial 'oneness'. Frantz Fanon described the quest for cultural identity and self-recovery as 'the whole body of efforts made by a people in the sphere of thought to describe, justify and praise action through which that people has created itself and keeps itself in existence'.[56] These efforts seek to negate white stereotypes of blacks and in their place insert a black worldview or standpoint. Of critical importance here are the dialogic racial representations effected by blacks themselves against negative representations—or more precisely, blacks' appropriation of the productive power of language for the purpose of resistance.[57]

Such a discursive rendering of race counters images of physical and psychical rupture with images of wholeness. Yet once again, race serves as myth and as a global sign, for it superimposes a 'natural' unity over a plethora of historical, socio-economic, and ideological differences among blacks themselves. This is not to understate the critical liberating intention implicit in blacks' own usage of the term 'the race', when referring to themselves as a group. But the characterization obscures rather than mirrors the reality of black heterogeneity. In fact, essentialist or other racialized conceptions of national culture hardly reflect paradigmatic consistency. Black nationalism itself has been a heteroglot conception, categorized variously as revolutionary, bourgeois reformist, cultural, religious, economic, or emigrationist.[58] Race as the sign of cultural identity has been neither a coherent nor static concept among African-Americans. Its perpetuation and resilience have reflected shifting, often monolithic and essentialist assumptions on the part of thinkers attempting to identify and define a black peoplehood or nation.

Acceptance of a nation-based, racialized perspective even appears in the work of black women scholars, who seek to ground a black feminist standpoint in the concrete experience of race and gender oppression. Notwithstanding the critical importance of this work in contesting racism and sexism in the academy and larger society, its focus does not permit sufficient exploration of ideological spaces of difference among black women themselves. For example, sociologist Patricia Hill Collins identifies an ethic of caring and an ethic of personal accountability at the root of Afrocentric values and particularly of Afrocentric feminist epistemology, yet she does not investigate how such values and epistemology are affected by differing class positions.[59] In short, she posits but does not account for the *singularity* of an Afro-American women's standpoint amid diverse and conflicting positions of enunciation.

The rallying notion of 'racial uplift' among black Americans during the late nineteenth and early twentieth centuries illustrates the problematic aspects of identifying a standpoint that encompasses all black women. Racial uplift was celebrated in the motto of the National Association of Colored Women—'lifting as we climb'. The motto itself expressed a paradox: belief in black womanhood's common cause and recognition of differential values and socio-economic positions. Racial uplift, while invoking a discursive ground on which to explode negative stereotypes of black women, remained locked within hegemonic articulations of gender, class, and sexuality. Black women teachers, missionaries, and club members zealously promoted values of temperance, sexual repression, and polite manners among the poor.

'Race work' or 'racial uplift' equated normality with conformity to white middle-class models of gender roles and sexuality. Given the extremely limited educational and income opportunities during the late nineteenth–early twentieth centuries, many black women linked mainstream domestic duties, codes of dress, sexual conduct, and public etiquette with both individual success and group progress.[60] Black leaders argued that 'proper' and 'respectable' behaviour proved blacks worthy of equal civil and political rights. Conversely, nonconformity was equated with deviance and pathology and was often cited as a cause of racial inequality and injustice. S. W. Layten, founder of the National League for the Protection of Colored Women and leader of one million black Baptist women, typified this attitude in her statement of 1904: 'Unfortunately the minority or bad Negroes have given the race a questionable reputation; these degenerates are responsible for every discrimination we suffer.'[61]

On a host of levels, racial uplift stood at odds with the daily practices and aesthetic tastes of many poor, uneducated, and 'unassimilated' black men and women dispersed throughout the rural South or newly huddled in urban centres.[62] The politics of 'respectability' disavowed, in often repressive ways, much of the expressive culture of the 'folk', for example, sexual behaviour, dress style, leisure activity, music, speech patterns, and religious worship patterns. Similar class and sexual tensions between the discourse of the intelligentsia (the 'New Negro') and that of the 'people' (the 'folk' turned proletariat in the northern urban context) appear in Hazel Carby's discussion of black women novelists of the Harlem Renaissance during the 1920s.[63]

Today, the metalanguage of race continues to bequeath its problematic legacy. While its discursive construction of reality into two opposing camps—blacks versus whites or Afrocentric versus Eurocentric standpoints—provides the basis for resistance against external forces of black subordination, it tends to forestall resolution of problems of gender, class, and sexual orientation internal to black communities. The resolution of such differences is also requisite to the liberation and well-being of 'the race'. Worse yet, problems deemed too far astray of respectability are subsumed within a culture of dissemblance. The AIDS crisis serves as a case in point, with AIDS usually contextualized within a Manichean opposition of good versus evil that translates into heterosexuality versus homosexuality or wholesome living versus intravenous drug use. At a time when AIDS is a leading killer of black women and their children in impoverished inner-city neighbourhoods, educational and support strategies lag far behind those of white gay communities.[64] Black women's groups and community organizations fail to tackle the problem with the priority it merits. They shy away from public discussion in large measure because of the historic association of disease and racial/sexual stereotyping.

CONCLUSION

By analysing white America's deployment of race in the construction of power relations, perhaps we can better understand why black women historians have largely refrained from an analysis of gender along the lines of the male/female dichotomy so prevalent among white feminists. Indeed, some black women scholars adopt the term *womanist* instead of *feminist* in rejection of gender-based dichotomies that lead to a false homogenizing of women. By so doing they follow in the spirit of black scholar and educator Anna J. Cooper, who in *A Voice from the South* (1892) inextricably linked her racial identity to the 'quiet, undisputed dignity' of her womanhood.[65] At the threshold of the twenty-first century, black women scholars continue to emphasize the inseparable unity of race and gender in their thought. They dismiss efforts to bifurcate the identity of black women (and indeed of all women) into discrete categories—as if culture, consciousness, and lived experience could at times constitute 'woman' isolated from the contexts of race, class, and sexuality that give form and content to the particular women we are.[66]

On the other hand, we should challenge both the overdeterminancy of race *vis-à-vis* social relations among blacks themselves and conceptions of the black community as harmonious and monolithic. The historic reality of racial conflict in America has tended to devalue and discourage attention to gender conflict within black communities and to tensions of class or sexuality among black women. The totalizing tendency of race precludes recognition and acknowledgment of intragroup social relations as relations of power. With its implicit understandings, shared cultural codes, and inchoate sense of a common heritage and destiny, the metalanguage of race resounds over and above a plethora of conflicting voices. but it cannot silence them.

Black women of different economic and regional backgrounds, of different skin tones and sexual orientations, have found themselves in conflict over interpretation of symbols and norms, public behaviour, coping strategies, and a variety of micropolitical acts of resistance to structures of domination.[67] Although racialized cultural identity has clearly served blacks in the struggle against discrimination, it has not sufficiently addressed the empirical reality of gender conflict within the black community or class differences among black women themselves. Historian E. Frances White makes this point brilliantly when she asserts that 'the site of counter-discourse is itself contested terrain'.[68] By fully recognizing race as an unstable, shifting, and strategic reconstruction, feminist scholars must take up new challenges to inform and confound many of the assumptions currently underlying Afro-American history and women's history. We must problematize much more of what we take for granted. We must bring to light and to coherence the one and the many that we always were in history and still actually are today.

Notes

1. See, e.g. Teresa de Lauretis, *Alice Doesn't: Feminism, Semiotics, Cinema* (Bloomington: Indiana University Press, 1984), and Teresa de Lauretis (ed.), *Feminist Studies, Feminist Criticism* (Bloomington: Indiana University Press, 1986); Toril Moi, *Sexual/Textual Politics* (New York: Routledge, 1985); Joan W. Scott, *Gender and the Politics of History* (New York: Columbia University Press, 1988); Judith Butler, *Gender Trouble: Feminism and the Subversion of Identity* (New York: Routledge, 1990).

2. By the early 1980s women of colour from various disciplines had challenged the notion of a homogeneous womanhood. A few include: Sharon Harley and Rosalyn Terborg-Penn (eds.), *The Afro-American Woman: Struggles and Images* (Port Washington, NY: Kennikat, 1978); Gloria T. Hull, Patricia Bell Scott, and Barbara Smith (eds.), *But Some of Us Are Brave* (Old Westbury, NY: Feminist Press, 1982); Barbara Smith (ed.), *Home Girls: A Black Feminist Anthology* (New York: Kitchen Table: Women of Color Press, 1983); Cherríe Moraga and Gloria Anzaldua (eds.), *This Bridge Called My Back: Writings by Radical Women of Color* (New York: Kitchen Table: Women of Color Press, 1983); Bonnie Thornton Dill, 'Race, Class, and Gender: Prospects for an All-Inclusive Sisterhood', *Feminist Studies*, 9 (Spring 1983), 131–50.

3. Charles Drew, in developing a method of blood preservation and organizing blood banks, contributed to the explosion of the myth that blacks were physiologically different from whites. See Charles E. Wynes, *Charles Richard Drew: The Man and the Myth* (Urbana: University of Illinois Press, 1988), 65–71; and C. R. Drew and J. Scudder, 'Studies in Blood Preservation: Fate of Cellular Elements and Prothrombin in Citrated Blood', *Journal of Laboratory and Clinical Medicine*, 26 (June 1941): 1473–8. Also see W. E. B. Du Bois, 'Races', *Crisis* (Aug. 1911), 157–8, and *Dusk of Dawn: An Essay toward an Autobiography of a Race Concept* (New York: Harcourt Brace, 1940), 116–17, 137; Oliver C. Cox, *Caste, Class and Race* (1948; repr., New York: Monthly Review Press, 1970), 317–20.

4. Michel Foucault, *History of Sexuality*, i. *An Introduction*, trans. Robert Hurley (New York: Vintage, 1980), 127, 146. Teresa de Lauretis criticizes Foucault for presenting a male-centred class analysis that disregards gender (see *Technologies of Gender* (Bloomington: Indiana University Press, 1987), 3–30). In both cases 'technology' is used to signify the elaboration and implementation of discourses (classificatory and evaluative) in order to maintain the survival and hegemony of one group over another. These discourses are implemented through pedagogy, medicine, mass media, etc.

5. For discussion of race and signification, see Robert Miles, *Racism* (New York: Routledge, 1989), 69–98; also, Michael Omi and Howard Winant, *Racial Formation in the United States from the 1960s to the 1980s* (New York: Routledge & Kegan Paul, 1986), 68.

6. *Jacobellis* v. *State of Ohio*, 378 US 184, 197 (1964).

7. Although Fields does not use the term 'trope', her discussion of race parallels that of Gates. Henry Louis Gates, Jr., ed., *'Race', Writing, and Difference* (Chicago: University of Chicago Press, 1986), esp. articles by Gates, Jr., 'Introduction: Writing "Race" and the Difference It Makes', 1–20; Anthony Appiah, 'The Uncompleted Argument: Du Bois and the Illusion of Race', 21–37; and Tzvetan Todorov, ' "Race", Writing, and Culture', 370–80. See also Barbara J. Fields, 'Ideology and Race in American History', in J. Morgan Kousser and James M. McPherson (eds.), *Region, Race, and Reconstruction: Essays in Honor of C. Vann Woodward* (New York: Oxford University Press, 1982), 143–7.

8. Michel Foucault describes the strategic function of the apparatus of power as a system of relations between diverse elements (e.g. discourses, laws, architecture, moral values, institutions) that are supported by types of knowledge: 'I understand by the "term" apparatus a sort of . . . formation which has its major function at a given historical moment that of responding to an *urgent need*. . . . This may have been, for example, the assimilation of a floating population found to be burdensome for an essentially mercantilist economy' (Colin Gordon (ed.), *Power/Knowledge: Selected Interviews and Other Writings, 1972–1977* (New York: Pantheon, 1980), 194–5).

9. Louis Althusser, 'Ideology and Ideological State Apparatuses (Notes toward an Investigation')', in his *Lenin and Philosophy, and Other Essays*, trans. Ben Brewster (New York: Monthly Review Press, 1972), 165.

10. Roland Barthes, *Mythologies*, trans. Annette Lavers (New York: Hill & Wang, 1972), 118, 120.

11. Ibid. 114–15.

12. Elizabeth V. Spelman, *Inessential Woman: Problems of Exclusion in Feminist Thought* (Boston: Beacon, 1988), 13, 80–113.

13. M. M. Bakhtin, *The Dialogic Imagination: Four Essays*, ed. Michael Holquist, trans. Caryl Emerson and Michael Holquist (Austin: University of Texas Press, 1981), 352.

14. Bakhtin argues: 'Language is not an abstract system of normative forms but rather a concrete heteroglot conception of the world'. For my purposes of discussion, 'race', therefore, would convey multiple, even conflicting meanings (heteroglossia) when expressed by different groups—the multiplicity of meanings and intentions not simply rendered between blacks and whites, but within each of these two groups. See Bakhtin on 'heteroglossia' (293, 352).

15. Fields, 'Race and Ideology in American History', 148–9.

16. Eugene D. Genovese, *Roll Jordan Roll: The World the Slaves Made* (New York: Pantheon, 1974), 3–7, 28.

17. Sojourner Truth's speech appears in Bert James Loewenberg and Ruth Bogin, *Black Women in Nineteenth Century American Life* (University Park: Pennsylvania State University Press, 1976), 235. For works on slave women, see Deborah Gray White, *Ar'n't I a Woman: Female Slaves in the Plantation South* (New York: Norton, 1985); Elizabeth Fox-Genovese, *Within the Plantation Household: Black and White Women of the Old South* (Chapel Hill: University of North Carolina Press, 1988), esp. chs. 3 and 6.

18. Fox-Genovese, 326.
19. A. Leon Higginbotham, Jr., notes: 'One of the ironies is that the master's estate was denied a profit from Celia's rape. Despite the court's "mercy" in delaying execution until the birth of the child, the record reflects that a Doctor Carter delivered Celia's child, who was born dead' ('Race, Sex, Education and Missouri Jurisprudence: Shelley v. Kraemer in a Historical Perspective', *Washington University Law Quarterly* 67 [1989], 684–5).
20. Gates, Jr., 'Introduction: Writing "Race" and the Difference It Makes' (n. 7 above), 5.
21. Fields, 'Ideology and Race in American History' (n. 7 above), 156.
22. Abram Harris and Sterling Spero, *The Black Worker: A Study of the Negro in the Labor Movement* (1931; repr., New York: Atheneum, 1968), 158–61, 167–81; Joe William Trotter, *Black Milwaukee: The Making of an Industrial Proletariat, 1915–45* (Urbana: University of Illinois Press, 1985), 13–14, 18, 39–79; Dolores Janiewski, *Sisterhood Denied: Race, Gender, and Class in a New South Community* (Philadelphia: Temple University Press, 1985), 152–78; Jacqueline Jones, *Labor of Love: Labor of Sorrow* (New York: Basic, 1985), 148, 168, 177–9.
23. See Sharon Harley, 'For the Good of Family and Race', *Signs: Journal of Women in Culture and Society*, 15/2 (Winter 1990), 340–1.
24. Patricia Hill Collins argues persuasively for the continued role of race in explaining social-class position in her analysis of studies of contemporary black low-income, female-headed families. In her critique of the Moynihan report and the televised Bill Moyers documentary on the 'vanishing black family', Collins argues that social class is conceptualized in both these studies as 'an outcome variable' of race and gender rather than the product of such structural factors as industrial flight, mechanization, inadequate schools, etc. ('A Comparison of Two Works on Black Family Life', *Signs* 14/4 (Summer 1989), 876–7, 882–4).
25. For discussion of 'female loaferism', see Jacqueline Jones, 45, 58–60.
26. Dolores Janiewski, 'Seeking, "a New Day and a New Way": Black Women and Unions in the Southern Tobacco Industry', in Carol Groneman and Mary Beth Norton (eds.), *'To Toil the Livelong Day': America's Women at Work, 1780–1980* (Ithaca, NY: Cornell University Press, 1987), 163.
27. *Mitchell v. United States*, 313 US 80 (1941), app.; also see Catherine A. Barens, *Journey from Jim Crow: The Desegregation of Southern Transit* (New York: Columbia University Press, 1983), 1–2.
28. See John R. Lynch's speech on the Civil Rights Bill of 1875 in US Congress, *Congressional Record* (3 Feb. 1875), 944–5.
29. *Railroad Co. v. Brown*, 84 US 445 (Wall) 445 (1873).
30. See Ida B. Wells-Barnett, *Crusade for Justice: The Autobiography of Ida B. Wells*, ed. Alfreda M. Duster (Chicago: University of Chicago Press, 1970), 18–20; for full discussion of this case and those of other black women on buses and street-cars, see Willie Mae Coleman, 'Black Women and Segregated Public Transportation: Ninety Years of Resistance', *Truth: Newsletter of the Association of Black Women Historians* (1986), repr. in Darlene Clark Hine (ed.), *Black Women in United States History* (Brooklyn: Carlson, 1990), 5:296–8.
31. For work by historians on sexuality's relation to class and race, see the essays in Kathy Peiss and Christina Simmons, with Robert Padgug (eds.), *Passion and Power: Sexuality in History* (Philadelphia: Temple University Press, 1989).

32. Foucault, *History of Sexuality*, i. 14, 140, 143, 145–6, and *Power/Knowledge* (n. 8 above), 210–11.

33. Nancy Cott calls attention to the role of evangelical Protestantism and, later, science in contributing to the image of 'passionlessness' for American northern women ('Passionlessness: An Interpretation of Victorian Sexual Ideology, 1790–1850', *Signs*, 4/2 (Winter 1978): 219–36); for changing Western representations, see Thomas Laqueur, *Making Sex: Body and Gender from the Greeks to Freud* (Cambridge, Mass.: Harvard University Press, 1990).

34. See discussion of Jefferson and larger discussion of Western views toward blacks in Winthrop D. Jordan, *White over Black: American Attitudes toward the Negro, 1550–1812* (New York: Norton, 1977), 24–40, 151, 154–9, 458–9.

35. See Sander L. Gilman, 'Black Bodies, White Bodies: Toward an Iconography of Female Sexuality in Late Nineteenth-Century Art, Medicine, and Literature', in Gates (ed.) (n 7 above), 223–40.

36. Jacquelyn Dowd Hall, *Revolt against Chivalry: Jessie Daniel Ames and the Woman's Campaign against Lynching* (New York: Columbia University Press, 1979), 129–57, 220; Ida Wells-Barnett, *On Lynching*, repr. (New York: Arno Press, 1969); Joel Williamson, *A Rage for Order* (New York: Oxford University Press, 1986), 117–51; Howard Smead, *Blood Justice: The Lynching of Mack Charles Parker* (New York: Oxford University Press, 1986).

37. 'Experiences of the Race Problem: By a Southern White Woman', *Independent*, 56 (17 Mar. 1904), as quoted in Annie Firor Scott, 'Most Invisible of All: Black Women's Voluntary Associations', *Journal of Southern History*, 56 (Feb. 1990), 10. Neil R. McMillen observes for the early twentieth century that courts did not usually convict white men for the rape of black women, 'because whites generally agreed that no black female above the age of puberty was chaste' (*Dark Journey: Black Mississippians in the Age of Jim Crow* (Urbana: University of Illinois Press, 1989), 205–6).

38. A number of writers have dealt with the issue of castration. For historical studies of the early slave era, see Jordan, 154–8, 463, 473; also discussing castration statutes as part of the slave codes in colonial Virginia, South Carolina, and Pennsylvania is A. Leon Higginbotham, Jr., *In the Matter of Color: Race and the American Legal Process* (New York: Oxford University Press, 1978), 58, 168, 177, 282, 413, n. 107. For discussion of castration during the twentieth century, see Richard Wright, 'The Ethics of Living Jim Crow: An Autobiographical Sketch', in his *Uncle Tom's Children* (1938; repr., New York: Harper & Row, 1965); and Trudier Harris, *Exorcising Blackness: Historical and Literary Lynching and Burning Rituals* (Bloomington: Indiana University Press, 1984), 29–68.

39. Bettina Aptheker, *Woman's Legacy: Essays on Race, Sex and Class in American History* (Amherst: University of Massachusetts Press, 1982), 53–77; Hazel V. Carby, ' "On the Threshold of Woman's Era': Lynching, Empire, and Sexuality in Black Feminist Theory', in Gates (ed.), 314–15.

40. James H. Jones, *Bad Blood: The Tuskegee Syphilis Experiment* (New York: Free Press, 1981), 11–29.

41. Ibid. 22. Elizabeth Fee argues that in the 1920s and 1930s, before a cure was found for syphilis, physicians did not speak in the dispassionate tone of term theory but, rather, reinforced the image of syphilis as a 'black problem' (see her study of Baltimore, 'Venereal Disease: The Wages of Sin?' in Peiss and Simmons (eds.) (n. 31 above), 182–4).

42. For a study of the social construction of venereal disease, from the late nineteenth century through the AIDS crisis of our own time, see Allan M. Brandt, *No Magic Bullet: A Social History of Venereal Disease in the United States since 1880* (New York: Oxford University Press, 1987); also see Doris Y. Wilkinson and Gary King, 'Conceptual and Methodological Issues in the Use of Race as a Variable: Policy Implications', *Milbank Quarterly*, 65 (1987), 68.

43. James H. Jones, 25, 28.

44. Darlene Clark Hine, 'Rape and the Inner Lives of Black Women in the Middle West: Preliminary Thoughts on the Culture of Dissemblance', *Signs*, 14/4 (Summer 1989), 915.

45. Bakhtin (n. 13 above), 293, 324.

46. On slave surnames, see Herbert G. Gutman, *The Black Family in Slavery and Freedom, 1750–1925* (New York: Pantheon, 1976), 230–56; also George P. Cunningham, ' "Called into Existence": Desire, Gender, and Voice in Frederick Douglass's Narrative of 1845', *Differences*, 1/3 (1989), 112–13, 117, 129–31.

47. Martin Robison Delany wrote in the 1850s of blacks in the United States: 'We are a nation within a nation;—as the Poles in Russia, the Hungarians in Austria, the Welsh, Irish, and Scotch in the British Dominions' (see his *The Condition, Elevation, Emigration and Destiny of the Colored People of the United States*, repr. (New York: Arno, 1969), 209; also W. E. Burghardt Du Bois, *The Souls of Black Folks* (New York: Washington Square Press, 1970), 3).

48. See, devoted to the subject of nationalism, John H. Bracey, Jr., August Meier, and Elliott Rudwick (eds.), *Black Nationalism in America* (New York: Bobbs-Merrill, 1970); Sterling Stuckey, *Slave Culture: Nationalist Theory and the Foundations of Black America* (New York: Oxford University Press, 1987), and *The Ideological Origins of Black Nationalism* (Boston: Beacon, 1972); Wilson Jeremiah Moses, *The Golden Age of Black Nationalism, 1850–1925* (Hamden, Conn.: Archon, 1978).

49. Pauline Hopkins, 'Heroes and Heroines in Black', *Colored American Magazine*, 6 (Jan. 1903), 211. The original publication of *Of One Blood* was serialized in issues of the *Colored American Magazine* between Nov. 1902 and Nov. 1903. See the novel in its entirety, along with Hazel Carby's introduction to the Oxford edition, in Pauline Hopkins, *Magazine Novels of Pauline Hopkins* (New York: Oxford University Press, 1988); also Hazel V. Carby, *Reconstructing Womanhood: The Emergence of the Afro-American Woman Novelist* (New York: Oxford University Press, 1987), 155–62.

50. See John Langston Gwaltney, 'A Nation within a Nation', in *Drylongso: A Self-Portrait of Black America*, ed. John Langston Gwaltney (New York: Random House, 1980), 3–23; and Patricia Hill Collins, 'The Social Construction of Black Feminist Thought', *Signs* 14/4 (Summer 1989), 765–80. For a critique of race and essentialism, see Diana Fuss, *Essentially Speaking: Feminism, Nature, and Difference* (New York: Routledge, 1989), 73–96.

51. Robert Miles (n. 5 above) argues that both race and nation are 'supra-class and supra-gender forms of categorisation with considerable potential for articulation' (89–90). Also, see Barbara Jeanne Fields, 'Slavery, Race, and Ideology in the United States of America', *New Left Review*, 181 (May/June 1990), 115.

52. See Benedict R. Anderson's discussion of nation as 'imagined' in the sense of its being limited (not inclusive of all mankind), sovereign, and a community, in his *Imagined Communities: Reflections on the Origin and Spread of Nationalism* (New York and London: Verso, 1983), 14–16.

53. Arthur Penrhyn Stanley, *The Life and Correspondence of Thomas Arnold, D.D.*, 12th edn. (London, 1881), ii. 324, quoted and cited in Reginald Horsman, *Race and Manifest Destiny: The Origins of American Racial Anglo-Saxonism* (Cambridge, Mass.: Harvard University Press, 1981), 66.

54. George Fredrickson discusses 'romantic racialism' within the context of 'benign' views of black distinctiveness. This view was upheld by romanticism, abolitionism, and evangelical religion and should be distinguished from 'scientific' explanations or cultural interpretations that vilified blacks as beasts and unworthy of human dignity (*The Black Image in the White Mind* (New York: Harper & Row, 1972), 97–9, 101–15, 125–6).

55. W. E. B. Du Bois stated: 'But while race differences have followed mainly physical race lines, yet no mere physical distinctions would really define or explain the deeper differences—the cohesiveness and continuity of these groups. The deeper differences are spiritual, psychical, differences—undoubtedly based on the physical but infinitely transcending them' ('The Conservation of Races', in *W. E. B. Du Bois Speaks: Speeches and Addresses, 1890–1919*, ed. Philip S. Foner (New York: Pathfinder, 1970), 77–9, 84); see also Appiah's critique of Du Bois (n. 7 above), 23–9.

56. Frantz Fanon offers this definition of national culture in contradistinction to one based on 'an abstract populism that believes it can discover the people's true nature' (*The Wretched of the Earth* (New York: Grove, 1968), 233).

57. Raymond Williams asserts: 'Language has then to be seen as a persistent kind of creation and re-creation: a dynamic presence and a constant regenerative process' (*Marxism and Literature* (New York: Oxford University Press, 1977), 31).

58. See Bracey, Meier, and Rudwick (eds.) (n. 48 above), xxvi–xxx; Winant and Omi (n. 5 above), 38–51.

59. E. Frances White's perceptive analysis of African-Americans' contestation of the discursive representation of Africa calls attention to the conservative implications of Afrocentric feminism. See E. Frances White, 'Africa on My Mind: Gender, Counter Discourse and African-American Nationalism', *Journal of Women's History*, 2 (Spring 1990), 90–4; Patricia Hill Collins, 'The Social Construction of Black Feminist Thought' (n. 50 above), 765–70, and *Black Feminist Thought: Knowledge, Consciousness, and the Politics of Empowerment* (Boston: Unwin Hyman, 1990), 10–11, 15. Also for a good critique, see bell hooks, *Yearning: Race, Gender, and Cultural Politics* (Boston: South End Press, 1990).

60. Evelyn Brooks Higginbotham, 'Beyond the Sound of Silence: Afro-American Women in History', *Gender and History*, 1 (Spring 1989), 58–9.

61. National Baptist Convention, *Journal of the Twenty-fourth Annual Session of the National Baptist Convention and the Fifth Annual Session of the Woman's Convention, Held in Austin, Texas, September 14–19, 1904* (Nashville: National Baptist Publishing Board, 1904), 324; also, I discuss the politics of respectability as both subversive and conservative in Evelyn Brooks Higginbotham, *Righteous Discontent: The Women's Movement in the Black Baptist Church, 1880–1920* (Cambridge, Mass.: Harvard University Press, 1992), ch. 7.

62. Houston A. Baker, Jr., in his discussion of the black vernacular, characterizes the 'quotidian sounds of black every day life' as both a defiant and entrancing voice (*Afro-American Poetics: Revisions of Harlem and the Black Aesthetic* (Madison: University of Wisconsin Press, 1988), 95–107); see also Houston A.

Baker, Jr., *Blues, Ideology and Afro-American Literature: A Vernacular Theory* (Chicago: University of Chicago Press, 1984), 11–13. Similarly, John Langston Gwaltney calls the 'folk' culture of today's cities a 'core black culture', which is 'more than *ad hoc* synchronic adaptive survival'. Gwaltney links its values and epistemology to a long peasant tradition. See Gwaltney (ed.) (n. 50 above), xv–xvii.

63. Carby, *Reconstructing Womanhood* (n. 49 above), 163–75; also Henry Louis Gates, Jr., 'The Trope of a New Negro and the Reconstruction of the Image of the Black', *Representations*, 24 (Fall 1988), 129–55.

64. See Bruce Lambert, 'AIDS in Black Women Seen as Leading Killer', *New York Times* (11 July 1990); Ernest Quimby and Samuel R. Friedman, 'Dynamics of Black Mobilization against AIDS in New York City', *Social Problems*, 36 (Oct. 1989): 407–13; Evelynn Hammonds, 'Race, Sex, Aids: The Construction of "Other" ', *Radical America*, 29 (Nov.–Dec. 1987), 28–36; also Brandt (n. 42 above), 186–92.

65. Anna Julia Cooper stated: 'When and where I enter in the quiet, undisputed dignity of my womanhood without violence and without suing or special patronage, then and there the whole Negro race enters with me' (*A Voice from the South*, repr. of 1892 edn. (New York: Negro Universities Press, 1969), 31).

66. Alice Walker, *In Search of Our Mothers' Gardens: Womanist Prose* (New York: Harcourt, Brace, Jovanovich, 1983), xi–xii; also see, e.g. Elsa Barkley Brown's introductory pages and historical treatment of Maggie Lena Walker, black Richmond banker in the early twentieth century, which reflect this perspective ('Womanist Consciousness: Maggie Lena Walker and the Independent Order of Saint Luke', ch. 16, this vol.

67. I am using 'micropolitics' synonymously with James C. Scott's term 'infrapolitics'. According to Scott, the infrapolitics of subordinate groups not only constitute the everyday, prosaic, 'unobtrusive' level of political struggle in contradistinction to overt protests but also constitute the 'cultural and structural underpinning' of more visible discontent (*Domination and the Arts of Resistance: Hidden Transcripts* (New Haven: Yale University Press, 1990), 183–92).

68. White (n. 59 above), 82.

Carnal Knowledge and Imperial Power: Gender, Race, and Morality in Colonial Asia

Ann Laura Stoler

Over the last fifteen years the anthropology of women has fundamentally altered our understanding of colonial expansion and its consequences for the colonized. In identifying how European conquest affected valuations of women's work and redefined their proper domains, we have sought to explain how changes in household organization, the sexual division of labour, and the gender-specific control of resources within it have modified and shaped how colonial appropriations of land, labour, and resources were obtained.[1] Much of this research has focused on indigenous gendered patterns of economic activity, political participation, and social knowledge, on the agency of those confronted with European rule—but less on the distinct agency of those women and men who carried it out.

More recent attention to the structures of colonial authority has placed new emphasis on the quotidian assertion of European dominance in the colonies, on imperial interventions in domestic life, and thus on the cultural prescriptions by which European women and men lived (Callan and Ardener 1984; Knibiehler and Goutalier

© 1991 The Regents of the University of California. The research for this paper was supported by an NSF Postdoctoral Fellowship for the International Exchange of Scientists (Grant No. IN-8701561), by a NATO Postdoctoral Fellowship in Science (Grant No. RCD-8751159), and by funding from the Centre National de la Recherche Scientifique in France. The Center for Asian Studies Amsterdam (CASA) and the Centre d'Etudes Africaines in Paris generously extended their facilities and collegial support. I owe particular thanks to the following people who have read various versions of this text and whose comments I have tried to take into special account here: Julia Adams, Etienne Balibar, Pierre Bourdieu, Robert Connell, Frederick Cooper, Linda Gordon, Lawrence Hirschfeld, Micaela di Leonardo, Gerda Lerner, George Mosse. A much shorter version of this paper has appeared under the title 'Making Empire Respectable: The Politics of Race and Sexual Morality in 20th Century Colonial Cultures', *American Ethnologist* 16/4: 634–60. The present paper is reprinted with permission from Micaela di Leonardo (ed.), *Gender at the Crossroad of Knowledge*, 51–101).

1985, 1987; Callaway 1987; Strobel 1987). Having focused on how colonizers have viewed the indigenous Other, we are beginning to sort out how Europeans in the colonies imagined themselves and constructed communities built on asymmetries of race, class, and gender—entities significantly at odds with the European models on which they were drawn.

Feminist attempts to engage the gender politics of Dutch, French, and British imperial cultures converge on some strikingly similar observations; namely that European women in these colonies experienced the cleavages of racial dominance and internal social distinctions very differently than men precisely because of their ambiguous positions, as both subordinates in colonial hierarchies and as active agents of imperial culture in their own right. (Callan and Ardener 1984; Knibiehler and Goutalier 1985; Reijs *et al.* 1986; Callaway 1987). Concomitantly, the majority of European women who left for the colonies in the late nineteenth and early twentieth centuries confronted profoundly rigid restrictions on their domestic, economic and political options, more limiting than those of metropolitan Europe at the time and sharply contrasting with the opportunities open to colonial men.[2]

In one form or another these studies raise a basic question: in what ways were gender inequalities essential to the structure of colonial racism and imperial authority? Was the strident misogyny of imperial thinkers and colonial agents a by-product of received metropolitan values ('they just brought it with them'), a reaction to contemporary feminist demands in Europe ('women need to be put back in their breeding place'), or a novel and pragmatic response to the conditions of conquest? Was the assertion of European supremacy in terms of patriotic manhood and racial virility an expression of imperial domination or a defining feature of it?

In this chapter I explore some of the ways in which imperial authority and racial distinctions were fundamentally structured in gendered terms. I look specifically at the administrative and medical discourse and management of European sexual activity, reproduction and marriage as it articulated with the politics of colonial rule. In this initial effort I focus primarily on the dominant male discourse (and less on women's perceptions of those constraints), on the evidence that it was the way in which women's needs were defined, not *by*, but *for* them which most directly accounted for specific policies.[3]

Focusing on French Indochina and the Dutch East Indies in the early twentieth century but drawing on other contexts, I suggest that the very categories of 'colonizer' and 'colonized' were secured through forms of sexual control that defined the domestic arrangements of Europeans and the cultural investments by which they identified themselves. In treating the sexual and conjugal tensions of colonial life as more than a political trope for the tensions of empire writ small, but as a part of the latter in socially profound and strategic ways, I examine how gender-specific sexual sanctions and prohibitions not only demarcated positions of power but prescribed the personal and public boundaries of race.

Colonial authority was constructed on two powerful but false premisses. The first was the notion that Europeans in the colonies made up an easily identifiable and discrete biological and social entity; a 'natural' community of common class interests, racial attributes, political affinities. and superior culture. The second was the related notion that the boundaries separating colonizer from colonized were thus self-evident and easily drawn (Stoler 1989). Neither premiss reflected colonial realities. Settler colonies such as those in Rhodesia and Algeria excepted—where inter-European conflicts were violent and overt—tensions between bureaucrats and planters, settlers and transients, missionaries and metropolitan policy-makers, *petits blancs* (lower-class whites), and monied entrepreneurs have always made Eurocolonial communities more socially fractious and politically fragile than many of their members professed (see, e.g. Cooper 1980; Drooglever 1980; Ridley 1981; Comaroff and Comaroff 1986; Kennedy 1987; Prochaska, 1989). Internal divisions developed out of competing economic and political agendas—conflicts over access to indigenous resources, frictions over appropriate methods for safeguarding European privilege and power, competing criteria for reproducing a colonial elite and for restricting its membership.

The shift away from viewing colonial elites as homogeneous communities of common interest marks an important trajectory in the anthropology of empire, signalling a major rethinking of gender relations within it. The markers of European identity and the criteria for community membership no longer appear as fixed but emerge as a more obviously fluid, permeable, and historically disputed terrain. The colonial politics of exclusion was contingent on constructing categories. Colonial control was predicated on identifying who was 'white', who was 'native', and which children could become citizens rather than subjects, designating who were legitimate progeny and who were not.

What mattered was not only one's physical properties but who counted as 'European' and by what measure.[4] Skin shade was too ambiguous; bank accounts were mercurial; religious belief and education were crucial but never completely sufficient. Social and legal standing derived from the cultural prism through which colour was viewed, from the silences, acknowledgements, and denials of the social circumstances in which one's parents had sex. Sexual unions based on concubinage, prostitution, or church marriage derived from the hierarchies of rule; but in turn, they were negotiated relations, contested classifications, which altered individual fates and the very structure of colonial society (Martinez-Alier 1974; Ming 1983; Taylor 1983). Ultimately inclusion or exclusion required regulating the sexual, conjugal, and domestic life of *both* Europeans in the colonies and their colonized subjects.

POLITICAL MESSAGES AND SEXUAL METAPHORS

Colonial observers and participants in the imperial enterprise appear to have had unlimited interest in the sexual interface of the colonial encounter. Probably no subject is discussed more than sex in colonial literature and no subject more frequently invoked to foster the racist stereotypes of European society (Pujarniscle 1931: 106; Loutfi 1971: 36). The tropics provided a site of European pornographic fantasies long before conquest was underway with lurid descriptions of sexual licence, promiscuity, gynaecological aberrations, and general perversion marking the Otherness of the colonized for metropolitan consumption (Loutfi 1971; Gilman 1985: 79).[5] Given the rigid sexual protocols of nineteenth-century Europe some colonial historians have gone so far as to suggest that imperial expansion itself was derived from the export of male sexual energy (Hyam 1986b) or at the very least 'a sublimation or alternative to sex [for European men]' (Gann and Duignan 1978: 240). The more important point, however, is that with the sustained presence of Europeans in the colonies, sexual prescriptions by class, race, and gender became increasingly central to the politics of empire and subject to new forms of scrutiny by colonial states.

The salience of sexual symbols as graphic representations of colonial dominance is relatively unambiguous and well-established. Edward Said, for example, argues that the sexual submission and possession of Oriental women by European men 'fairly *stands for* the pattern of relative strength between East and West, and the discourse about the Orient that it enabled' (1978: 6, my emphasis). He describes Orientalism as a 'male perception of the world', 'a male power-fantasy', 'an exclusively male province', in which the Orient is penetrated, silenced, and possessed (1978: 207). Sexuality, then, serves as a loaded metaphor for domination, but Said's critique is not (nor does it claim to be) about those relations between women and men. Sexual images illustrate the iconography of rule, not its pragmatics. Sexual asymmetries and visions convey what is 'really' going on elsewhere, at another political epicenter. They are tropes to depict other centres of power.

If Asian women are centrefold to the imperial voyeur, European women often appear in male colonial writings only as a reverse image—in so far as they do not fulfill the power fantasies of European men.[6] Whether portrayed as paragons of morality or as parasitic and passive actors on the imperial stage, these women are rarely the object of European male desire (Loutfi 1971: 108–9). In assuming that European men and women participated equally in the prejudices and pleasures which colonial privilege bestowed upon them, such formulations obscure the fact that European women engaged in the construction and consequences of imperial power in ways that imposed fundamentally different restrictions on them.

Sexual domination has been carefully considered as a discursive symbol, instrumental in the conveyance of other meanings, but has been less often treated as the substance of imperial policy. Was sexual dominance, then, merely a graphic substantiation of who was, so to speak, on the bottom and who was on the top? Was the medium the message, or did sexual relations always 'mean' something else, stand in for other relations, evoke the sense of *other* (pecuniary, political, or some possibly more subliminal) desires? This analytic slippage between the sexual symbols of power and the politics of sex runs throughout the colonial record—as well as through contemporary commentaries on it. Some of this may be due to the polyvalent quality of sexuality; symbolically rich and socially salient at the same time. But sexual control was more than a convenient metaphor for colonial domination; it was, as I argue here, a fundamental class and racial marker implicated in a wider set of relations of power.

Kenneth Ballhatchet's work on Victorian India points in a similar direction (1980). By showing that regulations on sexual access, prostitution, and venereal disease were central to segregationist policy, he links issues of sexual management to the internal structure of British rule. He convincingly argues that it was through the policing of sex that subordinate European military and civil servants were kept in line and that racial boundaries were thus maintained. his study then is about the relations of power between men and men; it has little to say about constraints on European colonial women since its emphasis is not on the relations of power between women and men.

As a critical interface of sexuality and the wider political order, the relationship between gender prescriptions and racial boundaries is a subject that still remains unevenly unexplored. Recent work on the oral history of colonial women, for example, shows clearly that European women of different classes experienced the colonial venture very differently from one another and from men, but we still know relatively little about the distinct investments they had in a racism they shared (Van Helten and Williams 1983; Knibiehler and Goutalier 1985; Callaway 1987; Strobel 1987).

In confronting some of these issues, feminists investigating colonial situations have taken a new turn, relating the real-life conditions of European and colonized women to imperial mentalities and to the cultural artifices of rule. Such efforts to sort out the distinct colonial experience of European women examine how they were incorporated into, resisted, and affected the politics of their men (Taylor 1983; Knibiehler and Goutalier 1985; Callan and Ardener 1984; Callaway 1987). Studies showing the intervention of state, business, and religious institutions in indigenous strategies of biological and social reproduction are now coupled with those that examine the work of European women in these programmes, the influence of European welfare programmes on colonial medicine, and the reproductive constraints on colonial women themselves (Knibiehler and Goutalier 1985; Hunt 1988).

Most of these contributions have attended to the broader issue of gender ideologies and colonial authority, not specifically to how sexual control has figured in the fixing of racial boundaries *per se.* Although feminist research across disciplines has increasingly explored the 'social embeddedness of sexuality', and the contexts that 'condition, constrain and socially define [sexual] acts' (Ross and Rapp 1980: 54), this emphasis has not been dominant in feminist studies of empire, nor has it refocused attention on the *racial* 'embeddedness of sexuality' in colonial contexts as one might expect. Important exceptions include recent work on Southern Africa where changing restrictions on colonial prostitution and domestic service were explicitly class-specific and directly tied racial policy to sexual control (Gaitskell 1983; Van Heyningen 1984; Schmidt 1987; Hansen 1989; White 1990; also see Ming 1983 and Hesselink 1987 for the Indies, and Engels 1983 for India).

The linkage between sexual control and racial tensions is both obvious and elusive at the same time. Although we can accept Ronald Takaki's (1977) assertion that sexual fear in nineteenth-century America was at base a racial anxiety, we are still left to understand why it is through sexuality that such anxieties are expressed. Winthrop Jordan contends that in the nineteenth-century American South, 'the sex act itself served as a ritualistic re-enactment of the daily pattern of social dominance' (1968: 141). More generally, Sander Gilman (1985) argues that sexuality is the most salient marker of Otherness and therefore figures in *any* racist ideology; like skin colour, 'sexual structures such as the shape of the genitalia, are always the antithesis of the idealized self's' (ibid. 25). If sexuality organically represents racial difference as Gilman claims, then we should not be surprised that colonial agents and colonized subjects expressed their contests—and vulnerabilities—in these terms.

This notion of sexuality as a core aspect of social identity has fig-ured importantly in analyses of the psychological motivation and consequences of colonial rule (Mannoni 1956; Fanon 1967; Nandy 1983). In this focus, sexual submission substantiates colonial racism, imposing essential limits on personal liberation. Notably, among colonized male authors, questions of virility and definitions of manliness are politically centrestage. The demasculinization of colonized men and the hypermasculinity of European males repre-sent principal assertions of white supremacy. But these studies are about the psychological salience of women and sex in the subordi-nation of men by men. They only incidentally deal with sex*ism* and racism as well as racism and sex.[7]

An overlapping set of discourses have provided the psychological and economic underpinnings for colonial distinctions of differ-ence, linking fears of sexual contamination, physical danger, cli-matic incompatability, and moral breakdown to a European national identity with a racist and class-specific core. In colonial scientific reports and the popular press we repeatedly come across statements varying on a common theme: 'native women bear con-tagions'; 'white women become sterile in the colonies'; 'colonial men are susceptible to physical, moral and mental degeneration when they remain in the tropics too long'. To what degree are these statements medically or politically grounded? We need to unpack what is metaphor, what is perceived as dangerous (is it disease, culture, climate, or sex?), and what is not.

In the sections that follow I look at the relationship between the domestic arrangements of colonial communities and their wider political structures. Part I draws on colonization debates over a broad period (sixteenth–twentieth century) in an effort to identify the long-term intervention of colonial authorities in issues of 'racial mixing', settlement schemes, and sexual control. In examining debates over European family formation, over the relationship between subversion and sex, I look at how evaluations of concubinage, and of morality more generally, changed with new forms of racism and new gender-specific expressions of them.

Part II treats the protection and policing of European women within the changing politics of empire. It traces how accusations of sexual assault related to new demands for political rights and restricted demarcations of social space in response to them. Part III examines what I call the 'cultural hygiene' of colonialism. Taking the early twentieth century as a breakpoint, I take up the convergent metropolitan and colonial discourses on health hazards in the tropics, race-thinking, and social reform as they related to shifts in the rationalization of rule. In tracing how fears of 'racial degeneracy' were grounded in class-specific sexual norms, I return to how and why racial difference was constituted and culturally coded in gendered terms.

PART I: SEX AND OTHER CATEGORIES OF COLONIAL CONTROL

> Though sex cannot of itself enable men to transcend racial barriers, it generates some admiration and affection across them, which is healthy, and which cannot always be dismissed as merely self-interested and prudential. On the whole, sexual interaction between Europeans and non-Europeans probably did more good than harm to race relations; at any rate, I cannot accept the feminist contention that it was fundamentally undesirable.
>
> (Hyam 1986a: 75)

The regulation of sexual relations was central to the development of particular kinds of colonial settlements and to the allocation of economic activity within them. Who bedded and wedded with whom in the colonies of France, England, Holland, and Iberia was never left to chance. Unions between Annamite women and French men, between Portuguese women and Dutch men, between Spanish men and Inca women produced offspring with claims to privilege, whose rights and status had to be determined and prescribed. From the early 1600s through the twentieth century the sexual sanctions and conjugal prohibitions of colonial agents were rigorously debated and carefully codified. It is in these debates over matrimony and morality that trading and plantation company officials, missionaries, investment bankers, military high commands, and agents of the colonial state confronted one another's visions of empire, and the settlement patterns on which it would rest.

In 1622 the Dutch East Indies Company (VOC) arranged for the transport of six poor but marriageable young Dutch women to Java, providing them with clothing, a dowry upon marriage, and a contract binding them to five years in the Indies (Taylor 1983: 12). Aside from this and one other short-lived experiment, immigration of European women to the East was consciously restricted for the next two hundred years. VOC shareholders argued against female emigration on several counts: the high cost of transporting married women and daughters (Blussé 1986: 161); the possibility that Dutch women (with stronger ties than men to the Netherlands?) might hinder permanent settlement by goading their burgher husbands to quickly lucrative but nefarious trade, and then repatriate to display their new found wealth (Taylor 1983: 14); the fear that Dutch women would enrich themselves through private trade and encroach on the company's monopoly;[8] and the prediction that their children would be sickly and force families to repatriate, ultimately depleting the colony of permanent and loyal settlers (Taylor 1983: 14).

The Dutch East Indies Company enforced the sanction against female migration by selecting bachelors as their European recruits and by promoting both extramarital relations and legal unions between low-ranking employees and imported slave women (Taylor 1983: 16).[9] Although there were Euro-Asian marriages, government regulations made concubinage a more attractive option by prohibiting European men with native wives and children from returning to Holland (Ming 1983: 69; Taylor 1983: 16; Blussé 1986: 173). The VOC saw households based on Euro-Asian unions, by contrast, as having distinct advantages; individual employees would bear the costs of dependants; children of mixed unions were considered stronger and healthier; and Asian women made fewer demands. Finally, it was thought that men would be more likely to settle permanently by establishing families with local roots.

Concubinage served colonial interests in other ways. It permitted permanent settlement and rapid growth by a cheaper means than the importation of European women. Salaries of European recruits to the colonial armies, bureaucracies, plantation companies, and trading enterprises were kept artificially low. This was possible not only because the transport of European women and family support was thereby eliminated, as was often argued, but because local women provided domestic services for which new European recruits would otherwise have had to pay. In the mid-nineteenth century, such arrangements were *de rigueur* for young civil servants intent on setting up households on their own (Ritter 1856: 21). Despite clerical opposition (the church never attained a secure and independent foothold in the Indies), by the nineteenth century concubinage was the most prevalent living arrangement for European men (van Marle 1952: 485). Nearly half of the Indies' European male population in the 1880s was unmarried and living with Asian women (Ming 1983: 70). It was only in the early twentieth century that concubinage was politically condemned (van Marle 1952: 486).

The administrative arguments from the 1600s invoked to curb the immigration of European women, on the one hand, and to condone sexual access to indigenous women, on the other, bear striking resemblance to the sexual politics of colonial capitalism three centuries later. Referred to as *nyai* in Java and Sumatra, *congai* in Indochina, and *petite épouse* throughout the French empire, the colonized woman living as a concubine to a European man formed the dominant domestic arrangement in colonial cultures through the early twentieth century. Unlike prostitution, which could and often did result in a population of syphilitic and therefore non-productive European men, concubinage was considered to have a stabilizing influence on political order and colonial health—a relationship that kept men in their barracks and bungalows, out of brothels and less inclined to 'unnatural' liaisons with one another.[10]

In Asia and Africa corporate and government decision-makers invoked the social services that local women supplied as 'useful guides to the language and other mysteries of the local societies' (Malleret 1934: 216; Cohen 1971: 122). The medical and cultural know-how of local women was credited with keeping many

European men alive in their initial confrontation with tropical life (Braconier 1933). Handbooks for incoming plantation employees bound for Tonkin, Sumatra, and Malaya urged men to find a bed-servant as a prerequisite to quick acclimatization (Nieuwenhuys 1959: 19; Dixon 1913: 77). In Malaysia, commercial companies encouraged the procurement of local 'companions' for psychological and physical well-being; to protect European staff from the ill-health that sexual abstention, isolation, and boredom were thought to bring (Butcher 1979: 200, 202).[11] Even in the British Empire, where the Colonial Office officially banned concubinage in 1910, it was tacitly condoned and practised long after (Hyam 1986b; Callaway 1987: 49; Kennedy 1987: 175). In the Indies a simultaneous sanction against concubinage among civil servants was only selectively enforced; it had little effect on domestic arrangements outside of Java and no perceptible impact on the European households in Sumatra's newly opened plantation belt where Javanese and Japanese *huishoudsters* (as Asian mistresses were sometimes called) remained the rule rather than the exception (Clerkx 1961: 87–93; Stoler 1985a: 31–4; Lucas 1986: 84).

Concubinage was a contemporary term which referred to the cohabitation outside of marriage between European men and Asian women. In fact, it glossed a wide range of arrangements that included sexual access to a non-European woman as well as demands on her labour and legal rights to the children she bore. Thus, to define concubinage as cohabitation perhaps suggests more social privileges than most women who were involved in such relations enjoyed.[12] Many colonized women combined sexual and domestic service within the abjectly subordinate contexts of slave or 'coolie' and lived in separate quarters. On the plantations in East Sumatra, for example, where such arrangements were structured into company policies of labour control, Javanese women picked from the coolie ranks often retained their original labour contracts for the duration of their sexual and domestic service (Lucas 1986: 186).

Although most of these Javanese women remained as servants, sharing only the beds of European staff, many *nyai* elsewhere in the Indies combined their service with some degree of limited authority. Working for wealthier men, these *huishoudsters* managed the businesses as well as the servants and household affairs of European men (Nieuwenhuys 1959: 17; Lucas 1986: 86; Taylor 1983).[13] Native women (like European-born women in a later period) were to keep men physically and psychologically fit for work, that is, marginally content without distracting them or urging them out of line (Chivas-Baron 1929: 103). Live-in companions, especially in remote districts and plantation areas, thus met the daily needs of low-ranking European employees without the emotional, temporal, and financial requirements that European family life were thought to demand.[14]

To say that concubinage reinforced the hierarchies on which colonial societies were based is not to say that it did not make those distinctions more problematic at the same time. In the first place, in such regions as North Sumatra grossly uneven sex ratios often made for intense competition among male workers and their European supervisors for indigenous women. *Vrouwen perkara* (disputes over women) resulted in assaults on white, new labour tensions, and dangerous incursions into the standards deemed essential for white prestige (Stoler 1985*a*: 33; Lucas 1986: 90–1). In the Netherlands Indies, more generally, an unaccounted number of impoverished Indo-European women, moving between prostitution and concubinage, disturbed the racial sensibilities of the Dutch-born elite (Hesselink 1987: 216). Metropolitan critics were particularly disdainful of these liaisons on moral grounds—all the more so when these unions *were* sustained an emotionally significant relationships, thereby contradicting the racial premiss of concubinage as an emotionally unfettered convenience.[15] But perhaps most important, the tension between concubinage as a confirmation and compromise of racial hierarchy was realized in the progeny that it produced, 'mixed bloods', poor 'Indos', and abandoned *métis* children who straddled the divisions of ruler and ruled and threatened to blur the colonial divide. These *voorkinderen* (literally, 'children from a previous marriage/union', but in this colonial context usually marking illegitimate children from a previous union with a non-European woman) were economically disadvantaged by their ambiguous social status and often grew up to join the ranks of the impoverished whites (Nieuwenhuys 1959: 21).

Concubinage was a domestic arrangement based on sexual service and gender inequalities which 'worked' as long as European identity and supremacy were clear. When either was thought to be vulnerable, in jeopardy, or less than convincing, at the turn of the century and increasingly through the 1920s, colonial elites responded by clarifying the cultural criteria of privilege and the moral premises of their unity. Structured sex in the politically safe context of prostitution, and where possible in the more desirable context of marriage between 'full-blooded' Europeans, replaced concubinage (Taylor 1977: 29). As in other colonial contexts as we shall see, the ban on concubinage was not always expressed in boldly racist language; on the contrary, difference and distance were often coded to mark race in culturally clear but nuanced terms.[16]

Restrictions on European Women in the Colonies

Colonial governments and private business not only tolerated concubinage but actively encouraged it—principally by restricting the emigration of European women to the colonies and by refusing employment to married male European recruits. Although most accounts of colonial conquest and settlement suggest that European women chose to avoid early pioneering ventures, the choice was rarely their own (cf. Fredrickson 1981: 109). In the Indies, a government ordinance of 1872 made it impossible for any soldier below the rank of sergeant-major to be married; and even above that rank, conditions were very restrictive (Ming 1983: 70). In the Indies army, marriage was a privilege of the officer corps, whereas barrack-concubinage was instituted and regulated for the rank and file. In the twentieth century, formal and informal prohibitions set by banks, estates, and government services operating in Africa, India, and South-East Asia restricted marriage during the first three to five years of service, while some simply prohibited it altogether. In Malaya, the major British banks required their employees to sign contracts agreeing to request prior permission to marry, with the understanding that it would not be granted in fewer than eight years (Butcher 1979: 138).

Many historians assume that these bans on employee marriage and on the emigration of European women lifted when specific colonies were politically stable, medically upgraded, and economically secure. In fact marriage restrictions lasted well into the twentieth century, long after rough living and a scarcity of amenities had become conditions of the past. In India as late as 1929, British employees in the political service were still recruited at the age of twenty-six and then prohibited from marriage during their first three probationary years (Moore-Gilbert 1986: 48). In the army, marriage allowances were also denied until the same age, while in the commercial houses restrictions were frequent but less overt (ibid. 48; Woodcock 1969: 164). On the Ivory Coast, employment contracts in the 1920s also denied marriage with European women before the third tour, which meant a minimum of five years' service, so that many men remained unmarried past the age of thirty (Tirefort 1979: 134).[17]

European demographics in the colonies were shaped by these economic and political exigencies and thus were enormously skewed by sex. Among the labouring immigrant and native populations as well as among Europeans in the late nineteenth and early twentieth centuries, the number of men was, at the very least, double that of women, and sometimes exceeded the latter by twenty-five times. Although in the Netherlands Indies, the overall ratio of European women to men rose from 47 : 100 to 88 : 100 between 1900 and 1930, representing an absolute increase from 4000 to 26 000 Dutch women (Taylor 1983: 128), in outlying islands such as Sumatra the ratios were kept far more uneven. Thus on Sumatra's plantation belt in 1920 there were still only 61 European women per 100 men (*Koloniale Verslag* quoted in Lucas 1986: 82). On Africa's Ivory Coast, European sex ratios through 1921 were still 1 : 25 (Tirefort 1979: 31). In Tonkin, European men sharply outnumbered European women as late as 1931 when there were 14 085 European men (including military) to 3083 European women (Gantes 1981: 138). While these imbalances are most frequently attributed to the physical hazards of life in the tropics, there are political explanations that are more compelling. In controlling the availability of European women and the sorts of sexual access allowed, colonial state and corporate authorities avoided salary increases as well as the proliferation of a lower-class European settler population. Such policies in no way muted the internal class distinctions within the European communities; they simply shaped the social geography of the colonies by fixing the conditions under which European privileges could be attained and reproduced.

Sex, Subversion and White Prestige: A Case from North Sumatra

The marriage prohibition was both a political and economic issue, defining the social contours of colonial communities and the standards of living within them (Butcher 1979). But, as importantly, it revealed how deeply the conduct of private life and the sexual proclivities individuals expressed were tied to corporate profits and the security of the colonial state. Nowhere was the connection between sex and subversion more openly contested than in North Sumatra in the early 1900s. Irregular domestic arrangements were thought to encourage subversion as strongly as acceptable unions could avert it. Family stability and sexual 'normalcy' were thus linked to political agitation or quiescence in very concrete ways.

Since the late nineteenth century, the major North Sumatran tobacco and rubber companies had neither accepted married applicants nor allowed them to take wives while in service (Schoevers 1913: 38; Clerkx 1961: 31–4). Company authorities argued that new employees with families in tow would be a financial burden, risking the emergence of a 'European proletariat' and thus a major threat to white prestige (*Kroniek 1917*: 50; *Sumatra Post* 1913). Low-ranking plantation employees protested against these company marriage restrictions, an issue that mobilized their ranks behind a broad set of demands (Stoler 1989*a*: 144). Under employee pressure, the prohibition was relaxed to a marriage ban for the first five years of service. This restriction, however, was never placed on everyone; it was pegged to salaries and dependent on the services of local women that kept the living costs and wages of subordinate and incoming staff artificially low.

Domestic arrangements thus varied as government officials and private businesses weighed the economic versus political costs of one arrangement over another, but such calculations were invariably meshed. Europeans in high office saw white prestige and profits as inextricably linked, and attitudes toward concubinage reflected that concern (Brownfoot 1984: 191). Thus in Malaya through the 1920s, concubinage was tolerated precisely because 'poor whites' were not. Government and plantation administrators argued that white prestige would be imperiled if European men became impoverished in attempting to maintain middle-class lifestyles and European wives. Colonial morality and the place of concubinage in it was relative, given the 'particular anathema with which the British regarded "poor whites" ' (Butcher 1979: 26). In late nineteenth-century Java, in contrast, concubinage itself was considered to be a major source of white pauperism; in the early 1900s it was vigorously condemned at precisely the same time that a new colonial morality passively condoned illegal brothels (Het Pauperisme Commissie 1901; Nieuwenhuys 1959: 20–3; Hesselink 1987: 208).

It was not only morality that vacillated but the very definition of white prestige—and what its defence should entail. No description of European colonial communities fails to note the obsession with white prestige as a basic feature of colonial mentality. White prestige and its protection loom as the primary cause of a long list of otherwise inexplicable colonial postures, prejudices, fears, and violences. As we have seen, what upheld that prestige was not a constant; concubinage was socially lauded at one time and seen as a political menace at another. White prestige was a gloss for different intensities of racist practice, gender-specific and culturally coded. Although many accounts contend that white women brought an end to concubinage, its decline came with a much wider shift in colonial relations along more racially segregated lines—in which the definitions of prestige shifted and in which Asian, creole, and European-born women were to play new roles.

Thus far I have treated colonial communities as a generic category despite the sharp demographic, social, and political distinctions among them. Colonies based on small administrative centres of Europeans (as on Africa's Gold Coast) differed from plantation colonies with sizable enclave European communities (as in Malaya and Sumatra), and still more from settler colonies (as in Algeria) with large and very heterogenous, permanent European populations. These 'types', however, were far less fixed than some students of colonial history suggest. Winthrop Jordan, for example, has argued that the 'bedrock demographics' of whites to blacks, and the sexual composition of the latter group, 'powerfully influenced, perhaps even determined the kind of society which emerged in each colony' (Jordan 1968: 141).[18] North Sumatra's European-oriented, overwhelmingly male colonial population, for example, contrasted sharply with the more sexually balanced mestizo culture that emerged in the seventeenth and eighteenth centuries in colonial Java. As we have seen, however, these demographics were not the bedrock of social relations from which all else followed. Sex ratios themselves derived from the particular way in which administrative strategies of social engineering collided with and constrained people's personal choices and private lives. While recognizing that these demographic differences, and the social configurations to which they gave rise, still need to be explained, I have chosen here to trace some of the common politically charged issues that a range of colonial societies shared; that is, some of the similar—and counterintuitive—ways in which the construction of racial categories and the management of sexuality were inscribed in new efforts to modernize colonial control.[19]

PART II: EUROPEAN WOMEN AND RACIAL BOUNDARIES

Perhaps nothing is as striking in the sociological accounts of European colonial communities as the extraordinary changes that are said to accompany the entry of white women. These adjustments shifted in one direction; toward European life-styles accentuating the refinements of privilege and new etiquettes of racial difference. Most accounts agree that the presence of European women put new demands on the white communities to tighten their ranks, clarify their boundaries, and mark out their social space. The material culture of European settlements in Saigon, outposts in New Guinea, and estate complexes in Sumatra were retailored to accommodate the physical and moral requirements of a middle-class and respectable feminine contingent (Malleret 1934; Gordon and Meggitt 1985; Stoler 1989*a*). Housing structures in the Indies were partitioned, residential compounds in the Solomon Islands enclosed, servant relations in Hawaii formalized, dress codes in Java altered, food and social taboos in Rhodesia and the Ivory Coast codified. Taken together these changes encouraged new kinds of consumption and new social services catering to these new demands (Boutilier 1984; Spear 1963; Woodcock 1969; Cohen 1971).

The arrival of large numbers of European women thus coincided with an embourgeoisment of colonial communities and with a significant sharpening of racial categories. European women supposedly required more metropolitan amenities than men and more spacious surroundings to allow it; they had more delicate sensibilities and therefore needed suitable quarters—discrete and enclosed. Women's psychological and physical constitutions were considered more fragile, demanding more servants for the chores they should be spared. In short, white women needed to be maintained at elevated standards of living, in insulated social spaces cushioned with the cultural artefacts of 'being European'.

Thomas Beidelman, for example, writes for colonial Tanganyika that 'European wives and children created a new and less flexible domestic colonialism exhibiting overconcern with the sexual accessibility or vulnerability of wives, with corresponding notions about the need for spatial and social segregation' (1982: 13). Whether women or men set these new standards and why they might have both done so for different reasons is left unclear. Who exhibited 'overconcern' and a 'need for' segregation? In Indo-China, male

225

doctors advised French women to have their homes built with separate domestic and kitchen quarters (Grall 1908: 74). Segregationist standards were what women 'deserved', and more importantly what white male prestige required that they maintain.

Racist But Moral Women, Innocent But Immoral Men

Recent feminist scholarship has challenged the universally negative stereotype of the colonial wife in one of two ways: either by showing the structural reasons why European women were racially intolerant, socially vicious, abusive to servants, prone to illness and bored, or by demonstrating that they really were not (Gartrell 1984; Knibiehler and Goutalier 1985; Callaway 1987). Several recent works have attempted to confront what Margaret Strobel calls the 'myth of the destructive female' to show that European women were not detriments to colonial relations but were in fact crucial to the bolstering of a failing empire, and charged with maintaining the social rituals of racial difference (Strobel 1987: 378–9).

Colonial rhetoric on white women was full of contradictions. At the same time that new female immigrants were chided for not respecting the racial distance of local convention, an equal number of colonial observers accused these women of being more avid racists in their own right (Spear 1963; Nora 1961). Allegedly insecure and jealous of the sexual liaisons of European men with native women, bound to their provincial visions and cultural norms, European women, it was and is argued, constructed the major cleavages on which colonial stratification rested. Thus Percival Spear, in commenting on the social life of the English in eighteenth-century India, asserted that women 'widened the racial gulf' by holding to 'their insular whims and prejudices' (1963: 140). Writing about French women in Algeria two hundred years later, the French historian Pierre Nora claimed that these 'parasites of the colonial relationship in which they do not participate directly, are generally more racist than men and contribute strongly to prohibiting contract between the two societies' (1961: 174). Similarly, Octavio Mannoni noted 'the astonishing fact' that European women in Madagascar were 'far more racialist than the men' (1964 (1950): 115). For the Indies 'it was jealousy of the dusky sirens . . . but more likely some say . . . it was . . . plain feminine scandalization at free and easy sex relations' that caused a decline in miscegenation (Kennedy 1947: 164).

Such bald examples are easy to find in colonial histories of several decades ago. Recent scholarship is more subtle but not substantially different. In the European community on the French Ivory Coast, ethnographer Alain Tirefort contends that 'the presence of the white woman separated husbands from indigenous life by creating around them a zone of European intimacy' (1979: 197). Gann and Duignan state simply that it was 'the cheap steamship ticket for women that put an end to racial integration in British Africa' (1978: 242; also see O'Brien 1972: 59). Lest we assume that such conclusions are confined to metropolitan men, we should note the Indian psychiatrist Ashis Nandy's observation—tying white women's racism to the homosexual cravings of their husbands—that 'white women in India were generally more racist because they unconsciously saw themselves as the sexual competitors of Indian men' (1983: 9–10).

What is most startling here is that women, these otherwise marginal actors on the colonial stage, are charged with dramatically reshaping the face of colonial society, imposing their racial will on, as in the case of Africa, a colonial world where 'relatively unrestrained social intermingling . . . had been prevalent in earlier years' (Cohen 1971: 122). Similarly, in Malaya the presence of European women put an end to 'free and easy social intercourse with [Malayan] men as well', replacing 'an iron curtain of ignorance . . . between the races' (Vere Allen 1970: 169). European women are not only the bearers of racist beliefs but hardline operatives who put them into practice. European women, it is claimed, destroyed the blurred divisions between colonizer and colonized, encouraging class distinctions among whites while fostering new racial antagonisms, formerly muted by sexual access (ibid. 168).[20]

Are we to believe that sexual intimacy with European men yielded social mobility and political rights for colonized women? Or even less likely, that because British civil servants bedded with Indian women, somehow Indian men had more 'in common' with British men and enjoyed more parity? Colonized women could sometimes parlay their positions into personal profit and small rewards, but these were *individual* negotiations with no social, legal, or cumulative claims. European male sexual access to native women was not a levelling mechanism for asymmetries in race, class, or gender (Strobel 1987: 378; Degler 1986: 189).

Male colonizers positioned European women as the bearers of a redefined colonial morality. But to suggest that women fashioned this racism out of whole cloth is to miss the political chronology in which new intensities of racist practice arose. In the African and Asian contexts already mentioned, the arrival of large numbers of

European wives, and particularly the fear for their protection, followed from new terms and tensions in the colonial contract. The presence and protection of European women was repeatedly invoked to clarify racial lines. It coincided with perceived threats to European prestige (Brownfoot 1984: 191), increased racial conflict (Strobel 1987: 378), covert challenges to the colonial order, outright expressions of nationalist resistance, and internal dissension among whites themselves (Stoler 1989*a*: 147–9).

If white women were the primary force behind the decline of concubinage as is often claimed, they did so as participants in a much broader racial realignment and political plan (Knibiehler and Goutalier 1985: 76). This is not to suggest that European women were passive in this process, as the dominant themes in many of their novels attest (Taylor 1977: 27). Many European women did oppose concubinage—not because they were categorically jealous of, and threatened by, Asian women as often claimed (Clerkx 1961), but, more likely, because of the double standard it condoned for European men (Lucas 1986: 94–5). Although some Dutch women in fact championed the cause of the wronged *nyai*, urging improved protection for non-provisioned women and children, they rarely went so far as to advocate for the legitimation of these unions in legal marriage (Taylor 1977: 31–2; Lucas 1986: 95). The voices of European women, however, had little resonance until their objections coincided with a realignment in racial and class politics in which they were strategic in both.

Race and the Politics of Sexual Peril

The gender-specific requirements for colonial living, referred to above, were constructed on heavily racist evaluations, which pivoted on images of the heightened sexuality of colonized men (Tiffany and Adams 1985). Although, as we have noted, in novels and memoirs European women were categorically absent from the sexual fantasies of colonial men, the very same men deemed them to be desired and seductive figures to men of colour. European women needed protection because men of colour had 'primitive' sexual urges and uncontrollable lust, aroused by the sight of white women (Strobel 1987: 379; Schmidt 1987: 411). In some colonies that sexual threat remained an unlabelled potential; in others it was given a specific name. The 'Black Peril' referred throughout Africa and much of the British Empire to the professed dangers of sexual assault on white women by black men.

In Southern Rhodesia and Kenya in the 1920s and 1930s preoc-cupations with the 'Black Peril' gave rise to the creation of citizens' militias, ladies' riflery clubs, and investigations as to whether African female domestic servants would not be safer to employ than men (Kirkwood 1984: 158; Schmidt 1987: 412; Kennedy 1987: 128–47; Hansen 1989). In New Guinea alleged attempted assaults on European women by Papuan men prompted the passage of the White Women's Protection Ordinance of 1926, which provided 'the death penalty for any person convicted for the crime of rape or attempted rape upon a European woman or girl' (Inglis 1975: vi). And in the Solomon Islands authorities introduced public flogging in 1934 as punishment for 'criminal assaults on [white] females' (Boutilier 1984: 197).

What do these cases have in common? First, the rhetoric of sex-ual assault and the measures used to prevent it had virtually no cor-relation with actual incidences of rape of European women by men of colour. Just the contrary: there was often no *ex post facto* evi-dence, nor any at the time, that rapes were committed or that rape attempts were made (Schmidt 1987; Inglis 1975; Kirkwood 1984; Kennedy 1987; Boutilier 1984). This is not to suggest that sexual assaults never occurred, but that their incidence had little to do with the fluctuations in anxiety about them. Moreover, the rape laws were race-specific; sexual abuse of black women was not clas-sified as rape and therefore was not legally actionable, nor did rapes committed by white men lead to prosecution (Mason 1958: 246–7). If these accusations of sexual threat were not prompted by the fact of rape, what did they signal and to what were they tied?

Allusions to political and sexual subversion of the colonial system went hand in hand. The term 'Black Peril' referred to sexual threats, but it also connoted the fear of insurgence, of some perceived non-acquiescence to colonial control more generally (van Onselen 1982; Schmidt 1987; Inglis 1975; Strobel 1987; Kennedy 1987: 128–47). Concern over protection of white women intensified during real and perceived crises of control—provoked by threats to the internal cohesion of the European communities or by infringements on its borders. Thus colonial accounts of the Mutiny in India in 1857 are full of descriptions of the sexual mutilation of British women by Indian men despite the fact that no rapes were recorded (Metcalf 1964: 290). In Africa too, although the chronologies of the Black Peril differ—on the Rand in South Africa peaking a full twenty years earlier than elsewhere—we can still identify a patterned *sequence* of events (van Onselen 1982). In New Guinea, the White

Women's Protection Ordinance followed a large influx of acculturated Papuans into Port Moresby in the 1920s. Resistant to the constraints imposed on their dress, movement, and education, whites
perceived them as arrogant, 'cheeky', and without respect (Inglis
1975: 8, 11). In post-World War I Algeria, the political unease of
pieds noirs (local French settlers) in the face of 'a whole new series
of [Muslim] demands' manifested itself in a popular culture newly
infused with strong images of sexually aggressive Algerian men
(Sivan 1983: 178).

Second, rape charges against colonized men were often based on
perceived transgressions of social space. 'Attempted rapes' turned
out to be 'incidents' of a Papuan man 'discovered' in the vicinity of
a white residence, a Fijian man who entered a European patient's
room, a male servant poised at the bedroom door of a European
woman asleep or in half-dress (Boutilier 1984: 197; Inglis 1975: 11;
Schmidt 1987: 413). With such a broad definition of danger in a
culture of fear, all colonized men of colour were threatening as sexual and political aggressors.

Third, accusations of sexual assault frequently followed upon
heightened tensions within European communities—and renewed
efforts to find consensus within them. Rape accusations in South
Africa, for example, coincided with a rash of strikes between
1890–1914 by both African and white miners (van Onselen 1982:
51). As in Rhodesia after a strike by white railway employees in
1929, the threat of native rebellion brought together conflicting
members of the European community in common cause where
'solidarity found sustenance in the threat of racial destruction'
(Kennedy 1987: 138).

During the late 1920s when labour protests by Indonesian workers and European employees were most intense, Sumatra's corporate elite expanded their vigilante organizations, intelligence
networks, and demands for police protection to ensure their
women were safe and their workers 'in hand' (Stoler 1985a). White
women arrived in large numbers during the most profitable years of
the plantation economy but also at a time of mounting resistance to
estate labour conditions and Dutch rule. In the context of a
European community that had been blatantly divided between low-
ranking plantation employees and the company elite, the community was stabilized and domestic situations were rearranged.

In Sumatra's plantation belt, subsidized sponsorship of married
couples replaced the recruitment of single Indonesian workers and
European staff, with new incentives provided for family housing

and *gezinvorming* ('family formation') in both groups. This recomposed labour force of family men in 'stable households' explicitly weeded out politically 'undesirable elements' and the socially malcontent. With the marriage restriction finally lifted for European staff in the 1920s, young men sought wives among Dutch-born women while on leave in Holland or through marriage brokers by mail. Higher salaries, upgraded housing, elevated bonuses, and a more mediated chain of command between colonized fieldworker and colonial staff served to clarify both national and racial affinities and to differentiate the political interests of European from Asian workers more than ever before (Stoler 1985*a*). With this shift, the vocal opposition to corporate and government directives, sustained by the independent Union of European Estate Employees (*Vakvereeniging voor Assistenten in Deli*) for nearly two decades, was effectively dissolved (*Kroniek 1933*: 85).

The remedies sought to alleviate sexual danger embraced new prescriptions for securing white control; increased surveillance of native men, new laws stipulating severe corporal punishment for the transgression of sexual and social boundaries, and the creation of areas made racially off-limits. These went with a moral rearmament of the European community and reassertions of its cultural identity. Charged with guarding cultural norms, European women were instrumental in promoting white solidarity. It was partly at their own expense, as they were to be nearly as closely policed as colonized men (Strobel 1987).

Policing European Women and Concessions to Chivalry

Although native men were the ones legally punished for alleged sexual assaults, European women were frequently blamed for provoking those desires. New arrivals from Europe were accused of being too familiar with their servants, lax in their commands, indecorous in their speech and in their dress (Vellut 1982: 100; Kennedy 1987: 141; Schmidt 1987: 413). In Papua New Guinea 'everyone' in the Australian community agreed that rape assaults were caused by a 'younger generation of white women' who simply did not know how to treat servants (Inglis 1975: 80). In Rhodesia as in Uganda, sexual anxieties persisted in the absence of any incidents and restricted women to activities within the European enclaves (Gartrell 1984: 169). The immorality act of 1916 'made it an offence for a white woman to make an indecent suggestion to a male native' (Mason 1958: 247). European women in Kenya in the 1920s were not only dissuaded from staying alone on their homesteads but strongly discouraged by rumours of rape from taking up farming on their own (Kennedy 1987: 141). As in the American South, 'the etiquette of chivalry controlled white women's behaviour even as [it] guarded caste lines' (Dowd Hall 1984: 64). A defence of community, morality, and white male power was achieved by increasing control over and consensus among Europeans, by reaffirming the vulnerability of white women, the sexual threat posed by native men, and by creating new sanctions to limit the liberties of both.

European colonial communities in the early twentieth century assiduously controlled the movements of European women and, where possible, imposed on them restricted and protected roles. This is not to say that European women did not work; French women in the settler communities of Algeria ran farms, rooming houses, and shops along with their men (Baroli 1967: 159; O'Brien 1972). On the Ivory Coast, married European women worked to 'supplement' their husbands' incomes (Tirefort 1979: 112), while in Senegal the 'supplementary' salary of French wives maintained the white standard (Mercier 1965: 292). Among women who were posted throughout the colonial empires as missionaries, nurses, and teachers, some openly questioned the sexist policies of their male superiors. However, by and large their tasks buttressed rather than contested the established racial order (Ralston 1977; Knibiehler and Goutalier 1985; Callaway 1987: 111; Ramuschack n.d.).

Particularly in the colonies with small European communities as opposed to those of large-scale settlement, there were few opportunities for women to be economically independent or to act politically on their own. The 'revolt against chivalry'—the protest of American Southern white women to lynchings of black men for alleged rape attempts—had no counterpart among European women in Asia and Africa (Dowd Hall 1984). French feminists urged women with skills (and a desire for marriage) to settle in Indo-China at the turn of the century, but colonial administrators were adamantly against their immigration. They not only complained of a surfeit of resourceless widows but argued that European seamstresses, florists, and children's outfitters could not possibly compete with the cheap and skilled labour provided by well-established Chinese firms (Lanessan 1889: 450; Corneau 1900: 12). In Tonkin in the 1930s, 'there was little room for single women, be they unmarried, widowed or divorced' (Gantes 1981: 45). Although some colonial widows, such as the editor of a major

Saigon daily, succeeded in their own ambitions, most were shipped out of Indo-China—regardless of skill—at the government's charge.[21]

Firmly rejecting expansion based on the 'poor white' (*petit blanc*) Algerian model, French officials in Indo-China dissuaded *colons* with insufficient capital from entry and promptly repatriated those who tried to remain.[22] Single women were seen as the quintessential *petit blanc*, with limited resources and shopkeeper aspirations, they presented the dangerous possibility that straitened circumstances would lead them to prostitution, thereby degrading European prestige at large. In the Solomon Islands lower-class white women were overtly scorned and limited from entry (Boutilier 1984: 179). Similarly, an Indies Army high commander complained in 1903 to the governor-general that lower-class European-born women were vastly more immodest than their Indies-born counterparts and thus posed a greater moral threat to European men (Ming 1983: 84–5). State officials themselves identified European widows as among the most economically vulnerable and impoverished segments of the Indies European community (Het Pauperisme onder de Europeanen 1901: 28).

Professional competence did not leave single European women immune from marginalization (Knibiehler and Goutalier 1985). Single professional women were held in contempt as were European prostitutes, with surprisingly similar objections.[23] White prostitutes threatened prestige, while professional women needed protection; both fell outside the social space to which European colonial women were assigned: namely, as custodians of family welfare and respectability, and as dedicated and willing subordinates to, and supporters of, colonial men. The rigor with which these norms were applied becomes more comprehensible when we see why a European family life and bourgeois respectability became increasingly tied to notions of racial survival, imperial patriotism, and the political strategies of the colonial state.

PART III: WHITE DEGENERACY, MOTHERHOOD, AND THE EUGENICS OF EMPIRE

de-gen-er-ate (adj.) [L. *degeneratus*, pp. of *degenerare*, to become unlike one's race, degenerate < *degener*, not genuine, base < *de-*, from + *genus*, race, kind: see *genus*]. 1. to lose

233

former, normal, or higher qualities. 2. having sunk below a
former or normal condition, character, etc.; deteriorated. 3.
morally corrupt; depraved- (n.) a degenerate person, esp. one
who is morally depraved or sexually perverted- (vi.) -*at'ed*,
-*at'ing*. 1. to decline or become debased morally, culturally,
etc. . . . 2. Biol. to undergo degeneration; deteriorate.

(*Webster's New World Dictionary* 1972: 371)

European women were essential to the colonial enterprise and the
solidification of racial boundaries in ways which repeatedly tied
their supportive and subordinate posture to community cohesion
and colonial security. These features of their positioning within
imperial politics were powerfully reinforced at the turn of the century by a metropolitan bourgeois discourse (and an eminently
anthropological one) intensely concerned with notions of 'degeneracy' (Le Bras 1981: 77).[24] Middle-class morality, manliness, and
motherhood were seen as endangered by the intimately linked fears
of 'degeneration' and miscegenation in scientifically construed
racist beliefs (Mosse 1978: 82).[25] Degeneration was defined as
'departures from the normal human type . . . transmitted through
inheritance and lead[ing] progressively to destruction' (Morel
quoted in Mosse 1978: 83). Due to environmental, physical, and
moral factors, degeneracy could be averted by positive eugenic
selection or, negatively, by eliminating the 'unfit' and/or the environmental and more specifically cultural contagions that gave rise
to them (Mosse 1978: 87; Kevles 1985: 70–84).

Eugenic discourse has usually been associated with Social
Darwinian notions of 'selection', with the strong influence of
Lamarckian thinking reserved for its French variant (Schneider
1982). However, the notion of 'cultural contamination' runs
throughout the British, US, French, and Dutch eugenic traditions
(Rodenwaldt 1928). Eugenic arguments used to explain the social
malaise of industrialization, immigration, and urbanization in the
early twentieth century derived from notions that acquired characteristics were inheritable and thus that poverty, vagrancy, and
promiscuity were class-linked biological traits, tied to genetic material as directly as night-blindness and blonde hair. As we shall see,
this Lamarckian feature of eugenic thinking was central to colonial
discourses that linked racial degeneracy to the sexual transmission of
cultural contagions and to the political instability of imperial rule.

Appealing to a broad political and scientific constituency at the
turn of the century, Euro-American eugenic societies included
advocates of infant welfare programmes, liberal intellectuals, con-

servative businessmen, Fabians, and physicians with social concerns. By the 1920s, however, it contained an increasingly vocal number of those who called for and put into law, if not practice, the sterilization of what were considered the mentally, morally, or physically unfit members of the British, German, and American underclass (Mosse 1978: 87; Stepan 1982: 122).[26] Feminist attempts to appropriate this rhetoric for their own birth-control programmes largely failed. Eugenics was essentially elitist, racist, and misogynist in principle and practice (Gordon 1976: 395; Davin 1978; Hammerton 1979). Its proponents advocated a pronatalist policy toward the white middle and upper classes, a rejection of work roles for women that might compete with motherhood, and 'an assumption that reproduction was not just a function but the purpose . . . of women's life' (Gordon 1974: 134). In France, England, Germany, and the United States, eugenics placed European women of 'good stock' as 'the fountainhead of racial strength' (Ridley 1981: 91), exhalting the cult of motherhood while subjecting it to the scrutiny of this new scientific domain (Davin 1978: 12).

As part of metropolitan class politics, eugenics reverberated in the colonies in predictable as well as unexpected forms. The moral biological, and sexual referents of the notion of degeneracy (distinct in the dictionary citation above), came together in the actual deployment of the concept. The 'colonial branch' of eugenics embraced a theory and practice concerned with the vulnerabilities of white rule and new measures to safeguard European superiority. Designed to control the procreation of the 'unfit' lower orders, eugenics targeted 'the poor, the colonized, or unpopular strangers' (Hobsbawm 1987: 253). The discourse, however, reached further. It permeated how metropolitan observers viewed the 'degenerate' life-style of colonials, and how colonial elites admonished the behaviour of 'degenerate' members among themselves (Koks 1931: 179–89). Whereas studies in Europe and the United States focused on the inherent propensity of the impoverished classes to criminality, in the Indies delinquency among 'European' children was biologically linked to the amount of 'native blood' children born of mixed marriages had inherited from their native mothers (Braconier 1918: 11). Eugenics provided not so much a new vocabulary as a new biological idiom in which to ground the medical and moral basis for anxiety over the security of European hegemony and white prestige. It reopened debates over segregated residence and education, new standards of morality, sexual vigilance, and the rights of *certain* Europeans to rule.

Eugenic influence manifested itself, not in the direct importation of metropolitan practices such as sterilization, but in a translation of the political *principles* and the social values that eugenics implied. In defining what was unacceptable, eugenics also identified what constituted a 'valuable life': 'a gender-specific work and productivity, described in social, medical and psychiatric terms' (Bock 1986: 274). Applied to European colonials, eugenic statements pronounced what kind of people should represent Dutch or French rule, how they should bring up their children, and with whom they should socialize. Those concerned with issues of racial survival and racial purity invoked moral arguments about the national duty of French, Dutch, British, and Belgian colonial women to fulfill an alternative set of imperial imperatives: to 'uplift' colonial subjects through educational and domestic management, to attend to the family environment of their colonial husbands, or sometimes to remain in the metropole and to stay at home. The point is that a common discourse was mapped onto different immediate exigencies of empire as variations on a gender-specific theme exalting motherhood and domesticity.

If in Britain racial deterioration was conceived to be a result of the moral turpitude and the ignorance of working-class mothers, in the colonies the dangers were more pervasive, the possibilities of contamination worse. Formulations to secure European rule pushed in two directions: on the one hand, away from ambiguous racial genres and open domestic arrangements, and on the other hand, toward an upgrading homogenization, and a clearer delineation of European standards; away from miscegenation toward white endogamy; away from concubinage toward family formation and legal marriage; away from, as in the case of the Indies, mestizo customs and toward metropolitan norms (Taylor 1983; Van Doorn 1985). As stated in the bulletin of the Netherlands Indies' Eugenic Society, 'eugenics is nothing other than belief in the possibility of preventing degenerative symptoms in the body of our beloved *moedervolken*, or in cases where they may already be present, of counteracting them' (Rodenwaldt 1928: 1).

Like the modernization of colonialism itself, with its scientific management and educated technocrats with limited local knowledge, colonial communities of the early twentieth century were rethinking the ways in which their authority should be expressed. This rethinking took the form of asserting a distinct colonial morality, explicit in its reorientation toward the racial and class markers of 'Europeanness', emphasizing transnational racial commonalities despite national differences—distilling a *homo europeaus* for whom superior health, wealth, and education were tied to racial endowments and a White Man's norm. Thus Pujarniscle, a novelist and participant-observer in France's colonial venture, wrote: 'one might be surprised that my pen always returns to the words *blanc* (white) or "European" and never to "Français" . . . in effect colonial solidarity and the obligations that it entails allies all the peoples of the white races' (1931: 72; also see Delavignette 1946: 41).

Such sensibilities coloured imperial policy in nearly all domains with fears of physical contamination, giving new credence to fears of political vulnerability. Whites had to guard their ranks—in qualitative and quantitative terms—to increase their numbers and to ensure that their members blurred neither the biological nor political boundaries on which their power rested.[27] In the metropole the socially and physically 'unfit', the poor, the indigent, and the insane, were either to be sterilized or prevented from marriage. In the colonies it was these very groups among Europeans who were either excluded from entry or institutionalized while they were there and eventually sent home (Arnold 1979; Vellut 1982: 97).

In sustaining a vision that good health, virility, and the ability to rule were inherent features of 'Europeanness', whites in the colonies had to adhere to a politics of exclusion that policed their members as well as the colonized. Such concerns were not new to the 1920s (Taylor 1983; Sutherland 1982). In the 1750s the Dutch East Indies Company had already taken 'draconian measures' to control pauperism among 'Dutchmen of mixed blood' (*Encylopedie van Nederland-Indie 1919*: 367). In the same period, the British East Indies Company legally and administratively dissuaded lower-class European migration and settlement, with the argument that it might destroy Indian respect for 'the superiority of the European character' (quoted in Arnold 1983: 139). Patriotic calls to populate Java in the mid-1800s with poor Dutch farmers were also condemned, but it was with new urgency that these proposals were rejected in the following century as successive challenges to European rule were more profoundly felt.

Measures were taken both to avoid poor white migration and to produce a colonial profile that highlighted the manliness, well-being, and productivity of European men. Within this equation, protection of manhood, national identity, and racial superiority were meshed (Loutfi 1971: 112–13; Ridley 1981: 104).[28] Thus British colonial administrators were retired by the age of fifty-five, ensuring that

no Oriental was ever allowed to see a Westerner as he ages and degenerated, just as no Westerner needed ever to see himself, mirrored in the eyes
of the subject race, as anything but a vigorous, rational, ever-alert young
Raj. (Said 1978: 42)

In the twentieth century, these 'men of class' and 'men of character'
embodied a modernized and renovated image of rule; they were to
safeguard the colonies against physical weakness, moral decay, and
the inevitable degeneration which long residence in the colonies
encouraged, and against the temptations that interracial domestic
situations had allowed.

Given this ideal, it is not surprising that colonial communities
strongly discouraged the presence of non-productive men. Colonial
administrators expressed a constant concern with the dangers of
unemployed or impoverished Europeans. During the succession of
economic crises in the early twentieth century, relief agencies in
Sumatra, for example, organized fundraisers, hill-station retreats,
and small-scale agricultural schemes to keep 'unfit' Europeans
'from roaming round' (*Kroniek 1917*: 49). The colonies were neither
open for retirement nor tolerant of the public presence of poor
whites. During the 1930s depression, when tens of thousands of
Europeans in the Indies found themselves without jobs, government and private resources were quickly mobilized to ensure that
they were not 'reduced' to native living standards (Cool 1938;
Veerde 1931; Kantoor van Arbeid 1935). Subsidized health care,
housing, and education complemented a rigorous affirmation of
European cultural standards in which European womanhood
played a central role in keeping men *civilisé*.

The Cultural Dynamics of Degeneration

The *colon* is, in a common and etymological sense, a barbar-
ian. He is a non-civilized person, a 'new-man', . . . it is he who
appears as a savage.

(Dupuy 1955: 188)

The shift in imperial thinking that we can identify in the early twentieth century focuses not only on the Otherness of the colonized but
on the Otherness of colonials themselves. In metropolitan France a
profusion of medical and sociological tracts pinpointed the colonial
as a distinct and degenerate social type, with specific psychological
and even physical characteristics (Maunier 1932; Pujarniscle
1931).[29] Some of that difference was attributed to the debilitating

results of climate and social milieu, from staying in the colonies too long:

The climate affects him, his surroundings affect him, and after a certain time, he has become, both physically and morally, a completely different man. (Maunier 1932: 169)

People who stayed 'too long' were in grave danger of overfatigue; of individual and racial degeneration (Le Roux 1898: 222); of physical breakdown (not just illness); of cultural contamination and neglect of the conventions of supremacy, and of *disagreement* about what those conventions were (Dupuy 1955: 184–5). What were identified as the degraded and unique characteristics of European colonials—'ostentation', 'speculation', 'inaction', and a general 'demoralization'—were 'faults' contracted from native culture, which now marked them as *décivilisé* (Maunier 1932: 174; Jaurequiberry 1924: 25).[30]

Colonial medicine reflected and affirmed this slippage between physical, moral, and cultural degeneracy in numerous ways. The climatic, social, and work conditions of colonial life gave rise to a specific set of psychotic disorders affecting *l'equilibre cerebral* and predisposing Europeans in the tropics to mental breakdown (Hartenberg 1910; Abatucci 1910). Neurasthenia was the most common manifestation, a mental disorder identified as a major problem in the French empire and accounting for more than half the Dutch repatriations from the Indies to Holland (Winckel 1938: 352). In Europe and America, it was 'the phantom disease . . . the classic illness of the late 19th century', encompassing virtually all 'psychopathological or neuropathological conditions', and 'intimately linked to sexual deviation and to the destruction of social order itself' (Gilman 1985: 199, 202).

Whereas in Europe neurasthenia was considered to be a consequence of 'modern civilization' and its high-pitched pace (Showalter 1987: 135), in the colonies its etiology took the *reverse* form. Colonial neurasthenia was allegedly caused by a *distance* from civilization and European community, and by proximity to the colonized. The susceptibility of a colonial (man) was increased by an existence 'outside of the social framework to which he was adapted in France, isolation in outposts, physical and moral fatigue, and modified food regimes' (Joyeux 1937: 335).[31]

The proliferation of hill-stations in the twentieth century reflected these political and physical concerns. Invented in the early nineteenth century as sites for military posts and sanatoria, hill-stations provided European-like environments in which colonials could recoup their physical and mental well-being by simulating the conditions 'at home' (Spencer and Thomas 1948; King 1976: 165). Isolated at relatively high altitudes, they took on new importance with the colonial presence of increasing numbers of European women and children who were considered particularly susceptible to anaemia, depression, and ill-health.[32] Vacation bungalows and schools built in these 'naturally' segregated surroundings provided cultural refuge and regeneration (Price 1939).

Some doctors considered the only treatment to be *le retour en Europe* (Joyeux 1937: 335; Pujarniscle 1931: 28). Others prescribed a local set of remedies, advising adherence to a bourgeois ethic of morality and work. This included sexual moderation, a 'regularity and regimentation' of work, abstemious diet, physical exercise, and *European* camaraderie, buttressed by a solid (and stolid) family life with European children and a European wife (Grall 1908: 51; Price 1939; also see Kennedy 1987: 123). Guides to colonial living in the 1920s and 1930s reveal this marked shift in outlook; Dutch, French, and British doctors now denounced the unhealthy, indolent life-styles of 'old colonials', extolling the energetic and engaged activities of the new breed of colonial husband and wife (Raptchinsky 1941: 46).[33] As women were considered most prone to neurasthenia, anaemia, and depression, they were exhorted to actively participate in household management and child-care, and divert themselves with botanical collections and 'good works' (Chivas-Baron 1929; Favre 1938).

Children on the Colonial Divide: Degeneracy and the Dangers of Métissage

> [Young colonial men] are often driven to seek a temporary companion among the women of colour; this is the path by which, as I shall presently show, contagion travels back and forth, contagion in all senses of the word.
>
> (Maunier 1932: 171)

Racial degeneracy was thought to have social causes and political consequences, both tied to the domestic arrangements of colonialism in specific ways. *Métissage* (interracial unions) generally, and concubinage in particular, represented the paramount danger to racial purity and cultural identity in all its forms. Through sexual contact with women of colour European men 'contracted' not only disease but debased sentiments, immoral proclivities, and extreme susceptibility to decivilized states (Dupuy 1956: 198).

By the early twentieth century, concubinage was denounced for undermining precisely those things that it was charged with fortify-ing decades earlier. The weight of competing discourses on local women shifted emphasis. Although their inherently dangerous, passionate, and evil characters previously had been overshadowed by their role as protectrices of European men's health, in the new equation they became the primary bearers of ill health and sinister influences. Adaptation to local food, language, and dress, once pre-scribed as healthy signs of acclimatization, were now the sources of contagion and loss of (white) self. The benefits of local knowledge and sexual release gave way to the more pressing demands of respectability, the community's solidarity, and its mental health. Increasingly, French men in Indo-China who kept native women were viewed as passing into 'the enemy camp' (Pujarniscle 1931: 107). Concubinage became the source not only of individual break-down and ill-health, but of the biological and social root of racial degeneration and political unrest. Children born of these unions were 'the fruits of a regrettable weakness' (Mazet 1932: 8), physi-cally marked and morally marred with 'the defaults and mediocre qualities of their mothers' (Douchet 1928: 10).

Concubinage was not as economically tidy and politically neat as colonial policy-makers had hoped. It was about more than sexual exploitation and unpaid domestic work; it was about children—many more than official statistics often revealed—and about who was to be acknowledged as a European and who was not. Concu-bine children posed a classificatory problem, impinging on politi-cal security and white prestige. The majority of such children were not recognized by their fathers, nor were they reabsorbed into local communities as authorities often claimed. Although some Euro-pean men legally acknowledged their progeny, many repatriated to Holland, Britain, or France and cut off ties and support to mother and children (Nieuwenhuys 1959: 23; Brou 1907; Ming 1983: 75). Native women had responsibility for, but attenuated rights over, their own offspring.[34] Although the legal system favoured a European upbringing, it made no demands on European men to provide it. The more socially asymmetric and perfunctory the rela-tionship between man and woman, the more likely the children were to end up as wards of the state, subject to the scrutiny and imposed charity of the European-born community at large.

Concubine children invariably counted among the ranks of the European colonial poor, but European paupers in the late nineteenth-century Netherlands Indies came from wider strata of colonial society than that of concubines alone (Het Pauperisme

Commissie 1903). Many Indo-Europeans including creole children born in the Indies of European parents, had become increasingly marginalized from strategic political and economic positions in the early twentieth century despite the fact that new educational facilities were supposed to have provided new opportunities for them. At the turn of the century, volumes of official reports were devoted to documenting and alleviating the proliferation on Java of a 'rough' and 'dangerous pauper element' among (Indo-)European clerks, low-level officials, and vagrants (*Encyclopedie van Nederland-Indie 1919*: 367). In the 1920s and 1930s Indies-born and educated youth were uncomfortably squeezed between an influx of new colonial recruits from Holland and the educated *inlander* (native) population with whom they were in direct competition for jobs (Mansvelt 1932: 295).[35]

European pauperism in the Indies reflected broad inequalities in colonial society, underscoring the social heterogeneity of the category 'European' itself. None the less, concubinage was still seen as its major cause and as the principal source of *blanken-haters* (white-haters) (Braconier 1917: 298). Concubinage became equated with a progeny of 'malcontents', of 'parasitic' whites, idle and therefore dangerous. The fear of concubinage was carried yet a step further and tied to the political fear that such Eurasians would demand economic access, political rights, and express their own interests through alliance with (and leadership of) organized opposition to Dutch rule (Mansvelt 1932; Blumberger 1939).

Racial prejudice against *métis* was often, as in the Belgian congo, 'camouflaged under protestations of "pity" for their fate, as if they were "*malheureux*" [unhappy] beings by definition' (Vellut 1982: 103). The protection of *métis* children in Indo-China was a *cause célèbre* of European women at home and abroad. The French assembly on feminism, organized for the colonial exposition of 1931, devoted a major part of its proceedings to the plight of *métis* children and their native mothers, echoing the campaigns for *la recherche de paternité* by French feminists a half-century earlier (Moses 1984: 208). The assembly called for 'the establishment of centres [in the colonies] where abandoned young girls or those in moral danger could be made into worthy women' (Knibiehler and Goutalier 1987: 37). European colonial women were urged to oversee the 'moral protection' of *métis* youths, to develop their 'natural' inclination toward French society, to turn them into 'collaborators and partisans of French ideas and influences' instead of revolutionaries (Chenet 1936: 8; Knibiehler and Goutalier 1987: 35; Sambuc 1931: 261). The gender breakdown was clear: moral instruction would avert sexual promiscuity among *métisse* girls and political precocity among *métis* boys who might otherwise become militant men.

Orphanages for abandoned European and Indo-European children were a prominent feature of Dutch, French, and British colonial cultures. In the Netherlands Indies by the mid-eighteenth century, state orphanages for Europeans were established to prevent 'neglect and degeneracy of the many free-roaming poor bastards and orphans of Europeans' (quoted in Braconier 1917: 293). By the nineteenth century, church, state, and private organizations had become zealous backers of orphanages, providing some education and strong doses of moral instruction. In India the military orphanages of the late eighteenth century expanded into a nineteenth-century variant in which European and Anglo-Indian children were cared for in civil asylums and charity schools in 'almost every town, cantonment and hill-station' (Arnold 1979: 108). In French Indo-China in the 1930s virtually every colonial city had a home and society for the protection of abandoned *métis* youth (Chenet 1936; Sambuc 1931: 256–72; Malleret 1934: 220).[36]

Whether these children were in fact 'abandoned' by their Asian mothers is difficult to establish; the fact that *métis* children living in native homes were sometimes *sought out* by state and private organizations and placed in these institutions suggests another interpretation (Taylor 1983). Public assistance in India, Indo-China, and the Netherlands Indies was designed not only to keep fair-skinned children from running barefoot in native villages but to ensure that the proliferation of European pauper settlements was curtailed and controlled.[37] The need for specific kinds of religious and secular education and socialization of children was symptomatic of a more general fear; namely, that these children would grow into *Hollander-haters*, patricides, and anti-colonial revolutionaries; that as adult women they would fall into prostitution; that as adult men with lasting ties to native women and indigenous society they would become enemies of the state, *verbasterd* (degenerate) and *décivilisé* (Braconier 1917: 293; Angoulvant 1926: 102; Pouvourville 1926; Sambuc 1931: 261; Malleret 1934).

European Women, Race and Middle-Class Morality

A man remains a man as long as he stays under the watch of a woman of his race.

(George Hardy quoted in Chivas-Baron 1929: 103)

Rationalizations of imperial rule and safeguards against racial degeneracy in European colonies merged in the emphasis on particular moral themes. Both entailed a reassertion of European conventions, middle-class respectability, more frequent ties with the metropole, and a restatement of what was culturally distinct and superior about how colonials ruled and lived. For those women who came to join their spouses or to find husbands, the prescriptions were clear. Just as new plantation employees were taught to manage the natives, women were schooled in colonial propriety and domestic management. French manuals, such as those on colonial hygiene in Indo-China, outlined the duties of colonial wives in no uncertain terms. As 'auxiliary forces' in the imperial effort they were to 'conserve the fitness and sometimes the life of all around them' by ensuring that 'the home be happy and gay and that all take pleasure in clustering there' (Grall 1908: 66; Chailley-Bert 1897). The *Koloniale School voor Meisjes en Vrouwen*, established in The Hague in 1920, provided adolescent and adult women with ethnographic lectures and short child-bearing courses to prepare them for their new lives in the Indies. Practical guides to life in the Belgian Congo instructed (and indeed warned) *la femme blanche* that she was to keep 'order, peace, hygiene and economy' (Favre 1938: 217), 'perpetuate a vigorous race', while preventing any 'laxity in our administrative mores' (ibid. 256; Travaux du Groupe d'Etudes coloniales 1910: 10).

This 'division of labour' contained obvious asymmetries. Men were considered more susceptible to moral turpitude than women, who were thus held responsible for the immoral states of men. European women were to safeguard prestige, morality, and insulate their men from the cultural and sexual contamination of contact with the colonized (Travaux . . . Coloniales 1910: 7). Racial degeneracy would be curtailed by European women charged with regenerating the physical health, the metropolitan affinities, and the imperial purpose of their men (Hardy 1929: 78).

At its heart was a reassertion of racial difference that harnessed nationalist rhetoric and markers of middle-class morality to its cause (Delavignette 1946: 47; Loutfi 1971: 112; Ridley 1981; Mosse 1978: 86). George Mosse has characterized European racism as a 'scavenger ideology', annexing nationalism and bourgeois respectability in such a way that control over sexuality was central to all three (1985: 10, 133–52). If the European middle-class sought respectability 'to maintain their status and self-respect against the lower-classes, and the aristocracy', in the colonies respectability was a defence against the colonized, and a way of more clearly defining themselves (ibid. 5). Good colonial living now meant hard work, no sloth, and physical exercise rather than sexual release, which had been one rationale for condoning concubinage and prostitution in an earlier period. The debilitating influences of climate could be surmounted by regular diet and meticulous personal hygiene over which European women were to take full charge. British, French, and Dutch manuals on how to run a European household in the tropics provided detailed instructions in domestic science, moral upbringing, and employer–servant relations. Adherence to strict conventions of cleanliness and cooking occupied an inordinate amount of women's time, while cleanliness itself served as a 'prop to a Europeanness that was less than assumed' (Riddle 1981: 77). Both activities entailed a constant surveillance of native nursemaids, laundrymen, and live-in servants, while demanding a heightened domesticity for European women themselves.

Leisure, good spirit, and creature comforts became the obligation of women to provide, the racial duty of women to maintain. Sexual temptations with women of colour would be curtailed by a happy, *gezellig* (cozy) family life, much as 'extremist agitation' among Javanese plantation workers was to be averted by selecting married recruits and providing family housing so that men would feel *senang* (happy/content) and 'at home' (Stoler 1985a: 42–4). Moral laxity would be eliminated through the example and vigilance of women whose status was defined by their sexual restraint and dedication to their homes and their men.

Imperial Priorities: Motherhood vs. Male Morality

> The European woman [in Indo-China] can only fulfill her duties to bear and breast-feed her children with great hardship and damage to her health.
>
> (Grall 1908: 65)

The perceptions and practice that bound women's domesticity to national welfare and racial purity were not confined to colonial women alone. Child-rearing in late nineteenth-century Britain was hailed as a national, imperial, and racial duty, as it was in France, Holland, the United States, and Germany at the same time (Davin 1978: 13; Smith-Rosenberg 1973: 351; Bock 1984: 274; Stuurman 1985). In France, where declining birth rates were of grave concern, fecundity itself had become 'no longer something resting with

245

couples' but with 'the nation, the state, the race . . .' (LeBras 1981: 90). Popular colonial authors such as Pierre Mille pushed the production of children as women's 'essential contribution to the imperial mission of France' (Ridley 1981: 90). With motherhood at the centre of empire-building, pronatalist policies in Europe forced some improvement in colonial medical facilities, the addition of maternity wards, and increased information and control over the reproductive conditions of both European and colonized women. Maternal and infant-health programmes instructed European women bound for the tropics in the use of milk substitutes, wet nurses, and breast-feeding practices in an effort to encourage more women to stay in the colonies and in response to the many more that came (Hunt 1988). But the belief that the colonies were medically hazardous for white women meant that motherhood in the tropics was not only a precarious but a conflicted endeavour.

Real and imagined concern over individual reproduction and racial survival contained and compromised white colonial women in a number of ways. Tropical climates were said to cause low fertility, prolonged amenorrhea, and permanent sterility (Rodenwaldt 1928: 3).[38] Belgian doctors confirmed that 'the woman who goes to live in a tropical climate is often lost for the reproduction of the race' (Knibiehler and Goutalier 1985: 92; Vellut 1982: 100). The climatic and medical conditions of colonial life were associated with high infant mortality, such that 'the life of a European child was nearly condemned in advance' (Grall 1908: 65). A long list of colonial illnesses ranging from neurasthenia to anaemia supposedly hit women and children hardest (Price 1939: 204).

These perceived medical perils called into question whether European-born women and thus the 'white race' could actually reproduce if they remained in the tropics for an extended period of time. An international colonial medical community cross-referenced one another in citing evidence of racial sterility by the second or third generation (Harwood 1938: 132; Ripley quoted in Stocking 1968: 54; Cranworth quoted in Kennedy 1987: 115). Although such a dark view of climate was not prevalent in the Indies, psychological and physical adaptation were never givens. Dutch doctors repeatedly quoted German physicians, not to affirm the inevitable infertility among whites in the tropics, but to support their contention that European-born women and men (totoks) should never stay in the colonies too long (Hermans 1925: 123). French observers could flatly state that unions among creole Dutch in the Indies were sterile after two generations (Angoulvant 1926: 101). Medical studies in the 1930s, such as that supported by the Netherlands Indies Eugenic Society, were designed to test whether fertility rates differed by 'racial type' between Indo-European and European-born women and whether 'children of certain Europeans born in the Indies displayed different racial markers than their parents' (Rodenwaldt 1928: 4).

Like the discourse on degeneracy, the fear of sterility was less about the biological survival of whites than about their political viability and cultural reproduction. These concerns were evident in the early 1900s, coming to a crescendo in the 1930s when white unemployment hit the colonies and the metropole at the same time. The depression made repatriation of impoverished Dutch and French colonial agents unrealistic, prompting speculation as to whether European working-classes could be relocated in the tropics without causing further racial degeneration (Winckel 1938; Price 1939).[39] Although white migration to the tropics was reconsidered, poor-white settlements were rejected on economic, medical and psychological grounds. Whatever the solution, such issues hinged on the reproductive potential of European women, invasive questionnaires concerning their 'acclimatization', and detailed descriptions of their conjugal histories and sexual lives.

Imperial perceptions and policies fixed European women in the colonies as 'instruments of race-culture' in what proved to be personally difficult and contradictory ways (Hammerton 1979). Child-rearing decisions faithfully followed the sorts of racist principles that constrained the activities of women charged with child-care (Grimshaw 1983: 507). Medical experts and women's organizations recommended strict surveillance of children's activities (Mackinnon 1920: 944) and careful attention to those with whom they played. Virtually every medical and household handbook in the Dutch, French, and British colonies warned against leaving small children in the unsupervised care of local servants. In the Netherlands Indies, it was the 'duty' of the *hedendaagsche blanke moeder* (the modern white mother) to take the physical and spiritual upbringing of her offspring away from the *babu* (native nursemaid) and into her own hands (Wanderken 1943: 173).

Precautions had to be taken against 'sexual danger', uncleanly habits of domestics, against a 'stupid negress' who might leave a child exposed to the sun (Bauduin 1941; Bérenger-Féraud 1875: 491). Even in colonies where the climate was not considered unhealthy, European children supposedly thrived well 'only up to the age of six' (Price 1939: 204) when native cultural influences came into stronger play. Thus in late nineteenth-century Hawaii, for example, native nursemaids commonly looked after American children until the age of five at which point 'prattlers' were confined to their mothers' supervision, prevented from learning the local language, and kept in a 'walled yard adjacent to the bedrooms . . . forbidden to Hawaiians' (Grimshaw 1983: 507).

In the Netherlands Indies, where educational facilities for European children were considered excellent, it was still deemed imperative to send them back to Holland to avoid the 'precocity' associated with the tropics and the 'danger' of contact with *Indische* youths not from 'full-blooded European elements' (Bauduin 1941: 63).

We Dutch in the Indies live in a country which is not our own. . . . We feel instinctively that our blonde, white children belong to the blonde, white dunes, the forests, the moors, the lakes, the snow. . . . A Dutch child should grow up in Holland. There they will acquire the characteristics of their race, not only from mother's milk but also from the influence of the light, sun and water, of playmates, of life, in a word, in the sphere of the fatherland. This is not racism. (Bauduin 1941: 63–4)

Such patriotic images culturally coded racial distinctions in powerful ways. Dutch identity was represented as a common (if contested) cultural sensibility in which class convention, geography, climate, sexual proclivity, and social contact played central roles.

In many colonial communities, school-age children were packed off to Europe for education and socialization, but this was rarely an unproblematic option. When children could not be left with family in the metropole, it meant leaving them for extended periods of time in boarding-schools or, when they attended day-schools, in boarding-houses catering to Indies youths. Married European women were confronted with a difficult set of choices that entailed separation either from their children or husbands (Angoulvant 1926: 101). Frequent trips between colony and metropole not only separated families but also broke up marriages and homes (Malleret 1934: 164; Grimshaw 1983: 507; Callaway 1987: 183–4).

Not surprisingly, how and where European children should be provided with a proper cultural literacy was a major theme addressed in women's organizations and magazines in the Indies and elsewhere right through de-colonization. The rise of specific programmes in home education (such as the *Clerkx-methode voor Huisonderwijs*) may have been a response to this new push for women to accommodate their multiple imperial duties; to oversee their husbands and servants while remaining in control of the cultural and moral upbringing of their children. The important point is that such conflicting responsibilities profoundly affected the social space European women (not only wives) occupied, the tasks or which they were valorized, and the economic activities in which they could feasibly engage.

The Strategies of Rule and Sexual Morality

The political etymology of colonizer and colonized was gender- and class-specific. The exclusionary politics of colonialism demarcated not just external boundaries but interior frontiers, specifying internal conformity and order among Europeans themselves. I have tried to show that the categories of colonizer and colonized were secured through notions of racial difference constructed in gender terms. Redefinitions of acceptable sexual behaviour and morality emerged during crises of colonial control precisely because they called into question the tenuous artifices of rule *within* European communities and what marked their borders. Even from the limited cases we have reviewed, several patterns emerge. First and most obviously, colonial sexual prohibitions were racially asymmetric and gender-specific. Sexual relations might be forbidden between white women and men of colour but not the other way around. On the contrary, interracial unions (as opposed to marriage) between European men and colonized women aided the long-term settlement of European men in the colonies while ensuring that colonial patrimony stayed in limited and selective hands. Second, interdictions against interracial unions were rarely a primary impulse in the strategies of rule. In India, Indo-China, and South Africa in the early centuries—colonial contexts usually associated with sharp social sanctions against interracial unions—'mixing' has been systematically tolerated and even condoned.

I have focused on late colonialism in Asia, but colonial elite intervention in the sexual life of their agents and subjects was by no means confined to this place or period. In sixteenth-century Mexico mixed marriages between Spanish men and Christianized Indian women were encouraged by the crown until mid-century, when colonists felt that 'the rising numbers of their own mestizo progeny threatened the prerogatives of a narrowing elite sector' (Nash 1980: 141). In eighteenth- and early nineteenth-century Cuba mild opposition to interracial marriage gave way to a 'virtual prohibition' from 1864 to 1874 when 'merchants, slave dealers and the colonial powers opposed [it] in order to preserve slavery' (Martinez-Alier 1974: 39).

Changes in sexual access and domestic arrangements have invariably accompanied major efforts to reassert the internal coherence of European communities and to redefine the boundaries of privilege between the colonizer and the colonized. Sexual union in itself, however, did not automatically produce a larger population legally classified as 'European'. On the contrary, even in early twentieth-century Brazil where miscegenation had made for a refined system of gradations, 'most mixing . . . [took] place outside of marriage' (Degler 1971: 185). The important point is that miscegenation signalled neither the presence nor absence of racial discrimination; hierarchies of privilege and power were written into the *condoning* of interracial unions, as well as into their condemnation.

Although the chronologies vary from one colonial context to another, we can identify some parallel shifts in the strategies of rule and in sexual morality. Concubinage fell into moral disfavour at the same time that new emphasis was placed on the standardization of European administration. Although this occurred in some colonies by the early twentieth century and in others later on, the correspondence between rationalized rule, bourgeois respectability, and the custodial power of European women to protect their men seems strongest during the interwar years. Western scientific and technological achievements were then in question (Adas 1989); British, French, and Dutch policy-makers had moved from an assimilationist to a more segregationist, separatist colonial stance. The reorganization of colonial investments along corporate and multinational lines brought with it a push for a restructured and more highly productive labour-force; and with it more strident nationalist and labour movements resisting those demands.

An increasing rationalization of colonial management produced radical shifts in notions of how empires should be run, how agents of empire should rule, and where, how, and with whom they should live. Thus French debates concerning the need to systematize colonial management and dissolve the provincial and personalized satraps of 'the old-time colon' invariably targeted and condemned the unseemly domestic arrangements in which they lived. British high officials in Africa imposed new 'character' requirements on their subordinates, designating specific class attributes and conjugal ties that such a selection implied (Kuklick 1979). Critical to this restructuring was a new disdain for colonials *too* adapted to local custom, too removed from the local European community, and too encumbered with intimate native ties. As we have seen in Sumatra, this hands-off policy distanced Europeans in more than one sense:

it forbade European staff both from personal confrontations with their Asian fieldhands and from the limited local knowledge they gained through sexual ties.

At the same time medical expertise confirmed the salubrious benefits of European camaraderie and frequent home leaves; of a *cordon sanitaire*, not only around European enclaves, but around each European man and his home. White prestige became redefined by the conventions that would safeguard the moral respectability, cultural identity, and physical well-being of its agents, with which European women were charged. Colonial politics locked European men and women into a routinized protection of their physical health and social space in ways that bound gender prescriptions to the racial cleavages between 'us' and 'them'.

It may be, however, that we should not be searching for congruent colonial chronologies (attached to specific dates) but rather for similar shifts in the *rhythms* of rule and sexual management, for similar internal patterns within specific colonial histories themselves.[40] For example, we know that the Great Rebellion in India in 1857 set off an entire restructuring of colonial morality in which political subversion was tied to sexual impropriety and was met with calls for middle-class respectability, domesticity, and increased segregation—all focusing on European women—nearly a half-century earlier than in colonies elsewhere. Looking to a somewhat longer *durée* than the colonial crises of the early twentieth century, we might consider British responses to the Mutiny not as an exception but as a template, thereby emphasizing the modular quality of colonial perceptions and policies that were built on new international standards of empire, specific metropolitan priorities, and that were always responsive to the local challenges of those who contested European rule.

I have focused here on the multiple levels at which sexual control figured in the substance, as well as the iconography, of racial policy and imperial rule. But colonial politics was not just about sex; nor did sexual relations reduce to colonial politics. On the contrary, sex in the colonies was about sexual access and reproduction, class distinctions and racial demarcations, nationalism and European identity—in different measure and not all at the same time. These major shifts in the positioning of women were not, as we might expect, signalled by the penetration of capitalism *per se* but by more subtle changes in class politics, imperial morality, and as responses to the vulnerabilities of colonial control. As we attempt broader ethnographies of empire, we may begin to capture how European culture and class politics resonated in colonial settings, how class and gender discriminations were transposed into racial distinctions and reverberated in the metropole as they were fortified on colonial ground. Such investigations should help show that sexual control was both an instrumental image for the body politic, a salient part standing for the whole, and itself fundamental to how racial policies were secured and how colonial projects were carried out.

Notes

1. See, for example, Etienne and Leacock (1980), Hafkin and Bay (1976), Robertson and Klein (1983), and Silverblatt (1987). For a review of some this literature in an African context see Bozzoli (1983), Robertson (1987), and White (1988).

2. This is not to suggest that there were not some women whose sojourns in the colonies allowed them to pursue career possibilities and independent lifestyles barred to them in metropolitan Europe at the time. However, the experience of professional women in South Asia and Africa highlights how quickly they were shaped into 'cultural missionaries' or, in resisting that impulse, were strongly marginalized in their work and social life (see Callaway 1987: 83–164; Ramuschack, n.d.).

3. In subsequent work, I focus explicitly on the contrasts and commonalities in how European women and men represented and experienced the social, psychological, and sexual tensions of colonial life.

4. See Verena Martinez-Alier's *Marriage, Class and Colour in Nineteenth-Century Cuba* (1974), which subtly analyses the changing criteria by which colour was perceived and assigned. For the Netherlands Indies, see Jean Taylor's (1983) exquisite study of the historical changes in the cultural markers of European membership from the seventeenth through the early twentieth centuries. Also see Van Marle's (1952) detailed description of racial classification, conjugal patterns, and sexual relations for the colonial Indies.

5. See Winthrop Jordan (1968: 32–40) on Elizabethan attitudes toward black African sexuality and Sander Gilman's analysis of the sexual iconography of Hottentot women in European art of the eighteenth and nineteenth centuries (1985: 76–108). On colonial sexual imagery see Malleret (1934: 216–41), Tiffany and Adams (1985), and the bibliographic references therein. 'The Romance of the Wild Woman', according to Tiffany and Adams, expressed critical distinctions drawn between civilization and the primitive, culture and nature, and the class differences between repressed middle-class women and 'her regressively primitive antithesis, the working-class girl' (1985: 13).

6. Thus in Dutch and French colonial novels of the nineteenth century, for example, heightened sensuality is the recognized reserve of Asian and Indo-European mistresses, and only of those European women born in the colonies and loosened by its moral environment (Daum 1984; Loutfi 1971).

7. The relationship between sexual control, racial violence, and political power has been most directly addressed by students of American Southern social history: see Jordan (1968), Lerner (1972), Dowd Hall (1984), and the analyses by turn-of-the-century Afro-American women intellectuals discussed in Carby

(1985). See Painter who argues that the treatment of rape as a symbol of male power was an interpretation held by both white and black male authors (1988: 59).

8. Fear of trade competition from European women is alluded to frequently in historical work on eighteenth-century colonies. In the French trading centres (factories) of the Middle East, for example, the Marseille Chamber of Commerce went to great lengths to ensure that no marriages would take place in their trading domain, fearing that European women and children would pose a threat to the French monopoly. In 1728 any French national married in a factory was prohibited from trading directly or indirectly with the royal government (Cordurie 1984: 42).

9. This exclusion of European-born women was also the case for much of the Portuguese empire from the sixteenth through eighteenth centuries (Boxer 1969: 129–30).

10. The references that Hyam (1986a) cites for homoerotic tendencies in British political biography are not, to my knowledge, paralleled for Dutch colonial officials in the Indies. Although the dangers of homosexuality are frequently invoked to justify prostitution among Chinese plantation workers and concubinage among common European soldiers, such arguments were rarely applied to higher-ranking European staff (Van den Brand 1904; Middendorp 1924: 51; Ming 1983: 69, 83).

11. The danger of sexual abstinence for young men was often invoked to licence both concubinage and government-regulated prostitution at different times (Hesselink 1987: 208–9).

12. As Tessel Pollman suggests, the term *njai* glossed several functions: household manager, servant, housewife, wife, and prostitute (1986: 100). Which of these was most prominent depended on a complex equation that included the character of both partners, the prosperity of the European man, and the local conventions of the colonial community in which they lived.

13. Some women were able to use their positions to enhance their own economic and political standing. In Indo-China and in the Indies a frequent complaint made by members of the European community was that local women provided employment to their own kin. There is far more evidence, however, that concubines exercised very few rights; they could be dismissed without reason or notice, were exchanged among European employers and, most significantly, as stipulated in the Indies Civil Code of 1848, 'had no rights over children recognized by a white man' (Taylor 1983: 148).

14. Although prostitution served some of the colonies for some of the time, it was medically and socially problematic. It had little appeal for those administrations bent on promoting permanent settlement (Kohlbrugge 1901, Ballhatchet 1980; Ming 1983) and venereal disease was difficult to check even with the elaborate system of lock hospitals and contagious-disease acts developed in parts of the British Empire. When concubinage was condemned in the 1920s in India, Malaysia, and Indonesia venereal disease spread rapidly, giving rise to new efforts to reorder the domestic arrangements of European men (Butcher 1979; Ming 1983; Taylor 1977; Ballhatchet 1980).

15. In the mid-nineteenth century these arrangements are described as a 'necessary evil' with no emotional attachments to native women, for whom 'the meaning of our word "love" is entirely unknown' (Ritter 1856: 21). This portrayal of concubinage as a loveless practical union contrasted sharply with the

image of the *nyai* in Chinese literature in the Indies. Bocquet-Siak argues that it was precisely the possibility of romantic love that made concubinage with Javanese or Sundanese women so attractive to Chinese men (1984: 8–9). Cf. Genovese's discussion of the categorical denial that love could enter into relations between slaveholder and slave in the American South: 'the tragedy of miscegenation lay not in its collapse into lust and sexual exploitation, but in the terrible pressure to deny the delight, affection, and love that so often grew from tawdry beginnings' (1976: 419).

16. In the case of the Indies, interracial marriages increased at the same time that concubinage fell into sharp decline (Van Marle 1952). This rise was undoubtedly restricted to *Indisch* Europeans (those born in the Indies) who may have been eager to legalize pre-existing unions in response to the moral shifts accompanying a more European cultural climate of the 1920s (Van Doorn 1985). It undoubtedly should not be taken as an indication of less closure among the highly endogamous European-born (*totok*) population of that period (I owe this distinction in conjugal patterns to Wim Hendrik).

17. In British Africa 'junior officers were not encouraged to marry, and wives' passages to Africa were not paid' (Gann and Duignan 1978: 240).

18. Degler makes a similar point, contrasting the shortage of European women in the Portuguese colonies to the family emigration policy of the British in North America; he argues that the former gave rise to widespread miscegenation and a vast population of mulattos, the 'key' to contrasting race relations in the United States and Brazil (1986: 226–38).

19. Similarly, one might draw the conventional contrast between the different racial policies in French, British, and Dutch colonies. However, despite French assimilationist rhetoric, Dutch tolerance of intermarriage, and Britain's overtly segregationist stance, the similarities in the actual maintenance of racial distinctions through sexual control in these varied contexts are perhaps more striking than the differences. For the moment, it is these similarities with which I am concerned. See, for example, Simon (1981: 46–8) who argues that although French colonial rule was generally thought to be more racially tolerant than that of Britain, racial distinctions in French Indo-China were *in practice* vigorously maintained. John Laffey also has argued that the cultural relativistic thinking tied to associationist rhetoric was used by Indo-China's French *colon* to uphold inequalities in law and education (1977: 65–81).

20. Degler also attributes the tenor of race relations to the attitudes of European women who, he argues, were not inherently more racist but able to exert more influence over the extramarital affairs of their men. Contrasting race relations in Brazil and the United States, he contends that British women in the English settlements had more social power than their Portuguese counterparts, and therefore slaveholding men could and did less readily acknowledge their mulatto offspring (1986 (1971): 238).

21. Archive D'Outre Mer, GG9903, 1893–1894; GG7663 'Emigration des femmes aux colonies 1897–1904'.

22. See the Archive d'Outre Mer, Series S.65, 'Free Passage Accorded to Europeans', including dossiers on 'free passage for impoverished Europeans', GG9925, 1897; GG2269, 1899–1903.

23. European prostitutes and domestics-turned-prostitutes were not banned from South Africa, where at the turn of the century there were estimated to be more than 1000. Van Onselen argues that their presence was secured by the

presence of a large, white, working-class population and a highly unstable labour market for white working-class women (1982: 103–62). Also see Van Heyningen who traces the history of prostitution among continental women in the Cape Colony, arguing that its prohibition was led by white middle-class women 'secure . . . in their respectability' and only came about with new notions of racial purity and the large-scale urbanization of blacks after the turn of the century (1984: 192–5).

24. On the intimate relationship between eugenics and anthropology see William Schneider on France (1982), H. Biervliet *et al.* on the Netherlands (1980), and Paul Rich on Britain (1984).

25. As George Mosse notes, the concept of racial degeneration had been tied to miscegenation by Gobineau and others by the mid-nineteenth century but gained common currency in the decades that followed, entering European medical and popular vocabulary at the turn of the century (1978: 82–8).

26. British eugenists petitioned to refuse marriage licences to the mentally ill, vagrants, and the chronically unemployed (Davin 1978: 16; Stepan 1982: 123). In the United States a model eugenic sterilization law from 1922 targeted among others 'the delinquent, the blind, orphans, homeless and paupers' (Bajema 1976: 138). In Germany during the same period 'sterilization was widely and passionately recommended as a solution to shiftlessness, ignorance, laziness in the work-force, . . . prostitution . . . illegitimate birth, the increasing number of ill and insane, . . . poverty; and the rising costs of social services' (Bock 1984: 27). However, in pro-natalist France, the sterilization of social deviants was never widely embraced (Leonard 1985).

27. The articles published in the bulletin of the Netherlands Indies Eugenics Society give some sense of the range of themes included in these concerns: these included discussions of 'bio-genealogical' investigations, the complementarity between Christian thought and eugenic principles, ethnographic studies of mestizo populations, and the role of Indo-Europeans in the anti-Dutch rebellions (see *Ons Nageslacht* from the years 1928–32).

28. See Mosse (1985) for an examination of the relationship between manliness, racism, and nationalism in a European context.

29. The linkage made between physical appearance and moral depravity was not confined to evaluations of European colonials alone. Eugenic studies abounded with speculations on the constellation of physical traits that signalled immorality in the European lower orders, while detailed descriptions of African and Asian indigenous populations paired their physical attributes with immoral and debased tendencies. See, for example, Simon (1977: 29–54) on French descriptions of physical features among Annamites in colonial Indo-China.

30. Historical analyses of earlier colonial ventures followed the same explanatory convention. Thus a 1939 publication of the American Geographical Society used the Portuguese colonies to 'illustrate the factors that defeated the whites in the eastern hemisphere':

The unbridled passions of the lower types of invaders, who included outlaws and prostitutes, brought scandal upon the Portuguese name. As few European women came out to India, miscegenation was common, and even the higher classes *degenerated*. . . . [L]ife in Goa became *orientalized*. The whites left all hard work to slaves and fell into luxury, vanity, and sloth . . . the whites adopted the enervating doctrines that trade disgraces a man and domestic work is beneath a woman's social status. These evils are still rampant in British India, as in most of the Eastern tropics where the Europeans hold sway. (Price 1939: 16)

31. Adherence to the idea that 'tropical neurasthenia' was a specific malady was not shared by all medical practitioners. Those who suggested that the use of the term be discontinued maintained that tropical neurasthenia was a psychopathology caused by social, not physiological, maladjustment (Culpin (1926) cited in Price 1939: 211).

32. On the social geography of hill-stations in British India and on the predominance of women and children in them, see King (1976: 156–79).

33. Contrast this thinking on appropriate colonial life-styles to that of a Jamaican historian writing in 1793 on the physical characteristics of 'tropical whites':

> The women lived calm and even lives, marked by habitual temperance and self-denial. They took no exercise . . . and had no amusement or avocation to compel them to much exertion of either mind or body. . . . Their mode of life and the hot oppressive atmosphere produced lax fibre and pale complexions. They seemed to have just risen from a bed of sickness. Their voices were soft and spiritless, and every step betrayed languor and lassitude. Eminently and deservedly applauded for heart and disposition, *no women on earth made better wives or better mothers.* (quoted in Price 1939: 31; my emphasis)

34. When children were recognized by a European father, a native mother could neither prevent them from being taken from her nor contest paternal suitability for custody.

35. The term *pauperism* was only applied in the Indies to those individuals legally classified as 'European' (Ming 1983). At the turn of the century it referred primarily to a class of Indo-Europeans marginalized from the educated and 'developed' elements in European society (Blumberger 1939: 19). However, pauperism was by no means synonymous with Eurasian status since 75 per cent of the 'Dutch' community were of mixed descent, some with powerful political and economic standing (Braconier 1917: 291). As Jacques van Doorn notes, 'It was not the Eurasian as such, but the "kleine Indo" [poor Indo] who was the object of ridicule and scorn in European circles' (1983: 8). One could pursue the argument that the denigration of 'poor Indos' coincided with a political bid for increased civil liberties among Eurasians at large; that it was as much the danger of Eurasian *empowerment* as pauperism that had to be checked.

36. Lest we assume that such support indicated a liberalization of colonial policy, it should be noted that such conservative colonial architects as van den Bosch (who instituted the forced cultivation system in Java) were among those most concerned that the government take responsibility for neglected European offspring (Mansvelt 1932: 292).

37. In colonial India, 'orphanages were the starting-point for a lifetime's cycle of institutions' (Arnold 1979: 113). 'Unseemly whites'—paupers, the sick, the aged, 'fallen women', and the insane were protected, secluded from Asian sight, and placed under European control. In Indonesia, *Pro Juventate* branches supported and housed together 'neglected and criminal' youth with special centres for Eurasian children. In French Indo-China, colonial officials debated the advantages of providing segregated education for *métis* youth 'to protect' them from discrimination.

38. Not everyone agreed with this evaluation. Cf. the following medical report from 1875: '[I]f the white race does not perpetuate itself in Senegal, one need

not attribute it to the weakened reproductive properties of the individuals, but to the thousands of other bad conditions against which they fight a desperate and incessant battle' (Bérenger-Féraud 1875: 491).

39. In search for some alleviation for metropolitan unemployment, a surge of scientific reports appeared reassessing the medical arguments against European settlement in the tropics (as in the proceedings of the 1938 International Congress of Geography).

40. I thank Barney Cohn for pressing me to engage this issue which I attend to more fully in subsequent work.

References

Abbatucci, Severin (1910), 'Le milieu africain consideré au point de vue de ses effets sur le système nerveux de l'européen', *Annales d'hygiène et de médecine coloniale*, 13: 328–35.

Adas, M. (1989), *Machines as the Measure of Men* (Ithaca: Cornell University Press).

Angoulvant, Gabriel (1926), *Les Indies Néelandaises* (Paris: Le Monde Nouveau).

Archive d'Outre-Mer, Aix-en-Marseille, France.

Arnold, David (1979), European Orphans and Vagrants in India in the Nineteenth Century, *Journal of Imperial and Commonwealth History*, 7/2: 104–27.

—— (1983), White Colonization and Labour in Nineteenth-Century India, *Journal of Imperial and Commonwealth History*, 11/2: 133–58.

Bajema, Carl (1976) (ed.), *Eugenics Then and Now* (Stroudsburg, Pa.: Dowden, Hutchinson & Ross).

Ballhatchet, K. (1980), *Race, Sex and Class under the Raj: Imperial Attitudes and Policies and Their Critics, 1793–1905* (New York: St. Martin's Press).

Baroli, March (1967), *La vie quotidienne des Français en Algérie* (Paris: Hachette).

Bauduin, D. C. M. (1941) (1927), *Het Indische Leven* (S-Gravenhage: H. P. Leopolds).

Beidelman, Thomas (1982), *Colonial Evangelism* (Bloomington: Indiana University Press).

Bérenger-Féraud, L. (1875), *Traité clinque des maladies des Européens au Sénégal* (Paris: Adrien Delahaye).

Biervliet, H. *et al.* (1980), Biologism, Racism and Eugenics in the Anthropology and Sociology of the 1930s, *Netherlands Journal of Sociology*, 16: 69–92.

Blumberger, J. Th. P. (1939), *De Indo-Europeesche Beweging in Nederlandsch-Indie* (Haarlem: Tjeenk Willink).

Blussé, Leonard (1986), *Strange Company: Chinese Settlers, Mestizo Women and the Dutch in VOC Batavia* (Dordrecht: Foris).

Bock, Gisela (1984), 'Racism and Sexism in Nazi Germany: Motherhood, Compulsory Sterilization, and the State', in *When Biology Became*

Destiny: Women in Weimar and Nazi Germany (New York: Monthly Review Press), 271–96.

Bocquet-Siek, M. (1984), 'Some Notes on the Nyai Theme in Pre-War Peranakan Chinese Literature', paper prepared for the Asian Studies Association of Australia, Adelaide University, 13 May 1984.

Boxer, C. R. (1969), *The Portuguese Seaborne Empire, 1415–1825* (New York: Knopf).

Bozzoli, Belinda (1983), Marxism, Feminism and South African studies', *Journal of Southern African Studies* 9/2: 139–71.

Boutilier, James (1984), European Women in the Solomon Islands, 1900–1942', in Denise O'Brien and Sharon Tiffany (eds.), *Rethinking Women's Roles: Perspectives from the Pacific* (Berkely, Los Angeles, London: University of California Press), 173–99.

Braconier, A. de (1913), 'Het Kazerne-Concubinaat in Ned-Indie', *Vragen van den Dag*, 28: 974–95.

—— (1917), 'Het Pauperisme onder de in Ned. Oost-Indie levende Europeanen', *Nederlandsch-Indie* (1st yr.): 291–300.

—— (1918), *Kindercriminaliteit en de verzorging van misdadig aangelegde en verwaarloosde minderjarigen in Nederlandsche-Indie* (Baarn: Hollandia-Drukkerij).

—— (1933), Het Prostitutie-vraagstuk in Nederlandsch-Indie, *Indisch Gids* 55/2: 906–28.

Brand, J. van den (1904), *Nogeens: De Millionen uit Deli* (Amsterdam: Hoveker & Wormser).

Brink, K. B. M. Ten (1920), *Indische Gezondheid* (Batavia: Nillmij).

Brou, A. M. N. (1907), Le Métis Franco-Annamite', *Revue Indochinois* (July 1907): 897–908.

Brownfoot, Janice N. (1984), 'Memsahibs in Colonial Malaya: A Study of European Wives in a British Colony and Protectorate 1900–1940', Hilary Callan and Shirley Ardener (eds.), *The Incorporated Wife* (London: Croom Helm).

Butcher, John (1979), *The British in Malaya, 1880–1941: The Social History of a European Community in Colonial Southeast Asia* (Kuala Lumpur: Oxford University Press).

Callan, Hilary, and Ardener, Shirley (1984) (eds.), *The Incorporated Wife* (London: Croom Helm).

Callaway, Helen (1987), *Gender, Culture and Empire: European Women in Colonial Nigeria* (London: Macmillan Press).

Carby, Hazel (1985), 'On the Threshold of Woman's Era: Lynching, Empire and Sexuality in Black Femnist Theory', *Critical Inquiry* 12/1: 262–77.

Chailley-Bert, M. J. (1897), *L'Emigration des femmes aux colonies*, Union Coloniale Française-conference, 12 Jan. 1897 (Paris: Armand Colin).

Chenet, Ch. (1936), 'Le role de la femme française aux Colonies; Protection des enfants métis abandonnés', *Le Devoir des femmes* (15 Feb. 1936), 8.

Chivas-Baron, C. (1929), *La Femme française aux colonies* (Paris: Larose).

Clerkx, Lily (1961), *Mensen in Deli* (Amsterdam: Sociologisch-Historisch Seminarium for Zuidoost-Azie).

Cock, J. (1980), *Maids and Madams* (Johannesburg: Ravan Press).

Cohen, William (1971), *Rulers of Empire: The French Colonial Service in Africa* (Stanford, Calif.: Hoover Institution Press).

—— (1980), *The French Encounter with Africans: White Response to Blacks, 1530–1880* (Bloomington: Indiana University Press).

Comaroff, John, and Comaroff, Jean (1986), 'Christianity and Colonialism in South Africa', *American Ethnologist* 13: 1–22.

Cool, F. (1938), 'De Bestrijding der Werkloosheidsgevolgen in Nederlandsch-Indie gedurende 1930–1936', *De Economist* 87: 135–47, 217–43.

Cooper, Frederic (1987), *On the African Waterfront* (New Haven: Yale Univeristy Press).

Cordurie, M. (1984), 'Résidence des Françaises et mariage des Français dan les echelles du Levant au XVIIIᵉ siècle', in *La femme dans les sociétés coloniales* (Aix-en-Provence: Institut d'Histoire des Pays d'Outre-Mer, Université de Provence), 35–47.

Corneau, Grace (1900), *La femme aux colonies* (Paris: Librairie Nilsson).

Courtois, E. (1900), 'Des règles hygiéniques que doit suivre l'Européen au Tonkin', *Revue Indo-chinoise*, 83: 539–41, 564–6, 598–601.

Daum, P. A. (1984), *Ups and Downs of Life in the Indies* (Amherst: University of Massachusetts Press).

Davin, Anna (1978), 'Imperialism and Motherhood', *History Workshop*, 5: 9–57.

Degler, Carl (1986), *Neither Black nor White* (Madison: University of Wisconsin Press [1971]).

Delavignette, Robert (1946), *Service Africain* (Paris: Gallimard).

Dixon, C. J. (1913), *De Assistent in Deli* (Amsterdam: J. H. de Bussy).

Doorn, Jacques van (1983), *A Divided Society: Segmentation and Mediation in Late-Colonial Indonesia* (Rotterdam: CASPA).

—— (1985), 'Indie als Koloniale Maatschappy', in F. L. van Holthoon (ed.), *De Nederlandse samenleving sinds 1815* (Assen: Maastricht).

Doucet, Robert (1928), *Métis et congaies d'Indochine* (Hanoi).

Dowd Hall, Jacquelyn (1984), ' "The Mind that Burns in Each Body": Women, Rape, and Racial Violence', *Southern Exposure*, 12/6: 61–71.

Drooglever, P. J. (1980), *De Vaderlandse Club, 1929–42* (Franeker: T. Wever).

Dupuy, A. (1955), 'La personnalité du colon', *Revue d'histoire économique et sociale* 33/1: 77–103.

Encyclopedie van Nederland-Indie (1919), (S-Gravenhage: Nijhoff and Brill).

Engels, Dagmar (1983), 'The Age of Consent Act of 1891: Colonial Ideology in Bengal', *South Asia Research* 3/2: 107–34.

Etienne, Mona, and Leacock, Eleanor (1980) (eds.), *Women and Colonization* (New York: Praeger).

Fanon, Franz (1967) (1952), *Black Skin, White Masks* (New York: Grove Press).

Favre, J.-L. (1938), *La vie aux colonies* (Paris: Larose).

Feuilletau de Bruyn, Dr. W. K. H. (1938), 'Over de Economische Mogelijkheid van een Kolonisatie van Blanken op Nederlandsch Nieuw-Guinea', in *Comptes Rendus du Congrès International de Géographie, Amsterdam* (Brill: Leiden), 21–9.

Fredrickson, George (1981), *White Supremacy: A Comparative Study in American and South African History* (New York: Oxford Unversity Press).

Gaitskell, Deborah (1983), 'Housewives, Maids or Mothers: Some Contradictions of Domesticity for Christian Women in Johannesburg, 1903–39', *Journal of African History*, 24: 241–56.

Gann, L. H., and Duignan, Peter (1978), *The Rulers of British Africa, 1870–1914* (Stanford, Calif.: Stanford University Press).

Gantes, Gilles de (1981), *La Population française au Tonkin entre 1931 et 1938*, Mémoire de Matrise (Aix-en-Provence: Université de Provence, Centre d'Aix: Institut d'Histoire des Pays d'Outre Mer).

Gartrell, Beverley (1984), 'Colonial Wives: Villains or Victims?' in Hillary Callan and Shirely Ardener (eds.), *The Incorporated Wife* (London: Croom Helm), 165–85.

Genovese, Eugene (1976), *Roll, Jordan, Roll: The World the Slaves Made* (New York: Vintage).

Gilman, Sander L. (1985), *Difference and Pathology: Stereotypes of Sexuality, Race, and Madness* (Ithaca: Cornell University Press).

Gordon, Linda (1976), *Woman's Body, Woman's Right: A Social History of Birth Control in America* (New York: Grossman).

Gordon, Robert, and Meggitt, Mervyn (1985), 'The Deline of the Kipas', in R. Gordon and M. Meggit (eds.), *Law and Order in the New Guinea Highlands: Encounters with Enga* (Hanover: University Press of New England), 39–70.

Grall, Ch. (1908), *Hygiène coloniale appliquée: Hygiène de l'Indochine* (Paris: Baillière).

Grimshaw, P. (1983), ' "Christian Woman, Pious Wife, Faithful Mother, Devoted Missionary": Conflicts in Roles of American Missionary Women in Nineteenth-Century Hawaii', *Feminist Studies*, 9/3: 489–521.

Hafkin, Nancy, and Bay, Edna (1976) (eds.), *Women in Africa: Studies in Social and Economic Change* (Stanford, Calif.: Stanford University Press).

Hammerton, James (1979), *Emigrant Gentlewomen: Genteel Poverty and Female Emigration 1830–1914* (London: Croom Helm).

Hansen, Karen Tranberg (1984), 'Negotiating Sex and Gender in Urban Zambia', *Journal of Southern African Studies* 10/2: 218–38.

—— (1989), *Distant Companions: Servants and Employers in Zambia, 1900–1985* (Ithaca: Cornell University Press).

Hardy, George (1929), *Ergaste ou la vocation coloniale* (Paris: Armand Colin).

Hartenberg, Paul (1910), 'Les troubles nerveux et mentaux chez les coloniaux (Paris).

Harwood, Dorothy (1938), 'The Possibility of White Colonization in the Tropics', in *Comptes Rendu de Congrès International de Géographie* (Leiden: Brill), 131–40.

Hermans, E. H. (1925), *Gezondscheidsleer voor Nederlandsche-Indie* (Amsterdam: Meulenhoff).

Hesselink, Liesbeth (1987), 'Prostitution: A Necessary Evil, Particularly in the Colonies: Views on Prostitution in the Netherlands Indies' in E. Locher-Scholten and A. Niehof (eds.), *Indonesian Women in Focus* (Dordrecht: Foris), 205–24.

Het Pauperisme Commissie (1901), *Het Pauperisme onder de Europeanen* (Batavia: Landsdrukkerij).

—— (1903), *Rapport der Pauperisme-Commissie* (Batavia: Landsdrukkerij).

Heyningen, Elizabeth Van B. (1984), 'The Social Evil in the Cape Colony 1868–1902: Prostitution and the Contagious Disease Acts', *Journal of Southern African Studies*, 10/2: 170–97.

Hobsbawm, Eric (1987), *The Age of Empire, 1875–1914* (London: Weidenfeld and Nicholson).

Hunt, Nancy (1988), 'Le bébé en brousse: European Women, African Birth-Spacing and Colonial Intervention in Breast-Feeding in the Belgian Congo', *International Journal of African Historical Studies*, 21/3.

Hyam, Ronald (1986a), 'Empire and Sexual Opportunity', *Journal of Imperial and Commonwealth History*, 14/2: 34–90.

—— (1986b), 'Concubinage and the Colonial Service: The Crewe Circular (1909)', *Journal of Imperial and Commonwealth History*, 14/3: 170–86.

Inglis, Amirah (1975), *The White Women's Protection Ordinance: Sexual Anxiety and Politics in Papua* (London Sussex University Press).

Jaurequiberry (1924), *Les Blancs en pays chauds* (Paris: Maloine).

Jordan, Winthrop (1968), *White over Black: American Attitudes Toward the Negro, 1550–1812* (Chapel Hill: University of North Carolina Press).

Joyeux, Ch., and Sice, A. (1937), 'Affections exotiques du système nerveux', *Précis de médecine coloniale* (Paris: Masson).

Kantoor van Arbeid (1935), *Werkloosheid in Nederlandsch-Indie* (Batavia: Landsdrukkerij).

Kennedy, Dane (1987), *Islands of White: Settler Society and Culture in Kenya and Southern Rhodesia, 1890–1939* (Durham, NC: Duke University Press).

Kennedy, Raymond (1947), *The Ageless Indies* (New York: John Day).

Kevles, Daniel (1985), *In the Name of Eugenics* (Berkeley, Los Angeles, London: University of California Press).

King, Anthony (1976), *Colonial Urban Development: Culture, Social Power and Environment* (London: Routledge & Kegan Paul).

Kirkwood, Deborah (1984), 'Settler Wives in Southern Rhodesia: A Case Study', in H. Callan and S. Ardener (eds.), *The Incorporated Wife* (London: Croom Helm).

Knibiehler, Yvonne, and Goutalier, Regine (1985), *La femme au temps des colonies* (Paris: Stock).

—— —— (1987), *'Femmes et colonisation': Rapport terminal au Ministère des Relations Extérieures et de la Cooperation* (Aix-en-Provence: Institut d'Histoire des Pays d'Outre-Mer).

Kohlbrugge, J. F. H. (1910), *Prostitie in Nederlandsch-Indie* (Indisch Genootschap of 19 Feb. 1901), 2–36.

Koks, Dr. J. Th. (1931), *De Indo* (Amsterdam: H. J. Paris).

Kroniek 1917, 'Oostkust van Sumatra-Instituut', (Amsterdam: J. H. de Bussy).

Kroniek 1933, 'Oostkust van Sumatra-Instituut', (Amsterdam: J. H. de Bussy).

Kuklick, Henrika (1979), *The Imperial Bureaucrat: The Colonial Administrative Service in the Gold Coast, 1920–1939* (Stanford, Calif.: Hoover Institution Press).

La femme dans les sociétés coloniales (1982), Table Ronde CHEE, CRHSE, IHPOM (Institut d'Histoire des Pays d'Outre-Mer, Université de Provence).

Laffey, John (1977), 'Racism in Tonkin Before 1914', *French Colonial Studies*, 8: 65–81.

Lanessan, J.-L. (1889), *Indochine française* (Paris: Felix Alcan).

Le Bras, Hervé (1981), 'Histoire secrète de la fécondité', *Le Débat*, 8: 76–100.

Leonard, Jacques (1985), 'Les origines et les conséquences de l'eugenique en France', *Annales de demographie historique*: 203–14.

Lerner, Gerda (1972), *Black Women in White America* (New York: Pantheon).

Le Roux (1898), *Je deviens colon* (Paris).

Loutfi, Martine Astier (1971), *Littérature et colonialisme* (Paris: Mouton).

Lucas, Nicole (1986), 'Trouwerbod, inlandse huishousdsters en Europese vrouwen: Het concubinaat in de planterswereld aan Sumatra's Oostkust 1860–1940', in J. Reijs *et al.*, *Vrouwen in de Nederlandse Kolonien* (Nijmegen: SUN), 78–97.

Mackinnon, Murdoch (1920), 'European Children in the Tropical Highlands', *Lancet* 199: 944–5.

Malleret, Louis (1934), *L'Exotisme Indochinois dans la littérature française depuis 1860* (Paris: Larose).

Mannoni, Octavio (1956), *Prospero and Caliban: The Psychology of Colonization* (New York: Praeger).

Mansvelt, W. (1932), 'De Positie der Indo-Europeanen', *Kolonial Studien*, 16: 290–311.

Marks, Schula (1987) (ed.), *Not Either an Experimental Doll: The Separate Worlds of Three South African Women* (Bloomington: Indiana University Press).

Marle, A. van (1952), 'De group der Europeanen in Nederlands-Indie', *Indonesie*, 5/2: 77–121; 5/3: 314–41; 5/5: 481–507.

Martinez-Alier, Verena (1974), *Marriage, Class and Colour in Nineteenth Century Cuba* (Cambridge: Cambridge University Press).

Mason, Philip (1958), *The Birth of a Dilemma* (New York: Oxford University Press).

Maunier, M. René (1932), *Sociologie coloniale* (Paris: Domat-Montchrestien).

Mazet, Jacques (1932), *La Condition juridique des métis* (Paris: Domat-Montchrestien).

McClure, John A. (1981), *Kipling and Conrad: The Colonial Fiction* (Cambridge, Mass.: Harvard University Press).

Mercier, Paul (1965), 'The European Community of Dakar', in Pierre van den Berghe (ed.), *Africa: Social Problems of Change and Conflict* (San Francisco: Chandler), 284–304.

Metcalf, Thomas (1964), *The Aftermath of Revolt: India, 1857–1870* (Princeton: Princeton University Press).

Middendorp, W. (1924), *De Poenale Sanctie* (Haarlem: Tjeenk Willink).

Ming, Hanneke (1983), Barracks-Concubinage in the Indies, 1887–1920', *Indonesia*, 35 (April): 65–93.

Moore-Gilbert, B. J. (1986), *Kipling and 'Orientalism'* (New York: St. Martin's).

Moses, Claire Goldberg (1984), *French Feminism in the Nineteenth Century* (Albany: SUNY Press).

Mosse, George (1978), *Toward the Final Solution* (New York: Fertig).

—— (1985), *Nationalism and Sexuality* (Madison: University of Wisconsin Press).

Nandy, Ashis (1983), *The Intimate Enemy: Loss and Recovery of Self under Colonialism* (Delhi: Oxford University Press).

Nash, J. (1980), 'Aztec Women: The Transition From Status to Class in Empire and Colony', in M. Etienne and E. Leacock, (eds.), *Women and Colonization: Anthropological Perspectives* (New York: Praeger), 134–48.

Nieuwenhuys, Roger (1959), *Tussen Twee Vaderlanden* (Amsterdam: Van Oorschot).

Nora, Pierre (1961), *Les Français d'Algerie* (Paris: Julliard).

O'Brien, Rita Cruise (1972), *White Society in Black Africa: The French in Senegal* (London: Faber & Faber).

Onselen, Charles van (1982), 'Prostitutes and Proletarians, 1886–1914', in *Studies in the Social and Economic History of the Witwatersrand 1886–1914*, i. (New York: Longman), 103–62.

Ons Nageslacht, Orgaan Van de Eugenetische vereeniging in Ned-Indie (Batavia).

Painter, N. I. (1988), ' "Social Equality": Miscegenation, Labor and Power', in N. Bartley (ed.), *The Evolution of Southern Culture* (Athens: University of Georgia Press).

Pollmann, Tessel (1986), 'Bruidstraantjes: De Koloniale roman, de njai en de apartheid', in Jeske Reijs *et al.*, *Vrouwen in de Nederlandse Kolonien* (Nijmegen: SUN), 98–125.

Pourvourville, Albert de (1926), 'Le Métis', in *Le Mal d'argent* (Paris: Monde Moderne), 97–114.

Price, Grenfell A. (1939), *White Settlers in the Tropics* (New York: American Geographical Society).

Prochaska, David (1989), *Making Algeria French: Colonialism in Bone, 1870–1920* (Cambridge: Cambridge University Press).

Pujarniscle, E. (1931), *Philoxène ou de la littérature coloniale* (Paris).

Ralston, Caroline (1977), *Grass Huts and Warehouses: Pacific Beach Communities of the Nineteenth Century* (Canberra: ANU Press).

Ramuschack, Barbara (n.d.), 'Cultural Missionaries, Maternal Imperialist, Feminist Allies: British Women Activists in India, 1865–1945', in *Women Studies International* (forthcoming).

Raptchinsky, B. (1941), *Kolonisatie van blanken in de tropen* (Den Haag: Bibliotheek van Weten en Denken).

Riejs, J., Kloek, E., Jansz, U., de Wildt, A., van Norden, S., and de Bat, M. (1986), *Vrouwen in de Nederlandse Kolonien* (Nijmegen: SUN).

Rich, P. (1984), 'The Long Victorian Sunset: Anthropology, Eugenics and Race in Britain', *c.*1900–48', *Patterns of Prejudice*, 18/3: 3–17.

Ridley, Hugh (1981), *Images of Imperial Rule* (New York: Croom Helm).

Ritter, W. L. (1856), *De Europeaan in Nederlandsch Indie* (Leyden: Sythoff).

Robertson, Claire, and Klein, Martin (1983) (eds.), *Women and Slavery in Africa* (Madison: University of Wisconsin Press).

Robertson, Claire (1987), 'Developing Economic Awareness: Changing Perspectives in Studies of African Women, 1976–85', *Feminist Studies*, 13/1: 97–135.

Rodenwaldt, Ernest (1928), 'Eugenetische Problemen in Nederlandsch-Indie', in *Ons Nageslacht*, Orgaan van de Eugenetische Vereeniging in Nederland-Indie (1928): 1–8.

Ross, Ellen, and Rapp, Rayna (1980), 'Sex and Society: A Research Note from Social History and Anthropology', *Comparative Studies in Society and History*, 22/1: 51–72.

Said, Edward W. (1978), *Orientalism* (New York: Vintage).

Sambuc (1931), 'Les métis Franco-Annamites en Indochine', *Revue du Pacifique*, 256–72.

Schneider, William (1982), 'Toward the Improvement of the Human Race: The History of Eugenics in France', *Journal of Modern History*, 54: 269–91.

Schoevers, T. (1913), 'Het leven en werken van den assistent bij de Tabakscultuur in Deli', *Jaarboek der Vereeniging 'Studiebelangen'* (Wageningen: Zomer), 3–43.

Schmidt, Elizabeth (1987), 'Ideology, Economics, and the Role of Shona women in Southern Rhodesia, 1850–1939', Ph.D. diss., University of Wisconsin.

—— (n.d.) 'Race, Sex and Domestic Labour: The Question of African Female Servants in Southern Rhodesia, 1900–1939', MS.

Showalter, Elaine (1987), *The Female Malady* (New York: Penguin).

Silverblatt, Irene (1987), *Moon, Sun, and Witches: Gender Ideologies and Class in Inca and Colonial Peru* (Princeton: Princeton University Press).

Simon, Pierre-Jean (1977), 'Portraits coloniaux des Vietnamiens (1858–1914)', *Pluriel*, 10: 29–54.

—— (1981), *Rapatriés d'Indochine: Un village franco-indochinois en Bourbonnais* (Paris: Harmattan).

Sivan, Emmanuel (1983), *Interpretations of Islam, Past and Present* (Princeton: Darwin Press).

Smith-Rosenberg, C., and Rosenberg, C. (1973), 'The Female Animal: Medical and Biological Views of Woman and Her Role in Nineteenth-Century America', *Journal of American History*, 60/2: 332–56.

Spear, Percival (1963), *The Nabobs* (London: Oxford University Press).

Spencer, J. E., and Thomas, W. L. (1948), 'The Hill-Stations and Summer Resorts of the Orient', *Geographical Review*, 38/4: 637–51.

Stepan, Nancy (1982), *The Idea of Race in Science: Great Britain, 1880–1960* (London: Macmillan).

Stocking, George (1982) (1968), *Race, Culture, and Evolution* (Chicago: University of Chicago Press).

Stoler, Ann (1985a), *Capitalism and Confrontation in Sumatra's Plantation Belt, 1870–1979* (New Haven: Yale University Press).

—— (1985b), 'Perceptions of Protest: Defining the Dangerous in Colonial Sumatra', *American Ethnologist*, 12/4: 642–58.

—— (1989a), 'Rethinking Colonial Categories: European Communities and the Boundaries of Rule', *Comparative Studies in Society and History*, 13/1: 134–61.

—— (1989b), 'Making Empire Respectable: The Politics of Race and Sexual Morality in 20th Century Colonial Cultures', *American Ethnologist*, 16/4: 634–60.

Strobel, Margaret (1987), 'Gender and Race in the Nineteenth- and Twentieth-Century British Empire', in *Becoming Visible: Women in European history* (Boston: Houghton Mifflin).

Stuurman, Siep (1985), *Verzuiling, Kapitalisme en Patriarchaat* (Nijmegen: SUN).

Sumatra Post (Medan, Sumatra).

Sutherland, Heather (1982), 'Ethnicity and Access in Colonial Macassar', in *Papers of the Dutch-Indonesian Historical Conference*, Dutch and Indonesian Steering Committees of the Indonesian Studies Programme (Leiden: Bureau of Indonesian Studies), 250–77.

Takaki, Ronald (1977), *Iron Cages* (Berkeley, Los Angeles, London: University of California Press).

Taylor, Jean (1977), 'The World of Women in the Colonial Dutch Novel', *Kabar Seberang*, 2: 26–41.

—— (1983), *The Social World of Batavia* (Madison: University of Wisconsin Press).

Tiffany, Sharon, and Adams, Kathleen (1985), *The Wild Woman: An Inquiry into the Anthropology of an Idea* (Cambridge, Mass.: Schenkman).

Tirefort, A. (1979), ' "Le Bon Temps": La Communauté française en Basse Cote d'Ivoire pendant l'entre-deux guerres, 1920–1940' (Troisième Cycle, Centre d'Etudes Africaines).

Travaux du Groupe d'Etudes Coloniales (1910), *La Femme blanche au Congo* (Brussels: Misch and Thron).

Treille, G. (1888), *De L'acclimatation des Europeens dan le pays chaud* (Paris: Octave Doin).

Union Géographique International (1938), *Comptes Rendus du Congres International de Géographie, Amsterdam 1938* (Leiden: Brill).

Van-Helten, Jean J., and Williams, K. (1983), ' "The Crying Need of South Africa": The Emigration of Single British Women to the Transvaal, 1901–1910', *Journal of South African Studies*, 10/1: 11–38.

Van Heyningen, Elizabeth B. (1984), 'The Social Evil in the Cape Colony 1868–1902: Prostitution and the Contagious Disease Act', *Journal of Southern African Studies*, 10/2: 170–97.

Veerde, A. G. (1931), 'Onderzoek naar den omvang der werkloosheid op Java (Nov 1930–June 1931), *Koloniale Studien*, 16: 242–73, 503–33.

Vellut, Jean-Luc (1982), 'Materiaux pour une image du Blanc dans la société coloniale du Congo Belge', in Jean Pirotte (ed.), *Stérotypes nationaux et préjugés raciaux aux XIXe et XXe siècles* (Leuven: Editions Nauwelaerts).

Vere Allen, J. de (1970), 'Malayan Civil Service, 1874–1941: Colonial Bureaucracy/Malayan Elite', *Comparative Studies in Society and History*, 12: 149–78.

Wanderken, P. (1943), 'Zoo leven onze kinderen', in *Zoo Leven Wij in Indonesia* (Deventer: Van Hoever), 172–87.

Wertheim, Willem (1959), *Indonesian Society in Transition* (The Hague: Van Hoeve).

White, Luise (1988), Book review, *Signs* 13/2: 360–4.

—— (1990), 'The Comforts of Home: Prostitution in Colonial Nairobi' (Chicago: University of Chicago Press).

Winckel, C. W. F. (1938), 'The Feasibility of White Settlements in the Tropics: A Medical Point of View', in *Comptes Rendus du Congrès International de Géographie, Amsterdam*, ii, sect. iiic. (Leiden: Brill), 345–56.

Woodcock, George (1969), *The British in the Far East* (New York: Antheneum).

9 Equality and difference in National Socialist racism

Gisela Bock

This essay aims to shed light on the conceptual couple 'equality' and 'difference' by looking from a historian's point of view at National Socialism in Germany. Two implications of this approach are particularly important. First, the crucial core of National Socialism and its crimes was racism, in both theory and practice. In this context, therefore, 'equality' and 'difference' concern not only gender relations, but also race relations, and the groups that were discriminated against on racial grounds included both women and men. Second, while racism was not confined to National Socialism or Germany, but was an international phenomenon, National Socialism carried all forms of racism to unprecedented extremes. This was possible because National Socialism politicized racism by extending it from the social to the political sphere, transforming it into race policy; and where 'politics are centred around the concept of race, the Jews will be at the centre of hostility'.[1] Racism was from the beginning institutionalized within the state, so that measures ranging from the legislative to the bureaucratic could be marshalled in support of the persecution of Jews and the policy of compulsory sterilization, beginning in 1933, and ultimately in support of the massacres which started six years later. The following reflections will therefore be concerned with the political sphere and with this pair of issues—racist sterilization and racist massacre—which were forms of compulsory intervention in the body and in life. To put them in perspective, I will first outline some of the current opinions held by historians and non-historians on the topic of women and National Socialism, particularly those regarding gender difference and gender equality. In the second section of the essay I shall deal with various gender dimensions of National Socialist policies on

First published as ch. 5 in Gisela Bock and Susan James (eds.), *Beyond Equality and Difference: Citizenship, Feminist Politics, and Female Subjectivity* (London: Routledge, 1992) and is reprinted with permission.

procreation and welfare, and in the third with some gender dimensions of National Socialist genocide.

VISIONS OF WOMEN AND NATIONAL SOCIALISM

According to one opinion, National Socialism favoured women. A first version of this view holds that, before 1933, 'equality' was emphasized, particularly by the women's movement, 'difference' was played down, and having children was scorned. National Socialism is supposed to have made child-bearing respectable again, to have rewarded mothers and upgraded the family, to have promoted not an illusory and undesirable 'equality' of women with men but their 'equal value'. Another version of the same position underlines a different link between the earlier women's movement and Nazi gender policies. The former supported women's distinctiveness and 'separate sphere', the centrality of maternity and demands for the improvement of the situation of mothers; National Socialism is said to have taken over this radical feminist programme.[2] A further and influential version argued that, regardless of countervailing ideologies, National Socialism produced for women 'a new status of relative if unconventional equality'. Women experienced improved job opportunities and rising wages and benefited from social policies related to maternity; their loss of political status did not differ from the same loss as experienced by men.[3]

A second opinion, for many years the prevailing one among feminists and non-feminists alike, evokes a similar picture but evaluates it differently, seeing it not as pro-women, but as anti-women. It deplores the fact that, before 1933, the women's movement had proclaimed the value of motherhood, corporal as well as spiritual, and argues that National Socialism adopted largely the same view. National Socialism is thus interpreted as having valorized motherhood in both moral and material terms, thereby reducing women to mothers. This is held to have been achieved in several ways: by the use of propaganda, by incentives such as child allowances and various other subsidies given to mothers, and by coercive means (*Gebärzwang*) such as firing women *en masse* from their jobs, excluding them from the universities, outlawing birth-control, tightening up the anti-abortion law and vastly increasing the number of convictions for abortion. These measures, designed to keep women out of the labour-force and to encourage them to bear as many children as possible, are seen as constituting a policy of extreme pro-natalism and a cult of motherhood, which are in turn interpreted as the essential and distinctive features of National Socialist sexism and of the regime's victimization of women.

Both these opinions are problematic, particularly with respect to the issues of maternity and female 'difference'. Their proponents often confuse propaganda with actual policies, take account of only selected parts of this propaganda and misrepresent historical facts. For example, the National Socialist image of women limited them much less to a 'separate sphere', to motherhood and housewifery, than, for instance, the image of women dominant in the United States of the 1930s.[4] Despite a number of Nazi and non-Nazi voices in 1933–4, women were not fired *en masse* during the National Socialist era and the number of employed women increased, particularly in the industrial labour-force and among married mothers. The decline in the number of women university students was not so much due to the regime's intervention as to economic developments—except for the exclusion of Jews of both sexes.[5] Financial incentives were paid not to women, but to men. The number of convictions for abortion did not increase, but decreased by one-sixth by comparison with the Weimar Republic period.[6]

Most important, however, is the fact that millions of women and men under the National Socialist regime were discouraged from having children at all. The National Socialist state did not abolish birth-control, but took it over. In 1933, prior to the introduction of any pro-natalist measures, it introduced a law ordering compulsory sterilization of those considered to be of 'inferior value', thus embarking on a policy of anti-natalism. This anti-natalist policy was designed to improve the 'quality' of the population, to bring about 'race regeneration' and 'racial uplift' (*rassische Aufartung*). In 1933–4, an enormous propaganda campaign attempted to render this policy popular, and around one and a half million people were officially declared to be 'unworthy of procreating' (*fortpflanzung-sunwürdig*). In 1935, abortion on medical and eugenic grounds was included in the sterilization law. In the same year, two laws intro-duced marriage prohibitions, one against marriages between Jews and non-Jews, the other between the eugenically 'inferior' and other (non-sterilized) Germans, with the aim of preventing 'racially inferior' offspring. From 1939 on, this anti-natalist policy receded into the background as mass murder and genocide took over. The female among the victims of these policies include otherwise very diverse groups. Between 1933 and 1945, almost 200 000 women were sterilized on eugenic grounds, one per cent of those of child-bearing age. The number of those prevented from marrying is as yet unknown. From 1933, about 200 000 German Jewish women were exiled, and after 1941 almost 100 000 of them were killed. From 1939, probably over 80 000 female inmates of mostly psychiatric institutions were killed, including all those who were Jewish. Over two million foreign women performed forced labour during the war, and hundreds of thousands of them had to undergo involuntary abortions and sterilizations. Several million non-German Jewish women were killed in the massacres during World War II, as were an unknown number of other women, mostly gypsies and Slavs.

In view of these figures and policies concerning the female victims of National Socialist racism, the assertion that the essence and distinctiveness of National Socialist policy towards women consisted in 'pro-natalism and a cult of motherhood' must be called into question. Equally problematic is the further assertion, common to both the opinions I have outlined, that in the National Socialist state gender relations were based not on 'equality' but on 'difference' between the sexes and that men and women were treated differently. On the one hand, within the groups that were racially discriminated against, both men and women of the racially discriminated groups were considered to be 'alien' and 'different' (*anders, fremd, artfremd*); they were treated as 'unequal' and above all as 'inferior' (*minderwertig*). On the other hand, both men and women of the racially privileged groups were considered and treated as 'equal' (*gleich, gleichartig, artgleich*) and above all as 'superior' (*wertvoll*). The race theorists of National Socialism held gender relations, and specifically conceptions of 'equality' and 'difference', to be different in different ethnic groups. Thus in their view only the women of 'superior' ethnic groups were 'different' from men and fit to occupy 'separate spheres'. The 'inferior' women and men, by contrast, whether Jews, blacks, or gypsies, were held to display 'sexual levelling' (*sexuelle Applanation*). According to one of these authors, 'the division into manly and womanly characteristics is a specific feature of the Nordic race, so that this race most purely embodies the manly and womanly essence', and Nordic men and women 'differ more sharply from each other' than the men and the women of other races.[7] Finally, and most importantly, National Socialist policy-makers by no means treated 'racially inferior' women 'differently' from the men of their groups, but 'equally'. Both men and women became victims of forced sterilization, forced labour, and massacre. For these women, there was no 'separate sphere'.

In order to revise prevailing opinions, we must include and place at the centre of our analysis racism both as theory and as practice. However, when we turn to research on National Socialist racism, on anti-Jewish and anti-gypsy policies, and on sterilization and euthenasia, we usually find that any discussion of gender relations is conspicuously absent.[8] Occasionally, we even find eminent historians of the genocide supporting, without any qualification, the view that 'women's emancipation' was considerably accelerated under the National Socialist regime.[9] Moreover, we find in this body of scholarship another common opinion which argues or implies that, in the context of National Socialist racism, the issue of women and gender relations is irrelevant or even inadmissible, because, on the one hand, not 'all women' became victims of National Socialist racism and, on the other, both men and women were equally its victims, numerically as well as in virtue of the equal treatment they received at its hands.[10] Racist policies, it is sometimes said, were not directed against women; their female victims became victims not 'as women', but irrespective of their sex, as gender-neutral members of certain racial groups. Yet the view that women's history is irrelevant to the history of racism is merely the obverse of the opinions already mentioned, which imply that the history of racism is irrelevant to the history of women. It condemns half the victims of racism to historical invisibility. But it also poses a series of questions: Does 'gender equality' or 'equal treatment' of the sexes among the victims actually mean gender neutrality? What has 'equality' come to mean in this context? Would a focus on the female victims of racism be legitimate only if all or most of its victims had been female, or if all women had been its victims (instead of a minority of hundreds of thousands of German and millions of non-German women), or if victimized women had been treated differently from victimized men?

There have indeed been attempts to overcome the limitations inherent in so much recent scholarship and to link women's history to National Socialist race policy and genocide. One resulting view focuses not on the female victims of National Socialist racism, nor on the minority of women who played an active part in the promotion of race policies, but on the majority of the women who belonged to the groups considered to be racially 'superior'. According to this view, these women were guilty of and responsible for genocide not just generally, because of the German nation's

271

collective guilt, but specifically and individually 'as women'—as mothers, wives and home-keepers. Their guilt is held to stem from the fact that they lived and believed in their female 'difference' and in the value of their 'separate sphere', thereby sharing and supporting Nazism's conception and treatment of women. Far from victimizing women, Nazi pro-natalism and its cult of motherhood drew upon women's own aspirations to be, and be valued as, mothers. Women willingly 'lent the healthy gloss of motherhood', of human and family values, to cover up a criminal regime and are therefore seen to be at the 'very centre' of 'Nazi evil'. The elaboration of ideas of gender difference, maternity, and separate spheres by males, females, and feminists since the late eighteenth century is said to have paved the way for the National Socialist massacres; the prescription of 'polarized identities for males and females'—among the victims as well as among those who were not—is held to be at the roots of the massacres. Precisely because of their 'difference' as a sex, German non-Jewish women are held to have been 'equally' guilty of genocide, 'no less than men' who are usually at the centre of historical studies of the Holocaust.[11]

This concept of equal guilt deriving from sexual 'difference' confronts us with another difficult sense of 'equality'. No less important in this context is the problematic fact that this view is based on the traditional picture of Nazism as a pro-natalist regime which fostered a cult of motherhood—an assumption which we have already seen to be fraught with contradiction and difficulty. A still further contradiction relates to the issue of women's power which is of course central to the argument of women being at the very centre of the Nazi crimes. On the one hand, female difference—expressed in motherhood and the separate sphere—is held to be the source of powerlessness, not even implying some 'invisible power' of women. On the other hand, it is held to have been a source of women's power to bring about genocide.[12] Another influential version of this view attempts to overcome the contradiction by claiming that, indeed, female 'difference' implied female power, the 'power of the mothers'; such 'power of the mothers' is then held to have been at the roots of genocide.[13] Although neither sources nor historical scholarship support this assumption, its function is obvious. It revives the old myth of Nazi 'pro-natalism and cult of motherhood', which is so thoroughly jeopardized by even a superficial glance at the depressing and contradicting facts of racism and genocide, by presenting it as a female version of genocide. Despite the problems of this approach, it poses important questions: What really was women's contribution to and guilt and responsibility for National Socialist race policy and genocide? Was it specific to the female sex and therefore grounded in female 'difference'? If not, was it equal to the contribution of men, and in what way? If so, how 'separate' actually were the 'separate spheres' under National Socialism?

I shall explore some of these issues by focusing on some gender and race dimensions of National Socialist policies of sterilization, of welfare, and of massacre. The exploration will conform to a methodological requirement which I consider indispensable: that in any adequate analysis of National Socialist racism, its agents and its victims must be central. No generalization can be valid unless it is also valid for these groups. It will emerge that National Socialist racism was by no means gender-neutral any more than National Socialist sexism was race-neutral. On both levels, in the sources as well as in historical analysis, the conceptual couple equality/difference has an essential place. At the same time, however, it is context dependent.

ANTI-NATALISM AND THE 'PRIMACY OF THE STATE IN THE SPHERE OF LIFE'

'Superiority' and 'inferiority', *Wert* and *Minderwertigkeit*, were the main categories common to all forms of Nazi racism. These terms were, moreover, intimately linked to the language of 'equality' and 'inequality'. The sterilization law of 1933, like the anti-Jewish laws, put into practice the classical racist demand, proclaimed in Germany specifically by the advocates of eugenic sterilization: 'Unequal value, unequal rights' (*ungleicher Wert, ungleiche Rechte*).[14] According to section 14 of the law, sterilization was forbidden to the 'healthy' members of both sexes, while according to section 12 it was compulsory for their 'inferior' members. In addition, these notions were linked to the language of the 'private' and the 'political'. The sterilization law was officially proclaimed, upon its enactment, as enforcing the 'primacy of the state over the sphere of life, marriage and family' (*Primat des Staates auf dem Gebiet des Lebens, der Ehe und der Familie*). It was thus through the policy of birth-prevention that the private sphere came to be subordinated to and ruled by the political sphere. The sterilization law was, according to its official commentators, an expression of the view that 'the private is political', and that any decision about the dividing line between private and political is in itself political.[15] Finally, this policy was linked to the concept of 'biology' which assumed a variety of meanings in this discourse. It referred not to the different bodies of men and women, but to a superior or inferior 'biological value' which was, for women and men alike, genetically transmitted. 'Biology' also, and most importantly, meant bodily intervention for the sake of social change. In this respect, the sterilization law went even further than the anti-Jewish laws of 1933, since it ordered compulsory bodily intervention and was thereby the first of the Nazi measures that sought to 'solve' social and cultural problems by what were referred to as 'biological' means. It was in these terms, rather than in the language of gender, that in 1936 Himmler praised the sterilization law to the Hitler Youth: 'Germans . . . have once again learned . . . to recognize bodies and to bring up this God-given body and our God-given blood and race according to its value or lack of value.'[16]

Forced and mass sterilization was pursued for the sake of 'uplifting the race' or 'the people', of 'eradicating inferior hereditary traits' by preventing 'inferior' people from having children and passing on their traits to posterity. The Nazi sterilization law, which was the culmination of the preceding international movement of eugenics or race hygiene, was an integral component of National Socialist racism as defined by the regime itself:

The German race question consists primarily in the Jewish question. In second place, yet no less important, there is the gypsy question . . . [But] degenerative effects on the racial body may arise not only from outside, from members of alien races, but also from inside, through unrestricted procreation of inferior hereditary material.[17]

The sterilization law established psychiatric grounds for sterilization, particularly feeble-mindedness, schizophrenia, epilepsy, and manic-depressive derangement. It did not specifically mention Jews, gypsies, blacks, or Poles and therefore seemed to be ethnically neutral. Interestingly, Hitler objected briefly to sterilizing persons of non-German ethnicity, on the grounds that they deserved no 'uplift' of their race. But this objection was soon overcome, and 'inferior' Germans and emotionally or mentally disabled persons of other ethnic groups were subjected to the law on equal terms. (After 1945, this fact was appealed to by those who claimed, defending the sterilization policy, that it had nothing to do with racism.)

None the less, ethnicity made a difference. Psychiatric theory and practice established various links between ethnicity and psychiatric constitution, for example that western Jews were more prone to schizophrenia than 'normal' people and eastern Jews more prone to 'feeble-mindedness'. Gypsies were likely to be classified as 'feeble-minded', and black people were thought to be more prone to both feeble-mindedness and schizophrenia. In 1937, all Afro-Germans who could be found were sterilized. Like many gypsies they were sterilized both within and outside the 1933 law. In 1941—the year when the deadly deportations from Germany to occupied Poland began—a Berlin Jewish woman was sterilized because she had been diagnosed as schizophrenic, a derangement 'proven' by the fact that she had 'depressions' and had attempted to commit suicide. From March 1942, Jews were exempted from the sterilization law, but by then the massacres did to them what sterilization would have done to their offspring—prevented them from living.[18]

Because neither women nor men were mentioned in the sterilization law it seemed to be gender-neutral and to affect the sexes equally. Yet even this apparent gender-neutrality was not self-evident but the subject of controversy. Interestingly, there was up to 1933 a public debate as to whether it might be unjust or unwise to sterilize women and men in equal numbers, since the operation on women (salpingectomy, including full anaesthesia, abdominal incision and the concomitant risk) was so much more dramatic than that on men (vasectomy), and the higher rate of complication and death might provoke resistance. In 1933, however, the Propaganda Ministry announced that just as many women as men would have to be sterilized, regardless of their sex, for reasons of 'justice' and the 'logic' of hereditary transmission. In fact, the 400 000 sterilization victims were about half women, half men.

None the less, gender made a difference, and the sterilization policy was anything but gender-neutral. Compulsory and mass sterilization of women meant violent intervention not only with the female body but also with female life. Probably about 5000 people died as a result of sterilization, and whereas women made up 50 per cent of those sterilized, they made up about 90 per cent of those who died in the process. Many of them died because they resisted right up to the operating table or because they rejected what had happened even afterwards.[19] An unknown number, mainly women, committed suicide. Hence, the first National Socialist massacre, scientifically planned and bureaucratically executed for the sake of 'racial uplift', was the result of anti-natalism, and its victims were mostly women. Historians have not noted it because women's bodily difference seemed to be unimportant, even in the case of a policy of bodily intervention.

There were also other respects in which sterilization was not gender-neutral. Childlessness, like having children, had a different meaning for women and for men. Their reactions and forms of resistance to sterilization consequently differed in many ways. Women as well as men protested against their stigmatization as 'second-class people'—in thousands of letters preserved among the documents of the sterilization courts—but women complained of the resulting childlessness more often than men. This was especially true for young women (the minimum age for being sterilized was 14). Many women attempted to become pregnant before sterilization. Their resistance was sufficiently important for the authorities to give the phenomenon a special name: 'protest pregnancies' (*Trotzschwangerschaften*). One girl emphasized that she had got pregnant in order 'to show the state that I won't go along with that'. These protest pregnancies were a major reason for the expansion of the sterilization law in 1935 into an abortion law, after which abortions could be performed on the same eugenic grounds as sterilizations. (This law also allowed abortion on the ground of a woman's state of health.) When abortions were performed for eugenic reasons, sterilization also was compulsory, and the number of such cases was about 30 000.[20]

Physically, sterilization means the separation of sexuality and procreation, and it had different meanings for women and men. A particularly important issue for male victims was the fear of castration, and here the medical authorities attempted to explain the difference and allay their anxieties. One doctor wrote about sterilized men in 1935: 'Happy that nothing can happen to them any more, that neither condoms nor douches are necessary, they fulfil their marital duties without restraint.' With respect to women a quite different aspect of sexuality was discussed in the professional press. Tens of thousands of women who, as one of them asserted, did 'not care at all about men' and had never had sexual intercourse, were sterilized because, according to the opinions of the all-male jurists and doctors, the possibility of pregnancy through rape had to be taken into consideration.[21] Therefore, the commentary to the law explicitly laid down that 'a different assessment of the danger of procreation is necessary for men and for women', and in the sterilization verdicts the following phrase, supported by government decree in 1936, regularly appeared. 'In the case of the female hereditarily sick, the possibility of abuse against her will must be taken into account.' Frequently, compulsory sterilization was advocated as a means of preventing the 'consequences' of a potential rape, namely pregnancy. The risk of 'inferior' women being raped was thus taken to be so high as to be a ground for the sterilization of women. At the same time, sterilized women often became objects of sexual abuse.

Those to be sterilized were denounced mostly by doctors, psychiatrists, and the heads of psychiatric institutions who handed to the authorities 80 per cent of the almost 400 000 denunciations in 1934 and 1935. Members of the same professional groups drew up the decisive applications for sterilizing specific persons; the most active agents here were 'state doctors', occupants of a position created in 1934 specifically for the purpose of searching for sterilization candidates. Sterilizations (and marriage prohibitions) were decided upon by about 250 specially created courts in which the judges were exclusively male doctors, psychiatrists, anthropologists, experts in human genetics, and jurists. This brought with it a highly important innovation: state power to decide on the subject of procreation was conferred on male doctors and scientists. However, women were also involved in the procedure. For instance, some social workers and female doctors (mostly, but not exclusively, those in the respective Nazi organizations) were among those who denounced possible candidates; their number seems to have declined as the 'state doctors' took over most of this activity.[22]

The courts decided on psychiatric diagnoses, using different criteria for women and men. Those for women measured their 'departure from the norm' against norms for the female sex, and those for men against norms for the male sex. To determine female 'inferiority', heterosexual behaviour was regularly investigated, and negatively evaluated when women frequently changed sexual partners or had more than one illegitimate child. The comparable behaviour of men was less investigated, and any findings carried little weight in the sterilization verdict. Women, not men, were tested on their inclination and capacity for housework and child-rearing (tests which were also applied to childless women). Women as well as men were assessed as to their inclination and capacity for extra-domestic employment. All these criteria were particularly prominent in the most crucial diagnosis, that of 'feeble-mindedness'. Indeed, whereas this diagnosis was the reason given for almost two-thirds of all sterilizations, women constituted almost two-thirds of the group sterilized on these grounds. About 10 per cent of the trials ended with acquittal;[23] women were let off when they could prove, to the satisfaction of the doctors and lawyers in court, who often came to inspect them at home and consulted their superiors at the extra-domestic work-place, that they did their work adequately inside as well as outside the home.

Unlike the later policy of extermination, the sterilization policy was not carried on secretly, but almost entirely in public view. In contrast to the impression given by many studies of women under National Socialism, the population was virtually bombarded with anti-natalist propaganda from 1933 on (before the Nazi rise to power, public sterilization propaganda was largely limited to the professional press). When in 1933–4 the Propaganda Ministry organized an aggressive campaign on 'population policy', Catholics were prevented from participating because of their pro-natalist and anti-sterilization stance, and the Catholic mothers' leagues were suppressed in 1935 on account of their anti-sterilization activities. Whereas in 1933 the 'women's page' of the *Völkischer Beobachter*, the official Nazi daily, dedicated 15 per cent of its space to the topic 'motherhood', it was reduced to 5 per cent by 1938.[24] National Socialism by no means wanted children at any cost and never propagated the slogan 'Kinder, Küche, Kirche' which has frequently, but wrongly, been ascribed to it;[25] equally, the biblical injunction 'Be fruitful and multiply' was explicitly rejected.[26] The Propaganda Ministry sharply denounced the misunderstanding that 'the state allegedly wants children at any cost' and reminded citizens that the goal was 'racially worthy, physically and mentally unaffected children of German families'. Official and influential authors estimated only a minority of somewhere between 10 and 30 per cent of German women to be 'worthy of procreating', and an equal percentage to be 'unworthy of procreating' (*fortpflanzungsunwürdig*).[27]

Often, propaganda was specifically addressed to the female sex, because it seemed to require more effort to make women understand the new anti-natalism than to get it across to men.[28] In 1934 the *Völkischer Beobachter* argued against women to 'see the value of their existence in having children' and proclaimed the sterilization law as the 'beginning of a new era' for women. Millions of pamphlets explained to women that 'the state's goal' was not prolific propagation but 'regeneration', and that they should present themselves and their children to the sterilization authorities if they felt that anything was wrong with them. Maternalism (*Mütterlichkeit*) became the target of vigorous polemics, many of them in journals for women and by female authors. According to one such writer, a medical doctor, there was 'a great danger arising from women precisely because of their maternalism', since 'it acts, like any egoism, against the race'. The 'unfortunate struggle between the sexes' was to be replaced by their common struggle for the 'future generation'. The traditional view that 'woman, because of all her physical and mental characteristics, is particularly close to all living beings, and has a particular inclination towards all life' was sharply criticized because it would encourage women to practise 'the worst sin against nature' ('nature' was understood as 'eradicating' the weak if left undisturbed by humane and charitable intervention).[29] Gertrud Scholtz-Klink, the 'Reich Women's Leader' who advocated sterilization and spoke against Catholic women workers' rejection of this policy, agreed with male Nazis on another aspect of 'female nature'. Like them, she insisted on the profound racial difference between 'German and un-German science', but denied that any differences of gender were relevant in this field: 'There is nothing like a specifically "female" knowledge, any more than a specifically "female" method', and 'no gender-based scholarship'.[30]

Such Nazi visions of nature, women, and anti-natalism contrasted sharply with the widespread maternalism of the moderate majority and a radical minority of the earlier women's movement. But ironically, whereas many historians have interpreted this maternalism as a precursor of the Nazi conceptions of gender, the voices of some radical feminists who, before 1933, advocated the sterilization of the 'inferior' (hoping thereby to render birth-control acceptable and respectable) are not usually regarded as precursors of Nazi policies.[31] Whatever the precise historical relationship turns out to be, it seems probable that the earlier feminist views on these issues—both maternalism and anti-natalism—did not influence the rise of National Socialist conceptions and policies. As to the latter, it is evident that never before had there been a state which, like the National Socialist regime, pursued an anti-natalist policy of such dimensions and efficiency in theory, in propaganda and in practice.

What, then, is the substance of Nazi pro-natalism and its alleged cult of motherhood? How did National Socialism conceive of gender relations in this area, and how is this area linked to anti-natalism and to race policy in general? Clearly, more 'German and healthy' babies were desired, but propaganda on this issue never failed to stress the contrasting policy of anti-natalism. In an important public speech of June 1933, the Minister of the Interior explained the hoped-for numerical relation between pro- and anti-natalism: 300 000 more children per year should be born (30 per cent of the birth rate), but 12 million Germans (20 per cent of the population) were suspected of being 'inferior'.[32] More importantly, no terror or compulsion was employed and no new bureaucracy developed for pro-natalist purposes. Rather, Nazism relied here on volition, tradition, and a range of welfare measures such as marriage loans (1933), tax rebates for the head of household in respect of wife and children (1934, 1939) and child allowances (1936). While these benefits did not succeed in raising the birth rate (its rise between 1933 and 1938 was rather due to increasing and then full employment), they resembled those introduced in most European countries as an integral component of the emerging welfare states, in contexts where pro-natalism was sometimes less, sometimes more rampant than in Nazi Germany.

National Socialist family subsidies nevertheless differed from those in other European countries in two significant respects: they were shot through with sexism and with racism. In connection with the first issue, studies of Nazi pro-natalism have overlooked the role of men, just as studies of Nazi anti-natalism have overlooked the role of women. As in the other masculinist dictatorships, Italy and Spain, Nazi state welfare privileged fathers over mothers, and glorified fatherhood as 'nature'; one Reich minister declared: 'The concept of fatherhood has been handed down through age-old processes of natural law', and 'the concept of the father in unambiguous and must be placed at the centre of financial measures for the family'. Race theorists insisted on the 'patriarchal spirit of the Nordic race'. Unlike female 'nature', male 'nature' seemed to require economic rewards. As the male head of the Nazi Party's organization Mother and Child emphasized:

There is no more beautiful image of selfless service than that of a mother with her children . . . who never thinks whether she is going to get anything in return . . . At the very moment at which she began to calculate returns, she would cease to be a good mother.[33]

Begetting children was considered more valuable than bearing and rearing them, and child allowances were paid to fathers, not to mothers; unmarried mothers obtained them only if the father of their child was known to the authorities. This gender policy differed sharply from that prevailing in the European democracies, where child allowances were paid to mothers, if only in response to the tenacious struggles of maternalist feminism.[34]

The second characteristic feature of Nazi family subsidies, its connection with racism, was unique, differing even from practice in the other dictatorships. All those classified as 'inferior'—such as eugenically 'unfit' parents and children, Jews, gypsies, and labourers from Eastern Europe—were denied benefits and discouraged from having children.

Thus, while state welfare for families and procreation was not in itself sexist or racist, National Socialism nevertheless linked the emergence of modern state welfare to sexism and racism by privileging men over women and 'valuable German' men over 'racially inferior' men. Welfare policy met its limits in race policy; the latter had priority over the former. Pro-natalism focused on fathers, and was shaped by the requirements of anti-natalism for the sake of 'racial uplift'. Hence, the unique and specific gender dimension of National Socialist population policy consisted not in 'pro-natalism and a cult of motherhood', but in anti-natalism and a cult of fatherhood and masculinity; whereas the latter was largely traditional, state anti-natalism was entirely novel. A historical continuity leads from there to the escalation of racism in the 1940s.

GENDER DIMENSIONS OF GENOCIDE

National Socialist race policy was directed, in both principle and practice, not only against men, but equally against women. Yet despite the equal treatment meted out to victims of both sexes, race policy was in many respects directed against women precisely as women. This is obvious in the case of racist anti-natalism, since when it comes to giving life human activities are obviously gender-based, and the anti-natalist 'primacy of the state in the sphere of life' assumed new features in the 1940s. But gender issues and gender difference were also important when it came to the 'primacy of the state in the sphere of death', particularly to genocide.

When war was declared in 1939, the practice of legalized sterilization was curtailed in order to liberate work-forces for war and massacre. Anti-natalism was now directed almost exclusively against women, particularly against those who had to perform forced labour and those in the concentration camps. Early in the war, Polish women who became pregnant were sent back east, and it seems that many took deliberate advantage of this policy in order to avoid forced labour. Their gesture was babies against war-work. But from 1941, when war was declared on Russia, the policy changed and pregnant Polish and Russian women had to stay in Germany. They were encouraged, and often forced, to undergo abortion and sterilization, and often had their children taken away from them. Pregnant Russian women were put to work at 'men's jobs' in the munitions industry so as to increase the chance that they would miscarry: a policy of war-work against babies. Around the same time, sterilization experiments were pursued under Himmler's command, particularly in Auschwitz and Ravensbrück, on Jews and gypsies . Originally they were meant for the future sterilization of those *Judenmischlinge* who were exempted from extermination, and the experiments were performed on both women and men. But they soon focused on women, who received injections into the uterus performed by doctors with previous experience of sterilization. Their aim now was to develop a technique for the mass sterilization of women who were considered 'inferior' on both ethnic and eugenic grounds. Jewish and gypsy women in the camps were used for the experimentation of a policy that in future was to overtake hundreds of thousands of ethnically and eugenically 'inferior' women all over Europe.[35] In all these instances, female difference was used to prevent maternity.

The pre-war sterilization policy was also a 'forerunner of mass murder',[36] of genocide as well as of 'euthanasia' (called Aktion T4), the massacre of the ill in which up to 200 000 ill, old and disabled people were killed between 1939 and 1945. Most of them were inmates of psychiatric clinics, women as well as men, and they included all Jews in such institutions. To kill them, gas was used for the first time. Anti-natalism anticipated certain features of this massacre in that, first, it had grown out of a mentality which saw sterilization not as a private and free choice, but as a 'humane' alternative to killing for the sake of the *Volkskörper*, as an 'elimination without massacre',[37] as a political substitute for 'nature' which 'naturally' (that is, without modern charity and medicine) prevented 'unfit' people from surviving. Second, it was through the policy of sterilization that the experts and authorities had already become used to dealing with bodily intervention and death, particularly in the case of women. Third, the very first victims of this massacre were 5000 disabled children aged 3 and under, precisely those whose mothers (and fathers) could not previously be identified as sterilization and abortion candidates (either because of the limits of bureaucracy or because the child's handicap was not hereditary). They were searched out through the channels of the sterilization bureaucracy. Finally, the activists of T4—mostly doctors and other medical personnel—had also been advocates and practitioners of compulsory sterilization, and many of them also played an important role in the genocide of the Jews.

Late in 1941, the T4 gas chambers and the male members of the teams who operated them were transferred from Germany to the death camps in the occupied East where they served for the systematic killing of millions of Jews and gypsies, women as well as men. This transfer was not just one of technology but had several significant gender dimensions. Before gas was used, hundreds of thousands of Jews had already been killed, mostly by mass shooting. The SS men involved seem to have experienced considerable 'psychological difficulties', particularly in shooting women and children, as was acknowledged, for instance, by the commandant of Auschwitz. Even Himmler became nervous while watching executions which included the killing of women and children. Soon after, gas technology was introduced not only as a means to accelerate killing, but also as 'a "suitable" method', a 'human' alternative to overt bloodshed, which would relieve the largely gender-specific scruples of the killers. Some of the first mobile gas vans used for killing Jews were used exclusively on women and children. Women were the majority of those who were delivered from the ghettos to be killed in the gas chambers of the death camps in occupied Poland. Nazi doctors in the death camps, who had turned from healers into killers, were able to function—sometimes over years—largely because of male bonding, heavy drinking, and their adaptation to an 'overall Nazi male ideal'.[38]

'Men, women and children' was the frequent description of the victims in many contemporary documents. In Auschwitz it was mostly Jewish women, and particularly those with children, who were selected for death as soon as they arrived in the camp ('every Jewish child meant automatic death to its mother'), whereas most able-bodied Jewish men were sent to forced labour. Almost two-thirds of the German Jews deported to and killed in the death camps were women, as were 56 per cent of the gypsies who were sent into the Auschwitz gas chambers.[39] The precise number of women among the other millions of dead will probably remain unknown. Hannah Arendt described the situation, the 'image of hell', as a massacre where no difference was made 'between men and women', a 'monstrous equality without fraternity or humanity', the 'darkest and deepest abyss of primal equality'.[40]

Historians have not yet explored this kind of 'equality' nor the meaning of the fact that the initiators, decision-makers and actors involved in these massacres were men, and that at least half of their victims were women. But the male massacre experts were by no means blind to such gender dimensions and did not consider this 'equal treatment' of the sexes among their victims as self-evident or self-explanatory. Rather, they felt that such murderous violence against women needed to be especially legitimized and its necessity particularly emphasized. Goebbels, in a widely broadcast radio speech of 1941 which explained why the Jews had to wear the Star of David, emphasized that Jewish women had to wear it too because they were just as dangerous as Jewish men, even though they 'may look utterly fragile and pitiful'.[41] But in Himmler's view, the justification for killing Jewish women was gender difference. In 1943, he felt the need to respond to a 'question which is certainly on people's minds. The question is: You know, I do understand that they kill adult Jews, but women and children . . .?' He addressed his SS men and other high officials, summarizing previous reflections and urging his audience 'only to listen but never to speak about what I am going to tell you here':

We came to the question: what about the women and children? I have decided to find a clear solution here too. In fact I did not regard myself as justified in exterminating the men—let us say killing them or having them killed—while letting avengers in the shape of children grow up.

Hence, Jewish women were killed as women, as child-bearers, and mothers of their people. But Himmler went further, placing female victims at the centre of his own definition of genocide:

When I was forced somewhere in some village to act against partisans and against Jewish commissars . . . then as a principle I gave the order to kill the women and children of those partisans and commissars too . . . Believe you me, that order was not so easy to give or so simple to carry out as it was logically thought out and can be stated in this hall. But we must constantly recognize that we are engaged in a primitive, primordial, natural race struggle.[42]

In this kind of 'logical thought',[43] in this—successful—attempt to override male scruples about a war of men against women, the most extreme form of the National Socialist 'natural' *Rassenkampf* was defined as a deadly struggle of men not just against men—as in a traditional military campaign—but particularly against women as mothers.

Occasionally, historians have perceived the centrality of the massacre of all Jewish women, boys and elderly men to the *Rassenkampf*; others consider it as self-evident and unworthy of specific mention.[44] Still others have singled out, as the most important gender dimension of the Holocaust, the notion that non-Jewish women participated in it by believing in female difference, particularly in motherhood, and by being mothers and wives. There were, in fact, many women who actively participated in Nazi race policies, but they do not correspond to this notion. They were a minority among the perpetrators and a minority among women at large, though a remarkably tough and efficient one, as their victims often emphasized. The more active among them were usually unmarried and without children; they were drawn from all social classes except the highest ones; and their participation in racist policies was mostly, as was often the case with comparable men, a function of their job or profession. Whereas the sterilization policy was entirely directed by men, some female social workers and medical doctors helped select the candidates. In the six T4 killing centres, female nurses assisted male doctors in selecting and killing. Female clerical workers worked alongside men in the offices and bureaucracies which dealt with race policies and genocide. Some women academics co-operated with their male superiors in gypsy studies and laid the groundwork for the selection and extermination of gypsies. Female camp guards who supervised women in the concentration camps came mostly from lower-class backgrounds and had volunteered for the job because it promised some upward mobility. Of all the women activists, they were closest to the centre of the killing operations and the most responsible for their functioning.[45] National Socialist racism was not only institutionalized as state policy, but also professionalized. Female participation in it, and responsibility for it, did not depend on a commitment to female difference, separate spheres, and motherhood, but on the extra-domestic adaptation of women to male-dominated and professionalized race policy. These women did not act as mothers, nor did they believe in maternalism as a feature of the female sex.

CONCLUSION

In this essay I have aimed to show why a range of prevailing opinions about the place of women in National Socialism are problematic. Many of their problems are due to traditional and simplified conceptions of the meaning of gender equality and gender difference for the National Socialist regime, particularly in the context of its racism and for the history of women under this regime. I have attempted to focus not only on some top Nazis' ritualized pronouncements on women, conjuring up 'the nobility of motherhood', but on the conceptions which were relevant to actual policy-making; not only on the majority of 'healthy German' women, but on the minorities which became victims of race policy—and which were soon to become much more than just a minority. Some of the results are summarized here.

The notions of gender equality and gender difference are context dependent. The context on which they depended in National Socialist theory and practice was, first of all, its racism. Race policy was what gave National Socialism its novelty and specificity. Moreover, this context is important because it applied the concepts 'equality' and 'difference' not only to gender relations, but also to race relations. Concepts and policies which focused on race relations also shaped National Socialism's visions of women and gender relations. Therefore, the latter were not traditional, simple and coherent, but in many ways novel, multiple, and contradictory.

There is no essential continuity between early twentieth-century feminist maternalism and National Socialist visions of women. Whereas in the feminist view, female 'difference' was the ground on which claims for women's 'equality' were based, National Socialist notions of race-based gender 'equality' and 'difference' were the ground on which 'racially inferior' women received a treatment which was equal to that of the men of their groups—persecution, sterilization, and death. Moreover, the National Socialist notions allowed a number of 'racially superior' women to participate in the development of the theory and practice of race policy. They did not act as mothers and wives, but acted on equal terms with the male agents of racism and in virtue of their extra-domestic roles. Hence, neither the female victims nor the female agents of National Socialist race policy inhabited a separate sphere dedicated to female 'difference'. Yet precisely this novel and 'monstrous equality' requires to be explored in terms of gender.

No image of essential female difference and no cult of motherhood were at the core of the National Socialist view and treatment of the female sex, nor was the image of women as mothers, where it appeared, specific to National Socialism. From its beginnings, National Socialism had broken with these images in many ways, most of all in its race policy. The essential and specific gender dimension of National Socialist birth policy did not consist in pronatalism and a cult of motherhood, but in anti-natalism and a cult of fatherhood and masculinity.

In particular, it is impossible to conceive a more profound contrast than that between Himmler's view of Jewish women doomed to death by virtue of being (potential) mothers, and the visions of motherhood developed by the strong German Jewish feminist movement before 1933, at a time when it constituted a pillar of the moderate German women's movement. Jewish feminists had often pointed to the parallels between women's emancipation and Jewish emancipation, and had claimed the right to be different both as women and as Jews. One of their crucial concerns, similar to that of other contemporary women's movements, was the value of motherhood; this was perceived as one form of female 'difference' which had not been sufficiently protected and empowered and which had not yet had a chance to develop its own cultural forms. Like all the other Western women's movements of that period, the German Jewish one had searched for a desirable relation between the recognition of women's equality and that of women's difference.[46]

National Socialism put an end to such efforts, a fact which suggests that modern racism and modern sexism have a parallel structure (even though Nazi sexism was largely traditional, whereas Nazi racism was both novel and deadly). Both deduce, from selected 'differences' among human beings, their 'inequality' in the sense of a hierarchy of values; and both measure 'inferiority' against the cultural norms of an allegedly 'superior' group. They deny the actually or allegedly different group not only the right to be 'equal', but also the right to be different without being punished for it: to live 'differently' in physical, emotional, mental—in short, in cultural—respects. As long as equality is understood as 'sameness' and difference as 'inferiority'—in terms of gender as well as of race—there is no space for human plurality, for the right and liberty to be different.

Notes

1. H. Arendt, *The Jew as Pariah: Jewish Identity and Politics in the Modern Age*, ed. R. H. Feldman (New York: Grover Press, 1978), 160. She emphasized the importance of the fact that for National Socialism, anti-Semitism and racism were not only social but eminently political issues; see H. Arendt, *The Origins of Totalitarianism* (New York: Harcourt, Brace & World, 1966).
2. For references to this view see K. Offen, 'Defining Feminism: A Comparative Historical Approach', *Signs*, 14 (1988), 154.
3. D. Schoenbaum, *Hitler's Social Revolution: Class and Status in Nazi Germany, 1933–1939* (Garden City, NY: Doubleday, 1967), 191–2.
4. L. J. Ruppl, *Mobilizing Women for War: German and American Propaganda, 1939–1945* (Princeton: Princeton University Press, 1978), esp. chs. 2, 3.
5. C. Huerkamp, 'Jüdische Akademikerinnen in Deutschland 1900–1938', forthcoming in *Geschichte und Gesellschaft* (1993). For women's employment see

D. Winkler, *Frauenarbeit im 'Dritten Reich'* (Hamburg: Hofmann & Campe, 1977); R. Hachtmann, *Industriearbeit im Dritten Reich* (Göttingen: Vandenhoeck & Ruprecht, 1989). For a comparable situation in the United Stated see A. Kessler-Harris, 'Gender Ideology in Historical Reconstruction: A Case-Study from the 1930s', *Gender and History*, 1 (1989), 31–49.

6. G. Bock, *Zwangssterilisation im Nationalsozialismus: Studien zur Rassenpolitik und Frauenpolitik* (Opladen: Westdeutscher Verlag, 1986), 160–1, 170–3.

7. H. F. K. Günther, 'Rassenkunde des jüdischen Volkes', app. to H. F. K. Günther, *Rassenkunde des deutschen Volkes* (Munich: Lehmann, 1923), 421–2; P. Schultze-Naumburg, 'Das Eheproblem in der nordischen Rasse', *Die Sonne*, 9/1 (1932), 25.

8. An exception is T. Wobbe (ed.), *Nach Osten: Die Verbrechen des Nationalsozialismus und die Verfolgung von Frauen* (Frankfurt: Neue Kritik, 1992).

9. S. Friedländer, 'Uberlegungen zur Historisierung des Nationalsozialismus', in D. Diner (ed.), *Ist der Nationalsozialismus Geschichte? Zu Historisierung und Historikerstreit* (Frankfurt: Fischer, 1987), 35.

10. See the discussion in M. Broszat (ed.), *Deutschlands Weg in die Diktatur: Internationale Konferenz zur nationalsozialistischen Machtübernahme im Reichstagsgebäude zu Berlin. Referate und Diskussionen* (Berlin: Siedler, 1984), 237–53.

11. C. Koonz, *Mothers in the Fatherland* (New York: St Martin's Press, 1987), 6, 17, 405, 419.

12. Ibid. 181–3, 218–19.

13. K. Windaus-Walser, 'Gnade der weiblichen Geburt?', *Feministische Studien*, 1 (1988), 131.

14. H. Burkhardt, *Der rassenhygienische Gedanke und seine Grundlagen* (Munich: Reinhardt, 1930), 93.

15. A. Gütt, E. Rüdin and F. Ruttke, *Gesetz zur Verhütung erbkranken Nachwuchses vom 14. Juli 1933* (Munich: Lehmann, 1934), 5, 176.

16. *Heinrich Himmler: Geheimreden 1933 bis 1945 und andere Ansprachen*, ed. B. F. Smith and A. F. Peterson (Frankfurt: Propyläen, 1974), 54–5.

17. W. Feldscher (Ministry of the Interior), *Rassen- und Erbpflege im deutschen Recht* (Berlin: Deutscher Rechtsverlag, 1943), 26, 118. See also K.-D. Bracher, 'Stufen der Machtergreifung', in K.-D. Bracher, W. Sauer, and G. Schultz, *Die nationalsozialistische Machtergreifung* (Opladen: Westdeutscher Verlag, 1960), 284–6; D. Majer, *'Fremdvölkische' im Dritten Reich* (Boppard: Bolt, 1981), 103 ff., 180–1.

18. R. Pommerin, *'Sterilisierung der Rheinlandbastarde': Das Schicksal einer farbigen deutschen Minderheit 1918–1937* (Düsseldorf: Droste, 1979); Bock, *Zwangssterilisation*, 358–60.

19. Information on these issues is available, among other sources, in around 200 doctoral dissertations accepted by medical faculties in the 1930s and 1940s which dealt with the sterilization mostly of women; see Bock, *Zwangssterilisation*, 181–2, 372–81.

20. See Ibid. 384–8.

21. The available sources do not tell if some among these women were lesbians. Among thousands of cases, I have found only one where this was an issue. For the documents see ibid. 389–401.

22. Ibid., chs. 4 and 5.

23. Hundreds of thousands of denunciations were not passed on to the sterilization courts, but were included in the 'hereditary census' of the German people; its files, which were said to comprise 10 million entries by 1941, focused on persons with 'negative hereditary traits'. Many of the cases not handed to the courts were postponed for the time after the war.

24. H. Kessler, *'Die deutsche Frau': Nationalsozialistische Frauenpropaganda im Völkischen Beobachter* (Cologne: Pahl-Rugenstein, 1981) 42 ff., 86 ff.

25. B. Friedan, *The Feminine Mystique* (New York, Dell, 1963), 32; T. Childers, *The Nazi Voter: The Social Foundation of Fascism in Germany, 1919–1933* (Chapel Hill, NC: North Carolina University Press, 1983), 174, 189.

26. One example is E. Rüdin (ed.), *Erbpflege und Rassenhygiene im völkischen Staat* (Munich: Lehmann, 1934), 8–9.

27. For documents see Bock, *Zwangssterilisation*, 24–5, 122–5, 456–61 (instructions from the Propaganda Ministry, the views of the blood-and-soil ideologue Richard Walther Darré, the head of the party's Race Office Walter Groß, *et al.*).

28. There were some good reasons for this belief. For instance, in 1934 the Kassel Secret Police reported that women were particularly hostile towards the sterilization law (Deutsches Zentralarchiv Potsdam, 15.01/26060, f. 297).

29. *Völkischer Beobachter*, 31 Jan. 1934; E. von Barsewisch, *Die Aufgaben der Frau für die Aufartung (=Schriften des Reichsausschusses für Volksgesundheitsdienst, no. 5)* (Berlin: Reichsdruckerei, 1933), 13–14; A. Bluhm, 'Das Gesetz zur Verhütung erbkranken Nachwuchses', *Die Frau*, 41 (1934), 529–38. For the journals of women's organizations see Bock, *Zwangssterilisation*, 130–1; for this propaganda see also Christa Wolf, *Kindheitsmuster* (Darmstadt: Luchterhand), 58–62.

30. G. Scholtz-Klink, *Die Frau im Dritten Reich: Eine Dokumentation* (Tübingen: Grabert, 1978), 364, 402, 379. For her speech see Bock, *Zwangssterilisation*, 208.

31. See A. T. Allen, 'German Radical Feminism and Eugenics, 1900–1918', *German Studies Review*, 11 (1989), 45–6.

32. W. Frick, *Bevölkerungs- und Rassenpolitik (Schriften zur politischen Bildung, no. 12/1)* (Langensalza: Beyer, 1933).

33. H. Frank, lecture to the committee for race and population policy in the Ministry of the Interior, 1937 (Bundesarchiv Koblenz, R 61/130); Günther, *Rassenkunde*, 274 ff., 345–6; Erich Hilgenfeldt to Bormann, reporting a conversation with Himmler in 1942 (Bundesarchiv Koblenz, NS 18/2427).

34. G. Bock and P. Thane (eds.), *Maternity and Gender Policies: Women and the Rise of the European Welfare States, 1880s–1950s* (London: Routledge, 1991).

35. Bock, *Zwangssterilisation*, 440–56.

36. R. J. Lifton, *The Nazi Doctors: Medical Killing and the Psychology of Genocide* (New York, Basic Books, 1986), 23.

37. H.-W. Schmuhl, *Rassenhygiene, Nationalsozialismus, Euthanasie: Von der Verhütung zur Vernichtung 'lebensunwerten' Lebens 1890–1945* (Göttingen: Vandenhoeck & Ruprecht, 1987), 40.

38. Lifton, *Nazi Doctors*, 159, 462 (quotes); R. Hilberg, *The Destruction of the European Jews*, 3 vols., rev. and definitive edn. (New York: Holmes & Meier, 1985), i. 332–4; ii. 690–1; iii. 871; J. M. Ringelheim, 'Verschleppung, Tod und Überleben: Nationalsozialistische Politik gegen Frauen und Männer im besetzten Polen', in Wobbe, *Nach Osten*.

39. L. Adelsberger, *Auschwitz: Ein Tatsachenbericht* (Berlin: Lettner, 1956), 127 (quote); J. Ficowski, 'Die Vernichtung', in Tilman Zülch (ed.), *In Auschwitz vergast, bis heute verfolgt: Zur Situation der Roma (Zigeuner) in Deutschland und Europa* (Reinbek: Rowohlt, 1979), 135–6; M. Richarz, *Jüdisches Leben in Deutschland*, iii. (Stuttgart: Deutsche Verlagsanstalt, 1982), 61; E. Kogon *et al.* (eds.), *Nationalsozialistische Massentötungen durch Giftgas* (Frankfurt: S. Fischer, 1986), 88–97, 105–8, 122, 131, 134, 158, 210–15.

40. H. Arendt, 'The Image of Hell', *Commentary*, 2–3 (1946) 291–5. For her reflections on the concept 'equality' see also her *Origins of Totalitarianism*, chs. 1, 9.

41. Quoted in H. G. Adler, *Der verwaltete Mensch: Studien zur Deportation der Juden aus Deustschland* (Tübingen: Mohr, 1974), 63–4.

42. *Heinrich Himmler*, 169, 201.

43. Himmer's 'logic' resembled that which had led to the sterilization of equal numbers of women and men which proved so fatal for women. This kind of 'logic' has been brilliantly analysed by Arendt, *Origins of Totalitarianism*, ch. 13.

44. E. Jäckel, 'Die elende Praxis der Untersteller', in *Historikerstreit* (Munich: Piper, 1987), 118/19; E. Nolte, 'Die Sache auf den Kopf gestellt', ibid. 229, argues that mentioning women here 'merely unfolds what can be more briefly expressed with the term "race murder" '.

45. For a different view—that these women 'did not affect the workings of the Nazi state'—see Koonz, *Mothers*, 405.

46. M. A. Kaplan, *The Jewish Feminist Movement in Germany: The Campaigns of the Jüdischer Frauenbund, 1904–1938* (Westport, Conn.: Greenwood Press, 1979); Offen, 'Defining Feminism'; Bock and Thane, *Maternity*; A. T. Allen, *Feminism and Motherhood in Germany, 1800–1914* (New Brunswick, NJ: Rutgers University Press, 1991).

Part IV. **Class**

10 Southern Honour, Southern Dishonour: Managerial Ideology and the Construction of Gender, Race, and Class Relations in Southern Industry

Dolores Janiewski

Southern employers behaved and spoke in ways designed to enhance awareness of racial and gender differences as they muted the recognition of any possible conflict between their own interests and those of white members of the labouring class. Tobacco planters in seventeenth-century Chesapeake initiated the process that created racial distinctions and reorganized pre-existing sexual divisions of labour. From these dominant practices antebellum and postbellum industrialists moulded an industrial labour force. Each successive group of employers contributed to a managerial ideology that deflected attention from class to gender and racial issues. These conceptions of race and gender became a part of the social conventions by which southern whites located men and women, blacks and whites, within their social order long after slavery had ended. If we can understand the development of those notions of essential racial and gender differences and inequalities, we are on our way to understanding how and why sexual and racial divisions have become so deeply entrenched in the labour force.

Research on the segmentation of the labour market has yielded important insights into the construction of differences between groups of workers, but its practitioners have often written as though managers operated freely in a cultural vacuum, guided only by their own economic interests. Identifying employers' motivations almost exclusively in class terms, they have ignored or downplayed gender and racial considerations.[1] Intent on explaining divisions among workers, they have concentrated on the work-place and the labour market—that is, on the sphere of production. While recognizing that workers bear other identities—racial and gender identities being among the most important—they have insisted, implicitly or explicitly, on the primacy of class. They have failed to give sufficient recognition to the dominant class interest in *reproducing* the members of their society as gendered and racially conscious beings. They have generally written 'labour' history rather than integrating their work into the comparative study of gender, race, and class and analysing the terms by which each of those relationships is represented by and to the members of each social group.[2]

Even Ruth Milkman's prize-winning, *Gender at Work* would be enhanced by more attention to issues that a study of the construction of southern labour markets and the sexual and racial divisions within them cannot avoid. Milkman's argument that ideology plays 'a central role in reproducing the sexual division of labor once it has crystallized in a particular labor market' needs to be extended to include the role of ideology in the initial creation of sexual and racial divisions of labour and their persistence despite such major shifts as emancipation and the wartime recruitment of women into 'men's jobs'.[3] Pre-existing assumptions about gendered labour, beyond the scope of Milkman's and similar work-place studies, shaped the managerial strategies she emphasizes and constrained the ability of unions and women workers to overcome them. An examination of one crucial aspect of the creation of a sexually and racially divided labour force in the South can help to trace the origins of conceptions of gendered labour which continue to influence twentieth-century labour relations outside as well as within the South.

Taking inspirations from appeals for labour historians to examine 'how people construct meaning' and 'how difference (and therefore sexual difference) operates in the construction of meaning', let us examine a language created by a dominant class that stressed 'identity' and 'difference'.[4] Emphasizing racial differences and gender differences among members of the 'dominant' race, the language fashioned by southern employers submerged the reality of class domination. Daniel A. Tompkins, one of the most prominent ideologues of the New South, wrote plainly in 1901: 'The white man loves to control, and loves the person willing to be controlled by him. The negro readily submits to the master hand, admires and even loves it.'[5] Having accentuated the masculinity of the 'master' race, Tompkins conflated a labour system with a sexual and racial system when he asserted that 'love' for the inferior was achieved at the cost of submission. A common inheritance 'naturally' endowed southern white men of every class with the right to dominate the 'naturally' subordinated members of southern society, who included all women and black men.[6] His language, like that of his fellow manufacturers, rendered invisible the control his class of white men exerted over the other white men, women, and children who worked in their factories.

ORIGINS

Tompkins deliberately used language that harkened back to the origins of labour relations in the South. Already acculturated into a society where a sexual division of labour allocated the major share of agricultural labour to men and domestic labour to women, the men who sought to establish a cash-crop economy in the southern colonies designated men as their primary labour supply. The original labour market involved a master's purchase of the labourer's person on a temporary or permanent basis. Slavery replaced indentured labour when the potential supply of European labour decreased and the price of African slaves declined. Slave owners embraced the idea of race as a way to represent the essential distinction between persons who could be enslaved and those who could not. Denying to Native Americans and Africans the rights of 'freeborn Englishmen', slave owners simultaneously raised the status of members of their own race above that of even a temporary 'unfree' person. They also lessened the danger arising from the expansion of a class of poor, recently freed indentured servants who were becoming a potentially rebellious class by the 1670s. Poorer whites, no longer required to perform the most servile labour, gained a stake in a system that replaced class with race as the primary form of identity and difference in the planter-generated labour and linguistic system.[7]

White male property owners, architects of southern law, created a social order in which they could exercise legitimate authority over the other, subordinated members of their society in racial and gender-specific forms. To ensure the creation and reproduction of two races, the laws necessarily regulated sexual, social, and productive relations. As gender relations among the dominant racial group developed into a form of domestic patriarchalism, white women concentrated on domestic labour, the reproductive work of bearing 'legitimate' heirs, and became the exclusive reproductive and sexual property of their fathers and husbands.[8] Simultaneously laws forbade white women to tend tobacco and refused to recognize them as productive labourers for purposes of taxation. Slaves, both women and men, became legally defined as productive and reproductive property whose labour and children belonged to their masters.[9] On one side of the racial divide, the law intervened directly to maintain the chastity of one group of women. On the other side, it offered no support for a slave woman's refusal of sexual access. Southern planters claimed exclusive control over sexual, productive, and reproductive property in racially and sexually distinct forms.[10]

Male members of the property-owning classes forged an ideological defence for the sexual and racial order they had constructed. They assumed the power to define and defend 'virtue and decency' as well as 'the barrier, which nature, as well as law, has erected between the white and black races'.[11] Especially among the lower classes, when familial discipline and social ostracism failed to prevent such transgressions, their judicial arm punished violators of the moral code.[12] Applying the rules that had evolved in other patriarchal caste systems, they insisted that white women's sexual restraint offered the only safeguard for the purity of the superior race in a system where children bore the racial identities of their mothers.[13] Defining black women as a 'class of females who set little value on chastity and afford easy gratification to the hot passions of men', they denied black women the honour they extolled in white women who possessed a reputation for chastity.[14] In effect pro-slavery ideologues portrayed slaves as a different order of being from themselves. Slaves were 'innately and immutably immoral', licentious, and perpetually childlike; their only legitimate 'family' was the one headed by the white planter.[15] As in other slave systems, for these slave women 'economic exploitation and sexual exploitation were ... linked' through the self-justifying language and actions of a male slave-owning group.[16] The logic of a patriarchal slave-holding society divided women into the respectable and the disreputable; the moral natures of these different sorts of women marked the classes and the races as made up of entirely different orders of being.

In a world ideally organized according to this model, labour would be performed only by the degraded caste—the slaves—and the superior group would act only as master. Indeed, labour itself would function as a mark of degradation. All whites would own slaves; all blacks would be enslaved. In the words of Linton Stephens, brother of the Confederate vice-president, 'menial services and manual labor' would be confined to a 'class of men defined by blood' rather than 'a class marked by poverty'.[17] All white women would be kept securely within the family economy and be supported by property-holding male protectors. Most southern whites, however, could not ascend into the ranks of slaveholders and planters. Many white males had to engage in 'the degradation of physical toil'. Sometimes they might be required to work for their economic superiors. Relatively prosperous non-slaveholders might still conform to an attenuated version of the slaveholder's ideal by keeping their womenfolk out of the fields and exercising authority over the family labour-force. But there were poor white women who had lost their male providers. Some white men could not even relieve their wives and daughters of 'those domestic drudgeries' that impaired 'delicate purity'.[18] Such class realities blurred the 'unerring lines' that were supposed to mark the 'distinction between the species' in a region whose leaders insisted 'that capital and labor . . . should be represented by the master and the slave'.[19] Somehow the frustrations of men unable to fulfill the social ideals had to be dealt with so that the labour and language system could remain compelling and mutually reinforcing.

The 'thousands of poor, degraded whites among us' posed a problem once they began 'to understand that they [had] rights'.[20] As a potential employer reported, a 'poor white man would feel affronted to be asked to engage in servile labor'. For white women the association of labour with degradation was intensified by slavery's linkage of sexual dishonour with economic exploitation. Any occupation that placed a white woman near a black labourer, male or female, inflicted 'a degree of degradation to which she could not condescend' and which her menfolk could not countenance. Wealthier whites, who sought to use the labour of white men and especially white women, faced a potential conflict between access to necessary labour and the maintenance of a racial and sexual hierarchy carefully constructed by the planters. Unless they could make work 'respectable for white persons', either racial chaos, class conflict, sexual disorder, or economic disaster might occur.[21] If southern employers were to use white labour without endangering 'our institutions', labour's 'symbolic load' must be overcome while poorer whites must be reassured that they were indeed raised to the 'general level' of other whites, as such planters as Jefferson Davis had promised them.[22]

CREATING AN INDUSTRIAL WORK-FORCE IN A SLAVE ECONOMY

So long as tobacco, sugar, and cotton earned prices high enough to subsidize the purchase of slaves, planters could avoid the ideological contradictions their labour and linguistic system had created. But men who sought to develop manufacturing in the South could not easily escape the dilemma. Depending on the 'size and character of the local labour pool, the regional price for slaves, the migratory patterns of whites, and the willingness of blacks and whites to enter the mills at prevailing wage rates, or even to work for wages', manufacturers decided on their own particular strategy.[23] Textile mills, needing water power and usually too undercapitalized to buy slaves, clustered in the Piedmont areas at the fall lines, where the available labour pool typically included white women and children unwanted in the agricultural economy. Tobacco factories gradually hired whites but the majority of their workers were slaves, purchased or hired. The numbers of white women and children in the industry increased in the 1850s, when the price of prime male slaves rose beyond the reach of manufacturers. But their employers maintained separate work sites for the newly hired whites and the remaining slaves.[24] Thus the sexual and racial divisions of labour developed by southern planters now shaped the choices of manufacturers.

Even as manufacturers conformed their recruitment policies to the 'size and character of the local labor pool', they sought to justify the social and political consequences of their decisions. Those who hired white workers claimed that the practice encouraged their recruits to become 'firm and uncompromising supporters of our institutions' by raising 'this class from want', 'beggary', and 'moral degradation to a state of ... moral and social respectability'.[25] William Gregg, a pioneering textile manufacturer in South Carolina, solicited votes in the 1840s on 'the ground that he had built a factory which gave work to poor white people'.[26] Yet such a rationale could be completely convincing only if employers demonstrated their commitment to 'the barrier which nature, as well as law, has erected between the white and black races'. They had to exclude slaves from their work-places so that whites would not be forced into degrading positions where they would compete with blacks'.[27] Providing additional reassurance, the supporters of the decision to hire white labour pointed to the dangers posed by the alternative choice. James Hammond, the last senator from South Carolina before the Civil War, argued that a slave mechanic was 'more than half freed' and warned that such a slave would become 'the most corrupt and turbulent of his class'.[28] The mill that relied heavily on the labour of white women and children would be a refuge for the 'afflicted' and would 'improve not only the physical but the moral and intellectual conditions of our citizens'. Children would be given 'light and honorable employment'. Any male hand 'who shall utter any slanderous word reflecting upon the good name of any female engaged in the establishment' was threatened with discharge from the mill of one particularly upright textile operator.[29] In short, employers could choose to make their jobs 'respectable for white persons' through ostentatious attention to their morality and the elimination of black workers from their factories. Adherents of this view insisted that slave labour should be confined to agriculture and white labour to manufacturing while predicting that a mixed-race labour force 'would be in hostile array to our institutions'.[30]

Employers who owned or hired slaves had to defend themselves against charges that industrial employment undermined slavery. Their defence of their policies harked back to Jefferson's warnings against the creation of a propertyless mob of white workers. Their spokesmen agreed with William Harper that such labourers, 'kept in strict subordination, will be less dangerous than . . . a class of what are called free laborers'.[31] They could point to the difficulties of persuading a sufficient number of whites to overcome their 'notable reluctance . . . to accept employment in the cotton mill'.[32] Yet the rising prices of slaves in the 1850s made their choice an expensive proposition.[33] Hampered by limited capital, the shortage of labour, and perplexing ideological dilemmas, southern manufacturers found it difficult to develop a successful labour recruitment strategy in the antebellum South.

AFTER EMANCIPATION

Emancipation removed the possibility of using slave labour and the ideological imperative of making a labour recruitment strategy appear compatible with slavery. Yet employers still needed great ideological dexterity. The war had shattered the social order into 'demoralized and trembling fragments of society and law';[34] defeat had brought impoverishment and the collapse of the labour system. They had to devise a recruitment strategy that would appear responsive to the political, economic, and social exigencies of the post Civil War South. An agricultural system in disarray promised to give them easier access to labour. At the same time it raised the question whether freed people had 'deteriorated as laborers'. Some employers insisted that 'young negroes are not equal to those of the older generation who were raised by whites'.[35] The decision to hire white widows and their children could make employers who recruited those victims of the war appear patriotic and charitable. But the strategy of using white labour also risked worsening class divisions already widened by the war. Denying that the nature of black labour had been radically altered by emancipation, some employers claimed to prefer a black worker because 'it is in his nature to submit to authority . . . and he does not want money or property enough to rise in rebellion against capital'.[36]

Southern manufacturers faced ideological pressure from an unaccustomed direction. As the *Vicksburg Republican* proclaimed in April 1868, 'The Republican Party is pledged to elevate labor, to educate the masses'. Thomas Settle, a leading Republican in North Carolina, campaigned for the support of poorer whites, whom he promised to rescue from 'moral servitude' to the power of planters and the degradation of labour the antebellum system had caused.[37] At the same time, southern manufacturers found it difficult to ignore the desires of planters, who still controlled most of the South's surviving resources. The planter spokesmen insisted that abolition should 'be limited, controlled', so as to 'make the change as slight as possible both to the white man and to the negro, the planter and the workman, the capitalist and the laborer'. Edmund Rhett insisted that freedmen be 'kept as near to the condition of slavery as possible and as far from the condition of the white man as is practicable'.[38] Though manufacturers loudly proclaimed the New South, they ignored the heirs to the Old South at their peril.[39] Emancipation had not freed manufacturers from dealing with the ideological conflicts between antebellum conceptions of appropriate gender, race, and labour relations and the 'free labor' ideology espoused by radical Republicans.

Manufacturers found it impossible to avoid involvement in the political arena. Republicanism appeared to offer the proper political vehicle for an aspiring industrial class. But southern Republicans were torn between a commitment to maintain a class of independent producers and a push toward an industrial economy of powerful employers and propertyless wage earners. They might best have pursued the first goal by promoting an interracial alliance between lower- and middle-class blacks and whites. But 'moderate' Republicans warned against the dangers of economic radicalism and black equality as they sought to promote a favourable business climate to lure capital southward. The Democratic party counter-attacked by proposing a cross-class alliance based on a common commitment to white supremacy which managed to 'redeem' the South from a party divided by the interests of entrepreneurs, yeomen, and freedmen. The Ku Klux Klan and similar paramilitary groups aided the success of the ideological appeal.

Manufacturers were not simply bystanders during this political and cultural counter-revolution. Some prominent manufacturers joined Democrats in preaching a new gospel that was more in tune with the interests of entrepreneurs. Henry W. Grady, the champion of this New South, boasted of a 'perfect democracy, the oligarchs leading in the popular movement' toward 'diversified industry'. In such a South blacks would be barred 'from no avenue in which their feet are fitted to tread' but would never be permitted to regain the 'negro supremacy' imposed during Reconstruction.[40] In the words of the *Manufacturers' Record*, 'business principles' would triumph over 'politics' in shaping the regional and national agenda.[41] By the 1890s Daniel Tompkins, another New South spokesman, declared that because 'the people of the North realize that an excess of zeal in the cause of freedom does injury, we are now all free in the South, free to enter upon manufacturing enterprises and to help develop American resources and promote American civilization'.[42] Combining ideological appeals to the dignity of labour, white supremacy, and economic development with attacks on 'agrarianism' and racial equality, prominent industrialists and Democrats sought to blend Old and New South ideologies into a political message that could cement an alliance between agrarian and industrial elites nationally while splitting members of the lower classes along racial lines.

Drawing on antebellum precedents, the agrarian elites and their commercial and industrial allies fashioned a language that would stir the emotions and inspire the loyalties of the embittered, impoverished white males whose families and whose labour they wished to use in their mills and factories and, increasingly, on tenant farms. The antebellum concern for racial purity served as a focal point for fears of a drastically altered sexual and political economy while it deflected attention from the actions of elites who were aiding and benefiting from the transformation. The loss of control over white women and fears about their exploitation as they entered the public work-place were translated into charges of assault by black rapists. Proclaiming themselves to be white women's protectors against the black menace, white men reasserted their control over white women and over blacks. Lynching and political campaigns for white supremacy reaffirmed white male solidarity through physical and rhetorical violence.[43]

Manufacturers joined in campaigns led by landed elites in the Black Belt to disfranchise black voters. E. C. Venable, of the Venable Tobacco Company, assured the Workingmen's Club of Petersburg, Virginia, that 'God had given the country to the white race and blacks were not going to rule any longer in Petersburg'.[44] The president of Erwin Cotton Mills granted permission for a parade in support of a disfranchisement amendment to the North Carolina constitution in 1900. The parade was led by a man holding a 'White Supremacy' banner and included a white float carrying sixteen young women dressed in white and bearing streamers with the slogan 'Protect us with your vote'.[45] Such explicit defences of white virgins against the 'black beast' expressed the anger of men whose masculinity was threatened by the dissolution of the patriarchal and racial foundations on which their identities rested. Symbolically ministering to the 'injuries of class', the elite rhetoric masked the actual shift of power from poorer to wealthier whites by the passage of many disfranchising statutes enacted in the name of white solidarity. Many of the laws drove the lower classes, white as well as black, from the southern electorate at the very time that the Populist movement was seeking, like the Republicans thirty years earlier, to create a class-based alliance.[46]

Yet, as Richard Edmonds of the *Manufacturers' Record* understood, manufacturers could never so enthusiastically embrace the cause of white supremacy as to exclude blacks altogether from the pool of potential workers. The danger of class conflict among whites could never be entirely eliminated. As one writer to the *Record* warned, 'White laboring men looking in the mirror and seeing in their lineaments a kinship of race and right with the ruling classes, clamor for a revolution.' The same writer welcomed black workers as allies against such dangers. 'The negro cannot do without us, and we cannot spare him. . . . He is an indispensable factor of our industrial system. . . . The negro, seeing in the color of his face the emblem of his inferiority, willingly submits to the menial pursuits of life.' Edmonds reluctantly printed opposing views demanding the expulsion of blacks from the South and encouraging 'white labour' to '[force] them all out of the State', but his New South could never become entirely a white man's country.[47] Farsighted businessmen avoided total endorsement of racial annihilation or removal because it obviously would limit their own options. Somehow labour recruiters in the New South must acknowledge the tenets of white supremacy while limiting its full implementation in its most virulent form.

TEXTILE AND TOBACCO RECRUITMENT STRATEGIES

In parallel with their political resolution of the post-war crisis, New South manufacturers resolved their ideological dilemmas by adapting pre-war recruitment strategies to post-war conditions. The textile industry continued to rely on the 'family labour system' and its ideological counterpart, industrial paternalism.[48] Such a strategy enabled mill owners to expand a white labour force by attracting women, girls, and young children, who had previously laboured only within the family economy. At the same time the supervisors found a welcome model for their efforts to discipline the workers in the patriarchal head of the farm family.[49] A continued commitment to a white labour force fitted the ideological and material interests of textile manufacturers. Interconnected labour processes made a homogeneous and unified labour force a major asset. Furthermore, this strategy enabled textile manufacturers and their allies to redefine the 'family' so as to exclude blacks. The 'coloured people' were 'with us still but they are not part of our families as they were then'.[50] Shifting from an interracial to an interclass 'family', textile officials reinforced the struggle for the same goal they were pursuing in the political arena.

Although a few efforts were made to use black labour in post-war mills, textile executives in the 1880s and 1890s were insisting that 'the question of the employment of colored labor in the finer processes of manufacturing' would be discussed only 'by those who know nothing about it'. The head of the Georgia school system testified before a Senate committee that because blacks lacked 'purity of life' and did not recognize the 'marriage relation', it was essential that they 'be under the control of the white race'. He considered black membership in a mill village family simply untenable. A Georgia mill executive provided another reason for excluding blacks: 'The whites won't work with the colored'. He also objected to using black workers in the mills because 'they think they are as good as you'.[51] In 1893, when the *Manufacturers' Record* polled its readers on the issue of 'colored mill help', the majority concluded that 'white labor will not work with the negro at the machine. You cannot mix them in a cotton mill. . . . You will not live to see a cotton mill run successfully by negro operatives'.[52] Statistical evidence revealed the results of these managerial beliefs. Whereas in 1890 14.2 per cent of southern textile operatives were black males and 2.95 per cent were black females, by 1910 only 1.33 per cent were black males and 0.76 per cent were black females.[53] As manufacturers anxiously sought to attract the 'better class' and increasingly avoided experiments with black labour or an integrated labour force, textile labour become defined ever more rigidly as white.[54]

This industrial strategy also eased the dangers that might arise from the presence of large numbers of white women who lacked the protection of an independent patriarchal family economy. Manufacturers averted a potential crisis in gender relations caused by conditions that forced white women into the public realm by giving them and their children employment that was 'well adapted to their strength' and by subjecting them 'to elevating social influences' in sheltered work-places where they visibly remained under white male protection and care.[55] Yeomen who could not control their own family economies on the land might thankfully come to a mill village, where they could personally ensure the respectability of their wives and daughters who laboured in the mill. The sons they reared in the mill village might aspire to as new patriarchal status as overseers and supervisors.[56] Certainly the racial and gender ideologies of the period would not permit 'the working of negroes, particularly negro men beside white women within walls. . . . No association which might permit the possible lessening of the negro's deference toward white women would be allowed'.[57] Now more than ever, textile manufacturers had to recognize that the 'right' labour was white.

Such a recruitment strategy made the textile industry less likely to be seen as bringing social degradation on its female workers even as it was being attacked for taking women away from the home.[58] When criticisms were voiced, textile manufacturers were quick to refute them. When Hugh Wilson of the *Abbeville* (SC) *Press and Banner* dared to suggest that a mill worker learned nothing of the 'duties and work of a womanly life—the life which nature and the laws of our civilization intended', manufacturers deplored his slander of the 'virtuous women who prefer to earn their bread by honest toil'.[59] Denunciations came just as rapidly in response to Clare de Graffenried's 'Georgia Cracker in the Cotton Mills', which appeared in *Century* in 1891. This report described mill families as huddled together 'irrespective of sex or relationship' in a society where 'moral distinctions' were unknown. While women and children laboured for long hours in the mills, de Graffenried reported, husbands sat 'sunning their big lazy frames'.[60] Richard Edmonds of the *Manufacturers' Record*, one of the leading proponents of the New South ideology, attacked de Graffenried's article for 'misrepresentation'.[61] Rebecca Felton, a leading Georgia suffragist and political activist, defended the 'industrious, honest, virtuous, well-behaved, law-abiding and God-fearing women' who had been unfairly accused of being 'indifferent to the moral law'. Felton denounced the charge of immorality as an 'outrage upon womanly virtue and modesty' which threatened to undermine white supremacy.[62] In the opinion of defenders of the textile industry, any suggestion that the mill village patriarch had failed his fatherly duty to defend the 'purity' of his 'daughters' or that white women could be guilty of sexual misconduct threatened to subvert the industry's claim to be an agent of white supremacy. White supremacists, such as Felton, vigorously denounced black depravity and allowed no one to place white mill workers at the same moral level as blacks.

Solid adherents of the sexual and racial assumptions of New South ideology, white workers vigorously objected whenever individual mill owners sought to hire black workers. They were outraged by any suggestion that their conduct or moral worth could be equated with that of blacks.[63] Managers frequently claimed that their white workers would never tolerate black labour in the mills.[64] In 1897 white workers at Fulton Bag and Cotton Factory attacked the 'nasty, black, stinkin' nigger wimmin' brought to work in the factory.[65] Charleston textile workers denounced the efforts of the 'negro-loving' president of the Vesta Cotton Mill to hire black workers as leading to 'either social degradation or starvation wages'. The head of the local textile union shared the white-supremacy podium with the president of Erwin Mills in the 1900 campaign to disenfranchise blacks in North Carolina. When a newspaper inadvertently referred to both mill workers and blacks in a sentence dealing with common health problems, the workers objected to the implication that they were 'some lower order of human beings'. Such resentment led the South Carolina legislature in 1915 to pass a law prohibiting the employment of blacks in the state's textile mills.[66] As Daniel Tompkins expressed it in an extended discussion of the feasibility of hiring black labour in the mills, 'The Anglo-Saxon laborer is . . . in possession of this industry, and it is yet to be proven whether the colored race can compete in it'.[67] Ironically, manufacturers' success in appealing to racial solidarity among their white workers limited their ability to play one group of workers off against another.

Because the textile industry came to represent the promises of the New South to impoverished white southerners, the need to maintain white solidarity constrained the recruitment strategies of mill owners to a greater extent than it did those of other manufacturers. Employers in other industries were better able to use black labour. Testimony at Senate hearings in 1883 made it clear that Alabama iron mills and Alabama mining companies could 'employ colored laborers . . . for ordinary laboring work, preferring them to whites'. A wealthy woman from Birmingham felt equally free to denounce poor whites as the 'most hopeless, helpless, trifling set of people in the entire South'; nothing could be done with those women except 'to employ them in factories'. Even blacks, she reported, considered themselves higher than 'poor white trash'.[68] Apparently industrial patterns in Alabama, and particularly in the iron and steel industry allowed employment policies and even public attitudes among the elites to differ significantly from those of the textile industry.

Given their considerably smaller labour requirements (one-half those of textile manufacturers in 1890, one-fifth in 1910), tobacco processors found it easier to recruit both black and white workers without running the risks that limited textile employers (see Tables 10.1 and 10.2). Practice of industrial slavery in the antebellum years gave them access to a pool of already trained black workers.[69] In addition, the processing of tobacco easily lent itself to two tiers of labour, those who prepared the leaf (the primary task before the war) and those who made the final products, whereas the work of the textile industry was more interconnected and horizontal. Tobacco manufacturers continued their antebellum tradition of using black labour in the non-mechanized parts of the process while increasing the number of white workers in newer parts of the industry, especially those being mechanized, which were not already identified with blacks.

As far as the virtue of their white female employees was concerned, tobacco manufacturers evidently felt the same compulsions as their counterparts in textiles. Allen & Ginter, the first company to produce cigarettes in the South, hired young white women in

Table 10.1. Percentages of textile employees who were black or female, 1890–1960

	1890	1910	1930	1940	1960
Total	482 110	898 992	1 183 400	1 170 014	963 040
Black	1.2%	1.3%	2.2%	2.1%	4.5%
Female	49.9%	45.6%	41.8%	40.8%	44.0%

Source: Richard L. Rowan, *The Negro in the Textile Industry, Report No. 20: The Racial Policies of American Industry* (Philadelphia: University of Pennsylvania Press, 1970), 54.

Table 10.2. Race and sex of tobacco workers in Kentucky, North and South Carolina, and Virginia, 1890–1940

	1890	1940
Total	16 977	43 516
White male	19.7%	30.7%
Female	8.2%	23.7%
Black male	47.4%	22.4%
Female	24.7%	23.1%

Source: US Department of Commerce, Bureau of the Census, Sixteenth Census, *The Labor Force* (Washington, DC: US Government Printing Office, 1942).

Richmond to roll cigarettes while pledging to provide 'clean' employment by avoiding the 'mingling of the sexes'. Their spokesmen reported that they hired only the daughters of 'respectable artisans' after carefully investigating their 'character and habits'.[70] The *Manufacturers' Record* rejoiced at the 'almost paternal care . . . exercised over . . . a hundred young girls' in the employ of W. Duke & Sons, and reported that 'immorality among them is absolutely unknown'.[71] The Dukes insisted that they guarded the 'moral purity' of their white female employees and required them to be 'self-respecting' and 'religious' in order to keep their jobs.[72] Into the 1930s the same factory continued to discharge white women whose sexual activities became the subject of gossip.[73] In that same decade a cigarette advertisement depicted white women standing in their white uniforms, like so many spotless vestal virgins, beside their machines. Manufacturers offered black female tobacco workers neither protection from sexual harassment nor the opportunity to represent the industry. Some foremen sought sexual favours from black women as the price of keeping their jobs. Other tobacco employers publicly boasted of treating black women roughly and rating them 'by their muscles' in language that clearly separated them from the virtuous white virgins who worked in other parts of the industry.[74] Perhaps impelled by the actual presence of black women in the industry, tobacco employers, like their contemporaries in textiles, symbolically placed white women in a higher moral class than black women.

Tobacco manufacturers reinforced the racial hierarchy within the tobacco factory. Segregation, while never legally enacted for the tobacco industry, divided the labour force spatially and ideologically.[75] In the New South black workers could be included in the tobacco industry only on a segregated basis.[76] Factory managers continued the antebellum practice of calling blacks by their first names while insisting that they be 'Mr. [Surname]' to black subordinates. Thus the factories were organized to honour 'the wise and beneficent purpose of keeping separate races which are, by nature, widely different in color, social qualities, and moral tendencies'.[77] Like other people marginalized by class, general, or racial hierarchies, black tobacco workers, particularly women, cleaned the dirt from the products of nature, becoming discoloured themselves in the process. White women, on the other side of the colour line, tended the machines of civilization, turning out cloth or cigarettes, while they wore white uniforms as testimony to their immunity to pollution. Like other dominant groups, southern manufacturers retained 'their stock of women within their control' while implicitly justifying 'social hierarchies and supremacy in terms of natural attributes', such as blackness, virginity, and dirt.[78]

The recruitment strategies of the tobacco and textile industries, which often coexisted in the same communities, complemented each other. Both industries carefully avoided excessive competition with agricultural employers. Each gained access to a plentiful and relatively cheap supply of labour through their access to the work of white children and young women. The tobacco industry had the additional advantage of hiring the still cheaper labour of black men, women, and children. For the most part both effectively kept their wage levels down while restricting better-paying occupations to experienced white males. Both strategies successfully accommodated industrial requirements to the demands of a racially and sexually stratified society.

HONOUR AND DISHONOUR IN TEXTILE AND TOBACCO FACTORIES

Weaving together the threads of honour and dishonour, southern manufacturers clothed their actual deviations from tradition in the garb of perfect fidelity to its racial and sexual practices. Like all employers, they could not operate purely from an economic calculus. Pre-existing divisions within the potential group of workers were recognized and reinforced because they suited the economic, political, and ideological interests of southern manufacturers and other elites. Treating all workers as interchangeable parts could have provoked widespread resistance to their power and perhaps subverted their authority. Like their slave-owning predecessors and their planter and merchant contemporaries, they feared the creation of a class-based alliance among the poorer members of their society. To avert that danger, they sought to instill a racial and gender consciousness while portraying themselves as defenders of white workers' interests.

The entrenchment of male authority appealed to patriarchal values already a familiar part of life. When workers referred to their employers as being 'like a daddy', they recognized the process by which they were being reared into a new way of working, for it echoed experiences of the past. Paternalism, a system of 'mutual obligations—duties, responsibilities, and ultimately even rights'— would bind white workers and employers together by transforming 'power relationships' into 'moral' obligations.[79] Employers offered their white male workers 'white skin' privilege in compensation for their loss of real control over human and economic resources. A brotherhood of white men bound together planter, industrialist, landlord, millworker, and tenant farmer in defence of an ideal that denied their conflicts of interest and disguised the real differences in power. Even as the private patriarchy of the yeoman's independent household dissolved, white men could take part in the symbolic construction of a public patriarchy that demonstrated their superiority over the subordinated members of southern society. Politicians, industrialists, and planters wielded power in the name of the white brotherhood while selected members of the lower classes exercised more limited authority in their behalf. Although an early advocate of this New South strategy had declared in 1881, 'In the fabric of thought and of habit which we have woven for a century we are no longer to dwell', textile and tobacco manufacturers clearly wove together old and new threads for the 'era of progressive enterprise' to which they were leading other southerners.[80]

That era began to unravel in the 1920s as the costs of the policy began to mount for the textile industry and as the tobacco industry grew more confident that it no longer needed to fear the consequences of a disgruntled labour force. Costly paternalism and family labour gave way to a more impersonal, bureaucratic managerial style that sought to raise productivity in the crisis-ridden textile industry. Emboldened by the Depression, the tobacco industry sought to speed up its workers, white and black alike, at a time when they apparently had little choice but to submit. Ironically, the forms of social cohesion reinforced or imposed by managerial strategy offered the workers a way to resist. Mill villages, once mobilized, could become class-conscious supporters of workers' actions. The violation of their sense of racial entitlement could radicalize white tobacco workers unwilling to accept conditions they likened to slavery. Perceiving the need for allies, black tobacco workers could seek aid from other members of their community and might even reach across racial lines to their newly enlightened white counterparts. Unions might gain adherents among white workers who felt betrayed when 'daddy' was revealed to be only a businessman.[81] Power relationships in the factory had begun to shed their moral, familial, fraternal, and racial disguise.

Managers were able to regain control through a series of concessions, innovations, and continuities. Mill owners sold village housing, scattering the cohesive working-class communities that had begun to challenge them. With the encouragement of employers and their unions, white tobacco workers continued to define certain jobs and departments as white and to maintain a racial and sexual differential in pay, promotion, and benefits. Black workers lost jobs to mechanization and to the segregation that denied their entrance to other occupations in the tobacco industry. When their unions too militantly addressed the issues of racism and corporate power, the government withdrew its protection and the more conservative labour movement turned its back. A feminist movement that could engage the loyalties of women across the racial and class boundaries did not emerge to mobilize women's energies or to redefine the 'virtuous woman'. Occupied by domestic concerns, a persistent legacy of the gender system, women could function as workers only by dividing their energy between two work-places. Male power remained firmly entrenched in union, factory, and the surrounding community, providing a useful foundation for modern hierarchies of power.

Workers nevertheless made some advances. Some black workers gained access to formerly all-white textile mills as the break-up of the village family removed one major barrier to blacks after World War II. Once installed, they became the major support for new union drives.[82] A combination of black agitation, the civil rights movement, and federal policy eventually forced the integration of the tobacco labour force and its union in the 1960s, after black workers had shrunk to a small minority of the work-force. Affirmative action altered some of the gender inequalities. Gradually the seniority lists and the occupational structure yielded to a more integrated labour-force, albeit primarily at the entry level. Racial and gender divisions narrowed but did not close.[83]

The fabric of control woven by planters and industrialists was ravelled and reworked in the transitions from the Old to the New South and now to the Sunbelt. Employers never recruited or managed workers as though they were colourless and sexless. They drew upon tradition to allocate work, power, honour, and resources while modifying the pre-existing patterns to their purposes. In the process they restricted their employees' ability to challenge their power but set limits on their own freedom of action. Obviously southern manufacturers displayed concern about the reproduction of a system of sexual, class, and racial domination that was not confined merely to their factories. Accentuating the issue of race in explosive connection with sex, they hindered the emergence of class-based alliances among the working and labouring groups in their society. Simultaneously they enhanced their own power as the dominant partners in three overlapping sets of relationships. Skilfully they mastered the craft of domination but they could never create an impenetrable fabric. While ultimately relying on power, they also had to resort to persuasion to secure allies for themselves. They always remained vulnerable to economic crisis, political challenge, and the possibility that the subordinate members of their society might somehow disentangle themselves.

Notes

1. For a pioneering effort in this literature, see Richard C. Edwards, Michael Reich, and David M. Gordon (eds.), *Labor-Market Segmentation* (Lexington, Mass.: D. C. Heath, 1975), and their later effort: David M. Gordon, Richard Edwards, and Michael Reich, *Segmented Work, Divided Workers: The Historical Transformation of Labor in the United States* (Cambridge: Cambridge University Press, 1982).
2. Joan Scott, 'On Language, Gender, and Working-Class History', *International*

Labor and Working-Class History, 31 (Spring 1987), 1–13, and the replies by Bryan D. Palmer and Christine Stansell in the same issue for a spirited discussion of the need for labour historians to engage in an encounter with poststructuralists and cultural anthropologists.

3. Ruth Milkman, *Gender at Work: The Dynamics of Job Segregation by Sex during World War II* (Urbana: University of Illinois Press, 1987), 157.

4. Scott, 'On Language, Gender, and Working-Class History', 1.

5. Daniel A. Tompkins, *Cotton and Cotton Oil* (Charlotte, NC: Published by the author, 1901), 47.

6. This emphasis on language should not be taken as total acceptance of Scott's position that language constructs either gender or class. Like her critics Bryan Palmer and Christine Stansell, I do not wish to privilege gender or language (or race) over the actual activities in which southerners, male and female, constructed their social existence. See Bryan D. Palmer, 'Response to Joan Scott', *International Labor and Working-Class History*, 31 (Spring 1987), 14–23, and Christine Stansell, 'A Response to Joan Scott', ibid. 24–9.

7. Edmund Morgan, in *American Slavery, American Freedom: The Ordeal of Colonial Virginia* (New York: Norton, 1975), makes these arguments about the shift from indentured white labour to enslaved black labour in Virginia.

8. See Alan Kulikoff, *Tobacco and Slaves: The Development of Southern Cultures in the Chesapeake, 1680–1800*, Institute of Early American History and Culture (Chapel Hill: University of North Carolina Press, 1985), 166, 382.

9. Winthrop Jordan, *White over Black: American Attitudes toward the Negro, 1550–1812* (New York: Norton, 1977), 167–78.

10. As discussed by Gerda Lerner in *The Creation of Patriarchy* (New York: Oxford University Press, 1986), 100.

11. John Campbell, 'Negro Mania—The Negro and Other Races of Man', in *Industrial Resources, Statistics, etc. of the U.S., and more particularly of the Southern and Western States*, 3 vols., comp. James D. B. De Bow, ii. 197 (1852–4; rpt. New York: A. M. Kelley, 1966); James H. Hammon, 'Progress of Southern Industry', in ibid. iii. 34–5.

12. See Victoria Elizabeth Bynum, 'Unruly Women: The Relationship between Status and Behavior among Free Women of the North Carolina Piedmont, 1840–1865' (Ph.D. diss., University of California, San Diego, 1987), 174–203.

13. William Harper, 'Memoir on Negro Slavery', in De Bow, *Industrial Resources*, iii. 220, 228; Mary Douglas, *Purity and Danger: An Analysis of the Concepts of Pollution and Taboo* (London: Routledge & Kegan Paul, 1966), 125–7.

14. Harper, 'Memoir on Negro Slavery', 220; Campbell, 'Negro Mania', 203.

15. Margaret A. Burnham, 'An Impossible Marriage: Slave Law and Family Law', *Law and Inequality: A Journal of Theory and Practice*, 5 (July 1987), 189.

16. Lerner, *Creation of Patriarchy*, 100.

17. Quoted in Lawrence Shore, *Southern Capitalists: The Ideological Leadership of an Elite, 1832–1885* (Chapel Hill: University of North Carolina Press, 1986), 44.

18. James D. B. De Bow and William Daniell, *American Cotton Planter*, Mar. 1854, quoted in Shore, *Southern Capitalists*, 35, 19.

19. Campbell, 'Negro Mania', 203; South Carolina Institute, *Second Annual Report*, Nov. 1850, quoted in Shore, *Southern Capitalists*, 37.

20. William Gregg, *Essays on Domestic Industry* (1844), and J. H. Taylor, 'Manufactures in South Carolina', *De Bow's Review*, Jan. 1850, both quoted in Shore, *Southern Capitalists*, 30, 34.

21. Charles T. James, 'Cotton and Cotton Manufactures at the South', in De Bow, *Industrial Resources*, i. 241.

22. Taylor, 'Manufactures in South Carolina', quoted in Shore, *Southern Capitalists*, 34; Douglas, *Purity and Danger*, 124, 227; Jefferson Davis, Mar. 1859, quoted in Shore, *Southern Capitalists*, 65.

23. Randall M. Miller, 'The Fabric of Control Slavery in Antebellum Southern Textile Mills', *Business History Review*, 55 (Winter 1981), 471–90.

24. Joseph Clarke Robert, *The Tobacco Kingdom: Plantation, Market, and Factory in Virginia and North Carolina, 1800–1860* (Gloucester, Mass.: Peter Smith, 1965), 197, 215–16.

25. James, 'Cotton and Cotton Manufactures', 241.

26. Tompkins, *Cotton Mill, Commercial Features*, 205.

27. Quoted in Peter Rachleff, 'Black, White, and Gray: Working-Class Activism in Richmond, Virginia, 1865–1890' (Ph.D. diss., University of Pittsburg, 1981).

28. Hammond, 'Progress of Southern Industry', 34–5.

29. Quoted in Gary Freeze, 'Poor Girls Who Might Otherwise Be Wretched: Society, Gender, and the Origins of Paternalism in North Carolina's Early Cotton Mills, 1836–1880', in Jeffrey A. Leiter *et al.*, 'Hanging by a Thread: Social Change in Southern Textiles', forthcoming.

30. South Carolina Institute, *Second Annual Report*, and Taylor, 'Manufactures in the South', quoted in Shore, *Southern Capitalists*, 37, 34.

31. Harper, 'Memoir on Negro Slavery', 234.

32. Quoted in Gavin Wright, *Old South, New South: Revolution in the Southern Economy since the Civil War* (New York: Basic Books, 1986), 128.

33. James, 'Cotton and Cotton Manufactures', 241.

34. Zebulon Vance to Joseph Brown, Jan. 1865, quoted in Shore, *Southern Capitalists*, 89.

35. R. Barnwell Rhett, Birmingham, 13 Nov. 1883, and Robert M. Patton, Birmingham, 12 Nov. 1883, in US Senate Committee on Education and Labor, *Capital and Labor Investigation*, iv. *Testimony* (Washington, DC: US Government Printing Office, 1885), 153, 48.

36. John W. Lapsley, planter and ironmaker, Birmingham, in ibid. 166.

37. Quoted in Shore, *Southern Capitalists*, 135, 141.

38. Quoted in ibid. 103.

39. See Jonathan M. Weiner, *Social Origins of the New South: Alabama, 1860–1885* (Balton Rouge: Louisiana State University Press, 1978) for the way planters thwarted industrial development in one southern state.

40. Henry W. Grady, 'The New South' (1886) and 'At the Boston Banquet' (1889), in Grady, *The South: Some Addresses* (Charlotte, NC: Observer Printing House, 1910).

41. 'A Southern Triumph', *Manufacturers' Record*, 18 (23 Aug. 1890).

42. D. A. Tompkins, 'Manufactures' (1899), in Grady, *The South*.

43. See Jacquelyn Dowd Hall, 'The Mind That Burns in Each Body: Women, Rape, and Racial Violence', in Ann Snitow, Christine Stansell, and Sharon Thompson (eds.), *Powers of Desire: The Politics of Sexuality* (New York: Monthly Review Press, 1983), 328–49, and Cal M. Logue and Howard Dorgan (eds.), *The Oratory of Southern Demagogues* (Baton Rouge: Louisiana State University Press, 1981).

44. Quoted in William D. Henderson, *Gilded Age City: Politics, Life, and Labor in*

Petersburg, Virginia, 1874–1889 (Lanham, Md.: University Press of America, 1980), 243.

45. Dolores E. Janiewski, *Sisterhood Denied: Race, Gender, and Class in a New South Community* (Philadelphia: Temple University Press, 1985), 91.

46. According to J. Morgan Kousser, *The Shaping of Southern Politics: Suffrage Restriction and the Establishment of the One-Party South* (New Haven: Yale University Press, 1974), the goal was to disfranchise poor whites and poor blacks.

47. C. J. Haden, 'Why Georgia Is the Empire State of the South', *Manufacturers' Record*, 24 (13 Oct. 1893); W. Silbert Wilson, 'Free Discussion of Southern Matters' and 'Correspondence: The Negro and Immigation' (24 Nov. 1893).

48. Philip Scranton, 'Varieties of Paternalism: Industrial Structures and the Social Relations of Production in American Textiles', *American Quarterly*, 36 (Summer 1984), 235–57.

49. William Lazonick argues that the family labour system offered the primary model for textile labour relations in England before the textile industry emerged in the United States: 'The Subjection of Labour to Capital: The Rise of the Capitalist System', *Review of Radical Political Economics*, 10 (Spring 1978), 6–9.

50. Gustavus J. Orr, Atlanta, 21 Nov. 1883, in US Senate, Committee on Education and Labor, *Capital and Labor Investigation*, 4:676.

51. Testimony in ibid. 589, 671, 539.

52. 'Colored Help for Textile Mills', *Manufacturers' Record*, 24 (22 Sept. 1893); 'Negroes Not Suited for Mill Work', ibid. (6 Oct. 1893); 'More Views about Colored Mill Help', ibid. (13 Oct. 1893).

53. Wright, *Old South, New South*, 178.

54. David Carlton, *Mill and Town in South Carolina, 1880–1920* (Baton Rouge: Louisiana State University Press, 1982), 115.

55. See e.g. Anne Firor Scott, *The Southern Lady: From Pedestal to Politics, 1830–1930* (Chicago: University of Chicago Press, 1970), chs. 4–6; *The Cotton Mills of South Carolina: Their Names, Locations, Capacity, and History* (Charleston, SC: News and Courier Book Presses, 1880), 22.

56. Wright, *Old South, New South*, 142.

57. Holland Thompson, *From the Cotton Field to the Cotton Mill: A Study of the Industrial Transition in North Carolina* (New York: Macmillan, 1906).

58. William P. Few, 'The Constructive Philanthropy of a Southern Cotton Mill', *South Atlantic Quarterly*, January 1909.

59. *Abbeville Press and Banner*, 22 Aug. 1883; *Charleston News and Courier*, 6 Sept. 1883.

60. Clare de Graffenried, 'The Georgia Cracker in the Cotton Mills', *Century*, Feb. 1891, 483–98. This article and the controversy it generated are fully explored by LeeAnn Whites in 'The de Graffenried Controversy: Class, Race, and Gender in the New South', *Journal of Southern History*, 54 (August 1988), 449–78.

61. *Manufacturers' Record*, 7 Feb. 1891.

62. *Augusta Chronicle*, 10 May 1891, as developed in Whites, 'De Graffenried Controversy'.

63. Melton A. McLaurin, *Paternalism and Protest: Southern Cotton Mill Workers and Organized Labor, 1875–1905* (Westport, Conn.: Greenwood, 1971), 60–1, 107.

64. 'Coloured Help for Textile Mills', *Manufacturers' Record*, 24 (22 Sept. 1893).

65. Wright, *Old South, New South*, 189.

66. Carlton, *Mill and Town in South Carolina*, 158–60, 245.

67. Daniel A. Tompkins, 'The Cultivation, Picking, Baling, and Manufacturing of Cotton from a Southern Standpoint', paper delivered to the New England Cotton Manufacturers' Association, Atlanta, 25 Oct. 1895.

68. Henry J. Evans, mayor of Chattanooga and iron manufacturer, and Mrs Ward, Birmingham, in US Senate Committee on Education and Labor, *Capital and Labor Investigation*, 4:169, 345.

69. See Robert S. Starobin, *Industrial Slavery in the Old South* (New York: Oxford University Press, 1970), 49, 211–12. Ironically for those historians who celebrate paternalism on the slave plantation, the industry that actually employed a higher percentage of slaves displayed fewer paternalistic tendencies than the one that relied on white labour. See e.g. Dweight Billings, Jr., *Planters and the Making of the 'New South': Class Politics and Development in North Carolina, 1865–1900* (Chapel Hill: University of North Carolina Press, 1979), 60–1, 101–4, 116–18.

70. *Richmond Industrial South*, 17 June 1882; *Frank Leslie's Illustrated Newspaper*, 10 Feb. 1883.

71. *Manufacturers' Record*, 19 (2 May 1891).

72. Washington Duke, quoted in *Raleigh News and Observer*, 5 Apr. 1896.

73. Janiewski, *Sisterhood Denied*, 97.

74. Emma L. Shields, 'A Half-Century of the Tobacco Industry', *Southern Workman*, Sept. 1922, 420–1.

75. John Cell, *The Highest Stage of White Supremacy: The Origins of Segregation in South Africa and the American South* (Cambridge: Cambridge University Press, 1982).

76. Howard Rabinowitz, *Race Relations in the Urban South, 1865–1890* (New York: Oxford University Press, 1978), argued that segregated labour was the only kind available to blacks from the time of emancipation. See also Janiewski, *Sisterhood Denied*, 95–126.

77. Quoted from *Baptist Missionary Herald*, Jan. 1874, in Rachleff, 'Black, White, and Gray'.

78. Leonore Davidoff, 'The Rationalization of Housework', in Diana Leonard Barker and Sheila Allen (eds.), *Dependence and Exploitation in Work and Marriage* (London: Longmans, 1976), draws on Mary Douglas's work on 'purity and danger' to analyse domestic service as a ritual of pollution and purity mediating between nature and culture. Members of the subordinate sex and class are required to do the cleaning; they themselves are 'unclean' and must be segregated lest they pollute members of the 'washed' classes. See also Kate Young, Carol Wolkowitz, and Roslyn McCullagh, *Of Marriage and the Market: Women's Subordination Internationally and Its Lessons* (London: Routledge & Kegan Paul, 1981), xix; Joel Williamson, *The Crucible of Race: Black–White Relations in the American South since Emancipation* (New York: Oxford University Press, 1984), 115–24, 249–58, 306–10, 418–22.

79. See Eugene D. Genovese, *Roll, Jordan, Roll: The World the Slaves Made* (New York: Random House, 1976), 5, for the first part of the definition Howard Newby, Colin Bell, David Rose, and Peter Saunders, *Property, Paternalism, and Power: Class and Control in Rural England* (Madison: University of Wisconsin Press, 1978), 28, for the second part.

80. *Charleston News and Courier*, 27 Dec. 1881.
81. Janiewski, *Sisterhood Denied*, 77, 153–78; George Sinclair Mitchell, *Textile Unionism in the South* (Chapel Hill: University of North Carolina Press, 1931); Herbert J. Lahne, *The Cotton Mill Worker* (New York: Farrar & Rinehart, 1944); Nannie Mae Tilley, *The R. J. Reynolds Tobacco Company* (Chapel Hill: University of North Carolina Press, 1985), 374–414; and Augusta V. Jackson, 'A New Deal for Tobacco Workers', *Crisis*, Oct. 1938, 322–4.
82. Harriet L. Herring, *Passing of the Mill Village: Revolution in a Southern Institution* (Chapel Hill: University of North Carolina Press, 1949); Richard L. Rowan, *The Negro in the Textile Industry, Report No. 20; The Racial Policies of American Industry* (Philadelphia: University of Pennsylvania Press, 1970), 69; Janiewski, *Sisterhood Denied*, 172–6; and Dolores Janiewski, 'Seeking a "New Day and a New Way"; Black Women and Unions in the Southern Tobacco Industry', in Carol Groneman and Mary Beth Norton (eds.), *'To Toil the Livelong Day': America's Women at Work, 1790–1980* (Ithaca: Cornell University Press, 1987), 161–78.
83. Mary Frederickson, 'Four Decades of Change: Black Workers in Southern Textiles, 1941–1981', *Radical America*, 16 (Nov.–Dec. 1982), 27–44; Mimi Conway, *Rise Gonna Rise: A Portrait of Southern Textile Workers* (Garden City, NY: Doubleday, 1979).

Sex and Skill: Notes Towards a Feminist Economics

Anne Phillips and Barbara Taylor

It is time the working females of England began to demand their long suppressed rights . . . In manufacturing towns, look at the value that is set on woman's labour, whether it be skilful (sic), whether it be laborious, so that woman can do it. The contemptible expression is, it is made by woman, and therefore cheap? Why, I ask, should woman's labour be thus undervalued? . . . Sisters, let us submit to it no longer . . . but unite and assert our just rights!

'A Bondswoman' (Frances Morrison) writing to a radical working class newspaper, *The Pioneer*, 12 April 1834.

Waged work in Britain, as in every other advanced capitalist country, is sharply differentiated along sexual lines. There may be few occupations left which are entirely the preserve of either men or women, but most men workers are employed in jobs where the work-force is at least ninety per cent male, while most women workers work in jobs which are at least seventy per cent female (Hakim, 1978). Even when men and women do work in the same industry, sexual demarcations are still rigidly maintained: women sew what men design and cut out; women serve what men cook; women run machines which men service; and so on and on . . . Everywhere we turn, we see a clear distinction between 'men's work' and 'women's work', with women's work almost invariably

Reprinted with permission from *Feminist Review*, 6 (1980), 79–88. This paper was originally written for presentation at the Nuffield Conference on De-skilling and the Labour Process, in November 1979, and later discussed by the Conference of Socialist Economists Sex and Class Group. We should like to thank Sue Himmelweit for her comments on the first drafts and for her encouragement to rewrite it for *Feminist Review*. In revising it we have gradually come to realize that it opens up many more questions than it resolves. We put it forward, therefore, not as a finished 'position' but as a way of sharing our questions with other feminists, in the hope that a wider dialogue may ensue.

characterized by lower pay, lack of craft traditions, weak union organization, and—above all—unskilled status.[1] Wherever women workers are, whatever jobs they do, they nearly always find themselves occupying the lowest rung on the skill ladder, earning wages which are commensurate, it is claimed, with the low level of training, ability or concentration required for the job.

In this paper we want to suggest that the classification of women's jobs as unskilled and men's jobs as skilled or semi-skilled frequently bears little relation to the actual amount of training or ability required for them. Skill definitions are saturated with sexual bias. The work of women is often deemed inferior simply because it is women who do it. Women workers carry into the work-place their status as subordinate individuals, and this status comes to define the value of the work they do. Far from being an objective economic fact, skill is often an ideological category imposed on certain types of work by virtue of the sex and power of the workers who perform it.

This hypothesis needs some qualification. Obviously it is true that there are jobs which require training, and it is also true that women workers (as well as some men workers, especially blacks or Asians) have generally been refused access to this training, thereby ensuring their exclusion from areas of work requiring more knowledge and initiative. Moreover domestic responsibilities— particularly childcare—curtail women's ability to enter training programmes even when these are open to them, as well as making it generally more difficult for women to climb up the job ladder. Part-time work and outwork, which are nearly always classified as unskilled, are often the only options open to women with small children. We are not denying this. But to suggest that the remarkable coincidence between women's labour and unskilled labour in our economy is solely the result of discriminatory training programmes, or even of home responsibilities, is surely naïve, since it implies that with educational upgrading and the provision of more day-nurseries women would take their place alongside skilled men workers, and gender-ghettos in waged work would disappear. We think the problem goes much deeper than this. In order to see how much deeper it goes, however, we must begin to rethink the meaning of skill itself and the economic categories through which skill has been defined.

How can we make sense of the rigid sexual segregation of waged work? At first glance, there seems to be nothing in the nature of capitalism itself which requires this division of labour on a sexual basis.

In principle, capitalism is the first mode of production which treats all members of society as equals. It does not divide up the species into those that are born free and those that are born slaves; it does not divide us into the complex hierarchy of ranks which characterized feudalism. For Marx and Engels it was this that gave capitalism its revolutionary nature. Here, they argued, was a form of social organization which would destroy these divisions and gradations, sweep away national, religious, sexual distinctions, reduce everything to the naked 'cash-nexus'. Capital is interested only in labour power—of whatever sex, race or rank in society—and selects its labour power on the purely quantitative basis of how much it can contribute to profits. How then do ghettos of 'women's work' arise?

When Marxist feminists first began to ask this question, they usually answered it in terms of the needs of capitalism itself. Employers benefit, it was argued, from the existence of a pool of cheap, unskilled labour which can be used to undercut men workers and fuel expansionist sectors. Women workers are particularly useful as this 'reserve army of labour' because their family responsibilities and (usually) partial dependence on a man's wage ensure that they are viewed (and often view themselves) as secondary workers, who can be pushed back into their primary sphere—the home—whenever they are not needed on the labour market. Women's family role makes them particularly vulnerable as workers, and their vulnerability is capital's strength. They are the super-exploitables.

In recent years, however, many Marxist feminists have become uneasy about the assumptions embodied in this style of argument. After all, 'if women's subordination within society predates capitalism, then surely one cannot hope to explain it in terms of the inherent logic of the capitalist system?' (Mackintosh, forthcoming).[2] More specifically, since work—whether waged or unwaged—has always been divided along sexual lines, surely we cannot hope to explain the sex segregation of capitalist waged work solely in terms of the profit imperatives of capitalism itself? Under the impact of radical feminism—which insists that women are oppressed by men, not just by systems of productive relations—some socialist women began searching for explanations which lay in the realm of family life, sexual relations, and the cultural formation of gender differences. The concept of 'patriarchy' began to be employed—not as a fully worked out theory of gender dominance, but as a way of indicating that such a theory was necessary; that it was no longer adequate to treat sexual oppression as a by-product of economic class relations. The construction and maintenance of gender hierarchy was argued to have its own 'laws of motion', and it is these which theorists of patriarchy have been attempting to explore.

These developments represent a major advance for feminist thinking. For until we shake ourselves loose of theoretical inhibitions and begin to explore freely the uncharted terrain of gender relations, we shall never make sense of the specificity of our experience as women. But there is a sense in which these developments have not been radical enough. For in attempting to push past the categories of Marxist economic analysis, we have left these categories untouched and unchallenged. In arguing against 'economism'—the reduction of sex oppression to capitalist economic imperatives—we have, in effect, left Marxism to the male Marxists, many of whom would very much like to believe that capitalist production relations have nothing to do with sexual relations and that the struggle between capital and labour is unconnected to—hence unchallenged by—the sex-struggle. This is surely not our aim. We do not want to find ourselves simply tacking the Woman Question onto a finished theory of the 'economy'. We want to take the issue of gender hierarchy into the heart of Marxist economic analysis itself.

A recent article by Heidi Hartmann (Hartmann, 1979) highlights this need to rethink economic categories in the light of feminism. According to Heidi Hartmann, the Marxist analysis of capitalism provides us only with a theory of the different 'places' required by capitalist production. It explains why a hierarchy of labour is necessary within the waged work-force, but tells us nothing about why *women* end up at the bottom of this hierarchy:

Marx's theory of the development of capitalism is a theory of the development of 'empty places' . . . Just as capital creates these places indifferent to the individuals who fill them, the categories of Marxist analysis, 'class', 'reserve army of labour', 'wage-labourer', do not explain why particular people fill particular places. They give us no clue about why *women* are subordinate to *men* inside and outside the family and why it is not the other way around. *Marxist categories, like capital itself, are sex-blind.* The categories of Marx cannot tell us who will fill the empty places (Hartmann, 1979: 7–8).

Hence the need for an additional theory of the patriarchal relations which assign women to subordinate places in the social hierarchy. Left to its own devices, capitalism might well have fulfilled the prophecies of Engels and others, and effectively destroyed sexual divisions within the family by drawing women indiscriminately into wage labour. But patriarchy intervened, and ensured through the development of the family wage system that women's subordinate position within the family be reproduced within waged labour.

Two assumptions lie behind this argument. The first is that sexual oppression can and must be theorized independently of the specific economic forms—capitalist or otherwise—in which it appears. Patriarchy has its own history, its own effects. As a working assumption, a starting-point for feminist investigation, that is a crucial presupposition. The second assumption, however, is more dubious. This is the idea that the capitalist economic system operates like an impersonal machine, geared to the extraction of surplus value, and indifferent to the sorts of people absorbed into its workings. As wage labourers, we are all just cogs in this machine: a 'variable capital' which is incorporated—regardless of sex, colour or nationality—into the remorseless cycle of capital accumulation. Heidi Hartmann points out that 'pure capitalism' in this form has never existed; that capitalism in its historical development encounters individuals who are already sex-stratified, and that this pre-existing structure of sexual stratification—patriarchy—then becomes harnessed to capital's need for different types of labour. But an understanding of this 'actual capitalism', she argues, will be based on our examination of the interaction of the two separate dynamics—that of patriarchy, for which we have as yet no developed analysis, and that of the capitalist economic machine, for which we can simply turn to the existing body of Marxist theory.

The particular interpretation of Marxism on which this argument is based is not, we should add, one which is unique to Heidi Hartmann. 'Economism', that is, the idea that capitalism develops through the mechanical operation of certain objective laws of material development, has been the dominant rendering of Marx since the late nineteenth century. It is an interpretation which has not only expelled gender as a determinate social factor, but—at its extreme limits—has managed to expel *all* social factors from its analysis, leaving instead only the relentless grinding through of an inner logic of capitalist development, in which the imperatives of profitability push capitalist society along a predestined route. On this account capitalism is not only 'sex-blind', but blind to the entire fabric of social existence in which it is historically located. It is, to mix our metaphors yet further, an economic train carrying us all in one direction, regardless of who we are or the historical baggage we carry.[3]

There have always been critics of this economistic interpretation of Marxism, and in recent years they have launched their attacks from a number of different directions. But in particular, there has been a spate of literature exploring the changing structure of capitalist work processes which has attempted to replace the Economic Machine view of Marxism with a dynamic, historical account of capitalist development, an account that undermines the dichotomy between 'objective laws' and 'subjective' consciousness which has been so prevalent in socialist thinking. These writings on the labour process have not been notable for their feminist content, but they do offer some basis for a reassessment of the relationship between sex and skill.

The 'labour process' discussions were generated partly by the publication of Harry Braverman's *Labour and Monopoly Capital* in 1974, which was quickly followed by a series of articles and books amplifying and extending his thesis; in Britain, most of this work has been carried out under the auspices of the Conference of Socialist Economists (Conference of Socialist Economists, 1976; Brighton Labour Process Group, 1977; Gorz, 1978). The innovative core of all these writings has been the insistence that capitalist production relations develop not as a mechanical logic of surplus extraction, but through a process of struggle, embedded in history. Changes in the organization of work cannot be treated simply as technological innovation demanded by capital's search for higher profits; they are the outcome of continuous tension between capitalists and workers—and, we would argue in extension of this thesis, of tensions between workers themselves, particularly between men and women workers. According to Harry Braverman and others, capitalism's capacity to make profits depends on the degree of command it can assert over its workers. Unless capital can directly control the organization of work—the labour process—it cannot dictate how much surplus value is produced. When knowledge and training are required to make a product, the worker who has that knowledge—who understands how things are made, and just what kind of operations must be performed to make things a certain way—also has power over the speed and quality of the work. If however, that craft knowledge can be transferred from the worker to the technical experts or managers, and the worker reduced to the performance of routine operations within a process she/he no longer fully comprehends, capitalist control over production is greatly increased. The worker becomes 'de-skilled', as the knowledge which was once part of the job becomes part of the power of capital itself. Changes in the production process are introduced, therefore, not as a way of achieving some abstract goal of economic 'efficiency', but as a way of breaking the control of powerful groups of workers who are able to obstruct the demands of profitability. However much capital might like to deal with workers as an abstract 'variable capital' which just produces surplus value on demand, it has been forced to deal with real people, with men and women who have had varying degrees of control over their work. And the continuing transformation of jobs under capitalism—the creation and re-creation of what Heidi Hartmann calls 'empty places'—arises out of the struggle for control between capital and these real workers, in which the power of the workers themselves becomes a key factor shaping and defining the jobs they do.

Interpreting capitalist development in this way leads directly into a redefinition of skill categories. In its attempts to assert its control over the labour process, Harry Braverman argues, capital has continually reduced the skill component in all forms of labour, making all work increasingly alike, and increasingly dull, dreary and degraded. This homogenization, he argues, has been masked by the multitude of distinctions foisted on us by government statisticians and academic sociology—blue-collar/white-collar, old working class/new working class, skilled, semi-skilled, unskilled—but the underlying reality is one of growing convergence. Office work and factory work, for example, have been subjected to the same dreary processes of routinization, to the point where any attempt to distinguish the former as mental labour from the latter as manual becomes almost entirely specious. The conventional view of the 'upgrading' of work in the twentieth century is thus an illusion, based partly on this assumption that the expanded sector of office work is more skilled than manual labour, and partly on the practice of classifying all machine operatives as semi-skilled, even when the content of their work may involve less judgement or require shorter training than jobs previously defined as unskilled general labour. Braverman is not denying that some skilled work remains, but is arguing that existing skill labels fool us into believing there is a great deal more of it around than is the case.

This scepticism with regard to skill classifications helps us as feminists to turn a more critical eye on divisions which have previously been taken for granted, and is something which anyone with an eye to the operations of the Equal Pay Act, with its recurrent downgrading of typically 'feminine' skills such as dexterity against typically 'masculine' qualities like strength, might already have concluded. Braverman himself is mainly concerned to dismiss skill categories as mystifying, but we would regard them as highly illuminating—not perhaps of the content of the work performed, but of the sexual hierarchy which permeates capitalism. If skill distinctions are not necessarily about real work differences, what are they about? Three examples help to illustrate the answer.

In a recent study (Rubery and Wilkinson, 1979) it is suggested that the skill distinctions between the work of producing paper boxes and that of producing cartons can only be understood as historical associations between typically 'male' work and skill. Paper boxes are produced by women working on hand-fed machines; the work is considered—and paid—as unskilled labour. Cartons are produced under a more automated process, and the work hence requires less individual concentration but it is treated as semi-skilled work. It is hard to escape the conclusion that it is because of the similarities between the work of men and women in the carton industry that women in carton production are considered more skilled than box workers. Men and women work in a similar process; men are recognized as semi-skilled rather than unskilled workers; therefore carton production must be semi-skilled. The women producing paper boxes are simply women producing paper boxes, and however much the work itself might seem to qualify for upgrading, it remains unskilled because it is done by typically unskilled workers—women (Craig, Rubery, Tarling, and Wilkinson, 1980).

In this example, the association between skill and sex is quite complex. Since both kinds of work are done by women, it seems to be the comparability between men's and women's jobs in the carton industry that forces a recognition of women in carton production as semi-skilled. Much more common than this is our second example, clerical work, where a new kind of labour is created which is defined as 'female' from its beginnings, and which is allowed no comparability with previous or existing men's jobs. The transformation of the male 'black-coated worker' of the nineteenth century into today's temp typist and file clerk occurred through the enormous expansion of all forms of office work in the period following World War I. The new class of clerical workers had little in common with the clerks of the previous century, and the skill component of their work was immediately downgraded into typically 'female' abilities—including as usual dexterity, ability to carry out repetitive tasks, and so on. In this case it was not that men's jobs were deskilled, and women drawn into them, but that a new category of work was created which was classified as 'inferior' not simply by virtue of the skills required for it but by virtue of the 'inferior' status of the women who came to perform it. It is interesting to speculate whether the downgrading of the newly created skills would have occurred with so little struggle if the thousands of young women who came to fill the offices in this century had instead been young men. We can at least state with some certainty that the entire personal service aspect of clerical labour (as in virtually all the service work performed by women) would not in this case have developed in the same way.

The third example, based on Ben Birnbaum's analysis of the English clothing industry (Birnbaum, n.d.), goes further in indicating how this identification of men with skilled and women with semi-skilled or unskilled status has been generated through the struggles of men workers to retain their dominance within the sexual hierarchy. Throughout this century, machining in the clothing trade has been done by both men and women. But where it was done by men it was classified as skilled; where it was done by women it was classified as semi-skilled. As in the previous examples, it was a supposed non-comparability between men's and women's work which made this distinction possible: the women worked in larger workshops, in a more subdivided labour process, machining men's garments, while the men worked in smaller shops machining women's garments. And in successive redefinitions of the basis for skill classification, differences were always employed in such a way as to ensure skilled status for the men and semi-skilled for the women. Initially the two sectors operated with different definitions of skill; predictably machining in the sector controlled by men turned out to be skilled, and machining in the sector controlled by women, semi-skilled. When in 1926 the wages council enforced a single basis for skill classification for the two sectors, it was drawn up in such a way as, once again, to confirm the men machinists as skilled and the women as semi-skilled. Ben Birnbaum argues that the distinctions cannot be rationalized in terms of the content of the work—it arose out of the struggle of men workers from the Russian, Jewish and Polish communities to retain their social status within the family, even when excluded by their position as immigrants from the 'skilled' jobs they might otherwise have done. Forced as they were to take on machining work usually done by women as semi-skilled, they fought to preserve their masculinity by redefining (their) machining as skilled labour. Within the clothing trade he concludes 'the only way to become skilled was to change one's sex'.

What all of these examples indicate is the extent to which skill has become saturated with sex. It is not that skill categories have been totally subjectified: in all cases *some* basis was found in the content of the work to justify the distinctions between men's and women's work. But the equations—men/skilled, women/unskilled—are so powerful that the identification of a particular job with women, ensured that the skill content of the work would be downgraded. It is the sex of those who do the work, rather than its content, which leads to its identification as skilled or unskilled.

Ben Birnbaum's analysis is also important because he suggests that the imperative operating to enforce skill distinctions in garment production was the need of men workers to retain domestic authority. The men were denied access to the skilled jobs they considered theirs by right. Faced with this they struggled to acquire skilled status and skilled rates of pay for jobs usually deemed semi-skilled. For them, craft status was identified with manhood, and the struggle to maintain their position in the upper level of the labour hierarchy was fuelled by a determination to maintain the traditional balance of power in families where men had always acted as primary breadwinners.

This pattern of development—the sexualization of skill labels following the actual de-skilling of work processes—is one which has been repeated throughout the course of the nineteenth and twentieth centuries. It has been closely interwoven with the continuous battle between organized craftsmen and employers over the control of production. The outcome of this battle has been uneven (though not for Harry Braverman, who tends to regard capital as all-powerful). But to the extent that capital has succeeded in demolishing the actual craft knowledge and abilities of men workers, it has eroded the material basis for skill distinctions, thereby creating a work-force with a thin layer of skilled men at the top and a mass of unskilled workers at the bottom. Men workers have fought long and hard against this process, fought to retain their craft position, and failing all else, at least their craft labels. And in these struggles, craft has been increasingly identified with masculinity, with the claims of the breadwinner, with the degree of union strength. Skill has been increasingly defined *against* women—skilled work is work that women don't do.

Historically, this outcome is hardly surprising. The main protagonists were after all capital and the organized male working class; it was the power of the craftsmen that capital was most concerned to break with its weapon of de-skilling, and it was these workers who were in the best position to defy the process. In this history capital has been far from sex-blind. Since it is concerned not just with a logic of surplus extraction, but with an assertion of command, it is necessarily sensitive to those social relations which make some workers already more subordinated than others. The women who machine fashion garments in their own home are not subjected to the employer's control over their every movement: they can stop the machine at any moment; they can work at any time of day or night; they can get up to make a cup of tea when they decide to. But they are less powerful than the most de-skilled of men machine operatives, because they are chained to the home by their young children, denied access to any other form of employment, made totally dependent on their employer's decisions about how much to pay them. For them it is what they are as women, rather than the way their work is organized, that brings them under capital's control. Or as one early textile manufacturer explained to a questioner during the struggle over factory hours in the early nineteenth century, he liked to employ married women who had 'families at home dependent on them for support' because they were 'attentive, docile' and 'compelled to use their utmost exertions to procure the necessaries of life' (Marx, 1976: 526 n). Since 'docility' could be induced in women by their economic and social subordination, it was primarily the more powerful and stroppier men workers who had to be countered with technical and organizational innovations aimed at de-skilling their jobs. This is not to say that women's jobs have been protected from the processes of de-skilling, but merely to emphasize that the confrontations over de-skilling have taken place on an already sexually defined terrain—between capital and skilled men workers.

In these struggles, the preservation of *masculine* skills became the issue which provided much of the force to workers' resistance. Where capital tried to undercut men's power by introducing women workers onto jobs previously defined as 'male'—as in textiles in the early nineteenth century, or engineering during World War I—hostility was open and fierce. It is an irony of great concern to feminists that one of the most celebrated episodes in the history of British class struggle—the Shop Stewards' Movement of World War I—drew its strength from the resistance of men workers to a dilution of their jobs by women. Here the battle against de-skilling was re-inforced and fuelled by the rejection of women's entry into men's jobs. The perpetuation of sexual hierarchy has been inextricably interwoven with the struggles against the real subordination to capital, as claims to skilled status have come to rely more and more on sex of the workers and less and less on the nature of the job.

The result is deeply contradictory for men workers, who thereby continually re-create for capital a group of 'inferior' workers who can be used to undercut them. But as well as this, the identification of 'women's work' with unskilled work has masked the process through which capitalist work in general has become more routinized, more deadening, more a denial of the humanity of those who perform it. The segregation of women's work from men's conceals from many men workers the ways in which we are all becoming 'women workers' now; all subject to (in Harry Braverman's phrase) a 'degradation of labour' which gives to all jobs the classic features of women's employment.

As feminists we face two tasks. The first is to re-think economic categories in the light of feminism; 'economics' cannot be left unchallenged by the feminist critique. Capitalist production relations develop in and through confrontations between capital and workers, and the form which these confrontations take is often dictated by the deep divisions within the working class between men and women. Gender hierarchy enters directly into the development of capitalist relations, and a Marxism which fails to recognize this will not be sufficient for us. The second task is to reorganize economic struggles themselves—a task which has long been understood by feminists who find themselves in an uneasy alliance with a trade union tradition whose concern with differentials, with the maintenance of existing skill hierarchies, seems to leave little space for feminist politics. We might suggest that it is only when the socialist movement has been freed from its ideology of masculine skills that it will be able to confront the nature of capitalist work itself, and make the transformation of that work the focus of a future strategy. Perhaps then—in a struggle to claim for both men and women the lives now given over, day-by-day, year-by-year, to the crippling dictates of capitalist production—a new basis for sexual unity might begin to be forged.

Notes

1. This process of identification of women with lack of skill seems if anything to be increasing. To give just one example; in 1911 women performed 24 per cent of all skilled jobs and 15.5 per cent of all unskilled; by 1971 they performed only 13.5 per cent of skilled manual work and just over 37 per cent of the unskilled (Bain and Price, 1972; cited in Hakim, 1978).

2. We are grateful to Maureen Mackintosh for letting us see her paper prior to publication.
3. Clearly at one level the argument that the capital–labour relation is not a gender relation is correct; inasmuch as the capital–labour relation is a *value relation* it is not a relation between people at all, but between abstract quantities of dead and living labour. The circuit of capital as a value-circuit is not the story of real men and women entering into concrete social relations with one another, but an account—*abstracted from these relations*—of changing value forms. The mechanism whereby this abstraction occurs is not, of course, a theoretician's brain, but the market—through which all qualitative relations become expressed in quantitative terms. But: 'the capitalist labour process is the unity of the processes of valorization and the real labour process on the adequate basis of a specific form of social organization of labour' (Brighton Labour Process Group, 1977: 6). As a process which occurs in time, over time, a capitalist labour process is embedded in history, in inherited social relations. As a *concrete historical* process, the capitalist labour process must situate itself within existing patterns of social dominance and subordination. As a use-value—that is, in its historic existence—labour is concrete labour, characterized as much by its femaleness as any other of its attributes—and in our society 'femaleness' is a condition of relative powerlessness. As a concrete material process, capitalist production employs labours which are 'male' and 'female', and hence in a relation of power to one another. There is no pure 'economics' free of gender hierarchy, no Marxist science which can direct its gaze where women are not.

References

Bain, G. S., and Price, R. (1972), 'Union Growth and Employment Trends in the United Kingdom 1964–1970', *British Journal of Industrial Relations*, 10 (Nov.).

Birnbaum, Ben (unpub. paper) 'Women, Skill and Automation: A Study of Women's Employment in the Clothing Industry 1946–1972'.

Braverman, Harry (1974), *Labour and Monopoly Capital* (New York: Monthly Review Press).

Brighton Labour Process Group (1977), 'The Capitalist Labour Process' *Capital and Class*, 1.

Conference of Socialist Economists (1976), *The Labour Process and Class Strategies* (London: Stage 1).

Craig, Christine, Rubery, Jill, Tarling, Roger, and Wilkinson, Frank (1980), 'Abolition and After: The Paper Box Wages Council', research paper by the Labour Studies Group Department of Employment.

Gorz, Andre (1978), (ed.), *The Division of Labour* (Brighton: Harvester Press).

Hakim, Catherine (1978), 'Sexual Division within the Labour Force: Occupational Segregation', Department of Employment Gazette (Nov.).

Hartmann, Heidi (1979), 'The Unhappy Marriage of Marxism and Feminism: Towards a more Progressive Union', *Capital and Class*, 8.

Mackintosh, Maureen (forthcoming) 'Gender and Economics: Debates on the Sexual Division of Labour' to be published in a forthcoming volume of papers from the 1978 Sussex Conference on the Subordination of Women in the Development Process.

Marx, Karl (1976), *Capital*, i. (Harmondsworth: Penguin).

Rubery, Jill, and Wilkinson, Frank (1979), 'Notes on the Nature of the Labour Process in the Secondary Sector', *Low Pay and Labour Markets Segmentation Conference Papers*, Cambridge 1979.

Part V. **Sexuality**

12 Discipline and Respectability: Prostitution and the Reformation in Augsburg

Lyndal Roper

'Here at Augsburg the Council did away with the brothel at the prompting of the Lutheran preachers'.[1] This laconic sentence—a notation under the year 1532 by the Catholic monk Clemens Sender—is the only reference made by any of the town's chroniclers to the closure of the city brothel, an event which they and historians since seem to have thought of little consequence in the turbulent years of the Reformation. Augsburg was not the only town at this time to close a city brothel which had been an established part of civic life for more than two centuries.[2] Such decisions marked a turning point in the organization of prostitution, attitudes to it and, indeed, to sexuality. As the chronicler knew, these changes were connected with the new ethos of the Reformation; but what remains obscure, then and now, is quite how the two were related, or what the altered sexual regime reveals of the nature of the Reformation.

Historians have often pointed to what they consider to be a shift in sexual values accomplished by the Reformation. It is generally considered to have brought about a new positive affirmation of marriage and married life. As one recent writer expressed it: 'While it cannot be claimed that Protestants were unique in achieving loving marriages, their new marriage laws ... became the most emphatic statement of the ideal of sharing, companionable marriage in the sixteenth century.'[3] Much less has been written about the movement to abolish city brothels, though this casts a different

Reprinted with permission from *History Workshop* Spring 1985, Issue 19, 3–28. Thanks to the Oxford History Workshop Activities Group, the London Feminist History Group, the German History Society; to Guy Boanas; and to Leonie Archer, Olwen Hufton, Margaret Pelling, Raphael Samuel, Bob Scribner, Anne Summers, Johannes Wilhelm, and Carol Willock. Research was made possible by grants from the German Historical Institute and the University of London Central Research Fund.

light on the new sexual ethic. Where it is mentioned, it frequently tends to be presented as yet another of the Reformation's purifying onslaughts on the corrupt and lascivious world of the late medieval city, as it established the values of marriage and fidelity. Yet the history of the campaign to end prostitution in Augsburg—a large, wealthy Imperial city—is far more contradictory, and its presuppositions more ambiguous, than such a black and white picture would suggest.

But what was the system of tolerated prostitution which the reformers found so ungodly? Its most distinctive feature was the municipal character of the city-run brothel. The brothel keeper was required, in most towns, to swear an annual oath of office to the Council like other civic officials; and its terms might describe his duties as (to quote the Ulm oath) 'to further the interest and piety of the city and its folk, and to warn and keep it from harm'.[4] Though the brothel keeper ran the business, and in some towns (as in Augsburg) owned the buildings, the civic authority might still be liable for repairs to the premises.[5] In return, the town made use of the brothel as a civic resource. During Imperial visits, the Emperor and his retinue might be given a complimentary night at the brothel; and their evening was celebrated with torchlight processions and luxurious feasting.[6] At Würzburg, visits by town officials on St John's Day, and at Frankfurt, invitations to the prostitutes for the Council's annual venison feast confirmed the brothel's role as part of the town's ceremonial resources, a means to demonstrate the power and hospitality of the commune.[7] The women, like other civic assets, were subject to inspection by civic officials; the latter were usually midwives (though to the brothel keeper's horror, the Ulm Council introduced inspection by male doctors, in the presence of the city employees responsible for patrolling beggars). The inspectors ensured that the brothel keeper was fulfilling his obligation to provide the city with 'suitable, clean and healthy women'.[8] These three adjectives encapsulate the Council's concerns: the women should be free from disease (syphilis is clearly one of its anxieties), should be of age and should be sound specimens. In formulating such ordinances and arranging annual inspections, the Council was declaring itself the adjudicator in disputes between prostitutes and brothel keeper, and adopting special responsibility for a trade which had no guild structure of its own.

It was therefore fully consistent with the brothel's place in civic society for the Council to speak of it as 'enhancing the good, piety and honour of the whole commune'.[9] But this language, and the manner in which the Council employed the brothel as show-piece, rested upon a male-defined understanding of who the term 'commune' included. The brothel offered a sexuality with which men could identify and the Council's rhetoric addressed the males who would have access to prostitutes. Just as only adult male citizens could enjoy full political rights and bear arms in defence of the commune, so here also, masculinity, virility, and membership of the polity were intimately connected. In theory, women too were supposed to benefit from the brothel because it made the city safe for 'respectable' women: yet here, they were referred to protectively in terms of their relations to men, as the wives and daughters of citizens, even though they could be citizens in their own right.

Though a public institution, the city brothel was not officially open to all men. Theoretically, married men were forbidden to visit it; and all cities threatened punishment for any married man found within its walls.[10] Restrictions were placed on clerics using the brothel: Nuremberg banned them outright, while Nördlingen more realistically forbade them only to stay overnight.[11] But in Augsburg at least, in the early years of the sixteenth century, there are suspiciously few cases of married men being caught in brothels, and in other towns, cases usually multiply in the wake of mandates against concubinage and adultery.[12] One has only to compare the numerous convictions of married men found in the Zurich brothel during the Reformation years, when the Council was determined to translate principle into practice.[13] Travellers, a group who brought much of the brothel's custom, could easily deny being married; and such niceties were forgotten during the Emperor's visits or at Imperial diets.

Brothels were designed for one particular group of men: journeymen and apprentices not yet married; and the 'free house', 'common house', or 'women's house', as it was variously known, was a central part of their cultural world. Richer men could afford the services of courtesans or retain a mistress, but in the city brothels, low prices ensured that ordinary apprentices and journeymen could afford to pay. A centre of popular entertainment of all kinds, brothels sold alcohol, board games were played, and the brothel keeper was supposed to watch out for professional cheats.[14] Its function , like that of taverns, as a focus of male entertainment, explains why (as the Ulm Council complained) young lads aged twelve or less were frequenting it[15]—for many, the excitement of going with a group of workmates, of looking, teasing, and fantasizing, comprised the amusement. The sale of food and alcohol was an important source of the brothel's profit, and in 1510 and 1512 the Ulm Council found it necessary to forbid the brothel keeper selling alcohol to take away, holding drinking sprees or forcing prostitutes and clients to buy alcohol at inflated prices.[16] Brothels were a stage for male bravado; and they were frequently the scene of fights, even though causing a disturbance in the brothel carried a double penalty.[17] The brothel's popularity exemplifies the distinctness of the leisure lives of young men and women: while men's entertainment involved spending money, drinking, or roaming the streets in bands at night to fight or perhaps to serenade the young women they fancied, women's social lives do not seem to have depended to the same extent on ready cash. They do not appear to have made much use of guild or local drinking rooms, and the indoor sewing circle under the watchful eye of elders was more important to their leisure. Women who walked the streets alone at night risked being mistaken for prostitutes. Dances, fairs, and church ales were the occasions where young men and women might meet; but sexual contact was not allowed.

Thus, through the institution of the brothel, the city was able to celebrate and encourage youthful male virility while at the same time insisting that these young men should not marry until, their craft training completed, they could support a wife and children. From this perspective, the argument that the brothel prevented anarchic sexual relations has a special point: the city fathers had long supported parents' right to a say in their children's marriages, even in spite of the Church's doctrine that marriage consisted solely in the mutual consent of the couple themselves. At dances, weddings, fairs, and church ales young people often did promise marriage 'secretly' or consummate illicit unions, upsetting the delicate balance between male sexual vigour and delayed marriage which the city elders wanted to maintain. As they saw it, the brothel forestalled such relationships and helped to keep the town's 'respectable' women sexually inaccessible.[18]

The prostitutes, on the other hand, were sexually available and were presented as objects of sexual fantasy and glamour; but they were not the social equals of their clients. When, in Nuremberg, the Council discovered that the prostitutes were preferring 'special beaux, whom they call their beloved men' over other customers, it was quick to order that this practice be stopped, and decreed that the women should be available to any man who paid.[19] As 'common women', they were not to develop disruptive preferences, relationships which might imperil the distinctions between on the one hand respectable young women who could become wives; and on the other the free, common women who, under Augsburg law, could not sue for paternity, and in some other towns could not even be raped, since they were owned by all men.[20] For youths, sexual experience with prostitutes was part of becoming a real man; but because its context was the milieu of young men's bands, and civic prostitutes were thought of as belonging to all men in common, it could also strengthen male bonding.[21]

From the prostitutes' point of view, the civic brothel might appear to be an institution which accorded them both respect and protection. Many measures served their interests: in Ulm, there was a separate bath for their use, and the food they were to receive was precisely prescribed; in Nördlingen, a weekly bath was included in the rent. But if it seemed a beneficent regime, it placed the prostitutes firmly under the brothel keeper's hand. In Ulm, his control of the women's labour power was so complete that he could require them to spin yarn during the day or else reimburse him for the lost earnings.[22] As we saw, the women did not have the right to refuse a client. From the brothel ordinances, which concern the keeper's provision of food, alcohol, clothing, baths, and rent, it is obvious there was little need for the woman to step outside the brothel to make any purchases. That this might amount to a total *de facto* curfew is evident from the many regulations forbidding the brothel keeper to prevent women leaving the brothel, especially if their purpose was to go to church.[23]

Economic pressures forced the women to keep working and made it hard for them to leave. In some towns, menstruating or sick women could choose not to work; while pregnant or seriously ill women were forbidden to do so.[24] On the eves of holy days and throughout Holy Week, the brothel was shut.[25] On these days they earned nothing, yet they still had to meet the costs of food, rent, and clothing. Many fell into a cycle of debt, for the brothel keepers would allow women to buy goods through them (at prices the keepers nominated) and deduct the money from their future wages. In Überlingen, for example, the keeper pocketed a third of each woman's earnings and then deducted debt repayments from the rest. In Ulm, the money the women made was put into a box and distributed each week, one third passing to the brothel keeper who also charged for rent and maintenance. Limits were imposed on how much he might lend the women or what he could sell them, though it is not clear whether these where effective. Though the women might scrutinize the pay out, their control of their earnings was reduced to a minimum. In Überlingen, only gifts and what the woman earned from an 'overnight' customer were paid directly to her. This system made it hard for her to forgo a night customer and crucial to please the client so that she could command those extra gifts. A bout of sickness could be enough to put the woman behind in repayments, thus compelling her to chalk up yet another debt against her future earnings.[26]

The vicious circle of indebtedness was aggravated by the practice of 'lending money' using the women as security. The documents are vague on the point, but the inescapable conclusion is that women were in effect being sold into the trade and compelled to repay the capital 'lent' through their labour. It was rumoured that there were prostitute markets where women were bought or exchanged by brothels. If these tales have the ring of fancy, they do demonstrate that there was some concern about methods of procurement.[27] Yet this had its limits. The 1428 ordinance of Augsburg, which accused the brothel keeper of 'piling sin upon sin' by refusing to permit indebted prostitutes to leave the brothel, reveals that the 'sin' lay not so much in purchasing prostitutes, but in preventing women from reforming.[28] In Ulm, where it was, interestingly enough, the Church which raised this complaint, the Council decreed that women should be free to leave the brothel, whether or not their debts had been settled, on payment of one gulden—not an easy sum for a woman to raise. When she left, she could take only the clothes with which she had come to the brothel. For a known prostitute, without means of support and usually without accumulated capital, finding a position and making a new life outside the brothel would have been extremely hard. But if she once returned to prostitution, the brothel keeper could reclaim her and demand payment of all debts.[29]

The so-called 'free women' thus had little power over their lives or their earnings, and would have found it nearly impossible to leave a brothel whose regime they found intolerable for another. As a form of labour, it was unlike any other within the town walls, where, as the boastful proverb had it, 'city air makes one free'. Though apprentices, servants, and journeymen too might be subject to restrictions on movement, might find it hard to leave an unpleasant master and might also fall into debt with him, prostitutes faced a far severer discipline. They had little or no chance of ever becoming brothel keepers themselves—in Augsburg, the brothel seems to have been run only by men in this period—and they might become indentured labour bound to work off debts which they had not even contracted. Ironically, the town brothel, used so often to represent the proud munificence of the free city, operated on a system which was the antithesis of the ideal of the free citizen controlling his own labour.

In addition to legal prostitution however, there were networks of free prostitution, tolerated to some extent by civic authorities. Nuremberg on occasion allowed civic prostitutes to attack and 'discipline' free prostitutes who detracted from their trade.[30] In Augsburg, a motley assortment of illegal prostitutes, their procurers and small brothel holders, were banished each year just after St Gall's day, the beginning of winter.[31] This fell a few weeks after St Michael's Day when those who had been banished previously, travelling folk and vagabonds, might freely enter the city; and it coincided with the meeting of the Large Council when the tax rate for the coming year would be fixed.[32] A ritual of purification, a public spectacle where those on the Galli list were marched out of town to the sound of the storm bell, it was hardly a serious measure of policing. The guilty would soon secure an intercession from some dignitary and gain a pardon.[33] Indeed, the same women appear regularly on the lists of offenders: 'Margaret the Court Virgin behind St Steven's' was listed nearly every year between 1515 and 1520.

Augsburg's policing, like that of other towns, concentrated instead on limiting noise and public disturbance from prostitutes who solicited on the streets, and distinguishing prostitutes from 'respectable' women. Prostitutes were required to wear a broad green stripe on their veil, forbidden to wear wreaths like maidens and were not allowed to wear silk cloth or rosaries.[34] They could not have a maid accompany them on the street. The distinguishing mark—whether a yellow stripe or a red beret as in other towns—classed prostitutes in a similar category to Jews, who were also compelled to wear some visible sign of difference. Both Jew and prostitute were believed to perform essential services for the commune, yet both groups were excluded from full membership of the city, and Jews even from residence after the mid-fifteenth century expulsions. Intercourse between Jew and Christian was theoretically punishable by death.[35] So also, ties with prostitutes were discouraged: women who befriended them might find themselves reputed prostitutes too; and men who had too close a relationship with such women, who had one 'hanging about him', might be threatened with expulsion from their craft union.[36] Prostitutes were supposed to be foreign women, and brothels were forbidden to employ local girls—though many women from the town certainly worked as free prostitutes.[37] Like the Jews, prostitutes were conceived of as foreign in some sense; and just as Jews were buried outside the city walls, so also in Frankfurt, the Council threatened the prostitutes with burial 'in the ditch', in unblessed earth.[38] Too intimate an association with either Jews or prostitutes could endanger the respectable citizen's civic existence.

Indeed, the symbolic position of the prostitute could be described as one of clearly defined marginality. Regulations made sure that 'the two species of the honourable and the dishonourable' were easily told apart.[39] Urban geography made the point: in Augsburg, the brothel was strategically placed near a minor city gate by the wall, only just within the town borders, yet conveniently close to the city centre. In Hamburg and Strasbourg the city councils restricted free prostitution to a few streets.[40] None the less, prostitutes formed part of urban culture, participating in races at the shooting carnivals and appearing at weddings and dances.[41] In Vienna, they partnered the young men in the St John's Day Fires dances, and at carnival time in Leipzig, they processed through the city to protect the town from plague and preserve women's fertility, as it was said.[42] Prostitutes had particular saints—St Affa of Augsburg had herself been forced into prostitution by her mother—and in Ulm, the prostitutes burnt a weekly candle in Our Lady's Church 'to the praise and honour of Mary, and as a comfort to all Christian souls'—a phrase which expresses the prostitutes' inclusion in the work of prayer and worship of the community.[43]

But this public acceptance was double-edged, serving also to imprison the women in their identity as prostitute, a separate species of woman. At the same time, the provision of brothels legitimated the social construction of male desire as a force which must have an outlet or cause chaos. The men who gained their first sexual experiences with prostitutes were distanced from them psychologically and socially. Prostitutes counted as dishonourable people who could pollute others. The extent of their dishonour was clearly manifested in the various systems devised to supervise the women. According to the 1276 civic code of Augsburg, prostitutes should be under the control of the hangman, the most dishonourable figure of the entire city.[44] So polluting and injurious to honour was contact with him or his work that the entire carpenters' guild had to repair the gallows together, in order that none should be more tainted than his fellow guildsmen.[45] In Regensburg, when the brothel-keeper died in 1532 he was buried under the gallows like a criminal, despite the considerable fortune he had amassed.[46] In Vienna, hangman and beadle were paid from the revenues of the brothel. All these regulations aligned prostitutes with the social outcasts, polluters, and dishonourable members of the city.

Such a marginal position also gave prostitutes a paradoxical kind of symbolic freedom. According to the folk customs of one area, prostitutes could attend weddings and they chased the groom, staging a mock capture and demanding money to let him go.[47] They could punish those who misbehaved sexually by ritually shaming them. Thus the Nuremberg Council permitted civic prostitutes to shame their free competitors; and on another occasion, prostitutes paraded a woman found committing fornication with her lover in the brothel through the streets.[48] Free prostitutes had more freedom to walk the streets at night than did 'respectable' women; and though their dress was supposed to be restricted, its style did not fit the strict categories to which 'respectable' women were subject according to their class position.

The Church too gave prostitution considerable sanction. The tradition of toleration derived from Augustine; and Aquinas justified the need for prostitutes in vivid analogy as well, comparing them to a cesspit for a palace. Though dirty in themselves, it is their function to purify a town—without them, it would soon become corrupt.[49] The image equated prostitutes with what was dirty and evil, while making men's sexuality appear an uncomplicated natural urge like defecation. It diagnosed the problem as prostitution, not male sexuality. These ideas could lead to the advocacy of prostitution by appealing to religious values. The ordinances of both Nördlingen and Nuremberg opened with prefaces defending the brothel's existence and noting that 'in Christendom common women are tolerated by the holy church in order to prevent worse evil'.[50] A Dominican preacher, Johannes Falkenberg, could even advise the city of Cracow to establish a brothel on precisely these grounds; and in some ecclesiastical towns, the Church derived revenues from the local brothel.[51]

In confessional manuals, visits by bachelors to prostitutes were ranked among the less serious sexual sins, and in one such manual, they were classed in the second of eight ascending categories, as 'whoring', worse only than fornication and on a par with intercourse on several occasions while single. Another published in Augsburg ranked 'the common and public sinning women' in the second of the eight categories too, above single folk who committed fornication but below adulterers, seducers, and masturbators. The author warned that fornication alone was 'sufficient for eternal damnation', but he noted that people thought little of it.[52]

Though prostitutes might have a representative presence in the church—witness the prostitutes' candle at Ulm—it is more difficult to determine whether they attended church and mass. The brothel ordinances insisted that they be free to do so, but the need for such a ruling suggests that in practice they were hindered or chose not to attend. Some towns ordered the women to sit separately in church so that 'respectable' women should not be offended—or men distracted. At Ulm, prostitutes were allowed an annual confession, but they were to be directed to a particular church by the officials in charge of beggars, a humiliating provision. Even in church, a prostitute was reminded that she was not like other women.[53]

Augsburg had not permitted its prostitutes to attend church until 1520, so their appearance at St Moritz's in a special area of the church to hear the sermon of Dr Speiser was a dramatic event.[54] By 1522 at the latest, Speiser was clearly identified with the evangelical camp. So, when Easter approached in 1526, and Augsburg's Lutheran preacher Johannes Frosch heard the confessions of the prostitutes, what better proof could there have been of the power of the preaching of God's Word? We do not know what Frosch preached, but we can assume that he would have exhorted them to leave their profession, not for the walls of a convent of Magdalenes, but to marry, just as the reformers were doing. The period before Easter in these early years of the Reformation was always especially charged. Easter, the occasion of the annual communion, was the festival where the reformers focused their demands to celebrate the Last Supper in both kinds, giving the Cup to the laity—or else carried out liturgical experiments, even without the permission of the civic authority. The exhortations to prostitutes to repent thus took place at a moment of intense popular piety and expectation. Though the Council was not to declare for the Reformation until eight years later, and did not introduce a full Reformation until 1537, on this occasion it identified itself publicly with Frosch's campaign, and awarded him an honorarium of one gulden.[55] And in the following years, as small numbers of prostitutes left the brothel, the Council showed its support for the reintegration of the women into respectable life by presenting them with an outfit of clothes—a gift both practical and symbolic, for the mock noble attire of prostitutes branded them as such.[56] One of the women at least married; but we do not know what became of the others.[57] In

1533, with the brothel shut, the turn against prostitution seemed complete when a former brothel-keeper's wife could write 'and we both spouses daily give God Almighty thanks, praise and honour because (the Council) has helped the above-mentioned my husband to leave this sinful state and condition'. Even the brothel-keeper appeared to have seen the error of his ways, an impression dented only by her shrewd assessment in the next line of this petition that my lords of the Council would not, in any case, permit the brothel to reopen.[58]

The evangelical preachers were closely associated with the campaign against prostitution which gained momentum in the 1520s and 1530s; but their rhetoric can be seen to pass through different stages and directions. At first, attacks on prostitution were part of a range of anti-clerical salvoes. Taking up elements of a long tradition hostile to monks and priests, they portrayed them as lecherous women-stealers.[59] In this propaganda, little distinction was made between allegations that monks frequently resorted to brothels, that they seduced married women and virgins, or that they kept concubines—all was 'whoring'. So Johannes Strauss, in a pamphlet on confession, urged men to be wary if their wives' sessions at confession lasted suspiciously long.[60] Unlike Protestant pastors, priests lacked wives; and therefore they endangered other men's women. Urbanus Rhegius, an evangelical preacher at Augsburg, went so far as to declare that 'every monk is a whorer, either in secret or in public'.[61]

These themes find pointed illustration in a woodcut of 1523 depicting 'The Monk and the Maiden'. At one level, the picture is a typical Reformation indictment of the lustful monk. The trusty peasant stands for the common man, supporter of the Reformation. He is the actor in the picture, and his discovery of the priest's seduction of his daughter is the drama. Yet at another level, the woodcut can be interpreted as a satire on prostitution, directed as much against the women characters as against the clergy. The mother who turns away from the scene is smiling as she holds her hand to her face; and the viewer is struck by her large, bulging purse. Her daughter seems captivated by the monk, despite her professed repentance of her loss of virginity. The mother's feet lead away from the monk as if, unlike her husband, she is departing: has she been paid off by the monk just as he now attempts to bribe the peasant? Drawing on a stock myth about prostitution, the artist implies that the women are in league for the monk's money.[62]

The linking of anti-clericalism and prostitution was not restricted to the level of a literary and pictorial device. By 1537, the

Council was ordering all men to separate from concubines and commanding the women to leave town.[63] Such edicts had been repeatedly promulgated throughout the fifteenth and sixteenth centuries,[64] but now the Council set about enforcing them, instituting a special court to deal with this and other offences, paying spies to report on 'suspicious persons' and fining heavily those men whom it found guilty. Particular concern was expressed about the 'whoring' of the priests as the Council made its first tentative steps to introduce the Reformation in 1534.[65] At the same time, a dramatic series of trials of prostitutes who confessed their dealing with clergy, and told how one young virgin had been hawked around to various clerics, fuelled the tendency to identify priests as the polluters and women-stealers of the town.[66]

Anti-clerical feeling of this type, however, rapidly shaded into attacks on prostitutes themselves. They came to be classed with the Catholic priests; and the concubines were the people exiled following the trials. As early as 1520, Luther had explicitly argued that in a Christian society, there should be no brothels:

Finally, is it not a lamentable thing that we Christians should openly tolerate in our midst common houses of ill-fame, though we all took the oath of chastity at our baptism? I am well aware of the frequent reply, that it is a custom not confined to any one people, that it would be difficult to stop, and that it is better to have such houses than that married women, or maidens, or others held in greater respect, should be dishonoured. Nevertheless, ought not the secular but Christian government to consider that that is not the way to get rid of a heathen custom?[67]

Here, Luther was engaging (albeit tentatively) with the time-honoured defence of brothels: that they protected the honour of respectable women. This argument became more sophisticated as reformers began to claim that brothels actually caused the ill they were supposed to contain.

As Johannes Brenz wrote, 'Some say one must have public brothels to prevent greater evil—but what if these brothels are schools in which one learns more wickedness than before?' Here, the reformers were questioning the cornerstone of the theory of male desire which justified prostitution because men's lust was an anarchic, uncontrollable force which could only be channelled in specific, less socially disruptive directions. At times, the reformers even seem to be grappling with the paradoxes of their society's sexual paradigms:

If the authorities have the power to allow a brothel and do not sin in this, where not only single men (who sin heavily) but also married men may go, and say this does no harm ... Why do they not also permit a women's brothel, where women who are old and weak and have no husbands may go?[68]

If women are indeed the more sensual sex, as sixteenth-century society held them to be, and if men, as more rational beings, are better able to control their lusts than women, why should women not be allowed brothels? The writer, Melchior Ambach, pushed the argument to this 'absurd' point to show the fallacious reasoning of those who supported brothels; but as he did so, he at least laid bare the contradictions in the sexual natures ascribed to women and men. Implicitly he was claiming that men, too, must be regarded as sexually responsible subjects.

However, the belief that sex was a force which is denied at society's peril returned in the demands that men and women ought to marry young. Indeed, in the passages cited earlier, the writers usually proceeded to praise marriage, the 'better way' instituted by God. Marriage was classed as the only possible context for sex for the Christian. But if the reformers rejected chastity as an ideal binding on all clerics, they did advocate chastity for those men and women who were not of an age to marry. Certainly, the pre-Reformation church did not advocate sexual experience for youths, but it did not assume that young men would be virgins when they married. Yet this was exactly what the new church held up as the ideal for all men—an interesting example of the ways in which the preoccupations of the reformers themselves, is heavily determined by the monastic experiences many had rebelled against, could lead them to advocate a monastic ideal for all. Even so, they did not believe that men or women could be expected to maintain this chastity for any length of time, and their consequent advocacy of early marriage to avoid the perils of unsatisfied lust led them into open conflict with secular tradition. The latter favoured late marriage and discouraged matches until the man had completed craft training.[69]

As the reformers' ethic was elaborated, prostitutes themselves began to be perceived as evil temptresses, figures of hate in their own right rather than as the satellites of the old priests. Worse than merely vain, selfish and luxurious, prostitutes came to be regarded as evil. It is surely significant that the reformers were drawn to the symbol of the Whore of Babylon to represent the Papacy.[70] The polemical images of the richly attired prostitute, dressed like a noble woman, and riding the seven-headed Beast, which adorned the Lutheran Bible and appeared as pamphlet illustrations, were also visions of the powerful woman flaunting her sexuality and the riches it has brought her. Perhaps the viewer was reminded of the depictions of women riding not animals but men—for example, that of Phyllis astride Aristoteles, made foolish by his love of a woman.[71] And the rhetoric which surrounded the theme of the Pope as Babylonian Whore was deeply imbued with the sense that these were the Last Days, the Prostitute-Pope a sign of the impending apocalypse. The prostitute was a menacing as well as a sinful character.

The various levels of the demonization of prostitutes can be seen coalescing in Luther's denunciation to his students of a group of prostitutes who had recently arrived near Wittenberg. He asked them to believe that 'the evil spirit sent these whores here' and calls them 'dreadful, shabby, stinking, loathsome and syphilitic'. These women, Luther says, are murderers, worse even than poisoners, for 'such a syphilitic whore can give her disease to ten, twenty, thirty, and more good people', and continues that, were he a judge, he should have them 'broken on the wheel and flayed'.[72]

Here there is no sympathy for the prostitute, and she, not the men who are her customers, is named as the source of sin. Disease is a metaphor of her nature, and she, not her clients, is the origin of the illness. Her infection is of little consequence: it is the transmission of the sickness to 'good people' which calls forth Luther's invective.

The argument that prostitutes caused syphilis was propounded by medical writers too, but it was not the chief or only ground they cited. Syphilis had become recognized as a major European epidemic in the late fifteenth and early sixteenth centuries, but there was considerable dispute as to its nature, cause, and cure. On the introduction of the disease to Germany there were several theories. Some held that German mercenary soldiers had imported it, one that it had been deliberately caused by French soldiers who had mixed leper's blood into the bread they fed the German soldiers. Others blamed Italian prostitutes, and one even named a single woman as the sole cause of the plague.[73] All these myths shared the assumption that it was some undesirable group, whether German mercenaries, who stood for the antithesis of settled bourgeois life, prostitutes, or the hated Southerners. As to the immediate causes of the disease, opinion was divided. Most mentioned intercourse with people suffering from the illness; and yet, as J. K. Proksch has pointed out, it was chiefly women whom the writers mentioned as a danger.[74] This is a linguistic slip in part because the writers assumed a male readership; but it meant that women as a sex could be regarded as a possible source of contagion. But 'bad air', the eating of infected pork (it was held that animals could contract the disease), medical bleeding, and even (some held) decayed menstrual blood could cause the illness.[75] In some writers, these themes merged into a general complaint against the 'times' and its morals, for which syphilis was seen as God's punishment.

The contradictions in popular attitudes to venereal disease and prostitution are nicely conveyed by Johannes Haselbergk's satirical poem 'On the Southern Pox', which begins in the form of a dialogue between a merchant and a citizen. The merchant is to blame for his own sufferings, the citizen tells him, for 'God has sent this plague because of our loose living' and 'You merchant folk travel far and wide|Well known to the Women Beautiful|With them you have your amusement|and they know how to entertain you|You forget your wife and child.' The link between prostitution and syphilis made here is as much moral as biological. Yet a major section of the poem is a lengthy list of all the brothels and prostitutes' haunts in every major German town, interspersed with puns and sexual jokes. It could clearly double as a guide book. The poem's apparent moralism is undercut by its fascination with prostitution, and syphilis simply adds a comic piquancy.[76]

Though worry about the disease contributed to the movement against prostitution, prostitutes were never regarded as the sole source of the illness. Nor did recognition of the connection between the two lead of itself to abolitionism. The Ulm Council seems to have believed the danger could be averted by a ban on women 'with the warts', frequent inspection of prostitutes, and special baths.[77] Furthermore, the thesis that prostitutes could be held responsible for the plague was as much a product of the turn against prostitution as a cause of it. We need to explain why prostitutes rather than, for example, mercenary soldiers should have come to be identified with the disease. As the strongly moral tone of so much of the medical literature against prostitution suggests, the equation of prostitute and disease was itself coloured by attitudes to women and their sexuality.

When the Augsburg Council came to close the brothel, pronouncements about the dangers to health it caused were notably absent;[78] and when, in the 1530s and 1540s, it campaigned to abolish free prostitution and punish those involved in it, no mention was made of venereal disease. Rather, it developed a new language to define sexual sin which was a fusion of elements of both civic moralism and religious rhetoric, all the more powerful for its ambiguity.

In 1537, it published a new, comprehensive Discipline Ordinance and established a special court to deal with discipline offences. The 1537 ordinance does not mention prostitution by name, but speaks instead of those who commit fornication and adultery. No longer a clearly identifiable trade, prostitution was subsumed under these sins; and the prostitute was not addressed as a separate class of woman. The sexual discipline which the whole citizenry were to adopt was both more all-embracing and less well defined than it had been before the Reformation. Now any sexual relationship outside marriage was counted sinful and any occasion where the sexes mingled, such as dances, might lead to sin. So absolute were the demands of the ideal that the Council was drawn inevitably to define marriage and the relations which ought to hold between husband and wife, parents and children, masters and servants as it articulated the concept of discipline. Parents ought to take responsibility for their children who, in turn, should obey their parents; masters should pay their servants while servants should be tractable. Indeed, the ordinance amounted to an attempt to order the household, to emphasize the distances which ought to exist between each of its members, and to define the rights and duties of each. The same ordinance also included an admonition to all citizens to wear clothing appropriate to their social position, so that each may 'be recognized for whom he or she is'.[79]

Prostitution had previously been regarded as the cure for the dangers of male lust, protecting (as all who favoured its existence insisted) the honour of wives and virgins. Such claims were of course related to concern about sexual anarchy within the household—the wives, daughters and maids for whom they feared were their own; the sexual threat derived from the young men of the house. Once the brothel was abolished, and prostitutes considered either fornicators or adulteresses like other women, it is not surprising that there should have been such care devoted to redrawing the boundaries within the household. Nor is it difficult to see why one of the Reformation's major concerns should have been with reworking the concept of incest, making it both a narrower but a far more strictly held set of rules.[80]

But it was as it was put into practice, in the investigations and interrogations of wrongdoers, that the meaning of the new ideal of discipline was worked out; and the trials of prostitutes gave the opportunity for its fullest expression. Instead of merely warning or banishing prostitutes, the Council now began to subject them to systematic interrogation; and the questioning increased in length and detail, frequently extended over more than one session, and more often involved the use of torture.[81] Less concerned with travelling prostitutes, who, in any case, were probably better able to slip the Council's net, the Council showed especial interest in women domiciled in the town, particularly those of the lower guild strata.

Above all, the prostitution trials of the second quarter of the sixteenth century reveal an obsession with the parental background of the accused woman. Thus, when Appolonia Strobel was suspected of prostitution, both her parents were summoned by the Council and interrogated. Her father was asked 'whether he had not noticed and known that his daughter went after dishonourable things', 'why he had allowed her to leave his house and be outside it day and night', 'why he had not punished her indiscipline in a fitting manner'. These were not ingenuous questions but accusations designed to impress upon him his failure as a father. The following day he was interrogated again under threat of torture and told that the Council refused to believe that he had not known all about his daughter's misdeeds. The questions put to Appolonia's mother were different. She was informed that 'it is well known that her daughter leads an unchristian dishonourable life' and asked 'why she had permitted and not interfered with this for some time past'. The Council tried to bring her to confess that she had been party to her daughter's prostitution and profited from it. At her second questioning, she was told that 'it is not to be believed that she knew nothing of her daughter's affairs' and admonished that 'if she were an honourable mother she could well have prevented such things'.[82]

Showing a genuine fascination with prostitution and its causes as an almost pathological condition, the Council was here locating the reasons for Appolonia's disgrace in her parents' failure to behave as true mother and father. The careful lines of questioning convict her mother of failing to safeguard her daughter's virtue and make it plain that this was her moral duty as an 'honourable mother'. Parents' duties were thus seen to involve religious duty, and the roles accorded father and mother were sharply differentiated. Lienhart Strobel, as befited a household head, was to observe his daughter's style of life and punish her for any moral lapses; while her mother's authority was conceived of as more personal and immediate. Her influence over her daughter was supposed to relate directly to sexual matters—she, rather than her husband, was chided for the loss of her daughter's virginity, and the Council pressed her to admit that she had acted as her daughter's procuress. Behind this accusation we might detect the belief that mothers are only too eager to entice their daughters into prostitution and that mother and daughter collude to profit from the business.

This was an essentially bourgeois conception of parental responsibility. Lienhart Strobel was not a craftsman but a day labourer and spent his working day in fields or in town, not in a workshop based in the house where he lived. His wife took in washing and did needlework while Appolonia also earned money sewing on contract. Each family member had to work independently for the household to survive. Lienhart Strobel explained that he could not know what went on in his house during the day, and he saw nothing unusual in his daughter staying out overnight or leaving home for a period while she was on a sewing engagement. Strobel could not be an ever-present patriarch, noting his daughter's activities and guarding her virginity, for his work was structured differently. Yet he had his own conception of good fatherhood—as his perplexed account of how he saw his duty puts it, 'He had always directed his daughter to the good', and 'if she had done something dishonourable despite this, he did not know about it'. His words lack the conviction of paternal authority, confident of its power to punish, and they reveal a willingness to allow his daughter her own life. His view of what was 'dishonourable' was inherently practical and related to meeting general social obligations rather than focusing on sexual behaviour. Repudiating suggestions that he had lived off his daughter's earnings, he maintained that 'he had always paid his round', and never profited from immoral earnings. 'Paying one's round', his practical metaphor for right living, was far removed from the Council's religious terminology: two rather different moral worlds were brought into collision.

Appolonia's mother also defended her behaviour as a parent, but her replies betray contradictory attitudes. She insisted that she did not at first know of her daughter's relationship with the patrician David Baumgartner and so could not be held responsible; and, she added, nothing dishonourable had ever taken place in her house. Yet she also admitted that once she discovered the situation she had warned Baumgartner that he ought to keep the promise he had made to compensate her daughter financially, and she threatened to write to his father. Her careful distinctions reveal her sense of discomfort—if she claimed not to be involved, she was determined that her daughter should receive financial compensation. Similarly, Anna Stockler's mother, a widow, asserted under interrogation that, like a dutiful parent, and acting in her father's place, she had admonished and beaten her daughter as soon as she discovered her involvement in prostitution. But, she explained, she was dependent on her daughter's earnings. If she were too strict, she feared Anna would desert her. In a casuistic argument, she claimed never to have touched a penny of her daughter's dishonest earnings but only what she was paid for her sewing; and if she had permitted her to go to the house of a client, that had been for the sole purpose of sewing, nothing more. Else Stockler placed trust in the man's promise not to leave her daughter in the lurch.[83] What she saw as maternal responsibility was ensuring her daughter a good match; and both women knew that their daughters could only hope to escape from the treadmill work of poorly paid sewing by offering their clients 'extra services' and saving a dowry.

But it was in the interrogations of the prostitutes themselves that the Council attempted most vigorously to arouse a sense of guilt. Using the religious language of sin, it robbed the women of their own words to define what happened. Let us return to the interrogation of Appolonia Strobel.[84] The first question she was asked was prefaced 'Since it is well known that for some time past she has led an undisciplined and ungodly life . . .' and asked her to name who had first involved her. These words were new: until the 1530s, a neutral word like 'trade', or the term *Buberei*, villainy, a term so broad as to cover any sort of misbehaviour and lacking religious connotations, would have been used to refer to prostitution.[85] The force of the word *unzuchtig* can hardly be caught in the English word 'undisciplined'. In essence a civil, moral term—the series of ordinances regulating citizens' moral behaviour were *Zuchtordnungen*—*unzuchtig* carried implications of disorder as well as sexual misbehaviour, and it represented the antithesis of the *Zucht*, the moral order, which the Council wished to inculcate. The word 'ungodly' added an explicitly religious dimension, echoing the religious injunction that no fornicator shall enter the Kingdom of Heaven.

The questioning centred on the occasion on which she had lost her virginity. 'Who was the first?' it asked Appolonia Strobel; and, doubting her answer, it tried to shake her statement at the second interrogation. The very expressions it used to refer to first intercourse—'robbed her of honour', 'brought her to fall', 'felled her', 'weakened her'—imply corruption and destruction of her integrity. By extracting a response to the question 'who had first brought her to fall?', the Council made the woman participate in her own condemnation.

'Because she is robbed of her virginity,' the Council told Katharina Ziegler, 'it is not to be supposed that she has remained pious since.'[86] Once fallen, promiscuity was inevitable, the Council believed. Prostitution was described as 'unchaste acts', 'sinful acts', 'the undisciplined life', 'dishonourable doings'. The central words from which these expressions derive are honour, discipline, and sin. Good women were 'honourable', 'disciplined', 'chaste', or *fromm*, pious. *Fromm*, as the Council used the word, meant right living, obeying the sexual code; but it also meant pious, right-believing. Piety began to merge with sexually orthodox behaviour.

The techniques involved derived from those of the confessional; but it was now the Council which required details of the events. The object of the interrogation was a complete revelation of the woman's sexual history, a kind of verbal undressing of the prostitute; leading to an acknowledgement, from her, of her sinfulness.[87] The new moralism made a very sharp distinction between married women and single women working as prostitutes. Married women were found guilty and punished for 'having committed adultery many times', as the placard read out and displayed at their punishment put it.[88] Single women were accused of multiple fornication. The moralization of the offence had the effect of denying the existence of prostitution as a trade—two separate types of immorality were distinguished. And conversely, there was now no clear distinction between prostitutes and adulteresses or fornicators.

The logical consequence of the redefinition was that the women's clients were equally sinners; and indeed, the Council did begin to take note of the names of all customers. In the 1540s, it proceeded to punish a number of men, including some quite prominent civic figures. It even maintained, consistently, that men who knowingly visited married prostitutes were guilty of adultery even if they were bachelors.[89]

Yet though there are reports that Martin Haid, civic notary, Gereon Sailer, humanist and civic doctor, and Ulrich Jung, doctor and patrician, were all found guilty of resort to prostitutes, all appear to have been fined and cautioned privately.[90] The group of about a dozen men found guilty in the 1540s and treated with what appears to have been exemplary firmness turn out, however, to have been connected with three men, Hans Gunzburger, Hans Eggenberger, and Anthoni Baumgartner.[91] The last two were members of the patriciate, while Gunzburger, a friend of the Baumgartner clan, was able to secure the intercession of Charles V's secretary on his behalf. The Baumgartner were a prominent

Catholic family, so one may suspect that motives other than the pursuit of sexual equity led the now firmly evangelical Council to act against them. Moreover, both Eggenberger and Baumgartner were known to have squandered their fortunes; and in 1544, Anthoni Baumgartner was to forfeit personal control of his assets.[92] Of the three, only Eggenberger faced the rigours of an interrogation, though torture was not used. The questions he faced had more to do with his financial mismanagement than with his sexual exploits.[93]

Though all these men faced very heavy fines and though the Council was determined that even when patricians were found guilty, 'it should be done this time as it is done to others in such cases', men were not in fact as severely punished as women. Men were more often able to convert imprisonment terms into fines;[94] and they found it easier for their offence to be treated as an aberration rather than as the occasion for a full investigation of the details of their 'sinful life'. Many men whom the Council listed as clients do not appear to have been summoned; and those it chose to proceed against follow a pattern; where first, priests had been identified as the source of the evil, now suspected Catholics and spendthrifts were its targets. But that it chose to prosecute clients at all did mark a major change in civic attitudes to prostitution.[95]

Prostitution, of course, was abolished neither by the closure of the brothel nor by the campaign against prostitutes and clients, riven as it was by contradictory attitudes to sexuality. Demographic pressures, low wages, and a declining job market for women ensured there was no shortage of women willing to work as prostitutes. Imperial Diets, where rich visitors and their retinues crowded the city, had always been magnets for prostitutes, foreign and local; yet in 1547 and 1548 when the Diet again met in Augsburg, the Council did not attempt a mass expulsion.[96]

Ironically, the closure of the city brothel encouraged the growth of small-scale brothel prostitution and free street-walking. It gave women greater control of their trade; and the dominance of women working as procurers, prostitutes, and brothel-keepers in the records stands in striking contrast to the long operation of the city brothel by men.[97] Women certainly lost the protection of the civic institution, where brothel-keeper and city guards were soon on hand to deal with rowdy young men; and the private brothels could exploit the women who worked in them even more mercilessly than the city enterprise. The chances of discovery were greater, and the punishments more severe.

The women interrogated, however, did not seem to regard what they were doing as a form of sexual delinquency, but as work. It is hard to distinguish what may be the scribe's bowdlerisations in a text which has already been transposed into the third person. But it is noticeable that the women never employed the moral terms of the Council, choosing instead neutral words, such as 'had to do with him', 'the matter', 'the business' to describe the sexual transaction.[98] This contrasts with the familiar affection with which men spoke of prostitutes, calling them 'the pretty ones', 'daughters', 'common women' and using their nicknames—language which denied that prostitution is work.[99]

If prostitution is indeed a transaction, then we need to place it in the context of the other exchanges of sex and money which took place in Augsburg if we are to understand its meaning. A clearly related exchange is the money which a virgin who had been seduced could claim not only for childbed and child support, but also for 'her honour', at a price which she determined.[100] Here there is the same conceptualization of the woman's honour as a material asset which can be sold; and which is distinct from the seller. This custom in turn derived its meaning from the institution of the morning gift, paid to the bride on the morning after the wedding night.[101] The seduced woman is thus a virgin who has sold her reputation once; and what she receives is calculated so that she may marry within her class, thus partially healing the wound to honour. The wife's virginity is also 'sold', but she has a new honour as a wife, which now rests upon her continued fidelity. In prostitution, the woman is classed as 'dishonourable'. She has severed the link between money and fidelity to one man; but the bond between money and sexual ownership remains, for she is owned by all men.

Prostitution, in common with other such exchanges in sixteenth-century society, represents sex as a transaction where men are the purchasers and women are the thing bought.[102] But what precisely were men buying? If we are to take seriously the claim that masculinity and femininity are historically constructed, then the answer to this question is by no means obvious. To say that, for example, men are seeking 'release from sexual tension', or that prostitution is a necessity in a society which delays marriage for its young men, confuses a theory about what male sexuality is like with a biological explanation; and masks the issues of power and aspects of fantasy involved. As a first step, we need to pay attention to the elements which seem to be involved in prostitution in different times and places.

Such a project is easy to propose: to carry it out is probably a foolhardy undertaking. What follows are some necessarily tentative remarks about some of the features of prostitution in Augsburg.

The first and most distinctive characteristic of late medieval prostitution was that visiting prostitutes was understood and sanctioned as a phase in a young man's life, part of his induction into manhood and marriage.[103] Older men who frequented brothels might be described as behaving 'like youths'. It reinforced male bonding and defined sexual virility as the essential male characteristic. The practices of prostitution, interestingly enough, seem to echo those of marriage: men could sleep overnight with civic prostitutes; and a man might say he was 'wedded to a prostitute for the night'. For youths, prostitution was understood through the prism of marriage; and it allowed them to learn and act out the 'masculinity' of married men.

A second aspect we might single out is the importance of clothes in sixteenth-century prostitution, both as a means of advertisement and as part of fantasy for client and prostitute alike. It is suggestive that town councils repeatedly tried to limit the finery a woman might wear, sometimes even attempting to force prostitutes to wear a uniform of short length, utterly divorced from the patterns of style and fashion within the town. Prostitutes' finery was a mockery of patrician or noble dress, favouring much jewellery, and dramatic berets or feathered hats in place of the wifely wimple. This love of luxury had always been one of the standard components of the image of the whore; but as the testimonies of the Augsburg prostitutes make plain, clothes had a very deep imaginative significance for them. Many mentioned the clothes they had earned, and one woman described in loving detail the cinnamon-coloured coat which a patrician had ordered to be made for her. Extravagant dress was a way of displaying one's wealth, showing oneself to be as good as a patrician and free of the drab dress of the 'honourable' women of one's own class. For the men, prostitution could also be a class fantasy, the brothel the place where identities were shed and emperor and apprentice could lie with the same woman. It offered the chance for men to dream of enjoying a woman of higher class— or indeed, of humiliating her.

Finally, virginity appears to have been a shared obsession within prostitution—hardly surprising, given its central role in the systems of marriage and the notions of paternal and maternal responsibility.

Women charged more for their first time; and procurers demanded a high price for virgins. In Augsburg, the brothel was known as the 'virgins' court'; and one prostitute was nicknamed 'Margaret the Court Virgin behind St Steven's'. But the heavy-handed irony of the slang perhaps suggests another element in the desires at play in prostitution. Just as the Council demanded of prostitutes 'Who was the first?', so the taking of a woman's virginity confirmed the man's masculinity, his ability to destroy her sexual intactness and determine her reputation. This was the ultimate confirmation of manhood, which men might dream of, even though an experienced prostitute could not fulfil it.[104]

Let us return to the question with which we began: the effect of the brothel's closure on attitudes to sexuality in Augsburg. The closure represented a recognition that men's sexual natures were not uncontrollable, and a faith that male lust could be educated and directed towards marriage. Prostitutes were no longer regarded as a separate category of dishonourable women to be tolerated and regulated: indeed, in the new moral language of the Council, prostitution was not even a term. But conversely, the implementation of the new ideal required far greater powers of surveillance. Between 1528 and 1548 there were at least 110 convictions for offences relating to prostitution, while in a further 58 cases, people were suspected of involvement and questioned.[105] The number of visitors a woman had, what kind of men and when they came, became indices of suspicious behaviour. The boundary between prostitute and non-prostitute became blurred. No longer a group of dishonourable women, clearly defined by where they lived and what they wore, there was little difference between prostitutes, fornicators, or adulteresses—indeed, any woman might be a prostitute.

But these shifts in attitude were always contested and never achieved total acceptance. By 1562, Augsburg was responding to Nuremberg's plea for advice on whether or not to close their brothel by admitting that some regretted the closure of Augsburg's brothel.[106] The familiar defence of prostitution as a protection for wives and daughters of 'respectable folk' was raised once more. Yet what does appear to have been an abiding legacy of the Reformation was the new obssession with women's sexual experience. Whereas the new church weakened or abolished individual confession, the Council now demanded a full and true account of the woman's sins. The whore had become a moral category, not a professional prostitute; and she stood for the lust of all women. If we might identify a more lasting transformation in sexual attitudes, it is located in the strengthening of the belief that women's lusts were to be feared as unbridled and demonic. The Reformation, which seemed at first to offer a sexual ethic identical for men and women, and appeared to bestow a new dignity on the married wife, suspected all women, single or married, of being ever ready to surrender themselves to their lust for debauchery.

Notes

1. *Die Chroniken der deutschen Städte*, 23 (Leipzig, 1894), 337.
2. On closures in other cities, see Iwan Bloch, *Die Prostitution*, 2 vols. (Berlin, 1912, 1925), ii. 260–2; and Susan Karrant-Nunn, 'Continuity and Change: Some Effects of the Reformation on the Women of Zwickau', *Sixteenth Century Journal*, 12/2 (1982), 16–42, p. 23.
3. Steven Ozment, *When Fathers Ruled: Family Life in Reformation Europe* (Harvard, 1983), 99.
4. Stadtarchiv Ulm (hereinafter cited as StAUlm) A 3988 Der frowen wiert ayd (hereafter referred to as 'oath') and see Stadtarchiv Augsburg (hereafter cited as StAA) Ratsbuch no. 277, 'Aidbuch' of the fifteenth century, fo. 18ᵛ, frowen wirt aid. I am grateful to Rolf Kiessling for this reference. Augsburg has few records on the brothel before the Reformation, so I have drawn on material relating to brothels in other cities. Surviving ordinances reveal a broadly similar organization. On Augsburg in the late medieval period, See Rolf Kiessling, *Bürgerliche Gesellschaft und Kirche in Augsburg im Spätmittelalter (Abhandlungen zur Geschichte der Stadt Augsburg*, 19) (Augsburg, 1971).
5. See G. L. Kriegk, *Deutsches Bürgerthum im Mittelalter*, 2 vols. (Frankfurt, 1868, 1871) ii. 308; Karl Obser, 'Zur Geschichte des Frauenhauses in Überlingen', *Zeitschrift für Geschichte des Oberrheins*, 70 (1916), 631–44; Dr von Posern-Klett, 'Frauenhäuser und freie Frauen in Sachsen', *Archiv für die sächsische Geschichte*, 12 (1874), 63–89, p. 67.
6. Carl Jäger, *Ulms Verfassungs-, bürgerliches und commercielles Leben im Mittelalter* (Heilbronn, 1831), 545; von Posern-Klett, 'Frauenhäuser und freie Frauen', 80; Max Bauer, *Liebesleben in deutscher Vergangenheit* (Berlin, 1924), 139; see also *Chroniken der deutschen Städte*, 11 (Leipzig, 1874), 464; and W. Rudeck, *Geschichte der öffentlichen Sittlichkeit in Deutschland* (Jena, 1897), 31–3.
7. Kriegk, *Deutches Bürgerthum*, ii. 327; Bauer, *Liebesleben*, 138. On the municipal nature of the brothel see also, for France, Jacques Rossiaud, sect. III of Jacques Le Goff (ed.), *La ville médiévale des Carolingiens à la Renaissance* (*Histoire de la France urbaine*, ii. ed. G. Duby) (Paris, 1980), 532.
8. Brothel-keeper's complaint: Staatsarchiv Ludwigsburg, B 207 Bü 68 no. 166. The doctor and the official in charge of beggars gave the women an internal examination ('besechent sy einwertz Jrs leibs') ('which no man has the right to do'). Clean women: StAUlm A 3669 (Zweites Gsatzbuch) fo. 416 ff., Newe frawen wierts ordnung 1512. I have found no evidence that German prostitutes were organized in guilds, though this claim is even repeated in modern literature: the 'guild of prostitutes' however, is used ironically to refer to the women.

9. StAUlm A 3988. Draft ordinance 1510. On prostitutes as an integral part of their community, see Mary Perry, ' "Lost Women" in Early Modern Seville: The Politics of Prostitution', *Feminist Studies* 4/1 (1978), 195–214; and Richard Trexler, 'La prostitution Florentine au xvᵉ siècle: Patronages et clientèles', *Annales E.S.C.*, 26, vi. (1981), 983–1015.

10. Bloch, *Die Prostitution*, i. 767. Note also StAA, Schätze 36 (1), Zuchtordnung 1472. This refers to the woman 'who goes to a married man's house and does not spare the wife within'; and threatens her with banishment. It suggests both that there were 'home calls' for married men and that this, rather than any recourse to prostitutes whatsoever by married men, was causing concern.

11. Bauer, *Liebesleben*, 134 (Metz, 1332), Joseph Baader, *Nürnberger Polizeiordnungen aus dem xiii bis xv Jahrhundert* (*Bibliothek des litterarischen Vereins in Stuttgart*, 63) (Stuttgart, 1861), 119; Wilhelm Reynizsch, *Uiber Truhten und Truhtensteine, Barden und Bardenliebe, Feste Schmaeuser und Gerichte der Teutschen* (Gotha, 1802), 31 (Nördlingen, 1472).

12. StAA Ratsbuch 13, fo. 83ᵛ, 1515; Strafbuch des Rats 1509–1526, p. 185, 20 Sept. 1526; and cases of married men punished for consorting with prostitutes, see for example pp. 19, 37, and 46.

13. Walter Köhler, *Zürcher Ehegericht und Genfer Konsistorium* (*Quellen und Abhandlungen zur schweizerischen Reformationsgeschichte*, vii and x) (Leipzig, 1932, 1942), i. 145–7.

14. StAUlm A 3988; (oath); A [6543] Aid- und Ordnugnsbuch B, fo. cccxvʳ; Bloch, *Die Prostitution*, i. 777.

15. Gottfried Geiger, *Die Reichsstadt Ulm vor der Reformation* (*Forschungen zur Geschichte der Stadt Ulm*, 11) (Ulm, 1971), 173–4.

16. StAUlm A 3988 (oath); Bloch, *Die Prostitution*, i. 767–70.

17. StAUlm A 3669 fo. 416 ff.; Bloch, *Die Prostitution*, i. 770; Reynizsch, *Uiber Truhten und Truhtensteine*, p. 31 (Nördlingen, 1472); fights in and around the brothel, StAA, Strafbuch des Rats 1509–26, p. 6, 30 Jan. 1510, p. 119, 10 Dec. 1521; Urgichtensammlung, 23 Sept. 1506; cautions against fighting, Kriegk, *Deutsches Bürgerthum*, ii. 307.

18. On the different social worlds of men and women, Rainer Beck, 'Voreheliche Sexualität auf dem Land', in R. van Dülmen and H. Heidrich (eds.), *Kultur der einfachen Leute: Bayerisches Volksleben vom 16. bis zum 19. Jahrhundert* (Munich, 1983); on secret marriages, Thomas Robischeaux, 'Peasants and Pastors: Rural Youth Control and the Reformation in Hohenlohe', *Social History*, 6 (1981), 281–300 and Thomas Safley, *Let No Man Put Asunder: The Control of Marriage in the German South-West: A Comparative Study* (Kirksville, 1984); and for cases of clandestine marriage promises at church ales, etc. Archiv des Bistums Augsburg, Protokolle des bischöflichen Konsistoriums 1535–6 (the one surviving 16th-century pre-Reformation volume) and StAA Ehegerichtsbuch 1537–46.

19. Baader, *Nürnberger Polizeiordnungen*, 121; Reynizsch, *Uiber Truhten und Truhtensteine*, 31 (Nördlingen, 1472); Gustav Wustmann, *Aus Leipzigs Vergangenheit*, 4 vols. (Leipzig, 1885–1909) iii. 120.

20. Christian Meyer, *Das Stadtbuch von Augsburg, insbesondere das Stadtrecht vom Jahre 1276* (Augsburg, 1872), 88, Art XXXI and 190, Art CXIII. Prostitutes unable to bring accusations of rape: Heath Dillard, 'Daughters of the Reconquest: Medieval Women in Castilian Town Society 1100–1300', Ph.D. diss, University of Virginia (1980), 508, 661–5; and at Ems, von Posern-Klett,

Frauenhäuser und freie Frauen', 75. Nor if a citizen 'disciplined' or beat a prostitute for her 'misdeeds' did this count as an assault: StAA Schätze 36(1) (Zuchtordnung, 1472).

21. See Jacques Rossiaud, 'Prostitution, Youth, and Society in the Towns of South-eastern France in the Fifteenth Century', in Robert Forster and Orest Ranum (eds.), *Deviants and the Abandoned in French Society: Selections from the Annales*, iv. trans. Elborg Forster and Patricia M. Ranum (Baltimore, 1978).
22. Bloch, *Die Prostitution*, i. 767–70; StAUlm A 3988 (Draft ordinance); A 3669 fo. 416 ff.
23. For example, Baader, *Nürnberger Polizeiordnungen*, 119; J. Brucker, *Strassburger Zunft- und Polizeiordnungen des 14. und 15. Jahrhunderts* (Strasbourg, 1889), 469.
24. Baader, *Nürnberger Polizeiordnungen*, 120; Bauer, *Liebesleben*, 128–9 (Würzburg). Both ordinances clearly allow the women to choose whether or not to work when menstruating; though intercourse with menstruating women was forbidden according to Christian precept and folk lore. In Ulm in 1512 (StAUlm A 3669 fo. 416 ff.) and in Überlingen in 1524, menstruating women were banned from working (Obser, 'Zur Geschichte des Frauenhauses in Überlingen', 634). On attitudes to menstruation, see Ian Maclean, *The Renaissance Notion of Woman: A Study in the Fortunes of Scholasticism and Medical Science in European Intellectual Life* (Cambridge, 1980), 39–40; and Patricia Crawford, 'Attitudes to Menstruation in Seventeenth-Century England', *Past and Present*, 91 (1981), 47–73.
25. Gustav Schönfeldt, *Beiträge zur Geschichte des Pauperismus und der Prostitution in Hamburg* (*Sozial-geschichtliche Forschungen, Ergänzungshefte zur Zeitschrift für Socialund Wirthschaftsgeschichte*, 11. Heft) (Weimar, 1897), 109; Bloch, *Die Prostitution*, i. 767. But note StAA Ratsbuch no. 277 fo. 18^{v}: the brothel keeper was merely warned to 'permit no disturbance' at these times.
26. Baader, *Nürnberger Polizeiordnungen*, 118–19; Brucker, *Strassburger Zunft- und Polizei-Verordnungen*, 469; Obser, 'Zur Geschichte des Frauenhauses in Überlingen', 638; StAUlm, A 3669 fo. 416 ff. It is difficult to see how the much vaunted 'social security' system for prostitutes at Ulm, to which each woman contributed a penny a week and the brothel-keeper two, could ever have been sufficient for the women's needs, since pregnant, sick and menstruating women were forbidden to work.
27. Rumour that the Ulm brothel-keepers were travelling to purchase prostitutes for twenty or thirty gulden: Staatsarchiv Ludwigsburg, B207, Bü 76; the Augsburg brothel-keeper punished for exchanging a woman to the Ulm brothel when she had arranged a marriage: StAA, Strafbuch des Rats 1509–1526, 124, 10 Mar. 1522; Complaints on buying and pawning woman: Baader, *Nürnberger Polizeiordnugnen*, 117 (only those who were not previously prostitutes might be sold). Brucker, *Strassburger Zunft- und Polizei-Verordnungen*, 468; Reynizsch, *Uiber Truhten und Truhtensteine*, 31; 'Whoreseller' as a profession, Kreigk, *Deutsches Bürgerthum* 318 (1390).
28. StAA, Ratsbuch 3, fo. 109^{r}/p. 107, 1428.
29. StAA Ratsbuch 3, fo. 109^{v}/p. 217, 1428; Baader, *Nürnberger Polizeiverordnungen*, 120, Obser, 'Zur Geschichte des Frauenhauses in Überlingen', 642–3. For a letter from the Ulm brothel-keeper objecting to even these provisions, see Staatsarchiv Ludwigsburg, B 207 Bü 68, no. 166.

30. *Chroniken der deutschen Städte*, 11 (Leipzig, 1874), 645–6, 695; Reynizsch, *Uiber Truhten und Truhtensteine*, 32–6 (Nuremberg, 1492); and StAUlm 3669 fo. 416 ff.

31. The Strafbücher of Augsburg contains records of these lists. The last banishment took place in 1534. See also Archivar Buff, 'Verbrechen und Verbrecher zu Augsburg in der zweiten Hälfte des 14. Jahrhunderts', *Zeitschrift des historischen Vereins für Schwaben und Neuburg*, 4, 1878, 160–232: though he states that petty thieves and vagabonds were also among those banished, by the 16th century, the lists are almost exclusively of people connected with prostitution. For a similar annual round-up of prostitutes in Hamburg, Schönfeldt, *Beiträge zur Geschichte des Pauperismus*, 99.

32. StAA Schätze 63, fo. 170^r; and fo. 8^v, 17^r; Claus Peter Clasen, *Die Augsburger Steuerbücher um 1600* (Augsburg, 1976), 17–18.

33. Thus in 1516 the banishments were delayed because of the Emperor's presence so that 'my lords' should not be overwhelmed by petitioners. StAA, Strafbuch des Rats, 1509–1526, 64.

34. StAA Ratsbuch 3, p. 464/fo. 406^v, 232^v; on prostitutes' clothing elsewhere, Bloch, *Di Prostitution*, i. 814–15; and for clothes in the colours of the city, see Wustmann, *Aus Leipzigs Vergangenheit*, 122; prostitutes forbidden to wear wreaths, von Posern-Klett, 'Frauenhäuser und freie Frauen', 84.

35. Meyer, *Das Stadtbuch von Augsburg*, 57, Art. XIX, s. 11; but see Buff, 'Verbrechen und Verbrecher'—the sentence was commuted. On distinguishing clothes for Jews, see Anton Binterim, *Pragmatische Geschichte der deutschen National-, Provinzial- und vorzüglichsten Diözesanconcilien von dem vierten Jahrhundert bis auf das Concilium zu Trient*, 7 vols. (Mainz, 1843–52), vii. 468 (Mainz, 1451), 481 (Cologne, 1452).

36. For an example, StAA, Urgichtensammlung, 27 Feb. 1532, Kunigund Schwaiher. On the threat prostitutes posed to honour, von Posern-Klett, 'Frauenhäuser und freie Frauen', 71; and Erich Maschke, 'Die Unterschichten der mittelalterlichen Städten Deutschlands', in Maschke and J. Sydow (eds.), *Gesellschaftliche Unterschichten in den südwestdeutschen Städten* (Stuttgart, 1967).

37. Baader, *Nürnberger Polizeiordnungen*, 119; and for punishment of brothel-keeper for doing precisely this, StAA Strafbuch des Rats 1509–26, 214, 10 Mar. 1522.

38. Kriegk, *Deutsches Bürgerthum*, ii. 329 and 394, n. 256 (Frankfurt, 1546). Compare Binterim, *Pragmatische Geschichte der deutschen Concilien*, vii. 469, Mainz 1451: priests' concubines were threatened with refusal of church burial by the Church.

39. Herman Hoffman, ed., *Würzburger Polizeisätze Gebote und Ordnungen des Mittelalters 1125–1495* (*Veröffentlichungen der Gesellschaft für fränkische Geschichte*, Reihe X, v. (Würzburg, 1955), 203; and see also H. Deichert, *Geschichte des Medizinalwesens im Gebiet des ehemaligen Konigsreichs Hannover* (*Quellen und Darstellungen zur Geschichte Niedersachsens*, 26) (Hanover and Leipzig, 1908), 243.

40. Schönfeldt, *Beitrage zur Geschichte des Pauperismus*, 99; Brucker, *Strassburger Zunft- und Polizei-Verordnungen*, 459, 465–6.

41. (Shootings:) Kriegk, *Deutsches Bürgerthum*, ii. 327; Max Radlkofer, 'Die Schützengesellschaften und Schützenfeste Augsburgs im 15. und 16. Jahrhundert', *Zeitschrift des historischen Vereins für Schwaben und Neuburg*, 21 (1894), 87–138, 103; (Weddings:) Bauer, *Liebesleben*, 137 (Rothenburg);

Kriegk; *Deutsches Bürgerthum*, ii. 327; (Dances:) Brucker, *Strassburger Zunft- und Polizei-Verordnungen*, 466 (prostitutes banned from attending); Josef Schrank, *Die Prostitution in Wien*, 2 vols. (Vienna, 1886), i. 105 (prostitutes banned *henceforth*).

42. Schrank, *Die Prostitution in Wien*, i. 105, Rudeck, *Geschichte der öffentlichen Sittlichkeit*, 35; Wustmann, *Aus Leipzigs Vergangenheit*, 129.

43. Though of course directing prostitutes to burn a candle to the Virgin may have an ironic point. I am grateful to Carol Willock for suggesting this. Geiger, *Die Reichsstadt Ulm vor der Reformation*, 173–4 StAUlm A 3669 fo. 416 ff.

44. Meyers, *Das Stadtbuch von Augsburg*, 71 Art. XXVII s. 3; p. 72, s. 8. In Vienna, the hangman and beadle were paid from the brothel's revenues, Kriegk, *Deutsches Bürgerthum*, ii. 298; in Leipzig, the executioner was in charge of the brothel as late as 1519. J. Glenzdorf and F. Treichel, *Henker, Schinder und arme Sünder*, 2 vols. (Bad Münster, 1970) i. 92–3; at Zwickau, the brothel was next to the hangman's house on the city wall, Karrant-Nunn, 'Continuity and Change: Some Effects of the Reformation on the Women of Zwickau', 21, and Bloch, *Die Prostitution*, i. 745.

45. StAA, Schätze 63, fo. 3ᵛ.

46. *Chroniken der deutschen Städte*, 15 (Leipzig, 1878), 108 (Leonhart Widmann's chronicle). On the concept of honour and the class of the 'Unehrlichen', dishonourables, see esp. Karl Lorenzen Schmidt, 'Beleidigungen in Schleswig-Holsteinsichen Städten im 16. Jahrhundert, soziale Norm und soziale Kontrolle in Städtegesellschaften', *Kieler Blätter zur Volkskunde*, 10 (1978), 5–20.

47. Sebastian Franck, *Weltbůch: Spiegel und bildtnisz des gantzen erdtbodens* (Tübingen, V. Morhart, 1534), fo. cxxviiiᵛ.

48. *Chroniken der deutschen Städte*, 11: 645–6.

49. James Brundage, 'Prostitution in the Medieval Canon Law', *Signs*, 1/4 (1976), 825–45; Bloch, *Die Prostitution*, i. 645.

50. Baader, *Nürnberger Polizeiordnungen*, 117; Reynizsch, *Uiber Truhten und Truhtensteine*, 29 (Nördlingen, 1472).

51. Bloch, *Die Prostitution*, i. 646.

52. *Spiegel des sünders* [Augsburg, 1480, A. Sorg] and *Beichtbüchlin* (Augsburg, 1491). See also Thomas Tentler, *Sin and Confession on the Eve of the Reformation* (Princeton, 1977), esp. 141; and note Binterim, *Pragmatische Geschichte der deutschen Concilien*, vi. 286 (Constance, 1328), 306–7 (Augsburg, 1355), 397 (Trier, 1310): intercourse with prostitutes is not classed as a 'reserved sin'; and note also vii. 302 (Eichstetten, 1453), 'some go so far as to say that simple fornication (*Hurerei*) is no serious sin', and advises confessional instruction to counteract this error.

53. *Chroniken der deutschen Städte*, 25 (Leipzig, 1896) 'Cronica newer Geschichten von Wilhelm Rem', 123: on the first occasion when the women went to the sermon at St Moritz's, two escaped. For Ulm, StAUlm, A 3669, fos. 416 ff. Prostitutes sitting in separate parts of the church: Brucker, *Strassburger Zunft- und Polizei-Verordnungen*, 406; warned to do so, Kreigk, *Deutsches Bürgerthum*, ii. 325; Prostitutes not to take communion, Binterim, *Pragmatische Geschichte der deutschen Concilien*, v. 367; must go on the Friday after Easter to avoid offence, v. 367; Prostitutes no longer to go in pairs to church, J. Siebenkees, *Materialien zur Nürnbergischen Geschichte*, 4 vols. (Nuremberg, 1792–4), iv. 592.

54. On the Reformation in Augsburg, see Friedrich Roth, *Augsburgs Reforationsgeschichte*, 4 vols. (Munich, 1901–11); and Philip Broadhead, 'Internal Politics and Civic Society in Augsburg During the Era of the Early Reformation 1518–1537', Ph.D. diss. (Kent, 1981); For the prostitutes' first attendance at sermons, *Chroniken der deutschen Städte* 25, 123; Roth, *Augsburgs Reformationsgeschichte*, i. 95–6.

55. StAA Baumeisterbuch 1526, fo. 67^v and Baumeisterbuch 1530, fo. 60^r.

56. StAA Baumeisterbuch 1529, fo. 66^r; Baumeisterbuch, 1530, fo. 60^r; Baumeisterbuch, 1532 fo. 67^v, and fos. 74^v, 75^v, fo. 80^r. Most seem to have left just after Easter.

57. StAA Baumeisterbuch 1529, fo. 67^r Note an early redemption, Baumeisterbuch 1513, fo. 53^v. In Nuremberg when the brothel was closed in 1562, however, the women were expelled from the city: Siebenkees, *Materialien zur Nürnbergischen Geschichte*, iv. 595.

58. StAA. Stadtkanzlei Urkundenkonzepte 2.75 Schuldbriefe, supplication Margaret Stegman. The brothel was eventually sold to the Council for debt. From the intricate series of documents surrounding the sale it emerges that the brothel-keeper usually paid off the purchase price through the brothel income, which was lucrative enough for one keeper to pay 2 gulden per week. The brothel itself was a valuable piece of property, worth 1050 gulden in 1531. See StAA, Stadtkanzlei Urkundenkonzepte 2.75 Schuldbriefe, 19 Oct. 1530; 6 Mar. 1531; post 18 Mar. 1533; 18 Mar. 1533; 26 Mar. 1533; Stadtgerichtsbuch, 1533, fos. 32b, 39a, 45a, 77b, 80a; Realitätensammlung, 16 June 1533, 16 Sept. 1533. The Imperial Ordinances of 1530 and 1548 and the Carolina of 1532 have sometimes been credited with bringing about the closure of city brothels; but since their provisions are directed against fornication, adultery, and procuring alone, and on restricting prostitutes' clothing, this seems unlikely. *Aller dess Heiligen Romischen Reichss gehaltener Reichstäg Ordnung . . . 1356 bis 1603* (Mainz, 1607, J. Albin), 218, 374, 688; and *Die Peinliche Gerichtsordnung Kaiser Karls V von 1532* (Carolina), ed A. Kaufman, 4th edn. (Munich, 1975), 80, 81.

59. For example, Anton Firn, *Supplication des Pfarrers vnnd der Pfarrkinder zů sant Thoman* [P. Ulhart, Augsburg], 1524; Johann Eberlin, *Die ander getrew vermanung an den Rath der stadt Vlm* [M. Ramminger, Augsburg], 1523; Jakob Strauss, *Ein Sermon in der deutlich angezaiget* [G. Nadler, Augsburg, 1523?], *Ein neüw wunderbarlich Beycht büechlin*, [S. Grimm, Augsburg, 1523].

60. Jakob Strauss, *Ein neüw wunderbarlich Beycht büechlin*, and see Steven Ozment, *The Reformation in the Cities* (Yale, 1975), 51–3. But the pre-Reformation church had also taken the problem seriously. Binterim, *Pragmatische Geschichte der deutschen Concilien*, vi. 412 (Trier, 1310), 'The confessions of women should be heard in a public, not a covered place; also one should not look in their faces, but either the headcloth should be held before the eyes or one should look away.'

61. Urbanus Rhegius, *Ernstliche erbietung der Euangelische Prediger* [P. Ulhart, Augsburg, 1524] and see also Jakob Fuchs, *Ain schöner Sendbrieff an Bischof vo Wirtzburg darinn Priester Ee beschirmbt wirdt* [H. Steiner, Augsburg, 1523]. For examples of hostile invective directed against the priests' concubines themselves, *Concubinarij. Vnderricht ob ein Priester ein beyschläferin haben mög* [J. Cammerlander, Strasbourg], 1545; fo. D; *Dialogus von Zweyen pfaffen Kochin* [M. Buchfürher, Erfurt, 1523]; Hans Kolb, (*Ein*) *Reformation not-*

durftig in der Christenheit mit den Pfaffen und ihren Mägden (n.d., n.pl.) (*Die Flugschriften des frühen 16. Jahrhunderts*, Microfiche series, ed. Hans-Joachim Köhler (Zug, 1978–) no. 328/924; *Von dem Pfründmarkt der Curtisanen und Tempelknechten* (1521, n. pl.), *Flugschriften Microfiche* 279/796.

62. Max Geisberg, *The German Single Leaf Woodcut 1500–1550*, 4 vols. (New York, 1974), i. 120. Artist Leonhard Beck, 1523, Berlin. On the Reformation and iconography, see R. W. Scribner, *For the Sake of Simple Folk. Popular Propaganda for the Reformation* (Cambridge, 1981).

63. StAA Zuchtordnung, 1537.

64. StAA Schätze 36(1) Zuchtordnung, 1472.

65. StAA Literalien 1534, Nachtrag I, no. 24 fo. 29ʳ and Nachtrag II, no. 29 (Kötzler) fos. 1ʳ–4ᵛ; see Philip Broadhead, 'Politics and Expediency in the Augsburg Reformation', in *Reformation Principle and Practice, Essays in Honour of A. G. Dickens*, ed. Peter N. Brooks (London, 1980) and K. Wohlfart, *Die Augsburger Reformation in den Jahren 1533–4* (Leipzig, 1901).

66. StAA Urgichtensammlung, 27 Feb. 1532 Kunigund Schwaiher, and see also 9 Sept. 1532, Ulrich Diether, Barbara Diether.

67. J. Dillenberger, ed. *Martin Luther: Selections from his Writings* (New York, 1961), 483.

68. Johannes Brenz as cited in Melchior Ambach, *Von Ehbruch vnd hurerey* (C. Iacob, Frankfurt, 1543) fo. H4ᵛ and Ambach, fo. A3ᵛ and throughout. See Ozment, *When Fathers Ruled*, 55–6.

69. See my 'Going to Church and Street: Weddings in Reformation Augsburg', *Past and Present*, 106 (1985), 62–102.

70. See Merry Wiesner, 'Luther and Women: the Death of Two Marys', forthcoming in J. Obelkevich, L. Roper and R. Samuel (eds.), *Religion and Society* (London, 1985) and on Luther's attitude to sexuality, Heiko Oberman, *Luther: Mensch zwischen Gott und Teufel* (Berlin, 1982).

71. Geisberg, *German Single Leaf Woodcut*, Artist Peter Flötner (detail of *The Power of Womanhood*), iii. 780, and for a literary equation of the prostitute, the 'free woman' with the powerful female, Johannes Diepolt, *Ein Sermon an Sankt Mariae Magdlenae Tag . . .* (n.pl., 1523), *Flugschriften Microfiche*, 456/1233.

72. Martin Luther, in *Luther: Letters of Spiritual Counsel*, ed. G. Tappert (*Library of Christian Classics*, 18) (London and Philadelphia, 1955), 292–4, p. 293.

73. See C. H. Fuchs, *Die ältesten Schriftsteller über die Lustseuche in Deutschland von 1495 bis 1510* (Göttingen, 1893); esp. 375, 377–8; and J. K. Proksch, *Die Geschichte der venerischen Krankheiten: Eine Studie*, 2 vols. (Bonn, 1895); Alfred Crosby, Jr., 'The Early History of Syphilis: A Reappraisal', *American Anthropologist*, 71 (1969), 218–27; Owsei Temkin, 'Zur Geschichte von "Moral und Syphilis" ', *Archiv für Geschichte der Medizin* 19 (1927), 331–48; and esp. Margaret Pelling, 'Appearance and Reality: Barbersurgeons, the Body and Disease in Early Modern London', in L. Beier and R. Finlay (eds.), *The Making of the Metropolis* (forthcoming).

74. Proksch, *Die Geschichte der venerischen Krankheiten*, i. 400.

75. Ibid. and ibid. 156–61.

76. Johannes Haselbergk, *Von den welschen Purppeln* [Ivo Schoeffer, Mainz], 1533.

77. StAUlm [3988] and see also Bloch, *Die Prostitution*, ii. 12 (Winterthur, 1503). On this point, see in particular, Judith Walkowitz, *Prostitution and Victorian Society. Women, Class and the State* (Cambridge, 1980).

78. But compare Karrant-Nunn, 'Continuity and Change: Some Effects of the Reformation on the Women of Zwickau', 23–4. The Council mentioned the danger of syphilis when it closed the brothel, but note her comments, p. 24, 'Venereal disease itself did not drive them to close the brothel. The Reformation did.'
79. StAA Zuchtordnung, 1537; and note the very lengthy edition of 1552.
80. See Köhler, *Zürcher Ehegericht und Genfer Konsistorium*; and Jack Goody, *The Development of the Family and Marriage in Europe* (Cambridge, 1983) on the Reformation's redefinition of incest.
81. See chapter 'Prostitution' in my forthcoming thesis, 'Gender and Society: Women and the Reformation in Augsburg' (Ph.D.., London) for figures.
82. StAA Urgichtensammlung, 28, 29 July 1542, Lienhart Strobel; 25, 28, 29 July 1542, Appolonia Strobel the elder.
83. Ibid. 27 April 1541, Els Stockler.
84. Ibid. 25, 28, 29 July 1542, Appolonia Strobel the younger.
85. For examples of this language, see Strafbücher des Rats. I am not arguing that 'sin' had never been used by the Council in relation to prostitution before the Reformation. But it is used infrequently, and without the consistency, clarity, and association with the concepts of honour and discipline.
86. StAA Urgichtensammlung, 8, 11 Aug. 1541, Katharina Ziegler.
87. Compare Annemarie Dross, *Die erste Walpurgisnacht* (Hamburg, 1981) on the interrogation of witches.
88. For example, StAA Strafbuch des Rats 1547, fo. 112^r, 20 Sept. (Ursula Niclin); Urgichtensammlung, 14, 18 July 1533 (Agnes Veiheler); Strafbuch 1547 fo. 113^v, 1 Sept. (Kunigund Geiger); Strafbuch, 1547, fo. 103^r 2 Apr. (Anna Beckh).
89. StAA Strafbuch der Zuchtherren, 21 Sept. 1541, p. 72 (Hans Eggenberger, Endris Degen); p. 73 (Philip Bloss); 7 Oct. 1541, p. 77 (three men); 11 Feb. 1542, p. 103 (Georg Beckh), 13 Feb. 1542, p. 104 (Jacob Ruff, Jacob Breising).
90. *Chroniken der deutschen Städte*, 13 (Sender), 404.
91. See the Urgichten of Barbara Scherer (9 July 1541), Barbara Riedhauser/Mair (19 Sept. 1541) and Emerenciana Hefeler (9 Feb. 1542): they implicated some men who were not, as far as we can tell, punished—see n. 89.
92. StAA Urkundensammlung, 30 Jan. 1544.
93. Ibid. 26, 27, 28 April 1541 (Hans Eggenberger).
94. For example, StAA Ratsbuch, 17, I, fo. 102^v 13 May 1543 (David Baumgartner); Strafbuch der Zuchtherren, 7 Oct. 1541 p. 77 (Marx Hartman, Hans Fockher); 21 Sept. 1541, p. 73 (Endris Degen); Ratsbuch 17, I, fo. 47^v, 15 Mar. 1543 (Anthoni Baumgartner fined the colossal sum of 400 gulden for the third offence). See, on the double standard, Keith Thomas, 'The Double Standard', *Journal of the History of Ideas*, 20 (1959), 195–216.
95. This raises the fascinating question of the Counter-Reformation's distinctive moralism and its attitude to prostitution—this cannot be discussed here. But see Bloch, *Die Prostitution*, ii.
96. A higher number than average (twelve) were convicted of involvement in prostitution and a further eighteen were suspected in 1547; while in 1548, nine were convicted and fourteen suspected. See chapter 'Prostitution' in my thesis, 'Gender and Society'. But this was insignificant in relation to the number of prostitutes working. Compare estimates of 1500 prostitutes at the Diet of Regensburg, 1471; 700 'public' and at least as many more 'secret' prostitutes

at the Council of Constance, Bloch, *Die Prostitution*, i. 710–11; and on sexual indulgence at the Diet in 1547–8, see Bartholomäus Sastrow's comments, V. Brosthaus, ed., *Bürgerleben im 16. Jahrhundert: Die Autobiographie des Stralsunder Bürgermeisters Bartholomäus Sastrow als kulturgeschichtliche Quelle* (Vienna 1972), 57.

97. On the control of prostitution by women in this period, see chapter 'Prostitution' in my thesis, 'Gender and Society': between 1528 and 1548, 97 women but only 13 men were convicted of involvement; and many of those men were married to women in the trade.

98. See StAA Urgichtensammlung.

99. These are expressions which occur in the Augsburg documents. For a list of all the known expressions, see Bloch, *Die Prostitution*, i. 732 ff.

100. For cases of compensation, see Ordinariatsarchiv, Augsburg, Protokolle des bischöflichen Konsistoriums (the volumes 1535–6 survive from the pre-Reformation period) and for records of the evangelical marriage court, StAA Ehegerichtsbuch, 1537–1546.

101. See Roper, 'Going to Church and Street'.

102. There is some evidence of male prostitution in Cologne and in Italy, see Bloch, *Die Prostitution*, i. 799.

103. Compare Rossiaud, 'Prostitution, Youth and Society'.

104. On the meaning of virginity, see Luisa Accati Levi, 'Il furto del desiderio', *Memoria*, 7 (1983), 7–16. On the images of the harlot and the virgin, see Perry, ' "Lost Women": Prostitution in Early Modern Seville', and for a fascinating account of the parallels between nuns and prostitutes, Nikki Harrison, 'Nuns and Prostitutes in Enlightenment Spain' (forthcoming).

105. 110 individuals were convicted of involvement in the trade of prostitution, 97 of them women; of 58 suspected and interrogated, 45 were women. Details in chapter 'Prostitution' in 'Gender and Society'. Figures were derived from StAA Urgichtensammlung, Ratsbücher, Strafbücher des Rats, Strafbücher der Zuchtherren since no one source was complete.

106. J. Siebenkees, *Materialien zur Nürnbergischen Geschichte*, iv. 593–6. I am grateful to Merry Wiesner for drawing my attention to this.

The Female World of Love and Ritual: Relations between Women in Nineteenth-Century America

Carroll Smith-Rosenberg

The female friendship of the nineteenth century, the long-lived, intimate, loving friendship between two women, is an excellent example of the type of historical phenomena which most historians know something about, which few have thought much about, and which virtually no one has written about.[1] It is one aspect of the female experience which consciously or unconsciously we have chosen to ignore. Yet an abundance of manuscript evidence suggests that eighteenth- and nineteenth-century women routinely formed emotional ties with other women. Such deeply felt, same-sex friendships were casually accepted in American society. Indeed, from at least the late eighteenth through the mid-nineteenth century, a female world of varied and yet highly structured relationships appears to have been an essential aspect of American society. These relationships ranged from the supportive love of sisters, through the enthusiasms of adolescent girls, to sensual avowals of love by mature women. It was a world in which men made but a shadowy appearance.[2]

Defining and analysing same-sex relationships involves the historian in deeply problematical questions of method and interpretation. This is especially true since historians, influenced by Freud's libidinal theory, have discussed these relationships almost exclusively within the context of individual psychosexual developments or, to be more explicit, psychopathology.[3] Seeing same-sex relationships in terms of

Research for this paper was supported in part by a grant from the Grant Foundation, New York, and by National Institutes of Health trainee grant 5 FO3 HD48800–03. I would like to thank several scholars for their assistance and criticism in preparing this paper: Erving Goffman, Roy Schafer, Charles E. Rosenberg, Cynthia Secor, Anthony Wallace. Judy Breault, who has just completed a biography of an important and introspective nineteenth-century feminist, Emily Howland, served as a research assistant for this paper and her knowledge of nineteenth-century family structure and religious history provided invaluable. Reprinted with permission from *Signs*, 1/1 (Autumn 1975), 1–29.

a dichotomy between normal and abnormal, they have sought the origins of such apparent deviance in childhood or adolescent trauma and detected the symptoms of 'latent' homosexuality in the lives of both those who later became 'overtly' homosexual and those who did not. Yet theories concerning the nature and origins of same-sex relationships are frequently contradictory or based on questionable or arbitrary data. In recent years such hypotheses have been subjected to criticism both from within and without the psychological professions. Historians who seek to work within a psychological framework, therefore, are faced with two hard questions: Do sound psychodynamic theories concerning the nature and origins of same-sex relationships exist? If so, does the historical datum exist which would permit the use of such dynamic models?

I would like to suggest an alternative approach to female friendships—one which would view them within a cultural and social setting rather than from an exclusively individual psychosexual perspective. Only by thus altering our approach will we be in the position to evaluate the appropriateness of particular dynamic interpretations. Intimate friendships between men and men and women and women existed in a larger world of social relations and social values. To interpret such friendships more fully they must be related to the structure of the American family and to the nature of sex-role divisions and of male–female relations both within the family and in society generally. The female friendship must not be seen in isolation; it must be analysed as one aspect of women's overall relations with one another. The ties between mothers and daughters, sisters, female cousins, and friends, at all stages of the female life-cycle constitute the most suggestive framework for the historian to begin an analysis of intimacy and affection between women. Such an analysis would not only emphasize general cultural patterns rather than the internal dynamics of a particular family or childhood; it would shift the focus of the study from a concern with deviance to that of defining configurations of legitimate behavioural norms and options.[4]

This analysis will be based upon the correspondence and diaries of women and men in thirty-five families between the 1760s and the 1880s. These families, though limited in number, represented a broad range of the American middle class, from hard-pressed pioneer families and orphaned girls to daughters of the intellectual and social elite. It includes families from most geographic regions, rural and urban, and a spectrum of Protestant denominations ranging from Mormon to orthodox Quaker. Although scarcely a comprehensive sample of America's increasingly heterogeneous population, it does, I believe, reflect accurately the literate middle class to which the historian working with letters and diaries is necessarily bound. It has involved an analysis of many thousands of letters written to women friends, kin, husbands, brothers, and children at every period of life from adolescence to old age. Some collections encompass virtually entire life-spans; one contains over 100 000 letters as well as diaries and account books. It is my contention that an analysis of women's private letters and diaries which were never intended to be published permits the historian to explore a very private world of emotional realities central both to women's lives and to the middle-class family in nineteenth-century America.[5]

The question of female friendships is peculiarly elusive; we know so little or perhaps have forgotten so much. An intriguing and almost alien form of human relationship, they flourished in a different social structure and amidst different sexual norms. Before attempting to reconstruct their social setting, therefore, it might be best first to describe two not atypical friendships. These two friendships, intense, loving, and openly avowed, began during the women's adolescence and, despite subsequent marriages and geographic separation, continued throughout their lives. For nearly half a century these women played a central emotional role in each other's lives, writing time and again of their love and of the pain of separation. Paradoxically to twentieth-century minds, their love appears to have been both sensual and platonic.

Sarah Butler Wister first met Jeannie Field Musgrove while vacationing with her family at Stockbridge, Massachusetts, in the summer of 1849.[6] Jeannie was then sixteen, Sarah fourteen. During two subsequent years spent together in boarding school, they formed a deep and intimate friendship. Sarah began to keep a bouquet of flowers before Jeannie's portrait and wrote complaining of the intensity and anguish of her affection.[7] Both young women assumed *nom de plumes*, Jeannie a female name, Sarah a male one; they would use these secret names into old age.[8] They frequently commented on the nature of their affection: 'If the day should come', Sarah wrote Jeannie in the spring of 1861, 'when you failed me either through your fault or my own, I would forswear all human friendship, thenceforth.' A few months later Jeannie commented: 'Gratitude is a word I should never use toward you. It is perhaps a misfortune of such intimacy and love that it makes one regard all kindness as a matter of course, as one has always found it, as natural as the embrace in meeting.'[9]

Sarah's marriage altered neither the frequency of their correspondence nor their desire to be together. In 1864, when twenty-
nine, married, and a mother, Sarah wrote to Jeannie: 'I shall be
entirely alone [this coming week]. I can give you no idea how desperately I shall want you. . . .' After one such visit Jeannie, then a
spinster in New York, echoed Sarah's longing: 'Dear darling Sarah!
How I love you & how happy I have been! You are the joy of my life.
. . . I cannot tell you how much happiness you gave me, nor how
constantly it is all in my thoughts. . . . My darling how I long for the
time when I shall see you. . . .' After another visit Jeannie wrote: 'I
want you to tell me in your next letter, to assure me, that I am your
dearest. . . . I do not doubt you, & I am not jealous but I long to hear
you say it once more & it seems already a long time since your voice
fell on my ear. So just fill a quarter page with caresses & expressions
of endearment. Your silly Angelina.' Jeannie ended one letter:
'Goodbye my dearest, dearest lover—ever your own Angelina.' And
another, 'I will go to bed . . . [though] I could write all night—A
thousand kisses—I love you with my whole soul—your Angelina.'

When Jeannie finally married in 1870 at the age of thirty-seven,
Sarah underwent a period of extreme anxiety. Two days before
Jeannie's marriage Sarah, then in London, wrote desperately:
'Dearest darling—How incessantly have I thought of you these
eight days—all today—the entire uncertainty, the distance, the long
silence—are all new features in my separation from you, grevious to
be borne. . . . Oh Jeannie. I have thought & thought & yearned over
you these two days. Are you married I wonder? My dearest love to
you wherever and *who*ever you are.'[10] Like many other women in
this collection of thirty-five families, marriage brought Sarah and
Jeannie physical separation; it did not cause emotional distance.
Although at first they may have wondered how marriage would
affect their relationship, their affection remained unabated
throughout their lives, underscored by their loneliness and their
desire to be together.[11]

During the same years that Jeannie and Sarah wrote of their love
and need for each other, two slightly younger women began a similar odyssey of love, dependence and—ultimately—physical,
though not emotional, separation. Molly and Helena met in 1868
while both attended the Cooper Institute School of Design for
Women in New York City. For several years these young women
studied and explored the city together, visited each other's families,
and formed part of a social network of other artistic young women.
Gradually, over the years, their initial friendship deepened into a

close intimate bond which continued throughout their lives. The tone in the letters which Molly wrote to Helena changed over these years from 'My dear Helena', and signed 'your attached friend', to 'My dearest Helena', 'My Dearest', 'My Beloved', and signed 'Thine always' or 'thine Molly'.[12]

The letters they wrote to each other during these first five years permit us to reconstruct something of their relationship together. As Molly wrote in one early letter:

I have not said to you in so many or so few words but I was happy with you during those few so incredibly short weeks but surely you do not need words to tell you what you must know. Those two or three days so dark without, so bright with firelight and contentment within I shall always remember as proof that, for a time, at least—I fancy for quite a long time—we might be sufficient for each other. We know that we can amuse each other for many idle hours together and now we know that we can also work together. And that means much, don't you think so?

She ended: 'I shall return in a few days. Imagine yourself kissed many times by one who loved you so dearly'.

The intensity and even physical nature of Molly's love was echoed in many of the letters she wrote during the next few years, as, for instance in this short thank-you note for a small present: 'Imagine yourself kissed a dozen times my darling. Perhaps it is well for you that we are far apart. You might find my thanks so expressed rather overpowering. I have that delightful feeling that it doesn't matter much what I say or how I say it, since we shall meet so soon and forget in that moment that we were ever separated. . . . I shall see you soon and be content'.[13]

At the end of the fifth year, however, several crises occurred. The relationship, at least in its intense form, ended, though Molly and Helena continued an intimate and complex relationship for the next half-century. The exact nature of these crises is not completely clear, but it seems to have involved Molly's decision not to live with Helena, as they had originally planned, but to remain at home because of parental insistence. Molly was now in her late twenties. Helena responded with anger and Molly became frantic at the thought that Helena would break off their relationship. Though she wrote distraught letters and made despairing attempts to see Helena, the relationship never regained its former ardour—possibly because Molly had a male suitor.[14] Within six months Helena had decided to marry a man who was, coincidentally, Molly's friend and publisher. Two years later Molly herself finally married. The letters toward the end of this period discuss the transition both women made to having male lovers—Molly spending much time reassuring Helena, who seemed depressed about the end of their relationship and with her forthcoming marriage.[15]

It is clearly difficult from a distance of 100 years and from a post-Freudian cultural perspective to decipher the complexities of Molly and Helena's relationship. Certainly Molly and Helena were lovers—emotionally if not physically. The emotional intensity and pathos of their love becomes apparent in several letters Molly wrote Helena during their crisis: 'I wanted so to put my arms around my girl of all the girls in the world and tell her . . . I love her as wives do love their husbands, as *friends* who have taken each other for life—and believe in her as I believe in my God. . . . If I didn't love you do you suppose I'd care about anything or have ridiculous notions and panics and behave like an old fool who ought to know better. I'm going to hang on to your skirts. . . . You can't get away from [my] love.' Or as she wrote after Helena's decision to marry: 'You know dear Helena, I really was in love with you. It was a passion such as I had never known until I saw you. I don't think it was the noblest way to love you.' The theme of intense female love was one Molly again expressed in a letter she wrote to the man Helena was to marry: 'Do you know sir, that until you came along I believe that she loved me almost as girls love their lovers. *I know I loved her so.* Don't you wonder that I can stand the sight of you.' This was in a letter congratulating them on their forthcoming marriage.[16]

The essential question is not whether these women had genital contact and can therefore be defined as heterosexual or homosexual. The twentieth-century tendency to view human love and sexuality within a dichotomized universe of deviance and normality, genitality and platonic love, is alien to the emotions and attitudes of the nineteenth century and fundamentally distorts the nature of these women's emotional interaction. These letters are significant because they force us to place such female love in a particular historical context. There is every indication that these four women, their husbands and families—all eminently respectable and socially conservative—considered such love both socially acceptable and fully compatible with heterosexual marriage. Emotionally and cognitively, their heterosocial and their homosocial worlds were complementary.

One would argue, on the other hand, that these letters were but an example of the romantic rhetoric with which the nineteenth century surrounded the concept of friendship. Yet they possess an emotional intensity and a sensual and physical explicitness that is difficult to dismiss. Jeannie longed to hold Sarah in her arms; Molly mourned her physical isolation from Helena. Molly's love and devotion to Helena, the emotions that bound Jeannie and Sarah together, while perhaps a phenomenon of nineteenth-century society were not the less real for their Victorian origins. A survey of the correspondence and diaries of eighteenth- and nineteenth-century women indicates that Molly, Jeannie, and Sarah represented one very real behavioural and emotional option socially available to nineteenth-century women.

This is not to argue that individual needs, personalities, and family dynamics did not have a significant role in determining the nature of particular relationships. But the scholar must ask if it is historically possible and, if possible, important, to study the intensely individual aspects of psychosexual dynamics. Is it not the historian's first task to explore the social structure and the world view which made intense and sometimes sensual female love both a possible and an acceptable emotional option? From such a social perspective a new and quite different series of questions suggests itself. What emotional function did such female love serve? What was its place within the hetero- and homosocial worlds which women jointly inhabited? Did a spectrum of love-object choices exist in the nineteenth century across which some individuals, at least, were capable of moving? Without attempting to answer these questions it will be difficult to understand either nineteenth-century sexuality or the nineteenth-century family.

Several factors in American society between the mid-eighteenth and the mid-nineteenth centuries may well have permitted women to form a variety of close emotional relationships with other women. American society was characterized in large part by rigid gender-role differentiation within the family and within society as a whole, leading to the emotional segregation of women and men. The roles of daughter and mother shaded imperceptibly and ineluctably into each other, while the biological realities of frequent pregnancies, childbirth, nursing, and menopause bound women together in physical and emotional intimacy. It was within just such a social framework, I would argue, that a specifically female world did indeed develop, a world built around a generic and unselfconscious pattern of single-sex or homosocial networks. These supportive networks were institutionalized in social conventions or rituals which accompanied virtually every important event in a woman's life, from birth to death. Such female relationships were frequently supported and paralleled by severe social restrictions on intimacy between young men and women. Within such a world of emotional richness and complexity devotion to and love of other women became a plausible and socially accepted form of human interaction.

An abundance of printed and manuscript sources exists to support such a hypothesis. Etiquette books, advice books on child rearing, religious sermons, guides to young men and young women, medical texts, and school curricula all suggest that late eighteenth- and most nineteenth-century Americans assumed the existence of a world composed of distinctly male and female spheres, spheres determined by the immutable laws of God and nature.[17] The unpublished letters and diaries of Americans during this same period concur, detailing the existence of sexually segregated worlds inhabited by human beings with different values, expectations, and personalities. Contacts between men and women frequently partook of a formality and stiffness quite alien to twentieth-century America and which today we tend to define as 'Victorian'. Women, however, did not form an isolated and oppressed subcategory in male society. Their letters and diaries indicate that women's sphere had an essential integrity and dignity that grew out of women's shared experiences and mutual affection and that, despite the profound changes which affected American social structure and institutions between the 1760s and the 1870s, retained a constancy and predictability. The ways in which women thought of and interacted with each other remained unchanged. Continuity, not discontinuity, characterized this female world. Molly Hallock's and Jeannie Fields's words, emotions, and experiences have direct parallels in the 1760s and the 1790s.[18] There are indications in contemporary sociological and psychological literature that female closeness and support networks have continued into the twentieth-century—not only among ethnic and working-class groups but even among the middle class.[19]

Most eighteenth- and nineteenth-century women lived within a world bounded by home, church, and the institution of visiting— that endless trooping of women to each others' homes for social purposes. It was a world inhabited by children and by other women.[20] Women helped each other with domestic chores and in times of sickness, sorrow, or trouble. Entire days, even weeks, might be spent almost exclusively with other women.[21] Urban and town women could devote virtually every day to visits, teas, or shopping trips with other women. Rural women developed a pattern of more extended visits that lasted weeks and sometimes months, at times even dislodging husbands from their beds and bedrooms so that dear friends might spend every hour of every day together.[22] When husbands travelled, wives routinely moved in with other women, invited women friends to teas and suppers, sat together sharing and comparing the letters they had received from other close women friends. Secrets were exchanged and cherished, and the husband's return at times viewed with some ambivalence.[23]

Summer vacations were frequently organized to permit old friends to meet at water spas or share a country home. In 1848, for example, a young matron wrote cheerfully to her husband about the delightful time she was having with five close women friends whom she had invited to spend the summer with her; he remained at home alone to face the heat of Philadelphia and a cholera epidemic.[24] Some ninety years earlier, two young Quaker girls commented upon the vacation their aunt had taken alone with another woman; their remarks were openly envious and tell us something of the emotional quality of these friendships: 'I hear Aunt is gone with the Friend and wont be back for two weeks, fine times indeed I think the old friends had, taking their pleasure about the country . . . and have the advantage of that fine woman's conversation and instruction, while we poor young girls must spend all spring at home. . . . What a disappointment that we are not together. . . .'[25]

Friends did not form isolated dyads but were normally part of highly integrated networks. Knowing each other, perhaps related to each other, they played a central role in holding communities and kin systems together. Especially when families became geographically mobile women's long visits to each other and their frequent letters filled with discussions of marriages and births, illness and deaths, descriptions of growing children, and reminiscences of times and people past provided an important sense of continuity in a rapidly changing society.[26] Central to this female world was an inner core of kin. The ties between sisters, first cousins, aunts, and nieces provided the underlying structure upon which groups of friends and their network of female relatives clustered. Although most of the women within this sample would appear to be living within isolated nuclear families, the emotional ties between non-residential kin were deep and binding and provided one of the fundamental existential realities of women's lives.[27] Twenty years after Parke Lewis Butler moved with her husband to Louisiana, she sent her two daughters back to Virginia to attend school, live with their grandmother and aunt, and be integrated back into Virginia society.[28] The constant letters between Maria Inskeep and Fanny Hampton, sisters separated in their early twenties when Maria moved with her husband from New Jersey to Louisiana, held their families together, making it possible for their daughters to feel a part of their cousins' network of friends and interests.[29] The Ripley daughters, growing up in western Massachusetts in the early 1800s, spent months each year with their mother's sister and her family in distant Boston; these female cousins and their network of friends exchanged gossip-filled letters and gradually formed deeply loving and dependent ties.[30]

Women frequently spent their days within the social confines of such extended families. Sisters-in-law visited each other and, in some families, seemed to spend more time with each other than with their husbands. First cousins cared for each other's babies— for weeks or even months in times of sickness or childbirth. Sisters helped each other with housework, shopped and sewed for each other. Geographic separation was borne with difficulty. A sister's absence for even a week or two could cause loneliness and depression and would be bridged by frequent letters. Sibling rivalry was hardly unknown, but with separation or illness the theme of deep affection and dependency re-emerged.[31]

Sisterly bonds continued across a lifetime. In her old age a rural Quaker matron, Martha Jefferis, wrote to her daughter Anne concerning her own half-sister, Phoebe: 'In sister Phoebe I have a real friend—she studies my comfort and waits on me like a child. . . . She is exceedingly kind and this to all other homes (set aside yours) I would prefer—it is next to being with a daughter.' Phoebe's own letters confirmed Martha's evaluation of her feelings. 'Thou knowest my dear sister', Phoebe wrote, 'there is no one . . . that exactly feels [for] thee as I do, for I think without boasting I can truly say that my desire is for thee.'[32]

Such women, whether friends or relatives, assumed an emotional centrality in each others' lives. In their diaries and letters they wrote of the joy and contentment they felt in each others' company, their sense of isolation and despair when apart. The regularity of their correspondence underlines the sincerity of their words. Women named their daughters after one another and sought to integrate dear friends into their lives after marriage.[33] As one young bride wrote to an old friend shortly after her marriage: 'I want to see you and talk with you and feel that we are united by the same bonds of sympathy and congeniality as ever.[34] After years of friendship one ageing woman wrote of another: 'Time cannot destroy the fascination of her manner . . . her voice is music to the ear. . . .'[35] Women made elaborate presents for each other, ranging from the Quakers' frugal pies and breads to painted velvet bags and phantom bouquets.[36] When a friend died, their grief was deeply felt. Martha Jefferis was unable to write to her daughter for three weeks because of the sorrow she felt at the death of a dear friend. Such distress was not unusual. A generation earlier a young Massachusetts farm woman filled pages of her diary with her grief at the death of her 'dearest friend' and transcribed the letters of condolence other women sent her. She marked the anniversary of Rachel's death each year in her diary, contrasting her faithfulness with that of Rachel's husband who had soon remarried.[37]

These female friendships served a number of emotional functions. Within this secure and empathetic world women could share sorrows, anxieties, and joys, confident that other women had experienced similar emotions. One mid-nineteenth-century rural matron in a letter to her daughter discussed this particular aspect of women's friendships: 'To have such a friend as thyself to look to and sympathize with her—and enter into all her little needs and in whose bosom she could with freedom pour forth her joys and sorrows—such a friend would very much relieve the tedium of many a wearisome hour. . . .' A generation later Molly more informally underscored the importance of this same function in a letter to Helena: 'Suppose I come down . . . [and] spend Sunday with you quietly,' she wrote Helena '. . . that means talking all the time until you are relieved of all your latest troubles, and I of mine. . . .'[38] These were frequently troubles that apparently no man could understand. When Anne Jefferis Sheppard was first married, she and her older sister Edith (who then lived with Anne) wrote in detail to their mother of the severe depression and anxiety which they experienced. Moses Sheppard, Anne's husband, added cheerful postscripts to the sisters' letters—which he had clearly not read—remarking on Anne's and Edith's contentment. Theirs was an emotional world to which he had little access.[39]

This was, as well, a female world in which hostility and criticism of other women were discouraged and thus a milieu in which women could develop a sense of inner security and self-esteem. As one young woman wrote to her mother's long-time friend: 'I cannot sufficiently thank you for the kind unvaried affection & indulgence you have ever shown and expressed both by words and actions for me. . . . Happy would it be did all the world view me as you do, through the medium of kindness and forbearance.'[40] They valued each other. Women, who had little status or power in the larger world of male concerns, possessed status and power in the lives and worlds of other women.[41]

An intimate mother–daughter relationship lay at the heart of this female world. The diaries and letters of both mothers and daughters attest to their closeness and mutual emotional dependency. Daughters routinely discussed their mother's health and activities with their own friends, expressed anxiety in cases of their mother's ill-health and concern for her cares.[42] Expressions of hostility which we would today consider routine on the part of both mothers and daughters seem to have been uncommon indeed. On the contrary, this sample of families indicates that the normal relationship between mother and daughter was one of sympathy and understanding.[43] Only sickness or great geographic distance was allowed to cause extended separation. When marriage did result in such separation, both viewed the distance between them with distress.[44] Something of this sympathy and love between mothers and daughters is evident in a letter Sarah Alden Ripley, at age sixty-nine, wrote her youngest and recently married daughter: 'You do not know how much I miss you, not only when I struggle in and out of my mortal envelop and pump my nightly potation and no longer pour into your sympathizing ear my senile gossip, but all the day I muse away, since the sound of your voice no longer rouses me to sympathy with your joys or sorrows. . . . You cannot know how much I miss your affectionate demonstrations.[45] A dozen ageing mothers in this sample of over thirty families echoed her sentiments.

Central to these mother–daughter relations is what might be described as an apprenticeship system. In those families where the daughter followed the mother into a life of traditional domesticity, mothers and other older women carefully trained daughters in the arts of housewifery and motherhood. Such training undoubtedly occurred throughout a girl's childhood but became more systematized, almost ritualistic, in the years following the end of her formal education and before her marriage. At this time a girl either returned home from boarding school or no longer divided her time between home and school. Rather, she devoted her energies on two tasks: mastering new domestic skills and participating in the visiting and social activities necessary to finding a husband. Under the careful supervision of their mothers and of older female relatives, such late-adolescent girls temporarily look over the household management from their mothers, tended their young nieces and nephews, and helped in childbirth, nursing, and weaning. Such experiences tied the generations together in shared skills and emotional interaction.[46]

Daughters were born into a female world. Their mother's life expectations and sympathetic network of friends and relations were among the first realities in the life of the developing child. As long as the mother's domestic role remained relatively stable and few viable alternatives competed with it, daughters tended to accept their mother's world and to turn automatically to other women for support and intimacy. It was within this closed and intimate female world that the young girl grew toward womanhood.

One could speculate at length concerning the absence of that mother–daughter hostility today considered almost inevitable to an adolescent's struggle for autonomy and self-identity. It is possible that taboos against female aggression and hostility were sufficiently strong to repress even that between mothers and their adolescent daughters. Yet these letters seem so alive and the interest of daughters in their mothers' affairs so vital and genuine that it is difficult to interpret their closeness exclusively in terms of repression and denial. The functional bonds that held mothers and daughters together in a world that permitted few alternatives to domesticity might well have created a source of mutuality and trust absent in societies where greater options were available for daughters than for mothers. Furthermore, the extended female network—a daughter's close ties with her own older sisters, cousins, and aunts—may well have permitted a diffusion and a relaxation of mother–daughter identification and so have aided a daughter in her struggle for identity and autonomy. None of these explanations are mutually exclusive; all may well have interacted to produce the degree of empathy evident in those letters and diaries.

At some point in adolescence, the young girl began to move outside the matrix of her mother's support group to develop a network of her own. Among the middle class, at least, this transition toward what was the same time both a limited autonomy and a repetition of her mother's life seemed to have most frequently coincided with a girl's going to school. Indeed education appears to have played a crucial role in the lives of most of the families in this study. Attending school for a few months, for a year, or longer, was common even among daughters of relatively poor families, while middle-class girls routinely spent at least a year in boarding school.[47] These school years ordinarily marked a girl's first separation from home. They served to wean the daughter from her home, to train her in the essential social graces, and, ultimately, to help introduce her into the marriage market. It was not infrequently a trying emotional experience for both mother and daughter.[48]

In this process of leaving one home and adjusting to another, the mother's friends and relatives played a key transitional role. Such older women routinely accepted the role of foster mother; they supervised the young girl's deportment, monitored her health, and introduced her to their own network of female friends and kin.[49] Not infrequently women, friends from their own school years, arranged to send their daughters to the same school so that the girls might form bonds paralleling those their mothers had made. For years Molly and Helena wrote of their daughters' meeting and worried over each others' children. When Molly finally brought her daughter east to school, their first act on reaching New York was to meet Helena and her daughters. Elizabeth Bordley Gibson virtually adopted the daughters of her school chum, Eleanor Custis Lewis. The Lewis daughters soon began to write Elizabeth Gibson letters with the salutation 'Dearest Mama'. Eleuthera DuPont, attending boarding school in Philadelphia at roughly the same time as the Lewis girls, developed a parallel relationship with her mother's friend, Elizabeth McKie Smith. Eleuthera went to the same school and became a close friend of the Smith girls and eventually married their first cousin. During this period she routinely called Mrs Smith 'Mother'. Indeed Eleuthera so internalized the sense of having two mothers that she causally wrote her sisters of her 'Mamma's' visits at her 'mother's' house—that is at Mrs Smith's.[50]

Even more important to this process of maturation than their mother's friends were the female friends young women made at school. Young girls helped each other overcome homesickness and endure the crises of adolescence. They gossiped about beaux, incorporated each other into their own kinship systems, and attended and gave teas and balls together. Older girls in boarding school 'adopted' younger ones, who called them 'Mother'.[51] Dear friends might indeed continue this pattern of adoption and mothering throughout their lives; one woman might routinely assume the nurturing role of pseudomother, the other the dependency role of daughter. The pseudomother performed for the other woman all the services which we normally associate with mothers; she went to absurd lengths to purchase items her 'daughter' could have obtained from other sources, gave advice, and functioned as an idealized figure in her 'daughter's imagination. Helena played such a role for Molly, as did Sarah for Jeannie. Elizabeth Bordley Gibson bought almost all Eleanor Parke Custis Lewis's necessities—from shoes and corset covers to bedding and harp strings—and sent them from Philadelphia to Virginia, a procedure that sometimes took months. Eleanor frequently asked Elizabeth to take back her purchases, have them redone, and argue with shopkeepers about prices. These were favours automatically asked and complied with. Anne Jefferis Sheppard made the analogy very explicitly in a letter to her own mother written shortly after Anne's marriage, when she was feeling depressed about their separation: 'Mary Paulen is truly kind, almost acts the part of a mother and trys to aid and *comfort me*, and also to *lighten my new cares*.'[52]

A comparison of the references to men and women in these young women's letters is striking. Boys were obviously indispensable to the elaborate courtship ritual girls engaged in. In these teenage letters and diaries, however, boys appear distant and warded off—an effect produced both by the girl's sense of bonding and by a highly developed and deprecatory whimsy. Girls joked among themselves about the conceit, poor looks, or affectations of suitors. Rarely, especially in the eighteenth and early nineteenth centuries, were favourable remarks exchanged. Indeed, while hostility and criticism of other women were so rare as to seem almost tabooed, young women permitted themselves to express a great deal of hostility toward peer-group men.[53] When unacceptable suitors appeared, girls might even band together to harass them. When one such unfortunate came to court Sophie DuPont she hid in her room, first sending her sister Eleuthera to entertain him and then dispatching a number of urgent notes to her neighbouring sister-in-law, cousins, and a visiting friend who all came to Sophie's support. A wild female romp ensued, ending only when Sophie banged into a door, lacerated her nose, and retired, with her female cohorts, to bed. Her brother and the presumably disconcerted suitor were left alone. These were not the antics of teenagers but of women in their early and mid-twenties.[54]

Even if young men were acceptable suitors, girls referred to them formally and obliquely: 'The last week I received the unexpected intelligence of the arrival of a friend in Boston,' Sarah Ripley wrote in her diary of the young man to whom she had been engaged for years and whom she would shortly marry. Harriet Manigault assiduously kept a lively and gossipy diary during the three years preceding her marriage, yet did not once comment upon her own engagement nor indeed make any personal references to her fiancé—who was never identified as such but always referred to as Mr Wilcox.[55] The point is not that these young women were hostile to young men. Far from it; they sought marriage and domesticity. Yet in these letters and diaries men appear as an other or out group, segregated into different schools, supported by their own male network of friends and kin, socialized to different behaviour, and coached to a proper formality in courtship behaviour. As a consequence, relations between young women and men frequently lacked the spontaneity and emotional intimacy that characterized the young girls' ties to each other.

Indeed, in sharp contrast to their distant relations with boys, young women's relations with each other were close, often frolicsome, and surprisingly long-lasting and devoted. They wrote secret missives to each other, spent long solitary days with each other, curled up together in bed at night to whisper fantasies and secrets.[56] In 1862 one young woman in her early twenties described one such scene to an absent friend: 'I have sat up to midnight listening to the confidences of Constance Kinney, whose heart was opened by that most charming of all situations, a seat on a bedside late at night, when all the household are asleep & only oneself & one's confidante survive in wakefulness. So she has told me all her loves and tried to get some confidences in return but being five or six years older than she, I know better. . . .'[57] Elizabeth Bordley and Nelly Parke Custis, teenagers in Philadelphia in the 1790s, routinely secreted themselves until late each night in Nelly's attic, where they each wrote a novel about the other.[58] Quite a few young women kept diaries, and it was a sign of special friendship to show their diaries to each other. The emotional quality of such exchanges emerges from the comments of one young girl who grew up along the Ohio frontier:

Sisters CW and RT keep diaries & allow me the inestimable pleasure of reading them and in turn they see mine—but O shame covers my face when I think of it; theirs is so much better than mine, that every time. Then I think well now I *will* burn mine but upon second thought it would deprive me the pleasure of reading theirs, for I esteem it a very great privilege indeed, as well as very improving, as we lay our hearts open to each other, it heightens our love & helps to cherish & keep alive that sweet soothing friendship and endears us to each other by that soft attraction.[59]

Girls routinely slept together, kissed and hugged each other. Indeed, while waltzing with young men scandalized the otherwise flighty and highly fashionable Harriet Manigault, she considered waltzing with other young women not only acceptable but pleasant.[60]

Marriage followed adolescence. With increasing frequency in the nineteenth century, marriage involved a girl's traumatic removal from her mother and her mother's network. It involved, as well, adjustment to a husband, who, because he was male came to marriage with both a different world view and vastly different experiences. Not surprisingly, marriage was an event surrounded with supportive, almost ritualistic, practices. (Weddings are one of the last female rituals remaining in twentieth-century America.) Young women routinely spent the months preceding their marriage almost exclusively with other women—at neighbourhood sewing-bees and quilting-parties or in a round of visits to geographically distant friends and relatives. Ostensibly they went to receive assistance in the practical preparations for their new home—sewing and quilting a trousseau and linen—but of equal importance, they appear to have gained emotional support and reassurance. Sarah Ripley spent over a month with friends and relatives in Boston and Hingham before her wedding; Parke Custis Lewis exchanged visits with her aunts and first cousins throughout Virginia.[61] Anne Jefferis, who married with some hesitation, spent virtually half a year in endless visiting with cousins, aunts, and friends. Despite their reassurance and support, however, she would not marry Moses Sheppard until her sister Edith and her cousin Rebecca moved into the groom's home, met his friends, and explored his personality.[62] The wedding did not take place until Edith wrote to Anne: 'I can say in truth I am entirely willing thou shouldst follow him even away in the Jersey sands believing if thou are not happy in thy future home it will not be any fault on his part. . . .'[63]

Sisters, cousins, and friends frequently accompanied newlyweds on their wedding night and wedding trip, which often involved additional family visiting. Such extensive visits presumably served to wean the daughter from her family of origin. As such they often contained a note of ambivalence. Nelly Custis, for example, reported homesickness and loneliness on her wedding trip. 'I left my Beloved and revered Grandmamma with sincere regret,' she wrote Elizabeth Bordley. 'It was sometime before I could feel reconciled to traveling without her.' Perhaps they also functioned to reassure the young woman herself, and her friends and kin, that though marriage might alter it, it would not destroy old bonds of intimacy and familiarity.[64]

Married life, too, was structured about a host of female rituals. Childbirth, especially the birth of the first child, became virtually a *rite de passage*, with a lengthy seclusion of the woman before and after delivery, severe restrictions on her activities, and finally a dramatic re-emergence.[65] This seclusion was supervised by mothers, sisters, and loving friends. Nursing and weaning involved the advice and assistance of female friends and relatives. So did miscarriage.[66] Death, like birth, was structured around elaborate unisexed rituals. When Nelly Parke Custis Lewis rushed to nurse her daughter who was critically ill while away at school, Nelly received support, not from her husband, who remained on their plantation, but from her old school friend, Elizabeth Bordley. Elizabeth aided Nelly in caring for her dying daughter, cared for Nelly's other children, played a major role in the elaborate funeral arrangements (which the father did not attend), and frequently visited the girl's grave at the mother's request. For years Elizabeth continued to be the confidante of Nelly's anguished recollections of her lost daughter. These memories, Nelly's letters make clear, were for Elizabeth alone. 'Mr. L. knows nothing of this,' was a frequent comment.[67] Virtually every collection of letters and diaries in my sample contained evidence of women turning to each other for comfort when facing the frequent and unavoidable deaths of the eighteenth and nineteenth centuries.[68] While mourning for her father's death, Sophie DuPont received elaborate letters and visits of condolence—all from women. No man wrote or visited Sophie to offer sympathy at her father's death.[69] Among rural Pennsylvania Quakers, death and mourning rituals assumed an even more extreme same-sex form, with men or women largely barred from the deathbeds of the other sex. Women relatives and friends slept with the dying woman, nursed her, and prepared her body for burial.[70]

Eighteenth- and nineteenth-century women thus lived in emotional proximity to each other. Friendships and intimacies followed the biological ebb and flow of women's lives. Marriage and pregnancy, childbirth and weaning, sickness and death involved physical and psychic trauma which comfort and sympathy made easier to bear. Intense bonds of love and intimacy bound together those women who, offering each other aid and sympathy, shared such stressful moments.

These bonds were often physical as well as emotional. An undeniably romantic and even sensual note frequently marked female relationships. This theme, significant throughout the stages of a woman's life, surfaced first during adolescence. As one teenager from a struggling pioneer family in the Ohio Valley wrote in her diary in 1808: 'I laid with my dear R[ebecca] and a glorious good talk we had until about 4[a.m.]—O how hard I do *love* her. . . .'[71]

Only a few years later Bostonian Eunice Callender carved her initials and Sarah Ripley's into a favourite tree, along with a pledge of eternal love, and then waited breathlessly for Sarah to discover and respond to her declaration of affection. The response appears to have been affirmative.[72] A half-century later urbane and sophisticated Katherine Wharton commented upon meeting an old school chum: 'She was a great pet of mine at school & I thought as I watched her light figure how often I had held her in my arms—how dear she had once been to me.' Katie maintained a long intimate friendship with another girl. When a young man began to court this friend seriously, Katie commented in her diary that she had never realized 'how deeply I loved Eng and how fully'. She wrote over and over again in that entry: 'Indeed I love her!' and only with great reluctance left the city that summer since it meant also leaving Eng with Eng's new suitor.[73]

Peggy Emlen, a Quaker adolescent in Philadelphia in the 1760s, expressed similar feelings about her first cousin, Sally Logan. The girls sent love poems to each other (not unlike the ones Elizabeth Bordley wrote to Nellie Custis a generation later), took long solitary walks together, and even haunted the empty house of the other when one was out of town. Indeed Sally's absences from Philadelphia caused Peggy acute unhappiness. So strong were Peggy's feelings that her brothers began to tease her about her affection for Sally and threatened to steal Sally's letter, much to both girls' alarm. In one letter that Peggy wrote the absent Sally she elaborately described the depth and nature of her feelings: 'I have not words to express my impatience to see My Dear Cousin, what would I not give just now for an hours sweet conversation with her, it seems as if I had a thousand things to say to thee, yet when I see thee, everything will be forgot thro' joy. . . . I have a very great friendship for several Girls yet it dont give me so much uneasiness at being absent from them as from thee. . . . [Let us] go and spend a day down at our place together and there unmolested enjoy each others company.[74]

Sarah Alden Ripley, a young, highly educated women, formed a similar intense relationship, in this instance with a woman somewhat older than herself. The immediate bond of friendship rested on their atypically intense scholarly interests, but it soon involved strong emotions, at least on Sarah's part. 'Friendship', she wrote Mary Emerson, 'is fast twining about her willing captive the silken hands of dependence, a dependence so sweet who would renounce it for the apathy of self-sufficiency?' Subsequent letters became far more emotional, almost conspiratorial. Mary visited Sarah secretly in her room, or the two women crept away from family and friends to meet in a nearby woods. Sarah became jealous of Mary's other young woman friends. Mary's trips away from Boston also thrust Sarah into periods of anguished depression. Interestingly, the letters detailing their love were not destroyed but were preserved and even reprinted in a eulogistic biography of Sarah Alden Ripley.[75]

Tender letters between adolescent women, confessions of loneliness and emotional dependency, were not peculiar to Sarah Alden, Peggy Emlen, or Katie Wharton. They are found throughout the letters of the thirty-five families studied. They have, of course, their parallel today in the musings of many female adolescents. Yet these eighteenth- and nineteenth-century friendships lasted with undiminished, indeed often increased, intensity throughout the women's lives. Sarah Alden Ripley's first child was named after Mary Emerson. Nelly Custis Lewis's love for and dependence on Elizabeth Bordley Gibson only increased after her marriage. Eunice Callender remained enamoured of her cousin Sarah Ripley for years and rejected as impossible the suggestion by another woman that their love might someday fade away.[76] Sophie DuPont and her childhood friend, Clementina Smith, exchanged letters filled with love and dependency for forty years while another dear friend, Mary Black Couper, wrote of dreaming that she, Sophie, and her husband were all united in one marriage. Mary's letters to Sophie are filled with avowals of love and indications of ambivalence toward her own husband. Eliza Schlatter, another of Sophie's intimate friends, wrote to her at a time of crisis 'I wish I could be with you present in the body as well as the mind & heart—I would turn your *good husband out of bed*—and snuggle into you and we would have a long talk like old times in Pine St.—I want to tell you so many things that are not *writable. . . .*'[77]

Such mutual dependency and deep affection is a central existential reality colouring the world of supportive networks and rituals. In the case of Katie, Sophie, or Eunice—as with Molly, Jeannie, and Sarah—their need for closeness and support merged with more intense demands for a love which was at the same time both emotional and sensual. Perhaps the most explicit statement concerning women's lifelong friendships appeared in the letter abolitionist and reformer Mary Grew wrote about the same time, referring to her own love for her dear friend and lifelong companion, Margaret Burleigh. Grew wrote, in response to a letter of condolence from another women on Burleigh's death: 'Your words respecting my beloved friend touch me deeply. Evidently . . . you comprehend and appreciate, as few persons do . . . the nature of the relation which existed, which exists, between her and myself. Her only surviving niece . . . also does. To me it seems to have been a closer union than that of most marriages. We know there have been other such between two men and also between two women. And why should there not be. Love is spiritual, only passion is sexual.[78]

How then can we ultimately interpret these long-lived intimate female relationships and integrate them into our understanding of Victorian sexuality? Their ambivalent and romantic rhetoric presents us with an ultimate puzzle: the relationship along the spectrum of human emotions between love, sensuality, and sexuality.

One is tempted, as I have remarked, to compare Molly, Peggy, or Sophie's relationships with the friendships adolescent girls in the twentieth century routinely form—close friendships of great emotional intensity. Helena Deutsch and Clara Thompson have both described these friendships as emotionally necessary to a girl's psychosexual development. But, they warn, such friendships might shade into adolescent and post-adolescent homosexuality.[79]

It is possible to speculate that in the twentieth century a number of cultural taboos evolved to cut short the homosocial ties of girlhood and to impel the emerging women of thirteen or fourteen toward heterosexual relationships. In contrast, nineteenth-century American society did not taboo close female relationships but rather recognized them as a socially viable form of human contact—and, as such, acceptable throughout a woman's life. Indeed it was not these homosocial ties that were inhibited but rather heterosexual leanings. While closeness, freedom of emotional expression, and uninhibited physical contact characterized women's relationships with each other, the opposite was frequently true of male–female relationships. One could thus argue that within such a world of female support, intimacy, and ritual it was only to be expected that adult women would turn trustingly and lovingly to each other. It was a behaviour they had observed and learned since childhood. A different type of emotional landscape existed in the nineteenth century, one in which Molly and Helena's love became a natural development.

Of perhaps equal significance are the implications we can garner from this framework for the understanding of heterosexual marriages in the nineteenth century. If men and women grew up as they did in relatively homogeneous and segregated sexual groups, then marriage represented a major problem in adjustment. From this perspective we could interpret much of the emotional stiffness and distance that we associate with Victorian marriage as a structural consequence of contemporary sex-role differentiation and gender-role socialization. With marriage both women and men had to adjust to life with a person who was, in essence, a member of an alien group.

I have thus far substituted a cultural or psychosocial for a psychosexual interpretation of women's emotional bonding. But there are psychosexual implications in this model which I think it only fair to make more explicit. Despite Sigmund Freud's insistence on the bisexuality of us all or the recent American Psychiatric Association decision on homosexuality, many psychiatrists today tend explicitly or implicitly to view homosexuality as a totally alien or pathological behaviour—as totally unlike heterosexuality. I suspect that in essence they may have adopted an explanatory model similar to the one used in discussing schizophrenia. As a psychiatrist can speak of schizophrenia and of a borderline schizophrenic personality as both ultimately and fundamentally different from a normal or neurotic personality, so they also think of both homosexuality and latent homosexuality as states totally different from heterosexuality. With this rapidly dichotomous model of assumption, 'latent homosexuality' becomes the indication of a disease in progress—seeds of a pathology which belie the reality of an individual's heterosexuality.

Yet at the same time we are well aware that cultural values can effect choices in the gender of a person's sexual partner. We, for instance, do not necessarily consider homosexual-object choice among men in prison, on shipboard, or in boarding schools a necessary indication of pathology. I would urge that we expand this relativistic model and hypothesize that a number of cultures might well tolerate or even encourage diversity in sexual and nonsexual relations. Based on my research into this nineteenth-century world of female intimacy, I would further suggest that rather than seeing a gulf between the normal and the abnormal we view sexual and emotional impulses as part of a continuum or spectrum of affect gradations strongly effected by cultural norms and arrangements, a continuum influenced in part by observed and thus learned behaviour. At one end of the continuum lies committed heterosexuality, at the other uncompromising homosexuality; between, a wide latitude of emotions and sexual feelings. Certain cultures and environments permit individuals a great deal of freedom in moving across this spectrum. I would like to suggest that the nineteenth century was such a cultural environment. That is, the supposedly repressive and destructive Victorian sexual ethos, may have been more flexible and responsive to the needs of particular individuals than those of mid-twentieth century.

Notes

1. The most notable exception to this rule is now eleven years old: William R. Taylor and Christopher Lasch, 'Two "Kindred Spirits": Sorority and Family in New England, 1839–1846', *New England Quarterly*, 36 (1963), 25–41. Taylor has made a valuable contribution to the history of women and the history of the family with his concept of 'sororial' relations. I do not, however, accept the Taylor–Lasch thesis that female friendships developed in the mid-nineteenth century because of geographic mobility and the breakup of the colonial family. I have found these friendships as frequently in the eighteenth century as in the nineteenth and would hypothesize that the geographic mobility of the mid-nineteenth century eroded them as it did so many other traditional social institutions. Helen Vendler, 'Review of *Notable American Women, 1607–1950*', *New York Times*, 5 Nov. 1972, sec. 7) points out the significance of these friendships.

2. I do not wish to deny the importance of women's relations with particular men. Obviously, women were close to brothers, husbands, fathers, and sons. However, there is evidence that despite such closeness relationships between men and women differed in both emotional texture and frequency from those between women. Women's relations with each other, although they played a central role in the American family and American society, have been so seldom examined either by general social historians or by historians of the family that I wish in this article simply to examine their nature and analyse their implications for our understanding of social relations and social structure. I have discussed some aspects of male–female relationships in two articles: 'Puberty to Menopause: The Cycle of Femininity in Nineteenth-Century America', *Feminist Studies*, 1 (1973), 58–72, and, with Charles Rosenberg, 'The Female Animal: Medical and Biological Views of Women in 19th Century America', *Journal of American History*, 59 (1973), 331–56.

3. See Freud's classic paper on homosexuality, 'Three Essays on the Theory of Sexuality', in *The Standard Edition of the Complete Psychological Works of Sigmund Freud*, trans. James Strachey (London: Hogarth Press, 1953), vii. 135–72. The essays originally appeared in 1905. Prof. Roy Shafer, Department of Psychiatry, Yale University, has pointed out that Freud's view of sexual behaviour was strongly influenced by nineteenth-century evolutionary thought. Within Freud's scheme, genital heterosexuality marked the height of human development (Schafer, 'Problems in Freud's Psychology of Women', *Journal of the American Psychoanalytic Association*, 22 (1974), 459–85).

4. For a novel and most important exposition of one theory of behavioural norms and options and its application to the study of human sexuality, see Charles Rosenberg, 'Sexuality, Class and Role', *American Quarterly*, 25 (1973), 131–53.

5. See e.g. the letters of Peggy Emlen to Sally Logan, 1768–72, Wells Morris Collection, Box 1, Historical Society of Pennsylvania; and the Eleanor Parke Custis Lewis Letters, Historical Society of Pennsylvania, Philadelphia.

6. Sarah Butler Wister was the daughter of Fanny Kemble and Pierce Butler. In 1859 she married a Philadelphia physician, Owen Wister. The novelist Owen Wister is her son. Jeannie Field Musgrove was the half-orphaned daughter of constitutional lawyer and New York Republican politician David Dudley Field. Their correspondence (1855–98) is in the Sarah Butler Wister Papers, Wister Family Papers, Historical Society of Pennsylvania.

7. Sarah Butler, Butler Place, SC, to Jeannie Field, New York, 14 Sept. 1855.

8. See e.g. Sarah Butler Wiser, Germantown, Pa., to Jeannie Field, New York, 25 Sept. 1862, 21 Oct. 1863; or Jeannie Field, New York, to Sarah Butler Wister, Germantown, 3 July 1861, 23 Jan. and 12 July 1863.

9. Sarah Butler Wister, Germantown, to Jeannie Field, New York, 5 June 1861, 29 Feb. 1864; Jeannie Field to Sarah Butler Wister 22 Nov. 1861, 4 Jan. and 14 June 1863.

10. Sarah Butler Wiser, London, to Jeannie Field Musgrove, New York, 18 June and 3 Aug. 1870.

11. See e.g. two of Sarah's letters to Jeannie: 21 Dec. 1873, 16 July 1878.

12. This is the 1868–1920 correspondence between Mary Hallock Foote and Helena, a New York friend (the Mary Hallock Foote Papers are in the Manuscript Division, Stanford University). Wallace E. Stegner has written a fictionalized biography of Mary Hallock Foote (*Angle of Repose* [Garden City, NY: Doubleday & Co., 1971]). See, as well, her autobiography: Mary Hallock Foote, *A Victorian Gentlewoman in the Far West: The Reminiscences of Mary Hallock Foote*, ed. Rodman W. Paul (San Marino, Calif.: Huntington Library, 1972). In many ways these letters are typical of those women wrote to other women. Women frequently began letters to each other with salutations such as 'Dearest', 'My Most Beloved', 'You Darling Girl', and signed them 'tenderly' or 'to my dear dear sweet friend, good-bye'. Without the least self-consciousness, one woman in her frequent letters to a female friend referred to her husband as 'my other love'. She was by no means unique. See e.g. Annie to Charlene Van Vleck Anderson, Appleton, Wis., 10 June 1871, Anderson Family Papers, Manuscript Division, Stanford University; Maggie to Emily Howland, Philadelphia, 12 July 1851, Howland Family Papers, Phoebe King Collection, Friends Historical Library, Swarthmore College; Mary Jane Burleigh to Emily Howland, Sherwood, NY, 27 Mar. 1872, Howland Family Papers, Sophia Smith Collection, Smith College; Mary Black Couper to Sophia Madeleine DuPont, Wilmington, Del.: n.d. [1834] (two letters), Samuel Francis DuPont Papers, Eleutherian Mills Foundation, Wilmington, Del.; Phoebe Middleton, Concordiville, Pa., to Martha Jefferis, Chester County, Pa., 22 Feb. 1848; and see in general the correspondence (1838–49) between Rebecca Biddle of Philadelphia and Martha Jefferis, Chester County, Pa., Jefferis Family Correspondence, Chester County Historical Society, West Chester, Pa.; Phoebe Bradford Diary, 7 June and 13 July 1832, Historical Society of Pennsylvania; Sarah Alden Ripley, to Abba Allyn, Boston, n.d. [1818–20], and Sarah Alden Ripley to Sophia Bradford, 30 Nov. 1854, in the Sarah Alden Ripley Correspondence, Schlesinger Library, Radcliffe College; Fanny Canby Ferris to Annie Biddle, Philadelphia, 11 Oct. and 19 Nov. 1811, 26 Dec. 1813, Fanny Canby to Mary Canby, 27 May 1801, Mary R. Garrigues

to Mary Canby, five letters n.d., [1802–8], Anne Biddle to Mary Canby, two letters n.d., 16 May, 13 July, and 24 Nov. 1806, 14 June 1807, 5 June 1808, Anne Sterling Biddle Family Papers, Friends Historical Society, Swarthmore College; Harriet Manigault Wilcox Diary, 7 Aug. 1814, Historical Society of Pennsylvania. See as well the correspondence between Harriet Manigault Wilcox's mother, Mrs Gabriel Manigault, Philadelphia, and Mrs Henry Middleton, Charleston, SC, between 1810 and 1830, Cadwalader Collection, J. Francis Fisher Section, Historical Society of Pennsylvania. The basis and nature of such friendships can be seen in the comments of Sarah Alden Ripley to her sister-in-law and long-time friend, Sophia Bradford: 'Hearing that you are not well reminds me of what it would be to lose your loving society. We have kept step together through a long piece of road in the weary journey of life. We have loved the same beings and wept together over their graves' (Mrs O. J. Wister and Miss Agnes Irwin (eds.), *Worthy Women of Our First Century* (Philadelphia: J. B. Lippincott & Co., 1877), 195).

13. Mary Hallock [Foote] to Helena, n.d. [1869–70], n.d. [1871–2], Folder 1, Mary Hallock Foote Letters, Manuscript Division, Stanford University.

14. Mary Hallock [Foote] to Helena, 15 and 23 Sept. 1873, n.d. [Oct. 1873], 12 Oct. 1873.

15. Mary Hallock [Foote] to Helena, n.d. [Jan. 1874], n.d. [Spring 1874].

16. Mary Hallock [Foote] to Helena, 23 Sept. 1873; Mary Hallock [Foote] to Richard, 13 Dec. 1873. Molly's and Helena's relationship continued for the rest of their lives. Molly's letters are filled with tender and intimate references, as when she wrote, twenty years later and from 2000 miles away: 'It isn't because you are good that I love you—but for the essence of you which is like perfume' (n.d. [1890s?]).

17. I am in the midst of a larger study of adult gender-roles and gender-role socialization in America, 1785–1895. For a discussion of social attitudes toward appropriate male and female roles, see Barbara Welter, 'The Cult of True Womanhood: 1820–1860', *American Quarterly*, 18 (Summer 1966), 151–74; Ann Firor Scott, *The Southern Lady: From Pedestal to Politics, 1830–1930* (Chicago: University of Chicago Press, 1970), chs. 1–2; Smith-Rosenberg and Rosenberg.

18. See e.g. the letters of Peggy Emlen to Sally Logan, 1768–72, Wells Morris Collection, Box 1, Historical Society of Pennsylvania; and the Eleanor Parke Custis Lewis Letters, Historical Society of Pennsylvania.

19. See esp. Elizabeth Botts, *Family and Social Network* (London: Tavistock Publications, 1957); Michael Young and Peter Willmott, *Family and Kinship in East London*, rev. edn. (Baltimore: Penguin Books, 1964).

20. This pattern seemed to cross class barriers. A letter than an Irish domestic wrote in the 1830s contains seventeen separate references to women and but only seven to men, most of whom were relatives and two of whom were infant brothers living with her mother and mentioned in relation to her mother (Ann McGrann, Philadelphia, to Sophie M. DuPont, Philadelphia, 3 July 1834, Sophie Madeleine DuPont Letters, Eleutherian Mills Foundation).

21. Harriett Manigault Diary, 28 June 1814, and *passim*; Jeannie Field, New York, to Sarah Butler Eister, Germantown, 19 Apr. 1863; Phoebe Bradford Diary, 30 Jan., 19 Feb., 4 Mar., 11 Aug. and 14 Oct. 1832, Historical Society of Pennsylvania; Sophie M. DuPont, Brandywine, to Henry DuPont, Germantown, 9 July 1827, Eleutherian Mills Foundation.

22. Martha Jefferis to Anne Jefferis Sheppard, 9 July 1843; Anne Jefferis Sheppard to Martha Jefferis, 28 June 1846; Anne Sterling Biddle Papers, *passim*, Biddle Family Papers, Friends Historical Society, Swarthmore College; Eleanor Parke Custis Lewis, Virginia, to Elizabeth Bordley Gibson, Philadelphia, 24 Nov. and 4 Dec. 1820, 6 Nov. 1821.

23. Phoebe Bradford Diary, 13 Jan., 16–19 Nov. 1832, 26 Apr. and 7 May 1833; Abigail Brackett Lyman to Mrs Catling, Litchfield, Conn., 3 May 1801, collection in private hands; Martha Jefferis to Anne Jefferis Sheppard, 28 Aug. 1845.

24. Lisa Mitchell Diary, 1860s, *passim*, Manuscript Division, Tulane University; Eleanor Parke Custis Lewis to Elizabeth Bordley [Gibson] 5 Feb. 1822; Jeannie McCall, Cedar Park, to Peter McCall, Philadelphia, 30 June 1849, McCall Section, Cadwalader Collection, Historical Society of Pennsylvania.

25. Peggy Emlen to Sally Logan, 3 May 1769.

26. For a prime example of this type of letter, see Eleanor Parke Custis Lewis to Elizabeth Bordley Gibson, *passim*, or Fanny Canby to Mary Canby, Philadelphia, 27 May 1801; or Sophie M. DuPont, Brandywine, to Henry DuPont, Germantown, 4 Feb. 1832.

27. Place of residence is not the only variable significant in characterizing family structure. Strong emotional ties and frequent visiting and correspondence can unit families that do not live under one roof. Demographic studies based on household structure alone fail to reflect such emotional and even economic ties between families.

28. Eleanor Parke Custis Lewis to Elizabeth Bordley Gibson, 20 Apr. and 25 Sept. 1848.

29. Maria Inskeep to Fanny Hampton Correspondence, 1823–60, Inskeep Collection, Tulane University Library.

30. Eunice Callender, Boston, to Sarah Ripley [Stearns], 24 Sept. and 29 Oct. 1803, 16 Feb. 1805, 29 Apr. and 9 Oct. 1806, 26 May 1810.

31. Sophie DuPont filled her letters to her younger brother Henry (with whom she had been assigned to correspond while he was at boarding school) with accounts of family visiting (see e.g. 13 Dec. 1827, 10 Jan. and 9 Mar. 1828, 4 Feb. and 10 Mar. 1832; also Sophie M. DuPont to Victorine DuPont Bauday, 26 Sept. and 4 Dec. 1827, 22 Feb. 1828; Sophie M. DuPont, Brandywine, to Clementina B. Smith, Philadelphia, 15 Jan. 1830; Eleuthera DuPont, Brandywine, to Victorine DuPont Bauday, Philadelphia, 17 Apr. 1821, 20 Oct. 1826; Evelina DuPont [Biderman] to Victorine DuPont Bauday, 18 Oct. 1816). Other examples, from the Historical Society of Pennsylvania, are Harriet Manigault [Wilcox] Diary, 17 Aug., 8 Sept., 19 and 22 Oct., 22 Dec. 1814; Jane Zook, Westtown School, Chester County, Pa., to Mary Zook, 13 Nov., 7 and 11 Dec. 1870, 26 Feb. 1871; Eleanor Parke Custis [Lewis] to Elizabeth Bordley [Gibson], 30 Mar. 1796, 7 Feb. and 20 Mar. 1798; Jeannie McCall to Peter McCall, Philadelphia, 12 Nov. 1847; Mary B. Ashew Diary, 11 and 13 July, 17 Aug., Summer and Oct. 1858, and, from a private collection, Edith Jefferis to Anne Jefferis Sheppard, Nov. 1841, 5 Apr. 1842; Abigail Brackett Lyman, Northampton, Mass., to Mrs Catling, Litchfield, Conn., 13 May 1801; Abigail Bracket Lyman, Northampton, to Mary Lord, 11 Aug. 1800. Mary Hallock Foote vacationed with her sister, her sister's children, her aunt, and a female cousin in the summer of 1874; cousins frequently visited the Hallock farm in Milton, NY. In later years Molly and her sister Bessie set up a joint household in Boise, Idaho (Mary Hallock Foote to Helena, July [1874?]

and *passim*). Jeannie Field, after initially disliking her sister-in-law, Laura, became very close to her, calling her 'my little sister' and at times spending virtually every day with her (Jeannie Field [Musgrove] New York, to Sarah Butler Wister, Germantown, 1, 8, and 15 Mar., and 9 May 1863).

32. Martha Jefferis to Anne Jefferis Sheppard, 12 Jan. 1845; Phoebe Middleton to Martha Jefferis, 22 Feb. 1848. A number of other women remained close to sisters and sisters-in-law across a long lifetime (Phoebe Bradford Diary, 7 June 1832, and Sarah Alden Ripley to Sophia Bradford, cited in Wister and Irwin, p. 195).

33. Rebecca Biddle to Martha Jefferis, 1838–49, *passim*; Martha Jefferis to Anne Jefferis Sheppard, 6 July 1846; Anne Jefferis Sheppard to Rachael Jefferis, 16 Jan. 1865; Sarah Foulke Farquhar [Emlen] Diary, 22 Sept. 1813, Friends Historical Library, Swarthmore College; Mary Garrigues to Mary Canby [Biddle], 1802–8, *passim*; Anne Biddle to Mary Canby [Biddle], 16 May, 13 July, and 24 Nov. 1806, 14 June 1807, 5 June 1808.

34. Sarah Alden Ripley to Abba Allyn, n.d., Schlesinger Library.

35. Phoebe Bradford Diary, 13 July 1832.

36. Mary Hallock [Foote] to Helena, 23 Dec. [1868 or 1869]; Phoebe Bradford Diary, 8 Dec. 1832; Martha Jefferis and Anne Jefferis Sheppard letters, *passim*.

37. Martha Jefferis to Anne Jefferis Sheppard, 3 Aug. 1849; Sarah Ripley [Stearns] Diary, 12 Nov. 1808, 8 Jan. 1811. An interesting note of hostility or rivalry is present in Sarah Ripley's diary entry. Sarah evidently deeply resented the husband's rapid remarriage.

38. Martha Jefferis to Edith Jefferis, 15 Mar. 1841; Mary Hallock Foote to Helena, n.d. [1874–5?]; see also Jeannie Field, New York, to Sarah Butler Wister, Germantown, 5 May 1863, Emily Howland Diary, Dec. 1879, Howland Family Papers.

39. Annie Jefferis Sheppard to Martha Jefferis, 29 Sept. 1841.

40. Frances Parke Lewis to Elizabeth Bordley Gibson, 29 Apr. 1821.

41. Mary Jane Burleigh, Mount Pleasant, SC, to Emily Howland, Sherwood NY, 27 Mar. 1872, Howland Family Papers; Emily Howland Diary, 16 Sept. 1879, 21 and 23 Jan. 1880; Mary Black Couper, New Castle, Del., to Sophie M. DuPont, Brandywine, 7 Apr. 1834.

42. Harriet Manigault Diary, 15, 21, and 23 Aug. 1814, Historical Society of Pennsylvania, Polly [Simmons] to Sophie Madeleine DuPont, Feb. 1822; Sophie Madeleine DuPont to Victorine Bauday, 4 Dec. 1827; Sophie Madeleine DuPont to Clementina Beach Smith, 24 July 1828, 19 Aug. 1829; Clementina Beach Smith to Sophie Madeleine DuPont, 29 Apr. 1831; Mary Black Couper to Sophie Madeleine DuPont, 24 Dec. 1828, 21 July 1834. This pattern appears to have crossed class lines. When a former Sunday school student of Sophie DuPont's (and the daughter of a worker in her father's factory) wrote to Sophie she discussed her mother's health and activities quite naturally (Ann McGrann to Sophie Madeleine DuPont, 25 Aug. 1832; see also Elizabeth Bordley to Martha, n.d. [1797], Eleanor Parke Custis [Lewis] to Elizabeth Bordley [Gibson], 13 May 1796, 1 July 1798; Peggy Emlen to Sally Logan, 8 Jan. 1786. All but the Emlen/Logan letters are in the Eleanor Parke Custis Lewis Correspondence, Historical Society of Pennsylvania).

43. Mrs S. S. Dalton, 'Autobiography', (Circle Valley, Utah, 1876), 21–2, Bancroft Library, University of California, Berkeley; Sarah Foulke Emlen Diary, Apr. 1809; Louisa G. Van Vleck, Appleton, Wis., to Charlena Van Vleck Anderson,

Göttingen, n.d. [1875], Harriet Manigault Diary, 16 Aug. 1814, 14 July 1815; Sarah Alden Ripley to Sophy Fisher [early 1860s], quoted in Wister and Irwin (n. 12 above), p. 212. The Jefferis family papers are filled with empathetic letters between Martha and her daughters, Anne and Edith. See e.g. Martha Jefferis to Edith Jefferis, 26 Dec. 1836, 11 Mar. 1837, 15 Mar. 1841; Anne Jefferis Sheppard to Martha Jefferis, 17 Mar. 1841, 17 Jan. 1847; Martha Jefferis to Anne Jefferis Sheppard, 17 Apr. 1848, 30 Apr. 1849. A representative letter is this of 9 Mar. 1837 from Edith to Martha: 'My heart can fully respond to the language of my own precious Mother, that absence has not diminished our affection for each other, but has, if possible, strengthened the bonds that have united us together & have had to remark how we had been permitted to mingle in sweet fellowship and have been strengthened to bear one another's burdens. . . .'

44. Abigail Brackett Lyman, Boston, to Mrs Abigail Brackett (daughter to mother), n.d. [1797], 3 June 1800; Sarah Alden Ripley wrote weekly to her daughter, Sophy Ripley Fisher, after the latter's marriage (Sarah Alden Ripley Correspondence, *passim*); Phoebe Bradford Diary, 25 Feb. 1833, *passim*, 1832–3; Louisa G. Van Vleck to Charlena Van Vleck Anderson, 15 Dec. 1873, 4 July, 15 and 29 Aug., 19 Sept. and 9 Nov. 1875. Eleanor Parke Custis Lewis's long correspondence with Elizabeth Bordley Gibson contains evidence of her anxiety at leaving her foster mother's home at various times during her adolescence and at her marriage, and her own long for her daughters, both of whom had married and moved to Louisiana (Eleanor Parke Custis [Lewis] to Elizabeth Bordley [Gibson]. 13 Oct 1795, 4 Nov. 1799, *passim*, 1820s and 1830s). Anne Jefferis Sheppard experienced a great deal of anxiety on moving two days' journey from her mother at the time of her marriage. This loneliness and sense of isolation persisted through her marriage until, finally a widow, she returned to live with her mother (Anne Jefferis Sheppard to Martha Jefferis, Apr. 1841, 16 Oct. 1842, 2 Apr., 22 May, and 12 Oct. 1844, 3 Sept. 1845, 17 Jan. 1847, 16 May, 3 June, and 31 Oct. 1849; Anne Jefferis Sheppard to Susanna Lightfoot, 23 Mar. 1845, and to Joshua Jefferis, 14 May 1854). Daughters evidently frequently slept with their mothers—into adulthood (Harriet Manigault [Wilcox] Diary, 19 Feb. 1815; Eleanor Parke Custis Lewis to Elizabeth Bordley Gibson, 10 Oct. 1832). Daughters also frequently asked mothers to live with them and professed delight when they did so. See e.g. Sarah Alden Ripley's comments to George Simmons, 6 Oct. 1844, in Wister and Irwin, p. 185: 'It is no longer "Mother and Charles came out one day and returned the next", for mother is one of us: she has entered the penetratice, been initiated into the mystery of the household gods, . . . Her divertisement is to mend the stockings . . . whiten sheets and napkins, . . . and take a stroll at evening with me to talk of our children, to compare our experiences, what we have learned and what we have suffered, and, last of all, to compete with pears and melons the cheerful circle about the solar lamp. . . .' We did find a few exceptions to this mother–daughter felicity (M. B. Ashew Diary, 19 Nov. 1857, 10 Apr. and 17 May 1858). Sarah Foulke Emlen was at first very hostile to her stepmother (Sarah Foulke Emlen Diary, 9 Aug. 1807), but they later developed a warm supportive relationship.

45. Sarah Alden Ripley to Sophy Thayer, n.d. [1861].

46. Mary Hallock Foote to Helena [winter 1873] (no. 52); Jossie, Stevens Point, Wis., to Charlena Van Vleck [Anderson], Appleton, Wis., 24 Oct. 1870; Pollie Chandler, Green Bay, Wis., to Charlena Van Vleck [Anderson], Appleton, n.d.

[1870]; Eleuthera DuPont to Sophie DuPont, 5 Sept. 1829; Sophie DuPont to Eleuthera DuPont, Dec. 1827; Sophie DuPont to Victorine Bauday, 4 Dec. 1827; Mary Gilpin to Sophie DuPont, 26 Sept. 1827; Sarah Ripley Starns Diary, 2 Apr. 1809; Jeannie McCall to Peter McCall, 27 Oct. [late 1840s]. Eleanor Parke Custis Lewis's correspondence with Elizabeth Bordley Gibson describes such an apprenticeship system over two generations—that of her childhood and that of her daughters. Indeed Eleanor Lewis's own apprenticeship was quite formal. She was deliberately separated from her foster mother in order to spend a winter of domesticity with her married sisters and her remarried mother. It was clearly felt that her foster mother's (Martha Washington) home at the nation's capital was not an appropriate place to develop domestic talents (13 Oct. 1795, 30 Mar. 13 May, and [summer] 1796, 18 Mar. and 27 Apr. 1797, Oct. 1827).

47. Education was not limited to the daughter of an Ohio Valley frontier farmer, for instance, attended day-school for several years during the early 1800s. Sarah Ripley Stearns, the daughter of a shopkeeper in Greenfield, Mass., attended a boarding school for but three months, yet the experience seemed very important to her. Mrs S. S. Dalton, a Mormon woman from Utah, attended a series of poor country schools and greatly valued her opportunity, though she also expressed a great deal of guilt for the sacrifices her mother made to make her education possible (Sarah Foulke Emlen Journal, Sarah Ripley Stearns Diary, Mrs S. S. Dalton, 'Autobiography').

48. Maria Revere to her mother [Mrs Paul Revere], 13 June 1801, Paul Revere papers, Massachusetts Historical Society. In a letter to Elizabeth Bordley Gibson, 28 Mar. 1847, Eleanor Parke Custis Lewis from Virginia discussed the anxiety her daughter felt when her granddaughters left home to go to boarding school. Eleuthera DuPont was very homesick when away at school in Philadelphia in the early 1820s (Eleuthera DuPont, Philadelphia, to Victorine Bauday, Wilmington, Del., 7 Apr. 1821; Eleuthera DuPont to Sophie Madeleine DuPont, Wilmington Del., Feb. and 3 Apr. 1821).

49. Elizabeth Bordley Gibson, a Philadelphia matron, played such a role for the daughters and nieces of her lifelong friend, Eleanor Parke Custis Lewis, a Virginia planter's wife (Eleanor Parke Custis Lewis to Elizabeth Bordley Gibson, 29 Jan. 1833, 19 Mar. 1836, and *passim* through the collection). The wife of Thomas Gurney Smith played a similar role for Sophie and Eleuthera DuPont (see e.g. Eleuthera DuPont to Sophie Madeleine DuPont, 22 May 1825; Rest Cope to Philema P. Swayne [niece] West Town School, Chester County, Pas., 8 Apr. 1829, Friends Historical Library, Swarthmore College). For a view of such a social pattern over three generations, see the letters and diaries of three generations of Manigault women in Philadelphia: Mrs Gabrielle Manigault, her daughter, Harriet Manigault Wilcox, and granddaughter, Charlotte Wilcox McCall. Unfortunately the papers of the three women are not in one family collection (Mrs Henry Middleton, Charleston, SC, to Mrs Gabrielle Manigault, n.d. [mid 1800s]; Harriet Manigault Diary, i; 1 Dec. 1813, 28 June 1814; Charlotte Wilcox McCall Diary, i. 1842, *passim*. All in Historical Society of Philadelphia).

50. Frances Parke Lewis, Woodlawn, Va., to Elizabeth Bordley Gibson, Philadelphia, 11 Apr. 1821, Lewis Correspondence; Eleuthera DuPont, Philadelphia, to Victorine DuPont Bauday, Brandywine, 8 Dec. 1821, 31 Jan. 1822; Eleuthera DuPont, Brandywine, to Margaretta Lammont [DuPont], Philadelphia, May 1823.

51. Sarah Ripley Stearns Diary, 9 and 25 Mar. 1810; Peggy Emlen to Sally Logan, Mar. and 4 July 1769; Harriet Manigault [Wilcox] Diary, vol. 1, 1 Dec. 1813, 28 June and 18 Sept. 1814, 10 Aug. 1815; Charlotte Wilcox McCall Diary, 1842, *passim*; Fanny Canby to Mary Canby, 27 May 1801, 17 Mar. 1804; Deborah Cope, West Town School, to Rest Cope, Philadelphia, 9 July 1828, Chester County Historical Society, West Chester, Pa.; Anne Zook, West Town School, to Mary Zook, Philadelphia, 30 Jan. 1866, Chester County Historical Society, West Chester, Pa.; Mary Gilpin to Sophie Madeleine DuPont, 25 Feb. 1829; Eleanor Parke Custis [Lewis] to Elizabeth Bordley [Gibson], 27 Apr., 2 July, and 8 Sept. 1797, 30 June 1799, 29 Dec. 1820; Frances Parke Lewis to Elizabeth Bordley Gibson, 20 Dec. 1820.
52. Anne Jefferis Sheppard to Martha Jefferis, 17 Mar. 1841.
53. Peggy Emlen to Sally Logan, Mar. 1769, Mount Vernon, Va.; Eleanor Parke Custis [Lewis] to Elizabeth Bordley [Gibson], Philadelphia, 27 Apr. 1797, 30 June 1799; Jeannie Field, New York, to Sarah Butler Wister, Germantown, 3 July 1861, 16 Jan. 1863, Harriet Manigault Diary, 3 and 11–13 Aug. 1814; Eunice Callender, Boston, to Sarah Ripley [Stearns], Greenfield, 4 May 1809. I found one exception to this inhibition of female hostility. This was the diary of Charlotte Wilcox McCall, Philadelphia (see e.g. her 23 Mar. 1842 entry).
54. Sophie M. DuPont and Eleuthera DuPont, Brandywine, to Victorine DuPont Bauday, Philadelphia, 25 Jan. 1832.
55. Sarah Ripley [Stearns] Diary and Harriet Manigault Diary, *passim*.
56. Sophie Madeleine DuPont to Eleuthera DuPont, Dec. 1827; Clementina Beach Smith to Sophie Madeleine DuPont, 26 Dec. 1828; Sarah Faulke Emlen Diary, 21 July 1808, 30 Mar. 1809; Annie Hethroe, Ellington, Wis., to Charlena Van Vleck [Anderson], Appleton, Wis., 23 Apr. 1865; Frances Parke Lewis, Woodlawn, Va., to Elizabeth Bordley [Gibson], Philadelphia, 20 Dec. 1820; Fanny Feris to Debby Feris, West Town School, Chester County, Pa., 29 May 1826. An excellent example of the warmth of women's comments about each other and the reserved nature of their references to men are seen in two entries in Sarah Ripley Stearn's diary. On 8 Jan. 1811 she commented about a young woman friend: 'The amiable Mrs White of Princeton . . . one of the loveliest most interesting creatures I ever knew, young fair and blooming . . . beloved by everyone . . . formed to please & to charm. . . .' She referred to the man she ultimately married always as 'my friend' or 'a friend' (2 Feb. or 23 Apr. 1810).
57. Jeannie Field, New York, to Sarah Butler Wister, Germantown, 6 Apr. 1862.
58. Elizabeth Bordley Gibson, introductory statement to the Eleanor Parke Custis Lewis Letters [1850s], Historical Society of Pennsylvania.
59. Sarah Foulke [Emlen] Diary, 30 Mar. 1809.
60. Harriet Manigault Diary, 26 May 1815.
61. Sarah Ripley [Stearns] Diary, 17 May and 2 Oct. 1812; Eleanor Parke Custis Lewis to Elizabeth Bordley Gibson, 23 Apr. 1826; Rebecca Ralston, Philadelphia, to Victorine DuPont [Bauday], Brandywine, 27 Sept. 1813.
62. Anne Jefferis to Martha Jefferis, 22 and 27 Nov. 1840, 13 Jan. and 17 Mar. 1841; Edith Jefferis, Greenwich, NJ, to Anne Jefferis, Philadelphia, 31 Jan., 6 Feb. and Feb. 1841.
63. Edith Jefferis to Anne Jefferis, 31 Jan. 1841.
64. Eleanor Parke Custis Lewis to Elizabeth Bordley, 4 Nov. 1799. Eleanor and her daughter Parke experienced similar sorrow and anxiety when Parke married and moved to Cincinnati (Eleanor Parke Custis Lewis to Elizabeth Bordley

Gibson, 23 Apr. 1826). Helena DeKay visited Mary Hallock the month before her marriage; Mary Hallock was an attendant at the wedding; Helena again visited Molly about three weeks after her marriage; and then Molly went with Helena and spent a week with Helena and Richard in their new apartment (Mary Hallock [Foote] to Helena DeKay Gilder [Spring 1874] (no. 61), 10 May 1874 [May 1874], 14 June 1874 [Summer 1874]. See also Anne Biddle, Philadelphia, to Clement Biddle (brother), Wilmington, 12 Mar. and 27 May 1827; Eunice Callender, Boston, to Sarah Ripley [Stearns], Greenfield, Mass., 3 Aug. 1807, 26 Jan. 1808; Victorine DuPont Bauday, Philadelphia, to Evelina DuPont [Biderman], Brandywine, 25 and 26 Nov., 1 Dec. 1813; Peggy Emlen to Sally Logan, n.d. [1769–80?]; Jeannie Field, New York, to Sarah Butler Wister, Germantown, 3 July 1861).

65. Mary Hallock to Helena DeKay Gilder [1876] (no. 81); n.d. (no. 83), 3 Mar. 1884; Mary Ashew Diary, ii. Sept.–Jan. 1860; Louisa Van Vleck to Charlena Van Vleck Anderson, n.d. [1875]; Sophie DuPont to Henry DuPont, 24 July 1827; Benjamin Ferris to WIlliam Canby, 13 Feb. 1805; Benjamin Ferris to Mary Canby Biddle , 20 Dec. 1825; Anne Jefferis Sheppard to Martha Jefferis, 15 Sept. 1884; Martha Jefferis to Anne Jefferis Sheppard, 4 July 1843, 5 May 1844, 3 May 1847, 17 July 1849; Jeannie McCall to Peter McCall, 26 Nov. 1847, n.d. [late 1840s]. A graphic description of the ritual surrounding a first birth is found in Abigail Lyman's letter to her husband Erastus Lyman, 18 Oct. 1810.

66. Fanny Ferris to Anne Biddle, 19 Nov. 1811; Eleanor Parke Custis Lewis to Elizabeth Bordley Gibson, 4 Nov. 1799, 27 Apr. 1827; Martha Jefferis to Anne Jefferis Sheppard, 31 Jan. 1843, 4 Apr. 1844; Martha Jefferis to Phoebe Sharpless Middleton, 4 June 1846; Anne Jefferis Sheppard to Martha Jefferis, 20 Aug. 1843, 12 Feb. 1844; Maria Inskeep, New Orleans, to Mrs Fanny G. Hampton, Bridgeton, NJ, 22 Sept. 1848; Benjamin Ferris to Mary Canby, 14 Feb. 1805; Fanny Ferris to Mary Canby [Biddle], 2 Dec. 1816.

67. Eleanor Parke Custis Lewis to Elizabeth Bordley Gibson, Oct.–Nov. 1820.

68. Emily Howland to Hannah, 30 Sept. 1866; Emily Howland Diary, 8, 11, and 27 Feb. 1880; Phoebe Brandford Diary, 12 and 13 Apr., and 4 Aug. 1833; Eunice Callender, Boston, to Sarah Ripley [Stearns], Greenwich, Mass., 11 Sept. 1802, 26 Aug. 1810; Mrs H. Middleton, Charleston, to Mrs Gabrielle Manigault, Philadelphia, n.d. [mid-1800s]; Mrs H. C. Paul to Mrs Jeannie McCall, Philadelphia, n.d. [1840s]; Sarah Butler Wister, Germantown, to Jeannie Field [Musgrove], New York, 22 Apr. 1864; Jeannie Field [Musgrove] to Sarah Butler Wister, 25 Aug. 1861, 6 July 1862; S. B. Raudolph to Elizabeth Bordley [Gibson], n.d. [1790s]. For an example of similar letters between men, see Henry Wright to Peter McCall, 10 Dec. 1852; Charles McCall to Peter McCall, 4 Jan. 1860, 22 Mar. 1864; R. Mercer to Peter McCall, 29 Nov. 1872.

69. Mary Black [Couper] to Sophie Madeleine DuPont, Feb. 1827 [1 Nov. 1834], 12 Nov. 1834, two letters [late Nov. 1834]; Eliza Schlatter to Sophie Madeleine DuPont, 2 Nov. 1834.

70. For a few of the references to death rituals in the Jefferis papers see: Martha Jefferis to Anne Jefferis Sheppard, 28 Sept. 1843, 21 Aug. and 25 Sept. 1844, 11 Jan. 1846, summer 1848, *passim*; Anne Jefferis Sheppard to Martha Jefferis, 20 Aug. 1843; Anne Jefferis Sheppard to Rachel Jefferis, 17 Mar. 1863, 9 Feb. 1868. For other Quaker families, see Rachel Biddle to Anne Biddle, 23 July 1854; Sarah Foulke Farquhar [Emlen] Diary, 30 Apr. 1811, 14 Feb. 1812; Fanny Ferris to Mary Canby, 31 Aug. 1810. This is not to argue that men and

women did not mourn together. Yet in many families women aided and comforted women and men, men. The same-sex death ritual was one emotional option available to nineteenth-century Americans.

71. Sarah Foulke [Emlen] Diary, 29 Dec. 1808.

72. Eunice Callender, Boston, to Sarah Ripley [Stearns] Greenfield, Mass., 24 May 1803.

73. Katherine Johnstone Brinley [Wharton] Journal, 26 Apr., 30 May, and 29 May 1856, Historical Society of Pennsylvania.

74. A series of roughly fourteen letters written by Peggy Emlen to Sally Logan (1768–71) has been preserved in the Wells Morris Collection, Box 1, Historical Society of Pennsylvania (see esp. 3 May and 4 July 1769, 8 Jan. 1768).

75. The Sarah Alden Ripley collection, the Arthur M. Schlesinger, Sr., Library, Radcliffe College, contains a number of Sarah Alden Ripley's letters to Mary Emerson. Most of these are undated, but they extend over a number of years and contain letters written both before and after Sarah's marriage. The eulogistic biographical sketch appeared in Wister and Irwin (n. 12 above). It should be noted that Sarah Butler Wister was one of the editors who sensitively selected Sarah's letters.

76. See Sarah Alden Ripley to Mary Emerson, 19 Nov. 1823. Sarah Alden Ripley routinely, and one must assume ritualistically, read Mary Emerson's letters to her infant daughter, Mary. Eleanor Parke Custis Lewis reported doing the same with Elizabeth Bordley Gibson's letters, *passim*. Eunice Callender, Boston, to Sarah Ripley [Stearns], 19 Oct. 1808.

77. Mary Black Couper to Sophie M. DuPont, 5 Mar. 1832. The Clementina Smith–Sophie DuPont correspondence of 1678 letters is in the Sophie DuPont Correspondence. The quotation is from Eliza Schlatter, Mount Holly, NJ, to Sophie DuPont, Brandywine, 24 Aug. 1834. I am indebted to Anthony Wallace for informing me about this collection.

78. Mary Grew, Providence, RI, to Isabel Howland, Sherwood, NY, 27 Apr. 1892, Howland Correspondence, Sophia Smith Collection, Smith College.

79. Helena Deutsch, *Psychology of Women* (New York: Grune & Stratton, 1944), i. chs. 1–3; Clara Thompson, *On Women*, ed. Maurice Green (New York: New American Library, 1971).

Creating Boundaries: Homosexuality
and the Changing Social Order in
France, 1830–1870

Victoria Thompson

Upon its publication in 1835, Théophile Gautier's *Mademoiselle de Maupin* caused a tremendous sensation. In his study on Gautier, the journalist Maxime du Camp recalled that upon reading the novel 'people covered their faces and asked, "alas! is it possible?"' [1] Preceded by an inflammatory preface in which Gautier attacked the French bourgeoisie for its alleged materialism and self-interest, the story itself was a tale of cross-dressing intrigue, in which characters explored the possibility of gender reversal and same-sex love.

Gautier's hero, d'Albert, was searching for a perfect love, one that would enable him to transcend the boundaries of the self and become one with his beloved. To evoke this union of two persons, Gautier used the image of the hermaphrodite, whom he described as 'two equal and separate beauties which form a whole superior to each separately'.[2] Combining male and female in one body, the hermaphrodite could be considered an ideal metaphor for heterosexual union. Yet Gautier chose instead to give this metaphor an interesting twist. D'Albert did come close, at least for a short time, to realizing his desire of losing himself in another, but not by meeting the perfect woman. Instead, d'Albert lost his sense of identity

Earlier versions of this article were presented at 'Homosexuality in Modern France', a conference sponsored by the Center for Lesbian and Gay Studies at the Graduate School and University Center of the City University of New York and funded by the Florence Gould Foundation, and at the 1995 Annual Meeting of the American Historical Association. I would like to thank all those who made very helpful comments on these two occasions, and in particular, Barry Bergen, Lynn Hunt, and Bonnie Smith. This article has greatly benefited from discussions with the other contributors to the volume *Homosexuality in Modern France*, and from the many careful readings of the volume's editors, Bryant T. Ragan and Jeffrey Merrick. I would also like to thank Joan Scott for her comments and suggestions, and Deborah Hamilton for her willingness to read, critique, and discuss many versions of this article. Reprinted with permission from Jeffrey Merrick and Bryant T. Ragan (eds.), *Homosexuality in Modern France* (New York: Oxford University Press, 1996).

only after admitting to himself that he had fallen in love with another man: 'everything within me is mixed-up and upside down; I no longer know who I am or who others are, I am unsure if I am a man or a woman . . . there are moments . . . when the sense of my existence abandons me altogether.'[3]

While the reader knows that the dashing Théodore de Serannes, the man who had stolen d'Albert's heart, was actually a woman in disguise, d'Albert does not suspect his love's true sex until much later in the story, after he has come to terms with his love for another man. Once that gender confusion is ironed out, Gautier throws in another twist: before riding off into the night, Madeleine (the cross-dressing *chevalier*) makes love not only to d'Albert, but to his mistress Rosette as well. We can well imagine what all the 'hubbub' over the novel was about![4]

Raising the possibility, in *Mademoiselle de Maupin*, of a love affair between two men or two women was more than an attempt to scandalize bourgeois readers.[5] *Mademoiselle de Maupin* can be placed within a larger debate over the social order occurring in mid-nineteenth-century France, a debate in which definitions of sexuality, linked to categories of class and gender, came to play an important role. While during the July Monarchy (1830–48), a period of tremendous social upheaval, sexuality and gender often appeared as fluid, by the 1850s and 1860s sexuality and gender were increasingly organized into rigidly defined categories.

This transformation paralleled changing attitudes toward issues such as social mobility and class relations. Occurring in the midst of the upheaval caused by urbanization and industrialization, the Revolution of 1830, which inaugurated the July Monarchy, seemed to many to mark the beginning of a new era. Many, including romantics and republicans seeking to forge a place for themselves in the new social and political order, considered the moment ripe for social reorganization, and advocated change as beneficial to society as a whole. Others, concerned with maintaining their positions, were less enthusiastic regarding the possibilities of social transformation. In either case, boundaries between different categories, including those of sexuality, gender, and class, seemed to many, for better or for worse, to be highly permeable during this period.

By contrast, the June Days of 1848, when conflict over the political and social structure of the new Second Republic culminated in bloodshed in the streets of Paris, resulted in a rejection of even limited acceptance of social change. The widespread loss of idealism that followed the June Days led to a desire, primarily on the part of the bourgeoisie, for the establishment and maintenance of order at all costs. As fluidity became identified with conflict and disorder, certain cultural categories—class, gender, and sexuality—became increasingly fixed. The result was a shift in perception that affected all aspects of French culture. In the words of literary critic Richard Terdiman, 'Once the dream of fraternity between the classes was shattered by the brutality of June 1848, it was as if what Marx named "classes" and "class struggle" suddenly became primary and incontrovertible perceptual structures. Divisions deepened.'[6]

As a result of this shift in perception, representations of sexuality lost their fluidity and were increasingly made to correspond to one of two categories (what we would call heterosexuality and homosexuality), while distinctions between different types of same-sex sexuality (for example, male versus female, or active versus passive) were developed into fixed definitions. This process corresponded to an increased awareness of class identity and was closely linked to the elaboration of distinct gender roles. As differences between 'masculine' and 'feminine' became more clearly elaborated, the 'hermaphrodite' of the 1830s and 1840s gave way to a proto-homosexual 'type', labelled alternatively pederast or *antiphysique* (for men), tribade or lesbian (for women). This early 'homosexual', not yet the medically-defined and criminalized 'invert' of the late nineteenth century, was increasingly used to symbolize a 'reversal of the regular order'.[7]

Working from the assumption formulated by Robert Padgug, that 'sexual categories . . . are the expression of active relations of entire groups and collectivities', this article explores the way in which representations of sexuality worked during this period to establish and support definitions of difference and hierarchy.[8] In particular, it examines four moments during which same-sex sexuality became an important metaphor for discussing the organization of society. In the first section, I discuss a number of novels from the 1830s in which same-sex sexuality was used to criticize July Monarchy society. In the second section, I examine concern over same-sex relationships in debates concerning prison reform in the 1840s. In the last two sections, which focus on the Second Empire, I examine first, the development of an increasingly negative discourse linking male homosexuality to crime, and second, the way in which lesbianism was used to criticize (in a very limited fashion) bourgeois self-interest. In comparing a variety of sources (including popular literature, police memoirs, writings on prison reform, prostitution, and legal medicine) over time, this article explores some of the links between images of sexuality and attitudes underpinning the social order, so as to suggest ways in which sexuality can be read historically within a broad cultural context.

SOCIAL BONDS, SOCIAL MOBILITY, AND SAME-SEX RELATIONSHIPS IN THE JULY MONARCHY

In his *Confessions*, author, journalist, and *mondain* Arsène Houssaye wrote that during the July Monarchy, 'Sappho was reborn in Paris, not knowing if she loved Phaon or Erinne.'[9] While Houssaye used this witticism to open a discussion of reputed love affairs between women during this time, his comment had a larger relevance. During the July Monarchy, cross-dressing, hermaphrodism, and same-sex love were hot topics.[10] In 1829, Henri de Latouche published his tale of an Italian hermaphrodite, *Fragoletta*. This influential novel is said to have inspired Honoré de Balzac's *Séraphîta*, the story of a Norwegian hermaphrodite, and *La Fille aux yeux d'or*, as well as Gautier's *Mademoiselle de Maupin*, all published in 1835. Balzac's Vautrin, a notorious member of what he called the 'third sex', appeared in *Le Père Goriot* (1834–5), the 1840 play *Vautrin*, and the novel *Splendeurs et misères des courtisanes* (1838–46). The inherent 'danger' of a relationship between two men formed the climax of Balzac's *Sarrasine* (1830), the story of a feminized Italian castrato. In the popular literature on Paris and the Parisians produced in abundance during this period, one of the most frequent recurring characters was the *lorette*, a woman, inspired perhaps by George Sand, who regularly appeared in public dressed as a man.[11] Moreover, social reformers expressed much concern about the effects of same-sex relationships among prisoners and prostitutes.

In these various sources, ambiguous gender and sexual identity functioned as a metaphor for a society in which social and economic boundaries were perceived as permeable. This apparent permeability had both positive and negative connotations for contemporaries. On the one hand, it was considered important in a liberal model of society, one based on the possibility of upward social mobility and led by a merit-based elite. On the other hand, social boundaries that become too fluid threatened to dissolve altogether, thus posing a constant threat to stability.[12]

Participation in Louis-Philippe's regime was in theory based on merit; yet merit was determined by wealth. Guizot's exhortation to those who demanded a widening of the income-based suffrage, 'enrichissez-vous', (get rich) was criticized by republicans and romantics alike. In their opinion, the regime's emphasis on material success encouraged self-interest and individualism, thereby threatening to destroy community. For writers and journalists in particular, struggling to make their way in an increasingly commercialized literary world, lauding material wealth rather than 'natural' talent as the key to social and political success was troubling. As a response, many writers attempted to elaborate a model of the social hierarchy that encouraged social mobility based on 'natural' talent rather than economic power. In several works of literature from the 1830s writers used fluid categories of gender and sexuality to critique the existing model of society, and to propose an alternative.

In these works we meet characters who have been unable to find true love because they have devoted themselves to achieving social recognition. The hero of *Mademoiselle de Maupin*, d'Albert, found no satisfaction with his mistress Rosette, since he wanted to 'possess' her in order to get ahead in society.[13] When we first meet d'Hauteville, the protagonist of *Fragoletta*, he is mourning the loss of Honorine, who committed suicide because d'Hauteville, searching not for devotion but for a 'trophy', spurned her love. In Balzac's *Séraphîta*, Wilfrid, one of Séraphîta's admirer's, came to the small Norwegian town where the novel is set after pursuing glory and advancement in Napoleon's army. Unfulfilled, the characters seek a love that would enable them to lose a sense of self(-interest). D'Albert, for example, tries repeatedly with Rosette to lose a sense of himself as a distinct individual, to 'rid myself of the idea that I was me'.[14] This loss of self is impossible, however, since, as Rosette herself remarks, lovers like d'Albert, 'only passed over me in order to achieve something else. I was a path for them, not a destination.'[15]

Similarly, Balzac's novel *La Fille aux yeux d'or* opens with the author's description of Parisian society as a never-ending search for pleasure, social recognition, and economic success. Workers, the bourgeoisie, the aristocracy, and artists all constantly seek advancement. For artists in particular, this need for success posed special difficulties:

Worn out by a need to produce, overtaken by their costly fantasies, fatigued by a devouring genius, famished for pleasure, the artists of Paris all want to make up through excessive work the holes left by laziness, and seek in vain to reconcile *le monde* and glory, money and art.[16]

In this way, Balzac invokes the conflict, in his opinion especially acute for artists, between social recognition and natural talent. According to Balzac, the need to produce so as to satisfy expensive tastes or 'fantasies' created by immersion in Parisian society comes into conflict with the natural ebb and flow of artistic creation. This constant need to pursue one's interests that Balzac considered characteristic of Parisian society, explained '[the] cadaverous physiognomy [of] . . . this exhumed people'.[17] The only escape was to live, '*à l'orientale*', that is, to remove oneself from society's endless quest for success and glory. Yet this alternative was only really possible for certain women, kept separate from the outside world, those who 'remain hidden, like rare plants who only open their petals at certain times'.[18]

The mysterious Pacquita in *La Fille aux yeux d'or* was such a woman, appearing only for brief walks in the park, always chaperoned and never allowed to speak. Balzac's protagonist, de Marsay, was immediately drawn to her; he saw her as a rare example of a woman unsullied by contact with the market:

She is the original of the delirious painting called *la femme caressant sa chimère* [the woman caressing her chimera], the hottest, the most infernal inspiration of ancient genius; a sacred poetry prostituted by those who have copied it for frescos and mosaics; for a crowd of bourgeois who see in this cameo only a trinket, and put it on their watch chains.[19]

De Marsay's desire for Pacquita can be read as a desire for love untainted by the exigencies of social mobility, or, by extension, as a desire for a social order in which wealth and financial skill would be replaced by 'natural' talent as the determinant of social status and power.[20]

Creating such a society would require a reconfiguration of the social order, and of social categories. This reconfiguration is symbolized in these novels by confused gender and sexual identities. Thus the attempt to move outside the realm of market relations, marked by the introduction of characters who are literally or figuratively 'hermaphrodites', is accompanied by a general confusion of sexual and gender identities among the protagonists.[21] D'Albert, for example, unable to find an ideal union with his mistress Rosette, first wishes to become a woman, then falls in love with a cross-dressing (and it turns out, 'bisexual') visitor to the château whom he sincerely believes to be another man.[22] De Marsay dresses as a woman to please and excite Pacquita, later learning that she is being 'kept' by a female lover.[23] D'Hauteville falls in love with Camille, a hermaphrodite who is first introduced as a female, and over the course of the story also comes to have strong feelings of attraction for someone he believes to be her 'brother' (actually her masculine side), Adriani.

This confusion of gender and sexual identities was not always portrayed in negative terms. Gautier's d'Albert, for example, came to accept his love for another man as natural:

What's strange is that I no longer think of his sex and I love him with a perfect security. Sometimes I try to persuade myself that this love is abominable, and I tell myself this as severely as possible; but it's something I say . . . and that I don't feel.[24]

Likewise in *Fragoletta*, d'Hauteville willingly confused his love for Camille with a sense of attraction to her 'brother' Adriani. During a carriage ride on a moonlit night, Adriani 'held out a white and effeminate hand [to d'Hauteville], and squeezed . . . with a more forceful and lengthy embrace than fraternal affection required'.[25] D'Hauteville, inspired by the romantic setting and by Adriani's admiration, sought to return to Adriani the 'same and affectionate caresses that he had just received'.[26] In *Séraphîta*, Minna, aware that Séraphîta appeared to everyone except her to be a woman, still pursued her.[27] Finally, in the play *Vautrin*, Balzac compared the love of the title character Vautrin for his young protege, Raoul, with the love of a mother for her son.[28]

While these examples of an implied acceptance of same-sex love are interesting and noteworthy, the purpose of introducing, in these works, a character whose sexuality is ambiguous was not necessarily to argue for the acceptance or toleration of alternate forms of sexual behaviour.[29] Rather, such a character symbolizes a situation in which boundaries are in flux. After passing through this period of confusion, these novels end with the re-establishment of harmony and stability on a 'higher' plane, symbolized by the loving, heterosexual couple. In *Séraphîta*, for example, the death of the hermaphrodite leaves her two young suitors, Minna and Wilfrid, united in love and spirituality. The departure of Théodore/ Madeleine, the cross-dressing character in *Mademoiselle de Maupin*, serves much the same function; sleeping with both the hero, d'Albert, and his mistress, Rosette, in the same night, Théodore/Madeleine leaves them with the advice to 'Love each other in memory of me, whom you have both loved, and say sometimes my name in a kiss.'[30]

The endings of *Fragoletta* and *La Fille aux yeux d'or* are somewhat more ambiguous, yet both novels ultimately convey a similar sense of possible, if more difficult, unity. In *Fragoletta*, Camille/Adriani falls to her/his death after struggling with d'Hauteville. As the hermaphrodite plunges off the cliff into the sea, her/his final words prompt the main character to think of the woman who killed herself out of love for him: 'The memory of Honorine crossed d'Hauteville's mind like a sharp dart.'[31] D'Hauteville's crime, to which Camille/Adriani alluded before dying, was to have spurned Honorine's love for conquests that would give him greater social recognition. The hermaphrodite's death therefore underscored the message that unity required a repudiation of self-interest (here described as vanity). Likewise, Pacquita's murder in *La Fille aux yeux d'or*, although violent, brings de Marsay and Pacquita's female lover together, allowing them to realize that they are brother and sister.[32] The creation of a new social order, while still possible in these texts, entails struggle and violent death.

The passage of the novels' characters through a period characterized by ambiguous gender and sexual identity, and the sacrifice of the bisexual/hermaphrodite character, result in the creation of a new order. Self-interest and individualism, qualities which romantics and republicans portrayed as detrimental to social harmony and community, are replaced by love and the complementarity of 'natural' gendered distinctions. In this sense, these novels convey a vision of society similar to that of the Saint-Simonians, who believed that social stability could only be brought about through the harmonious and loving co-operation of male and female, worker and employer. Whereas the ultimate message of these novels—that the ideal social order should reflect the 'natural' complementarity of the heterosexual couple—is by no means revolutionary, what is significant is the role that same-sex relations played in establishing this ideal order. The necessity of passing through a period of unstable or permeable boundaries, including those of gender and sexuality, opened up the possibility for imagining same-sex relationships in a somewhat positive manner.

Balzac's *Sarrasine* provides an interesting counter-example to the novels discussed above. On one level, *Sarrasine*, the tale of a sculptor who falls in love with someone he believes to be a woman, but who turns out to be a highly feminized castrato, seems to contain a condemnation of same-sex relationships. Sarrasine, the sculptor, reacts with horror upon learning the true sex of Zambinella, the singer to whom he had professed his strong love and admiration. As an old man protected by his wealthy Parisian relatives, Zambinella serves as a constant reminder of death. Yet on another level, *Sarrasine* is, as Roland Barthes remarked, 'not the story of a castrato, but of a contract'.[33] The 'desire to exchange' that Barthes argued structured the narrative, manifested in the relationship between the narrator and the marquise, is, I would argue, precisely what Balzac wished to condemn.[34] Zambinella wished to find a love untainted by material interest or base passion, to be loved, 'purely', but he was the only character who felt this way.[35] Unlike d'Albert, Sarrasine never abandoned his sense of self-interest. Even in his love for the castrato, he was driven by ambition, hoping that finding the perfect female form would allow him to realize his desire to 'engrave his name between those of Michelangelo and Mister Bouchardon [his teacher]'.[36] One could argue that it was this ambition that led him to ignore Zambinella's request that he not pursue him, and thus led to the crisis of the story. Zambinella, condemned never to find the 'pure' love he sought, was forced to dedicate himself to his career; the castrato's voice was, we learn at the end of the story, the mysterious and inglorious source of the family's immense wealth. Thus Zambinella's condemnation of men is echoed in the reaction of the marquise upon hearing the story, when she seems to include both herself and Zambinella among the ranks of women betrayed by the perfidies of a society that cares only for wealth: 'Mothers, our children kill us either by their bad behaviour or their lack of affection. Wives, we are betrayed. Lovers [*amantes*], we are left behind, abandoned. Friendship! does it exist? . . . Leave me alone.'[37] The reaction of the marquise to Zambinella's tragedy indicates that Balzac's condemnation here was not directed against same-sex relationships (indeed, such an argument would contradict his depictions of same-sex relationships in other works), but was instead directed against excess ambition and a devotion to wealth that destroyed the possibility of pure love. Zambinella was associated with death not because, as a castrato, he was extremely feminine in appearance, but because men's ambition trapped him in a world without love.

While these literary works used same-sex relationships and ambiguous gender and sexual identities to convey a message regarding the desirability of political and social change, the depiction and meaning of same-sex relationships in writings on prison reform reflect a growing concern with social stability.[38] In the 1840s increased awareness of the social and economic consequences of industrialization—poverty, urban overcrowding, and popular unrest—resulted in the questioning of liberal ideals. While many still considered upward social mobility and a merit-based social hierarchy the central legacies of the Revolution of 1789, for others, growing social conflict created a fear of instability. In writings on prison reform, hopes and fears regarding the nature of social bonds crystallized around representations of same-sex relationships. In these writings, prison society functioned as a mirror of liberal society, reflecting its potential for both good and bad. On the one hand, reformers portrayed prison society as organized by a natural hierarchy based on talent, in which relationships between inmates were close, based on love and respect, and virtually indestructible. On the other hand, however, reformers depicted the close bonds that they believed were formed between prisoners as symbolizing the possibility of a complete dissolution of social distinctions. In these writings, as in the novels discussed above, same-sex sexuality functioned as a way of discussing the ability of French society to create and maintain categories and boundaries during a time of rapid and extreme social, political, and economic change.

For reformers, prison was defined by constant contact with others that made the development of close relationships inevitable. It was a life in which 'men . . . are continually together, . . . working elbow to elbow for years, . . . eating at the same table, sleeping thirty centimeters apart in the same dormitory . . .'.[39] Reformers believed that relationships between prisoners formed very rapidly:

It is, in fact, proven, that a condemned man is in prison no more than five days when all his companions in captivity [already] know his name, his history, the nature and length of his punishment; it takes no longer than a month to make acquaintances and intimate friends.[40]

Such relationships, usually believed to be instigated by more experienced inmates, were portrayed as offering newcomers a means of integrating themselves into the community. In the long term, these relationships were also considered an avenue to 'improvement', as the weaker or less experienced of the two became stronger and more knowledgeable with the help of his/her new partner. Josephine Mallet, a reformer concerned with women's prisons, painted the following scenario:

the stronger of the two offers her arm to the weaker, in order to help her walk; and despite the active surveillance of which they are the object, during the long hours of walking in the room, then in the courtyards . . . the most intimate confidences take place. . . . The more depraved of the two corrupts her companion, initiates her into all sorts of crimes. . . .[41]

Larcenaire, the literary criminal who was the talk of Parisian society in 1835, portrayed this process as a conscious effort on the part of newcomers to find a role model in order to increase their status in prison society. According to Lacenaire, the newcomer, 'models himself on the best specimens he sees around him, the best of this particular kind. He adopts their tone and manners; he imitates them, in two days he finds himself able to speak their jargon.'[42]

Such descriptions of relationships among prisoners reveal a belief that prison society was organized according to a hierarchy of knowledge and talent. According to reformers, this hierarchy, although immediately evident to those newly incarcerated, was nevertheless somewhat fluid, as it allowed for the integration and upward mobility of newcomers. Larcenaire's enormous popularity rested in part on his ability to play to this assumption regarding the functioning of the criminal underworld. Presenting himself as the 'dandy' of prison society, and as one who had risen rapidly through the prison hierarchy, Larcenaire appealed to Parisians as a symbol of successful upward social mobility.

In reformers' writings, prison was depicted as a site of solidarity among those who fell outside the norms of mid-nineteenth-century society. In their rapidly established relationships, prisoners reportedly found the love, respect, and acceptance that they were deprived of in the outside world. According to Joséphine Mallet, it was a sense of common suffering that brought prisoners together and accounted for their intense relationships: 'suffering experienced in common is for women the most powerful bond of sympathy, the only one that cancels out all sentiments of competition'.[43] It was for this reason, reformers believed, that criminals looked forward to incarceration as an 'eagerly awaited punishment'.[44]

Reformers thus depicted prison society as a mirror of the ideal liberal society. In this view of prison life, conflict was replaced by sympathy and love, as 'natural' leaders emerged within a universally recognized and respected hierarchy. These leaders, however, never forgot or ignored their obligations toward those who followed and looked up to them. For Larcenaire, this sense of mutual respect and loyalty that was so much a part of prison life was one of its most positive characteristics:

make no mistake, there are such things as respect and contempt even in the galleys, a fact that explains why certain convicts are better off in gaol than in a society that has nothing for them but contempt.[45]

In the final section of *Splendeurs et misères des courtisanes*, written in the late 1840s, Balzac reproduced many of the themes found in reformers' works, while making the sexual nature of prison relationships more explicit.[46] Balzac's protagonist, Vautrin, also symbolized successful upward mobility; he was, in his role as banker for the criminal 'Society of Ten Thousand', the underworld counterpart of the financier Nucingen. Vautrin's superior intellectual and criminal talents made him the 'natural' leader of prison society. In the novel, Vautrin enters the prison of the Conciergerie under the watchful eyes of police inspector Bibi-Lupin, who had hoped that the prison inmates would reveal the disguised criminal's true identity. Yet from the moment they laid eyes upon Vautrin, the other inmates immediately support his charade of pretending to be a Spanish abbot. Vautrin, 'the same as Napoleon recognized by his soldiers, obtained obedience and respect from the three criminals'.[47] Vautrin's fictional success, which culminated in his appointment, by the end of the novel, to chief of the Paris *Sûreté*, or special police, was much more enduring than that of the real-life criminal Larcenaire, who, despite his popularity, was guillotined for his crimes. Vautrin's talent with disguises, his role as both thief and banker, his ability to move in a variety of social circles, and finally his passage from the world of criminality to that of law and order all functioned to indicate his symbolic importance as a figure able to cross boundaries and move among and through social categories. It is not surprising, therefore, to learn that Vautrin, described by Balzac as a member of the 'third sex', had affective relationships exclusively with men.

Whereas intimacy between prisoners was depicted in reformers' writings in non-sexual terms, in Balzac's description of prison life the strongest ties among prisoners were between those who were or had been lovers, and this special bond between past lovers was recognized by the prison population. When Vautrin's three comrades saw him in the prison yard, they immediately assumed that the reason for his presence at the Conciergerie was to rescue his former lover Théodore from imminent execution. They surmised that Vautrin 'wants to see his *tante* who is supposed to be executed soon'.[48] Describing Théodore as a *tante*, a common slang term for someone who engaged in homosexual relationships in prison and heterosexual relationships on the outside, indicated the likelihood that the two men had a sexual relationship.

Vautrin's plan to save Théodore, developed once he learned of the impending execution, hinged on the co-operation of one of his comrades, La Pouraille. Balzac provides numerous indications that La Pouraille was meant to be identified as another of Vautrin's former lovers. The feminized name 'La Pouraille' signals that he too was a *tante*. La Pouraille 'knew' Vautrin 'intimately', and he alone among the prisoners is addressed by Vautrin as 'my love'.[49] This past intimacy between the two explains the special influence Vautrin seemed to have over La Pouraille, who, once addressed lovingly by Vautrin, professed his complete loyalty: 'You are and you will always be our *dab* [boss], I will never have secrets from you.'[50]

Rather than criticizing self-interest or individualism, as the novelists discussed earlier had done, reformers focused on the intimacy of prison relationships as a source of danger. Intimate relationships between prisoners led, according to reformers, to a complicity between the two partners that signalled the dissolution of barriers between them. This complicity was often represented as the ability to speak a secret language that police and prison surveillants could not understand, an even more hidden form of the special slang, or *argot*, used by prisoners. In Balzac's novel, while all the prisoners speak slang, Vautrin and Théodore alone communicate in Italian, under the frustrated eyes of Bibi-Lupin. La Pouraille supported Vautrin's plan to save Théodore when Vautrin gave him a special, silent look. Joséphine Mallet also believed that women prisoners who established intimate relationships could communicate through silent looks alone. According to Mallet, the two partners, 'no longer need words to communicate their thoughts, a look suffices'.[51]

The melding of the two partners, represented by the ability to communicate in secret, was extremely troubling to contemporaries. Such relationships were based on close, unbreakable, and impenetrable ties that contemporaries believed formed the foundation of a criminal underworld that threatened to infiltrate and corrupt 'honest' society.[52] In the words of one observer, 'What especially inspires a sense of terror are those associations that form in prison amongst evil-doers, associations whose frightful danger is revealed to us each day by the *cours d'assises*, and whose primary cause, relationships formed in captivity, can never be destroyed by the communal regime.'[53] Reformers argued that ties formed in prison seemed to subsist in the face of all obstacles and functioned equally well in or outside of prison. It was well known, for example, that Larcenaire's accomplice in his deadly crime was someone with whom he had been 'intimately associated' in the prison of Poissy.[54] When Vautrin re-established contact with Théodore in the Conciergerie, they immediately re-established their former intimacy as well; Théodore, who had been involved with a woman outside of prison, excused himself by saying that Vautrin was no longer with him, and exclaimed, 'Ah! if I want to live, it is now more for you than for her.'[55] Intimate ties, especially those between lovers, were seen as the strongest links in the underground criminal network that many were certain existed in Paris.

As a way to counter this threat, reformers recommended isolating prisoners from each other so as to avoid the establishment of close relationships. According to historian Patricia O'Brien, the desire to prevent 'promiscuous' sexual behaviour was 'one of the most potent arguments in favor of the single cell'.[56] Already in July 1843, similar fears regarding the morality of female prostitutes, no doubt influenced by public-hygiene expert Parent-Duchâtelet's discussion of 'tribadism' in his 1836 treatise on Parisian prostitutes, had resulted in a police ruling that made it illegal for prostitutes not housed in brothels to share an apartment.[57] In making such rulings and recommendations, contemporaries hoped not only to prevent the establishment of close relationships between prisoners or prostitutes, but also to prevent the more dangerous consequence of such relationships: the loss of social distinctions. For Joséphine Mallet, prison was dangerous because 'prisoners of different categories of the [prison] population sleep, work, in short live and pervert each other in common'.[58] The potential for prison relationships to dissolve social distinctions led reformers to denounce the communal regime as 'a danger that is immoral to allow . . . any longer'.[59]

In writings concerning prison society, homosexuality signified the blurring of categories and the permeability of boundaries. A positive view of prison society, one in which bonds between individuals were based on love, respect, and mutual aid, was opposed in reformers' writings by a fear that such a society existed only as an ideal, and that attempts to reorganize the social structure could lead to the complete dissolution of distinctions. While the theme of same-sex relationships that ran throughout these writings did not have exclusively negative connotations (for example, reformers revealed mixed attitudes toward upward social mobility), these writings ultimately convey a fear that social mobility, and the permeability of social categories that it implied, could lead to the disintegration of social boundaries. One reformer, in explaining how prisoners were able to escape surveillance and become intimate, highlighted this fear of mobility. He argued that prisoners, under careful watch most of the time, took advantage of moments of transition, for example in moving from the prison to the courtyard, to form intimate relationships. It was thus these moments of, 'general comings and goings when there is always a little confusion', that posed the most danger.[60] By the late 1840s, in a climate of growing political and economic unrest, mobility had become increasingly suspect.

TOWARD THE DEVIANT 'HOMOSEXUAL': MAINTAINING THE CATEGORIES OF BOURGEOIS LIFE

After 1848, the fear regarding the consequences of reconfiguring the social order that permeated writings on prison reform became more pronounced. At the same time, even limited acceptance of permeable boundaries, and of gender and sexual confusion, virtually disappeared. With the establishment of its new moral order, Second Empire society encouraged, indeed demanded, the eradication of confused boundaries as a precondition for social stability. As medical experts such as Ambroise Tardieu sought to categorize and define same-sex sexuality, legal experts increasingly linked homosexuality to criminality in an exclusively negative sense. During this period, male homosexuality in particular, linked increasingly to the crime of blackmail, served as a symbol of social disorder. Representations of male homosexuality during this time also reveal a hardening of class and gender boundaries.

In 1857 a respected expert in legal medicine, Ambroise Tardieu, published his *Etude médico-légale sur les attentats aux mœurs*, a highly influential and extremely popular work based on his observations as legal expert in numerous rape cases. According to historian Antony Copley, it was 'one of the most widely read, and indeed just about the only work of its kind available on the subject of homosexuality until the 1920s'.[61] Tardieu was the first in France to devote considerable attention to homosexual rape.[62] While the French penal code specified that rape could involve persons of either sex, earlier studies had devoted almost no attention to homosexual rape since their authors believed that sodomy rarely left physical traces.[63] Tardieu, in contrast, argued that practitioners of sodomy could and should be identified, since, in his opinion, a penchant for sodomy (which was not illegal) indicated a tendency to engage in criminal behaviour. Examining the genital organs of prisoner after prisoner, Tardieu sought to transform, with his categories and system of signs, a sexuality that had seemed fluid during the July Monarchy into one whose definitions and boundaries were fixed and clearly observable.

During the July Monarchy exclusive homosexual preference was rarely portrayed. (Vautrin was in this sense an exception.) During the Second Empire, in contrast, representations of 'bisexuality' virtually disappear. Tardieu's analysis is interesting in part for its attempt to transform what we might call 'bisexual' preference into homosexual preference. Tardieu attempted to separate out, among men who had sexual relationships with people of both sexes, those who were, in Tardieu's words, 'true pederasts'.[64] To make this distinction, Tardieu implicitly differentiated between desire and behaviour. While he portrayed sexual behaviour as fluid (for example, it was possible, according to his schema, to have sex with both men and women), he depicted desire as exclusively heterosexual or homosexual in nature. While the *tante*, for example, sought homosexual relationships under certain circumstances (for example, to fulfil a need for companionship in prison, or to earn money through prostitution), his primary affective object, was, according to Tardieu, a woman. The 'true' pederast, in contrast, even if married or 'associated with women of easy virtue', had a preference for men.[65] In drawing such distinctions, Tardieu began to move away from the notion of a continuum of sexual desire, represented in earlier sources by the hermaphrodite, and emphasized instead the dominance of either 'homosexual' or 'heterosexual' desire within individuals.

The further division of 'true' pederasts into the categories of 'active' or 'passive' was, for Tardieu, the key to their successful identification by legal authorities. While Tardieu recognized that some men moved back and forth between roles, he believed that most men had a preference for one or the other, and could thus be characterized as predominantly either 'active' or 'passive'. He argued that if earlier observers had been unable to find definite physical signs indicating sexual activity between men, it was because they had not established such clear categories. He maintained that, 'the absence of positive signs is a very rare exception; and I am very inclined to think that if we have believed and proclaimed the opposite, it is because we have constantly neglected to make an important distinction between pederasts. . . . However, and this is a capital point in this study, pederasty encompasses in some sense two roles.'[66] Tardieu exhorted his colleagues and readers, 'never to lose sight of this capital difference'.[67]

413

Tardieu was not interested in the causes of homosexual desire. While he hazarded the hypothesis that homosexual preference was the result of extreme cynicism and debauchery, he was more interested in classifying and naming male pederasts than in understanding their behaviour.[68] This strong desire to classify and to develop a complete system of signs can be considered a counter-measure to what he regarded as one of the greatest dangers of same-sex sexuality, the disorder it created through the blurring of boundaries.

For Tardieu, one of the most troubling aspects of homosexuality was that it often involved a confusion, or even reversal, of class positions. Tardieu was shocked by the existence of sexual contact between men 'apparently distinguished by education and fortune', and those characterized by 'profound degradation, [and] revolting filth'.[69] Like his contemporary, the novelist Ernest Feydeau, who in *La Comtesse de Chalis, ou les mœurs du jour*, described a scandalous alliance between a courtesan and an aristocratic woman, Tardieu saw homosexual behaviour as contributing to a dangerous blurring of class distinctions that threatened public order.[70] Although sodomy was not a crime in France at this time, the association frequently made between same-sex sexuality and confused boundaries contributed to the development of the idea that same-sex sexuality was an important pre-condition to crime, and eventually, a type of crime in itself.[71] Writers such as Tardieu were not necessarily motivated, in making such associations, by a desire to 'criminalize' homosexual behaviour. Rather, decreased tolerance for the blurring of social categories made same-sex sexuality seem dangerous.

This threat to order was most often expressed by linking male homosexuality to the crime of blackmail. According to police descriptions, blackmailers typically operated in pairs. One of the blackmailers enticed an apparently wealthy man to engage in homosexual sex in a public place. When the sex act had begun, the other appeared, disguised as a police officer, and invoked Article 330 of the penal code, which outlawed acts of public exhibitionism. The victim, fearing a public scandal, would agree to pay the 'police officers' in order to avoid a public scandal.

In this blackmail scenario, criminality and transgression are linked to homosexuality, an association that became more frequent over the course of the nineteenth century. The central aspect of Article 330, according to legal theorists of the 1830s, was the transgression of the boundary between public and private, since it was the *public* nature of acts regulated by Article 330, rather than the acts themselves, that made them criminal: 'Hidden, they have not the least criminal aspect; public, they become crimes.'[72] During the Second Empire, this transgression of the public–private divide was increasingly conflated with male homosexuality. As a result, by the 1880s, Article 330 was identified exclusively with male homosexual activity. According to one commentator, 'Sodomy, attempted or consummated in a place open to the public constitutes the crime of public offence against decency.'[73] At the same time, blackmail was also increasingly linked to male homosexuality. Carlier, chief of the *service des mœurs* in the 1860s, wrote in his *Les Deux prostitutions*, a study of male and female prostitution in Paris, that most serious blackmail operations involved male homosexuals: 'It is especially in the matter of pederasty that the offence takes on the most odious nature and acquires worrisome proportions.'[74]

The association made between same-sex sexuality, criminality, and the transgression of boundaries conveyed the idea that sexual relationships between men posed a danger to the social order. In the blackmail scenario, this danger was indicated in part by the confusion between criminal and police officer (both in that the blackmailer disguised himself as a police officer, and in that the person being blackmailed believed the officer would accept a bribe). Blackmail also entailed a transgression of the boundaries between public and private life, since the victim agreed to be blackmailed because he feared the scandal that would result from his private sexual desires becoming public knowledge. Such a scandal was described in Jules Méry's 1859 novel *Monsieur Auguste*.[75] In this novel, Auguste, a man with exclusive homosexual preferences, attempts to win the beautiful Louise in marriage as an act of revenge against Octave, who has spurned his companionship. Just when it seems as if Auguste will be able to carry out his plan, an ex-lover who possesses a number of letters written to him by Auguste enters the scene and threatens Auguste with blackmail. In this scene, the dangers of the public realm of economic self-interest (the blackmailer hoped to exchange the letters for money) are brought into the sphere of the home, and there is a general role reversal among the characters. Auguste collapses, helpless and in tears, while a female friend of the family stands up to the blackmailer, like a man, and chases him away. The collapsing of boundaries between public and private and the concomitant reversal of gender roles was so dangerous that it sent Louise into a life-threatening nervous crisis. Needless to say, the wedding was called off.

The blackmail scene serves to bring about Auguste's banishment from the family grouping. While the author justified the publication of the novel by arguing that it could serve as a warning to fathers of families, alerting them to the necessity of ensuring that prospective sons-in-law were what they appeared to be, the real warning here was for those who were tempted to cross boundaries of class, gender, or sexuality.[76] Scandal and ostracism were presented as the punishments awaiting any man who, by engaging in homosexual sex, endangered the boundaries of public and private, and thus called into question the organization of society as a whole. The message of such accounts was that transgression inevitably led to disaster. For even if blackmail did not result in public scandal, it could ruin a man by depleting his fortune, an event that also led to social disorder; since the blackmailer was always of a lower social class than his victims, blackmail transferred wealth across class lines.

Public scandal and financial ruin, the consequences of homosexual sex, could only be avoided if homosexuals created and maintained a way of differentiating between public and private life, something done in heterosexual relationships through the use of gender distinctions. Police-Inspector Canler, for example, related the story of a wealthy older man who was not vulnerable to blackmail because the life he and his young lover led reinforced the divide between public and private through the manipulation of gender roles. In public, they appeared to be two sober male friends; in private, their roles replicated those of a heterosexual couple:

[the older man] spent his days shut up in his apartment, where his young man, dressed as a woman, was occupied in some type of needlework, either embroidery or tapestry. At the dinner hour, the so-called nephew put on again his masculine attire, and, the meal finished, the two inseparables got in their carriage to go to the café.[77]

These two men, already distinguished by a difference in age, used distinctions based on gender to reinforce boundaries of public and private. In so doing, they succeeded, in Canler's eyes at least, in protecting themselves from the threat of blackmail. They were all the more successful because they belonged to the same social class. Thus while establishing certain distinctions within the couple (male/female and public/private) diminished some of the danger associated with male homosexuality, crossing class boundaries would render such precautions null.

According to a variety of sources from the Second Empire, men risked social ostracism and financial ruin if they crossed lines of class, gender, and sexuality. Women, however, were faced with death, damnation, or imprisonment. In the 1870 novel *Madem-*

oiselle Giraud, ma femme, for example, Paule Giraud marries Adrien, but refuses to consummate the marriage, and continues instead a sexual relationship with her friend from convent school, Madame de Blangy. By the end of the novel, Paule repents, but only just before expiring from a nervous disorder. Madame de Blangy is drowned by Adrien on the fashionable Normandy coast. In *La Comtesse de Chalis, ou les mœurs du jour*, the title character neglects her family and instead pursues a life of pleasure that leads her to meet Florence, a courtesan with whom she begins an affair. When the countess's husband learns of this scandal, he commits his wife to a sanatorium. Shortly thereafter, he and her two children die, presumably as a result of her transgression. In *Mademoiselle Giraud* homosexuality signalled a disruption of the gendered order of the family, and in particular a challenge to male dominance. In *La Comtesse de Chalis* class distinctions were called into question. In describing her desire to meet Florence, the Countess stressed the similarity between women of high society and those who, like Florence, belonged to the margins of this society, saying, 'when I found myself in front of her, I couldn't resist the desire to try a little bit and find out what kind of woman she was . . . there is almost no difference between her and . . . and us.'[78] For women such as the countess or Paule Giraud, meant to be guardians of the family and of morality, homosexual love was disastrous, since it upset the gendered and class-based order upon which society was supposed to be based.

While the theme of male homosexuality, linked increasingly to crime, was used to warn against transgressing social boundaries, representations of lesbianism functioned in the literature of the Second Empire in a more ambiguous fashion.[79] They served as a vehicle for both a critique and a reification of the existing social order. While 'honest' middle-class women endangered themselves and their families by becoming sexually involved with other women, the lesbian love affairs of women who were already outside the family, such as prostitutes, were portrayed more sympathetically, even considered a 'natural' reaction to a life spent almost exclusively in the society of men.[80] Stories of courtesans who turned to women as a result of prolonged contact with men's ambitions and self-interest became an extremely popular theme in literature during this period.

Théodore de Banville's *Les Parisiennes de Paris* (1867), for example, relates the story of Lucille, a virtuous girl of the popular classes whose mother sends her across the street to buy milk.[81] In this cautionary tale concerning the dangers presented to women when they enter the public and commercial spaces of the city, Lucille never arrives at the milk merchant; instead she finds herself 'in a dressing gown of quilted silk . . . in an apartment hung with gilded paper. . . . Sitting all around her, [were] false gentlemen.' She has become, in short, a courtesan. Despite Lucille's success in the *demi-monde*—voyaging to London and Baden, stopping at all the Parisian hot spots of this milieu—she is disgusted by the life she leads. Then she meets a woman:

a sister, a friend, and this one wouldn't flee; she was a woman like herself, a victim like herself, a martyr dedicated to the crowd, to champagne. . . . They met and recognized each other. 'So, since love is a lie, let's try friendship, let's live together. Never separating, hand in hand, jealous, wild, faithful, with a friendship that will be the hatred and shame of everyone!'[82]

In their fierce loyalty and their desire to escape their status as objects of men's desires, Lucille and her 'friend' resemble the tribades described earlier by Parent-Duchâtelet in his study of Parisian prostitution.[83] Yet while the women he described in 1836 spent, for all we know, long and happy lives together, in accounts from the Second Empire, women like Lucille who looked for love with other women were destined for disappointment, death, or damnation. Lucille's lover, Paule, 'did not . . . know how to love Lucille' and left her.[84] Lucille, disillusioned by this loss, returns to her mother, with the milk, but also with the conclusion that 'life is a horrible thing and . . . men are cruel beasts'.[85] Such accounts were meant to symbolize the moral decay and corruption of a society consumed by self-interest.

While earlier novels had also used the theme of same-sex sexuality as part of a larger critique of self-interest, in works from the Second Empire, this theme becomes more negative and pessimistic, often expressed by reference to the brutality, especially the sexual brutality, of men. In these later accounts, men are almost universally condemned for treating women as no more than objects to be used to satisfy their own desires and ambitions. In *Mademoiselle Giraud*, a critique of male dominance is linked to the issue of spousal rape. Paule's love for Madame de Blangy gave her the courage to defy her husband's wishes; after repeatedly refusing her husband entry to her bedroom, Paule proposed that they live together as brother and sister. Adrien refused, but Paule was adamant, and asked him to leave her alone, saying, 'and if you have pretensions of being a husband, at least, I imagine, you would not want to be a tyrant'.[86] Adrien proved that he was, in fact, capable of violence, when he attempted that same night to rape Paule and later forced her to leave France for Algeria. Adrien's actions and Paule's condemnation of male tyranny and brutality, constitute a theme in the novel that is common to most, if not all, representations of lesbianism during this period. Lucille, for example, recounts that the men she associated with talked incessantly of 'the names of women they had overpowered, worn out, and brutalized for money'.[87] The narrator of *La Comtesse de Chalis* concluded that an affair between women of different social classes was only possible in a society in which men lacked the 'cult of women' and 'knew only venal love'.[88] This theme reappeared in Zola's work, most specifically in *Nana* (1880), but also in *La Curée* (1871); in both cases, it served as an integral part of Zola's condemnation of the excessive focus on material greed that he believed characterized the Second Empire. In these accounts, lesbianism was a sign for, and symbol of, the violent underside of bourgeois rule, a theme that was further developed by decadent writers.

This critique, however, was ultimately a limited one, since these accounts conveyed the message that escape from the existing social order was not only disastrous, but impossible. Adrien married Paule Giraud, for example, because he wanted to escape the demands of social convention. Despite meeting many women who were more 'suitable' in that they belonged to the same social class as he, Adrien insisted on marrying a woman without a dowry. While Adrien ultimately succeeded in eliminating the female couple, and by extension the implied threat to male dominance that they posed, it was at the expense of his own future. Adrien's brush with lesbianism left him a broken man; no longer a husband and condemned never to be a father, Adrien was denied a place in the social order. Likewise Charles, the narrator of *La Comtesse de Chalis* ruined a brilliant academic career when he got involved with the countess. In their attempts to escape the restrictions placed upon them by participating by the maintenance of bourgeois power, these characters found not the harmonious love of a hermaphrodite, but an infinite abyss, the destruction of the social order. Baudelaire's condemnation, in his poem 'Femmes damnées', of Delphine and Hippolyte, women who wanted to avoid the 'cruel kisses' of a 'stupid fiancé', applies equally well to all who attempted, in literary works from the Second Empire, to escape male brutality, self-interest, or ambition.[89] While according to Christine Buci-Glucksmann, the lesbian constituted for Baudelaire a symbol of 'heroic protest against . . . modernity', the price of that protest was high.[90] As with Delphine and Hippolyte, those who attempted to change or deny the existing social and economic order would not only fail, but would be banished:

> Far from the living, condemned wanderers,
> Run like wolves across the deserts;
> Make your destiny, disordered souls,
> And flee the infinite that you carry inside![91]

Any attempt to flee the demands imposed upon individual freedom by the need to maintain the social order led to exile, chaos, and the destruction of society altogether.

Whereas writers of the July Monarchy had hoped to create a new social order based on love and harmony, and expressed this desire through the image of the hermaphrodite, Second-Empire writers, despite the critique of self-interest that they shared with their predecessors, seemed to conclude that no alternatives were possible, since any attempt at social reorganization would result in the complete dissolution of society. Second-Empire sources clearly warned that crossing boundaries of gender, class, and sexuality led to disorder, that unity was a chimera, and that social stability depended upon respecting distinctions and divisions in society. Those who wished to live and prosper in society had to respect the boundaries and distinctions that were part of bourgeois life. As Charles, the narrator of *La Comtesse de Chalis*, concluded, somewhat sadly, the stability of the social order itself depended upon respecting such distinctions:

Virility is every day, all one's life, creating two parts of one's time: the first for one's family, the second for society. It's not enjoyable, perhaps; but it is on this condition alone that we become and remain a people.[92]

CONCLUSION

According to Peter Brooks, the sexualized body functions in modern narratives as 'a source and a locus of meanings', and sexual desire constitutes, in these same narratives, 'the desire to know'.[93] By extension, the sexualized body constitutes a privileged site for the elaboration of discourses that seek to define and make comprehensible a definition not only of the self, but of the social order as well. French society in mid-century, shaken by political revolution and industrialization, was undergoing an economic, social, and political transformation. With old-regime barriers to upward social mobility gone, contemporaries during this period attempted to elaborate a new model of the social hierarchy, one that could incorporate movement while at the same time ensure stability. Abandoning categories of blood and birth as a means of creating and maintaining social distinctions, they sought new ways of describing difference. Due in large part to its ability to naturalize difference, gender became, as Joan Scott has argued, a primary means of 'legitimiz[ing] and construct[ing] social relationships', during the nineteenth century.[94] Working in close conjunction with, and as an integral part of, discourses on gender difference, representations of sexuality produced during this time were used to elaborate and define divisions within the social order, divisions of male and female, rich and poor, public and private.

A common theme in sources from both the July Monarchy and the Second Empire was a perceived conflict between self-interest and social unity; excess, in the form of either extreme individualism or a lack of social differentiation, was considered dangerous. Throughout this period, the perfect balance of individualism and social unity was expressed through the metaphor of a balance of 'masculine' and 'feminine' qualities. In the aftermath of the French Revolution, the idea that a stable society must be based on distinct gender roles became a central aspect of French culture.[95] As an organizing principle, gender provided a means of reconciling conflicting impulses of liberty and order, since it could allow for upward social mobility and limited individualism (in a realm defined as 'masculine') while at the same time incorporating a notion (in the realm of the 'feminine') of stability, timelessness, and community.[96]

Definitions of sexuality played an important role in the articulation of this gender-based model, since, as Robert Nye has argued, heterosexual attraction reinforced the binary division of genders that was considered the necessary foundation of society.[97] Whereas during the July Monarchy it was possible to represent gender in a somewhat fluid manner, during the Second Empire distinctions based on gender became more clearly elaborated. The categorization of sexuality that accompanied this transition paved the way for the elaboration of the 'homosexual' as a type outside of heterosexuality. According to Eve Sedgwick, the invention of the homosexual as a clearly-defined type was also the invention of 'a new and immensely potent tool that had become available for the manipulation of every form of power that refracted through the gender system—that is, in European society, of virtually every form of power'.[98] The homosexual, as someone who threatened the gender balance that was at the basis of all other social distinctions, thus became a symbol of disorder. The gradual definition and exclusion of the 'homosexual' over the course of the nineteenth century can be seen, from this perspective, as a counterpart to the creation of bourgeois economic, political, and social hegemony.[99]

Yet just as the creation of a bourgeois order was the result of much conflict and struggle, the development of the 'homosexual' as a sign for deviance was the result of a specific historical evolution. Both processes were uneven, subject to negotiation, and both were inextricably linked.[100] In the process of replacing one model of the social hierarchy with another, there arose an opportunity for negotiating the meaning of 'difference', an opportunity that created a possibility of imagining the social order differently, and of imagining same-sex sexuality in a more fluid, and more positive, manner.[101] Rather than reject change, writers such as Gautier embraced it, and explored its many possibilities. Théodore/Madeleine's sentiment in his/her parting letter, 'to remain in the same spot is to move backwards', would be shared by many who believed that questioning received ideas concerning categories of class, gender, and sexuality was a necessary component of social change.[102]

Notes

1. Maxine du Camp, *Théophile Gautier*, trans. J. E. Gordon (1893; repr., Freeport, NY: Books for Libraries Press, 1971), 156.
2. Théophile Gautier, *Mademoiselle de Maupin* (Paris: Garnier-Flammarion, 1966), 212. On the hermaphrodite as a symbol of perfection in romantic literature see Michel Crouzet, '*Mademoiselle de Maupin* ou l'Eros romantique', *Romantisme*, 8 (1974), 2–21; Lucienne Frappier-Mazur, 'La Structure symbolique de *Séraphîta* et le mythe de l'androgyne', *L'Année Balzacienne 1973*, 235–77. For a more negative nineteenth-century view of the hermaphrodite see Michel Foucault (ed.), *Herculine Barbin: Being the Recently Discovered Memoirs of a Nineteenth-Century Hermaphrodite*, trans. Richard McDougall (New York: Pantheon Books, 1980).
3. Gautier, *Mademoiselle de Maupin*, 195. For an interesting comparison, see Dennis Allen's discussion of Oscar Wilde's use of homosexuality to indicate the dissolution of the distinction between subject and object in *The Picture of Dorian Gray* in Dennis W. Allen, *Sexuality in Victorian Fiction* (Norman, Okla.: University of Oklahoma Press, 1994).
4. du Camp, *Théophile Gautier*, 155.

5. Lillian Faderman argues that a desire to shock the bourgeoisie was responsible for the popularity of lesbian themes in nineteenth-century French literature. See Lillian Faderman, *Surpassing the Love of Men: Romantic Friendship and Love between Women from the Renaissance to the Present* (London: The Women's Press, 1981), 264.

6. Richard Terdiman, 'Class Struggles in France', in Denis Hollier (ed.), *A New History of French Literature* (Cambridge, Mass.: Harvard University Press, 1989), 707.

7. *Littré medical* (1866), quoted in Brigitte Lhomond, 'Between Man and Woman: The Character of the Lesbian', in Rommel Mendès-Leite and Pierre-Olivier de Busscher (eds.), *Gay Studies from the French Cultures: Voices from France, Belgium, Brazil, Canada and the Netherlands*, 65.

8. Robert A. Padgug, 'Sexual Matters', in Kathy Peiss and Christina Simmons (eds.), *Passion and Power: Sexuality in History* (Philadelphia: Temple University Press, 1989), 22.

9. Arsène Houssaye, *Les confessions: Souvenirs d'un demi-siècle* (Paris: Librairie Dentu, n.d.), ii:13.

10. The popularity of some of these themes in romantic literature is discussed in Mario Praz, *The Romantic Agony*, 2nd edn., trans. Angus Davidson (London: Oxford University Press, 1951).

11. On the *lorette* see Lucette Czyba, 'Paris et la lorette', in Roger Bellet (ed.), *Paris au XIXe siècle: Aspects d'un mythe littéraire* (Lyon: Presses universitaires de Lyon, 1984), 107–22.

12. For an analysis of how this same conflict was played out during the French Revolution in images of the family see Lynn Hunt, *The Family Romance of the French Revolution* (Berkeley: University of California Press, 1992).

13. Gautier, *Mademoiselle de Maupin*, 68.

14. Ibid. 113. In a very interesting article, Michael Warner discusses how the problem of establishing boundaries between 'self' and 'other' was played out in the writings of Henry Thoreau through the use of metaphoric sexual imagery, and links Thoreau's conflicted attitude toward the possibility of 'losing' the self within the other to the paradox of liberalism, with its need to establish difference while professing sameness. Unlike Thoreau, however, d'Albert does not wish to retain the self/other distinction, but wants to move beyond it altogether (a state symbolized by the hermaphrodite). This difference reflects, perhaps, a difference in national attitudes towards the relationship between the individual and society. In general, the French novels reveal a great unease with individualism, and favour instead a corporate vision of social organization. See Michael Warner, 'Thoreau's Bottom', *Raritan*, 11/3 (Dec. 1992), 53–79.

15. Ibid. 169.

16. Honoré de Balzac, *La Fille aux yeux d'or* (Paris: Garnier-Flammarion, 1988), 220.

17. Balzac, *La Fille*, 209.

18. Ibid. 209, 225.

19. Ibid. 237.

20. My interpretation of Pacquita differs from that of Camille Paglia, who sees her as the embodiment of 'Paris and its vices'. See Camille Paglia, *Sexual Personae: Art and Decadence from Nefertiti to Emily Dickinson* (London and New Haven: Yale University Press, 1990), 395.

21. These characters either possess the genitalia of both sexes, or they engage in sexual relations with both men and women.

22. For the sake of convenience, I am using the term 'bisexual', placing it in quotation marks, to describe a person who had sexual and/or affective relationships with both men and women. Although both writers and readers during the July Monarchy were aware that a person could have lovers of both sexes, they did not use the term 'bisexual', and would not have recognized it as a category of either sexual behaviour or identity as we do today.

23. Isabelle de Courtivron has argued that the gender confusion in *Mademoiselle de Maupin* and *La Fille aux yeux d'or* reveals a desire of 'eluding the trappings of the societally defined "masculine role"'. I am building in part on this insight, and widening its implications, arguing that fulfilling this masculine role included meeting the demands of market-based upward social mobility. See de Courtivron, 'Weak Men and Fatal Women: The Sand Image', in George Stambolian and Elaine Marks (eds.), *Homosexualities and French Literature* (Ithaca: Cornell University Press, 1979), 218.

24. Gautier, *Mademoiselle de Maupin*, 212.

25. Latouche, Hyacinthe-Joseph-Alexandre-Thabaude de, *Fragoletta* (1829, repr. in *Œuvres complètes de H. de Latouche*, new edn., Paris: Michel Lévy, frères, 1867), 243.

26. Ibid. 243–4. When d'Hauteville responds to Adriani's advances, Adriani jumps away and starts to kiss violently d'Hauteville's sister. The sister also establishes a somewhat ambiguous relationship to the hermaphrodite, who appears to her as a man, but acts like a woman, and uses shared interest in 'female' pursuits such as needlework to seduce her.

27. Honoré de Balzac, *Séraphita* (Paris: Berg International Editeurs, 1986).

28. Honoré de Balzac, *Vautrin in Théâtre de H. de Balzac* (Paris: D. Giraud and J. Dagneau, 1853), 112.

29. Charges of homosexuality could just as easily be used against a public figure to ruin his reputation. For an example of this, see Bonnie G. Smith, 'The Rise and Fall of Eugène Lerminier', *French Historical Studies* XII, 3 (Spring 1982), 377–400.

30. Gautier, *Mademoiselle de Maupin*, 375.

31. Latouche, *Fragoletta*, 342.

32. Camille Paglia describes the relationship between brother and sister, both of whom are sleeping with Pacquita as 'displaced incest'; she considers the relationship between Minna and Wilfrid in *Séraphita* incestuous as well (Paglia, *Sexual Personae*, 400, 403). According to Mario Praz, the theme of incest was popular in romantic literature (Praz, *Romantic Agony*, 109–10). While I have not developed this theme, it is relevant in that incest is one way of imagining bonds between individuals in society, as Lynn Hunt demonstrated in *The Family Romance*. For the mid-nineteenth century, Naomi Schor discusses the theme of incest in the work of George Sand, and links Sand's rejection of incest after June 1848 to an increased concern with establishing gender differentiation. See Naomi Schor, 'Reading Double: Sand's Difference', in Nancy K. Miller (ed.), *The Poetics of Gender* (New York: Columbia University Press, 1986), 249–69. Following Schor's analysis, then, the relatively greater acceptance of incest in literature before June 1848 is yet another example of greater tolerance for blurred boundaries during this period.

33. Roland Barthes, *S/Z*, trans. Richard Miller (New York: Hill and Wang, 1974), 90.

34. Ibid. The narrator offers to tell the marquise the story of the old man in exchange for an invitation to her home. Barthes interprets this, correctly I think, as an offer to exchange the story for sex.

35. Honoré de Balzac, *Sarrasine*, in *La Comédie Humaine* (1844: repr., Paris: Les Bibliophiles de l'Originale, 1966), 10: 114. My analysis here is different from that of Barthes, who sees in Zambinella's desire for a pure love, and in the reaction of the marquise to the story of the castrato, an 'equivocation', an attempt to be 'exile[d]', in one case, or to 'retreat', in the other, from sex. Barthes, *S/Z*, 161, 212.

36. Ibid. 106.

37. Ibid. 120.

38. On prison reform in nineteenth-century France see Michel Foucault, *Discipline and Punish: The Birth of the Prison*, trans. Alan Sheridan (New York: Vintage Books, 1979); Michelle Perrot (ed.), *L'Impossible Prison* (Paris: Seuil, 1980); Patricia O'Brien, *The Promise of Punishment: Prisons in Nineteenth-Century France* (Princeton: Princeton University Press, 1982).

39. A. Cerfberr de Médelsheim, *La Vérité sur les prisons: Lettres à M. de Lamartine* (Paris: Mansut, 1844), 24.

40. Ibid.

41. Josephine Mallet, *Les Femmes en prison: Causes de leurs chutes, moyens de les relever. Dédié à S.A.R. Madame la princesse Adélaide d'Orléans* (Paris: Moulins, 1843), 196–7.

42. Quoted in H. B. Irving, *Studies of French Criminals of the Nineteenth Century* (London: William Heinemann, 1901), 11.

43. Mallet, *Les Femmes en prison*, 196.

44. Médelsheim, *La Vérité*, 37.

45. Quoted in Irving, *Studies of French Criminals*, 11.

46. On the subject of Vautrin's 'homosexuality', in and outside of prison, see Philippe Berthier, 'Balzac du coté de Sodom', *L'Année Balzacienne 1979*, 147–77.

47. Honoré de Balzac, *Splendeurs et misères des courtisanes* (Paris: Garnier-Flammarion, 1968), 523.

48. Ibid. 521.

49. Ibid. 508, 555.

50. Ibid.

51. Mallet, *Les Femmes en prison*, 197.

52. Louis Chevalier, *Classes laborieuses et classes dangereuses à Paris, pendant la première moitié du XIXe siècle* (Paris: Librairie Générale Française, 1978).

53. Médelsheim, *La Vérité*, 24.

54. Canler, *Mémoires de Canler, ancien chef de la service de Sûreté*, 3rd edn. (Paris, J. Hetzel, n.d.), 99.

55. Balzac, *Splendeurs*, 545.

56. O'Brien, *The Promise of Punishment*, 94.

57. Alexandre-Jean-Baptiste Parent-Duchâtelet, *De La Prostitution dans la ville de Paris, considérée sous le rapport de l'Hygiène Publique, de la morale et de l'administration* (Paris: J-B Ballière, 1836). On prostitution in Paris see, Alain Corbin, *Les Filles de noce: Misère sexuelle et prostitution (19e et 20e siècle)* (Paris: Aubier-Montaigne, 1978), and Jill Harsin, *Policing Prostitution in Nineteenth-Century Paris* (Princeton: Princeton University Press, 1985).

58. Mallet, *Les Femmes en prison*, 148.

59. Médelsheim, *La Vérité*, 37.
60. Ibid. 41.
61. Antony Copley, *Sexual Moralities in France, 1780–1980: New Ideas on the Family, Divorce, and Homosexuality* (London: Routledge, 1989), 105.
62. J. P. Aron and Roger Kempf characterized this innovation as 'staggering', in their *La Bourgeoisie, le sexe et l'honneur* (Paris: Editions Complexe, 1984), 48.
63. Alphonse Devergie, *Médecine légale, théorique et pratique: Avec le texte et l'interprétation des lois relatives à la médecine légale*, revised and annotated by J. B. F. Dehaussy de Robécourt (Paris: J-B Ballière, 1836), i: 337.
64. Ambroise Tardieu, *Etude médico-légale sur les attentats aux mœurs*, 4th edn. (Paris: J-B Ballière et fils, 1862), 157.
65. Ibid. 202.
66. Ibid. 164.
67. Ibid. 165.
68. Ibid. 161.
69. Ibid. 162.
70. Ernest Feydeau, *La Comtesse de Chalis, ou les mœurs du jour* (Paris: Michel Lévy frères, 1868).
71. On the link between homosexuality and criminality in France, see Copley, *Sexual Moralities in France*, and Guy Hocquenghem, *Le Désir homosexuel*, 2nd edn. (Paris: Editions Universitaires, 1972).
72. Devergie, *Médicine-légale*, 334.
73. F. Brager, *Dictionnaire général de police administrative et judiciaire*, 2nd edn. (Paris, chez l'auteur, n.d.), i: 848.
74. F. Carlier, *Les deux prostitutions: Étude de pathologie sociale* (Paris: E. Dentu, 1887), 235.
75. Jules Méry, *Monsieur Auguste* (Paris: Librairie nouvelle, 1859).
76. Ibid. 1–2.
77. Canler, *Mémoires*, 268.
78. Feydeau, *La Comtesse*, 262.
79. Three studies of representations of lesbianism in nineteenth-century France with very different approaches are Jean-Pierre Jacques, *Les Malheurs de Sapho* (Paris: Grasset, 1981); Marie-Jo Bonnet, *Un Choix sans équivoque: Recherches historiques sur les relations entre femmes XVIe–XXe siècle* (Paris: Denoël, 1981), ch. 3; Joan DeJean, *Fictions of Sappho, 1546–1937* (Chicago: University of Chicago, 1989), ch. 3.
80. Elaine Marks notes that a sympathetic view of, or 'apology' for, lesbianism as a theme in modern French literature appeared first, and most fully, in the 1778 work 'Apologie de la secte anandryne'. See Elaine Marks, 'Lesbian Intertextuality', in Stambolian and Marks (eds.), *Homosexualities and French Literatures*, 359. For the late nineteenth century, see also Jacques, *Les Malheurs de Sapho*, 236–49.
81. Théodore de Banville, *Les Parisiennes de Paris*, new edn. (Paris: Michel Lévy, frères, 1867).
82. Ibid. 316–17.
83. Parent-Duchâtelet, *De la prostitution*.
84. De Banville, *Les Parisiennes*, 317.
85. Ibid. 317, 321.
86. Adolphe Belot, *Mademoiselle Giraud, ma femme* (1870; repr. Paris: Garnier, 1978), 94.

87. De Banville, *Les Parisiennes*, 319.
88. Feydeau, *La Comtesse*, 332, 331.
89. Charles Baudelaire, 'Femmes damnées (Delphine et Hippolyte)', *Les Fleurs du mal*, in *Œuvres complètes*, ed. Yves Florenne (Paris: Le Club Français du livre, 1966), i. 878.
90. Christine Buci-Glucksmann, 'Catastrophic Utopia: The Feminine as Allegory of the Modern', in Catherine Gallagher and Thomas Laqueur, *The Making of the Modern Body: Sexuality and Society in the Nineteenth Century* (Berkeley: University of California Press, 1987), 222.
91. Baudelaire, *Œuvres complètes*, i. 879.
92. Feydeau, *La Comtesse*, 334.
93. Peter Brooks, *Body Work: Objects of Desire in Modern Narrative* (Cambridge, Mass.: Harvard University Press, 1993), xii. 5.
94. Joan W. Scott, *Gender and the Politics of History* (New York: Columbia University Press, 1988), 46.
95. On the increased importance of a binary system of gender as a means to organize society during and after the French Revolution see Joan Landes, *Women and the Public Sphere in the Age of the French Revolution* (Ithaca, NY: Cornell University Press, 1988); Dorinda Outram, *The Body and the French Revolution: Sex, Class, and Political Culture* (New Haven: Yale University Press, 1989); Hunt, *The Family Romance*. On how this shift was constructed in medical and scientific discourses see Londa Schiebinger, *The Mind Has No Sex? Women in the Origins of Modern Science* (Cambridge: Harvard University Press, 1989); Thomas Laqueur, *Making Sex: Body and Gender from the Greeks to Freud* (Cambridge: Harvard University Press, 1990).
96. Among the many works that discuss the various meanings of 'masculine' and 'feminine' in nineteenth-century France are, Jean-Paul Aron (ed.), *Misérable et glorieuse: La Femme du XIXe siècle* (Paris: Fayard, 1980); Bonnie G. Smith, *Ladies of the Leisure Class: The Bourgeoises of Northern France in the Nineteenth Century* (Princeton: Princeton University Press, 1981); Scott, *Gender and the Politics of History*; Geneviève Fraisse and Michelle Perrot (eds.), *Histoire des femmes en occident: iv. Le XIXe siècle* (Paris: Plon, 1991).
97. Robert A. Nye, *Masculinity and Male Codes of Honor in Modern France* (New York: Oxford University Press, 1993).
98. Eve Kosofsky Sedgwick, *Between Men: English Literature and Male Homosocial Desire* (New York: Columbia University Press, 1985), 87.
99. Guy Hocquenghem has argued that capitalist society created both the 'homosexual', and the 'proletariat' in order to define its own limits. He dates this process from the 1830s. See Hocquenghem, *Le désir homosexuel*, 13. For Michel Foucault, the classification of sexuality was one component of the imposition of bourgeois rule in the nineteenth century. See Michel Foucault, *The History of Sexuality: i. An Introduction*, trans. Robert Hurley (New York: Vintage Books, 1980).
100. Likewise, in discussing the transformation in medical models of sexual differentiation, Thomas Laqueur has noted that the shift from a one-sex to a two-sex model was brought about through endless 'micro-confrontations', and that the 'play of difference never came to rest'. Laqueur, *Making Sex*, 193.
101. The work of Mikhail Bakhtin and of Richard Terdiman (himself strongly influenced by Bakhtin) have contributed greatly to my thinking on how this process of cultural negotiation might work. See M. M. Bakhtin, *The Dialogic*

Imagination: Four Essays, ed. M. Holquist, trans. C. Emerson and M. Holquist (Austin: Texas University Press, 1981); Richard Terdiman, *Discourse/Counter-Discourse: The Theory and Practice of Symbolic Resistance in Nineteenth-Century France* (Ithaca, NY: Cornell University Press, 1985).

102. Gautier, *Mademoiselle de Maupin*, 375.

15   Female Desires: The Meaning of World War II

Marilyn Lake

'I expressed a desire', confided a twenty-year-old teachers' college student to her diary in 1942, 'to silly Jack P. for a Yank boyfriend (Melb. & in fact all Austr. is swarming with them—since Xmas—& I felt I'd missed life, not having even met one—Else and I spoke to some one night in the dark of Swanston St. but didn't pick them up, as most girls do now.' A few weeks later she was pleased to record her own war victory: 'Anyway, I can tell my Grandchildren at least that during those momentous days when Austr. was rapidly accumulating thousands upon thousands of Yanks, when Melb. went bad, & every girl discussed her "pick-ups" I too had a little experience.'[1] The meaning of Australian women's experience during and immediately following World War II has been the subject of much historical writing, but I wish to suggest that the approach adopted by historians so far, by ignoring female subjectivity, has obscured significant aspects of women's experience. Most importantly, historians of World War II have generally failed to grasp the changing structure of femininity itself, the interplay of cultural forms and self-definition, and the way that changes in discourse were secured by the specificity of wartime conditions.

In studying the effects of war on the position of women in Australian society, historians have tended to measure the impact in terms of women's entry into the world of paid work. Within this framework, the experiences of women on the Australian home-front during World War II, and after, are usually represented as opportunities cruelly cancelled, doors closed, hopes and dreams dashed— one step forwards, two steps backwards. 'The expectations the war

Earlier versions of this paper were delivered to the 5th Annual Conference of the Stout Research Centre for the Study of New Zealand Society, History and Culture, 'A Warlike People? War in New Zealand Experience', 1–3 July 1988 and to the Melbourne Feminist History Conference, 28–9 May 1988. Reprinted with permission from *Australian Historical Studies*, 21/95 (Oct. 1990), 267–84.

had nurtured', observed Penelope Johnson in her study of the equal pay campaign, 'had not been realised'.[2]

In her path-breaking exploration of gender ideology in the *Australian Women's Weekly* Andree Wright observed in 1973:

Although some women welcomed the post-war chance to return to the home, other women wished to consolidate on their gains, and some might have been persuaded to do so had a magazine such as the *Weekly* taken the lead. But after the war the magazine refocused its attention on the traditional sphere of feminine interests, always following old trends, rather than innovating new ones.[3]

In her suggestion of a dichotomy between the old and the new, traditional femininity and modern gains, Wright expressed what would become a common understanding of women's position. Thus most women's experience of the post-war years is conceptualized as a retreat, a surrender, a return to old ways, familiar patterns, traditional roles. There is often an implied criticism of women's failure to consolidate their 'gains'. Instead, women went home. 'As the war was ending', wrote Anne Summers, 'old ideas about what was appropriate for women began to be reasserted.'[4] Or as Edna Ryan and Anne Conlon put it: 'After the war . . . many women surrendered their wartime jobs and returned to a domestic role.'[5] And in her study of plans for post-war housing Carolyn Allport reached the same conclusion: the end of the war saw 'the reassertion of the traditional role of women as mothers, housekeepers and child-minders'.[6]

The problem with these accounts of the reassertion of the 'traditional role' is that they fail to see the historically changing structure of femininity itself. I wish to argue that the equation of the 'feminine' with the 'traditional' in these accounts is highly misleading, in that it obscures the emergence, in the 1930s, of a new understanding of femininity, one which revolved around sexuality, sexual attractiveness and youthfulness. Furthermore, I would suggest that this reconceptualization of femininity was reinforced by women's experience of World War II.[7]

Femininity (and masculinity) are, as many feminist historians and theorists have pointed out, historical constructions, the products of diverse practices across a variety of sites or social domains— the work-place, the legislature, the schoolroom, the media. There is no one discrete 'sex role' dispensed by a master dramaturge, but rather competing, often conflicting, definitions of femininity. The task of the historian of women is, then, twofold: first, to identify the variety of discourses in force at any one time and second, to explain why particular groups of women, in particular historical circumstances, were more likely to respond to some representations of their identity and experience than others. I shall present my argument in four stages—first, a brief summary of the meaning of women's new work experiences during World War II; second, an exploration of the transformation of femininity in the 1930s and 1940s; third, a consideration of how the conduct of the war itself sexualized the Australian female population and finally, suggest how different groups of women understood their lives, and negotiated their experiences in terms of these developments. It is often argued that the main differentiator of women in these processes was class; I wish to point to the significance of age.

Australia's participation in World War II led to a widescale mobilization of 'manpower', which meant concerted efforts to woo, and then conscript, women into industrial labour. Faced with conflicting arguments from employers and trade unions about the desirable level of the wages of women in 'men's jobs', the Curtin Labor government established the Women's Employment Board (WEB) in 1942 to regulate the wages and conditions of those women doing men's work, for the 'duration' only. Numerous women benefited from the new guidelines, often receiving double the income of women who remained, stuck, in traditional female jobs, for example, in the textile and clothing industry. With higher wages, doing men's work and with male relatives away fighting, a number of women enjoyed a new sense of independence, self-reliance, and autonomy. Clarice McNamara writing in the *Labor Digest* in 1945 likened these women to 'the lion that tasted blood'.[8]

In doing men's jobs, women also demystified them and the operation of the wartime economy generated refreshing acknowledgment of female capability. As Judge Foster of WEB exclaimed:

To all of us it was an amazing revelation to see women who were yesterday working in beauty salons or who had not previously worked outside their own homes or who had come from the counters of retail stores or a dozen other industries rendered superfluous by war, who now stood behind mighty machines operating them with a skill and mastery that was little short of marvellous![9]

But rather than resulting in a blurring of gender distinctions, these transgressions prompted strenuous reaffirmations of sexual difference: 'When doing our job on munitions we don't neglect our appearance—but still keep our feminine charm by always having our Escapade lipstick with us'.[10] And in the process, femininity itself was being redefined as a sexual condition. Thus, I would argue, women were not so much pressured to return to old, traditional 'roles', as historians have usually asserted: rather they were invited to step into an alluring, exciting future. In place of the adventure of economic independence, women were offered the adventure of sexual romance.

The meaning of sexual difference and thus of femininity had been undergoing significant transformations during the decades preceding the outbreak of World War II. One new, modern, pervasive and invasive cultural form that played a prominent part in the construction of femininity in these years was advertising. Another was, of course, the cinema. The secret of the success of advertising, and the accompanying rise in consumerism, was its promise to secure sexual fulfilment and identity. Advertising simultaneously incited sexual desire and promised its gratification. To men it promised potency or power; to women sexual attractiveness or desirability. The advertising message was that femininity and masculinity could be secured through the purchase of commodities.

A number of historians have alluded briefly to the changing structure of femininity in the middle years of twentieth-century Australia. Jill Matthews in *Good and Mad Women* has pointed to a shift away from an understanding of femininity shaped by a populationist ideology, entailing a conception of woman as 'mother of the race', towards a femininity linked to the culture of 'permissive consumerism' in the 1950s.[11] Her later work on the British physical-culture movement has explored the modernizing of the female body in the interwar years. Leslie Johnson in a study of 'The Teenage Girl' has also identified a change: by the mid 1950s 'femininity became a question of glamour and charm'.[12] Rosemary Pringle in her study of secretaries has linked the replacement of the refined office wife by the 'sexy secretary' as the ideal secretary type in the 1950s to the changing structure of femininity.[13] A study of magazine advertisements between 1920 and 1950 enables us to identify more closely the ingredients of that charm and glamour, so central to 1940s and 1950s femininity, and to locate these discursive changes in the decades preceding the 1950s.

By the 1940s femininity was increasingly defined in terms of (hetero)-sexual attractiveness. One important dynamic in this process was the work of sexologists such as Sigmund Freud, Havelock Ellis, Marie Stopes, and Norman Haire. While much of their writing seemed to have the effect of locking women ever more tightly into sexual relationships with men, of stigmatizing the reluctant as 'frigid', as Sheila Jeffreys has suggested,[14] it also opened up a discursive space in which, as Ann Curthoys has argued with regard to Marion Piddington, women could argue for their own sexual rights, for their rights to sexual pleasure.[15] This 'sexualization of women', then, was profoundly ambiguous in its implications for women. In a heterosexual context, 'sexual freedom' might simply give new form and lend greater intensity to women's dependence on men. And yet it was a necessary advance. As Jill Matthews has observed of the physical-culture movement:

Here was a new and in some ways shocking attitude, which emphasised the role of wife and sexual partner, not mother, as the pinnacle of female ambition. Moreover it was an attitude that valued youth, and insisted upon woman's responsibility for her own life to the point of self-transformation and renewal if not self-creation. The argument that a woman must be fit and beautiful both for herself and in order to catch and keep a husband, as well as or instead of to raise healthy children, presented itself as the modern way . . .[16]

It was advertising's role to identify for women the means of their modern self-creation.

The task of advertisements, as Judith Williamson has pointed out, is to persuade the consumer of the differences between products that are essentially alike.[17] Advertisements directed at women between 1920 and 1950 argued that their product could more effectively secure 'feminine charm'. But as the years passed, the components of that charm were transformed. Woman's special charm, observed Ada Holman in *Everylady's Journal* in 1916 was 'grace and refinement'.[18] Advertisers agreed. In 1920 the promoters of 'Odo-ro-no' deodorant declared 'the loveliest charm a woman can have is daintiness'.[19] But by the late 1930s the prize for female consumers was 'sex-appeal'.[20] Femininity as an attribute of class distinction (emphasizing white hands, soft skin, refinement, daintiness, and other ladylike qualities) was succeeded by a sexualized femininity, democratically available (indeed, like voting in Australia, compulsory) for all women. These changes were symbolized in the emergence of a new social ritual in these years: the beauty contest. Opposing versions of femininity (those revolving around 'the mother of the race', for example), still jostled for attention, of course, but increasingly all femininities had to accommodate themselves to the modern emphasis on sexual allure. 'Wives should always be lovers too.' The capitulation to the new imperative is evident in the words of popular songs, but also in the words of women themselves as they struggled to negotiate competing demands. 'The husband of today wishes his wife to be a mother and a sweetheart and he is in his rights,' commented a woman in the 1940s.[21] A husband 'wishes to come home to a woman who is smart in appearance . . . not a back number', said another.[22]

In the visual representation of modern, up-to-date femininity in the advertisements of the interwar years the impact of Hollywood is clear as the image of woman surveying herself in a mirror is replaced by woman scrutinized by men. The male gaze is made explicit within the frame with the men positioned as subjects offering their judgements of women in speech balloons. There is, of course, continuity as well as change in these representations. Throughout the period women are constituted as objects to be looked at, as sights. It is clear, as Margaret Betterton has argued, that the visual has long been central to definitions of femininity.[23] As the woman in the advertisement for Schumann's Salts says, 'I know how essential it is to have an appearance.'[24] Thus all personal products in these decades promise an outcome of beauty, relieving women of 'unsightly' blotches, freckles, flesh, roughness of skin, mousy hair, or perspiration stains. Under this new regime the most unlikely products were found to have aesthetic dimensions, including tablets for period pain: Myzone tablets were called 'Beauty Tablets'. Betty Bright, modern business girl, kept her job with Myzone tablets, as her beauty was unspoiled by menstrual cramps.[25] Similarly, Siltex Sanitary Napkins were promoted as 'form-fitting, never betraying their presence even when worn with the closest clinging frocks and the lightest lingerie'.[26]

But the changes in the structure of femininity are perhaps more significant. By the 1930s it was essential not just to have an appearance, but to have a youthful appearance. Femininity was the 'charm of youth'. It is striking, given later developments and assumptions, that the earliest ads for face creams and similar products omitted considerations of age. Among the first to insist that beauty was youthful was Helena Rubinstein in promotions for her Valaze range of products: 'Pretty Women Die Twice. The rose dies in its fading, as well as its fall.'[27] In 1923 'Palmolive' was warning women to keep that 'schoolgirl complexion'.[28] By the 1930s, the promoters of Le Charme blackhead cream (for the removal of 'unsightly disfigurements') could announce: 'Remember that Youthfulness is a Social Necessity. Not a Luxury'.[29] And it was not sufficient to be young; one had to *look* young. For the woman/object appearances were all important, as an ad. for Schumann's Salts in 1933 made clear:

'How old Isobel looks'. Yes, she had heard that stinging remark and the bitter truth was all she could bear. She was young—as young as her friends, yet time and again, people whispered things that hurt her terribly. At last some kind person told her about P.B.S. Poisoned Blood Stream.[30]

One of the most striking transformations in the advertisements over twenty-five years is the change in visual codes from the woman gazing into mirrors of all shapes and sizes to the woman explicitly scrutinized by men. In the 1920s, the text reinforced the significance of the mirror: 'Do you look your best? Are you worried about your appearance? When you look in the mirror do you find your hair dull, brittle . . .?'[31] The mirror renders woman an object of vision to herself. Men's entry into the frame signifies an important shift as femininity is explicitly defined in terms of heterosexual desirability. Women are incited to be attractive, alluring, exciting— objects to men's positioning as subjects. Men look at women in the images and speak to and about them; women either look into men's eyes (in surrender) or avert their gaze. By the late 1930s women's bodies are being scrutinized, piece by piece, and they are increasingly rendered as palpable and physical, rather than merely aesthetic, objects: they become 'caressable', 'kissable' or offensively odorous. Their bodies are invested with the prized new quality of 'sex-appeal', guaranteed to the purchasers of the right product. The promoters of Sta-Blond Shampoo believed this quality could be measured by scientists: 'Recent scientific tests show that light fair-haired girls have 47 per cent more sex-appeal than the dark "Fairs".'[32] Sexual relations transgress the usual spatial barriers maintained by individuals. They enable a close-up view: so skin needed to be 'flawless'; teeth 'dazzlingly white'. But the proximity of bodies could offend senses other than sight. It was no longer sufficient for women to look right; they had to please men's nostrils. An absence of smell had to be purchased, as the promoters of Odo-Ro-No made clear in their story of Marion:

'Just the girl that I've been waiting for!' men thought when they first *saw* Marion. They'd cluster around for introductions but they'd rarely dance more than one dance. For though Marion carefully bathed and dressed, she neglected the simple precaution—and trusted her bath alone to keep her safe from underarm odour. Fatal Error![33]

By the late 1930s, representations of femininity—the new discourses on femininity—were increasingly an incitement to sexual pleasure, which in turn was constructed as excitement, adventure, and danger: 'Fair Girls Ought to be Doubly Careful'; 'Every Fair Girl Should Try Everything Once'.[34] Femininity was beginning to cast off its passivity as the logic of the incitement to pleasure took its course. Women take to the dance floor or embrace in passionate kisses. The bodies move. Lipstick brands proliferated in the 1930s and 1940s, promising lips that were 'seductive' and 'provokingly appealing'. A tension becomes apparent between women's positioning as sexual objects and their constitution as sexual subjects. The image of an active engagement in sexual pleasure (the strenuous kiss) is qualified by the caption that advises 'romance comes to the mouth that's kissable'. But the incitement to action becomes more insistent. Savage lipsticks offered 'new, more stirring lip colour . . . that stirs excitement for lips that wear it . . . all evening . . . until . . .!' Tattoo lipsticks had five South Sea Shades 'each aglow with reckless, red adventure'.[35] The background images of palm trees beckon women to try exotic, foreign pleasures.

That thousands of Australian women did try foreign pleasures in the 1940s in the form of sexual relationships with American servicemen was well recognized. Women's seemingly unrestrained sexual activity provoked responses as diverse as feminist campaigns, Vice Squad raids, Christian warnings, Albert Tucker's censorious series of paintings 'Images of Modern Evil', physical violence between Australian and American servicemen and the well-known 'Australian' joke that 'the trouble with the Yanks is that they are overpaid, oversexed and over here'.[36]

War, it is clear, is a gendering activity.[37] War restructures gender relations in ways that must be taken account of after the war. More specifically, I would argue that the stationing of foreign troops in a country has the effect of sexualizing the local female population. Just as Australian servicemen rendered Egyptian, French, and English women during World War I the objects of their desire, so too did the American based in Australian cities during World War II. Over one million American servicemen passed through Australia in those years, most arriving in 1942. And war conditions, as concerned contemporaries told each other, undermined traditional restraints and disciplines. Faced with an uncertain future, people lived for the day, seizing pleasure when and where they might find it. Thus the discursive construction of femininity as sexual, the incitement to pleasure and adventure, took place in circumstances increasingly conducive to sexual activity.

There is much evidence of young women's avid pursuit of sexual pleasure during wartime, in particular of their attraction to American servicemen. Though cautioned to 'discount the moonlight and the music and the war's urgency and the uniform', many young women had been prepared by Hollywood to see romantic heroes in the American visitors. 'The girls out here are just crazy about Hollywood,' reported one American soldier.[38] Their constitution as sex objects—'superbly tailored beige-pinks, olive-drabs and light khakis'—encouraged women to position themselves as subjects in the sexual drama.[39] The Americans were generous with gifts and compliments, but perhaps more important, many seemed to really enjoy the company of women. 'Americans have the gift of making the girls they escort feel like the finest ladies in the land' testified an Australian woman.[40] Australian women commented with surprise about these men who felt at ease with women, even liked women.

Witnesses to the wartime turmoil were alarmed and perplexed by women's and girls' active pursuit of sexual pleasure, by the prospect of girls, of all social classes, 'out of control'. Dr Cooper Booth, Director of Social Hygiene in Sydney, reporting the increase in venereal disease in young women between the ages of sixteen and twenty, told a meeting of the Housewives' Association: 'Don't get the idea that these girls are of one class only. Many of them come from the best homes and have a good education . . . The girls simply have a desire for sexual life.'[41] On another occasion, Dr Booth commended Newcastle on its superior moral standards: 'Newcastle to me seems a much saner place than Sydney. I didn't see anything like the number of corn-silk, peroxide-haired girls that I do in Sydney.'[42] Was Sta-Blond shampoo unobtainable, one wonders, in Newcastle?

The sexually active woman, neither prostitute nor married woman, defied old categories and could not easily be accommodated in prevailing discourses. A new name was coined: the 'amateur'. The army magazine *Salt* joined other authorities in warning soldiers against her:

These amateurs represent all classes of the community, cannot generally be classed as 'bad', and their only common traits are sex ignorance and promiscuity. Many of them genuinely like the man himself, as well as the act . . .[43]

In Sydney, it was reported that health and social workers estimated there were 7000 'amateurs' ('adventurous types of girls who seek no cash reward') in the metropolitan area.[44] Because women were deemed to be the source of venereal disease, the 'khaki-mad dabbler in sex', that is the sexually active woman, was declared by army authorities to be Public Enemy No. 1.[45] Col. Geoff Calway of the United States Army observed that girls in Melbourne were 'developed' at fifteen years and waited on street corners to catch Americans: 'They don't seem reluctant to play. Naturally a soldier on leave says to himself "Why shouldn't I? What have I got to lose?" '[46]

Though impelled to categorize and name these women as a special type of womanhood—the 'amateur'—authorities were forced to recognize the diversity of women involved. On the one hand, there was abundant evidence of teenage 'underage' activity; on the other 'young married women whose husbands are away' were the major culprits.[47] On the one hand, they were 'vagrants' with no regular employment; on the other they were 'Jekyll and Hydes', shop and office workers by day and sexual adventurers by night.[48] Dr Lucy Gullett, addressing the United Associations of Women, preferred to cast men as the active (guilty) subjects, but allowed that 'many young girls' found it difficult to resist appeals from soldiers and resistance was further weakened by the amount of drink which was available.[49]

Official responses to the 'sexual epidemic' seemed as much motivated by a desire to punish women for their sexual assertiveness, their 'immorality', as by a desire to curb the spread of venereal disease.[50] Thus hundreds of women in Sydney found in the company of American soldiers and sailors were arrested and gaoled for vagrancy. But often the Vice Squad had to admit many of the women picked up in raids were not in fact vagrants, but women in employment.[51] The minority found on examination to have venereal disease were gaoled for treatment. The new National Security Regulations of 1942 gave police unlimited powers to arrest suspected carriers of venereal disease, although, as a Federal Health department officer admitted, the new regulations impinged on women and girls more than men. When the National Health and Medical Research Council drew up recommendations to curb the spread of venereal disease it targeted young women:

The Council urges that serious consideration be given by the appropriate authorities to severe restriction on the sale of alcohol for consumption by women, especially young girls and stricter control by public authorities of laxity of conduct, especially by young women in public places.[52]

Such were the observations of witnesses. An investigation of women's diaries and letters of this period provides some evidence of the terms in which young women themselves made sense of their experiences, of the ways they shaped their actions in terms of the available discourses. As Rosalind Coward has noted women (and men) must form their identities within available discourses, or, with difficulty, against them.[53] In women's diaries and letters we glimpse the ways in which the language of love and romance resonates in the minds of the targets of that discourse. One woman who committed her aspirations and anxieties to paper in 1942 was Patricia Jones, a twenty-year-old teachers' college student. Her diary self-consciously marks her pleasure at being young, recording the '1st flutterings of Youth'. She is grateful for the 'opportunities to be young' afforded her by student life (living away from home and mixing with both sexes), dreading 'the blind complacency of middle age' which must follow, and worse, 'cold old age'. She hopes that her life, as told in her diary, will constitute a 'nice romantic story' and all her energies seem to be directed to that end. She records her romantic outings (skating, the pictures, the Palais, the beach), her '1st real kiss' and 'falling in love'. She has a succession of boyfriends: one 'got to the stage of even saying "The Words" '. But she 'felt reckless', was looking for 'novelty' especially in the form of a 'Yank boyfriend', all the while competing with 'rivals', including 'attractive Ivy Baker' and Audrey Lang, 'an attractive little piece with all the necessary backchat'.[54]

Kissing is the significant sexual activity here—'Stan got romantic and kissed me once'; 'Jack finally kissed me. I did enjoy it! More than Doug's technique—more experience I suppose'; 'I didn't quite understand what he meant by that kiss'. In July 1943, in the 'Letterettes' column of the *Daily Telegraph*, a debate erupted on the subject of the comparative talents of 'men' and 'girls' as 'kissers'. One correspondent opined that Australian girls were 'poor kissers', to which another countered that the problem was that they had too much practice and had become careless.[55] In this exchange the women's engagement was usually constructed in active terms (women were 'kissers') and it may be that, as Rosalind Coward suggests, for women kissing represents the 'consummation of sexual attraction and desire' and further, that 'kissing is a voracious activity, an act of mutual penetration'.[56] Recognizing women's investment in kissing, some men knew how to frustrate women's desires. 'Marg. makes some excuse for me to accompany her to a store', wrote an American serviceman in his diary, 'I figure she wants me to kiss her. I do not comply with her desires . . . She apparently is angry'.[57]

Patricia Jones was preoccupied by the presence of American ser-vicemen, but declines to 'pick-up' as many as her friends, Delma and Arlette, the 'Yank hunters' do. She is pleased, however, as has been noted, to record her one 'little experience' with an American soldier. She wonders why sexual relationships are so preoccupying and refers to psychology books she has read on the 'problem'. Marriage represents paradoxically both the culmination of youth-ful romance and its transcendence in 'maturity'—a much favoured term.

Another diarist, Marion Crawford, recorded her amorous adven-tures in similar terms.[58] 'Have got a pash on Eric Young. Only had 2 dances with him but boy he's a beaut dancer.' Returning from another dance with Jack: 'He insisted on bringing me home. Talk about funny. "Kiss me goodnight". I kissed him on the forehead.' After parting with Blue: 'Can't believe I've lost Blue but have a feel-ing he really kissed me for the last time.' As in the case of Patricia Jones, Marion Crawford divided her time between a variety of pleasurable activities: the pictures ('Jane Eyre', 'Fantasia', 'Irene', 'Rebecca', 'Sandy is a Lady', 'Dear Ruth', 'The Woman in the Window', 'The Valley of Indecision'), Luna Park, the Palais, swim-ming, dances and playing board and card games. She also pondered long and hard on whether she was really in love, an important mat-ter to decide, for it meant marriage, a life-long commitment: 'I think maybe I'll marry Bill after all.' Romantic love was not only the basis for marriage in the 1940s, but for women it was meant to sup-ply the meaning of life. Thus Marion Crawford wrote in April 1948: 'Something happened that I've been living my life through for—but didn't know it. If only I could believe it was true. Max kissed me!' But one week later everything was thrown in doubt: 'I know tonight that I don't love Max—I don't know what I feel really I'm too con-fused.'

In one entry in her diary, Marion Crawford wrote revealingly that she went to Myers and 'rode up and down on escalators—for my pleasure'. Hers was a generation of pleasure-seekers, intent on excitement and adventure. In their romantic adventures, they con-sidered themselves the privileged beneficiaries of freedom and youth. They had a sense of themselves as the agents of their lives, 'picking-up' and discarding men at will. They were of course painfully aware that 'love' needed to be reciprocated and castigated themselves for 'imaginitis'. As the lucky inhabitants of the self-styled 'World of Youth', they were largely unresponsive to the cau-tionary voices of 'cold old age', voices that included those of feminists in organizations such as the National Council of Women, the Women's Christian Temperance Union, and the United Associations of Women (UAW).

Feminists interpreted the world in different terms. In the young women's 'opportunities', feminists saw only danger and exploitation. The 'epidemic of sexuality' occasioned by the war, as Gail Reekie has shown for Western Australia, led to a widespread feminist mobilization aimed at protecting women from male 'vice', from venereal disease, unwanted pregnancies, abortion, and rape.[59] Reekie's primary interest is in the relationship of feminism to class. Arguing that middle-class feminist campaigns 'often translated politically into efforts to restrict working-class women's sexual activity', she is therefore surprised to find the extent of cross-class unity among feminists that is evident in the wartime campaigns around sexuality.[60] Unfortunately, her focus on class divisions obscures the emergence of an arguably more significant division between women—evident in the discourse on femininity—a distinction based on age. It is not 'working class sexual values' of which these middle-aged feminists disapprove, but 'the moral standard of our young people', as the president of the Women's Justices Association made clear.[61]

Nor is it true to say that women's campaigns were 'unrelated to any cohesive theory of women's position in society'.[62] Indeed quite the reverse is true: the feminist concern about, and response to, the 'epidemic of sexuality' arose quite logically from established feminist positions. Jessie Street's intervention illustrates this well. In May 1943 fifty-four-year-old Street, as president of the UAW, wrote to the *Daily Telegraph* deploring the 'cesspool of vice' that was Sydney. She regretted that the authorities had opted to make 'sex indulgence' safe rather than preventing it and she called for the punishment of 'the seducers of young girls' instead of 'those seduced'. The 'debauchers', she said, should be removed from society.[63] For Street, the more sexualized women were, the more degraded. Economic independence would free women from their condition as creatures of sex.[64] Her vision of female emancipation could not include sexual freedom: chastity rather than 'sex indulgence' was the necessary pre-condition for women's 'advancement'. The double standard that punished women, while it let men go free, was thus the major target of feminist campaigns.

Street's analysis represented a development of the de-sexualization strategy of nineteenth-century feminism.[65] Significantly, Street was a member of the British Association for Moral and Social

Hygiene founded in 1870 by Josephine Butler, the crusader against contagious diseases legislation, and there is much evidence to suggest that Street's experiences of working with prostitutes in the United States in 1915 were formative for her feminism.[66] For Street, as for nineteenth-century feminists, prostitution was the paradigmatic female condition: women reduced to their sex.

Although feminism reached a high point during World War II— the Australian Women's Charter Conference, representing ninety women's organizations, was the largest feminist conference yet held in Australia—feminists, many in their forties and fifties by World War II, were ageing and losing touch with the aspirations of young women.[67] The feminist Charter for Equality, emphasizing economic and political opportunity, could not accommodate female sexual desire. Street and others continued to speak of 'vice' and 'seduction'. There is evidence of indifference and resistance to feminist overtures among younger women. Organizers of the Women for Canberra movement, for example, despaired at young women's lack of interest: they 'were not seized with the seriousness of the matter'.[68]

Though differently motivated, feminists (concerned about the position of women) and Christian moralists (concerned to preserve Christian values) joined together in trying to curb the 'promiscuous' sexual activity of young women.[69] The Australian Women's Charter of 1943 advocated strict controls on the sale of liquor, the prohibition of 'literature calculated to stimulate crime and sexual laxity' and the provision of 'ample facilities for healthy recreation'. The Charter, like the churches and the Director of the Army Medical Corps, also called for the removal of obstacles to early marriage'.[70] While feminists sought to domesticate sexual pleasure, young women themselves embraced early marriage as a defiant expression of the freedom and sexual orientation of youth.[71] Some 12 000 Australian women married American servicemen. Marriage was seen as the gateway to sexual fulfilment, as a union of sweethearts.

These new understandings of marriage are present in women's diaries. They are also evident in the testimonies of Melbourne women who wrote to Dr V. H. Wallace in 1943 and 1944 about birth control, and of the 1400 women who responded in 1944 to the invitation from the National Health and Medical Research Council (NHMRC) to Australian women to say why they were limiting their families. After analysing the letters from those who limited their families to two children, the NHMRC concluded: 'There are several important and quite genuine motives influencing this decision. Perhaps the two most important of these are the desire to retain the companionship of the husband and the happiness of married life, and the desire to see that the two children are properly equipped for their later life.'[72] 'I believe a happy marriage', a patient told Dr Wallace, 'is based on a happy sexual life between husband and wife.'[73] The women's letters to the NHMRC and to Dr Wallace in Melbourne spoke of the difficulty of reconciling motherhood with the new imperatives of femininity. 'Desiring a normal marital relationship with my husband', explained a Surrey Hills wife and mother to Dr Wallace, 'I had no wish to bear children indiscriminately or too frequently'.[74] Mothers, wrote one to the NHMRC, 'still have an urge for an evening entertainment or a much-earned holiday with only an attentive and loving husband'.[75] Another mother of two children suggested that the exhaustion consequent upon housework meant that it was difficult to be a sweetheart, too: 'washing up, wiping up, and a spot of darning, etc., then bed, feeling as if you could only fall into bed and sleep, but have to be a good wife to husband'.[76] Yet another considered that if she had the five or six children society apparently required 'I would have no time to spend with my husband, and to be a real companion to him.'[77] 'Women with too many children attend to the children (if they are real mothers) [and] neglect their husband [sic] then he goes elsewhere for companionship'.[78] 'Companion' was becoming code for sexual partner: '[The wife] ceases to be a companion to her husband in the later months of pregnancy and the early months after the baby arrives.'[79] One solution to the contradictions experienced by these women lay in the use of contraceptives. With the free availability of contraceptives, a woman might 'safely retain her husband's love without the fear of a dozen children'.[80] Contraceptives, all were agreed, offered 'freedom from fear'. They also offered unimagined pleasures. The combination of a new (second) husband and reliable contraceptives gave one woman 'more satisfaction and happiness than [she] ever thought possible'.[81] It seems clear from the testimonies of these women that by the 1940s the use of artificial contraceptives, in particular condoms, pessaries, and diaphragms, was becoming widespread.[82] Many participants in the national survey expressed anxiety about the possibility of the NHMRC recommending their prohibition. The majority of Dr Wallace's patients expressed satisfaction with his recommended pessary: 'it is a great pity that birth control cannot be taught free to the masses', proclaimed one happy beneficiary.[83]

In explaining their refusal to bear more children, many women also complained of the 'disfigurement' of pregnancy—the 'sacrifice' of woman's figure. 'This is the woman's point of view. She marries, she has a child, she loses her figure . . .'[84] 'Another reason for restricting families', wrote another, was the 'appearance' of the pregnant woman.[85] The Council's summary of the responses noted the regularity of references to the 'inconveniences, humiliations and physical distress of pregnancy': 'many women dwelt at length on this aspect'.[86] The incompatibility of motherhood with modern femininity was stressed by Dame Enid Lyons in a radio debate on the decline in the birth rate on the ABC in 1944: 'There is one other point of importance which I think women find to be a great deterrent to having many children. That is our standard today of feminine beauty . . . Who are those whose beauty today is extolled? Those who have kept the extreme slimness and suppleness of early youth.'[87] A similar point was made by Mrs J. Bowie to a women's meeting in Sydney when she suggested beauty contests were responsible for over-emphasizing the bodily aspect of woman's personality.[88] Lyons regretted that sex had become an 'end in itself', while the child was regarded as of not very great importance.

The solution to the conflict was straightforward for one respondent to the national enquiry: 'glamorize motherhood'.[89] The National Health and Medical Research Council produced numerous recommendations for reforms to make mothering less expensive, less arduous and less alienating. But none of the recommendations really addressed the heart of the matter. As marriage came to be seen increasingly as an institution to secure sexual pleasure, for the gratification of heterosexual desire, for women as well as men, so the advent of children came to represent not the purpose of, but a direct threat to, marital happiness. 'The mental and physical adjustments [required by marriage] require time,' wrote one respondent to Dr Wallace, 'and when a child is born too soon those adjustments are delayed, and possibly never made.'[90] Children intruded upon the 'privacy' of the married couple as they increasingly expected 'time together alone'.[91]

Rather than characterize the triumph of marriage and domesticity in the 1940s and 1950s as a conservative retreat, a return to old ways, we should rather understand these phenomena as the triumph of modern femininity, youthful adventurism and a path embarked on by women attempting to live as female sexual subjects and explore the possibilities of sexual pleasure. Women began to enter marriage with high expectations of personal pleasure and it is not surprising that the marriage boom of the 1940s produced a 'divorce boom' in the 1950s. Interestingly, in his chapter on 'Marriage Breakdown' for A. P. Elkin's book on *Marriage and the Family in Australia*, W. G. Coughlan attributed much marital instability in the 1950s to the high incidence of 'heavy petting' preceding marriage:

Petting is taken for granted and expected from mid-adolescence, and is widespread among senior secondary school pupils, university students, apprentices and workers in every occupation. 'Heavy' petting and petting to climax figure in the case histories of most of the marriage counsellors' clients . . .[92]

Experienced in kissing and 'petting', the majority of young unmarried women were still, it would seem from surveys conducted by Dr Lotte Fink in the early 1950s, strangers to sexual intercourse: this was the novelty of marriage.[93]

Sexual satisfaction was now taken for granted as an adult right in the 'disease-free' 1950s and 1960s. Sexual relationships could be explored with relative impunity, though the costs were always greater for women. There could be no return to the old order at the end of the war. Indeed by the 1950s it was becoming clear that the tensions generated by the changing structure of femininity and by the concomitant wartime stimulation of female desire had created havoc with 'traditional roles'. A restlessness had been unleashed that could not be easily assuaged.

World War II saw both the triumph and demise of the old feminism.[94] The 1943 Charter Conference, the equal pay campaigns, the campaigns for the government provision of child care and the Women for Canberra movement together represent a peak of achievement; by the time of the second Charter Conference in 1946, however, feminism was on the defensive, branded anachronistic, prudish, and divisive. Whereas the 1943 Charter included a separate section titled 'Woman as Mother and/or Home Maker', by 1946 this had been reduced to a sub-section of, subsumed under, 'The Family, the Home and the Community'. The mutuality of women's and men's interests and needs, emphasized by the dominant discourse on sexual partnership, came to be represented in the ascendant concept of 'the Family', a metaphor for woman's sphere that gradually and significantly eclipsed the earlier designation, the Home. But women's interest in, and right to, sexual pleasure had been established, so that when the new feminism—women's liberation—emerged in the late 1960s, sexual freedom and its assumed preconditions of abortion on demand and free contraception were key demands. Lesbianism, not chastity, was the choice of those eschewing sexual relations with men. Female desire was put on the political agenda.

Notes

1. Diary, original in author's possession. Entry, ' "1942": Emergence into Full Youth'. I wish to express my thanks to Katie Holmes for sharing the two personal diaries, quoted in this article, with me. The names of the diarists have been changed to protect their anonymity.
2. P. Johnson, 'Gender, Class and Work: The Council of Action for Equal Pay and the Equal Pay Campaign in Australia During World War II', *Labour History*, 50 (May 1986), 146.
3. A. Wright, 'The *Women's Weekly*: Depression and War years Romance and Reality', *Refractory Girl*, 3 (Winter 1973), 12.
4. A. Summers, *Damned Whores and God's Police* (Melbourne 1975), 149.
5. E. Ryan and A. Conlon, *Gentle Invaders. Australian Women at Work* (Melbourne 1989), 139.
6. C. Allport, 'The Princess in the Castle: Women and the New Order Housing', in Third Women and Labour Conference Collective (eds.), *All her Labours: Embroidering the Framework* (Sydney 1984), 149. See also K. Darian-Smith, 'A City in War: The Home Front in Melbourne 1939–1945', Ph.D. thesis, University of Melbourne 1987, 140: at the end of the war 'the past . . . reigns supreme' and Kay Saunders and Helen Taylor, 'To Combat the Plague: The Construction of Moral Alarm and State Intervention in Queensland during World War II', *Hecate* 14/1 (1988) where (p. 26) the end of the war sees 'traditional' values 'ultimately reinforced'.
7. Aspects of this argument are anticipated in M. Lake, 'The War Over Women's Work', in V. Burgmann and J. Lee (eds.), *A Most Valuable Acquisition* (Melbourne 1988).
8. C. McNamara, 'Must Women Return to the Kitchen?', *Labor Digest* (April 1945), 49.
9. Foster quoted in C. Larmour, 'Women's Wages and the WEB' in A. Curthoys *et al.* (eds.), *Women at Work* (Canberra 1975), 50–1.
10. Quoted in Wright, op. cit. 12.
11. J. J. Matthews, *Good and Mad Women: The Historical Construction of Femininity in Twentieth-Century Australia* (Sydney 1984), 89–90; J. J. Matthews, 'Building the Body Beautiful: the Femininity of Modernity', *Australian Feminist Studies*, no. 5 (Summer 1987).
12. L. Johnson, 'The Teenage Girl: The Social Definition of Growing Up for Young Australian Women 1950 to 1965', *History of Education Review*, 18/1 (1989), 6.
13. R. Pringle, *Secretaries Talk Sexuality, Power and Work* (Sydney 1988), 6–15, 193.
14. S. Jeffreys, *The Spinster and her Enemies: Feminism and Sexuality 1880–1930* (London 1985), ch. 9; also Stephen Heath, *The Sexual Fix* (London 1982). Judith Allen, *Sex and Secrets: Crimes Involving Australian Women Since 1880* (Melbourne 1990), points to the implications of sexological discourse for rape

victims, pp. 152–3. Norman Haire, a leading sexologist in Britain and Australia, was prominent in Australia during World War II, expounding on the imperative of the 'sex urge' and advocating, like many sex reformers, eugenicist thinking.

15. Ann Curthoys, 'Eugenics, Feminism and Birth Control: The Case of Marion Piddington', *Hecate* 15/1 (1989). See also Alison Mackinnon and Carol Bacchi, 'Sex, Resistance and Power: Sex Reform in South Australia *c.*1905', *Australian Historical Studies*, 23/90 (Apr. 1988).
16. Jill Matthews, 'Building the Body Beautiful'.
17. Judith Williamson, 'Decoding Advertisements' in Rosemary Betterton (ed.), *Looking on Images of Femininity in the Visual Arts and Media* (London 1987), 49. See also Matthews, *Good and Mad Women*, 98–9, and Stuart Ewen, *Captains and Consciousness: Advertising and the Social Roots of the Consumer Culture* (New York 1976).
18. *Everylady's Journal*, 6 Apr. 1916, 208.
19. Ibid. 6 Apr., 6 Aug. 1920; also the 'Oatine Face Cream' and 'Use it to be Dainty' advertisements 6 July 1920.
20. See, for example, 'Sta-Blond' advertisement, *New Idea*, 24 Mar. 1939.
21. National Health and Medical Research Council, *Reports on the Decline in the Birth Rate*, Analysis of the Contents of the Letters Received, 18th Session, Canberra, 22–4 Nov. 1944, p. 73.
22. Dr V. H. Wallace Papers, 'Their Comments on Contraception', letter from Murrumbeena, 21 Mar. 1944. University of Melbourne Archives.
23. Betterton, op. cit. 7.
24. *Everylady's Journal*, 19 May 1926.
25. New Idea, 2 Dec. 1932.
26. Ibid. 29 July 1932.
27. *Everylady's Journal*, 6 May 1920.
28. Ibid. 6 Mar., 5 May, 20 July 1923. See also ad. for Kilma Cream, 6 Jan. 1923.
29. *New Idea*, 23 Mar. 1934.
30. Ibid. 8 Sept. 1938.
31. *Everylady's Journal*, 20 Aug. 1927.
32. *New Idea*, 24 Mar. 1939.
33. Ibid. 16 Sept. 1938.
34. Ibid. 24 Mar. 1938.
35. Ibid. 8 Jan., 24 Mar. 1938.
36. Two recent studies of the relationships between Australian women and American servicemen in Queensland are R. Campbell's *Heroes and Lovers: A Question of National Identity* (Sydney 1989), which, as the subtitle suggests, is concerned with the impact of the relationships on the 'national identity'; and M. Sturma's article 'Loving the Alien: The Underside of Relations between American Servicemen and Australian Women in Queensland, 1942–1945', *Journal of Australian Studies* (24 May 1989), which explores the 'darker side' of American relations with Australian women. Both studies position the Americans as the main subjects of their stories: women are the objects of *their* desires. Kay Saunders and Helen Taylor in 'To Combat the Plague' present women, especially working-class women, as victims of an aggrandising and punitive capitalist state. Women's general vulnerability to male violence in wartime is the theme of Judith Allen, op. cit. 218–25. It should be noted that the famous 'Australian' joke is also claimed as a New Zealand and British joke.

37. This is a point made in the Introduction to M. R. Higonnet *et al.* (ed.), *Behind the Lines: Gender and the Two World Wars* (New Haven 1987), 4, but it should be noted that Carmel Shute made the same point, in different language, in Australia as early as 1975. See C. Shute, 'Heroines and Heroes: Sexual Mythology in Australia 1914–1918', *Hecate* 1/1 (1975).

38. Dymphna Cusack and Florence James, *Come in Spinner* (Sydney 1973 (first pub. 1951)), 29. Cusack and James also wrote of the Americans' 'Hollywood love-making'.

39. E. Daniel Potts and Annette Potts, *Yanks Down Under 1941–5: The American Impact on Australia* (Melbourne 1985), 330, 341.

40. Ibid. 342, 344–5.

41. *Daily Telegraph*, 10 Apr. 1943.

42. Ibid. 8 May 1943.

43. *Salt*, 6/7 (7 June 1943), quoted in Darian-Smith, *op. cit.* 303. See also report of conference of United States and Australian Army medical officers. *Daily Telegraph*, 18 Apr. 1943.

44. *Daily Telegraph*, 30 Jan. 1943.

45. Darian-Smith, op. cit. 303.

46. Ibid. 305.

47. Dr Cooper Booth in *Daily Telegraph*, 29 June 1943.

48. Ibid. 14 Jan. 1943.

49. Women's News Column, *Sydney Morning Herald*, 23 Apr. 1945.

50. See Sturma, op. cit. 11; Saunders and Taylor, op. cit.; also K. Daniels and M. Murnane (eds.), *Uphill All the Way: A Documentary History of Women in Australia* (St Lucia 1980), 106–12.

51. *Daily Telegraph*, 15 July 1943.

52. *Sydney Morning Herald*, 31 May 1943.

53. Rosalind Coward, *Female Desire: Women's Sexuality Today* (London 1984).

54. This section of the diary is the record of the first part of 1942, entitled 'Emergence into Full Youth', written in May 1942. All quotes are from this record, which is not differentiated into daily entries.

55. *Daily Telegraph*, 3, 7, 8, 9 July 1943.

56. Coward, op. cit. 95–6.

57. Potts and Potts, op. cit. 345.

58. Diary of Marion Crawford, entries from 1943 until 1948. Original in possession of diarist.

59. Gail Reekie, 'War, Sexuality and Feminism: Perth women's organisations 1938–1945', *Historical Studies*, 21/85 (Oct. 1985).

60. Ibid. 576. Reekie's surprise at the cross-class unity of feminists ironically echoes the surprise of contemporaries confronted with the sexual activity of young women from all classes.

61. Ibid. 580.

62. Ibid. 577.

63. *Daily Telegraph*, 20 May 1943.

64. M. Lake, 'Jessie Street and "Feminist Chauvinism" ', in Heather Radi (ed.), *Jessie Street* (Sydney 1990). See especially Street to *News Chronicle*, London, 27 Oct. 1956, Jessie Street Papers, ANL, MS 2683/3/525.

65. See, for example, J. Walkowitz, 'Male Vice and Female Virtue: Feminism and the Politics of Prostitution in Nineteenth Century Britain', in A. Snitow, *et al.* (eds.), *Desire: The Politics of Sexuality* (London 1984); see also L. Gordon and

E. DuBois, 'Seeking Ecstasy on the Battlefield: Danger and Pleasure in Nineteenth Century Feminist Sexual Thought', in *Feminist Review* (ed.), *Sexuality: A Reader* (London 1987).

66. Jessie Livingstone to Kenneth Street, 20 Apr. 1915, Street Papers, MS 2683/1/6; Jessie Street interview with Hazel de Berg, 18 Mar. 1967, Tape 197, Oral History Collection, ANL.

67. For example, Jessie Street and Lucy Woodcock were 54 in 1943, Bessie Rischbieth was 60, Millicent Preston Stanley was 60, Muriel Heagney was 58.

68. *Sydney Morning Herald*, 9 Feb. 1943.

69. Ibid. See, for example, 'The Pulpit' column, 18 Jan. 1943, 8 Mar. 1943; and Women's News Column, 24 Feb. 1943, 26 Feb. 1943.

70. *Australian Women's Charter*, Nov. 1943, Sydney, 14–15; see also report of Dr Lucy Gullett addressing the United Nations of Women on 'early marriage as a protection against venereal disease', *Sydney Morning Herald*, 23 Apr. 1945 and Darian-Smith, op. cit. 138.

71. Marriage rates climbed during World War II and continued to do so until 1955. See P. McDonald, *Marriage in Australia* (Canberra 1975), 188, 192, and Gordon Carmichael, *With This Ring* (Canberra 1988), 11, 14, 28–9.

72. *National Health and Medical Research Council Reports on the Decline in the Birth Rate*, Analysis of the Contents of the Letters Received, 18th Session, Canberra, 22–4 Nov. 1944, 73.

73. Letter from Newport, 28 Nov. 1943, Wallace letters.

74. Letter from Surrey Hills, 13 Dec. 1943, ibid.

75. *NHMRC*, Letters Received, 72.

76. Ibid.

77. Ibid. 82.

78. Letter from Finley, 13 Oct. 1943, Wallace letters.

79. *NHMRC*, Letters Received, 83.

80. Ibid. 81.

81. Letter from East Brunswick, 12 Oct. 1943, Wallace letters.

82. See also Judith Allen, op. cit. 224.

83. Letter from Carrum, 12 Nov. 1943, Wallace letters.

84. *NHMRC*, Letters Received, 72, 83, 91, 92, 93.

85. Ibid. 81

86. Ibid. 75, 84, 89.

87. Ibid. 84.

88. *Daily Telegraph*, 14 Mar. 1943.

89. Australian Broadcasting Commission, *The Nation's Forum of the Air*, 23 Aug. 1944.

90. Letter from Brighton Beach, 17 Dec. 1943, Wallace letters.

91. Letter from Parkdale, 16 Oct. 1943, ibid.

92. W. G. Coughlan, 'Marriage Breakdown', in A. P. Elkin (ed.), *Marriage and the Family in Australia* (Sydney 1957), 133.

93. Lotte A. Fink, 'Premarital Sex Experience of Girls in Sydney', *International Journal of Sexology* 8/1 (Aug. 1954), 10–11.

94. This point is elaborated in Marilyn Lake, 'Jessie Street and "Feminist Chauvinism" ', in Heather Radi, op. cit.

Part VI. Feminisms

16 Womanist Consciousness: Maggie Lena Walker and the Independent Order of Saint Luke

Elsa Barkley Brown

In the first decades of the twentieth century Maggie Lena Walker repeatedly challenged her contemporaries to 'make history as Negro women'. Yet she and her colleagues in the Independent Order of Saint Luke, like most black and other women of colour, have been virtually invisible in women's history and women's studies. Although recent books and articles have begun to redress this,[1] the years of exclusion have had an impact more significant than just the invisibility of black women, for the exclusion of black women has meant that the concepts, perspectives, methods, and pedagogies of women's history and women's studies have been developed without consideration of the experiences of black women. As a result many of the recent explorations in black women's history have attempted to place black women inside feminist perspectives which by design, have omitted their experiences. Nowhere is this exclusion more apparent than in the process of defining women's issues and women's struggle. Because they have been created outside the experiences of black women, the definitions used in women's history and women's studies assume the separability of women's struggle and race struggle. Such arguments recognize the possibility that black women may have both women's concerns and race concerns, but they insist upon delimiting each. They allow, belatedly, black women to make history as women or as Negroes but not as 'Negro women'. What they fail to consider is that women's issues may be race issues, and race issues may be women's issues.[2]

Rosalyn Terborg-Penn, in 'Discontented Black Feminists: Prelude and Postscript to the Passage of the Nineteenth Amendment', an essay

My appreciation is expressed to Mary Kelley, Deborah K. King, Lillian Jones, and the participants in the Community and Social Movements research group of the 1986 Summer Research Institute on Race and Gender, Center for Research on Women, Memphis State University, for their comments on an earlier draft of this article. Reprinted with permission from *Signs*, 14/3 (Spring 1989), 610–33.

on the 1920s black women's movement, of which Walker was a part, persuasively discusses the continuing discrimination in the US women's movement and the focus of black women on 'uplifting the downtrodden of the race or . . . representing people of color throughout the world'. Subsequently she argues for the 'unique nature of feminism among Afro-American women'. The editors of *Decades of Discontent: The Women's Movement, 1920–1940*, the 1983 collection on post-Nineteenth Amendment feminism, however, introduce Terborg-Penn's article by mistakenly concluding that these black women, disillusioned and frustrated by racism in the women's movement, turned from women's issues to race issues. Using a framework that does not conceive of 'racial uplift, fighting segregation and mob violence' and 'contending with poverty' as women's issues, Lois Scharf and Joan Jensen succumb to the tendency to assume that black women's lives can be neatly subdivided, that while we are both black and female, we occupy those roles sequentially, as if one cannot have the two simultaneously in one's consciousness of being.[3] Such a framework assumes a fragmentation of black women's existence that defies reality.

Scharf and Jensen's conclusion is certainly one that the white feminists of the 1920s and 1930s, who occupy most of the book, would have endorsed. When southern black women, denied the right to register to vote, sought help from the National Woman's Party, these white feminists rejected their petitions, arguing that this was a race concern and not a women's concern. Were they not, after all, being denied the vote not because of their sex but because of their race?[4]

Black women like Walker who devoted their energies to securing universal suffrage, including that of black men, are not widely recognized as female suffragists because they did not separate their struggle for the women's vote from their struggle for the black vote. This tendency to establish false dichotomies, precluding the possibility that for many racism and sexism are experienced simultaneously, leads to discussions of liberation movements and women's movements as separate entities.

Quite clearly, what many women of colour at the United Nations Decade for Women conference held in Nairobi, Kenya, in 1985, along with many other activists and scholars, have argued in recent years is the impossibility of separating the two and the necessity of understanding the convergence of women's issues, race/nationalist issues, and class issues in women's consciousnesses.[5] That understanding is in part hampered by the prevailing terminology: femi-

nism places a priority on women; nationalism or race consciousness, a priority on race. It is the need to overcome the limitations of
terminology that has led many black women to adopt the term
'womanist'. Both Alice Walker and Chikwenye Okonjo Ogunyemi
have defined womanism as a consciousness that incorporates racial,
cultural, sexual, national, economic, and political considerations.[6]
As Ogunyemi explains, 'black womanism is a philosophy' that concerns itself both with sexual equality in the black community and
'with the world power structure that subjugates' both blacks and
women. 'Its ideal is for black unity where every black person has a
modicum of power and so can be a 'brother' or a 'sister' or a 'father'
or a 'mother' to the other. . . . [I]ts aim is the dynamism of wholeness and self-healing.'[7]

Walker's and Ogunyemi's terminology may be new, but their
ideas are not. In fact, many black women at various points in history had a clear understanding that race issues and women's issues
were inextricably linked, that one could not separate women's
struggle from race struggle. It was because of this understanding
that they refused to disconnect themselves from either movement.
They instead insisted on inclusion in both movements in a manner
that recognized the interconnection between race and sex, and they
did so even if they had to battle their white sisters and their black
brothers to achieve it. Certainly the lives and work of women such
as Anna Julia Cooper, Mary Church Terrell, and Fannie Barrier
Williams inform us of this. Cooper, an early Africanamerican womanist, addressed the holistic nature of the struggle in her address to
the World's Congress of Representative Women:

Let woman's claim be as broad in the concrete as in the abstract. *We take
our stand on the solidarity of humanity, the oneness of life*, and the unnatu-
ralness and injustice of all special favoritisms, whether of sex, race, country, or condition. If one link of the chain be broken, the chain is broken. . . .
We want, then, as toilers for the universal triumph of justice and human
rights, to go to our homes from this Congress, demanding an entrance not
through a gateway for ourselves, our race, our sex, or our sect, but a grand
highway for humanity. The colored woman feels that woman's cause is
one and universal; and that not till . . . race, color, sex, and condition are
seen as the accidents, and not the substance of life; . . . not till then is
woman's lesson taught and woman's cause won—not the white woman's,
nor the black woman's, nor the red woman's, but the cause of every man
and of every woman who has writhed silently under a mighty wrong.
*Woman's wrongs are thus indissolubly linked with all undefended woe, and
the acquirement of her 'rights' will mean the final triumph of all right over*

might, the supremacy of the moral forces of reason, and justice, and love in the government of the nations of earth.[8]

One of those who most clearly articulated womanist conscious-ness was Maggie Lena Walker. Walker (1867–1934) was born and educated in Richmond, Virginia, graduating from Colored Normal School in 1883. During her school years she assisted her widowed mother in her work as a washerwoman and cared for her younger brother. Following graduation she taught in the city's public schools and took courses in accounting and sales. Required to stop teaching when she married Armstead Walker, a contractor, her coursework had well prepared her to join several other black women in founding an insurance company, the Woman's Union. Meanwhile, Walker, who had joined the Independent Order of Saint Luke at the age of fourteen, rose through the ranks to hold several important positions in the order and, in 1895, to organize the juvenile branch of the order. In addition to her Saint Luke activ-ities, Walker was a founder or leading supporter of the Richmond Council of Colored Women, the Virginia State Federation of Colored Women, the National Association of Wage Earners, the International Council of Women of the Darker Races, the National Training School for Girls, and the Virginia Industrial School for Colored Girls. She also helped direct the National Association for the Advancement of Colored People, the Richmond Urban League, and the Negro Organization Society of Virginia.[9]

Walker is probably best known today as the first woman bank president in the United States. She founded the Saint Luke Penny Savings Bank in Richmond, Virginia, in 1903. Before her death in 1934 she oversaw the reorganization of this financial institution as the present-day Consolidated Bank and Trust Company, the oldest continuously existing black-owned and black-run bank in the country. The bank, like most of Walker's activities, was the out-growth of the independent Order of Saint Luke, which she served as Right Worthy Grand Secretary for thirty-five years.

The Independent Order of Saint Luke was one of the larger and more successful of the many thousands of mutual benefit societies that have developed throughout Africanamerican communities since the eighteenth century. These societies combined insurance functions with economic development and social and political activities. As such they were important loci of community self-help and racial solidarity. Unlike the Knight of Pythias and its female auxiliary, the Courts of Calanthe, societies like the Independent

Order of Saint Luke had a non-exclusionary membership policy; any man, woman, or child could join. Thus men and women from all occupational segments, professional/managerial, entrepreneurial, and working-class, came together in the order. The Independent Order of Saint Luke was a mass-based organization that played a key role in the political, economic, and social development of its members and of the community as a whole.[10]

Founded in Maryland in 1867 by Mary Prout, the Independent Order of Saint Luke began as a women's sickness and death mutual benefit association. By the 1880s it had admitted men and had expanded to New York and Virginia. At the 1899 annual meeting William M. T. Forrester, who had served as Grand Secretary since 1869, refused to accept reappointment, stating that the order was in decline, having only 1080 members in fifty-seven councils, $31.61 in the treasury, and $400.00 in outstanding debts. Maggie Lena Walker took over the duties of Grand Worthy Secretary at one-third of the position's previous salary.[11]

According to Walker, her 'first work was to draw around me *women*'.[12] In fact, after the executive board elections in 1901, six of the nine members were women: Walker, Patsie K. Anderson, Frances Cox, Abigail Dawley, Lillian H. Payne, and Ella O. Waller.[13] Under their leadership the order and its affiliates flourished. The order's ventures included a juvenile department, an educational loan fund for young people, a department store, and a weekly newspaper. Growing to include over 100 000 members in 2010 councils and circles in twenty-eight states, the order demonstrated a special commitment to expanding the economic opportunities within the black community, especially those for women.

It is important to take into account Walker's acknowledgement of her female colleagues. Most of what we know about the Order of Saint Luke highlights Walker because she was the leader and spokeswoman and therefore the most visible figure. She was able, however, to function in that role and to accomplish all that she did not merely because of her own strengths and skills, considerable though they were, but also because she operated from the strength of the Saint Luke collective as a whole and from the special strengths and talents of the inner core of the Saint Luke women in particular. Deborah Gray White, in her work on women during slavery, underscores the importance of black women's networks in an earlier time period: 'Strength had to be cultivated. It came no more naturally to them than to anyone. . . . If they seemed exceptionally strong it was partly because they often functioned in groups and derived strength from numbers. . . . [T]hey inevitably developed some appreciation of one another's skills and talents. This intimacy enabled them to establish the criteria with which to rank and order themselves.' It was this same kind of sisterhood that was Walker's base, her support, her strength, and her source of wisdom and direction.[14]

The women of Saint Luke expanded the role of women in the community to the political sphere through their leadership in the 1904 streetcar boycott and through the *St. Luke Herald's* pronouncements against segregation, lynching, and lack of equal educational opportunities for black children. Walker spearheaded the local struggle for women's suffrage and the voter registration campaigns after the passage of the Nineteenth Amendment. In the 1920 elections in Richmond, fully 80 per cent of the eligible black voters were women. The increased black political strength represented by the female voters gave incentive to the growing movement for independent black political action and led to the formation of the Virginia Lily-Black Republican Party. Walker ran on this ticket for state superintendent of public instruction in 1921.[15] Thus Walker and many other of the Saint Luke women were role models for other black women in their community activities as well as their occupations.

Undergirding all of their work was a belief in the possibilities inherent in the collective struggle of black women in particular and of the black community in general. Walker argued that the only way in which black women would be able 'to avoid the traps and snares of life' would be to 'band themselves together, organize, . . . put their mites together, put their hands and their brains together and make work and business for themselves'.[16]

The idea of collective economic development was not a new idea for these women, many of whom were instrumental in establishing the Woman's Union, a female insurance company founded in 1898. Its motto was 'The Hand That Rocks the Cradle Rules the World'.[17] But unlike nineteenth-century white women's rendering of that expression to signify the limitation of woman's influence to that which she had by virtue of rearing her sons, the idea as these women conceived it transcended the separation of private and public spheres and spoke to the idea that women, while not abandoning their roles as wives and mothers, could also move into economic and political activities in ways that would support rather than conflict with family and community. Women did not have to choose between the two spheres; in fact, they necessarily had to occupy both. Indeed, these women's use of this phrase speaks to their understanding of the totality of the task that lay ahead of them as black women. It negates, for black women at least, the public/private dichotomy.

Saint Luke women built on tradition. A well-organized set of institutions maintained community in Richmond: mutual benefit societies, interwoven with extended families and churches, built a network of supportive relations.[18] The families, churches, and societies were all based on similar ideas of collective consciousness and collective responsibility. Thus, they served to extend and reaffirm notions of family throughout the black community. Not only in their houses but also in their meeting-halls and places of worship, they were brothers and sisters caring for each other. The institutionalization of this notion of family cemented the community. Community/family members recognized that this had to be maintained from generation to generation; this was in part the function of the juvenile branches of the mutual benefit associations. The statement of purpose of the Children's Rosebud Fountains, Grand Fountain United Order of True Reformers, clearly articulated this:

> Teaching them . . . to assist each other in sickness, sorrow and afflictions and in the struggles of life; teaching them that one's happiness greatly depends upon the others. . . . Teach them to live united. . . . The children of different families will know how to . . . talk, plot and plan for one another's peace and happiness in the journey of life. Teach them to . . . bear each other's burdens . . . to so bind and tie their love and affections together that one's sorrow may be the other's sorrow, one's distress be the other's distress, one's penny the other's penny.[19]

Through the Penny Savings Banks the Saint Luke women were able to affirm and cement the existing mutual assistance network among black women and within the black community by providing an institutionalized structure for these activities. The bank recognized the meagre resources of the black community, particularly black women. In fact, its establishment as a *penny* savings bank is an indication of that. Many of its earliest and strongest supporters were washerwomen, one of whom was Maggie Walker's mother. And the bank continued throughout Walker's leadership to exercise a special commitment to 'the small depositor'.[20]

In her efforts Walker, like the other Saint Luke women, was guided by a clearly understood and shared perspective concerning the relationship of black women to black men, to the black community, and to the larger society. This was a perspective that acknowledged individual powerlessness in the face of racism and sexism and that argued that black women, because of their condition and status, had a right—indeed, according to Walker, a special duty and incentive—to organize. She argued, 'Who is so helpless as the Negro woman? Who is so circumscribed and hemmed in, in the race of life, in the struggle for bread, meat and clothing as the Negro woman?'[21]

In addition, her perspective contended that organizational activity and the resultant expanded opportunities for black women were not detrimental to the home, the community, black men, or the race. Furthermore, she insisted that organization and expansion of women's roles economically and politically were essential ingredients without which the community, the race, and even black men could not achieve their full potential. The way in which Walker described black women's relationship to society, combined with the collective activities in which she engaged, give us some insight into her understanding of the relationship between women's struggle and race struggle.

Walker was determined to expand opportunities for black women. In fulfilling this aim she challenged not only the larger society's notions of the proper place of blacks but also those in her community who held a limited notion of women's proper role. Particularly in light of the increasing necessity to defend the integrity and morality of the race, a 'great number of men' and women in Virginia and elsewhere believed that women's clubs, movements 'looking to the final exercise of suffrage by women', and organizations of black professional and business women would lead to 'the decadence of home life'.[22] Women involved in these activities were often regarded as 'pullbacks, rather than home builders'.[23] Maggie Walker countered these arguments, stressing the need for women's organizations, saying, 'Men should not be so pessimistic and down on women's clubs. They don't seek to destroy the home or disgrace the race.'[24] In fact, the Richmond Council of Colored Women, of which she was founder and president, and many other women's organizations worked to elevate the entire black community, and this, she believed, was the proper province of women.

In 1908 two Richmond men, Daniel Webster Davis and Giles Jackson, published *The Industrial History of the Negro Race of the United States*, which became a textbook for black children throughout the state. The chapter on women acknowledged the economic and social achievements of black women but concluded that 'the Negro Race Needs Housekeepers ... wives who stay at home, being supported by their husbands, and then they can spend time in the training of their children'.[25] Maggie Walker responded practically to those who held such ideas: 'The bold fact remains that there are more women in the world than men; . . . if each and every woman in the land was allotted a man to marry her, work for her, support her, and keep her at home, there would still be an army of women left uncared for, unprovided for, and who would be compelled to fight life's battles alone, and without the companionship of man.'[26] Even regarding those women who did marry, she contended, 'The old doctrine that a man marries a woman to support her is pretty nearly threadbare to-day.' Only a few black men were able to fully support their families on their earnings alone. Thus many married women worked, 'not for name, not for glory and honor—but for bread, and for [their] babies'.[27]

The reality was that black women who did go to work outside the home found themselves in a helpless position. 'How many occupations have Negro Women?' asked Walker. 'Let us count them: Negro women are domestic menials, teachers and church builders.' And even the first two of these, she feared, were in danger. As Walker perceived it, the expansion of opportunities for white women did not mean a corresponding expansion for black women; instead, this trend might actually lead to an even greater limitation on the economic possibilities for black women. She pointed to the fact that white women's entry into the tobacco factories of the city had 'driven the Negro woman out', and she, like many of her sisters throughout the country, feared that a similar trend was beginning even in domestic work.[28]

In fact, these economic realities led members of the Order of Saint Luke to discuss the development of manufacturing operations as a means of giving employment and therefore 'a chance in the race of life' to 'the young Negro woman'.[29] In 1902 Walker described herself as 'consumed with the desire to hear the whistle on our factory and see our women by the hundreds coming to work'.[30] It was this same concern for the economic status of black women that led Walker and other Saint Luke women to affiliate with the National Association of Wage Earners (NAWE), a women's organization that sought to pool the energies and resources of housewives, professionals, and managerial, domestic, and industrial workers to protect and expand the economic position of black women. The NAWE argued that it was vital that all black women be able to support themselves.[31] Drawing on traditional stereotypes in the same breath with which she defied them, Walker contended that it was in the self-interest of black men to unite themselves with these efforts to secure decent employment for black women: 'Every dollar a

461

woman makes, some man gets the direct benefit of same. Every woman was by Divine Providence created for some man; not for some man to marry, take home and support, but for the purpose of using her powers, ability, health and strength, to forward the financial . . . success of the partnership into which she may go, if she will. . . . [W]hat stronger combination could ever God make—than the partnership of a business man and a business woman.'[32]

By implication, whatever black women as a whole were able to achieve would directly benefit black men. In Walker's analysis family is a reciprocal metaphor for community: family is community and community is family. But this is more than rhetorical style. Her discussions of relationship networks suggest that the entire community was one's family. Thus Walker's references to husbands and wives reflected equally her understandings of male/female relationships in the community as a whole and of those relationships within the household. Just as all family members' resources were needed for the family to be well and strong, so they were needed for a healthy community/family.

In the process of developing means of expanding economic opportunities in the community, however, Walker and the Saint Luke women also confronted white Richmond's notions of the proper place of blacks. While whites found a bank headed by a 'Negress' an interesting curiosity,[33] they were less receptive to other business enterprises. In 1905 twenty-two black women from the Independent Order of Saint Luke collectively formed a department store aimed at providing quality goods at more affordable prices than those available in stores outside the black community, as well as a place where black women could earn a living and get a business education. The Saint Luke Emporium employed fifteen women as salesclerks. While this may seem an insignificant number in comparison to the thousands of black women working outside the home, in the context of the occupational structure of Richmond these women constituted a significant percentage of the white-collar and skilled working-class women in the community. In 1900 less than 1 per cent of the employed black women in the city were either clerical or skilled workers. That number had quadrupled by 1910, when 222 of the more than 13 000 employed black women listed their occupations as typists, stenographers, bookkeepers, salesclerks, and the like. However, by 1930 there had been a reduction in the numbers of black women employed in clerical and sales positions. This underscores the fact that black secretaries and clerks were entirely dependent on the financial stability of black businesses and in this regard the Independent Order of Saint Luke was especially important. With its fifty-five clerks in the home office, over one-third of the black female clerical workers in Richmond in the 1920s worked for this order. The quality of the work experience was significantly better for these women as compared to those employed as labourers in the tobacco factories or as servants in private homes. They worked in healthier, less stressful environments and, being employed by blacks, they also escaped the racism prevalent in most black women's work-places. Additionally, the salaries of these clerical workers were often better than those paid even to black professional women, that is, teachers. While one teacher, Ethel Thompson Overby, was receiving $18 a month as a teacher and working her way up to the top of the scale at $40, a number of black women were finding good working conditions and a $50-per-month paycheck as clerks in the office of the Independent Order of Saint Luke. Nevertheless, black women in Richmond, as elsewhere, overwhelmingly remained employed in domestic service in the years 1890–1930.[34]

Located on East Broad Street, Richmond's main business thoroughfare, the Saint Luke Emporium met stiff opposition from white merchants. When the intention to establish the department store was first announced, attempts were made to buy the property at a price several thousand dollars higher than that which the Order of Saint Luke had originally paid. When that did not succeed, an offer of $10 000 cash was made to the order if it would not start the emporium. Once it opened, efforts were made to hinder the store's operations. A white Retail Dealers' Association was formed for the purpose of crushing this business as well as other 'Negro merchants who are objectionable . . . because they compete with and get a few dollars which would otherwise go to the white merchant'. Notices were sent to wholesale merchants in the city warning them not to sell to the emporium at the risk of losing all business from any of the white merchants. Letters were also sent to wholesale houses in New York City with the same warning. These letters charged that the emporium was underselling the white merchants of Richmond. Clearly, then, the white businessmen of Richmond found the emporium and these black women a threat; if it was successful, the store could lead to a surge of black merchants competing with white merchants and thus decrease the black patronage at white stores. The white merchants' efforts were ultimately successful: the obstacles they put in the way of the emporium, in addition to the lack of full support from the black community itself, resulted in the department store's going out of business seven years after its founding.[35] Though its existence was short-lived and its demise mirrors many of the problems that black businesses faced from both within and without their community, the effort demonstrated the commitment of the Order of Saint Luke to provide needed services for the community and needed opportunities for black women.

Maggie Walker's appeals for support of the emporium show quite clearly the way in which her notions of race, of womanhood, and of community fused. Approximately one year after the opening of the emporium, Walker called for a mass gathering of men in the community to talk, in part, about support for the business. Her speech, 'Beniah's Valour; An Address for Men Only', opened with an assessment of white businessmen's and officials' continuing oppression of the black community. In her fine rhetorical style she queried her audience. 'Hasn't it crept into your minds that we are being more and more oppressed each day that we live? Hasn't it yet come to you, that we are being oppressed by the passage of laws which not only have for their object the degradation of Negro manhood and Negro womanhood, but also the destruction of all kinds of Negro enterprises?' Then, drawing upon the biblical allegory of Beniah and the lion, she warned, 'There is a lion terrorizing us, preying upon us, and upon every business effort which we put forth. The name of this insatiable lion is PREJUDICE. . . . The white press, the white pulpit, the white business associations, the legislature—all . . . the lion with whom we contend daily . . . in Broad Street, Main Street and in every business street of Richmond. Even now . . . that lion is seeking some new plan of attack.'[36]

Thus, she contended, the vital question facing their community was how to kill the lion. And in her analysis, 'the only way to kill the Lion is to stop feeding it.' The irony was that the black community drained itself of resources, money, influence, and patronage to feed its predator.[37] As she had many times previously, Walker questioned the fact that while the white community oppressed the black, 'the Negro . . . carries to their bank every dollar he can get his hands upon and then goes back the next day, borrows and then pays the white man to lend him his own money.'[38] So, too, black people patronized stores and other businesses in which white women were, in increasing numbers, being hired as salesclerks and secretaries while black women were increasingly without employment and the black community as a whole was losing resources, skills, and finances.[39] Walker considered such behaviour racially destructive and believed it necessary to break those ties that kept 'the Negro . . .

so wedded to those who oppress him'.[40] The drain on the resources of the black community could be halted by a concentration on the development of a self-sufficient black community. But to achieve this would require the talents of the entire community/family. It was therefore essential that black women's work in the community be 'something more tangible than elegant papers, beautifully framed resolutions and pretty speeches'. Rather, 'the exercising of every talent that God had given them' was required in the effort to 'raise . . . the race to higher planes of living'.[41]

The Saint Luke women were part of the Negro Independence Movement that captured a large segment of Richmond society at the turn of the century. Disillusioned by the increasing prejudice and discrimination in this period, which one historian has described as the nadir in US race relations, black residents of Richmond nevertheless held on to their belief in a community that they could collectively sustain.[42] As they witnessed a steady erosion of their civil and political rights, however, they were aware that there was much operating against them. In Richmond, as elsewhere, a system of race and class oppression including segregation, disfranchisement, relegation to the lowest rungs of the occupational strata, and enforcement of racial subordination through intimidation was fully in place by the early twentieth century. In Richmond between 1885 and 1915 all blacks were removed from the city council; the only predominantly black political district, Jackson Ward, was gerrymandered out of existence; the state constitutional convention disfranchised the majority of black Virginians; first the railroads and streetcars, and later the jails, juries, and neighbourhoods were segregated; black principals were removed from the public schools and the right of blacks to teach was questioned; the state legislature decided to substitute white for black control of Virginia Normal and College and to strike 'and College' from both name and function; and numerous other restrictions were imposed. As attorney J. Thomas Hewin noted, he and his fellow black Richmonders occupied 'a peculiar position in the body politics':

He [the Negro] is not wanted in politics, because his presence in official positions renders him obnoxious to his former masters and their descendants. He is not wanted in the industrial world as a trained handicraftsman, because he would be brought into competition with his white brother. He is not wanted in city positions, because positions of that kind are always saved for the wardheeling politicians. He is not wanted in State and Federal offices, because there is an unwritten law that a Negro shall not hold an office. He is not wanted on the Bench as a judge, because he would have to pass upon the white man's case also. Nor is he wanted on public conveyances, because here his presence is obnoxious to white people.[43]

Assessing the climate of the surrounding society in 1904, John Mitchell, Jr., editor of the *Richmond Planet*, concluded, 'This is the beginning of the age of conservatism.'[44] The growing movement within the community for racial self-determination urged blacks to depend upon themselves and their community rather than upon whites: to depend upon their own inner strengths, to build their own institutions, and thereby to mitigate the ways in which their lives were determined by the white forces arrayed against them. Race pride, self-help, racial co-operation, and economic development were central to their thinking about their community and to the ways in which they went about building their own internal support system in order to be better able to struggle within the majority system.

The Saint Luke women argued that the development of the community could not be achieved by men alone, or by men on behalf of women. Only a strong and unified community made up of both women and men could wield the power necessary to allow black people to shape their own lives. Therefore, only when women were able to exercise their full strength would the community be at its full strength, they argued. Only when the community was at its full strength would they be able to create their own conditions, conditions that would allow men as well as women to move out of their structural isolation at the bottom of the labour market and to overcome their political impotence in the larger society. The Saint Luke women argued that it was therefore in the self-interest of black men and of the community as a whole to support expanded opportunities for women.

Their arguments redefined not only the roles of women but also the roles and notions of manhood. A strong 'race man' traditionally meant one who stood up fearlessly in defence of the race. In her 'Address for Men' Walker argued that one could not defend the race unless one defended black women. Appealing to black men's notions of themselves as the protectors of black womanhood, she asked on behalf of all her sisters for their 'FRIENDSHIP, . . . LOVE, . . . SYMPATHY, . . . PROTECTION, and . . . ADVICE': 'I am asking you, men of Richmond, . . . to record [yourselves] as . . . the strong race men of our city. . . . I am asking each man in this audience to go forth from this building, determined to do valiant deeds for the Negro Women of Richmond.'[45] And how might they offer their friendship, love, and protection; how might they do valiant deeds for Negro womanhood? By supporting the efforts of black women to exercise every talent;[46] by 'let[ting] woman choose her own vocation, just as man does his';[47] by supporting the efforts then underway to provide increased opportunities—economic, political, and social—for black women.[48] Once again she drew upon traditional notions of the relationship between men and women at the same time that she countered those very notions. Black men could play the role of protector and defender of womanhood by protecting and defending and aiding women's assault on the barriers generally imposed on women.[49] Only in this way could they really defend the race. Strong race consciousness and strong support of equality for black women were inseparable. Maggie Walker and the other Saint Luke women therefore came to argue that an expanded role for black women within the black community itself was an essential step in the community's fight to overcome the limitations imposed upon the community by the larger society. Race men were therefore defined not just by their actions on behalf of black rights but by their actions on behalf of women's rights. The two were inseparable.

This was a collective effort in which Walker believed black men and black women should be equally engaged. Therefore, even in creating a woman's organization, she and her Saint Luke associates found it essential to create space within the structure for men as well. Unlike many of the fraternal orders that were male or female only, the Order of Saint Luke welcomed both genders as members and as employees. Although the office force was all female, men were employed in the printing department, in field-work, and in the bank. Principal offices within the order were open to men and women. Ten of the thirty directors of the emporium were male; eight of the nineteen trustees of the order were male. The Saint Luke women thus strove to create an equalitarian organization, with men neither dominant nor auxiliary. Their vision of the order was a reflection of their vision for their community. In the 1913 Saint Luke Thanksgiving Day celebration of the order, Maggie Walker 'thank[ed] God that this is a *woman's* organization, broad enough, liberal enough, and unselfish enough to accord equal rights and equal opportunity to men'.[50]

Only such a community could become self-sustaining, self-sufficient, and independent, could enable its members to live lives unhampered by the machinations of the larger society, and could raise children who could envision a different world in which to live

467

and then could go about creating it. The women in the Order of Saint Luke sought to carve a sphere for themselves where they could practically apply their belief in their community and in the potential that black men and women working together could achieve, and they sought to infuse that belief into all of black Richmond and to transmit it to the next generation.

The Saint Luke women challenged notions in the black community about the proper role of women; they challenged notions in the white community about the proper place of blacks. They expanded their roles in ways that enabled them to maintain traditional values of family/community and at the same time move into new spheres and relationships with each other and with the men in their lives. To the larger white society they demonstrated what black men and women in community could achieve. This testified to the idea that women's struggle and race struggle were not two separate phenomena but one indivisible whole. 'First by practice and then by precept'[51] Maggie Lena Walker and the Saint Luke women demonstrated in their own day the power of black women discovering their own strengths and sharing them with the whole community.[52] They provide for us today a model of womanist praxis.

Womanism challenges the distinction between theory and action. Too often we have assumed that theory is to be found only in carefully articulated position statements. Courses on feminist theory are woefully lacking on anything other than white, Western, middle-class perspectives; feminist scholars would argue that this is due to the difficulty in locating any but contemporary black feminist thought. Though I have discussed Maggie Lena Walker's public statements, the clearest articulation of her theoretical perspective lies in the organization she helped to create and in her own activities. Her theory and her action are not distinct and separable parts of some whole; they are often synonymous, and it is only through her actions that we clearly hear her theory. The same is true for the lives of many other black women who had limited time and resources and maintained a holistic view of life and struggle.

More important, Maggie Lena Walker's womanism challenges the dichotomous thinking that underlies much feminist theory and writing. Moist feminist theory poses opposites in exclusionary and hostile ways: one is black and female, and these are contradictory/problematical statuses. This either/or approach classifies phenomena in such a way that 'everything falls into one category or another, but cannot belong to more than one category at the same time'.[53] It is precisely this kind of thinking that makes it difficult to see race, sex, and class as forming one consciousness and the resistance of race, sex, and class oppression as forming one struggle. Womanism flows from a both/and world-view, a consciousness that allows for the resolution of seeming contradictions 'not through an either/or negation but through the interaction' and wholeness. Thus, while black and female may, at one level, be radically different orientations, they are at the same time united, with each 'confirming the existence of the other'. Rather than standing as 'contradictory opposites', they become 'complementary, unsynthesized, unified wholes'.[54] This is what Ogunyemi refers to as 'the dynamism of wholeness'. This holistic consciousness undergirds the thinking and action of Maggie Lena Walker and the other Saint Luke women. There are no necessary contradictions between the public and domestic spheres; the community and the family; male and female; race and sex struggle—there is intersection and interdependence.

Dichotomous thinking does not just inhibit our abilities to see the lives of black women and other women of colour in their wholeness, but, I would argue, it also limits our ability to see the wholeness of the lives and consciousnesses of even white middle-class women. The thinking and actions of white women, too, are shaped by their race and their class, and their consciousnesses are also formed by the totality of these factors. The failure, however, to explore the total consciousness of white women has made class, and especially race, non-existent categories in much of white feminist theory. And this has allowed the development of frameworks which render black women's lives invisible. Explorations into the consciousnesses of black women and other women of colour should, therefore, be a model for all women, including those who are not often confronted with the necessity of understanding themselves in these total terms. As we begin to confront the holistic nature of all women's lives, we will begin to create a truly womanist studies. In our efforts Maggie Lena Walker and black women like her will be our guide.

Notes

1. The recent proliferation of works in black women's history and black women's studies makes a complete bibliographical reference prohibitive. For a sample of some of the growing literature on black women's consciousness, see Evelyn Brooks, 'The Feminist Theology of the Black Baptist Church, 1880–1900', in Amy Swerdlow and Hanna Lessinger (eds.), *Class, Race, and Sex: The Dynamics of Control* (Boston: G. K. Hall, 1983), 31–59; Hazel V. Carby, *Reconstructing Womanhood: The Emergence of the Afro-American Woman*

Novelist (New York: Oxford University Press, 1987); Elizabeth Clark-Lewis, ' "This Work Had a' End": The Transition from Live-In to Day Work', *Southern Women: The Intersection of Race, Class, and Gender Working Paper no. 2* (Memphis, Tenn.: Memphis State University, Center for Research on Women, 1985); Patricia Hill Collins, 'The Social Construction of Black Feminist Thought', *Signs: Journal of Women in Culture and Society*, 14/4 (Summer 1989); Cheryl Townsend Gilkes, ' "Together and in Harness": Women's Traditions in the Sanctified Church', *Signs*, 10/4 (Summer 1985), 678–99; Deborah Gray White, *Ar'n't I a Woman? Female Slaves in the Plantation South* (New York: Norton, 1985). Also note: *Sage: A Scholarly Journal on Black Women*, now in its fifth year, has published issues that focus on education, health, work, mother–daughter relationships, and creative arts.

2. On a contemporary political level, this disassociation of gender concerns from race concerns was dramatically expressed in the 1985 United Nations Decade for Women conference held in Nairobi, Kenya, where the official US delegation, including representatives of major white women's organizations but not one representative of a black women's organization, insisted upon not having the proceedings become bogged down with race and national issues such as apartheid so that it could concentrate on birth control and other 'women's' issues. Delegates operating from such a perspective were unable to see African, Asian, and Latin American women who argued for discussion of national political issues as anything other than the tools of men, unfortunate victims unable to discern true women's and feminist struggles. For a discussion of the ways in which these issues were reflected in the Kenya conference, see Ros Young, 'Report from Nairobi: The UN Decade for Women Forum', *Race and Class*, 27/2 (Autumn 1985), 67–71; and the entire issue of *African Women Rising*, 2/1 (Winter–Spring 1986).

3. See Rosalyn Terborg-Penn, 'Discontented Black Feminists: Prelude and Postscript to the Passage of the Nineteenth Amendment', 261–78; Lois Scharf and Joan M. Jensen, 'Introduction', 9–10, both in Lois Scharf and Joan M. Jensen (eds.), *Decades of Discontent: The Women's Movement, 1920–1940* (Westport, Conn.: Greenwood, 1983).

4. Terborg-Penn, 267. A contemporary example of this type of dichotomous analysis is seen in much of the discussion of the feminization of poverty. Drawing commonalities between the experiences of black and white women, such discussions generally leave the impression that poverty was not a 'feminine' problem before white women in increasing numbers were recognized as impoverished. Presumably, before that black women's poverty was considered a result of race; now it is more often considered a result of gender. Linda Burnham has effectively addressed the incompleteness of such analyses, suggesting that they ignore 'class, race, and sex as *simultaneously* operative social factors' in black women's lives ('Has Poverty Been Feminized in Black America?' *Black Scholar*, 16/2 (Mar./Apr. 1985), 14–24 [emphasis mine]).

5. See e.g. Parita Trivedi, 'A Study of "Sheroes",' *Third World Book Review*, 1/2 (1984), 71–2; Angela Davis, *Women, Race, and Class* (New York: Random House, 1981); Nawal el Saadawi, *The Hidden Face of Eve: Women in the Arab World*, trans. Sherif Hetata (Boston: Beacon, 1981); Jenny Bourne, 'Towards an Anti-Racist Feminism', *Race and Class*, 25/1 (Summer 1983), 1–22; Bonnie Thornton Dill, 'Race, Class, and Gender: Prospects for an All-Inclusive Sisterhood', *Feminist Studies*, 9/1 (Spring 1983), 131–50; Evelyn Nakano

Glenn, *Issei, Nisei, War Bride: Three Generations of Japanese American Women in Domestic Service* (Philadelphia: Temple University Press, 1986); Audre Lorde, *Sister/Outsider: Essays and Speeches* (Trumansburg, NY: Crossing Press, 1984); Barbara Smith, 'Some Home Truths on the Contemporary Black Feminist Movement', *Black Scholar*, 16/2 (Mar./Apr. 1985), 4–13; Asoka Bandarage, *Toward International Feminism: The Dialectics of Sex, Race and Class* (London: Zed Press, forthcoming). For a typology of black women's multiple consciousness, see Deborah K. King, 'Race, Class, and Gender Salience in Black Women's Feminist Consciousness' (paper presented at American Sociological Association annual meeting, Section on Racial and Ethnic Minorities, New York, Aug. 1986).

6. Alice Walker's oft-quoted definition is in *In Search of Our Mothers' Gardens: Womanist Prose* (New York: Harcourt, Brace, Jovanovich, 1983), xi–xii: 'Womanist. 1. . . . Responsible. In Charge. *Serious*. 2. . . . Appreciates . . . women's strength. . . . Committed to survival and wholeness of entire people, male *and* female. Not a separatist, except periodically, for health. Traditionally universalist. . . . Traditionally capable. . . . 3. . . . Loves struggle. *Loves* the Folk. Loves herself. *Regardless*. 4. Womanist is to feminist as purple is to lavender.' Cheryl Townsend Gilkes's annotation of Alice Walker's definition ('Women, Religion, and Tradition: A Womanist Perspective' (paper presented in workshop at Summer Research Institute on Race and Gender, Center for Research on Women, Memphis State University, June 1986)) has been particularly important to my understanding of this term.

7. Chikwenye Okonjo Ogunyemi, 'Womanism: The Dynamics of the Contemporary Black Female Novel in English', *Signs*, 11/1 (Autumn 1985), 63–80.

8. May Wright Sewall (ed.), *World's Congress of Representative Women* (Chicago, 1893), 715, quoted in Bert James Loewenberg and Ruth Bogin (eds.), *Black Women in Nineteenth-Century American Life: Their Words, Their Thoughts, Their Feelings* (University Park: Pennsylvania State University Press, 1976), 330–1 [emphasis mine]. See also Anna Julia Cooper, *A Voice from the South: By a Black Woman of the South* (Xenia, Oh.: Aldine, 1892), esp. 'Part First'.

9. Although there exists no scholarly biography of Walker, information is available in several sources. See Wendell P. Dabney, *Maggie L. Walker and The I.O. of Saint Luke: The Woman and Her Work* (Cincinnati: Dabney, 1927); Sadie Iola Daniel, *Women Builders* (Washington, DC: Associated Publishers, 1931), 28–52; Sadie Daniel St. Clair, 'Maggie Lena Walker', in *Notable American Women, 1607–1960* (Cambridge, Mass.: Harvard University Press, Belknap, 1971), 530–1; Elsa Barkley Brown, 'Maggie Lena Walker and the Saint Luke Women' (paper presented at the Association for the Study of Afro-American Life and History 69th annual conference, Washington, DC, Oct. 1984), and ' "Not Alone to Build This Pile of Brick": The Role of Women in the Richmond, Virginia, Black Community, 1890–1930' (paper presented at the Midcontinental and North Central American Studies Association joint conference, University of Iowa, Apr. 1983); Lily Hammond, *In the Vanguard of a Race* (New York: Council of Women for Home Missions and Missionary Education Movement of the United States and Canada, 1922), 108–18; A. B. Caldwell, (ed.), *Virginia Edition, History of the American Negro*, v. (Atlanta: A. B. Caldwell, 1921), 9–11; Rayford Logan, 'Maggie Lena Walker', in Rayford W. Logan and Michael R. Winston (eds.), *Dictionary of American Negro*

Biography (New York: Norton, 1982), 626–7; Gertrude W. Marlowe, 'Maggie Lena Walker: African-American Women, Business, and Community Development; (paper presented at Berkshire Conference on the History of Women, Wellesley, Mass., 21 June 1987); Kim Q. Boyd, ' "An Actress Born, a Diplomat Bred": Maggie L. Walker, Race Woman' (M.A. thesis, Howard University, 1987); Sallie Chandler, 'Maggie Lena Walker (1867–1934: An Abstract of Her Life and Activities', 1975 Oral History Files, Virginia Union University Library, Richmond, Va., 1975; Maggie Lena Walker Paper, Maggie L. Walker National Historic Site, Richmond, Va. (hereafter cited as MLW Papers). Fortunately, much of Walker's history will soon be available; the Maggie L. Walker Biography Project, funded by the National Park Service under the direction of Gertrude W. Marlow, anthropology department, Howard University, is completing a full-scale biography of Walker.

10. Noting the mass base of mutual benefit societies such as the Independent Order of Saint Luke, August Meier has suggested that the activities of these organizations 'reflect the thinking of the inarticulate majority better than any other organizations or the statement of editors and other publicists' (*Negro Thought in America, 1880–1915: Racial Ideologies in the Age of Booker T. Washington* (Ann Arbor: University of Michigan Press, 1963), 130).

11. *50th Anniversary Golden Jubilee Historical Report of the R. W. G. Council I. O. St. Luke, 1867–1917* (Richmond, Va.: Everett Waddey, 1917), 5–6, 20 (hereafter cited as *50th Anniversary*).

12. Maggie L. Walker, 'Diary', 6 Mar. 1928, MLW Papers. My thanks to Sylvester Putman, superintendent, Richmond National Battlefield Park, and Celia Jackson Suggs, site historian, Maggie L. Walker National Historic Site, for facilitating my access to these unprocessed papers.

13. *50th Anniversary*, 26.

14. White (n. 1 above), 119–41. Although I use the term 'sisterhood' here to refer to this female network, sisterhood for black women, including M. L. Walker, meant (and means) not only this special bond among black women but also the ties amongst all kin/community.

15. Of 260 000 black Virginians over the age of twenty-one in 1920, less than 20 000 were eligible to vote in that year's elections. Poll taxes and literacy tests disfranchised many; white Democratic election officials turned many others away from the polls; still others had given up their efforts to vote, realizing that even if they successfully cast their ballots, they were playing in 'a political game which they stood no chance of winning' (Andrew Buni, *The Negro in Virginia Politics, 1902–1965* (Charlottesville: University of Virginia Press, 1967), 77–88). The high proportion of female voters resulted from whites' successful efforts to disfranchise the majority of black male voters, as well as the enthusiasm of women to exercise this new right; see e.g. *Richmond News-Leader* (Aug.–Oct. 1920); *Richmond Times-Dispatch* (Sept.–Oct., 1920). Rosalyn Terborg-Penn (n. 3 above, 275) reports a similarly high percentage of black female voters in 1920s Baltimore. In Richmond, however, black women soon found themselves faced with the same obstacles to political rights as confronted black men. Independent black political parties developed in several southern states where the lily-white Republican faction had successfully purged blacks from leadership positions in that party; see e.g. George C. Wright, 'Black Political Insurgency in Louisville, Kentucky: The Lincoln Independent Party of 1921', *Journal of Negro History*, 68 (Winter 1983), 8–23.

16. M. L. Walker, 'Addresses', 1909, MLW Papers, cited in Celia Jackson Suggs, 'Maggie Lena Walker', *TRUTH: Newsletter of the Association of Black Women Historians*, 7 (Fall 1985), 6.

17. Four of the women elected to the 1901 Saint Luke executive Board were board members of the Woman's Union, which had offices in Saint Luke's Hall; see advertisements in *Richmond Planet* (Aug. 1898–Jan. 3, 1903).

18. Some of the societies had only women members, including some that were exclusively for the mutual assistance of single mothers. For an excellent discussion of the ties among the societies, families, and churches in Richmond, see Peter J. Rachleff, *Black Labor in the South: Richmond, Virginia, 1865–1890* (Philadelphia: Temple University Press, 1984).

19. W. P. Burrell and D. E. Johnson, Sr., *Twenty-Five Years History of the Grand Fountain of the United Order of True Reformers, 1881–1905* (Richmond, Va.: Grand Fountain, United Order of True Reformers, 1909), 76–7.

20. Saint Luke Penny Savings Bank records: Receipts and Disbursements, 1903–9; Minutes, Executive Committee, 1913; Cashier's Correspondence Book, 1913; Minutes, Board of Trustees, 1913–15, Consolidated Bank and Trust Company, Richmond, Va.; *Cleveland Plain Dealer* (28 June 1914), in Peabody Clipping File, Collis P. Huntington Library, Hampton Institute, Hampton, Va. (hereafter cited as Peabody Clipping File), no. 88, i. See also Works Progress Administration, *The Negro in Virginia* (New York: Hastings House, 1940), 299.

21. This analysis owes much to Cheryl Townsend Gilkes's work on black women, particularly her 'Black Women's Work as Deviance: Social Sources of Racial Antagonism within Contemporary Feminism', working paper no. 66 (Wellesley, Mass.: Wellesley College Center for Research on Women, 1979), and '"Holding Back the Ocean with a Broom": Black Women and Community Work', in LaFrances Rodgers-Rose (ed.), *The Black Woman* (Beverly Hills, Calif.: Sage, 1980). Excerpt from speech given by M. L. Walker at 1901 annual Saint Luke convention, *50th Anniversary* (n. 11 above), 23.

22. The prevailing turn-of-the-century stereotype of black women emphasized promiscuity and immorality; these ideas were given prominent in a number of publications, including newspapers, periodicals, philanthropic foundation reports, and popular literature. The attacks by various segments of the white community on the morality of black women and the race at the turn of the century are discussed in Beverly Guy-Sheftall, '"Daughters of Sorrow": Attitudes toward Black Women, 1880–1920' (Ph.D. diss., Emory University, 1984), 62–86; Darlene Clark Hine, 'Lifting the Veil, Shattering the Silence: Black Women's History in Slavery and Freedom', in Darlene Clark Hine (ed.), *The State of Afro-American History: Past, Present, and Future* (Baton Rouge: Louisiana State University Press, 1986), 223–49, esp. 234–8; Willi Coleman, 'Black Women and Segregated Public Transportation: Ninety Years of Resistance', *TRUTH: Newsletter of the Association of Black Women Historians*, 8/2 (1986), 3–10, esp. 7–8; and Paula Giddings, *When and Where I Enter: The Impact of Black Women on Race and Sex in America* (New York: William Morrow, 1984), 82–6. Maggie Walker called attention to these verbal attacks on Negro womanhood in her speech, 'Beniah's Valour: An Address for Men Only', Saint Luke Hall, 1 Mar. 1906, MLW Papers (n. 9 above). It was in part the desire to defend black women and uplift the race that initiated the formation of the National Federation of Black Women's Clubs.

23. Charles F. McLaurin, 'State Federation of Colored Women' (n.p., 10 Nov. 1908), Peabody Clipping File, no. 231, i.
24. Chandler (n. 9), 10–11.
25. Daniel Webster Davis and Giles Jackson, *The Industrial History of the Negro Race of the United States* (Richmond: Virginia Press, 1908), 133. Similar attitudes expressed in the *Virginia Baptist* in 1894 had aroused the ire of the leading figures in the national women's club movement. The *Baptist* had been particularly concerned that women, in exceeding their proper place in the church, were losing their 'womanliness' and that 'the exercise of the right of suffrage would be a deplorable climax to these transgressions'; see discussion of the *Baptist* in *Women's Era*, 1/6 (Sept. 1894), 8.
26. M. L. Walker, 'Speech to Federation of Colored Women's Clubs', Hampton Va., 14 July 1912, MLW Papers (n. 9).
27. M. L. Walker, 'Speech to the Negro Young People's Christian and Educational Congress', Convention Hall, Washington, DC, 5 Aug. 1906, MLW Papers.
28. Quotations are from M. L. Walker, 'Speech to the Federation of Colored Women's Clubs'. These ideas, however, were a central theme in Walker's speeches and were repeated throughout the years. See e.g. 'Speech to the Negro Young People's Christian and Educational Congress' and 'Beniah's Valour' (n. 2 above). See also the *St. Luke Herald's* first editorial, 'Our Mission' (29 Mar. 1902), repr. in *50th Anniversary* (n. 11 above), 26.
29. Excerpt from speech given by M. L. Walker at 1901 annual Saint Luke convention, *50th Anniversary*, 23.
30. See 'Our Mission' (n. 28 above).
31. The NAWE, having as its motto 'Support Thyself—Work', aimed at making 'the colored woman a factor in the labor world'. Much of its work was premised upon the belief that white women were developing an interest in domestic science and other 'Negro occupations' to such an extent that the prospects for work for young black women were becoming seriously endangered. They believed also that when white women entered the fields of housework, cooking, and the like, these jobs would be classified as professions. It therefore was necessary for black women to become professionally trained in even domestic work in order to compete. Container 308, Nannie Helen Burroughs Papers, Manuscript Division, Library of Congress.
32. M. L. Walker, 'Speech to Federation of Colored Women's Clubs' (n. 28).
33. See e.g. 'Negress Banker Says If Men Can, Women Can', *Columbus Journal* (16 Sept. 1909), Peabody Clipping File (n. 20 above), no. 231, vii; see also Chandler (n. 9 above), 32.
34. In 1900, 83.8 per cent of employed black women worked in domestic and personal service; in 1930, 76.5 per cent. US Bureau of the Census, *Twelfth Census of the United States Taken in the Year 1900, Population Part 1* (Washington, DC: Census Office, 1901), *Thirteenth Census of the United States Taken in the Year 1910*, iv: *Population 1910: Occupuation Statistics* (Washington, DC: Government Printing Office, 1914), 595, and *Fifteenth Census of the United States: Population*, iv: *Occupations, by States* (Washington, DC: Government Printing Office, 1933); Benjamin Brawley, *Negro Builders and Heroes* (Chapel Hill: University of North Carolina Press, 1937), 267–72; US Bureau of the Census, *Fourteenth Census of the United States Taken in the Year 1920*, iv: *Population 1920: Occupations* (Washington, DC: Government Printing Office, 1923); Ethel Thompson Overby, ' "It's Better to Light a Candle than to Curse

the Darkness": The Autobiographical Notes of Ethel Thompson Overby' (1975), copy in Virginia Historical Society, Richmond.

35. The business, which opened the Monday before Easter, 1905, officially closed in Jan. 1912. Information on the emporium is found in *50th Anniversary* (n. 11 above), 55, 76–7; *New York Age*, 16 Mar. 1905, Peabody Clipping File, no. 88, i, 'Maggie Lena Walker Scrapbook', MLW Papers (n. 9 above); Daniels (n. 9 above), 41. The most detailed description of the opposition to the emporium is in M. L. Walker, 'Beniah's Valour' (n. 22 above), quote is from this speech.

36. M. L. Walker, 'Beniah's Valour'.

37. Ibid.

38. Chandler (n. 9 above), 30.

39. M. L. Walker, 'Beniah's Valour'.

40. Chandler, 30.

41. *New York Age* (22 June 1909), Peabody Clipping File, no. 231, i.

42. Rayford W. Logan, *The Betrayal of the Negro from Rutherford B. Hayes to Woodrow Wilson* (New York: Collier, 1965; originally pub. in 1954 as *The Negro in American Life and Thought: The Nadir*).

43. J. Thomas Hewin, 'Is the Criminal Negro Justly Dealt with in the Courts of the South?' in D. W. Culp (ed.), *Twentieth Century Negro Literature, or a Cyclopedia of Thought on the Vital Topics Relating to the American Negro* (Toronto: J. L. Nichols, 1902), 110–11.

44. *Richmond Planet* (30 Apr. 1904).

45. M. L. Walker, 'Beniah's Valour' (n. 22 above).

46. *New York Age* (22 June 1909), Peabody Clipping File, no. 231, i.

47. M. L. Walker, 'Speech to the Federation of Colored Women's Clubs' (n. 26 above).

48. M. L. Walker, 'Beniah's Valour'. This appeal for support of increased opportunities for black women permeated all of Walker's speeches. In her last speeches in 1934 she continued her appeal for support of race enterprises (newspaper clipping (n.p., n.d.), 'Maggie Laura Walker Scrapbook', MLW Papers [n. 9 above]). Maggie Laura Walker is Walker's granddaughter.

49. W. E. B. DuBois, who explored extensively the connection between race struggle and women's struggle in 'The Damnation of Women', also challenged men's traditional roles: 'The present mincing horror of a free womanhood must pass if we are ever to be rid of the bestiality of a free manhood; *not by guarding the weak in weakness do we gain strength, but by making weakness free and strong*' (emphasis mine; *Darkwater, Voices from within the Veil* (New York: Harcourt, Brace, & Howe, 1920), 165).

50. M. L. Walker, 'Saint Luke Thanksgiving Day Speech', City Auditorium, 23 Mar. 1913, MLW Papers (n. 9 above).

51. M. L. Walker, 'Address: Virginia Day Third Street Bethel AME Church', 29 Jan. 1933, MLW Papers.

52. Ogunyemi (n. 7 above; 72–3) takes this idea from Stephen Henderson's analysis of the role of the blues and blues women in the Africanamerican community.

53. The essays in Vernon J. Dixon and Badi G. Foster (eds.), *Beyond Black or White: An Alternate America* (Boston: Little, Brown, 1971) explore the either/or and the both/and world-view in relation to Africanamerican systems of analysis; the quote can be found in Dixon, 'Two Approaches to Black-White Relations', 23–66, esp. 25–6.

54. Johnella E. Butler explores the theoretical, methodological, and pedagogical implications of these systems of analysis in *Black Studies: Pedagogy and Revolution: A Study of Afro-American Studies and the Liberal Arts Tradition through the Discipline of Afro-American Literature* (Washington DC: University Press of America, 1981), esp. 96–102.

17 Gender in the Critiques of Colonialism and Nationalism: Locating the 'Indian Woman'

Mrinalini Sinha

Kumkum Sangari and Sudesh Vaid's excellent analysis of the historical processes which reconstituted patriarchy in colonial India provides both a definition and an example of the potential of feminist historiography. They provide a definition of feminist historiography that goes much beyond an exclusively 'women's history'. According to Sangari and Vaid, 'a feminist historiography rethinks historiography as a whole and discards the idea of women as something to be *framed* by a context, in order to be able to think of gender difference as both structuring and structured by the wide set of social relations.'[1] Hence they argue, on the one hand, that feminist historiography is neither a choice, as in the choice of an area or field of study, nor a simple inclusion of women, nor an evaluation of their participation in particular movements, but rather a mode of questioning that must undergird all attempts at historical reconstruction. On the other hand, they also suggest that 'patriarchies are not . . . systems either predating or superadded to class and caste but are intrinsic to the very formation of, and changes within, these categories'.[2] Feminist historiography, conceived in these terms, recognizes that all aspects of reality are gendered and that the very experience of gender changes according to race, class/caste, nation, and sexuality.

This double move is also being reflected in feminist theory in general. This is evident, for example, in the bid to go beyond the simple enumeration of gender, race, class/caste, nationality, and sexuality, as parallel or co-equal axes along which oppression, identity, and subjectivity are organized, to a recognition of the ways in which these axes are mutually determining and necessarily implicated in one another. For, as Chandra Mohanty puts it, 'no one "becomes a woman" (in Simone de Beauvoir's sense) purely

Reprinted with permission from Ann-Louise Shapiro (ed.), *Feminist Revision History* (New Brunswick, NJ: Rutgers University Press, 1994).

because she is female. . . . It is the intersections of the various sys-
temic networks of class, race, (hetero)sexuality and nation . . . that
position us as "women".' This, according to Teresa de Lauretis,
marks the crucial shift in feminist consciousness brought about by
the interventions made by women of colour and lesbians. It has led,
she suggests, to a redefinition of the feminist subject as 'not [just]
unified or *simply divided* between positions of masculinity and femininity, but *multiply organized* across positionalities along several
axes and across mutually contradictory discourses and practices'.
This recognition of the interrelatedness and co-implication of various other categories, such as race, class, nation, and sexuality, in
gender and in one another, has made possible the redefinition of the
'feminist subject . . . as much less pure, as indeed ideologically com-
plicitous with "the oppressor" whose position [the feminist sub-
ject] may occupy in certain sociosexual relations (though not in
others), on one or another axis'.[4]

It is from within the challenges of feminist historiography as
defined by Sangari and Vaid, and the redefinition of the feminist
subject as outlined by Teresa de Lauretis, that I pose the problem of
locating 'Indian womanhood' and the politics of feminism in colonial India. I will approach this question through a discussion of a
particular historical controversy in India, occasioned by the 1927
publication of the American-born writer Katherine Mayo's *Mother
India*.[5] *Mother India* was ostensibly an exposé of the condition of
women in India. Although Mayo's book focuses on the various
inequities imposed upon women, such as child marriage and pre-
mature maternity, by a patriarchal Hindu culture, it includes a
more wide-ranging discussion of India's various social, economic,
and political ills, for which Mayo held Hindu culture responsible.
Mayo arrived at the conclusion that far from being ready for political self-determination, India needed the continued 'civilizing'
influence of the British. Her connections with the official British
propaganda machine quickly discredited Mayo's credentials as a
champion of women's issues in India. For nationalists, however,
Mother India's attack on the political and cultural project of Indian
nationalism, made under the pretext of a discussion of the condition of women in India, could not be left unchallenged.[6] Indeed, the
book generated a tremendous controversy, the impact of which was
felt in India, Britain, and the United States.

My interest in this particular controversy as an Indian feminist
grew out of an earlier effort to reconstruct the Indian woman as
subject in the debate in which both sides used the Indian woman as

the object of their starkly opposed evaluations of Indian society. My attempt was to highlight the contributions of individual women and of the women's movement in India to the *Mother India* debate. Here, I return to my earlier reading of the emergence in this controversy of what Sarojini Naidu and her other middle-class/upper caste contemporaries identified as the 'authentic voice of modern Indian womanhood'[7] in order to explore the particular discursive strategies by which a subject position was created enabling the Indian woman to speak. I will explore the opportunity that such a reading offers for locating the Indian woman and the politics of middle-class Indian feminism.

My earlier inclination had been simply to read women's responses, following Joanna Liddle and Rama Joshi's analysis of the women's movement in India, as naturally occupying a space from which both male nationalist patriarchy and imperialist feminism could be critiqued in order to disrupt imperialist–nationalist invocations of the Indian woman in the *Mother India* controversy.[8] However the responses of the individual women and of the organized women's movement were not readily amenable to such an analysis. A nationalistic critic of imperialism and/or imperialist feminism could very easily interpret the women's responses as a triumph of the general nationalist critique of *Mother India*. For a feminist critic of nationalism, however, the women's responses could be read just as easily as a co-optation of Indian women by nationalist politics.[9] Such possible interpretations proved to be inadequate in one crucial way. To paraphrase Chandra Mohanty, reading women's responses simply in terms of their 'achievements' or their 'failures' in relation to some ideal effectively removes them and the ideal from history, and freezes them in time and space.[10] I was forced to recognize that any interpretation that hoped to historicize women's responses or the ideals against which they are measured must refuse to take as given or self-evident either the gender politics of colonialism and nationalism which framed the *Mother India* controversy or the self-constitution of the Indian woman herself in women's responses to the controversy. Such a reading would have to take into account both the historical context which made possible the identity of the Indian woman and the particular strategies by which women learned to speak in the voice of the Indian woman.

The historical context in which the identity of the Indian woman emerged has been written about extensively, but comparatively little work gas been done on women's own self-constitution within this context.[11] Here, therefore, my efforts to locate Indian woman-hood and the politics of middle-class Indian feminism in the *Mother India* controversy will shift between a survey of some recent scholarship on the gender politics of colonialism and nationalism and an examination of the voice of Indian womanhood itself. This survey in no way pretends to be exhaustive, but touches primarily on those issues that may enhance a reading of Indian women's voices in the *Mother India* controversy. I will return to the responses of Indian women themselves via a brief discussion of gender in some critiques of colonialism and nationalism in India.

Chandra Mohanty's introduction to *Third World Women and the Politics of Feminism* identifies three symptomatic characteristics of imperial rule: the ideological construction and consolidation of white masculinity as normative, and the corresponding racialization and sexualization of colonized peoples; the effects of colonial institutions and policies in transforming indigenous patriarchies and consolidating hegemonic middle-class cultures in metropolitan and colonized areas; and the rise of feminist politics and consciousness in this historical context within and against the framework of national liberation movements.[12] These aspects of imperial rule mark both Mayo's *Mother India* and the imperialist–nationalist controversy following the book's publication. I will briefly make a note of some of these elements in the framing of *Mother India* and the subsequent controversy, but will focus mainly on the impact of imperial rule on the emergence of a hegemonic middle-class Indian culture and its implications for the mobilization of women in the *Mother India* controversy.

Ann Stoler, in an article on the colonial cultures of French Indo-China and the Dutch East Indies, makes the important point that the very categories of 'colonizer' and 'colonized', essential for the exercise of imperial authority, were never stable, but needed to be secured through various policies and practices that constructed and regulated particular, historically specific, gendered, and racialized identities.[13] Stoler's analysis has implications for understanding why the construct of the 'manly Englishman' as the liberator of helpless Indian women and other oppressed groups becomes such a crucial element in Mayo's defence of imperial rule. Mayo's use of such old colonial stereotypes as the enlightened and reform-minded British official and the indolent and selfish Indian male who was the nemesis of helpless Indian women, however, also limited her discussion of Indian women. Consequently, in *Mother India* the Indian woman appears either as the object of the benevolent salvation of British imperialists or the object of the Indian male's cruel and barbaric practices.

Various scholars have also pointed out the collusion between imperialist and indigenous patriarchies in nineteenth-century debates over the 'woman's question' in India. Lata Mani's and Uma Chakravorty's analyses of debates about women in social-reform and protonationalist movements in India have provided illuminating insights into the simultaneous proliferation of discourses about women and their surprising marginalization in these same discourses.[14] Lata Mani's study of the official discourse on the regulation and the eventual abolition of the practice of widow immolation (sati) in the early nineteenth century clearly demonstrates that women were seldom the major concern of the various groups in this debate; instead, women were merely the sites on which competing views of tradition and modernity were debated. The legacy of these nineteenth-century debates about women was felt in many ways in the Mother India controversy. The understanding of tradition and modernity, for example, that framed the responses to child marriage and early sexuality were particularly colonial constructs; the arguments for and against the practice of child marriage were made, as Lata Mani has so brilliantly identified, in the context of the early nineteenth-century debate over sati, on the basis of a selective, textualized construct of Hindu culture and tradition. In such a context, the debate over child-marriage reforms shifted attention from the historical and material conditions for such practices to an evaluation of Indian culture. Both imperialists and nationalists invoked the position of the Indian woman to buttress their opposing evaluations of Indian culture. Uma Chakravorty, for example, has demonstrated that the upper-caste/class concept of the Indian/Arya woman was crucial to the modern re-invention of traditions for the protonationalist and nationalist project of national regeneration. Not surprisingly, therefore, the image of the Indian woman featured prominently in the Mother India debate: both sides invoked her in their battle over the nature of 'India'.

The image of the Indian woman as simply the object of imperialist–nationalist debates, however, was further complicated by the broader nationalist agenda. The re-articulation of middle-class Indian womanhood had been necessary for the emergence of a new middle-class public and private sphere in colonial India; this same ideal of womanhood also offered a space for the mobilization of middle-class women themselves. The significance of the ideal of womanhood to the consolidation of a hegemonic middle-class culture has been examined by several scholars. Sangari and Vaid, drawing upon the works of Partha Chatterjee and Sumanta Banerjee, suggest that the definition of Indian womanhood was closely tied to the class polarization that accompanied the development of the middle class, and to the anxieties of colonial nationalism. Sumanta Banerjee argues that the need for sharper differentiation between the classes provided the context for the regulation of women's popular culture in the nineteenth century, and for the creation of a new public space for the respectable *bhadramahila* (new, educated middle-class woman) who was now defined in opposition to women from the lower economic strata.[15]

According to Partha Chatterjee, a re-articulation of Indian womanhood was crucial in the resolution of the 'constitutive contradiction' in the formation of an Indian identity.[16] The central problem for Indian nationalism, he suggests, was the problem of modernizing the nation on Western terms while at the same time retaining an essential national identity as the basis for a political claim to nationhood. Nationalist thought dealt with this contradiction by distinguishing the spiritual from the material and the inner from the outer. Nationalists could now afford to imitate the West in the outer or material sphere while retaining the spiritual or the inner sphere as an 'uncolonized space' wherein the essence of Indianness could be located. This dichotomy was related, he suggests, to the socially prescribed roles for men and women. Women as the guardians of the inner or spiritual sphere of the nation were now regarded as the embodiments of an essentialized 'Indianness'.

The re-articulation of the Indian woman for the self-definition of the nationalist bourgeoisie provided the context for the 'modernizing' of certain indigenous patriarchal modes of regulating women in orthodox Indian society.[17] Although the critique of orthodox indigenous patriarchy did afford a limited agenda for the emancipation and self-emancipation of women, its emancipatory politics were severely constrained within the modernizing project of Indian nationalism. The models for modernization, for example, drew upon notions of bourgeois domesticity and the ideals of Victorian womanhood introduced via British rule in India; yet they were crucially modified to suit the particular needs of the nationalist bourgeoisie. Dipesh Chakrabarty suggests, drawing upon Chatterjee's work, that the 'originality' of the Indian middle-class project of modernization was constituted by the nationalist 'denial of the bourgeois private': the cultural norm of a patriarchal, patrilineal, patrilocal extended family was counterposed to the bourgeois patriarchal ideals of companionate marriage.[18] This reconfiguration of the middle-class 'home', he suggests, was part of the history of the development of the modern individual in India. Indeed, it was central in marking the difference between what was 'Indian' and what was 'European/English'.

We can see the impact that nationalist modifications of bourgeois domesticity had on the construct of the Indian woman in Chakrabarty's analysis of the word 'freedom' in debates about women's education in nineteenth-century India. He suggests that while freedom in the West was defined as the right to self-indulgence, freedom in India was defined as the capacity to serve and obey voluntarily. Hence, unlike the ultra-free Western/Westernized woman who was selfish and shameless, the 'modern' Indian woman was defined as educated enough to contribute to the larger body politic but yet 'modest' enough to be un-self-assertive and unselfish.[19] The ideological construct of the modern Indian woman as 'superior' to orthodox, uneducated women, to women of the lower castes/class, and to the Western/Westernized woman was key to the emerging social order in India, characterized by the consolidation of the nationalist bourgeoisie. At the same time, however, the construct of the modern Indian woman also created the climate both for women's reforms and for women's entry, under male patronage, to the male-dominated public sphere. The impact of this was evident in the unprecedented mobilization of middle-class women on behalf of the Gandhi-led nationalist movement, as well as in the all-India women's organizations and movements in the early twentieth century.

The question that we might legitimately raise at this point is that, given the ideological structures of domination outlined above, how can any reading of women's responses, as those in the *Mother India* controversy, hope to reconstruct the Indian woman as the subject of the controversy? In other words, do the ideological constructs that condition women's participation predetermine the nature of women's responses and make any interrogation of the consciousness and agency of women themselves irrelevant? I contend that a focus on the voice or the agency of women themselves does not have to be opposed to an examination of the ideological structures from which they emerged. I focus on women's responses during the *Mother India* controversy, not because they make visible the voice of the modern Indian woman that was always there, simply waiting to be expressed, but because these responses make visible the particular strategies by which a subject position was created, in a certain historical moment, from which the Indian woman could speak.

The question of the Indian woman's voice was clearly critical to the narrativization of the *Mother India* controversy. In the midst of the controversy, for example, *The Times* of London carried a piece with the provocative title: 'Indian Women: Are They Voiceless?'[20] Indian nationalists were happy to be able to give a resounding no to that question. The male author of *Sister India*, a book written in response to Mayo's *Mother India*, reported, with barely concealed satisfaction, that while Mayo considers herself a champion of women in India 'the women of India have held meetings in every part of India and have unanimously protested against *her* descriptions of their troubles'.[21] Prominent women leaders, such as Sarla Devi Chaudhrani, Latika Basu, and Jyotirmoyee Ganguly, were conspicuously present at the large protest meetings held against the book.[22] In separate women's meetings, such as the Mahila Samitis in Bengal and similar women's associations all over the country, women met to discuss the 'insult' to Indian womanhood contained in *Mother India*. Fairly typical of resolutions passed at such meetings was one proposed by Mrs Mirza Ismail at the Mysore Women's Education conference. The resolution declared Mayo's book to be 'at variance with the ideals of Indian womanhood, which inspire Indian women to lead much happier lives than appear to be led by women of other countries'.[23] Similarly, Maya Das's letter compared the nature and extent of the sexual exploitation of women in Britain unfavourably with the situation in India, provoking a long controversy in the *Pioneer*, a semi-official British newspaper in India.[24] Books written by women in response to *Mother India* also expressed feelings of nationalist outrage against Mayo. Chandravati Lakhanpal's *Mother India Ka Jawab* (A Reply to Mother India) and Charulata Devi's *The Fair Sex of India: A Reply to Mother India* pursued a line of argument also found in the numerous books written by men. Lakhanpal's, for instance, was a *tu quoque* response; she focused on the 'depraved sexuality' of Western societies just as Mayo had focused on sexual practices in India.[25] Charulata Devi, on the other hand, made no mention of Mayo or any of the points raised in *Mother India*, but simply provided sketches of eminent Indian women that countered Mayo's dismal portrait.[26]

The voices of women in India alluded to above may be read as contributing to the general nationalist outrage against *Mother India*. Of particular interest to me, however, are the discursive strategies through which a subject position was created for the Indian woman to speak. I turn, therefore, to the strategies that enabled the emergence of an 'authentic voice of modern Indian womanhood'. I will begin by examining the different strategies exemplified in the responses of four women: Cornelia Sorabji, Uma Nehru, Sarojini Naidu, and Dhanvanthi Rama Rau. My aim in analysing the array of positions represented by these women is to identify the particular conditions that enabled a so-called distinctive Indian woman's position on the controversy—a position to be contrasted not only with the imperialist/imperialist-feminist positions, but also with the allegedly gender-neutral nationalist positions. I will also explore the emergence of a politics of middle-class Indian feminism in this context.

CORNELIA SORABJI

Cornelia Sorabji was the only Indian woman who had been cited at some length in *Mother India*. Sorabji and Mayo maintained a warm relationship, through private communications, for years after the *Mother India* controversy. Yet Sorabji's complicated attitude toward Mayo's imperialist project precluded any possibility for the emergence of an Indian woman's position critical of either indigenous or imperialist patriarchy. At the time, Sorabji was one of the leading female legal practitioners in India and had developed a considerable reputation as the legal adviser to orthodox Hindu women in *purdanashin* (veiled seclusion).[27] Sorabji's main interest in the women's question was in social service, embodied in her scheme for an Institute for Social Service in India. Her role models came from an earlier generation of strong female reformers, such as Pandita Ramabai, Ramabai Ranade, and her own mother, Francina Sorabji. She was also an ardent supporter of the female ascetic Mataji Tapashwini who had started a school for women along orthodox Hindu lines in Calcutta.[28] Sorabji herself adopted a cautious, or even conservative, attitude toward female reform; she, for example, often defended the practice of *purdah* among upper-caste Hindu women. As a self-confessed loyalist of the British Raj, she was particularly sceptical of the new generation of women activists who, according to Sorabji, were advocating overly hasty political and social reforms for women. These women, in turn, regarded Sorabji as far too 'individualist' and far too critical of India.[39]

Despite Sorabji's close ties to Mayo and her prominence as an advocate for social reform in India, she remained a shadowy figure in the debate over *Mother India*. Apart from a review of *Mother India* which appeared in the Calcutta-based newspaper the *Englishman*, Sorabji's views on the book were confined to private communications to Mayo and to a handful of British women in Britain.[30] Even Mayo's efforts to portray Sorabji as an example of the 'enlightened' woman's position in India came to naught. Sorabji was forced to write to Mayo's secretary, Henry Field, urging him to request that Mayo refrain from using Sorabji's name in public. She later wrote to Mayo directly requesting that Mayo write to the Indian press absolving her of any complicity in the writing of *Mother India*. Mayo's disclaimer along these lines appeared in the Calcutta *Statesman* and in the Swarajist newspaper, the *Forward*.[31] Sorabji's sensitivity no doubt had been prompted by the flurry of criticism directed against her from nationalist quarters in India. She was publicly denounced at nationalist meetings held to protest Mayo's book. The *Forward* accused Sorabji of supplying Mayo with all her ammunition against India, while C. S. Ranga Iyer, a Swarajist member of the legislative assembly, denounced Sorabji in his *Father India*, written as a rejoinder to *Mother India*. Iyer had described Sorabji's work, from which Mayo had quoted extensively, as the 'vapourings of an unbalanced and unstructured mind'.[32] Even Sorabji's younger sister Dr Alice Pennell had disagreed with her sharply on her evaluation of Mayo's politics and on Mayo's contributions to the cause of Indian women. The most hurtful attack, one which Sorabji herself recorded with great bitterness, came from the young women graduates of the Federation of University Women in India, of which she was honorary president. The younger university women in India circulated a virulent petition, behind Sorabji's back, attacking her for her conciliatory stand toward Mayo's *Mother India*.[33]

If Sorabji's public position in the controversy was fraught, her private position was equally problematic. Even though Sorabji had praised Mayo for writing about the condition of women in India, she was, at first, careful to distance herself from Mayo's general political conclusions. This was in essence the position she had adopted both publicly, in her review of *Mother India*, and in her private communications with Mayo in which she expressed regret that Mayo had not eschewed all 'politics'. She even advised Mayo, although to no avail, to change the title of her book in subsequent editions so that it did not appear as an indictment of all of India or of Indian political aspirations.[34] As an advocate of social reform, Sorabji's initial concern was to use the controversy as an opportunity to draw attention to the need for a social service institute in which the conditions of women could be discussed in a less charged political atmosphere. This position, however, was abandoned quickly in favour of an anti-nationalist and pro-imperialist position. Later Sorabji, acknowledging her secret collaboration with Mayo, saw her role in the controversy only as a 'Scarlet Pimpernel', who supplied Mayo with information for her subsequent anti-Indian books. Sorabji's direct collaboration with Mayo, however, had to be kept a secret because, as she herself acknowledged, her association with such anti-Hindu diatribes, like that in Mayo's subsequent book *The Face of Mother India*, might end up alienating Sorabji's Hindu wards.[35]

Sorabji's role in the Mayo controversy was marked by contradictions and shrouded in secrecy. Sorabji found it impossible, from a position of support for Mayo and her imperialist politics, to articulate a subject position for/by the Indian woman in the controversy. Even Sorabji's initial sympathy for the Indian woman as the object of benevolent salvation, either by the British or by her own Institute for Social Service, provided only a limited appeal for an Indian women's position in the controversy. Her subsequent endorsement of Mayo's pro-imperialist politics, moreover, caused her to abandon all efforts at trying to describe a space from which the Indian woman could become the subject of the controversy. The only other Indian woman to be cited in *Mother India*, Mona Bose, had recognized the impossibility of speaking either for or as an Indian woman from within Mayo's pro-imperialist politics. Bose, therefore, publicly denied the views that were attributed to her in *Mother India*.[36] In contrast, Sorabji learnt through bitter experience that her pro-imperialist defence of Mayo could not provide a subject position from which the Indian woman could address either the British or male nationalists in India.

UMA NEHRU

For very different reasons, Uma Nehru also failed in her efforts to articulate a subject position for the Indian woman in the *Mother India* controversy. Although Nehru was an uncompromising critic of certain patriarchal assumptions in male nationalist discourse, she responded to Mayo's book from the general nationalist perspective. Indeed, her response to *Mother India* reflected the power of the nationalist discourse to contain even those voices that were critical of its particular nationalist resolution of the women's question. Nehru long had been a powerful advocate for women's rights through her articles in the Hindi journal *Stri Darpan* (*Women's Mirror*), edited by her sister-in-law Rameshwari Nehru. Her articles had addressed the hypocrisy of male nationalist discourse in prescribing models of ideal Indian womanhood for modern Indian women that were drawn from the legendary figures of Sita-Sati-Savitri.[37] Not surprisingly, Nehru was considered as far too 'Westernized', even in the anglicized Nehru family into which she was married.[38] Yet, in the imperialist–nationalist controversy over *Mother India*, Nehru responded to Mayo from the allegedly unmarked position of the 'Indian'.

Nehru's *Mother India Aur Uska Jawab* is a Hindi translation of Mayo's book meant, most probably, for Hindi-speaking women.[39] In the preface Nehru writes that her aim is 'to use this book meant to insult us to instil pride among us'. Her translation of *Mother India* was preceded by an imaginary dialogue with Mayo. *Mother India Aur Uska Jawab* was true to Nehru's earlier reservations about the nationalist ideal of modern Indian womanhood: it refrained from invoking the glorious tradition of Indian womanhood in responding to Mayo's criticism of the position of women in India. Deprived of the countervailing argument about the ideals of Indian womanhood, however, Nehru's dialogue with Mayo deals largely with the political and economic issues raised in *Mother India*. Nehru avoided discussing the particular implications of Mayo's book for the women's question. She missed, for instance, the opportunity to respond to Mayo's taunt to India's women leaders. In her second book on India, *The Slaves of the Gods*, Mayo had written that her aim was 'to awaken [Indian women's] intelligent patriotism and the consciousness of [their] men, by making inescapable the contrast between, on the one hand, florid talk of devotion and "sacrifice" poured out before an abstract figure, and, on the other hand, the consideration actually accorded to the living woman, mother of the race'.[40] Nehru's desire to present a strong nationalist argument against *Mother India*, even though she was herself critical of the attitudes towards women in male nationalist discourse, led her to avoid a detailed discussion of the special emphasis that Mayo had placed on women's issues in her attack on India. Nehru's critique of *Mother India*, therefore, was made from the supposedly neutral, or non-gendered, position of the Indian nationalist: it could not become the site for the elaboration of the gendered subject position of the Indian woman.

SAROJINI NAIDU

Ironically, the consolidation of a distinct Indian woman's position in the controversy could occur only within the male nationalist discourse. This is evident in the response of Sarojini Naidu, one of the most prominent women in the nationalist and the women's movements of the time. Naidu, by combining 'modern' political activism with 'traditional' Indian roots, embodied the nationalist ideals of middle-class Indian womanhood.[41] Her response to the *Mother India* controversy reflects the ways in which the Indian woman could arrogate a subject position for herself from which to address both the British and the male nationalists in India. In one of Naidu's earliest responses, she referred to *Mother India* only to urge Indian men to give up their prejudices against women and to educate their wives, mothers, and sisters if they sincerely wished to neutralize the impact of Mayo's book. Mayo would later use extracts from this speech to endorse her own views about the hypocrisy of male nationalists.[42] Yet there was no mistaking Naidu's sharp criticism of Mayo's imperialist politics. Her telegram to the famous Calcutta Town Hall meeting, organized by the nationalist Mayor J. N. Sengupta, summed up her attitude towards Mayo: 'The mouths of liars rot and perish with their own lies, but the glory of Indian womanhood shines pure and as the morning star.'[43] Unlike some of her male colleagues, however, Naidu's main concern was not to prove that oppressive practices against women did not exist in India, but to show that the women of India were capable of redeeming themselves.

Naidu's invocation of the glorious ideals of Indian womanhood and her elaboration of the nationalist Sati-Savitri model for the Indian woman did not simply reflect a co-optation by male nationalist discourse, but was also critical in legitimating the interventionary practices of Indian women themselves. Naidu's challenge to Mayo was directed at the latter's right to speak for Indian womanhood. Naidu stated this in no uncertain terms in her 1928 Kamala Lectures at the Calcutta University Senate in a speech on the 'Ideals of Indian Womanhood':

The women of India should answer all those who come in the guise of friendship to interpret India to the world and exploit their weakness and expose the *secrets of the home* [my emphasis], with the words 'whether we are oppressed, treated as goods and chattels and forced on the funeral pyres of our husbands, our redemption is in our hands. We shall break through the walls that imprison us and tear the veils that stifle. We shall do this by the miracle of our womanhood. We do not ask any friend or foe in the guise of a friend, to come merely to exploit us while they pretend to interpret, succour and solace our womanhood.'[44]

The accent on the 'secrets of the home' in Naidu's speech signals the ambivalence at the heart of the identity of the Indian woman. On the one hand, her speech recalls the nationalist effort at reformulating the new middle-class 'home' as an insulated space in which patriarchal authority remained intact and, on the other, its vigorous arguments for the potential of Indian woman's own agency in correcting the roots of their domination also leave open the possibility of challenging the patriarchal closure of the 'home' as a site for women's struggle.

Naidu's intervention demonstrates that although the nationalist ideal of the Indian woman ensured that middle-class women's entry into the public space was under male patronage, the same ideal also enabled a relatively liberal space for women at least partly of their own making. The popular representation of the nation as Mother India as well as the figure of the Indian woman as the essence of Indianness had also opened up new arenas for women's activism. The potential of such an ideal was evident in the radical claim that Naidu, as a prime example of the 'new woman' in India, had the unique distinction of representing, not only the Indian woman, but the entire Indian nation. Gandhi, for example, would recognize Naidu's claim as the unofficial ambassador for India/Indian women. In the wake of the *Mother India* controversy, he was persuaded to send Naidu to the United States as the spokesperson for India and the Indian woman. Officially Naidu was a representative of the All India Women's Conference at the Pan-Pacific Women's Conference in Honolulu, but as her extensive lecture tour demonstrates, her trip was meant to educate the American people about the 'real' Mother India.[45] Naidu lectured in the United States on 'The Interpretation of Indian Womanhood' and 'The Political Situation in India', topics on which she seemed uniquely qualified to speak. As the symbolic figure of nationalist India and of Indian women, she hoped to dispel the image of an unregenerate patriarchal Indian nationalism and of the downtrodden Indian woman found in Mayo's book. Therefore, she felt no compulsion to debate the specifics of the book with a Western audience.[46] Despite the sustained efforts of Mayo and her supporters to discredit Naidu as simply a mouthpiece for Gandhi, her trip was an immense public relations success, especially with the more liberal US women's organizations.[47] Indeed, it was precisely because Naidu had offered a strategy for articulating the Indian woman's position within male nationalist discourse that she was able to appropriate a unique subject position for the middle-class Indian woman in the *Mother India* controversy.

How does a discourse of the Indian woman as a figure of essentialized Indianness, however, enable a subject position for the 'Indian woman'? To recall Partha Chatterjee's analysis, the modern Indian could create a subject position from which to address the British only by elaborating an ahistorical and essentialized notion of Indian womanhood. Chatterjee, for example, argues that a marked '*difference* in the degree and manner of westernization of women, as distinct from men' was essential for the subject position of the Indian.[48] However, the entry of women into the male-dominated public sphere in the early twentieth century made it increasingly difficult to maintain this essential difference in the westernization of women, and created new demands on the gendered subject position of the Indian. In the context of rapid westernization of women, modern/westernized women, like Naidu, could, through service to the nation, also appropriate a subject position from which to address the West as Indian. They did this by positing an essential difference in the degree and manner of westernization of the truly modern Indian woman, as distinct from the merely westernized Indian woman. The essential difference lay in the fact that the modern Indian woman, unlike her merely westernized counterpart, claimed 'traditional' ideals of Indian womanhood *on behalf of the modernizing project of nationalism*. Naidu's strategy of negotiation in the *Mother India* controversy, therefore, reflected the particular conditions under which even the modern/westernized woman could address the West as Indian. This particular moment of an Indian female subjectivity, however, rested on an uneasy resolution of the modern Indian woman as both subject and as object of the nationalist discourse of essentialized Indianness.

DHANVANTHI RAMA RAU

Dhanvanthi Rama Rau's interventions in the Mayo controversy further illustrate how a subject position for the modern Indian woman was assigned within male nationalist discourse. Rau's contributions to the controversy lay in her struggle to establish the claim of Indian women and their organizations, against the rival claims of Western women's organizations, as the legitimate crusaders for the rights of all women in India. The argument for the special role of the modern Indian woman received its legitimacy from a nationalist discourse that papered over the very real class/caste contradictions in the particular imagining of the national community.

Following *Mother India*, women's organizations, especially in the United States and in Britain, demonstrated a great interest in the 'upliftment' of women in India. In the United States it was the more conservative women's groups, like the Daughters of the American Revolution, which openly endorsed Mayo's book, and started a fund for the helpless child brides of India.[49] More direct intervention on behalf of the women in India was left to British women's organizations, especially under the direction of Eleanor Rathbone. Rathbone acknowledged a 'great tidal wave of responsibility' for the helpless women of India.[50] As an imperialist, Rathbone was equally impressed by the political implications of Mayo's revelations in *Mother India*. Rathbone, therefore, urged Mayo to issue a cheaper edition of her book to be distributed among members of the Labour Party in Britain which 'badly need the corrective of [*Mother India*] because of their tendency to espouse self-government anywhere'.[51] In response to Mayo's description of women in India, Rathbone petitioned the British parliament to appoint two members of the National Union of Societies for Equal Citizenship (NUSEC), of which she was president, to the parliamentary commission, popularly known as the Simon Commission. This all-white commission was later boycotted in India by all the major political parties and by the all-India women's organizations for its exclusion of Indians and of women. Rathbone's proposal to the commission, as it was about to undertake an inquiry into the political conditions in India, was that British women appointed to the commission could provide information about that part of Indian society 'hidden behind the veil'. Rathbone's scheme, however, was met with scepticism from some Indian women. The wife of a distinguished Muslim leader from India wrote to the London *Times*,

'Indian women are not voiceless. They received the franchise, and those among them who are able and willing to take advantage of it are aware of the needs of their own people.'[52]

The most sustained criticism of Rathbone's efforts to get British women's organizations to assume responsibility for the women of India, however, came from Dhanvanthi Rama Rau, an active member of three of the all-India women's organizations. Rathbone, inspired by the revelations made in Mayo's book, had organized two large conferences in London on 'Women in India'. At the second conference, which was held in Caxton Hall on 7 and 8 October 1929, Rau attacked the remarks of the various speakers at the conference as variations of the 'white man's burden', and hotly 'disputed the right of British women to arrange a conference on Indian social evils, when all the speakers were British and many of them had never even visited India'.[53] On the request of some prominent British feminists, Rathbone was forced to provide Rau a platform to present her views to the conference. In her speech Rau outlined the work being done in India by Indian women's organizations and reiterated that British women could give only moral support: the practical work had to be done in India and by Indians. Despite the interventions of Rau and other Indian women, the resolution that British women's organizations had a special responsibility for Indian women was passed with only a few Indian women present dissenting. Sir M. F. Dywer, a former British official in India, concluded that the 'great meeting of British Women's Association' held at Caxton Hall could do much good to improve the status of Indian women because, at present, the 'Hindu women [themselves] were Dumb'.[54]

Although frustrated by the outcome of the conference, Rau did not leave unchallenged the claim that British women's organizations had a special responsibility for the condition of women in India. Rau, along with some British and Indian women associated with the Lyceum Club in London, wrote a letter to *The Times* accusing Rathbone's conference for promoting 'racial cleavage'. She boldly reiterated that while 'India welcomes co-operation [she] will not tolerate any form of patronage or philanthropy which will rob her of her self-esteem'.[55] Rau's various interventions served to attack the patronizing politics of Western women's organizations, and to secure recognition for the role of the modern Indian woman as the true representative of all her oppressed sisters in India. Henceforth, Rathbone and the NUSEC would be forced to work through the modern Indian woman as the representative of the women of India.

The consolidation of the nationalist bourgeoisie in India allowed the women of this class to emerge as the true champion of all women in India. Hence the modern Indian woman came to be seen as the liberator of all other women in India. To paraphrase Dipesh Chakrabarty's observations made in a slightly different context, the Indian woman, as a member of the modernizing elite, stood for an 'assumed unity called the "Indian people" that is always split into two—a modernizing elite and a yet-to-be-modernized peasantry'.[56] Within the modernizing project of nationalism, therefore, the modern Indian woman was also always the subject of modernity, the transmitter of the fruits of modernization to all other women in India. The self-constitution of the 'Indian woman', as simultaneously the subject and the object of nationalist discourse, however, exemplifies the contradictions in the subject positions available to women in all patriarchies.[57]

THE WOMEN'S MOVEMENT

The particular history of the self-constitution of the Indian woman in nationalist discourse also had implications for the politics of middle-class Indian feminism. The political struggles of the Indian women's movement in the *Mother India* controversy provided an arena for middle-class Indian women's engagement with feminism. For the fledgeling women's movement, the controversy afforded an opportunity to consolidate a feminist agenda for women's issues. Women activists and the women's movement, therefore, admitted the urgent need for the reform of women's position in India, even as they challenged Mayo's description of the Indian woman in *Mother India*. Kamala Sathianadhan, editor of the *Indian Ladies Magazine*, wrote:

We honour Miss Mayo for her courage in not caring for resentments and accusations; we congratulate her on her public spirit in 'shouldering the task' of 'holding the mirror' to that part of the human race which is a 'physical menace' to the world; we do not question her ability or her cleverness in writing this book; but we do deny her the presumption that she is 'in a position to present conditions and their bearing', and we do not for a minute admit her 'plain speech' as the 'faithful wounds of a friend': for she is no friend of ours.[58]

Women's organizations carefully distanced themselves from Mayo's imperialist propaganda, but used the attention that the controversy created to facilitate their own campaign for child-marriage reform and other legislation for women. The Women's Indian Association (WIA), a pioneer of the all-India women's movement, issued the following statement on Mayo's book: 'while we repudiate the book as a whole we must turn every ounce of our zeal towards the rooting out of those social evils which are undoubtedly in our midst'.[59] At Triplicane in Madras, the association organized the largest protest meeting of women against the book. This meeting was chaired by Dr Muthulakshmi Reddy, the first Indian woman to be nominated to the Provincial legislatures. The meeting passed the following two resolutions: first, it denied that 'Indian womanhood as a whole is in a state of slavery, superstition, ignorance and degradation which Miss Mayo affirms'; and, second, they called upon the legislative assembly and legislative council to enact measures that would legally prohibit child marriage, early parentage, enforced widowhood, dedication of girls to temples, and 'commercialized immorality'. This was also the position of the *Stri Dharma* (*Woman's Duty*), the paper of the Women's Indian Association.[60]

An episode at the annual meeting of the Indian National Social Conference held on 27 December 1927 indicates the context in which women activists conducted their successful campaign for child-marriage reform.[61] At the conference prominent men and women, while advocating the urgent need for child-marriage reform, denounced Mayo's *Mother India*. Only one speaker introduced a discordant note. S. N. Arya, the only representative from the Non-Brahmin Youth League present, referred to Mayo as a champion of women's reform in India. Pandemonium broke out at the mention of her name. Arya's comments, despite the pro-imperialist politics which he shared with some groups in the Non-Brahmin Movement of the 1920s and 1930s, served to question the consensus over women's issues secured within the upper-caste/-class politics of the nation-state.[62] The politics of the nation-state, however, also privileged the understanding of women of dominant classes/castes on women's reforms, and allowed the middle-class women's movement to set the agenda for women's reform in India. Dr Muthulakshmi Reddy, who chaired the conference, persuaded the delegates to ignore Arya's disruption and redirected their attention to women's reform.

The issue around which the all-India women's organizations mobilized in the *Mother India* controversy, that of the upper-caste/-class child bride rather than the underpaid *dhai*, or midwife, also mentioned in Mayo's book, reveals the elitist character of the early women's movement. It also reveals, however, the special conditions under which women's organizations could conduct a successful political campaign for women. The issue of child-marriage reform was not fundamentally opposed to the 'modernizing' efforts of the social reform and nationalist movements. The legacy of such male-sponsored reforms meant that the women's movement could mount a campaign for the modernization of the Indian home by urging child-marriage legislation without necessarily attacking male authority in the home. Rameshwari Nehru, for example, who was active in the campaign for child-marriage legislation, considered herself to be an advocate of women's rights, but not an advocate of sexual equality in the home. She wrote: 'I do not think that the home should be made a forum for women's battles.'[63]

This should not, however, make us overlook the contributions of the women's organizations in getting child-marriage legislation passed in the face of governmental indifference and orthodox male opposition. The women's movement had an uphill battle to gain recognition for their own contributions in getting child-marriage legislation passed in India. The issue of child-marriage reform had been a major concern of the women's movement in India even before the publication of *Mother India*. The very first meeting of the All-India Women's Conference (AIWC) held in Poona in 1926 had committed its support, not only to a bill on the age of consent— then languishing in the legislative assembly partly due to official indifference, but also to the eventual abolition of child marriage in India. The Mayo controversy speeded up the women's demand for child-marriage reform.[64] On 11 February 1928 a delegation of nineteen members of the AIWC led by the Rani of Mandi met the Viceroy and leaders of all the major Indian political parties to urge the passage of the Sarda Bill in the legislative assembly. The delegation also secured the appointment of one of its members, Rameshwari Nehru, to the age-of-consent committee appointed by the government on 25 June 1928. Rameshwari Nehru later wrote that it was in dealing with private bills on age-of-marriage and consent that the government had appointed this committee. Significantly, she made no mention of the publicity created by the Mayo controversy.[65] The report of the committee, which Mayo later used to write her sequel to *Mother India* and to validate the claims of her previous book, testified to the need for marriage reforms.[66] Women witnesses to the committee meetings were among the strongest advocates for the abolition of child marriage.

Following the report of the age-of-consent committee, women

activists launched a lobbying effort with Indian legislators and British officials to ensure the passage of the Sarda Child-Marriage Bill. Kamaladevi Chattopadhyay, on behalf of the AIWC, orchestrated the work of getting support for the bill from Indian legislators in Delhi. Dhanvanthi Rama Rau, as secretary of the Child-Marriage Abolition League, worked among the wives of British government officials urging them to persuade their husbands to support the child-marriage legislation.[67] On the day of the final debate on the Sarda Bill in the legislative assembly, approximately 300 AIWC activists attended to ensure support of the measure. The AIWC would later see the passage of the Child-Marriage Restraint Act in 1929 as a triumph of their own fledgeling organization.

Yet the contributions of the Indian women's movement in getting child-marriage reform in India did not receive automatic recognition. International opinion, for example, gave all the credit for the appointment of the age-of-consent committee and the passage of the Sarda Bill to Mayo's *Mother India*. The *New York Times* even carried a piece entitled 'Miss Mayo's Book on India Gets Action on Child Marriage'.[68] Mayo and her supporters were in great part responsible for popularizing the view that Indians had been shamed into supporting legislative reforms for women as a result of her brave exposé in *Mother India*. A letter which Mayo received from India chided her for taking credit for the passage of the child-marriage legislation:

speaking for every woman in India, I want to say to you that when you claim for yourself the credit of an 'attempt to raise the marriage age of females', because the U.S., as you explain, had accepted your book as truth—that you have betrayed yourself into a perfect illustration of what Dr Besant, Dr Tagore, Gandhi and others have called your perversion of facts. Such attempts have been going on for a number of years now.[69]

It should come as no surprise that the women actually involved in the campaign for child-marriage legislation make little or no mention of the role of Mayo or *Mother India* in getting the legislation passed.[70]

It is in the act of constructing themselves as the agents or subjects in the discourse about Indian women that we can locate the origins of middle-class Indian women's activism. Indian feminism emerged in the context of middle-class women's challenge to orthodox indigenous patriarchy. The very success of this challenge, however, also strengthened the new nationalist patriarchy and the class/cast stratification of Indian society. This ambivalence has led some scholars, like Kumari Jayawardena, to the pessimistic conclusion that the nationalist struggle did not permit 'a revolutionary feminist consciousness' in India.[71] Yet this desire for a 'pure' feminist consciousness or agency serves, in the end, to remove the feminist subject from the history of her production within interconnected axes of gender, race, class/caste, nation, or sexuality. A more useful way of locating middle-class Indian feminism is offered in Sangari and Vaid's observation that 'nowhere can or have reforms been directed at patriarchies alone, but they have also been involved in realigning patriarchy with social stratification (both existing and emerging) and with changing political formations'.[72]

As R. Radhakrishnan points out, Sangari and Vaid's observation has the potential for the reconceptualization of historiography as a whole. According to Radhakrishnan, implicit in Sangari and Vaid's comment, is the recognition that the categories of gender, race, nationality, sexuality, or class can neither be made to speak for the totality nor for one another, but are rather relationally implicated in one another. This notion of 'relational articulation', he suggests, make a feminist, nationalist, or class-based historiography, pursued entirely from within itself, highly questionable.[73] Discrete feminist, nationalist, or class-based historiographies arbitrarily fix the boundaries of the 'totality' or the total social formation that is the object of their study according to the different priorities that each assigns to gender, nation, or class as distinct categories. Radhakrishnan's notion of a truly critical historiography, however, suggests a new understanding of 'totality', not as the product of fixed or given boundaries, demarcated by distinct categories, but as the product of several different relational articulations. Hence, Sangari and Vaid's feminist historiography, conceived within such a radical rethinking of 'totality', does not claim to offer a new and improved paradigm for the flawed nationalist understanding of India, but locates its challenge clearly within that nationalist paradigm even as it critiques its very terms.

This reconceptualization of historiography not only emphasizes the need to historicize the conditions in which politics and identities emerge, but also draws attention to the writing of history itself as an interventionary practice that recreates the past for the present. It, therefore, opens up new possibilities for conceptualizing the problem of locating the Indian woman and the politics of middle-class Indian feminism. For example, such a reconceptualization enables me, as an Indian feminist, to see my reading of the 'Indian woman' and middle-class Indian feminism in the *Mother India* controversy as not just a retrieval of some lost historical past, but as an intervention in the historical present. The range of women's responses in the *Mother India* controversy indicates that there was nothing necessarily inevitable or predetermined about the voice of the modern Indian woman. In fact, the particular discursive strategies that gave rise to the subject position of the 'modern Indian woman' and the politics of middle-class Indian feminism were produced by, and meant to intervene in, a certain historical moment.

This understanding of the historical specificity of the Indian woman allows us to recognize an ideological continuity in the contemporary re-articulation of the Indian woman as the figure of some essentialized identity. In recent years, various communalist and nativist movements in India have engaged in constituting and reconstituting the Indian/Hindu woman as subjects and as objects of virulently anti-democratic discourses.[74] By insisting on historicizing the identity of the Indian woman, we can begin to critique the implications of the resurgence of an essentialized and ahistorical identity, divorced from the political and economic contexts in which it is produced and which it helps sustain.

Notes

1. Kumkum Sangari and Sudesh Vaid, 'Recasting Women: An Introduction: in K. Sangari and S. Vaid (eds.), *Recasting Women: Essays in Indian Colonial History* (New Brunswick, NJ, 1990), 2–3.
2. Ibid. 1.
3. Chandra Talpade Mohanty, 'Cartographies of Struggle' in C. Mohanty, A. Russo, and L. Torres (eds.), *Third World Women and the Politics of Feminism* (Bloomington, Ind., 1991), 12–13.
4. Teresa de Lauretis, 'Displacing Hegemonic Discourses: Reflections on Feminist Theory in the 1980s', *Inscriptions*, 3/4 (1988), 136.
5. Katherine Mayo, *Mother India* (New York, 1927).
6. For a detailed study of Mayo's imperialist politics, see Manoranjan Jha, *Katherine Mayo and India* (New Delhi, 1971).
7. The actual quotation is from the foreword, written by Sarojini Naidu, one of the most famous Indian women of the time, for a collection of essays by Indian women, Evelyn C. Gedge and Mithan Choksi (eds.), *Women in Modern India, Fifteen Papers by Indian Women Writers* (Bombay, 1929).
8. See Joanna Liddle and Rama Joshi, 'Gender and Imperialism in British India', *South Asia Research*, 5/2 (Nov. 1985), 147–65.
9. This tendency of evaluating women's mobilization in India along one or another of these lines is referred to in Geraldine Forbes, 'The Politics of Respectability: Indian Women and the Indian National Congress' in D. A. Low (ed.), *Congress, Centenary Hindsights* (Delhi, 1988), 54–97.
10. Chandra Mohanty, 'Cartographies of Struggle', 5–6.

11. For some exceptions, see Himani Bannerji, 'Fashioning a Self: Educational Proposals for and by Women in Popular Magazines in Colonial Bengal', *Economic and Political Weekly* 26/43 (26 Oct. 1991), ws50–ws62 and Susie Tharu and K. Lalitha, 'Literature of the Reform and Nationalist Movement' in *Women Writing in India*, i (New York, 1991), 143–86. Also useful are Susia Tharu, 'Women Writing in India', *Journal of Arts and Ideas*, 20–1 (March 1991), 49–66; and Lata Mani, 'Cultural Theory, Colonial Texts: Reading Eyewitness Accounts of Widow Burning' in Lawrence Grossberg, Cary Nelson, and Paula Treichler (eds.), *Cultural Studies* (New York, 1992), 392–408.

12. Chandra Mohanty, 'Cartographies of Struggle', 15.

13. See Ann Stoler, 'Making Empire Respectable: The Politics of Race and Sexuality in 20th Century Colonial Cultures', *American Ethnologist*, 16/4 (Nov. 1989), 634–60. Also 'Rethinking Colonial Categories', *Comparative Studies in Society and History*, 31/1 (Jan. 1989), 134–61.

14. Lata Mani, 'The Production of an Official Discourse on Sati in Early 19th Century Bengal', *Economic and Political Weekly* (Apr. 1987), 32–40 and 'Contentious Traditions: The Debate on Sati in Colonial India', *Cultural Critique*, 7 (1987), 119–56. Uma Chakravorty, 'Whatever Happened to the Vedic Dasi? Orientalism, Nationalism and a Script for the Past', in Sangari and Vaid (eds.), *Recasting Women*, 27–87.

15. Sumanta Banerjee, 'Marginalization of Women's Popular Culture in Nineteenth Century Bengal', in Sangari and Vaid (eds.), *Recasting Women*, 127–79 and *The Parlour and the Streets* (Calcutta, 1989). For the following discussion, I have drawn from Sangari and Vaid, 'Recasting Women: An Introduction', 1–26.

16. Partha Chatterjee, 'The Nationalist Resolution of the Women's Question', in Sangari and Vaid (eds.), *Recasting Women*, 233–53 and 'Colonialism, Nationalism and Colonized Women: The Contest in India', *American Ethnologist*, 16/4 (Nov. 1989), 662–83. For Chatterjee's analysis of Indian nationalist thought in general, see *Nationalist Thought and the Colonial World: A Derivative Discourse?* (London, 1986).

17. Sangari and Vaid in 'Recasting Women: An Introduction' distinguish between what they call the 'modernizing' of gender relations in the social reform and nationalist movements and the 'democratizing' of gender relations in mass peasant movements, 19–24.

18. Dipesh Chakrabarty, 'Postcoloniality and the Artifice of History: Who Speaks for "Indian" Pasts?', *Representations*, 37 (Winter 1992), 17.

19. Ibid. 11–14.

20. The article, written by a British doctor who had served in India, was reprinted in the Calcutta *Statesman* (30 Mar. 1928), 8.

21. World Citizen [S. G. Warty], *Sister India: A Critical Examination of and a Reasoned Reply to Miss Katherine Mayo's 'Mother India'* (Bombay, 1928), 143.

22. See *Bombay Daily Mail*, 5 Sept. 1927 in India, vol. 2 in folder no. 207, series 4, box 37, Katherine Mayo Papers, manuscript group no. 35 at Sterling Memorial Library, Yale University (henceforth: K. M. Papers). For details of this meeting see *Bengalee* (6 Sept. 1927), 3.

23. Cited in *Indian Social Reformer* in India, vol. 2 in folder 207, series 4, box 37 in K. K. Papers. For some examples of the women's protest meetings held all over India see the report of the protest of 'ladies' at Noakhali in *Amrita Bazar*

Patrika, 17 Sept. 1927, 5; Lahore 'ladies' protest, *Amrita Bazar Patrika*, 13 Dec. 1927, 10; protest of Comilla Mahila Samiti Meeting, *Bengalee*, 8 Sept. 1927, 3. Several other protest meetings were reported in the *Statesman*, *Bengalee*, and *Amrita Bazar Patrika* during the period September to December 1927.

24. For the exchange occasioned by Maya Das's letter, see *Pioneer*, 5 May 1928; 10 May 1928; 18 May 1928; and 31 May 1928 in India, vol. 3 in folder no. 207, series 4, box 37, K. M Papers.

25. Mrs C. Lakhanpal, *Mother India Aur Uska Jawab* (Dehradun, 1928). I was unable to trace this book; however, I had access to a brief translation of the book in a letter from Wolsey Haig to Mayo's secretary, Henry Field, letter, dated 22 June 1928 in folder no. 47, series 1, box 6, K. M. Papers. Although Haig declares the book to be poorly written, the Indian papers give it a more favourable review. See *Bombay Daily Mail*, 14 Jan. 1928 in India, vol. 3 in folder no. 207, series 4, box 37, K. M Papers.

26. Charulata Devi, *The Fair Sex of India* (Calcutta, 1929).

27. Mayo had quoted from Cornelia Sorabji's *Between the Twilights* (London, 1908). Biographical information on Sorabji is available in her prolific writings; see especially *India Calling: The Memoirs of Cornelia Sorabji* (London, 1934); *'Therefore': An Impression of Sorabji Kharshedji Langrana and his wife Francina* (London, 1924); and *Susia Sorabji: Christian-Parsee Educator of Western India* (London, 1932). For a brief sketch of Sorabji's early career, also see Mrs E. F. Chapman, *Sketches of Some Distinguished Indian Women with a Preface by the Marchioness of Dufferin and Ava* (London, 1891), 121–38.

28. See Cornelia Sorabji, 'The Position of Hindu Women Fifty Years Ago', in Shyam Kumari Nehru (ed.), *Our Cause: A Symposium of Indian Women* (Allahabad, 1938). Also letter from Sorabji to Mayo, dated 29 Jan. 1927, in folder no. 36, series 1, box 5, K. M. Papers.

29. For Sorabji's views on this matter see her *The Purdanashin* (Calcutta, 1917) and *India Recalled* (London, 1937). For critical assessments of Sorabji by her female contemporaries, see Margaret Cousins, *Indian Womanhood Today* (Kitabistan, 1941), 145; Kamaladevi Chattopadhyay, *Indian Women's Battle for Freedom* (New Delhi, repr. 1983), 51; and for Kamala Sathianadan's view, see Padmini [Sathianadan] Sengupta, *The Portrait of an Indian Woman* (Calcutta, 1956), 41.

30. Cornelia Sorabji, 'Mother India—The Incense of Service: What Sacrifice Can We Make?' *Englishman*, pt. 1, 31 Aug. 1927, 6–9, and pt. 2, 1 Sept. 1927, 6–9.

31. Letter from Sorabji to Mayo, dated 21 Nov. 1928 in folder no. 50, series 1, box 7, K. M. Papers. Mayo's letter to the *Statesman* appeared on 5 Mar. 1929, 18.

32. C. S. Ranga Iyer, *Father India: A Reply to Mother India* (London, 1928 repr.), 72–3. Ramananda Chatterjee, editor of the *Modern Review*, addressed a large gathering of Indians at which he accused Sorabji of providing Mayo with all her information on India, *Bengalee*, 8 Sept. 1927, 3; *Amrita Bazar Patrika*, 15 Nov. 1927, 5.

33. Letter from Sorabji to Mayo, 10 June 1928, in folder no. 47, series 1, box 6, K. M. Papers. For Alice Pennell's position, see the letter from Miss Hotz to Mayo, dated 1 Jan. 1936 in folder no. 78, series 1, box 10, K. M Papers.

34. See letters from Sorabji to Mayo, dated 6 Sept. 1927 and 1 Sept. 1927 in folder no. 38, series 1, box 5, and letter of 10 June 1928 in folder no. 47, series 1, box 6, K. M. Papers.

35. Katherine Mayo, *The Face of Mother India* (New York, 1935); letter from Sorabji to Mayo, dated 2 May 1935 in folder no. 75, series 1, box 9, and 31 Dec. 1935 in folder no. 76, series 1, box 10, K. M. Papers.

36. Bose's denial appeared in an article written by a British Y.M.C.A. official, in the *Indian Witness*, 7 Sept. 1927 cited in Henry Field, *After 'Mother India'* (New York, 1929), 140. For Mayo's concern about Bose's denial, see letter from Mayo to Ellen Stanton, 17 Dec. 1927 in folder no. 41 and Moyca Newell [Mayo's partner] to Col. Baltye, 25 Feb. 1928 in folder no. 43, series 1, box 6, K. M. Papers.

37. For a discussion of Nehru's journalistic contributions see Vir Bharat Talwar, 'Feminist Consciousness in Women's Journals in Hindi, 1910–1920' in Sangari and Vaid (eds.), *Recasting Women*, 204–32. See also Uma Nehru, 'Whither Women', in S. K. Nehru (ed.), *Our Cause*, 403–19.

38. Nehru was married to the journalist Shyamlal Nehru, uncle of the famous Jawaharlal Nehru. For an assessment of Nehru as too 'Westernized' see Vijaylakshmi Pandit (Uma Nehru's niece by marriage), *The Scope of Happiness: A Personal Memoir* (New York, 1979), 194–5 and interview with Indira Gandhi (Nehru's grand-niece) in Promilla Kalhan, *Kamala Nehru: An Intimate Biography* (Delhi, 1973), 133.

39. *Miss Mayo ki 'Mother India' (Sachitra Hindi Unuwad) jis me Srimati Uma Nehru likhit 'Bhumika' tatha paschimi samajyawad ke vishay me 'Miss Mayo se do do bate'* (Allahabad, 1928).

40. Katherine Mayo, *Slaves of the God* (New York, 1929), 237.

41. For a discussion of Naidu in these terms, see Geraldine Forbes, 'The Women's Movement in India: Traditional Symbols and New Roles', in M. S. A. Rao (ed.), *Sectarian, Tribal and Women's Movements*, ii. *Social Movements in India* (Delhi, 1979), 149–65; and Meena Alexander, 'Sarojini Naidu: Romanticism and Resistance', *Economic and Political Weekly*, 20/43 (26 Oct. 1985); ws68–ws71.

42. Naidu's speech was reported in *The Times* (London), 5 Sept. 1927, 5. For an extract of Mayo's interview in which she quotes from Naidu's speech, see folder no. 38, series 1, box 5, K. M. Papers.

43. For Naidu's telegram to the Calcutta meeting, see *Forward*, 7 Sept. 1927 in India, vol. 2 in folder no. 207, series 4, box 37, K. M. Papers.

44. Quoted in the *Statesman*, 24 Jan. 1928, 6. See also *Hindi*, 24 Jan. 1928 in India, vol. 2 in folder no. 207, series 4, box 37, K. M. Papers.

45. See *Statesman*, 30 Jan. 1929, 10.

46. For Naidu's refusal to discuss Mayo in the USA, see Tara Ali Baig, *Sarojini Naidu* (New Delhi 1974), 99–100; and Padmini Sengupta, *Sarojini Naidu* (Bombay, 1966), 209–11.

47. Naidu's triumphant US trip is covered in the *New York Times*, 14 Oct. 1928, 14; 28 Oct. 1928, 6; and 3 Mar. 1929, 15. For the efforts of Mayo and her supporters to sabotage Naidu's reception in the USA see letter from Sutton to Mayo, dated 22 Sept. 1930 in folder no. 56 in series 1, box 8, K. M. Papers. Also see the publication of Henry Field's (Mayo's secretary), *After 'Mother India'*, with is unfounded charge that Naidu had attempted to bribe an American woman who had been killed in a Gandhi-led demonstration in Bombay.

48. Chatterjee, 'The Nationalist Resolution', 243.

49. Mayo was now seen as an authority on Indian women in some women's circles abroad; she was invited by the League of Nation's Fellowship branch to

head the Indian delegation on Child Health. See letter from Miss Gail Barker, dated 9 Sept. 1927, in folder no. 38, series 1, box 5, K. M. Papers. For the Daughters of the American Revolution, and other conservative women's groups' support for Mayo, see the Colony Club meeting of women's groups in the USA held on 27 Nov. 1927, letter from Field to Mrs Henry Loomis, 19 Oct. 1927, in folder 39, series 1, box 5; copy of the resolutions passed at this meeting, see folder 42, series 1, box 6, K. M. Papers.

50. Rathbone's sense of 'responsibility' for the condition of women in India is discussed in Barbara Ramusack, 'Cultural Missionaries, Maternal Imperialists, Feminist Allies: British Women Activists in India 1865–1945', *Women's Studies International Forum*, 13/4 (1990), 309–21. For the significance of the condition of women in India for the self-identity of British feminism in the nineteenth century, see Antoinette Burton, 'The White Woman's Burden: British Feminists and "The Indian Woman" 1865–1915', *Women's Studies International Forum*, 13/4 (1990): 245–308.

51. Letter from Rathbone to Mayo, 24 Aug. 1927, in folder no. 37, series 1, box 5, K. M. Papers.

52. Mrs I. Ameer Ali's letter to *The Times* is quoted in *Statesman*, 14 Dec. 1927, 12. Ali's letter also provoked a response from a 'Rani of India' who argued that women behind the veil were indeed voiceless.

53. The second two-day conference was reported in *The Times*, 8 Oct. 1929, 9 and 9 Oct. 1929, 9. The report of the conference in the *Statesman* appeared under the heading 'Indian Women Lively', 9 Oct. 1929, 9. The details of the conflict between Rathbone and Rau is discussed in Mary D. Stocks, *Eleanor Rathbone: A Biography* (London, 1949), esp. 137 and Dhanvanthi Rama Rau, *An Inheritance: The Memoirs of Dhanvanthi Rama Rau* (London, 1977), esp. 170–2.

54. See his 'Mother India-Swaraj and Social Reform', *Fortnightly Review*, 122/633 (2 Jan. 1928), 182.

55. Letter signed by Dhanvanthi Rama Rau, Hannah Sen, and others appeared in *The Times*, 22 Oct. 1929, 12. Rathbone's reply was published on 24 Oct. 1929, 12. A letter supporting Rathbone's complaint that Indian women were politicizing women's issues appeared under the name Eva Mary Bell on 31 Oct. 1929, 10.

56. Chakrabarty, 'Postcoloniality and the Artifice of History', 18.

57. This point has been made in the context of discourses about nineteenth-century property and marriage legislation in Britain in Rosemary Hennessey and Rajeshwari Mohan, 'The Construction of Women in Three Popular Texts of Empire: Towards a Critique of Materialist Feminism', *Textual Practice*, 3/3 (Winter 1989), 323–59.

58. Quoted in Sengupta, *The Portrait of an Indian Woman*, 179–80.

59. The statement of Margaret Cousins, an Irish woman and pioneer of the all-India women's organizations, on behalf of the WIA, was quoted in the *Indian National Herald*, 17 Sept. 1927 in India, vol. 2 in folder no. 207, series 4, box 37, K. M. Papers.

60. For the report of the WIA protest meeting, see *Hindu*, 29 Sept. 1927 in India, vol. 2 in folder 207, series 4, box 37, K. M. Papers.

61. The events of the meeting have been reconstructed from the *Bombay Daily Mail*, 27 Dec. 1927 and the letter-to-editor in the *Hindu*, 12 Jan. 1927 in India, vol. 3 in folder no. 207, series 4, box 37, K. M. Papers.

62. For a background of the Non-Brahmin movement, see Gail Omvedt, *Cultural Conflict in a Colonial Society: The Non-Brahmin Movement in Western India, 1873–1830* (Poona, 1976).

63. See Rameshwari Nehru, *Gandhi is My Star: Speeches and Writings of Smt. Rameshwari Nehru*, comp. and ed. Somanth Dhar (Patna, 1950), 52.

64. For a history of child-marriage and age-of-consent reforms, see Geraldine Forbes, 'Women and Modernity: The Issue of Child Marriage in India', *Women's Studies International Quarterly*, 2 (1979), 407–19. For a general history of the AIWC, see Bharati Ray, *Women's Struggle: A History of the All India Women's Conference 1927–1990* (New Delhi, 1990).

65. Rameshwari Nehru, 'Early Marriage', in R. Nehru (ed.), *Our Cause*, 256–67.

66. Katherine Mayo, *Volume 2* (London, 1931).

67. See Kamaladevi Chattopadhyay, *Inner Recesses, Outer Spaces: Memoirs* (New Delhi, 1986), 113–17 and Rau, *An Inheritance*, 151.

68. See *New York Times*, 10 Feb. 1928, 13.1 Papers in Britain, like the *Edinburgh Evening News*, 10 Feb. 1928; *Star*, 10 Feb. 1928; *Reynolds Illustrated News*, 12 Feb. 1928; among others, gave sole credit to Mayo's book, see Great Britain, vol. 2 in folder no. 207, series 4, box 38, K. M. Papers. The view continues today; see the biographic entry on Mayo by William E. Brown Jr. in vol. 30 of *Encylcopedia of American Biographies*, 20, K. M. Papers. Historians also continue to differ in their evaluations of Mayo's contribution to women's reform; William W. Emilsen, 'Gandhi and Mayo's *Mother India*', *South Asia*, 10/1 (1 June 1987): 69–82 credits Mayo with the reform, ignoring entirely the women's movement in India. R. K. Sharma, *Nationalism, Social Reform and Indian Women: A Study in the Interaction between the National Movement and the Movement of Social Reform among Indian Women 1921–1937* (Patna, 1981), 198–212, argues that Mayo had no role in getting reform legislation passed.

69. Letter from Blanche Wilson, no date, in folder no. 42, series 1, box 6, K. M. Papers.

70. For some examples, see Jahan Ara Shahnawaz, *Father and Daughter* (Lahore, 1971), 97–8; Hansa Mehta, *Indian Women* (Delhi, 1981), 63; Amrit Kaur, *Challenge to Women* (Allahabad, 1946), 5; and the collection of essays in Kamaladevi Chattopadhyay *et al.* (eds.), *The Awakening of Indian Women* (Madras, 1939).

71. Kumari Jayawardena, *Feminism and Nationalism in the Third World* (London, 1986), 107–9. This point has been made in Mary John, 'Postcolonial Feminists in the Western Intellectual Field: Anthropologists and Native Informants?', *Inscriptions*, 5 (1989), 49–74.

72. Sangari and Vaid, 'Recasting Women: An Introduction', 19.

73. R. Radhakrishnan, 'Nationalism, Gender and Narrative', in Andrew Parker *et al.* (eds.), *Nationalisms and Sexualities* (New York, 1992), esp. 79–82.

74. The importance that such questions hold for our sense of the contemporary historical situation in India is spelled out in Kumkum Sangari, 'Introduction: Representations in History', *Journal of Arts and Ideas*, 17 and 18 (June 1989), 3–7. For an excellent example of the currency of the Indian/Hindu woman in some contemporary communal discourses in India, see Tanika Sarkar, 'The Woman as Communal Subject: Rashtrasevika Samiti and Ram Janmabhoomi Movement', *Economic and Political Weekly*, 26/35 (31 Aug. 1991), 2057–62.

In the early days of this wave of the women's movement, I sat in a weekly consciousness-raising group with my friend A. We compared notes recently: What did you think was happening? How did you think our own lives were going to change? A. said she had felt, 'Now I can be a woman; it's no longer so humiliating. I can stop fantasizing that secretly I am a man, as I used to, before I had children. Now I can value what was once my shame.' Her answer amazed me. Sitting in the same meetings during those years, my thoughts were roughly the reverse: 'Now I don't have to be a woman anymore. I need never become a mother. Being a woman has always been humiliating, but I used to assume there was no exit. Now the very idea "woman" is up for grabs. "Woman" is my slave name; feminism will give me freedom to seek some other identity altogether.'

On its face this clash of theoretical and practical positions may seem absurd, but it is my goal to explore such contradictions, to show why they are not absurd at all. Feminism is inevitably a mixed form, requiring in its very nature such inconsistencies. In what follows I try to show first, that a common divide keeps forming in both feminist thought and action between the need to build the identity 'woman' and give it solid political meaning and the need to tear

Reprinted with permission from Marianne Hirsch and Evelyn Fox Keller (eds.), *Conflicts in Feminism* (London: Routledge, 1990). I am indebted to the hard-working readers of an earlier draft, who are nevertheless not to blame for the times I have failed to profit from their excellent advice: Nancy Davidson, Adrienne Harris, Temma Kaplan, Mim Kelber, Ynestra King, Susana Leval, Eunice Lipton, Alix Kates Shulman, Alan Snitow, Nadine Taub, Meredith Tax, Sharon Thompson, and Carole Vance. A shorter version of this article ('Pages from a Gender Diary') appeared in *Dissent* (Spring 1989); a longer verion ('A Gender Diary') is in Adrienne Harris and Ynestra King (eds.), *Rocking the Ship of State: Toward a Feminist Peace Politics* (Boulder, Col.: Westview Press, 1989).

down the very category 'woman' and dismantle its all-too-solid history. Feminists often split along the lines of some version of this argument, and that splitting is my subject. Second, I argue that though a settled compromise between these positions is currently impossible, and though a constant choosing of sides is tactically unavoidable, feminists—and indeed most women—live in a complex relationship to this central feminist divide. From moment to moment we perform subtle psychological and social negotiations about just how gendered we choose to be.

This tension—between needing to act as women and needing an identity not overdetermined by our gender—is as old as Western feminism. It is at the core of what feminism is. The divide runs, twisting and turning, right through movement history. The problem of identity it poses was barely conceivable before the eighteenth century, when almost everyone saw women as a separate species. Since then absolute definitions of gender difference have fundamentally eroded, and the idea 'woman' has become a question rather than a given.

In the current wave of the movement, the divide is more urgent and central a part of feminism than ever before. On the one hand, many women moved by feminism are engaged by its promise of solidarity, the poetry of a retrieved worth. It feels glorious to 'reclaim an identity they taught [us] to despise'. (The line is Michelle Cliff's.) Movement passion rescues women-only groups from contempt; female intimacy acquires new meanings and becomes more threatening to the male exclusiveness so long considered 'the world'.

On the other hand, other feminists, often equally stirred by solidarity, rebel against having to be 'women' at all. They argue that whenever we uncritically accept the monolith 'woman', we run the risk of merely relocating ourselves inside the old closed ring of an unchanging feminine nature. But is there any such reliable nature? These feminists question the eternal sisterhood. It may be a pleasure to be 'we', and it may be strategically imperative to struggle as 'we', but who, they ask, are 'we'?[1]

This diary was begun to sort out my own thoughts about the divide. I have asked myself, is the image of a divide too rigid, will it only help to build higher the very boundaries I seek to wear down? Yet I keep stumbling on this figure in my descriptions of daily movement life. Perhaps the problem is my own. But others certainly have shared the experience of 'division'. Maybe the image works best as a place to start, not as a conclusion. A recurring difference inside feminism seems to lie deep, but it is also mobile, changing in emphasis, not (I'm happy to say) very orderly.

Take as an example my checkered entries about the women's peace movement. A number of feminists, myself included, felt uneasy about the new wave of women-only peace groups of the early 1980s. As feminist peace activist Ynestra King characterized the new spirit: 'A feminist peace sensibility is forming; it includes new women's culture and traditional women's culture.'[2] Some saw such a fusion between traditional female solidarity and new women's forms of protest as particularly powerful. Others felt that the two were at cross-purposes. Might blurring them actually lead to a watering down of feminism? The idea that women are by definition more nurturant, life-giving, and less belligerent than men is very old; the idea that such gender distinctions are social, hence subject to change, is much more recent, fragile, counterintuitive, and contested. Can the old idea of female specialness and the newer idea of a female outlook forged in social oppression join in a movement? And just how?

A study group met for a time in 1983 to talk about women's peace politics.[3] I was the irritating one in our group, always anxious about the nature of our project. I was the one who always nagged, 'Why a women's peace movement?'

I argued with a patient Amy Swedlow that women asking men to protect the children (as Women Strike for Peace asked Congress in 1961) was a repetition of an old, impotent, suppliant's gesture. Men had waged wars in the name of just such protection. And besides, did we want a world where only women worried about the children?[4] 'So what's your solution?', the good-tempered group wanted to know. 'Should women stop worrying about the children? Who trusts men to fill the gap?' Amy described how the loving women, going off to Washington to protest against nuclear testing, filled their suburban freezers with dinners so their families would miss them less.

I tried to explain the source of my resistance to the motherly rhetoric of the women's peace movement. During the 1960s, some of us had angrily offered to poison men's private peace, abort men's children. We proposed a bad girl's exchange: We'd give up protection for freedom, give up the approval we got for nurturance in exchange for the energy we'd get from open anger.

Of course, I knew what the group would ask me next, and rightly, too: 'Whose freedom? Which rage? Isn't abandoning men's project of war rage enough? And is women's powerlessness really mother's fault?' Although I reminded the group that the new wave of feminists never blamed motherhood as much as the media claimed, we did run from it, like the young who scrawled the slogan on Paris walls in 1968: 'Cours, camarade, le vieux monde est derrière toi.' ('Run, comrade, the past is just behind you.')

This scene is caricature, but it begins to get at the mood of our group. Fractious, I was always asking the others if they didn't agree that peace is assumed to be a women's issue for all the wrong reasons. I argued that if there is to be no more 'women-only' when it comes to emotional generosity or trips to the laundry, why 'women-only' in the peace movement? Maybe the most radical thing we could do would be to refuse the ancient women–peace connection? The army is a dense locale of male symbols, actions, and forms of association, so let men sit in the drizzle with us at the gates of military installations. Even if theorists emphasize the contingent and the historical and say that peace is an issue that affects women *differently* from men because of our different social position, we are trapped again in an inevitably oversimplified idea of 'women'. Are *all* women affected the same way by war? Or is class or age or race or nationality as important a variable? What do we gain, I asked the group, when we name the way we suffer from war as a specifically *women's* suffering? And so it went.

Until one day Ynestra King tactually suggested that perhaps I was seeking a mixed group to do my peace activism. (Mixed is a code word for men and women working together.) I was horrified. We were laughing, I'm pleased to recall, as I confessed myself reluctant to do political work in mixed groups. The clichés about women in the male Left making the coffee and doing the xeroxing were all literally true in my case. (I blame myself as well; often I chose those tasks, afraid of others.) Only by working with women had I managed to develop an intense and active relationship to politics at all. Not only had my political identity been forged in the women-only mould, but the rich networks I had formed inside feminism were the daily source of continued activism. My experience of the women-only peace camp at Greenham Common, England, was to become a source of continued political energy and inspiration. Women-only (the abstraction) was full of problems; women-only (the political reality in my life) was full of fascination, social pleasure, debates about meaning in the midst of actions taken, even sometimes, victories won.

The political meaning of these sides changes, as does the place they hold in each woman's life. But no matter where each feminist finds herself in the argument about the meaning of women-only, all agree that in practical political work, separate women's groups are necessary. Whatever the issue, feminists have gained a great deal by saying, 'We are "women", and this is what "women" want.' This belief in some ground of shared experience is the social basis from which any sustained political struggle must come.

Even feminists like myself, anxious about any restatement of a female ideal—of peacefulness or nurturance or light—are constantly forced in practice to consider what activists lose if we choose to say peace is *not* a women's issue. We keep rediscovering the necessity to speak specifically as women when we speak of peace because the female citizen has almost no representation in the places where decisions about war and peace are made—the Congress, the corporation, the army.

In 1979, President Jimmy Carter fired former congresswoman Bella Abzug from her special position as co-chair of his National Advisory Commission for Women because the women on the commission insisted on using that platform to talk about war and the economy. These, said the President, were not women's issues; women's role was to support the President. Carter was saying in effect that women have no place in general social debate, that women, as we learned from the subsequent presidential campaign, are a 'special interest group'.

What a conundrum for feminists: Because women have little general representation in Congress, our demand to be citizens—gender unspecified—can be made only through gender solidarity; but when we declare ourselves separate, succeed, for example, in getting our own government commission, the President turns around and tries to make that power-base into a ghetto where only certain stereotypically female issues can be named. So, however separate we may choose to be, our 'separate' has to be different from his 'separate', a distinction it's hard to keep clear in our own and other minds, but one we must keep trying to make.

This case may seem beside the point to radicals who never vested any hope in the federal government in the first place. But the firing of Bella Abzug was a perfect public embodiment of the puzzle of women's situation. The idea that 'women' can speak about war is itself the unsettled question, requiring constant public tests. It is no coincidence that Bella Abzug was one of the organizers of Women Strike for Peace in 1961. She must have observed the strengths and weaknesses in the public image of mothers for peace; then, on the coat-tails of feminism, she tried to be an insider, a congresswoman presumably empowered to speak—as a woman, or for women, or for herself—on any public topic. People with social memory were able to witness the problem that arises

for the public woman, no matter what her stance. Feminism is poten-
tially radical in almost all its guises precisely because it interprets this
injustice, makes the Abzug impasse visible. Once visible, it begins to
feel intolerable.[5]

By travelling along the twisted track of this argument, I have
made what I think is a representative journey, what feminist historians such as Joan Kelly and Denise Riley have called an 'oscillation',
which is typical of both feminist theory and practice.[6] Such oscillations are inevitable for the foreseeable future. In a cruel irony that
is one mark of women's oppression, when women speak *as women*
they run a special risk of not being heard because the female voice
is by our culture's definition that-voice-you-can-ignore. But the
alternative is to pretend that public men speak for women or that
women who speak inside male–female forums are heard and
heeded as much as similarly placed men. Few women feel satisfied
that this neutral (almost always male) public voice reflects the par-
ticulars of women's experience, however varied and indeterminate
that experience may be.

Caught between not being heard because we are different and not
being heard because we are invisible, feminists face a necessary
strategic leap of nerve every time we shape a political action. We
weigh the kinds of powerlessness women habitually face; we choose
our strategy—as women, as citizens—always sacrificing some part
of what we know.

Because 'separate' keeps changing its meaning depending on
how it is achieved and in what larger context its political forms
unfold, there is no fixed progressive position, no final theoretical or
practical resting place for feminists attempting to find a social voice
for women. Often our special womanness turns into a narrow space
only a moment after we celebrate it; at other times, our difference
becomes a refuge and source of new work, just when it looked most
like a prison in which we are powerless. And finally, although
women differ fundamentally about the meaning and value of
'woman', we all live partly in, partly out of this identity by social
necessity. Or as Denise Riley puts it, 'Women are not women in all
aspects of their lives.'[7]

Peace is *not* a woman's issue; at the same time, if women don't
claim a special relationship to general political struggles, we will
experience that other, more common specialness reserved for those
named women: we will be excluded from talking about and acting
on the life and death questions that face our species.

NAMES FOR A RECURRING FEMINIST DIVIDE

In every case, the specialness of women has this double face, though often, in the heat of new confrontations, feminists suffer a harmful amnesia; we forget about this paradox we live with. Feminist theorists keep renaming this tension, as if new names could advance feminist political work. But at this point new names are likely to tempt us to forget that we have named this split before. In the service of trying to help us recognize what we are fated—for some time—to repeat, here is a reminder of past taxonomies.

Minimizers and Maximizers

The divide so central as to be feminism's defining characteristic goes by many names. Catharine Stimpson cleverly called it the feminist debate between the 'minimizers' and 'maximizers'.[8] Briefly, the minimizers are feminists who want to undermine the category 'woman', to minimize the meaning of sex difference. (As we shall see, this stance can have surprisingly different political faces.) The maximizers want to keep the category (or feel they can't do otherwise), but they want to change its meaning, to reclaim and elaborate the social being 'woman', and to empower her.

Radical Feminists and Cultural Feminists

In *Daring to Be Bad: A History of the Radical Feminist Movement in America, 1967–1975*, Alice Echols sees this divide on a time-line of the current women's movement, with 'radical feminism' more typical of the initial feminist impulse in this wave succeeded by 'cultural feminism'. Echols's definition of the initial bursts of 'radical feminism' shows that it also included 'cultural feminism' in embryo. She argues that both strains were present from the first—contradictory elements that soon proclaimed themselves as tensions in sisterhood. None the less, the earlier groups usually defined the commonality of 'women' as the shared fact of their oppression by 'men'. Women were to work separately from men not as a structural ideal but because such separation was necessary to escape a domination that only a specifically feminist (rather than mixed, Left) politics could change. Echols gives as an example Kathie Sarachild, who disliked the women's contingents at peace marches against the Vietnam War: 'Only if the *stated* purpose of a women's group is to fight *against* the relegation of women to a separate position and status, in other words, to fight for women's liberation, only then does a separate women's group acquire a revolutionary character. Then separation becomes a base for power rather than a symbol of powerlessness.'[9]

On the other side stands Echols's category, 'cultural feminism'. In her depiction of the divide, the cultural feminist celebration of being female was a retreat from 'radical feminism': '[I]t was easier to rehabilitate femininity than to abolish gender.'[10] She offers as a prime example of the growth of cultural feminism the popularity of Jane Alpert's 'new feminist theory', published in *Ms.* magazine in 1973 as 'Mother Right':

[F]eminists have asserted that the essential difference between women and men does not lie in biology but rather in the roles that patriarchal societies (men) have required each sex to play. . . . However, a flaw in this feminist argument has persisted: *it contradicts our felt experience of the biological difference between the sexes as one of immense significance.* . . . The unique consciousness or sensibility of women, the particular attributes that set feminist art apart, and a compelling line of research now being pursued by feminist anthropologists all point to the idea that *female biology is the basis of women's powers.* Biology is hence the source and not the enemy of feminist revolution.[11]

Echols concludes that by 1973, 'Alpert's contention that women were united by their common biology was enormously tempting, given the factionalism within the movement.'[12]

Ironically, then, the pressure of differences that quickly surfaced in the women's movement between lesbians and straight women, between white and black, between classes, was a key source of the new pressure towards unity. The female body offered a permanence and an immediately rich identity that radical feminism, with its call to a long, often negative struggle of resistance, could not.

As her tone reveals, in Echols's account, 'radical feminism' is a relatively positive term and 'cultural feminism' an almost entirely negative one. As I'll explain later, I have a number of reasons for sharing this judgement. Finally, though, it won't help us to understand recurring feminist oppositions if we simply sort them into progressive versus reactionary alignments. The divide is nothing so simple as a split between truly radical activists and benighted conservative ones, or between real agents for change and liberal reformers, or between practical fighters and sophisticated theorists. The sides in this debate don't line up neatly in these ways. Maximizers and minimizers have political histories that converge and diverge. But a pretence of neutrality won't get us anywhere either. I'm describing a struggle here, and every account of it contains its overt or covert tropism toward one side or the other.

Essentialists and Social Constructionists

We have only to move from an account of movement politics to one of feminist theory in order to reverse Echols's scenario of decline. In academic feminist discussion, the divide between the 'essentialists' and the 'social constructionists' has been a rout for the essentialists. Briefly, essentialists (like Alpert, above) see gender as rooted in biological sex differences. Hardly anyone of any camp will now admit to being an essentialist, since the term has become associated with a naïve claim to an eternal female nature. All the same, essentialism, like its counterpart, cultural feminism, is abundantly present in current movement work. When Barbara Deming writes that 'the capacity to bear and nurture children gives women a special consciousness, a spiritual advantage rather than a disadvantage', she is assigning an enduring meaning to anatomical sex differences. When Andrea Dworkin describes how through sex a woman's 'insides are worn away over time, and she, possessed, becomes weak, depleted, usurped in all her physical and mental energies . . . by the one who occupies her', she is asserting that in sex women are immolated as a matter of course, in the nature of things.[13]

Social construction—the idea that the meaning of the body is changeable—is far harder to embrace with confidence. As Ellen Willis once put it, culture may shape the body, but we feel that the body has ways of pushing back.[14] To assert that the body has no enduring, natural language often seems like a rejection of common sense. Where can a woman stand—embodied or disembodied—in the flow of this argument?

Writing not about gender in general but about that more focused issue of bodies and essences, sexuality, Carole Vance has raised questions about the strengths and vicissitudes of social construction theory. She observes that the social constructionists who try to discuss sexuality differ about just what is constructed. Few would go so far as to say that the body plays no part at all as a material condition on which we build desire and sexual mores. But even for those social constructionists who try to escape entirely from any a priori ideas about the body, essentialism makes a sly comeback through unexamined assumptions. For example, how can social constructionists confidently say they are studying 'sexuality'? If there is no essential, transhistorical biology of arousal, then there is no unitary subject, 'sexuality', to discuss: 'If sexuality is constructed differently at each time and place, can we use the term in a comparatively meaningful way? . . . [H]ave constructionists undermined their own categories? Is there an "it" to study?'[15]

In the essentialist-versus-social constructionist version of the divide, one can see that one term in the argument is far more stable than the other. Essentialism such as Jane Alpert's in 'Mother Right' assumes a relatively stable social identity in 'male' and 'female', while as Carole Vance argues, social construction is at its best as a source of destabilizing questions. By definition social construction theory cannot offer a securely bounded area for the study of gender; instead it initiates an inspiring collapse of gender verities.

Cultural Feminists and Poststructuralists

The contrast between more and less stable categories suggests yet another recent vocabulary for the feminist divide. In 'Cultural Feminism versus Post-Structuralism: The Identity Crisis in Feminist Theory', Linda Alcoff puts Echols's definition of 'cultural feminism' up against what she sees as a more recent counter-development: feminist poststructural theory. By speaking only of 'the last ten years', Alcoff lops off the phase of 'radical feminism' that preceded 'cultural feminism' in movement history, leaving the revisionist image of extreme essentialism (such as Mary Daly's in *Gyn/Ecology*) as the basic matrix of feminist thought from which a radical 'nominalism' has more recently and heroically departed, calling all categories into doubt.[16] It is no accident that with attention to detail, Alice Echols can trace a political decline from 'radical feminism' to 'cultural feminism' between 1967 and 1975 while Linda Alcoff can persuasively trace a gain in theoretical understanding from 'cultural feminism' to 'poststructuralism' between 1978 and 1988. Put them together and both narratives change: instead of collapse or progress, we see one typical oscillation in the historical life of the divide.

These two accounts are also at odds because they survey very different political locations: Echols is writing about radical feminist activism, Alcoff about developments in academic feminist theory. Though political activism has developed a different version of the central debate from that of the more recent academic feminism, both confront the multiple problems posed by the divide. Nor will a model that goes like this work: *thesis* (essentialism, cultural feminism), *antithesis* (poststructuralism, deconstruction, Lacanian psychoanalysis), *synthesis* (some stable amalgam of women's solidarity that includes radical doubts about the formation, cohesion, and potential power of the group).

Instead, the divide keeps forming *inside* each of these categories. It is fundamental at any level one cares to meet it: material, psychological, linguistic. For example, US feminist theorists don't agree about whether poststructuralism tends more often toward its own version of essentialism (strengthening the arguments of maximizers by recognizing an enduring position of female Other) or whether poststructuralism is instead the best tool minimalists have (weakening any universalized, permanent concept such as Woman).[17] Certainly poststructuralists disagree among themselves, and this debate around and inside poststructuralism should be no surprise. In feminist discourse a tension keeps forming between finding a useful lever in female identity and seeing that identity as hopelessly compromised.

I'm not regressing here to the good old days of an undifferentiated, under-theorized sisterhood, trying to blur distinctions others have usefully struggled to establish, but I do want to explore a configuration—the divide—that repeats in very different circumstances. For example, in an earlier oscillation, both radical feminism and liberal feminism offered their own versions of doubt about cultural feminism and essentialism. Liberal feminists refused the idea that biology should structure women's public and sometimes even their private roles. Radical feminists saw the creation and maintenance of gender difference as the means by which patriarchs controlled women.[18] Though neither group had the powerful theoretical tools later developed by the poststructuralists, both intimated basic elements in poststructuralist work: that the category 'woman' was a construction, a discourse over which there had been an ongoing struggle; and that the self, the 'subject', was as much the issue as were social institutions. To be sure, these early activists often foolishly ignored Freud; they invoked an unproblematic 'self' that could be rescued from the dark male tower of oppression; and they hourly expected the radical deconstruction of gender, as if the deconstruction of what had been constructed was relatively easy. None the less, radical, philosophical doubts about the cohesion of 'woman' have roots that go all the way down in the history of both liberal and radical feminism.

Recently I asked feminist critic Marianne DeKoven for a piece she and Linda Bamber wrote about the divide for the Modern Language

Association in 1982. 'Feminists have refined our thinking a great deal since then,' she said. Yes, no doubt; but there is not much from the recent past that we can confidently discard. In fact, the Bamber–DeKoven depiction of the divide remains useful because we are nowhere near a synthesis that would make these positions relics of a completed phase. One side of the divide, Bamber says in her half of the paper, 'has been loosely identified with American feminism, the other with French feminism'.

But in fact these labels are inadequate, as both responses can be found in the work of both French and American feminists. Instead of debating French vs. American feminism, then, I want to define the two poles of our responses nonjudgementally and simply list their characteristics under Column A and Column B.

Column A feminism is political, empirical, historical. A Column A feminist rebels against the marginalization of women and demands access to 'positions that require knowledge and confer power'. A Column A feminist insists on woman as subject, on equal pay for equal work, on the necessity for women to be better represented in political life, the media, history books, etc. Column A feminism assumes, as Marks and de Courtivron put it, 'that women have (always) been present but invisible and if they look they will find themselves'.

The Column B feminist, on the other hand, is not particularly interested in the woman as subject. Instead of claiming power, knowledge, and high culture for women, Column B feminism attacks these privileged quantities as 'phallogocentric'. . . . The feminine in Column B is part of the challenge to God, money, the phallus, origins and ends, philosophical privilege, the transcendent author, representation, the Descartian cogito, transparent language, and so on. The feminine is valorized as fragment, absence, scandal. . . . Whereas the Column A feminist means to occupy the center on equal terms with men, the Column B feminist, sometimes aided by Derrida, Lacan, Althusser, Levi-Strauss, and Foucault, subverts the center and endorses her own marginality.[19]

No doubt Bamber and DeKoven would restate these terms now in the light of eight more years of good, collective feminist work, but I am trying to write against the grain of that usually excellent impulse here, trying to suggest a more distant perspective in which eight years become a dot.

Alcoff is only the latest in a long line of frustrated feminists who want to push beyond the divide, to be done with it. She writes typically: 'We cannot simply embrace the paradox. In order to avoid the serious disadvantages of cultural feminism and post-structuralism, feminism needs to transcend the dilemma by developing a third course. . . .'[20] But 'embracing the paradox' is just what feminism cannot choose but do. There is no transcendence, no third course. The urgent contradiction women constantly experience between the pressure to be a woman and the pressure not to be one will change only through a historical process; it cannot be dissolved through thought alone.

This is not to undervalue theory in the name of some more solid material reality but to emphasize that the dualism of the divide requires constant work; it resists us. It's not that we can't interrupt current patterns, not that trying to imagine our way beyond them isn't valuable, but that such work is continual.[21] What is more, activists trying to make fundamental changes, trying to push forward the feminist discourse and alter its material context, don't agree about what sort of synthesis they want. Nor can activists turn to theorists in any direct way for a resolution of these differences. Activism and scholarship have called forth different readings of the divide, but neither of these locations remains innocent of the primary contradiction. There is no marriage of theoretical mind and activist brawn to give us New Feminist Woman. The recognition that binary thinking is a problem doesn't offer us any immediate solution.

In other words, neither cultural feminism nor poststructuralism suggests a clear course when the time comes to discuss political strategy. Though we have learned much, we are still faced with the continuing strategic difficulty of *what to do*. As Michèle Barrett puts it: 'It does not need remarking that the postmodernist point of view is explicitly hostile to any political project behind the ephemeral.'[22] The virtue of the ephemeral action is its way of evading ossification of image or meaning. Ephemerally, we can recognize a possibility we cannot live out, imagine a journey we cannot yet take. We begin: The category 'woman' is a fiction; then, poststructuralism suggests ways in which human beings live by fictions; then, in its turn, activism requires of feminists that we elaborate the fiction 'woman' as if she were not a provisional invention at all but a person we know well, one in need of obvious rights and powers. Activism and theory weave together here, working on what remains the same basic cloth, the stuff of feminism.

Some theorists like Alcoff reach for a synthesis, a third way, beyond the divide, while others like Bamber and DeKoven choose instead the metaphor of an inescapable, irreducible 'doubleness'— a word that crops up everywhere in feminist discussion. To me, the metaphor of doubleness is the more useful: it is a reminder of the unresolved tension on which feminism continues to be built. As

Alice Walker puts it in her formal definition of a 'womanist' (her word for a black feminist): 'Appreciates and prefers women's culture, women's emotional flexibility . . . committed to survival and wholeness of entire people, male and female. Not a separatist, except periodically, for health.'[23]

This is not to deny change but to give a different estimate of its rate. Mass feminist consciousness has made a great difference; we have created not only new expectations but also new institutions. Yet, inevitably, the optimism of activism has given way to the academic second thoughts that tell us why our work is so hard. For even straightforward, liberal changes—like equal pay or day-care—are proving far more elusive than feminists dreamed in 1970. We are moving more slowly than Western women of the late twentieth century can easily accept—or are even likely to imagine.

Motherists and Feminists

If the long view has a virtue beyond the questionable one of inducing calm, it can help feminists include women to whom a rapid political or theoretical movement forward has usually seemed beside the point—poor women, peasant women, and women who for any number of reasons identify themselves not as feminists but as militant mothers, fighting together for survival. In a study group convened by Temma Kaplan since 1985, Grass Roots Movements of Women, feminists who do research about such movements in different parts of the world, past and present, have been meeting to discuss the relationship among revolutionary action, women, and feminist political consciousness. As Meredith Tax described this activism:

There is a crux in women's history/women's studies, a knot and a blurry place where various things converge. This place has no name and there is no established methodology for studying it. The things that converge there are variously called: community organizations, working-class women's organizations, consumer movements, popular mass organizations, housewives' organizations, mothers' movements, strike support movements, bread strikes, revolutions at the base, women's peace movements. Some feminist or protofeminist groups and united front organizations of women may be part of this crux. Or they may be different. There is very little theory, either feminist or Marxist, regarding this crux.[24]

The group has been asking: under what class circumstances do women decide to band together as women, break out of domestic space, and publicly protest? What part have these actions actually played in gaining fundamental political changes? How do women define what they have done and why? Does it make any sense to name feminist thinking as part of this female solidarity? Is there reason to think some kind of feminist consciousness is likely to emerge from this kind of political experience? Is the general marginality of these groups a strength or a weakness?

Almost all the women we have been studying present themselves to the world as mothers (hence, 'motherists') acting for the survival of their children. Their groups almost always arise when men are forced to be absent (because they are migrant workers or soldiers) or in times of crisis, when the role of nurturance assigned to women has been rendered impossible. Faced with the imperatives of their traditional work (to feed the children, to keep the family together) and with the loss of bread, or mobility, or whatever they need to do that work, women can turn into a military force, breaking the shop-windows of the baker or the butcher, burning the pass-cards, assembling to confront the police state, sitting-in where normally they would never go—on the steps of the governor's house, at the gates of the cruise-missile base.

As feminists, it interested us to speculate about whether the women in these groups felt any kind of criticism of the social role of mother itself, or of the structural ghettoization of women, or of the sexism that greets women's political efforts. As Marysa Navarro said of the women she studies, the Mothers of the Plaza de Mayo, who march to make the Argentine government give them news of their kidnapped, murdered children: 'They can only consider ends that are mothers' ends.'[25] The surfacing of political issues beyond the family weakened the Mothers of the Plaza de Mayo. Some wished to claim that party politics don't matter and that their murdered children were innocent of any interest in political struggle. Others felt political activism had been their children's right, one they now wished to share. These argued that their bereavement was not only a moral witnessing of crime and a demand for justice but also a specific intervention with immediate and threatening political implications to the state.

This kind of difference has split the mothers of the Plaza de Mayo along the feminist divide. To what extent is motherhood a powerful identity, a word to conjure with? To what extent is it a patriarchal construction that inevitably places mothers outside the realm of the social, the changing, the active? What power can women who weep, yell, mourn in the street have? Surely a mother's grief and rage removed from the home, suddenly exposed to publicity, are powerful, shocking. Yet as Navarro also points out, the unity of this image was misleading; its force was eventually undermined by differences a group structured around the monolith 'mother' was unable to confront.

But, finally, to give the argument one more turn, many Plaza de Mayo women experienced a political transformation through their mothers' network. No group can resolve all political tensions through some ideal formation. The mothers of the disappeared, with their cross-party unity, have been able to convene big demonstrations, drawing new people into the political process. Women can move when a political vacuum develops; by being women who have accepted their lot, they can face the soldiers who have taken their children with a sense of righteous indignation that even a usually murderous police find it hard to dispute. On whatever terms, they have changed the political climate, invented new ways to resist state terrorism.

Using examples like these, the Grass Roots study group gave rise to a particularly poignant exploration of the feminist divide. In each member's work we saw a different version of how women have managed the mixed blessing of their female specialness. Actions like bread riots are desperate and ephemeral, but also effective. With these street eruptions, women put a government on notice; they signal that the poor can be pushed no further. It is finally women who know when the line has been crossed to starvation. But what then? Prices go down; the women go home—until the next time.

Women's movements for survival are like fire storms, changing and dissolving, resistant to political definition. We asked: Would a feminist critique of the traditional role of women keep these groups going longer? Or might feminist insights themselves contribute to the splits that quickly break down the unity shared during crisis? Or, in yet another shift of our assumed values, why *shouldn't* such groups end when the crisis ends, perhaps leaving behind them politicized people, active networks, even community organizations capable of future action when called for? If the left were to expand its definition of political culture beyond the state and the workplace more often, wouldn't the political consciousness of women consumers, mothers, and community activists begin to look enduring in its own way, an important potential source of political energy? Perhaps, our group theorized, we are wrong to wish the women to have formed ongoing political groups growing out of bread riots or meat strikes. Maybe we would see more if we redefined political life to include usually invisible female networks.

The more we talked, the more we saw the ramifications of the fact that the traditional movements were collectivist, the feminist ones more individualistic. Women's local activism draws on a long history of women's culture in which mutual support is essential to life, not (as it often is with contemporary urban feminists) a rare or fragile achievement. The community of peasant women (or working women, or colonized women, or concerned mothers) was a given for the motherists; crisis made the idea of a separate, private identity beyond the daily struggle for survival unimportant. Here was another face of the divide: Collectivist movements are powerful but they usually don't raise questions about women's work. Feminism has raised the questions, and claimed an individual destiny for each woman, but remains ambivalent toward older traditions of female solidarity. Surely our group was ambivalent. We worried that mothers' social networks can rarely redefine the *terms* of their needs. And rich as traditional forms of female association may be, we kept coming on instances in which the power of societies organized for internal support along gender lines was undermined by the sexism of that very organization.

For example, historian Mrinalini Sinha's research describes how the Bengali middle class of nineteenth-century India used its tradition of marrying and bedding child brides as a way of defining itself against a racist, colonial government.[26] The British hypocritically criticized Bengali men as effeminate because they could not wait. Bengali men answered that it was their women who couldn't wait: the way to control unbounded female sexuality—in which, of course, the British disbelieved—was to marry women at first menstruation.

In Sinha's account one rarely hears the voices of Bengali women themselves, but the question of which sexism would control them—the British marriages of restraint or the Bengali marriages of children—raged around these women. Neither side in the quarrel had women's autonomy or power at heart. Both wanted to wage the colonial fight using women as the symbolic representatives of their rivalry. Because Bengali men wanted control of their women just as much as the British wanted control of Bengali men, the anticolonial struggle had less to offer women than men. In general, our group found that sexism inside an oppressed or impoverished community—such as rigidity about gender roles, or about male authority over women, or about female chastity—has cost revolutionary movements a great deal. Too often, gender politics goes unrecognized as an element in class defeat.[27]

Our group disagreed about the women's solidarity we were studying: was it a part of the long effort to change women's position and to criticize hierarchy in general, or did motherist goals pull in an essentially different direction from feminist ones? And no matter where each one of us found herself on the spectrum of the group's responses to motherist movements, no resolution emerged of the paradox between mothers' goals and the goals of female individuals no longer defined primarily by reproduction and its attendant tasks. We saw this tension in some of the groups we studied, and we kept discovering it in ourselves. (Indeed, some of us were part of groups that used motherist rhetoric, as Ynestra King and I were of women's peace networks, or Amy Swerdlow had been of Women Strike for Peace.)

Drawing hard lines between the traditional women's movements and modern Western feminist consciousness never worked, not because the distinction doesn't exist but because it is woven inside our movement itself. A motherist is in some definitions a feminist, in others not. And these differing feminisms are yoked together by the range of difficulties to be found in women's current situation. Our scholarly distance from the motherists kept collapsing. The children's toy-exchange network that Julie Wells described as one of the political groupings that build black women's solidarity in South Africa couldn't help striking us urban women in the United States as a good idea.[28] We, too, are in charge of the children and need each other to get by. We, too, are likely to act politically along the lines of association our female tasks have shaped. We sometimes long for the community the women we were studying took more for granted, although we couldn't help remarking on the ways those sustaining communities—say of union workers, or peasants, or ghettoized racial groups—used women's energy, loyalty, and passion as by right, while usually denying them a say in the group's public life, its historical consciousness.

Culture offers a variety of rewards to women for always giving attention to others first. Love is a special female responsibility. Some feminists see this female giving as fulfilling and morally powerful. Others see it as a mark of oppression and argue that women are given the job of 'life', but that any job relegated to the powerless is one undervalued by the society as a whole. Yet in our group there was one area of agreement: Traditional women's concerns—for life, for the children, for peace,—*should* be everyone's. Beyond that agreement the question that recreates the feminist divide remained: *How* can the caring that belong to 'mother' travel out to become the responsibility of everyone? Women's backs hold up the world, and we ached for the way women's passionate caring is usually taken for granted, even by women themselves. Some Western feminists, aching like this, want above all to recognize and honour these mothers who, as Adrienne Rich writes, 'age after age, perversely, with no extraordinary power, reconstitute the world.'[29] Others, also aching, start on what can seem an impossible search for ways to break the ancient, tireless mother's promise to be the mule of the world.

EQUALITY AND DIFFERENCE

By now anyone who has spent time wrangling with feminist issues has recognized the divide and is no doubt waiting for me to produce the name for it that is probably the oldest, certainly the most all-encompassing: 'equality' versus 'difference'. Most feminist thought grapples unavoidably with some aspect of the equality–difference problem at both the level of theory and of strategy. In theory, this version of the divide might be stated: Do women want to be equal to men (with the meaning of 'equal' hotly contested),[30] or do women see biology as establishing a difference that will always require a strong recognition and that might ultimately define quite separate possibilities inside 'the human'?

Some difference-feminists would argue that women have a special morality, or aesthetic, or capacity for community that it is feminism's responsibility to maximize. Others would put the theoretical case for difference more neutrally and would argue that woman, no matter *what* she is like, is unassimilable. Because she is biologically and therefore psychologically separable from man, she is enduring proof that there is no universally representative human being, no 'human wholeness'.[31] In contrast, the equality-feminists would argue that it is possible for the biological difference to wither away as a basis for social organization, either by moving men and women toward some shared centre (androgyny) or toward some experience of human variety in which biology is but one small variable.

Difference theory tends to emphasize the body (and more recently the unconscious where the body's psychic meaning develops); equality theory tends to de-emphasize the body and to place faith in each individual's capacity to develop a self not ultimately circumscribed by a collective law of gender. For difference theorists the body can be either the site of pain and oppression or the site of orgasmic ecstasy and maternal joy. For equality theorists neither extreme is as compelling as the overriding idea that the difference between male and female bodies is a problem in need of solution. In this view, therefore, sexual hierarchy and sexual oppression are bound to continue unless the body is transcended or displaced as the centre of female identity.

At the level of practical strategy, the equality–difference divide is just as ubiquitous as it is in theory. Willingly or not, activist lawyers find themselves pitted against each other because they disagree about whether 'equal treatment' before the law is better or worse for women than 'special treatment', for example, in cases about pregnancy benefits or child custody. (Should pregnancy be defined as unique, requiring special legal provisions, or will pregnant women get more actual economic support if pregnancy, when incapacitating, is grouped with other temporary conditions that keep people from work? Should women who give birth and are almost always the ones who care for children therefore get an automatic preference in custody battles, or will women gain more ultimately if men are defined by law as equally responsible for children, hence equally eligible to be awarded custody?)[32] Sometimes activists find themselves pressured by events to pit the mainstreaming of information about women in the school curriculum against the need for separate programmes for women's studies. Or they find themselves having to choose between working to get traditionally male jobs (for example in construction) and working to get fair pay in the women-only jobs they are already doing.

One rushes to respond that these strategic alternatives should not be mutually exclusive, but often, in the heat of local struggles, they temporarily become so. No matter what their theoretical position on the divide, activists find themselves having to make painfully unsatisfactory short-term decisions about the rival claims of equality and difference.[33]

Regrettably, these definitions, these examples flatten out the oscillations of the equality–difference debate; they obscure the class struggles that have shaped the development of the argument; they offer neat parallels where there should be asymmetries. Viewed historically, the oscillation between a feminism of equality and one of difference is a bitter disagreement about which path is more progressive, more able to change women's basic condition of subordination.

In this history each side has taken more than one turn at calling the other reactionary and each has had its genuine vanguard moments. 'Difference' gained some working women protection at a time when any social legislation to regulate work was rare, while 'equality' lay behind middle-class women's demand for the vote, a drive Ellen DuBois has called 'the most radical program for women's emancipation possible in the nineteenth century'. At the same time, bourgeois women's demands that men should have to be as sexually pure as women finessed the divide between difference and equality and gave rise to interesting cross-class alliances of women seeking ways to make men conform to women's standard, rather than the usual way round—a notion of equality with a difference.[34] As DuBois points out, it is difficult to decide which of these varied political constructions gave nineteenth-century women the most real leverage to make change:

My hypothesis is that the significance of the woman suffrage movement rested precisely on the fact that it bypassed women's oppression within the family, or private sphere, and demanded instead her admission to citizenship, and through it admission to the public arena.[35]

In other words, at a time when criticism of women's separate family role was still unthinkable, imagining a place outside the family where such a role would make no difference was—for a time—a most radical act.

Equality and difference are broad ideas and have included a range of definitions and political expressions. Equality, for example, can mean anything from the mildest liberal reform (this is piece-of-the-pie feminism, in which women are merely to be included in the world as it is) to the most radical reduction of gender to insignificance. Difference can mean anything from Mary Daly's belief in the natural superiority of women to psychoanalytic theories of how women are inevitably cast as 'the Other' because they lack penises.[36]

Just now equality—fresh from recent defeats at the polls and in the courts—is under attack by British and U.S. theorists who are developing a powerful critique of the eighteenth- and nineteenth-century roots of feminism in liberalism. In what is a growing body of work, feminists are exploring the serious limitations of a tradition based on an ideal of equality for separate, independent individuals acting in a free, public sphere—either the market or the state. This liberalism, which runs as an essential thread through Anglo-American feminism, has caused much disappointment. Feminists have become increasingly aware of its basic flaws, of the ways it splits off public and private, leaves sexual differences entirely out of its narrative of the world, and pretends to a neutrality that is nullified by the realities of gender, class, and race. A feminism that honours individual rights has grown leery of the liberal tradition that always puts those rights before community and before any caring for general needs. Liberalism promises an equal right to compete, but as bell hooks puts it: 'Since men are not equals in white supremacist, capitalist, patriarchal class structure, which men do women want to be equal to?'[37]

These arguments against the origins and tendencies of equality feminism are cogent and useful. They have uncovered unexamined assumptions and the essential weakness in a demand for a passive neutrality of opportunity. But there are cracks in the critique of equality-feminism that lead me back to my general assertion that neither side of the divide can easily be transcended. The biggest complaint against a feminist demand of 'equality' is that this construction means women must become conceptual men, or rather that to have equal rights they will have to repress their biological difference, to subordinate themselves in still new ways under an unchanged male hegemony.[38] In this argument the norm is assumed to be male and women's entry into public space is assumed to be a loss of the aspects of experience they formerly embodied— privacy, feeling, nurturance, dailiness. Surely, though, this argument entails a monolithic and eternal view both of public space and of the category 'male'. How successfully does public space maintain its male gender markers, how totally exclude the private side of life? (The city street is male, yet it can at times be not only physically but also conceptually invaded, say, by a sense of neighbourhood or by a demonstration of mass solidarity.)[39] Does male space sometimes dramatically reveal the fact of women's absence? How well does the taboo on public women hold up under the multiple pressures of modernity? Even if public and private are conceptually absolutes, to what extent do individual men and women experience moments in both positions.

Or, if one rejects these hopeful efforts to find loopholes in the iron laws of gender difference, the fear that women will become men still deserves double scrutiny. Is the collapse of gender difference into maleness really the problem women face? Or are we perhaps quite close to men already at the moment when we fear absorption into the other?

None of this is meant as a refutation of the important current work that brings scepticism to the construction of our demands.

When health activist Wendy Chavkin notes that making pregnancy disappear by calling it a 'disability' is one more way of letting business and government evade sharing responsibility for reproduction, she is right to worry about the invisibility of women's bodies and of our work of reproduction of which our bodies are one small part. When philosopher Alison Jaggar gives examples of how male norms have buried the often separate needs of women, she is sounding a valuable warning. When critic Myra Jehlen describes how hard it is for the concept of a person to include the particular when that particular is female, she is identifying the depth of our difficulty, men's phobic resistance to the inclusion of women into any neutral or public equation.[40]

None the less, I want to reanimate the problem of the divide, to show the potential vigour on both sides. On the one hand, an abstract promise of equality is not enough for people living in capitalism, where everyone is free both to vote and to starve. On the other, as Zillah Eisenstein has pointed out in *The Radical Future of Liberal Feminism*, the demand for equality has a radical meaning in a capitalist society that claims to offer it but structurally often denies it. Feminism asks for many things the patriarchal state cannot give without radical change. Juliet Mitchell's rethinking of the value of equality-feminism reaches a related conclusion: When basic rights are under attack, liberalism feels necessary again. At best, liberalism sometimes tips in action and becomes more radical than its root conceptions promise. Certainly, no matter which strategy we choose—based on a model of equality or of difference—we are constantly forced to compromise.[41]

It's not that we haven't gotten beyond classical liberalism in theory but that in practice we cannot *live* beyond it. In their very structure, contemporary court cases about sex and gender dramatize the fact of the divide, and media questions demand the short, one-sided answer. Each 'case', each 'story' in which we act is different, and we are only at moments able to shape that difference, make it into the kind of 'difference' we want.[42]

THE DIVIDE IS NOT A UNIVERSAL

After having said so much about how deep the divide goes in feminism, how completely it defines what feminism *is*, I run the risk of seeming to say that the divide has some timeless essence. In fact,

I want to argue the opposite, to place Western feminism inside its two-hundred-year history as a specific possibility for thought and action that arose as one of the possibilities of modernity.

When Mary Wollstonecraft wrote one of the founding books of feminism in 1792, *A Vindication of the Rights of Women*, she said what was new then and remains fresh, shocking, and doubtful to many now: that sex hierarchy—like ranks in the church and the army or like the then newly contested ascendancy of kings—was social, not natural. Though women before her had named injustices and taken sides in several episodes of an ancient *quarrelle des femmes*, Wollstonecraft's generation experienced the divide in ways related to how feminists experience it now. At one and the same time she could see gender as a solid wall barring her way into liberty, citizenship, and a male dignity she envied, and could see how porous the wall was, how many ways she herself could imagine stepping through into an identity less absolute and more chaotic.

Modern feminists often criticize her unhappy compromise with bourgeois revolution and liberal political goals, but if Wollstonecraft was often an equality-feminist in the narrowest sense, eager to speak of absolute rights, of an idealized male individualism, and to ignore the body, this narrowness was in part a measure of her desperation.[43] The body, she felt, could be counted on to assert its ever-present and dreary pull; the enlightenment promised her a mind that might escape. She acknowledged difference as an absolute— men are stronger—and then with cunning, she offered men a deal:

Avoiding, as I have hitherto done, any direct comparison of the two sexes collectively, or frankly acknowledging the inferiority of women, according to the present appearance of things, I shall only insist that men have increased that inferiority till women are almost sunk below the standard of rational creatures. Let their faculties have room to unfold, and their virtues to gain strength, and then determine where the whole sex must stand in the intellectual scale.[44]

Wheedling a bit, Wollstonecraft made men the modest proposal that if women are inferior, men have nothing to fear; they can generously afford to give women their little chance at the light. This is a sly, agnostic treatment of the issue of equality versus difference. Experimental and groping spirit, Wollstonecraft *didn't know* how much biological difference might come to mean; but that she suffered humiliation and loss through being a woman she did know, and all she asked was to be let out of the prison house of gender identity for long enough to judge what men had and what part of that she might want.

When Wollstonecraft wrote, difference was the prevailing wind, equality the incipient revolutionary storm. She feared that if women could not partake in the new civil and political rights of democracy, they would 'remain immured in their families groping in the dark'. To be sure this rejection of the private sphere made no sense to many feminists who came after her and left modern feminists the task of recognizing the importance of the private and women's different life there, yet it is a rejection that was absolutely necessary as one of feminism's first moves. We in turn have rejected Wollstonecraft's call for chastity, for the end of the passionate emotions 'which disturb the order of society';[45] we have rejected her confidence in objective reason and her desire to live as a disembodied self (and a very understandable desire, too, for one whose best friend died in childbirth and who was to die of childbed fever herself), but we have not gotten beyond needing to make the basic demands she made—for civil rights, education, autonomy.

Finally, what is extraordinary in *A Vindication* is its chaos. Multivalent, driven, ambivalent, the text races over most of feminism's main roads. It constantly goes back on itself in tone, thrilling with self-hatred, rage, disappointment, and hope—the very sort of emotions it explains are the mark of women's inferiority, triviality, and lascivious abandon. Though its appeals to God and virtue are a dead letter to feminists now, the anger and passion with which Wollstonecraft made those appeals—and out of which she imagined the depth of women's otherness, our forced incapacity, the injustice of our situation—feel thoroughly modern. Her structural disorganization derives in part from a circular motion through now familiar stages of protest, reasoning, fury, despair, contempt, desire.[46] She makes demands for women, then doubles back to say that womanhood should be beside the point. Her book is one of those that mark the start of an avalanche of mass self-consciousness about gender injustice. So, in the midst of the hopeful excitement, the divide is there, at the beginning of our history.

If the divide is central to feminist history, feminists need to recognize it with more suppleness, but this enlarged perspective doesn't let one out of having to choose a position in the divide. On the contrary, by arguing that there is no imminent resolution, I hope to throw each reader back on the necessity of finding where her own work falls and of assessing how powerful that political decision is as a tool for undermining the dense, deeply embedded oppression of women.

529

By writing of the varied vocabularies and constructions feminists have used to describe the divide, I do not mean to intimate that they are all one, but to emphasize their difference. Each issue calls forth a new configuration, a new version of the spectrum of feminist opinion, and most require an internal as well as external struggle about goals and tactics. Though it is understandable that we dream of peace among feminists, that we resist in sisterhood the factionalism that has so often disappointed us in brotherhood, still we must carry on the argument among ourselves. Better, we must actively embrace it. The tension in the divide, far from being our enemy, is a dynamic force that links very different women. Feminism encompasses central dilemmas in modern experience, mysteries of identity that get full expression in its debates. The electricity of its internal disagreements is part of feminism's continuing power to shock and involve large numbers of people in a public conversation far beyond the movement itself. The dynamic feminist divide is about difference; it dramatizes women's differences from each other—and the necessity of our sometimes making common cause.

A GENDER DIARY: SOME STORIES, SOME DIALOGUES

If, as I've said, the divide offers no third way, no high ground of neutrality, I certainly have not been able to present this overview so far without a constant humming theme beneath, my own eagerness to break the category 'woman' down, to find a definition of difference that pushes so far beyond a settled identity that 'being a woman' breaks apart.

Though sometimes I have found the theoretical equality arguments I have described blinkered and reactive, when it comes to strategy, I almost always choose that side, fearing the romance of femaleness even more than the flatness and pretence of undifferentiated, gender-free public space.

I suspect that each one's emphasis—equality or difference—arises alongside and not after the reasons. We criticize Wollstonecraft's worship of rationality, but how willing are we modern ones to look at the unconscious, the idiosyncratic, the temperamental histories of our own politics? It is in these histories—private, intellectual, and social—that we can find why some women feel safer with the equality model as the rock of their practice (with difference as a necessary condition imposed on it), while other women feel more true to themselves, more fully expressed, by difference as their rock (with equality a sort of bottom-line call for basic reforms that cannot ultimately satisfy).

Why do I decide (again and again) that being a woman is a liability, while others I know decide (again and again) that a separate female culture is more exciting, more in their interests, more promising as a strategic stance for now than my idea of slipping the noose of gender, living for precious moments of the imagination outside it? An obvious first answer is that class, race, and sexual preference determine my choices, and surely these play their central part. Yet in my experience of splits in the women's movement, I keep joining with women who share my feminist preferences but who have arrived at these conclusions from very different starting points.

This is not to understate the importance of class, race, and sexual preference but merely to observe that these important variables don't segment feminism along the divide; they don't provide direct keys to each one's sense of self-interest or desire nor do they yield clear directions for the most useful strategic moves. For example, lesbian and straight women are likely to bring very different understandings and needs to discussions of whether or not women's communities work, whether or not the concept is constricting. Yet in my own experience, trust of women's communities does not fall out along the lines of sexual preference. Instead, up close, the variables proliferate. What was the texture of childhood for each one of us? What face did the world beyond home present?

In the fifties, when an earlier, roiled life of gender and politics had subsided and the gender messages seemed monolithic again, I lived with my parents in the suburbs. My mother's class and generation had lived through repeated, basic changes of direction about women, family, and work, and my own engaged and curious mother passed on her ambivalent reception of the world's mixed messages to me in the food. With hindsight, I can see that of course gender, family, and class weren't the settled issues they seemed then. But the times put a convincing cover over continuing change. Deborah Rosenfelt and Judith Stacey describe this precise historical moment and the particular feminist politics born from it:

[T]he ultradomestic nineteen fifties [was] an aberrant decade in the history of US family and gender relations and one that has set the unfortunate terms for waves of personal and political reaction to family issues ever since. Viewed in this perspective, the attack on the breadwinner/homemaker nuclear family by the women's liberation movement may have been an over-reaction to an aberrant and highly fragile cultural form, a family system that, for other reasons, was already passing from the scene. Our devastating critiques of the vulnerability and cultural devaluation of dependent wives and mothers helped millions of women to leave or avoid these domestic traps, and this is to our everlasting credit. But, with hindsight, it seems to us that these critiques had some negative consequences as well. . . . [F]eminism's over-reaction to the fifties was an antinatalist, antimaternalist moment. . . .[47]

I am the child of this moment, and some of the atmosphere of rage generated by that hysterically domestic ideology of the fifties can now feel callow, young, or ignorant. Yet I have many more kind words to say for the reaction of which I was a part in the early seventies than Rosenfelt and Stacey seem to: I don't think the feminism of this phase would have spoken so powerfully to so many without this churlish outbreak of indignation. Nothing we have learned since about the fragility of the nuclear family alters the fundamental problems it continues to pose for women. It is not really gone, though it is changing. And although feminism seeks to preside over the changes, other forces are at work, half the time threatening us with loneliness, half the time promising us rich emotional lives if we will but stay home—a vicious double-punch combination. In this climate, feminist resistance to pronatalism—of either the fifties *or* the nineties—continues to make sense.

It's hard to remember now what the initial feminist moves in this wave felt like, the heady but alarming atmosphere of female revolt. As one anxious friend wondered back then, 'Can I be in this and stay married?' The answer was often 'no', the upheaval terrifying. Some of us early ones were too afraid of the lives of our mothers to recognize ourselves in them. But I remember that this emotional throwing off of the mother's life felt like the only way to begin. Black women whose ties to their mothers were more often a mutual struggle for survival rarely shared this particular emotion. As Audre Lorde has said, '[B]lack children were not meant to survive',[48] so parents and children saw a lifeline in each other that was harder for the prosperous or the white to discern. The usually white and middle-class women who were typical members of early women's consciousness-raising groups often saw their mothers as desperate or depressed in the midst of their relative privilege. Many had been educated like men and had then been expected to become . . . men's wives. We used to agree in those meetings that motherhood was the divide. Before it, you could pretend you were just like everyone else; afterward, you were a species apart—invisible and despised.

But if motherhood was despised, it was also festooned—then as now—with roses. Either way, in 1970, motherhood seemed an inevitable part of my future, and the qualities some feminists now praise as uniquely women's were taken for granted as female necessities: everyone wanted the nice one, the sweet one, the good one, the nurturant one, the pretty one. No one wanted the women who didn't want to be women. It's hard to recover how frightening it was to step out of those ideas, to resist continuing on as expected; it's hard to get back how very naked it made us feel. Some of the vociferousness of our rhetoric, which now seems unshaded or raw, came partly from the anxiety we felt when we made this proclamation, that we didn't want to be women. A great wave of misogyny rose to greet us. So we said it even more. Hindsight has brought in its necessary wisdom, its temporizing reaction. We have gotten beyond the complaint of the daughters, have come to respect the realities, the worries, and the work of the mothers. But to me 'difference' will always represent a necessary modification of the initial impulse, a reminder of complexity, a brake on precipitate hopes. It can never feel like the primary insight felt, the first breaking with the gender bargain. The immediate reward was immense, the thrill of separating from authority.

Conversation with E. She recalls that the new women's movement meant to her: you don't have to struggle to be attractive to men anymore. You can stop working so hard on that side of things. I was impressed by this liberation so much beyond my own. I felt the opposite. Oppressed and depressed before the movement, I found sexual power unthinkable, the privilege of a very few women. Now angry and awake, I felt for the first time what the active eroticism of men might be like. What men thought of me no longer blocked out the parallel question of what I thought of them, which made sexual encounters far more interesting than they had once been. Like E., I worried about men's approval less, but (without much tangible reason) my hopes for the whole business of men and women rose. For a brief time in the early seventies, I had an emotional intimation of what some men must feel: free to rub up against the world, take space, make judgements. With all its hazards, this confidence also offered its delight—but only for a moment of course. The necessary reaction followed at once: women aren't men in public space. There is no safety. Besides, I had romanticized male experience; men are not as free as I imagined. Still, I remember that wild if deluded time—not wanting to be a man but wanting the freedom of the street. The feminist rallying cry 'Take Back the Night' has always struck me as a fine piece of movement poetry. We don't have the night, but we want it, we want it.

533

*Another memory of the early seventies: an academic woman sym-
pathetic to the movement but not active asked what motivated me to
spend all this time organizing, marching, meeting. (Subtext; Why
wasn't I finishing my book? Why did I keep flinging myself around?)*

*I tried to explain the excitement I felt at the idea that I didn't have
to be a woman. She was shocked, confused. This was the motor of my
activism? She asked, 'How can someone who doesn't like being a
woman be a feminist?' To which I could only answer, 'Why would anyone who likes being a woman need to be a feminist?'*

*Quite properly my colleague feared woman-hating. She assumed
that feminism must be working to restore respect and dignity to
women. Feminism would revalue what had been debased, women's
contribution to human history. I, on the other hand, had to confess: I
could never have made myself lick all those stamps for a better idea of
what womanhood means. Was this, as my colleague thought, just a
new kind of misogyny? I wouldn't dare say self-hatred played no part
in what I wanted from feminism from the first. But even back then, for
me, woman-hating—or loving—felt beside the point. It was the idea
of breaking the law of the category itself that made me delirious.*

*The first time I heard 'women' mentioned as a potentially political
contemporary category I was already in graduate school. It was the
mid-sixties and a bright young woman of the New Left was saying how
important it was to enlist the separate support of women workers in
our organizing against the Vietnam War. I remember arguing with
her, flushed with a secret humiliation. What good was she doing these
workers, I asked her, by addressing them and categorizing them separately? Who was she to speak so condescendingly of 'them'? Didn't she
know that the inferior category she had named would creep up in the
night and grab her, too?*

*I'm ashamed now to admit that gender solidarity—which I lived
inside happily, richly every day in those years—first obtruded itself on
my conscious mind as a threat and a betrayal. So entirely was I
trapped in negative feelings about what women are and can do that I
had repressed any knowledge of femaleness as a defining characteristic
of my being.*

*I can see now that women very different from me came to feminist
conclusions much like my own. But this is later knowledge. My feminism came from the suburbs, where I knew no white, middle-class
woman with children who had a job or any major activities beyond the
family. Yet, though a girl, I was promised education, offered the pretence of gender neutrality. This island of illusions was a small world,
but if I seek the source for why cultural feminism has so little power to*

draw me, it is to this world I return in thought. During the day, it was safe, carefully limited, and female. The idea that this was all made me frantic.

S. reads the gender diary with consternation. In Puerto Rico, where she grew up, this fear of the mother's life would be an obscenity. She can't recognize the desire I write of—to escape scot free from the role I was born to. Latina feminists she knows feel rage, but what is this shame, she wants to know. In her childhood both sexes believed being a woman was magic.

S. means it about the magic, hard as it is for me to take this in. She means sexual power, primal allure, even social dignity. S. became a feminist later, by a different route, and now she is as agnostic about the meaning of gender as I am. But when she was young, she had no qualms about being a woman.

After listening to S., I add another piece to my story of the suburbs. Jews who weren't spending much of our time being Jewish, we lived where ethnicity was easy to miss. (Of course it was there; but I didn't know it.) In the suburbs, Motherhood was white bread, with no powerful ethnic graininess. For better and worse, I was brought up on this stripped, denatured product. Magical women seemed laughably remote. No doubt this flatness in local myth made girls believe less in their own special self, but at the same time it gave them less faith in the beckoning ideal of mother. My gifted mother taught me not the richness of home but the necessity of feminism. Feminism was her conscious as well as unconscious gift.

It is not enough for the diary to tell how one woman, myself, came to choose—again and again—a feminism on the minimalizers' side of the divide. Somehow the diary must also tell how this decision can never feel solid or final. No one gets to stay firmly on her side; no one gets to rest in a reliably clear position. Mothers who believe their daughters should roam as free as men find themselves giving those daughters taxi fare, telling them not to talk to strangers, filling them with the lore of danger. Activists who want women to be very naughty (as the women in a little zap group we call 'No More Nice Girls' want women to be) none the less warn them there's a price to pay for daring to defy men in public space.[49] Even when a woman chooses which shoes she'll wear today—is it to be the running shoes, the flats, the spikes?—she's deciding where to place herself for the moment on the current possible spectrum of images of 'woman'. Whatever our habitual position on the divide, in daily life we travel back and forth, or, to change metaphors, we scramble for whatever toe-hold we can.

Living with the divide: in a room full of feminists, everyone is say-ing that a so-called surrogate mother, one who bears a child for others, should have the right to change her mind for a time (several weeks? months?) after the baby is born. This looks like agreement. Women who have been on opposite sides of the divide in many struggles con-verge here, outraged at the insulting way one Mary Beth Whitehead has been treated by fertility clinics, law courts, and press. She is not a 'surrogate', we say, but a 'mother' indeed.

The debate seems richer than it's been lately. Nobody knows how to sort out the contradictions of the new reproductive technologies yet, so for a fertile moment there's a freedom, an expressiveness in all that's said. Charged words like 'birth' and 'mothering' and 'the kids' are spilling all around, but no one yet dares to draw the ideological line defining which possibilities belong inside feminism, which are anti-thetical to it. Some sing a song of pregnancy and birth while others offer contrapuntal motifs of child-free lesbian youth, of infertility, all in different keys of doubt about how much feminists may want to make motherhood special, different from parenting, different from caring—a unique and absolute relation to a child.

But just as we're settling in for an evening that promises to be fraught, surprising, suggestive, my warning system, sensitive after twenty years of feminist activism, gives a familiar twitch and tug. Over by the door, one woman has decided: surrogacy is baby-selling and ought to be outlawed. All mothering will be debased if motherhood can be bought. Over by the couch, another woman is anxiously respond-ing: why should motherhood be the sacred place we keep clean from money, while men sell the work of their bodies every day? Do we want women to be the special representatives of the moral and spiritual things that can't be bought, with the inevitable result that women's work is once again done without pay?

Here it is then. The metaconversation that has hovered over my political life since 1970, when I joined one of the first women's con-sciousness-raising groups. On the one hand, sacred motherhood. On the other, a wish—variously expressed—for this special identity to wither away.

Only a little later in the brief, eventful history of this ad hoc *Mary Beth Whitehead support group, a cleverly worded petition was circu-lated. It quoted the grounds the court used to disqualify Whitehead from motherhood—from the way she dyed her hair to the way she played pattycake—and ended: 'By these standards, we are all unfit mothers.' I wanted to sign the petition, but someone told me, 'Only mothers are signing.' I was amazed. Did one have to be* literally *a mother in order to speak authentically in support of Whitehead? Whether I'm a mother or not, the always obvious fact that I am from the mother half of humanity conditions my life.*

But after this initial flash of outrage at exclusion, I had second thoughts: Maybe I should be glad not to sign. Why should I have to be assumed to be a mother if I am not? Instead of accepting that all women are mothers in essence if not in fact, don't I prefer a world in which some are mothers—and can speak as mothers—while others are decidedly not?

To make a complicated situation more so, while I was struggling with the rights and wrongs of my being allowed to sign, several other women refused *to sign. Why? Because the petition quoted Whitehead's remark that she knew what was best for her child because* she was the mother. *The non-signers saw this claim as once again imputing some magic biological essence to motherhood. They didn't want to be caught signing a document that implied that mother always knows best. They supported Whitehead's right to dye her hair but not her claim to maternal infallibility.*

I saw the purity of this position, recognized these non-signers as my closest political sisters, the ones who run fast because the old world of mother-right is just behind them. But in this case I didn't feel quite as they felt. I was too angry at the double standard, the unfair response to Whitehead's attempts to extricate herself from disaster. I thought that given the circumstances of here, of now, Mary Beth Whitehead was as good an authority about her still-nursing baby as we could find anywhere in the situation. It didn't bother me at all to sign a petition that included her claim to a uniquely privileged place. The press and the court seemed to hate her for that very specialness; yet they all relegated her to it, execrating her for her unacceptable ambivalence. Under such conditions she was embracing with an understandable vengeance the very role the world named as hers. Who could blame her?

Eventually, I signed the petition, which was also signed by a number of celebrities and was much reported in the press. It is well to remember how quickly such public moments flatten out internal feminist debates. After much feminist work, the newspapers—formerly silent about feminism's stake in surrogacy questions—began speaking of 'the feminist position'. But nothing they ever wrote about us or our petition came close to the dilemma as we had debated it during the few intense weeks we met. Pro-surrogacy and anti-surrogacy positions coexist inside feminism. They each require expression, because neither alone can respond fully to the class, race, and gender issues raised when a poor woman carries a child for a rich man for money.

Over time I've stopped being depressed by the lack of feminist accord. I see feminists as stuck with the very indeterminacy I say I long for. This is it then, the life part way in, part way out. One can be recalled to 'woman' anytime—by things as terrible as rape, as trivial as a rude shout on the street—but one can never stay inside 'woman', because it keeps moving. We constantly find ourselves beyond its familiar cover.

Gender markers are being hotly reasserted these days—US defence is called 'standing tough' while the Pope's letter on women calls motherhood woman's true vocation. Yet this very heat is a sign of gender's instabilities. We can clutch aspects of the identity we like, but they often slip away. Modern women experience moments of free fall. How is it for you, there, out in space near me? Different, I know. Yet we share—some with more pleasure, some with more pain—this uncertainty.

Notes

1. The 'we' problem has no more simple solution than does the divide itself, but in spite of its false promise of unity the 'we' remains politically important. In this piece, 'we' includes anyone who calls herself a feminist, anyone who is actively engaged with the struggles described here.
2. MARHO Forum, John Jay College, New York, 2 Mar. 1984. For feminist critiques of the new peace activism see *Breaching the Peace: A Collection of Radical Feminist Papers* (London: Onlywomen Press, 1983) and Ann Snitow, 'Holding the Line at Greenham', in *Mother Jones* (Feb./Mar. 1985), 30–47.
3. Lourdes Beneria and Phyllis Mack began the study group, which was initially funded by the Institute on Women at Rutgers University. Other members were: Dorothy Dinnerstein, Zala Chandler, Carol Cohn, Adrienne Harris, Ynestra King, Rhoda Linton, Sara Ruddick, and Amy Swerdlow.
4. See Amy Swerdlow, 'Pure Milk, Not Poison: Women Strike for Peace and the Test Ban Treaty of 1963', in *Rocking the Ship of State*, 225–37. (This book grew from the study group above.)
5. Bella Abzug and Mim Kelber, *Gender Gap* (Boston: Houghton Mifflin, 1984). According to Kelber, Carter was outraged that the women of the commission were criticizing his social priorities; they were supposed to be on his side. Most of the commission resigned when Carter fired Abzug. When he reconstituted the commission somewhat later, the adjective national had been dropped from its name and it became the President's Advisory Commission for Women, with restricted powers and no lobbying function.
6. 'In the United States, we oscillate between participating in, and separating from, organizations and institutions that remain alienating and stubbornly male dominant' (Joan Kelly, 'The Doubled Vision of Feminist Theory', in Joan Kelly (ed.), *Women, History and Theory: The Essays of Joan Kelly* (Chicago: University of Chicago Press, 1984), 55). Also see Denise Riley, *War in the Nursery: Theories of the Child and Mother* (London: Virago, 1983).

7. Denise Riley, talk at the Barnard Women's Center, New York, 11 Apr. 1985.
8. Catharine R. Stimpson, 'The New Scholarship About Women: The State of the Art', *Annals of Scholarship* 1/2 (1980), 2–14.
9. Alice Echols, *Daring to Be Bad: A History of the Radical Feminist Movement in America, 1967–1975* (Minneapolis: University of Minnesota Press, forthcoming), typescript, p. 81.
10. Ibid. 273.
11. Ibid. 270.
12. Ibid. 273.
13. Barbara Deming, 'To Those Who Would Start a People's Party', *Liberation*, 18/4 (Dec. 1973), 24, cited in Echols, *Daring*, 272; Andrea Dworkin, *Intercourse* (New York: The Free Press, 1987), 67. Dworkin is not a biological determinist in *Intercourse* but she sees culture as so saturated with misogyny that the victimization of women is seamless, total, as eternal in its own way as 'mother right'.
14. Ellen Willis, remarks at the NYU Symposium on the publication of *Power of Desire: The Politics of Sexuality*, New York, 2 Dec. 1983.
15. Carole S. Vance, 'Social Construction Theory: Problems in the History of Sexuality', in Anja van Kooten Niekerk and Theo van der Meer (eds.), *Homosexuality, Which Homosexuality?* (Amsterdam: An Dekker, Imprint Schorer, 1989).
16. Linda Alcoff, 'Cultural Feminism Versus Post-Structuralism: The Identity Crisis in Feminist Theory', *Signs*, 13/3 (Spring 1988), esp. 406.
17. Linda Alcoff sees poststructuralism as anti-essentialist; in contrast, in *Feminist Studies*, 14/1 (Spring 1988), the editors Judith Newton and Nancy Hoffman introduce a collection of essays on deconstruction by describing differences *among* deconstructionists on the question of essentialism as on other matters.
18. See New York Radical Feminists, 'Politics of the Ego: A Manifesto for N.Y. Radical Feminists; in Anne Koedt, Ellen Levine, and Anita Rapone (eds.), *Radical Feminism* (New York: Quadrangle, 1973), 379–83. The vocabulary of the manifesto, adopted in December 1969, seems crude now, its emphasis on 'psychology' jejune; but the document begins with the task feminists have taken up since—the analysis of the interlocking ways in which culture organizes subordination.
19. Linda Bamber and Marianne DeKoven, 'Metacriticism and the Value of Difference' (paper presented at the MLA panel 'Feminist Criticism: Theories and Directions', Los Angeles, 28 Dec. 1982), 1–2.
20. Alcoff, 'Cultural Feminism', 421.
21. One might make a separate study of third-course thinking. Sometimes this work is an important and urgent effort to see the limiting terms of a current contradiction, to recognize from which quarter new contradictions are likely to develop. Third-course writing at its best tries to reinterpret the present and offer clues to the future. (British theorists have called this prefigurative thinking.) But often this work runs the risk of pretending that new terms resolve difficulties, and, more insidiously, it often falls back covertly into the divide it claims to have transcended. I admire, although I am not always persuaded by, the third-course thinking in such pieces as Angela Miles, 'The Integrative Feminine Principle in North American Radicalism: Value Basis of a New Feminism', *Women's Studies International Quarterly*, 4/4 (1981), 481–95. I have more doubts about pieces such as Ann Ferguson, 'Sex War: The Debate

Between Radical and Libertarian Feminists', and Ilene Philipson, 'The Repression of History and Gender: A Critical Perspective on the Feminist Sexuality Debate', *Signs*, 10/1 (Autumn 1984), 106–18. These essays claim a higher ground, 'a third perspective' (Ferguson, p. 108) that is extremely difficult to construct; their classifications of the sides of the divide reveal a tropism more unavoidable than they recognize.

22. Michèle Barrett, 'The Concept of "Difference" ', *Feminist Review*, 26 (Summer 1987), 34.

23. Alice Walker, *In Search of Our Mother's Gardens* (San Diego: Harcourt Brace Jovanovich, 1983), p. xi (epigraph). Also see, for example, Kelly, 'The Doubled Vision of Feminist Theory'; and Adrienne Rich, 'Compulsory Heterosexuality and Lesbian Existence', in Adrienne Rich (ed.), *Blood, Bread and Poetry* (New York: Norton, 1986), 60 ff. Rich also uses the metaphor of the continuum to describe the range in women's lives among different levels of female community. In *The Daughter's Seduction: Feminism and Psychoanalysis* (Ithaca, NY: Cornell University Press, 1982), Jane Gallop describes Julia Kristeva's effort to think beyond dualism: 'A constantly double discourse is necessary, one that asserts and then questions' (p. 122).

24. Meredith Tax, 'Agenda for Meeting at Barnard, May 3, 1986', 1. Members of the study group, convened at the Barnard Women's Center: Margorie Agosin, Amrita Basu, Dana Frank, Temma Kaplan, Ynestra King, Marysa Navarro, Ann Snitow, Amy Swerdlow, Meredith Tax, Julie Wells, and Marilyn Young.

25. Marysa Navarro, Grass Roots Meeting, 3 May 1986. Also see Shirley Christian, 'Mothers March, but to 2 Drummers', *New York Times*, 21 Feb. 1987.

26. Mrinalini Sinha, 'The Age of Consent Act: The Ideal of Masculinity and Colonial Ideology in 19th Century Bengal', *Proceedings*, Eighth International Symposium on Asian Studies (1986), 1199–214; and Mrinalini Sinha, 'Gender and Imperialism: Colonial Policy and the Ideology of Moral Imperialism in Late 19th Century Bengal', in Michael S. Kimmel (ed.), *Changing Men: New Directions in Research on Men and Masculinity* (Newbury Park, Calif.: Sage, 1987), 217–31.

27. At the Grass Roots study group, Julie Wells and Anne McClintock offered the example of Crossroads in South Africa, a squatter community of blacks largely maintained by women but finally undermined by, among other things, a colonialism that placed paid black men in charge. Also see descriptions of ways in which women become connected with revolutionary movements in Maxine Molyneux, 'Mobilization Without Emancipation? Women's Interests, the State, and Revolution in Nicaragua', *Feminist Studies*, 11/2 (Summer 1985), 227–53; Temma Kaplan, 'Women and Communal Strikes in the Crises of 1917–1922', in Renate Bridenthal, Claudia Koonz, and Susan Stuard, (eds.), *Becoming Visible: Women in European History*, 2nd edn. (Boston: Houghton Mifflin, 1987), 429–49; and Temma Kaplan, 'Female Consciousness and Collective Action: The Case of Barcelona, 1910–1918', *Signs*, 7/3 (1982), 545–66.

28. Julie Wells, 'The Impact of Motherist Movements on South African Women's Political Participation', (paper presented at the Seventh Berkshire Conference on the History of Women, 19 June 1987).

29. Adrienne Rich, 'Natural Resources', in Adrienne Rich (ed.), *The Dream of a Common Language: Poems, 1974–1977* (New York: Norton, 1978), 67.

30. Alison M. Jaggar gives an account of the contemporary feminist debate about the meaning and value of the demand for 'equality' in 'Sexual Difference and Sexual Equality', in Deborah L. Rhode (ed.), *Theoretical Perspectives on Sexual Differences* (New Haven: Yale University press, forthcoming). For some general accounts of the debate, also see Josephine Donovan, *Feminist Theory* (New York: Frederick Ungar, 1985); Hester Eisenstein, *Contemporary Feminist Thought* (Boston: G. K. Hall, 1983); Hester Eisenstein and Alice Jardine (eds.), *The Future of Difference* (Boston: G. K. Hall, 1980); Zillah R. Eisenstein, *Feminism and Sexual Equality: Crisis in Liberal America* (New York: Monthly Review Press, 1984); Juliet Mitchell, *Women's Estate* (New York: Pantheon, 1971); Juliet Mitchell and Ann Oakley (eds.), *What is Feminism?* (New York: Pantheon, 1986). The debates about Carol Gilligan's *In a Different Voice: Psychological Theory and Women's Development* (Cambridge, Mass.: Harvard University Press, 1982), often turn on the equality/difference problem. See John Broughton, 'Women's Rationality and Men's Virtues: A Critique of Gender Dualism in Gilligan's Theory of Moral Development', *Social Research*, 50/3 (Autumn 1983), 597–624; Linda K. Kerber, Catherine G. Greeno, and Eleanor E. Maccoby, Zella Luria, Carol B. Stack, and Carol Gilligan, 'On *In a Different Voice*: An Interdisciplinary Forum', *Signs*, 11/2 (Winter 1986), 304–33; *New Ideas in Psychology* (special issue on Women and Moral Development) 5/2 (1987); and Seyla Benhabib, 'The Generalized and the Concrete Other: The Kohlberg-Gilligan Controversy and Feminist Theory', in Seyla Benhabib and Drucilla Cornell (eds.), *Feminism as Critique* (Minneapolis: University of Minnesota Press, 1987), 77–95. Similarly, the feminist response to Ivan Illich, *Gender* (New York: Pantheon, 1982), has tended to raise these issues. See, for example, Lourdes Benería, 'Meditations on Ivan Illich's *Gender*', in B. Gustavsson, J. C. Karlsson, and C. Rafregard (eds.), *Work in the 1980s* (London: Gower Publishing, 1985).
31. The phrase 'human wholeness' comes from Betty Friedan, *The Second Stage* (New York: Summit Books, 1981), and the concept receives a valuable and devastating critique in Myra Jehlen, 'Against Human Wholeness: A Suggestion for a Feminist Epistemology' (MS).
32. For the pregnancy issue, see 'Brief of the American Civil Liberties Union *et al.*' *amici curiae*, *California Federal Savings and Loan Association et al.* v. *Mark Guerra et al.*, Supreme Court of the United States, October Term, 1985, Joan E. Bertin, Counsel of record; Wendy Chavkin, 'Walking a Tightrope: Pregnancy, Parenting, and Work', in Wendy Chavkin (ed.), *Double Exposure: Women's Health Hazards on the Job and at Home* (New York: Monthly Review Press, 1984); Lise Vogel, 'Debating Difference: The Problem of Special Treatment of Pregnancy in the Work-place', (paper presented at the Women and Society Seminar of Columbia University, New York, 24 Jan. 1988); Kai Bird and Max Holland, 'Capitol Letter: The Garland Case', *The Nation* (July 5–12), 1986, 8; Wendy Williams, 'Equality's Riddle: Pregnancy and the Equal Treatment/Special Treatment Debate', *N.Y.U. Review of Law and Social Change*, 13 (1984–5); Herma Hill Kay, 'Equality and Difference: The Case of Pregnancy', *Berkeley Women's Law Journal*, 1 (1985). For the custody issue, see Katharine T. Bartlett and Carol B. Stack, 'Joint Custody, Feminism and the Dependency Dilemma', *Berkeley Women's Law Journal* (Winter 1986–7), 501–33; Phyllis Chesler, *Mothers on Trial: The Battle for Children and Custody* (Seattle: Seal Press, 1986); Lenore J. Weitzman, *The Divorce Revolution: The*

Unexpected Social and Economic Consequences for Women and Children in America (New York: Macmillan, 1985). The work of Nadine Taub, director of the Women's Rights Litigation Clinic, School of Law, Rutgers/Newark, has frequent bearing on both issues and on the larger questions in equality/difference debates. See Nadine Taub, 'Defining and Combatting Sexual Harassment', in Amy Swerdlow and Hannah Lessinger (eds.), *Class, Race and Sex: The Dynamics of Control* (Boston: G. K. Hall, 1983), 263–75; Nadine Taub, 'Feminist Tensions: Concepts of Motherhood and Reproductive Choice', *Gender and Transition* (forthcoming); Nadine Taub, 'A Public Policy of Private Caring', *The Nation* (31 May 1986), 756–8; Nadine Taub and Wendy Williams, 'Will Equality Require More Than Assimilation, Accommodation or Separation from the Existing Social Structure?' *Rutgers Law Review*, 37/4 (Summer 1985), 825–44. The burgeoning feminist work on the new reproductive technologies also reproduces the divide. For complete references to all aspects of these debates, see Nadine Taub and Sherrill Cohen, *Reproductive Laws for the 1990s* (Clifton, NJ: Humana Press, 1989).

33. If I had to come up with an example of a feminist strategy that faced the power of the divide squarely yet at the same time undermined the oppression the divide represents, I'd choose recent feminist comparable worth legislation. Humble and earthshaking, comparable worth asserts two things: First, because women and men do different work, the concept 'equal pay' has little effect on raising women's low wages; and, second, if work were to be judged by standards of difficulty, educational preparation, experience, and so on (standards preferably developed by workers themselves), then anti-discrimination laws might enforce that men and women doing work of comparable worth be paid the same. (Perhaps nurses and automechanics? Or teachers and middle managers?) The activists who have proposed comparable worth have singularly few pretensions. They are the first to point out that on its face, the proposal ignores the work women do in the family, ignores the non-economic reasons why women and men have different kinds of jobs, ignores what's wrong with job hierarchies and with 'worth' as the sole basis for determining pay. Yet this little brown mouse of a liberal reform, narrow in its present political potential and limited by its nature, has a touch of deconstructive genius. Without hoping to get women doing men's work tomorrow, the comparable-worth model erodes the economic advantages to employers of consistently undervaluing women's work and channelling women into stigmatized work ghettos where pay is always lower. With comparable worth, the stigma might well continue to haunt women's work, but women would be better paid. Men might start wanting a 'woman's' job that paid well, while women might have new psychological incentives to cross gender work categories. Who knows, perhaps stigma might not catch up as categories of work got rethought and their gender markers moved around. And if the stigma clung to women's work, if men refused to be nurses even if nurses were paid as well as construction workers, a woman earning money is an independent woman. She can change the family; she can consider leaving it. Comparable worth asserts the divide, yet, slyly, it goes to work on the basic economic and psychological underpinnings of the divide; it undermines the idea that all work has a natural gender. See Sara M. Evans and Barbara J. Nelson, *Wage Justice; Comparable Worth and the Paradox of Technocratic Reform* (Chicago: University of Chicago Press, 1989). The mixtures of progressive and conservative impulses

that have characterized both sides of the divide at different moments get a nuanced reading from Nancy F. Cott in her historical study of American feminism, *The Grounding of Modern Feminism* (New Haven,: Yale University Press, 1987).

34. See, for example, Judy R. Walkowitz, *Prostitution and Victorian Society: Women, Class, and the State* (Cambridge: Cambridge University Press, 1980).

35. Ellen DuBois: 'The Radicalism of the Women Suffrage Movement: Notes Toward the Reconstruction of Nineteenth-Century Feminism', in Anne Phillips (ed.), *Feminism and Equality* (New York: New York University Press, 1987), 128.

36. See Mary Daly, *Gyn/Ecology: The Metaethics of Radical Feminism* (Boston: Beacon Press, 1978). Maggie McFadden gives an account of this range in her useful taxonomy piece, 'Anatomy of Difference: Toward a Classification of Feminist Theory', *Women's Studies International Forum*, 7/6 (1984), 495–504. Adrienne Harris has pointed out to me that essentialism comes and goes in feminist psychoanalytic discussions of the penis: 'The concept slips, moves and breaks apart'.

37. bell hooks, 'Feminism: A Movement to End Sexist Oppression', in Phillips (ed.), *Feminism and Equality*, 62.

38. Taken together, Alison Jaggar's essays on the equality/difference debate offer a poignant (and I think continuingly ambivalent) personal account of how one feminist theorist developed doubts about the equality position. See Jaggar, 'Sexual Difference and Sexual Equality'; Alison Jaggar, 'Towards a More Integrated World: Feminist Reconstructions of the Self and Society', (talk at Douglass College, New Brunswick, NJ, Spring 1985); Alison Jaggar, 'Sex Inequality and Bias in Sex Differences in Research' (paper for the symposium on Bias in Sex Differences Research, American Association for the Advancement of Science Annual Meeting, Chicago, 14–18 Feb. 1987).

39. See, for example, Christine Stansell, *City of Women: Sex and Class in New York, 1789–1860* (New York: Knopf, 1986).

40. For Chavkin, Jaggar, and Jehlen see nn. 30, 31, 32, and 38 above.

41. Eisenstein (New York: Longman, 1981); Mitchell, 'Women and Equality' (1976), reprinted in Phillips.

42. The feminist scandal of the Sears case offers a particularly disturbing example of the divide as it can get played out within the exigencies of a court case. See Ruth Milkman, 'Women's History and the Sears Case', *Feminist Studies*, 12 (Summer 1986), 375–400; and Joan W. Scott, 'Deconstructing Equality-Versus-Difference: Or the Uses of Poststructuralist Theory for Feminism', *Feminist Studies*, 14/1 (Spring 1988), 33–50. In her introduction to *Feminism and Equality*, Anne Phillips offers a useful instance of how, in different contexts, the feminist ambivalence about liberalism emerges; she observes that in the United States, feminism began with equality models that revealed their inadequacy in practice, while in Britain, feminists began with a socialist critique of liberal goals that their own disappointments have modified in the equality direction.

43. See the now classic restoration of Mary Wollstonecraft by Juliet Mitchell, 'Women and Equality'. Also see two more recent, subtle readings of Wollstonecraft: Patricia Yeager, 'Writing as Action: *A Vindication of the Rights of Women*', *The Minnesota Review*, 29 (Winter 1987), 67–80; Cora Kaplan 'Wild Nights: Pleasure/Sexuality/Feminism', (1983), repr. in Nancy

Armstrong and Leonard Tennenhouse (eds.), *The Ideology of Conduct: Essays on Literature and the History of Sexuality* (New York: Methuen, 1987), 160–84. An instance of Wollstonecraft's contemporaneity: Linda Nochlin makes precisely her arguments about gender; Nochlin sees it as a variable changeable as class or vocation in her ground-breaking essay, 'Why Have There Been No Great Women Artists?' (1971), repr. in Thomas B. Hess and Elizabeth C. Baker (eds.), *Art and Sexual Politics: Why Have There Been No Great Women Artists?* (New York: Macmillan, 1971), 1–39.

44. Mary Wollstonecraft, *A Vindication of the Rights of Women*, ed. Carol H. Poston (New York: Norton, 1975), 35.

45. Ibid. 5, 30.

46. Shulamith Firestone, *The Dialectic of Sex: The Case for Feminist Revolution* (New York: William Morrow, 1970), strikes me as offering the best instance of this mixture of tones in contemporary feminism. Firestone dedicates her book to de Beauvoir, but her political fervour comes much closer to Wollstonecraft's.

47. Deborah Rosenfelt and Judith Stacy, 'Second Thoughts on the Second Wave', *Feminist Studies*, 13/2 (Summer 1987), 350–1.

48. Audre Lorde, talk at the MLA.

49. Since the Hyde Amendment restricting Medicaid abortions in 1979, No More Nice Girls has done occasional, *ad hoc* street events in New York City to dramatize new threats to women's sexual autonomy.

Part VII. **History**

19 Historiography, Objectivity, and the Case of the Abusive Widow

Bonnie G. Smith

'What is an author?' the philosopher Michel Foucault asked some two decades ago, and although this question has fascinated literary theorists, it has barely interested historians, who are more absorbed by such disciplinary issues as objectivity.[1] Since the nineteenth century the profession of history has taken pride in its ability to purge itself of biases arising from class, gender, race, and politics; and these claims continue to be made and disputed. With each generation the discourse of objectivity is revitalized, most recently and notably at the hands of Peter Novick, who has woven the story of this 'noble dream' into a popular saga of origins, testing and challenge, and ultimately rescue by a heroic historian. In his and other accounts the founding myth of objectivity is constantly reworked, refurbished, and thus reborn through challenges from those with political, gendered, racial, or other concerns.

The story of objectivity, as Novick and others tell it, is one in which individual historians, though perhaps acting collectively, subject the founding dream to abuse or rescue it from its challengers. Thus, the virtue of objectivity is unquestioningly attributed to great historians, technically expert and visionary geniuses who soar beyond the passions and interests of ordinary people in ways that allow them to produce compelling if not always perfect history. Studies of one or two great historians per generation often serve to make up historiography, but while we examine 'objectivity', we rarely consider the shape of historiography itself and what it has meant to the profession to have its achievements exemplified in the biographies of a handful of great authors. What is the use to which these biographies are put and, how have these lives of great historians served to fortify the founding

© 1992 Wesleyan University. Reprinted with permission from *History and Theory*, *Beiheft* 31 (1992), 15–32. I thank Donald R. Kelley, Susan Kingsley Kent, and Ann-Louise Shapiro for their contributions to this article, and the ACLS and the National Humanities Center for supporting the early stages of this research.

myth of objectivity? Why has the story of the scholar who wrestles with the political, sexual, and social conditions of everyday life to free his genius been so much more central an ingredient of professionalization than even objectivity and so much less explored? In this connection 'What is an author?' would indeed be a useful question for historians to ask.

The status of the great historian first became pertinent to my own work in historiography when I stumbled on an insistent French fixation—the puzzling case of Michelet's widow, outlined in an appendix to Arthur Mitzman's *Michelet, Historian*.[2] Mitzman presented a long history of excoriation of Athénaïs Michelet, captured in the phrase 'abusive widow'. In 1936 Anatole de Monzie, a lawyer and author who had successively been minister of public works, of finance, and of education, coined this term, oddly enough, not for outrageously famous consorts like Catherine de Medici, who could be said to exemplify female 'misrule', but for spouses of intellectuals. He accused these women of criminally meddling in the literary or artistic legacies of men like Claude Bernard, Lev Tolstoy, and Jules Michelet. Each of them either managed a dead husband's reputation, edited his work, or claimed an independent intellectual status for herself; but of all the offenders Monzie took Athénaïs Mialaret-Michelet as 'the model for these excessive, inopportune. and abusive widows'.[3] A little more investigation showed a consistent pattern of diatribes: Gabriel Monod and Daniel Halévy opened the attack early in the century just a year or so after her death in 1899, while some fifty years later Roland Barthes's *Michelet lui-même* maintained that she 'falsified Michelet's manuscripts, stupidly falsifying the themes, i.e. Michelet himself'.[4] Chosen by Lucien Febvre to edit Michelet's collected works after World War II, Paul Viallaneix, Claude Digeon, and associated editors since the mid-1950s have spent hundreds of pages across multiple volumes repetitiously discrediting Mme Michelet's role in her husband's life and works, finally damning her as not a collaborator, but a mere researcher and copyist. This fixation invites us not only to consider why Athénaïs Michelet has been so crucial to historiography and the status of its great practitioners but to ponder the role that gender may actually play in establishing the centrality of objective authorship.

Literary scholars are more accustomed than historians to these extended fits of pique against wives and widows. *The Ordeal of Mark Twain*, according to Van Wyck Brooks, was that 'his wife not only edited his works but edited him'.[5] The widow of T. S. Eliot allegedly denies access to his papers, while Orwell's widow has also been accused of abusively tending his memory. But the historiography business is far from immune to seeing sober and wise men take exquisite pains to blacken a widow's reputation or make her look ridiculous. Harriet Grote, who wrote several books including the biography of her husband, the Greek historian George Grote, 'seldom underrated her husband, and never herself', quipped Arnaldo Momigliano in a typically witty dismissal of a historian's bluestocking widow.[6] Was Michelet's or Quinet's wife responsible for the break between the two inseparable historians, and who was worse when it came to producing posthumous accounts of her husband's life? Such questions and such scorn are an important part of historiography and of the lives of great historians, as we will surely recognize, but what part is it?

Athénaïs Michelet was among the many wives of historians who wrote books themselves or who assiduously worked on their husbands' projects. Indeed, during the course of nineteenth-century professionalization and even into the late twentieth century much historical writing and research was familial. Family members were researchers, copyists, collaborators, editors, proofreaders, and ghostwriters, and much writing took place at home. Sister combinations such as the Stricklands were almost as common as female dynasties such as that of Sarah Taylor Austin, her daughter (Lucie Duff Gordon), and granddaughter (Janet Ross), or Julia Cartwright and Cecilia Ady. François Guizot and his daughters, Pauline Guizot de Witt and Henriette Guizot de Witt, were another commonplace author team of history; but equally pervasive were husband–wife collaborations such as those of Alice Stopford Green and J. R. Green, Barbara and J. H. Hammond, Mary Ritter Beard and Charles Beard. Despite the modern ethos of separate spheres for men and women, historical writing was implicated in domesticity, the family, and sexuality—all of which were rich in possibilities for authorial confusion and unprofessional influences.

History thus had author teams that worked in household workshops in an age of professionalization, but conventions generally assumed authorship to be singular and male. For instance, in reviews of a work by a husband and wife, custom dictated attributing collaborative works to the men alone. This could be done in reviews by talking, say, about Charles Beard's *Rise of American Civilization* series or by noting 'the assistance of his wife' and then proceeding as if Charles Beard were the sole author. A compliment to the tender muse who inspired this man of genius was a wink to a knowing readership that the wife's contribution had been negligible. These conventions, veiling the complex authorship of many works, produced ambiguity because historical authorship was so conflicted anyway by the demands of scientific history.[7]

Beginning in the nineteenth century the shift from literary to scientific history ostensibly dealt the historical author a nasty blow by casting suspicion on the authorial presence. Ideally, professional history became a scientific enterprise in which a historical text containing verified facts was constructed into a narrative of the past. Originating in the assiduous research of a well-trained and self-abnegating historian, the best historical accounts contained their own positive truth because the author had put aside politics, class, gender, and other passions and interests, as well as concerns for literary drama, in order to achieve an autonomous, universally valid text. This autonomous text displayed its own verification in an ever increasing proportion of footnotes (*Anmerkungswissenschaft*) to support its assertions, and attained its universal status by purporting to describe the 'Past' purified of the contingencies of the present. 'Gentlemen, it is not I who speak', as the historian Fustel de Coulanges so famously put it, 'but History that speaks through me.' Nothing so clearly sets forth not only the pure voice of history but also the subordinate or questionable status of the author.

These claims to scientific impersonality, however, were made during the course of history's professionalization into a discipline that not only abided by a set of standards but that existed in the richly human institutions of the university, archives and libraries, and professional journals and associations. Professional life further comprised such diverse ingredients as offices at home and work, research assistants, copyrights and royalties, translations, editions, editors, and readers, and always the academic hierarchy of flesh and blood human beings which reinforced professorial authority. While professional standards invoked impersonality, professionalism developed as an arena charged with human affect and fantasy. When Leopold von Ranke imagined a new set of archival documents, he fancied them 'so many fairy princesses living under a curse and waiting to be free'.[8] The scientifically minded French scholar Gabriel Monod confessed that a review of Gregorovius's *Lucrecia Borgia* had 'made my mouth water' for a 'more intimate acquaintance with this "loose, amiable" ' woman.[9] Though critical of Michelet's historical methods, Monod could 'not escape the contagion of his enthusiasm, his hopes, and his youthful heart'.[10] Seminars taught lessons in palaeography, epigraphy, and other techniques for the scientific scrutiny of documents—'principles', in the words of another reformer, 'that are transmitted from the fathers to the sons'.[11] Scientific historians variously referred to the reformed academic community as a fraternity, an army, a monastery, a workshop, where the most important quality was 'deference toward their masters'.[12] And history, as the metaphors of princesses, loose women, masters, and fraternities show, was not unrelated to masculine identity: 'I study history', R. G. Collingwood wrote, 'to learn what it is to be a man.' In other words, alongside claims to impersonality, the professionalization of history provoked the expression of human sentiments, the development of close relationships, the unfolding of fantasies, and the investment of emotions across the enterprise.[13]

Few historians expressed so many wide-ranging passions and so complex an authorial experience as Jules Michelet, especially in his relationship to Athénaïs Mialaret, whom he married in 1849. Michelet's first wife, Pauline Rousseau, died in 1839, having given birth to two children and having lived much ignored during her husband's prodigious efforts to have an important career. Unlike the comparatively clean separation with Pauline, Jules's marriage to Athénaïs Mialaret was a complicated, literary experience. For one thing, Mialaret was already a studious woman, who at the time of her first contact with Michelet in 1848 tutored the children of the Princess Cantacuzène in Vienna. Their relationship began with her letter asking his moral advice because her reading of his *Du prêtre, de la femme, et de la famille* had left her in need of guidance. Each soon fell to writing the other about the revolutionary politics of 1848, which she reported from Vienna and he from Paris. When Athénaïs first visited his apartment in the fall of 1848, their interview took place in his study, and he reciprocated by delivering a copy of *Histoire de la révolution* to her hotel. Their relationship thus began and progressed as a literary one, and it remained so throughout twenty-six years of marriage. According to both their accounts Athénaïs Michelet did research and reported on it, wrote sections of his books, discussed projects and recorded details of their daily conversations on topics for books, and offered her judgements on the work that was published under Jules's name. She wrote books of her own, one of them a story of her childhood, and he drafted an unpublished manuscript ('Mémoires d'une jeune fille honnête') of her young adulthood, while she published selections from his journal and a story of his youth after his death as well as a posthumous edition of their love letters. Meanwhile, Michelet recorded many incidents in their work life and descriptions of her personal feelings in his journal.

Athénaïs was 22 at the time of their meeting and Jules, at 50, was passionately attracted to her. But the marriage, despite his extreme sexual arousal, was consummated only with difficulty and then after Jules had taken his young wife to consult with several physicians. These matters too were literary, for he recorded the course of the consultations in his letters and journal, noted her menstrual periods for more than two decades, and wrote about both their thwarted and successful sexual relations. Literary events constructed and even permitted Michelet's final conquest of his wife. Before their marriage he noted his growing desire, which was crushed on their wedding night: 'all was refused me. By her? No, her good little heart burned to make me happy.'[14] On 20 March 1849, eight days after their marriage, Jules noted that the couple had worked together for the first time, but 'physically, it's impossible to be less married'.[15] This pattern continued for some time, with work during the day followed by 'insoluble difficulties' at night.[16] Michelet alternated reports of his increasing sexual despair with moments of 'very tender abandon', 'of certain sweet and kindly signs that . . . her poor young body, so suffering and charming, is none the less not insensitive to the breath of May', all of them concentrating desire on Athénaïs and building an extraordinary, almost gothic literary drama of pursuit and escape.[17] 'My sweetheart, very sweetly, received me for a moment in her bed.'[18] Finally, on 8 November 1849, 'in the morning, before my work', the couple had sex: 'I penetrated her fully . . . very hard as my doctor indicated.'[19]

Michelet fashioned his journal into a sexual saga, and after this consummation his account of the marriage continued to charge domestic study and writing with sexual negotiation. Looking back over eight years of marriage at his remembrances of their best sex, he picked a date in 1850, 'near the end of the fourth volume of the *Révolution (Death of Danton's Wife)*, a vivid, nervous emotion. She was moved also . . . and calmed this storm in an act of tender humility.'[20] This was written in 1857, a year of particularly intense intellectual discussion surrounding composition of the book *The Insect* and a year in which Michelet filled his journal with sexual detail. 'After menstruation, extreme passion. I long to plunge myself into this fountain of life. . . . She herself is burning, delectable, tasty.'[21] These heady descriptions did not indicate intercourse, according to Jules's account, at more than a ten-day interval, but it often happened after reading and writing. While Athénaïs cut flowers to study for their work, he read from the draft of *The Insect*; later, 'she came to me like a little lamb and was very good.'[22] Two days later, he describes her reading another section, 'and in an isolated alleyway, the second behind the grand canal, she showed me a great deal of friendship.'[23] By this time, Michelet had written more than once of their intertwined endeavours—sexual and intellectual—and of their intertwined personalities. The ideal marriage, and one he often claimed to have, displayed constant impregnation with the other partner, a transformation and movement, in which 'she, imbibing of him, is him while remaining herself.'[24] He found himself absorbed in her, but he tried to prevent that absorption from being complete. Writing gave him some sense of individuation, but he also struggled 'to maintain a point apart from her where I can be strong.'[25]

Michelet further complicated his interpretation of their marriage by constantly referring to it as an incestuous one in which he consciously played the role of father to her role of daughter. With Athénaïs virtually the same age as his own daughter Adèle, Michelet wrote of her as 'my child' even before they were married and continued to refer to her in that way thereafter. '*The most permitted of incests.* Marriages of people unequal in age have a sweetness when the older resembles the father or mother of the younger and can thus be loved as such.'[26] Even while noting his wife's orgasms, he referred to her as a little girl, her innocence: 'All [her] pleasure . . . is true tenderness, affection, simultaneously conjugal and filial, and even more.' And a few days later: 'God forgive me for having been and for being so in love with a woman . . . and yet with a child. I was greedier and greedier for her sweet and wise words and for her virginal body; and the more I entered it, the more I left full of desire.'[27] For her part Athénaïs reportedly frolicked like a young colt, making saucy faces for Jules's paternal observation. Two layers of family relationships—father/daughter and husband/wife—enveloped these literary lives.

Thus the collaboration of Jules and Athénaïs Michelet on such works of 'natural' history as *The Bird* (1856), *The Insect* (1857), *The Sea, The Mountain,* and other writing was fraught with the ambiguities of domestic literary production.[28] Although published under Michelet's name, he himself opened the question of authorship, first by dedicating *The Bird* to her as the product of 'the foyer, of our sweet nightly conversations'.[29] The work, Michelet explained, issued from domestic 'hours of leisure, afternoon conversations, winter reading, summertime chats', and other joint efforts.[30] A reviewer in the *Moniteur* was not alone in acknowledging the hint of collaboration by citing the work as having 'the style of a superior man softened by the grace and delicate sensitivity of a woman',[31] and Michelet wrote to journalists suggesting its familial origins and asking them 'to take this into account' in their reviews. The next year Michelet reported the authorship of *The Insect* somewhat differently to an Italian journalists as 'in reality the work of my wife, but composed and edited by me'.[32] Victor Hugo offered his praise for the complimentary copy of *The Insect*: 'Your wife is in it, and I've sensed her pass in these subterranean corridors like a fairy, like your *luciole* guiding your genius with her ardent light. . . .'[33] In his two testaments of 1865 and 1872 Michelet accorded Athénaïs literary rights to his books and papers, not only because she had served as secretary, researcher, and proof-reader, but because she had 'written considerable sections of these books'.[34]

When Michelet died in 1874, his widow put aside some of the projects on which she had been working with special interest. She sorted out the papers remaining from those he himself had destroyed and used them as the basis for several books, including a summary of his youth, an abridged version of his journal, a history, a travel book, and a biography. Jules's son-in-law—a literary figure of some influence and reputation—and grandchildren contested his legacy to Athénaïs in court, but she won, ultimately taking as her patron in these publishing endeavours Gabriel Monod, one of the founders of the *Revue historique*, a pioneer in making historical writing more scientific in France, and a friend of the family. Monod introduced selections from Michelet's work, wrote an appreciation of him in *Renan, Taine, Michelet* (which also paid tribute to Mme Michelet's devotion to her husband's memory and to her continuation of his work), wrote a biography, and gave a course on Michelet's historical writing at the Collège de France. At her death, Athénaïs Michelet gave Monod control over the disposition of many of Michelet's papers. With that her real troubles began.

From Monod to Lucien Febvre and beyond, attention to Jules Michelet swelled among the most prominent French intellectuals, but it has invariably involved extraordinary invective toward Athénaïs, growing ever more pronounced over the course of the twentieth century. Monod, who during Athénaïs's lifetime acknowledged her contribution to Jules's work ('faithful trustee of his ideas'),[35] and particularly the publication of many posthumous papers, deftly changed course. Practitioner of a different, more scientific history, Monod attributed his choice of career to Michelet, but 'the feelings I have for him are not those of a disciple for a master whose doctrine one adopts'.[36] Michelet embodied a French historical spirit, 'a sympathy for the untolled dead, who were our ancestors'[37] and as such served as the model historian of French nationalism, so deeply important to Monod's generation of scientific historians.[38] In fact many scientifically oriented historians in this era of professionalization, although disavowing political interests and aiming to purge it from their work, were unabashedly nationalistic, had friends in politics, or engaged in politics themselves, especially (but not only) during the Dreyfus Affair. As with the case of Monod, a love of the nation-state was constitutive of the historical mind in this era,[39] but these scientific historians projected that patriotism back onto an earlier generation, conserving nationalism for history while divorcing it from scientific practice through frank discussions of patriotism and objective portraits of biased, dead historians.

Monod's first work on Michelet thus avoided a full discussion of Michelet's method but touted the connection between patriotic sentiment and history. In 1905 Monod wrote *Jules Michelet: Etudes sur sa vie et ses œuvres*, which began sketching the outlines of the 'historical Michelet'—one useful to the scientific aspirations of the profession. Invoking the study of history based on the scientific evaluation of documents, Monod published a few of Michelet's papers that had so recently fallen into his hands. The book opened by posing the question of authorship in Michelet's work, citing rumours that not he but his wife had actually written much appearing under his name. Monod used the introduction to start defining what was written by Jules, what by Athénaïs in the work written during their marriage and in Jules's posthumously published writings. He pointed to the liberties Athénaïs had taken in certain posthumous works and he affirmed Jules's genius in the strongest possible terms, but in general his judgement was positive about her contribution. The book additionally published intimate parts of their journals to show the complexities of their relationship and of Michelet's relationship with other members of his family. For all its measure, Monod's work was crucial to analysing Michelet's authorship in 'scientific terms', singling him out as the representative figure of romantic historiography, and clearly delineating the contours of an autonomous Michelet, the great historian. Chapters on two of Michelet's children and material on his first wife enlarged public knowledge of his family circle, diminishing the place of his second wife to one among these many supporting actors. During these years Monod also gave a course on Michelet at the Collège de France, and these further filled in the profile of Michelet scholarship by exhaustively examining the origins of his historical writing and establishing an interpretative precedent that his most important work had been done during his first marriage and before the Revolution of 1848.[40]

Monod had begun to separate Jules from his wife, but never definitively did so. He had neither ruptured the bond celebrated in Michelet's journal nor completely discredited the sense of fusion Athénaïs had additionally promoted in handling posthumous publications. Other authors were bolder. In 1902 Daniel Halévy published a widely read article in the *Revue de Paris* on 'Michelet's Marriage' that followed the line of asserting Michelet's utter failure after his dismissal from all his positions by Napoleon III (and by implication after his marriage).[41] But he also attributed this failure to Athénaïs, who, he maintained, 'suffered from spiritual frigidity' that contrasted sharply with Jules's 'feverish mysticism and enthusiasm'.[42] Distinct but also disturbed, she aimed for total and unnatural domination of her husband: 'from the bedroom, because that was an essential step, to the worktable. It was the table she aspired to and Michelet at first defended it, while she controlled the bed. For several months, the marriage was chaste. Finally Michelet got the bed and soon after Athénaïs the worktable.'[43] Halévy thus painted a chaotic, disordered domestic scene, from which he as historian could constantly rescue Jules's character, traced in bold, clear lines that further distinguished him from the surrounding cast of characters: not only were he and Athénaïs opposites, her rule separated him from family and isolated him from friends, making him 'the most miserable of modern men'.[44] Whereas Michelet professed to have profited from the blurred authorship of domestic collaboration, subsequent biographers and editors rewrote the scenario as sexual inversion and misrule. The drastic overhaul of Michelet's scripting of a tender, erotic, and collaborative domestic life was underway, maintaining the whiff of sexual secrets that motivated research while clarifying authorship.

Thus dragged onto the historiographical stage, the widow served an important literary function by helping set the boundaries around the historical author and by acting as double with whom the hero struggles in a classical *agon* of self-definition. Instead of being the dutiful daughter to a dominant father, Athénaïs became 'one of those women who avariciously dispenses her sex', with Jules locked in battle to get more of it.[45] Monzie converted their fraught sexualities (as reported in both their journals) into an evil repression by the wife, the result of which was to turn what he believed to be Jules's innate puritanism into an obsession with women that ruined his historical sense. Monzie made the observation of George Sand (Michelet was 'incapable of alluding to women without lifting their petticoats over their heads'[46]) into the fault of his wife's parsimonious control of the conjugal bed. Any weaknesses in his writing resulted from her authority over sex, but also from her interference in writing. A quote in Athénaïs's travel diary, in which she described exactly the food she apportioned to Jules, Monzie took as typical of her '*vue comptable*'. Widowed, however, and freed from his sanguine influence, she showed her true colours, when gathering quotes from his journals and letters, she 'mixes this hash with passages from the *Hundred Years' War*, stirs the whole thing, seasons it with oil and vinegar like a salad, then serves the dish to guests at the republican table with this tasty title: *Sur les chemins de l'Europe*'. This account contrasted Michelet's intellectual stature with the domestic 'hash' the 'widow-cook', as Monzie called her, served up as history.[47] Monzie's tactic in his pairing of intellectuals and their abusive consorts contrasted, for instance, Rousseau's partner Thérèse Levasseur's tendency to interrupt his learned discourses with questions about 'the soup or the laundry' with his regal response. 'He would have ennobled a piece of cheese had he spoken of it.'[48] Sexuality and domestic detail were part of the wife's character, and detachment and ennoblement part of the authorial husband's, as the distinctions between the two grew greater when the discourse of separate spheres was put into service.

Monzie's and Halévy's characterizations seem rough, crude even, but they were no more so than the portrait of the 'abusive widow' solidified by the legendary intellectuals who next took up the project of confirming Michelet's stature and who further rescripted his life. Monzie, minister of education in the 1920s, was a friend and mentor of Lucien Febvre, student of Gabriel Monod, co-founder of the *Annales*, and Monzie's choice to edit the massive *Encyclopédie française*—a work designed to compete with Soviet and British encyclopedias by substituting a conceptual organization for the conventional alphabetical one. In 1946 Febvre published a sampling of Michelet's historical writing, a sampling whose introduction was lengthier than the material it presented. Febvre's *Michelet* served to announce the post-war era of freedom in the series 'The Classics of Liberty'. 'Why Michelet,' Febvre asked rhetorically, 'his history full of errors . . . a superpatriot, a liberal: a crybaby domesticated by a shrew?'[49] Having endured immense deprivation in a family that struggled each day not for such luxuries as liberty but for daily bread, Michelet was the perfect symbol of all the French had endured during the war. But he also represented 'the France of twenty-five centuries . . . eternal France'.[50] For Michelet embodied 'history' or what Febvre saw (following Michelet) as the 'successive victory of human liberty over the fatality of nature'.[51] Under the Napoleonic Empire and the Restoration, censorship and political repression had prevented France from having any history at all. Then came the Revolution of 1830, when, according to Febvre, Michelet suddenly used the new freedom to start writing the first history in modern times. The deprived Parisian struggling to teach his students thus became the 'Father of History'.[52] In making Michelet relevant for 'those who today have experienced Munich, the disasters of 1940, of 1942, of 1944',[53] Febvre had wilfully to discount the careful scholarship of his mentor, Monod, whose detailed work on Michelet's texts had shown his *Universal History* of 1830 to be the work of the preceding six years and its introduction to have been written on the whole in the months preceding the 'Trois Glorieuses',[54] that is, before the so-called era of freedom had begun. Constructing a usable author took precedence over scholarly accuracy, and Febvre would constantly refer to Michelet in his work, ultimately writing an article 'How Michelet Invented the Renaissance'.

Taking command of the post-war project of publishing a scholarly edition of Michelet's papers and works, Febvre chose Paul Viallaneix and Claude Digeon as the editors, himself oversaw the project, and continued his great interest in Michelet. The volumes that have thus far appeared contain (among others) Michelet's journal, his youthful writings, and the collaborative works with his wife, all of them featuring conspicuous attacks on any claims that Athénaïs had a substantive or even minor role in their authorship. Proving this point has taken several forms, all of them accepted as part of the 'scientific' method. First, manuscripts of *The Birds* and other of the natural history writings were scrutinized for their handwriting. Anything in Jules's handwriting indicated to the editors his authorship, Athénaïs's script led to an opposite conclusion: that she was a 'simple copyist'. The editors allowed that she had done much of the preparatory work of research and drafting the outlines of the book, but they undercut that single, generous attribution by citing notes to indicate the 'importance of [Jules's] personal work of documentation'. Finally, the editors juxtaposed her copious first drafts with the final version of the book and judged that in contrast to her 'verbosity', the final version was so 'definitively' stamped with Michelet's 'originality' that his wife's ideas and thus any claims to authorship were completely eradicated. Thus, ' "the collaboration" of Mme. Michelet . . . ceases to be a problem. . . .'[55] Professing to be scientific, the editors saw Michelet's 'creative spirit' firmly stamped on the work. 'Her contribution to *The Birds* was effectively limited to the preparation. . . .' Transformed by his 'vast design', her 'childish book became an epic'.[56] The editors constructed authorship out of handwriting and even then applied gendered standards to what that indicated. In no instance could they admit to substantive collaboration between husband and wife, but rather they cast the book as the product of a struggle between male and female in which male genius triumphed, giving the world another masterpiece.

Retelling Michelet's story, the editors dropped Monod's progressive but qualified disapproval of Athénaïs's authorship and instead constructed an utterly negative account of her 'false' literary productions. Published after Michelet's death, these included the editions of Michelet's youthful writings, excerpts from his journal, travel writings, and his love letters to Athénaïs. The scholarly edition (1959) of Michelet's *Ecrits de jeunesse* opens with a description of the inspiration taken from an early version of this work both by young innocents, who receive the book from their schoolmasters, and by more sophisticated youth, who see in Michelet's friendships the noble relationships they have drawn from their study of the classics. But going to the Michelet archives, both groups of readers would find that despite helpful lessons in the book, they had been betrayed and were the 'blissful dupes of a fraud'.[57] What is the nature of this fraud? Instead of revealing it and its perpetrator immediately, the editors hold the readers in suspense by switching to the inspiring story of Michelet's life, which they represent as passed in a 'mental fever' of preparing his various histories. Toward the end of his life, 'considering his *Ecrits de jeunesse* as a relic', Michelet began destroying many of his other papers. Although Jules describes the destruction in the first person singular as his own doing, the editors add Athénaïs to the scene of destruction and provocatively ask: 'To what extent did his young wife, gripped by a kind of retrospective jealousy, herself censor these vestiges of a passionate life in which she had not been queen?'[58] Besides suggesting that she, not he, had burned the papers, thus rewriting Michelet's own journal, the authors scorned her publication of selections from the various early writings in a lone book, *Ma jeunesse*, as a travesty. Yet the editors themselves proceeded by gathering up what they admit are random notes, mixed reading lists and observations, drafts, notes, and sketchy essays and by making them into an integrated volume for which they devised a similar title—*Ecrits de jeunesse*. Moreover, Michelet had expressly written that one section of his early writings 'should never be published, but may be excerpted', a condition to which Athénaïs adhered far more faithfully than the twentieth-century editors,[59] who prided themselves on publishing everything.

Another edition of Michelet's writing entitled *Journal* by the same editors contains, according to their own admission, dispersed papers of different sorts, an intimate journal, various travel journals, and random notes from his course outlines assembled in chronological order. Holding Athénaïs in contempt for omitting vivid sexual detail, the edition of Viallaneix sees to it that from Michelet's jottings, notebooks, and other scraps of writing paragraphs are made, spelling and punctuation corrected, and other 'problems eliminated'—'We didn't think that accuracy demanded us to respect those.'[60] Thus the men who accused Athénaïs of eliminating those phrases that failed to coincide with her values explain away their own changes where Michelet fails to meet their own, different criteria. The editors have in fact created from fragments and assorted writings a 'unique and complete' account, an integrated and whole Michelet separated from his perfidious wife. This Michelet was none the less, over the multiple volumes of these *Complete Works*, their own production.[61]

Arthur Mitzman's recent study of Michelet has generously tried to absolve Athénaïs Michelet of many of these charges by explaining that she had no training as a scholar.[62] Moreover, as Mitzman points out and as his own work shows, this 'abusive widow', even though she may have suppressed some sexually explicit material, still left so much that Michelet's obsessions are more than amply documented. He also notes that the modern editors' version of Jules's love letters (a 'sacred relic', the editors claim, sacralizing Jules) omit Athénaïs's, which she had used in the original edition, often making his letters unintelligible. Mitzman continues to refer to the 'false Michelet' created by his widow, but he acknowledges the interactive nature at least of the posthumous publications.

Feminist scholarship would seem to support Mitzman's sympathetic treatment of a woman author, endorse an appreciation for her work, and strive to achieve at least a historically accurate contextualization of her accomplishments. However, this scholarship also runs the risk of replicating the historiographical problem of authorship, if, for instance, one argued that Athénaïs was an equal genius to her husband or tried to carve her out as a distinct author. Devising some way of treating Athénaïs as historian or author is not the intent of this paper. Rather, I intend to broach the subject of her authorship in order to suggest (along with Mitzman) its dialogic and collaborative qualities, to indicate the way in which she edited passages in the travel journals to describe women instead of men, and to note that a major part of the much condemned editing of Jules's love letters involved omitting those letters in which he discussed her sexual and physiological state and the doctors' opinions of it.

The attacks on Athénaïs Michelet's authorship are interesting in themselves because in using gender to create a historical author they help define the historical field: in another example Michelet's editors ask whether she 'reconciled her literary pretensions and her wifely love without asking herself if literary genius wasn't profoundly individual, if the most faithful writer doesn't find himself alone with his conscience and his talent when he writes and if the first duty of fidelity toward his memory isn't to respect to the letter the work he has left behind'.[63] Such statements remind us that the language of scholarship combines passages listing archival citations and professions of 'respect to the letter' with emotionally packed or sexually loaded phrases. Despite Hayden White's insight about the 'middle-brow' and 'genial' rhetorical style of scientific history, in fact it has simultaneously been highly charged, contentious, loaded with gendered fantasy, passion, and outrage. The case of Michelet's widow shows all of these being deployed to establish the scientific confines of history at whose bounds she menacingly stood.[64]

Second, the great author, created in so gendered a way, has served the authorial dilemmas of other historians. For example, Lucien Febvre's direction of the project to publish a new edition of Jules's work and his post-war devotion to and creation of the cult of Michelet covered ambiguities in is own authorship of the *Annales* and other works during the 1930s and World War II. Febvre cofounded the *Annales* with Marc Bloch, and their collaboration was never easy, as many historians point out. From the mid-1930s funding from the *Encyclopédie française* paid for Febvre to have an assistant, Lucie Varga, a young Austrian historian and regular contributor to the *Annales*. Febvre, who was also married to the scholar Suzanne Dognon Febvre, relied on Varga for research, and her detailed summaries and observations on books allowed him rapidly to produce book reviews. By the late 1930s Varga had lost her job because Febvre's growing romantic attachment to her threatened his marriage and career.[65] A second dilemma emerged under the occupation, as Natalie Davis has pointed out, when Febvre and Bloch were embattled over whether the journal should appear without Bloch's Jewish name on the cover. To Bloch's insistence that they resist Nazi policies for ridding the scholarly world of Judaism, Febvre responded 'One name only on the cover, so what? It's the enterprise that counts.'[66] Davis illuminates the difficulties of authorship during the Occupation, citing the many alternatives, compromises, and resistances possible. Febvre chose neither to collaborate openly nor to resist openly but rather took a middle way that would allow him to continue to appear an important historical author. Michelet's authorship firmly established in the gendered historiographical discourse of the preceding decades, Febvre consolidated his own by incanting the ritualized attacks on the abusive widow and by overseeing a project one of whose major outcomes would be a definitive destruction of her claims to authorship.

Establishing the bounds of history and the authorial identity of generations of subsequent historians, the saga of Jules and Athénaïs Michelet may even have opened onto questions of French identity and the shape of its history. Twentieth-century France was particularly tried by issues of nationalism, gender, and history. While Monod and Halévy were outlining a story of female misrule in the Michelet household, the falling birth rate, the feminist movement, and the new woman had already raised questions of gender and provoked fears of the declining virility of French men. Since 1870 the French had faced a world turned upside-down by defeat, reparation, and annexation after the Franco-Prussian War. Only after 1920, however, did the discourse of the 'abusive widow' take full and effective shape as France struggled with its hundreds of thousands of war widows and with a gender order troubled by the effects of war and economic depression. Those men who returned from the war were often deeply disturbed; others found that their wives had abandoned them, and a confident feminist movement demanded rights equal to those of men. Misrule—the 'decline of the Third Republic', most historians of France would have it—led to the defeat in 1940 and to lingering malaise after World War II. The 'abusive widow' offered a timely explanation wherein her stupidity, inferiority, and frigidity symbolized an inversion of all that French intellectuals took as their defining characteristics.[67]

If, as Hayden White suggests, factual storytelling or narrativity 'moralizes reality', then Michelet scholarship had a direct relationship to the political reality of French history. Michelet's biography as a historian recapitulated the story of post-revolutionary France, using gender as its trope. Before 1848 Michelet engaged in heroic struggles for greatness as a historian, muting other attachments, but that revolutionary year was a watershed for him as it was for France, entrancing him, even enslaving him to an illegitimate ruler. Michelet continued to be productive, even opening new avenues of research, but his enslavement was continually wearing. Michelet died in 1874, and with the advent of republicanism born of military defeat came French decline as well as the abuse of his writings, an erosion of his genius. But the interwar period launched his rebirth as well as that of history and of France, culminating in the triumph of scientism, planning, technocracy, and the professions that would rehabilitate France as they rehabilitated Michelet's reputation. Narrating Michelet, an enormous project of the post-war French Academy, moralized the story of France, using gender to make out where science ended and error began. If France were destitute economically and defeated militarily, its tradition of individual genius would help it survive.

These conclusions about Michelet and the history of modern France are truly speculative and secondary to my real concerns about the relationship between gender and historiography, between authorship and objectivity. Recently Lionel Gossman has proposed a 'middle ground' between claims that history corresponds to reality (or objectivity) and claims that history may be relative or arbitrary ('decisionism').[68] Instead of saying that history is commensurable with reality, Gossman suggests that good historical accounts have some degree of commensurability among themselves, while in place of arbitrariness, decisionism, or relativity, he invokes 'the ability to change one's mind for good reason'.[69] In trying these hypotheses on the case of Michelet's widow, I find myself in agreement with the objective conclusions about her scholarly inadequacy—that is, in all good faith I could also write a commensurable account about her inadequacy as a historical writer. In addition the changing evaluations of Michelet as author make perfectly good sense, allowing both commensurability and relativity their day. But Gossman's criteria still fail to account for the repetitious attention to someone so insignificant as Athénaïs Michelet; only exploring the ways in which gender may be constitutive of history can do that.

Michelet has been useful to individual careers not so much for the way he provides a nationalist refuge to those like Febvre, who may have unconsciously worried about their own decisions during the unbelievably difficult time of war and holocaust, but for the way he has helped construct the individual fantasy life of the scientific historian entranced by achievements of 'great' predecessors. Wrapped in the mantle of science and impartiality, the saga of Michelet mutilated by his widow and rescued by heroic researchers is a melodrama whose psychological dimensions we should begin attending to, if only to understand the world of history better. Like most professionals, the surviving co-founder of the *Annales*—so deeply indebted to Michelet's work on mountains and seas, to the sense of the local in the Michelet travel journals, and to the complicated relationship between historical actors and their environments on which Michelet pondered—fantasized unique and singular authors as the forefathers of and contributors to his new school of history, and he worked to script it that way as had many before him. The category 'author', as Foucault proposed, has helped organize the discipline around the classification of historical writing and the development of other critical procedures that the invocation of a single author facilitates, allowing for such genealogies of influence and parentage to arise. What is a historian? we ask, altering Foucault's query. Until now a historian has been the embodiment of universal truth, who, constructed from bits of psychological detail and having passed through the purifying trials dealt by the contingencies of daily life, human passion, and devouring women, emerges a genderless genius with a name that radiates extraordinary power in the profession and in the mind of the individual practitioner. It is time to begin thinking about the ways in which this authorial presence has in fact been gendered as masculine and how it comes into being through repetitious pairings of a male 'original' with a female 'copy(ist)' or 'falsifier' or 'fake'. Such a consistent pairing suggests that historical science with its aspirations to objectivity is grounded in the rhetorical tradition of classical misogyny.[70]

Notes

1. Michel Foucault, 'Qu'es-ce que c'est l'auteur', *Bulletin de la société française de philosophie*, 64 (1969), 73–104.
2. Arthur Mitzman, *Michelet, Historian: Rebirth and Romanticism in Nineteenth-Century France* (New Haven, 1990), 284–5, 'Appendix A: Michelet's Second Wife'.

3. Anatole de Monzie, *Les veuves abusives*, 6th edn. (Paris, 1936), 126.
4. Roland Barthes, *Michelet lui-même*, trans. Richard Howard (1954, repr. New York, 1987), 206.
5. Van Wyck Brooks, *The Ordeal of Mark Twain* (1920, repr. New York, 1970), 138.
6. Arnaldo Momigliano, *George Grote and the Study of Greek History* (London, 1952), 7.
7. Jack Stillinger, *Multiple Authorship and the Myth of Solitary Genius* (New York, 1990) calls for a more complex view of authorship that would acknowledge the work of editors, but his book tends to reinforce the view that men were geniuses whose editors and wives made no 'substantive' contributions. For instance, although John Stuart Mill calls the 'whole mode of thinking' in *On Liberty* his wife's, Stillinger says that scholars should really focus on Harriet's editorial role (p. 66) and stop worrying about whether she had ideas—she didn't, he implies. Ultimately, he describes her role as 'the middle-aged Mill being spruced up by his wife for attractive autobiographical presentation' (p. 182). Although appreciative of Stillinger's concern that some term be born to cover editorial contributions, I take a different view of the matter of historical authorship.

Another fascinating recognition of authorial complexity comes in Lionel Gossman's *Toward a Rational Historiography*, Transactions of the American Philosophical Society (Philadelphia, 1989) which sympathetically describes the community of criticism absorbed into scholarly publications. Yet Gossman, except for the first mention, comes to cite a work with three authors exclusively as that of Steven Toulmin even referring to it as 'Toulmin's' thought, argument, thesis, and so on.
8. Leopold von Ranke, *Briefwerke*, quoted in Leonard Krieger, *Ranke: The Meaning of History* (Chicago, 1977), 104–5.
9. Letter to Gaston de Paris, 6 Aug. 1874, in Bibliothèque nationale, Manuscrit Nouvelle acquisition française 24450, Fonds Gaston de Paris, ff. 131–2.
10. Gabriel Monod, *Renan, Taine, Michelet*, 5th edn. (Paris: n.d.), 178.
11. Victor Duruy, quoted in William R. Keylor, *Academy and Community: The Foundation of the French Historical Profession* (Cambridge, Mass., 1975), 70.
12. Ernest Lavisse quoted in ibid. 70–1.
13. See Bonnie Smith 'Gender and the Rise of Scientific History', in Wolfgang Natter (ed.), *Objectivity and Its Other* (Lexington, Ky., forthcoming).
14. Jules Michelet, *Journal*, ed. Paul Viallaneix (Paris, 1962), ii. 32.
15. Ibid., 34.
16. Ibid. 35.
17. Ibid. 37, 47.
18. Ibid. 73.
19. Ibid. 75. Athénaïs Michelet's prolonged virginity has been attributed to vaginismus by Jeanne Calo, to wilful frigidity by Halévy, Monzie, and Michelet's editors (among others), and to various ailments and physical fragility by Michelet. See Jeannne Calo, *La création de la femme chez Michelet* (Paris, 1975).
20. Ibid. 326.
21. Ibid. 329.
22. Ibid. 330.
23. Ibid. 331.

24. Ibid.
25. Ibid. 127.
26. Ibid. 323.
27. Ibid. 343, 345.
28. On these works and their very important connection to Michelet's evolving conceptualization of historical issues see Linda Orr, *Jules Michelet: Nature, History, and Language* (Ithaca, NY, 1976).
29. Jules Michelet, *Œuvres complètes*, ed. Paul Viallaneix (Paris, 1986), xvii. 45.
30. Ibid.
31. Ibid. 41.
32. Ibid. 279.
33. Ibid. 280.
34. Testament of 1872 quoted in ibid. 188.
35. Monod, *Renan, Taine, Michelet*, 289.
36. Ibid. 179.
37. Ibid. 178.
38. Keylor, *Academy and Community*, 43–4 and *passim*.
39. See 'Gender, Objectivity, and the Professionalization of History', in *Objectivity and Its Other*.
40. Gabriel Monod, *La Vie et la pensée de Jules Michelet 1798–1852: Cours professé au Collège de France*, 2 vols. (Paris, 1923). This posthumous publication clearly influenced Arthur Mitzman's engaging psychological interpretation, which ends in 1854 even though Michelet lived two more decades, wrote abundantly, and produced works of natural history that would influence Febvre and other historians of the *Annales* school.
41. Daniel Halévy, 'Le Mariage de Michelet', *Revue de Paris*, 15/9 (1 Aug. 1902), 557–79.
42. Ibid. 577.
43. Daniel Halévy, *Jules Michelet* (Paris, 1928), 133.
44. Halévy, 'Le Mariage de Michelet', 579.
45. Monzie, *Les veuves abusives*, 105.
46. Ibid. 111.
47. Ibid. 114, 118.
48. Ibid. 35.
49. Lucien Febvre (ed.), *Michelet* (Geneva and Paris, 1946), 11.
50. Ibid. 82–3.
51. Ibid. 58.
52. Ibid.
53. Ibid. 30.
54. Monod, *Vie et pensée*, i. 185–7. Febvre surely knew Monod's careful scholarship on Michelet's work that showed the *Introduction to Universal History* not to have been 'écrits sur les pavés brulants . . . d'un incroyable élan, d'un vol rapide', as Michelet would claim forty years later.
55. Michelet, *Œuvres complètes*, xvii. 187.
56. The quotes refer specifically to the editors' discussion of *The Birds*: Michelet, *Œuvres complètes*, xvii. 187–206.
57. Jules Michelet, *Ecrits de jeunesse*, ed. Paul Viallaneix, 5th edn. (Paris, 1959), 10.
58. Ibid. 17.
59. Ibid. 10.
60. Michelet, *Journal*, i. 31.

61. Those with further interest in the editors' relationship to Michelet might consult the introductions to his 'journal' and other work. Many of them rely on purple writing; the introduction to Vol. 2, for instance, is a dramatic imagining of Michelet's life with Athénaïs, written in the second person plural: 'You leave without your companion. She is out of sorts today, "a sick person, a wounded one" like all women. You pass your friend Quinet's door without knocking. You haven't the heart to expound on the future of democracy. The sky is too pure, the light too warm. This September evening is given to you freely. It requires meditation.' Ibid. ii. p. XI.

62. Mitzman, *Michelet, Historian.* Mitzman's two appendices excusing Athénaïs provided the inspiration for this article.

63. Michelet, *Journal,* i. 25.

64. In this regard readers can consult the way in which Novick uses such words as 'sexy', 'hot', and 'fashionable' to discredit certain groups of historians. In this case we see the language of bad history as the language of women, while in others employed by Novick ('Clio is going to be just a gal around town on whom anyone with two bits of inclination can lay claim') metaphors of prostitution are used to nail down a point about the impending end of historical standards. See also Hayden White, *The Content of the Form: Narrative Discourse and Historical Representation* (Baltimore, 1987), 71.

65. See Peter Schöttler, *Lucie Varga: Les autorités invisible* (Paris, 1991). Schöttler has done an extraordinary job discovering the details of Varga's obscure life and reprinting her essays and articles. He outlines Bloch's misogynous attitude toward women and intellectuals, but more important Bloch's distress at finding Febvre's and his collaboration still further complicated by Varga's work. Schöttler was loath to reveal the extent of Varga's and Febvre's personal relationship: 'La vie scientifique et l'amour . . . are not considered pertinent in accounts of the life of a scholar.' None the less, Schöttler considered it necessary to reveal the romance because 'its consequences were sufficiently determining that one could not keep it quiet without falsifying history' (57, n. 142). This ambiguous statement may refer to Varga's exile from the profession, forcing her into subsequent employment selling vacuum cleaners, working in a factory, and then in an advertising agency after which under Vichy her utter destitution kept her from getting the necessary medicine to treat her diabetes. She died at the age of 36 in 1941. Natalie Zemon Davis, 'Women and the World of the *Annales*', *History Workshop Journal*, 33 (1992), 121–37, describes the contributions of Suzanne Dognon Febvre to Lucie Febvre's work as well as considers the important part played by Paule Braudel in Fernand Braudel's work. I thank Professor Davis for communicating this article to me before publication.

66. Lucien Febvre to Marc Bloch, 1941, quoted in Natalie Davis, 'Rabelais among the Censors', *Representations*, 32 (Fall 1990), 5.

67. This part of my argument relies on Mary Louise Roberts's important thesis, 'The Great War, Cultural Crisis, and the Debate on Women in France, 1919–1924' (unpub. Ph.D. diss., Brown University, 1991).

68. Lionel Gossman, *Towards a Rational Historiography* (Philadelphia, 1989), 61–2.

69. Ibid. 62 and *passim.*

70. On this point see R. Howard Bloch, 'Medieval Misogyny', *Representations*, 20 (Fall 1987), 1–24.

20 Women's Culture and Women's Power: Issues in French Women's History

**Cécile Dauphin, Arlette Farge, Geneviève Fraise,
Christiane Klapisch-Zuber, Rose-Marie Lagrave,
Michelle Perrot, Pierrette Pézsert, Yannick Ripa,
Pauline Schmitt-Pantel, and Danièle Voldman**

The trials and tribulations of women's history and its current forms clearly reveal its place within the discipline of history. These explain in part the current choice of topics studied by historians and the specific methods they use. In the past ten years important shifts in how to identify and analyse historical material have taken place. Within this large movement, so far hardly subjected to critical analysis, women's history has met with widely divergent systems of exclusion, tolerance and, today, banalization that should be brought to light. Doing so would achieve two objectives: to remain critical towards women's history's own formulations and to raise different questions about the necessary relationship between this particular field and history as a whole. This represents an ambitious project whose difficulty we acknowledge, for it is always easier to ask questions than to answer them. But history is not just the production of new knowledge, it is also the formulation of questions. The questions it raises and that are asked of it constitute a specific site of research that urgently calls for open discussion. The choice of *Annales* as a forum is neither fortuitous nor indicative of a desire to carve out a niche in a journal which at first did not readily accept women's history, although it did not ignore it.[1] Rather, this choice offers an opportunity to openly question the methods used to analyse *rôles sexuels*,[2] methods often expounded in *Annales: E.S.C.*,

Ch. 6 in Karen Offen, Ruth Roalch Pierson, and Jane Rendall (eds.), *Writing Women's History: International Perspectives*. From the French 'Culture et pouvoir des femmes', published in *Annales: Economies, Sociétés, Civilisations*, 2 (Mar.–Apr. 1986). The original English translation by Camille Garnier, funded by the American Association of University Women, was published in the *Journal of Women's History*, 1/1 (Spring 1989) and is used here by permission. In this revised version some spellings and punctuation have been altered by the editors and a number of phrases have been retranslated. Explanatory footnotes have been embedded in the endnotes, and corrections have been made in the footnotes.

and to query how a certain recent strain of historiography has managed to appropriate the field of study of female–male relationships.
What follows is a brief description of the history of women's history, whose twists and turns have not been perceived by everyone.
Women's history really took off in 1970, with the realization that it
had been neglected and denied. It was helped along by the explosion
of the feminist movement, the progress made by anthropology and
the history of 'mentalités',[3] the new knowledge produced by social
history and the new studies on popular consciousness. This was a key
period when feminist activists were writing women's history before
women historians themselves. After this initial impulse, French universities initiated research groups and instituted new topics and
themes. This intense intellectual activity was governed by two principles: giving women a central place in a history which so far had
neglected differentiation by sex, and demonstrating their exploitation and oppression under male domination. In this particular context, where ideology and identification are part and parcel of the
object under examination, women's history is an addition to general
history. At times, male historians have added a chapter of women's
history but this was a mere token offering to a feminism that was
overtaking them. Feminism but not the history of feminism: the confusion between them is cleverly maintained when a distinction
should be drawn, since these are two separate entities. Is one a subcategory of a category that the discipline of history is already so
reluctant to recognize? Or is their relationship not more complex in
so far as feminism historically exceeds women's history by the very
questions it raises? At any rate, as the facts show, women's history
remains for the most part a women's task, a task either tolerated or
viewed as marginal by a discipline on which it has no direct impact.

As soon as this new area of research became more organized and
more important, some female historians realized the grave danger of
intellectual isolation which could only lead to excessively tautological
studies. Since they wanted to reach the whole discipline, they had to
hone their concepts and critically evaluate their works. The time has
come to assess what has been done so far, to create groups of critics[4]
and, with government help, an ongoing colloquium[5] and to set up a
Centre for the Study of Women and Feminism at the Centre National
de la Recherche Scientifique (CNRS).[6] For some women's historians,
this official recognition made the questions they had about the usage
of their concepts more urgent and reawakened their fear that women's
history might never become the spearhead for the discipline of history, or even a gadfly, because of its weaknesses. These include:

(1) the still noticeable preference for certain topics such as the female body, sexuality, motherhood, female physiology, and occupations closely related to a feminine 'nature';

(2) the continual use of the dialectic of domination/oppression which can scarcely get beyond a tautological statement, unless it can be shown how such domination exerts its power in different periods and places;

(3) too many studies on prescriptive discourses, which hardly take into account social practices and the forms of resistance to these discourses. Such studies sometimes lead to a sort of hypnotic auto-fascination with misfortune;

(4) a poor knowledge of the history of feminism and its connections with political and social history;

(5) lack of methodological and especially theoretical reflection.

Along with these uncertainties, history itself was changing in ways that were not always obvious at the time, except for the sudden and noteworthy male contribution to research on the differentiation of *rôles sexuels* by historians and anthropologists such as Maurice Godelier and Georges Duby, whose work exemplifies a more general awareness.[7] This consciousness evolved along a direction common to historical research, which today no longer finds very fashionable the history of '*mentalités*' and the unearthing of new topics such as sexuality, criminality, death, food, and deviance. These topics, so much in vogue just a little while back, do not attract much attention today, although the problems studied then are very far from being solved. New encompassing themes have emerged, such as fear, sin, and links between private and public life, which threaten to blur the analysis of social relations. At the same time, a new area of research, the history of social and cultural representations, and to a lesser degree, that of political representations, is developing. In this context the concept of 'women's culture' has emerged, through which gestures and practices are analysed as such.

There is no doubt that the success of cultural history and that of representations, plus the increasing contribution of ethnology and anthropology, have taken research on *rôles sexuels* in a new direction. This new direction needs to be examined all the more intently since it is becoming more and more important and since it is backed by a brilliant and innovative historiographical trend. In attempting to describe women's roles, a certain number of specific practices have been discerned and out of these practices, through a pattern of compensations, interferences or symbolic meanings, the traits of a women's culture have been sketched, without which the social fabric itself would disappear.[8] Similarly, the ever-changing interplay of symbolic oppositions between feminine and masculine, whose shifts in meaning vary according to given periods and themes, indicates that *rôles sexuels* are strongly constituted as a means to fight against all forms of undifferentiated roles, which are considered fatal to societies. Although we do not plan systematically to question this approach, we must nevertheless point out its limitations and its deleterious effects. We must also propose a methodological analysis capable of revealing its contributions as well as its limitations.

HAVING 'SOME' POWER

The Cultural Approach to the Sexes

It is accurate to say that belonging to one or the other sex colours one's attitudes, beliefs, and codes in a given society. It is also accurate to point out that such attributions differentiate societies from one another. This parameter has opened up new areas of research that have already yielded stimulating results. Among these are the identification of objects, places and behaviours deemed specifically female, and the slightly different inflections of the concept male domination/female oppression, which used to underlie any study of *rôles sexuels*.

Naming, identifying, and measuring women's presence in places, situations, and roles which are theirs, seemed to be a necessary and long overdue step. The categories of the masculine and feminine, blurred of late by a kind of gender neutrality that only benefited men, were thus clearly established. Since modes of masculine sociability, such as *abbayes de jeunesse*,[9] military conscription, cafés, *chambrettes*,[10] or hunting parties had been studied, it became legitimate to study feminine sociability, using the same criterion of separation between the sexes. This produced insightful studies on communal laundries and ovens, on the market-place and the household, and certain insights about these female sites that are more or less connected with productive tasks, whereas male sites are, for the most part, related to leisure activities. Work such as Yvonne Verdier's[11] was also done on the significant events in life (birth, marriage, or even death). This ethnologist showed how socially and symbolically coherent were the gestures of the laundress, the seamstress, and the cook. She also identified the strand (a sort of Ariadne's thread) that wove together in a coherent way the conversations, gestures, techniques, and roles played by women in a Burgundian village. At the very heart of women's culture lay the extraordinary power of their bodies, characterized as a series of prohibitions and of privileged relations with time.

Similarly, Agnès Fine described clearly, in her study on women's trousseaux, how the objects they contained were identified with their owners.[12] Using a slightly different approach, Jacques Gélis[13] focused on the rituals surrounding birth from the fifteenth to the nineteenth century, and thus came up with an inventory of numerous collective and individual gestures meant to encourage life and to repel death's threat. In this survey of specific female sites and behaviours, works on convent life and women's associations must also be included.[14]

On the other hand, some works suffered from a restricted and restrictive approach which focused solely on the dialectics of domination and oppression, without any attention being paid to existing systems of frequent and complex variations or to exclusively feminine forms of power. Relations between the sexes cannot be reduced to a single, unalterable and universal explanation, that is to men's supremacy. Indeed, if women have their own view of the *sens social*, if they are allowed practices meant to help the entire community pass from birth to death, they obviously have 'some' power. And such a power should change the direction of the general debate, and open up new possibilities for interpretation. It could lead to studies free from paralysing tautology and capable of explaining a reality that is ever-changing.

Take, for example, the work of Martine Segalen,[15] which deals with nineteenth-century rural society. This author clearly shows how male authority and female powers jointly structure space, work, sexual life, and the couple's relationship with the community, and are inscribed in rituals as well as in representations. In the same vein, the anthropologist Annette Weiner, re-examining an archetypical case (the Trobriand Islands),[16] freshly observed the exchange of traditional objects belonging to women (banana leaves) during mourning ceremonies. She questioned her predecessors' interpretation of how wealth circulates and discovered a new system of social explanation based on a knowledge of female roles, previously undetected. This emphasis on female powers represents a definite plus, enriching the inventory of private life as described by nineteenth-century historians and researchers through a rereading in terms of power and an analysis of the real and symbolic confrontations between public and private life.

However, this emphasis on female powers is fraught with danger—that of using it too freely or in a somewhat fallacious fashion. To realize that women possess powers within the framework of culture can lead to the espousal of an attitude of appeasement, juxtaposing the two cultures as at once diverse yet complementary, while forgetting that relations between the sexes are also fraught with violence and inequality. Only theoretical rigour can prevent the emergence of new stereotypes, hidden behind modern formulations.

Dead ends

The concept of complementarity utilized in many rural studies[17] has been so successful that it has led to a definitive representation of the partition of space, time, and daily activities, and rituals between men and women, and has presented a world in equilibrium in which roles and tasks are neither antagonistic nor competitive. Social life seemed to be organized around two apparently equivalent poles: male authority on the one hand, and female powers on the other. Even though it has sometimes been demonstrated that the sexual division of tasks is not fixed, and that there are overlapping zones of intersection and exchange that disrupt the opposition between female domestic work and male production work, the notion of complementarity is quite ambiguous. For example, domestic tasks are never performed by men: dealing with water, fire, and food preparation are female activities that are devalued when men perform them. Men do not try to take them over, in any case, either materially or symbolically. Conversely, it so happens that the chores usually performed by men do require women's participation for their completion. In this instance, women do not acquire any extra prestige, the necessary feminine 'touch' said to be innate in nature offsetting any value attributable to skill acquired through apprenticeship. This kind of reasoning is at the basis of all the classifications of contemporary professions and activities. In short, women are not 'disqualified', they are never 'qualified'.

Indeed, complementarity can account for real instances in which female–male association is necessary, but it also erases the fact that the distribution of tasks has, after all, a positive and a negative pole and contains implicitly a hierarchical system. The roles may be complementary, but one is subordinate to the other. The concept of complementarity should have, at the very least, taken into account the distinction between complementarity of subordination and complementarity of emulation made by Lucienne Roubin as early a 1970.[18] Consider the case of agriculture where the technical division of labour between the two sexes (men plough and sow, women weed and harvest) can be analysed in terms of complementarity, if we consider it only at the technological level. However, since peasant society encodes and values this technical complementarity differently, 'ploughing and sowing' are seen as noble tasks whereas 'weeding and harvesting' are seen as subordinate ones. Complementarity thus becomes a principle for hierarchical organization of roles; we are clearly confronting here a complementarity of subordination or a 'complementary opposition', which leaves intact the husband's and wife's divergent or convergent interests, their inequalities before the law and their contradictory relations as a couple.[19] From now on, as these studies and others suggest, one must take into account not only the technical division of chores but also the values and symbols that go with it.

This pattern can be illustrated by further examples. The trousseau may be a long task involving mother and daughter, the cooking of pig's blood may be as essential as the stabbing of the animal, still no one can deny the existence of a hierarchical difference between activities attributed to men and to women. This difference may also entail a certain kind of violence, as exemplified by the killing of pigs. Even if the cooking of the animals' blood does represent some form of nurturing, it nevertheless can be performed only after the killing on whose accomplishment it depends.

Similarly Jacques Gélis conveys to the reader, with his thorough inventory of daily rituals and customs surrounding birth, an overall impression of great violence apparently unbeknownst to the author himself, because he does not deal with it and does not seem to realize its full extent. Yet he shows how a woman in labour is dominated by the effort she must put forth, and how she tackles the physical and the supernatural elements involved in order to give birth successfully. Burdened by precepts that constantly seek to bring about a perfect order between her and the cosmos, which will ensure her success, she ends up haunted by the fear of failure. She has to engage in ceaseless activity so that neither God nor nature will betray her. The situation of the woman in labour, incompletely described in as much as the author omits behaviours not in compliance with the norm, suggests a permanent state of imbalance which she must redress most often alone, in order not to appear inadequate. Obviously there is no complementarity in this instance, only violence and fear which shape female rituals and behaviours, and which are rarely mentioned in the literature.

The shadow of contestation is kept at bay by the very reassuring concept of complementarity which neutralizes this threat ahead of time, in order to avoid the recognition of its modalities and its specific manifestations. Women's sweetness and peace-keeping qualities are sovereign in such a context, and the analysis of the masculine and the feminine comes to a dead end, the possibilities of tension and conflict, of rivalry or accession to power being pushed under the rug. The study of '*mentalités*' as practised by some, can encourage such a view. The cultural definition of female and male worlds can lead to the statement of a real and symbolic balance between them, from that confrontations and violence are absent. Consequently, the assumed need that these two symbolic and practical positions have of each other within a system of equivalent values blurs somewhat the stakes at hand (e.g. compensation, consent, confrontation). Formulated in this way, the daily reality with its difficulties and contrasts becomes hidden, and a slippage easily occurs from the notion of gender difference (*différence des sexes*) to the view of a binary structure of society which masks the sharpness of this difference. Although tempting, this approach is reductive.

The shift towards the recognition of a 'women's culture' took place in the wake of studies dealing with moments in history when such a culture still existed and could be recorded. In these studies, stereotypically rural society enjoys a special status and is described with few references to its historical context, or to the crucial changes that occurred in the nineteenth and the beginning of the twentieth centuries (railways, postal services, schools, 'universal' suffrage,[20] migrations, wars, urbanization), or to internal factors of mutation such as technical innovations and the price of land. Although the culture in question was a culture already on the wane, it was presented as a stable ahistorical society, one that leaves the reader with a strange sensation of timelessness. In these studies, the 'historical facts', purged both of events and conflicts, acquire their meaning from the repetition of gestures, rites, statements that bring to light constants, even universals, which are used to characterize the relationship between the sexes. By regarding village society as frozen, researchers chose to use only data that could be included in a mythological discourse. Works by specialists in folklore, literary or plastic representations, prescriptive discourses, even proverbs, all raise a problem of validity since they describe rural culture in a temporal vacuum and without giving voice to the peasants themselves. They mix innocence and nature, animal sexuality and human sexuality, salacious turn of mind and women's submission. The origin of these stereotypes, the way they are transmitted, their specificity to nineteenth-century rural society are hardly touched upon. Incorporating the teachings of ethnographers, this view of rural culture, and of its female–male relations prefers to focus on unchanging structures rather than on moments of evolutionary flux, of confrontation or questioning.

At best, the history of relations between the sexes can be seen as part of the '*longue durée*' or long-term history,[21] but the few attempts to distinguish between 'long-term' and 'short-term' history have not been too successful. Agnès Fine, in the conclusion of her article on the trousseau, uses two such notions of history to analyse the relations between the sexes. According to her, the political, economic, and social conditions of women's place in a given society belong to a precise chronology, that is a short-term chronology, whereas the system of sexual symbols, the sexes' perception of their relations, belong to long-term history. The latter aspects thus fall within the domain of permanence rather than that of change. This distinction is not without its problems.

The dialectic between the short-term and the long-term, familiar to historians of the past two decades, most often deals with separate topics. But, in this particular instance, it operates within the same field, that of the relations between the sexes. How, then, can one combine a 'symbolic of the sexes', static by nature, with a practice of sexual division that is subject to change? Logically, in the logic of a theory of representations which emphasizes, no matter how complex, the relations between the imagination and socio-political structures, such a combination is unthinkable. Either nothing changes —neither women's place nor the thinking about the division of the sexes—or everything changes. From a methodological point of view, such a distinction between real time dominated by history, and the time of '*mentalités*' set more or less outside history, is not really satisfactory. The distinction between two temporal 'levels of analysis' remains strictly formal and the insertion of the concept of 'women's culture' into a long-term history remains the privileged approach.

Even from this perspective, however, things remain obscure. Let us examine seriously the insertion of 'women's culture' in light of Michel Vovelle's critical analysis which reveals all the risks entailed.[22] According to him, all the domains pertaining to long-term history (history of the family, the couple, child, love) are precisely those that bring the *différence des sexes* (gender difference) into play most frequently; but attention is not paid directly to this difference. In other words, if we feel reticent about this approach involving the '*longue durée*', it is because none of the studies in anthropological history on themes related to the *différence des sexes* nor any of the studies that focus more specifically on women, has managed to analyse differently and historically the problem of the relations between the sexes—despite the fact that their authors have opted for a long-term approach.

Rethinking women's culture

We will now go beyond reconstructing specifically feminine discourses and knowledge and even beyond attributing to women some forgotten power. We must analyse how a women's culture evolves within a system of unequal relations, how it hides this system's flaws, how it reactivates conflicts, how it maps time and space, and finally how it views its own particularities and its relationship with society as a whole. Two works which we consider exemplary will help to do so.

In her study on bourgeois women in nineteenth-century northern France, Bonnie Smith shows how these women, excluded after 1860 from the management of businesses in which they had until then been associates, significantly changed their roles in society.[23] They had henceforth to supervise their households, composed of a large family and, of servants and, thus, had to change the image of themselves, especially in fiction, which their social group came to control. They also had to invent their own values, often in opposition to the male ideology of the time. Thus, for example, they advocated faith against reason, charity against capitalism, domestic matriarchy against economic management, acute moral awareness against money.

Is women's misfortune men's happiness? This is the question asked by Marie-Elisabeth Handmann about a small Greek village in the 1960s.[24] She shows how sexual antagonism lies at the heart of both men's and women's identities; yet this antagonism does not create sex solidarity, especially among women. Isolated and confined to their homes, they have only cunning left to help them survive man's violence. In a society that is economically closed and subjected to rigid socio-cultural codes, the two-faceted instrument of human misfortune functions in a cultural manner: the denial of any liberty for women and their subjugation to permanent sexual control become sources of frustrations for men. The latter's virility cannot be experienced in a climate of mutual exchange and often is expressed violently since it must follow the principle of domination. Consequently, a woman's identity remains confined to the necessarily unhappy status of wife and mother, from which she cannot deviate, transgression being punished by exclusion or by a violence that sometimes proves fatal.

Lessons can be drawn from these two periods, two societies, two cultures, two approaches to the history of women. One must first accept the heritage of the double meaning of the word culture. In the standard usage, it encompasses intellectual faculties and the products of the mind. Conversely, the anthropological meaning refers to discourse or behaviour having the least to do with 'culture': inherited models rooted in symbols and in all the forms of expression that enable individuals to communicate, retain and develop their knowledge and attitudes about life.[25] In studies on women, the shift from a standard meaning to an anthropological one is an implicit way of getting around a problem, since the refusal to consider women within the realm of intellectual activities does away with the need to analyse the mechanisms by which they are excluded from intellectual activities, and especially to 'consider sexual differences (*les différences de sexe*) in the same abstract theoretical light as kinship, political, and economic issues'.[26]

Then—all that remains on this deserted beach are gestures, techniques, and discourses from the past.[27] Simply giving significance to daily activities cannot explain the mechanisms by which some became specific to one or the other sex nor can it explain the 'disqualification' that took place when one of these activities is reassigned to the other sex. It is more important to analyse the pattern made by the different cultural elements. Consequently, the problem of whether to call 'feminine' what is created by women or what is assigned to them becomes a pseudo-problem.

In the study of the Greek village, the relevance of M. E. Handmann's approach is clear. She analysed the mechanisms by which categories of fundamental thought can become internalized schemes, as in the case of male domination which perpetuates itself from generation to generation thanks to women's internalization of this domination. Among the bourgeoisie of northern France, the triumphant figures of women ruling over their households go hand-in-hand with a fragile system of signs that is complex, rigid, intelligible to them alone. Women's presence, strong, yet contained within the family, invades public and private imaginations. This contradictory combination can be seen in practices and norms, as well as in fiction. Thus, the following question arises: how can a mental world so dominated by the feminine element exist in a society where only men have power?

The consensus by which members of a community live and which is inherently contained in the anthropological definition of culture, establishes the existence and the vitality of that culture. In this sense, women's culture indeed concerns the whole community, but each cultural element must be analysed in terms of dependence on and relationship to the other sex, to the social group, to the political and economic context, to the overall culture. It is important to determine the positions of each sex, since sexual division is never neutral, and since a value system based on division is not automatically based on equivalence. Thus, stressing the importance of women's roles should not overshadow the crucial problem of male domination. In the contemporary Greek village as well as in the towns of nineteenth-century northern France, a relationship of inequality indeed lies at the heart of unspoken masculine forms of resistance, just as it lies at the heart of accusations and alibis by those women who found themselves torn between their aspirations and their assigned roles.

The history of women's culture cannot set aside existing conflicts and contradictions. It must, on the contrary, focus on them since, as any other culture, women's culture evolves amid tensions that produce symbolic equilibria, contracts and compromises of a more or less temporary nature. Specific practices as well as mere silence or absence organize these conflicts, which at times legitimize, reorient, or control the logic of the powerful,[28] and which finally must be accounted for by historians.

HAVING POWER

'Women, how powerful!'[29] This near aphorism is not just meant to be a consolation prize for women. It also expresses a conviction felt by most people in the past as well as by most contemporary historians who believe that 'mores', that is, private and public domains, are after all more important than political events or the state. Contemporary ideologies and events, marked by the failure of volunteerism and by the forces of inertia, view the social as more important than 'the illusion of the political'. Consequently, the movements associated with the 1968 revolt emphasized the determining role played by peripheral groups, such as dissidents, minorities, and women, and the creative invention of everyday life. This type of analysis, possessing considerable heuristic value and fitting perfectly within long-term socio-cultural history, nevertheless presents the drawback of eliminating existing conflicts and tension, including class and sexual struggles. This return to a certain kind of 'political history' rather than to a 'history of the political' (*histoire du politique*)[30] does not mean a return to an account in which events are central, but rather a reflection on the stakes, the agents, the forms of mobilization, and on consent as well as seduction and resistance. The gender dimension of such an analysis is not, however, obvious at first glance. As a participant in a recent colloquium strongly insisted: 'political relationships can exist only between social groups'.[31] How, then, can we introduce this dimension and at the same time enrich women's history with the new insights such an approach brings to history?

The modalities of male domination

To answer the above question, we can first remind readers that the relations between the sexes are social relations since they are not natural but social constructions. Hence, they should be studied like other relations, equal or unequal, between social groups. From this perspective, male domination is just one form among others of unequal relations. This inequality, not specific to the Western world, can be found in many societies, whatever their development may be, and to unmask it wherever it exists does not constitute an act of exaggerated ethnocentrism.[32] The Amazons notwithstanding, 'no irrefutable proof of the existence of societies exempt from male domination has so far been forthcoming'.[33] The phenomenon of male domination does not stem from some moral judgment but from scientific observation. This is widely known but at the same time repeatedly questioned.

We expressed our concern that the concept of male domination and its corollary, female subordination, may constitute an impasse for women's history, a concern not alleviated by the new notion of women's culture. And now this concept re-emerges at the very centre of the description of sexual relations as a form of social relationship. However, in the perspective adopted here, male domination is not an invariable 'constant', but the expression of an unequal social relationship whose mechanism can be understood and whose characteristics, changing with time, can be analysed. As such, male domination represents an indispensable tool for understanding the overall logic of all social relations. It can even be said that the relations of the sexes and their expression, male domination, are closely connected to other types of inequalities, and that their interconnectedness must be kept in mind. Since there is no need to add to the already long list of the manifestations and modalities of male domination in the abstract, a few examples will suffice to recall the connections between this type of domination and other unequal forms of social relations.

When one analyses the mechanisms, concrete or symbolic, by which male domination is exercised, one realizes that it is not accomplished in a straightforward manner, but rather by defining or re-defining social positions or roles related, not specifically to women, but to the reproduction system of the entire society. For example, in nineteenth-century Greece, the assignment of women to domesticity, and its periodic valorization, are the surreptitious results of a re-definition of children's status[34] and the transformation undergone by Greek cities at the time. Male domination manifests itself in places and ways which at first glance have nothing to do with relations between the sexes. Unfortunately, there are not yet enough studies to deepen our knowledge of these mechanisms, which are less easy to detect than the violence that accompanies direct confrontation.

Both in pre-capitalist and industrialized societies, male domination cannot be dissociated from a mode of production of goods that denies women the benefit of their labour. In domestic production, women are exploited as workers and as child-bearers since the products of their labour belong to their legal guardian and procreation is under the control of the community. Thus, women become a 'consumer good', a situation not specific to archaic societies alone. This mode of domestic production continues, in other forms, in capitalist societies, as exemplified in family-based modes of production[35] in craft, commercial, or agricultural enterprises. Whether in the bakery trade[36] or in agriculture, male domination can be seen in the taking over by men of the status, the techniques of a trade which they also inherit as males.[37] The history of the dowry offers another example of women's 'dispossession' that is structurally linked to the inequality between the sexes and to society's mode of production. Finally, the social division of labour among salaried workers, need we repeat, is simultaneously a sexual division of labour.[38]

If we reposition male domination within an ensemble of unequal social relations and examine its specificity and its banality (since it so often combines with class domination in order to maintain the *status quo*), we can study it, and thus grasp what has all too often been regarded as unavoidable and ineluctable. We now must squarely confront it in order to better understand it, but as we shall see, the confrontation of male domination has in the past already elicited many different strategies. We will now discuss some of these earlier responses.

COMPENSATIONS AND RESISTANCES

As a result of male domination, women are, especially as procreators (*agent de la reproduction*), subjected to government manipulation. Such manipulation is not uniform, but takes on different nuances as evidenced by varied practices and discourses which have at heart the interests of the family, society, and the state. The level of constraint exercised upon women varies from one time period to another. But at the same time women derive from the system all kinds of compensations, including a certain number of powers, which may explain the degree to which they consent to a system that would not function without such consent.

For example, in contemporary industrialized societies, women's 'weakness' and 'maternal capital' have brought them a degree of protection in the form of specific labour legislation. French women stopped working underground in mines as early as 1850.[39] They were forbidden to work at night or to work long hours, but these restrictions also served to exclude them from certain factory jobs. During World War I, their entry in great numbers into armaments factories led to improved sanitation of the premises and the creation of a new supervisory position: that of female factory overseer. This ambiguous protection had perverse effects since it led to sexist discriminations and to the temporary retreat of women to what were supposedly less dangerous and more 'feminine' sectors such as sweated labour. Still, women were spared the brutality of heavy industry just as they were spared war and military service.

Women's exceptional longevity probably stems from this formal and informal protection rather than from a biological advantage which diminishes as they adopt a masculine life-style. The gap between men's and women's death rates in industrialized societies keeps increasing. In France, it has reached eight percentage points, among women of all classes. Could French women be 'more modern than their male counterparts? Why is it increasingly the weaker sex, especially in France, the sex that tradition keeps thinking of as the stronger one?' asks the demographer M. L. Levy.[40] As survivors and often as managers of family fortunes, women as widows remain for many years (often the years of their greatest power) the guardians of family memory, whereas other women live in increasing loneliness and poverty.[41]

Women's weakness has also justified a presumed irresponsibility which, at least in the nineteenth century, earned them the leniency of the courts. According to Michelet, 'Women are not punishable.' This, of course, does not entirely explain women's lower delinquency rate, as contemporary criminologists, such as Lombroso in his 1895 study, *Criminal Women*, tried to do in terms of 'nature'. Their lack of mobility and the supposed violence that characterizes their forms of expression and vengeance offer equally convincing explanations. Nevertheless, the idea that women are minors who, as such, 'deserve' paternal treatment, weighs on the deliberations, even in trials for infanticide or abortion which very often ended in acquittal. The fact that their bodies were viewed as sources of fertility may have also reduced the sentences inflicted upon them since few women were condemned to hard labour and even fewer received capital punishment.[42] In 1911, a law abolished the death penalty for crimes of infanticide. A low crime rate and lenient sentences thus became the hallmarks of women's penal situation in industrialized societies, a fact which had intrigues Tocqueville in America in the 1830s. No matter how surprising it may seem, the present claim by women for the right to violence and retribution must be understood in the light of their espousal of equal responsibility for both sexes. But, for most women, to be able to escape police involvement and jail, even suspicion, represented instead a privilege which they used and were sometimes asked to use, as was the case in the resistance movements against occupying forces.

Gallantry, that bastardized form of courtship ritual, the many stratagems of seduction, the subtle games of flattery and love please not only men. Women find compensations in awaiting a love declaration, in being the one to be conquered, 'adored, spoiled, fulfilled', to use the nineteenth-century phrase of Baudelaire. And for many of them, these compensations became their main concern, their delights and dreams. These slave's pleasures were—and still are—attractive. Even social obligations, which seem so fastidious to us, offered sources of satisfaction to leisure-class women. Often being unaware of the inherent traps, women revelled in touching shimmering fabrics, selecting cashmeres for wedding presents, wearing a dress for the first time, or brightening up men's sombre world, as the Impressionists have so masterfully showed us. Can we plot the economy of human desire? In fact, it would be an act of courage to undertake it since the complete silence imposed upon it by feminist movements has helped no one, least of all feminism itself. So far, it has been studied only in terms of women as sex objects or as temptresses.

The history of women's and men's seduction and sexual desire, illustrated for example by the history of physical appearance,[43] make-up, clothing, cooking, housing, or even advertising, should show that both men and women are caught in a complex game whose keys belong to neither sex alone. Yet, the precise code, which can be deciphered and recovered, changes quickly from age to age, revealing not only where the sexes stand in relation to each other but also how a society views sexual attraction and conquest. There is no reason not to consider them as historical materials, as has been done for taste, intimacy, or privacy.

Women's invasion of men's imagination, the celebration of 'famous women' during the Renaissance, the nineteenth-century worshipping of the Muse and the Madonna,[44] and Marianne and the Modern Style New Eve[45] represented also compensation for women's eviction, if not from public space, at least from the political arena which was more than ever dominated by the Father. Many women derived satisfaction from playing the roles of Muses or fairies—queens of the night—preferring the comfort of working in the shadows to the inevitably harsh competition with men. At the turn of the century, such preferences drove many feminists such as Madeleine Pelletier to despair.

The compensations received by women were not entirely of a passive nature. They also enjoyed some power, delegated or not, especially in the home, where their influence became so entrenched that they expressed their resentment at men's participation in cooking and cleaning. Even today, lower-class female factory workers remain unwilling to share household chores and insist on retaining the management of the budget, a privilege they acquired in the nineteenth century, probably after a fierce battle. They exercised their power first on their children, especially their daughters. In so far as children became more important in the nineteenth century, requiring a greater investment, the mother's role was reinforced, often to the detriment of the father.[46] Maternal power became inflated as is evidenced by tyrannical mothers such as Baudelaire's, Flaubert's, and Mauriac's, or literary mothers such as Madame Vingtras in Jules Vallès' *The Child* or Madame Lepic in Jules Renard's *Poil de Carotte*, both largely autobiographical novels. They constitute the constellation of mothers (the Milky Way) that made André Breton shiver. These mothers, especially those from the petty bourgeoisie, so eager for recognition and distinction, became scrupulous guardians of morality and propriety after internalizing the goals of social mobility. Overwhelmed with rules, duties, feelings of shame and culpability, they turned themselves into paragons of virtue and became cogs in a power system which could only satisfy them if they submitted to it, the price for rebellion often being insanity itself.

Maternal power, perhaps at its peak at the turn of the century, served as justification for men's 'virile' rebellions against mothers and against the blandness of women. This phenomenon can be seen in men's literary magazines from which mothers are absent,[47] as well as in detective stories which represent a reaction against sentimental serialized novels.[48] It is even more blatant in militantly anti-feminist literature,[49] as well as in J. Le Rider's essay which equates the feminine principle with an absence of strength.[50] Richard Sennett, in his way, also makes this point his own.[51]

This power can also be exercised over other women—over the servants in bourgeois households[52] where female solidarity disappears, over daughters and daughters-in-law in large, extended families[53] where patriarchal authority perches on a pyramid of subsequent or adjacent powers.[54] In this instance, some kind of domestic career for women seems possible, a career capable of stifling rebellions and fulfilling aspirations, since these oppressed women will eventually reign, as mothers-in-law or widows, in their turn. This 'turn over' in power, which lends itself to manipulation, shatters women's solidarity. The status of widow deserves special attention. In *Les Gynographes* (published in 1777), Restif de la Bretonne depicted widows as the moral power within the community. But access to this recognized power required both the death of their own sex (menopausal women supposedly are no longer in the sexual game) and the death of their husbands. What a lugubrious victory to look forward to![55]

What changed in the relationship between the private and the public in the nineteenth century was the glorification of a 'social power', at first mostly masculine[56] but progressively conceded to women who were invited to go beyond the sweet pleasures of the home and enter the outside world. Both the churches and the republic state exalted the 'social power of women',[57] regarded as essential to the development of the welfare state. In Germany, it took the form of a veritable 'social motherhood'.[58] Upper-middle-class women then assisted, educated, and controlled poor working women. Fired up by philanthropic associations, they changed from 'visitors to the poor' (Gérando's phrase) to volunteer investigators, from lady do-gooders to social assistants, the precursors of social workers. During the war (1914–18), the female factory supervisors introduced by the socialist Minister of War, Albert Thomas, came from and would continue to come from the leisured classes.[59] Similarly, doctors used women as their allies in the fight for better hygiene, which also provided a means of moralizing the misery hidden behind the filth. Many women found in this kind of work an outlet for their energies and the bad consciences they had about their idleness in a society that increasingly valued usefulness and work.

How did women take advantage of the powers given to them, of the portions accorded to them, of the missions entrusted to them? How was their potential identity crushed in the process? How did they know, at a given time, in a given circumstance, how to get around prohibitions, how to use trickery—the weapon of the weak—which they supposedly utilize so often and which has been shown by M. E. Handmann and Susan Rogers to eventually void male domination of its real content? To answer these questions, one would have to examine the subtle interplay of powers and counter-powers that constitute the secret web of the social fabric by using an approach—largely inspired by Michel Foucault—that would introduce the dimension of the relations between the sexes. Such a new but difficult approach would go beyond simplistic dichotomies and make possible a history of power—familial, social and political—viewed from the inside.

Obviously, women's response to domination lies not only in an indifferent, resigned or joyful consent, but also in a resistance whose forms have just begun to be analysed. Over the course of time, open revolts against masculine power have assuredly been rare. The battle of the sexes has little to do with confrontation between orders or classes, and, except in a few radical utopias (whose timing, even whose cycles, would be fascinating to study), the victory of one cannot be accomplished by the extermination of the other!

Women's interventions in public life have usually been extension of their family function, as can be seen in the food riots which have been the main form of public action by women in traditional societies and in France until the mid-nineteenth century. Women acted in the name of moral economics to redress a destructive imbalance which they attributed to the greed of merchants. They valued this role, and the disappearance of such disturbances, due to a more orderly market, partly explains why women withdrew from public life during the second half of the nineteenth century. During the troubles ensuing from the high cost of living in the early twentieth century (1910–11), the unions forced women to remain silent or to adopt more formal, and more 'virile' methods of organization, with the consequence that this housewives' rebellion was aimed not only at the merchants but also at men's intention of taking women's place in the market riots that had, since time immemorial, been their prerogative.

Frequently, however, women acted as men's assistants in the more or less conscious hope of obtaining some recognition of their identity and rights, but such hopes were more often than not dashed during wars or struggles for national independence.[60] These disappointments have had a considerable impact on women's developing consciousness of their sex; Hirschman's theories on the role of disappointment in public/private cycles[61] could surely be applied to the feminist movements.

Even the strictly feminist interventions, the direct expressions of women's rights, are the recent products of liberal and democratic societies whose logical continuation they somehow represent (if women are individuals, then they must be born free and equal in rights) and they take place most often in the void left by the weakening of political systems, or by the flaws of revolutions or governmental crises. It is as if a latent claim seized the opportunity to make itself known.

We will return to the radical novelty of feminism and to its importance, which is more political than social. In the past, women's resistance and revolts expressed themselves in civil society. They took on private, even secret forms, or joined together in such a way as to make the checking of male domination possible. For example, the demand made by nineteenth-century housewives to manage their husbands' wages gave them the right to oversee their work. This informal 'feminism' sometimes carried enormous stakes, such as birth control. McLaren sees in the increasing number of abortions undergone by married women with several children in late nineteenth-century France the emergence of a popular 'feminism'. And if Algerians were often hostile to their wives' becoming cleaning women in the households of Europeans, it was certainly out of national pride, but it was also because they feared that their wives would learn about these 'deadly secrets', and thus about the control of procreation, which had been considered the foundation *par excellence* of male power.[62]

Latent conflicts and open violence permeate family intimacy and the relations between the sexes. As stakes in the system of honour, women are more often than men the victims of vengeance.[63] But at the heart of women's 'misfortune', we often find a clash of wills. In her study on so-called crimes of passion in the nineteenth century, Joëlle Guillais-Maury depicts the vitality and forcefulness of lower-class Parisian women's desires and the retribution they engendered from men who were unable to accept free and strong-willed women.[63] When the arbitration of the law replaced husbands' violence, thanks to legislation permitting separation or divorce (between 1792 and 1816, and again in 1884), observers were amazed that those who took advantage of it were in the great majority women.[65]

It is obvious from the above pages that we have ceased to view the relations between the sexes as the harmonious complementarity of nature or duty; the 'invisible hand' is no more at work here than in the social or political order.

THE POLITICAL STAKES

In women's history, the political stakes are not obvious; where can we situate the politics and how can we describe them? In using the concept of domination and in stating its universality and its effects, that is, women's exclusion from politics, we offer an observation but certainly not an analysis. If one stops here, it may be because the emphasis on domination through oppression and rebellion prevents our understanding of it as a dialectical relationship. Most of the time, we go no further than the confrontation between dominant/dominated, which sheds little light on its mechanism and none on its causes. However, by affirming that the relations between the sexes are social relations, we are led to make a distinction between what is social and what is political, and thus to refine the concept of domination. Indeed, if what is political finds its origins in what is social, what makes the former different from the latter is its specific function, that is the making of common rules to govern society. But if it seems rather easy to identify political power, it proves more difficult to understand how, in so far as it structures, regulates, co-ordinates, and controls society, the political element defines and apportions what, historically, belongs to public or private life. Is it enough to state that men have been assigned to deal with public matters and women with private ones, then to add that the private sphere is subject to political influence? In fact, it should perhaps be asked how political change has come to be seen as determining the definition and distribution of power. Thus, we would go beyond the mere opposition between social and political, which has been seen as incorporating the opposition between private and public, when in fact these two oppositions should perhaps be considered in conjunction with each other. To see this theoretical problem as particularly relevant to the history of women constitutes in itself a new methodological approach.

By reintroducing a political dimension in the study of feminine/masculine, more importance is given to what is public in so far as it implies the consideration of the social, the economic, and the political, without discarding, however, the importance of private life. The opposite approach, which would infer the public from the private, proves to be nearly impossible. The feminist Jeanne Deroin told Proudhon, the famous advocate of women's 'confinement' to the home, that since men already possessed the public arena *and* the family, women also could add the public arena to the family.[66] She emphasized that women's presence in the outside world left the family intact whereas their absence from it had always been purported to offer a satisfactory representation of feminine life.

Instead of underscoring women's absence from political life or adhering to accounts which systematically minimize women's interventions, we suggest a re-evaluation, from a political perspective, of the various historical events in which women have taken part. We will re-evaluate, that is to say, we will consider as political intervention acts that are usually regarded as social, or in other words, we will perceive women in a historical framework where the uniqueness of an event is as important as the repetition of cultural facts. By using this approach, we can reformulate women's role in an eighteenth-century riot or in nineteenth-century social struggles, or in twentieth-century feminist actions. As an immediate result, women's history would no longer be thought of in terms of a more or less progressive evolution of a 'feminine condition'.

Women live with decisions they have not made, and which they cannot make. The political arena has been built around the decision to refuse making political subjects of women. Such a statement adds another dimension to any feminine intervention outside women's traditionally assigned place and to any historical event in which they take part. We are aware that it also indicates our return to a concept of power that 'crowns' the multiple powers which social scientists, since Michel Foucault and others, have sought to describe, as well as to a 'return of the event' which has been acknowledged in the last few years. This represents a necessary and salutary approach in a field of research where the ambiguous use of the various meanings of the word *power* translates all too easily into a system of compensation.

Should we associate the concept of power only with political thinking? Here again, we face a question of method: what would happen if instead of asking questions about women's power, we talked about women's freedom? We would probably be forced to change our system of representation and to give up present categories of hierarchy or compensation. As the history of feminism shows, we encounter not only the problem of women's power, but also that of their emancipation and liberation. To what re-evaluation of the public and political aspects would this lead?

Indeed, it is interesting to emphasize the similarities between Athens and nineteenth-century France at the crucial moments when both were forging autonomous political systems, and this despite major temporal and geographical differences. Both thought about public life in terms of individual citizenship and political responsibility; both represented, under the cover of a generic universality, the right of the individual to participate in the exercise of power. But in thinking universally both 'forgot' women, since such an exercise of citizenship was impossible inside the gynaeceum and since the 'universal' suffrage of 1848 concerned only men. How could there be universality in such circumstances, cut in half as it were? Besides, this political exclusion of women was not directly expressed in political terms. For example, in nineteenth-century France, it was deduced from civil rights.[67] Consequently, the concept of universality functioned as the 'unthought' of in a binary sexual partition of society. Meanwhile, the representation of the difference between the sexes continued to function at different levels of social life. This paradoxical situation in democratic societies needs to be rethought as problematic.

In addition, a contrary movement, stemming from the very status of the individual in contemporary democratic societies, allows us to speak of women's 'inclusion' in public and political life. On the one hand, we can describe how women's condition has been improved during the last few centuries and, on the other, how feminist struggles have forced democracies and industrialized societies to include women, thus putting an end to the binary division of so-called sex roles and allowing individuals to exercise their right to choose for themselves. This leads to a new problem, that is, the temptation, from now on, to neutralize the difference between the sexes. Such a prospect frightens Ivan Illich who sees unisex triumphing in the new society.[68] Objecting to women's exclusion might lead to the production of a 'neuter'; achieving equality might provoke the loss of sexual identity.

To think in such terms betrays a certain confusion, for if the neuter could be thought of as an opportunity to include women in a reinterpretation of universal categories, the difference between the sexes will still remain where it matters, namely in the relationship between one sexed person and another. It also means going in the opposite direction to that taken by history, which by creating the difference between the sexes at the social level destroyed it symbolically at the political level by excluding women. This neuter category is useful only in so far as it is temporary and operational. In any case, it has the merit of provoking a reassessment of the public and the political in such a way as to reintroduce later the real division between the public and private, but in a more original and less traditional way.

A WORKING HYPOTHESIS

In the face of a historical cataclysm, how does the difference between the sexes function? In the case of a significant event, a juridical, technological, economic or political watershed, how does either sex represent and redefine itself and is relationship to the other? Analysing the causes and effects of some of these historical watersheds or ruptures should lead to a better understanding of how women, and the difference between the sexes, can be inscribed in historical time. Then, cross-checking masculine chronology, which has always been in existence, with the history of women's interventions would be possible and productive. Women's history would necessarily have to be rewritten in a form at once less global and less atomized. By preferring the term 'watershed' (*une rupture*) to that of 'event' we could avoid the questionable opposition between long-term and short-term history and from neglecting one for the other. Furthermore, we would be able to go beyond the study of women as agents of a given historical moment (a problem particular to the history of feminism)[69] as well as remaining mindful of their intervention, however minimal, and of their participation and reactions within the social, political, and 'cultural' arena as it was redefined earlier in this article.

This working hypothesis poses several sets of questions, methodologically as well as theoretically. Based on the study of certain ruptures—transformations or upheavals—involving women directly or indirectly, we could then inquire about the subsequent evolution of the relations between the sexes, and study the eventual modification of the representational systems then in place. This should enable us to better identify all the parameters that compose these relations, and more specifically to ascertain which ones stem from a push for equality, from oppression, from women's desire for revenge or from all of these at once. Should these relations evolve, we could determine the causes, consequences and goals of the evolution in question. In the final analysis, this kind of study would stimulate a re-interpretation of history in general and of women's history in particular.

Now let us consider a few examples concerning social, political, economic and professional life, examples that will clarify this working hypothesis. Take, for instance, a new law, a judicial event bearing directly on women's lives, such as the institution of the dowry during the late Middle Ages or the right to divorce between 1792 and 1816, or an event not involving the difference between the sexes directly, such as the French Revolution which, however, can be interpreted in various ways depending on whether the point of view is Man's, men's, or women's. Can we say that this social and political upheaval viewed and accepted as progress by some, was necessarily experienced and interpreted as such by nineteenth-century women? By introducing into the analysis contradictions, or at lest paradoxes of this kind, we create the opportunity to place historical facts in an entirely different light. The institution of the dowry has commonly been recognized as a positive development in women's condition, but a study of its practical consequences in fact reveals that women derived only apparent economic power from it, since they could lose it through misappropriation either by management or by inheritance. We see also that by granting women a symbolic importance, subtle mechanisms of identification are established, which lead women to accept a domination whose strategies are not always easily detectable.

The erratic history of the right to divorce, once granted, then taken back and re-granted in 1884, offers an opportunity to analyse in depth the acts of liberation or consent it engendered within a few decades. These juridical hesitations reveal perhaps less a fear of women's independence (which would be understandable since they filed for divorce in much greater numbers than men) than anxiety about seeing private and public spheres blend—since the act of divorce makes what is private public. Here was a burning issue if ever there was one in the nineteenth century, an issue that has relevance far beyond the writing of a chapter in women's history. Finally, let us consider the right to vote granted to French women in 1944. Once we accept the fact that it was inevitable and that France lagged behind other countries in this matter, we can reflect upon women's intervention in politics. Although the consequences of this law are still debated, the way it came about may be even more interesting. Written as it were as an addendum to a legislative bill that bore no direct relation to women's lives, it appears on the surface to have little or no connection with the feminist struggles that contributed to obtaining it.

The act of researching what preceded and succeeded an event that caused a profound change makes one far more aware of what really happened. It also challenges the idea, which is still alive in the minds of historians both male and female, that women's history has been one of steady improvement. In short, we are calling for contrasting and contradictory historical perspectives.

Notes

1. A systematic inventory of articles on women and the masculine/feminine in *Annales: E.S.C.* (between 1970 and 1982) was published in Arlette Farge's article, 'Pratique et effets de l'histoire des femmes', in Michelle Perrot (ed.), *Une Histoire des femmes est-elle possible?* (Marseilles: Rivages, 1984), 18–35.
2. The French '*rôles sexuels*' has been left in the translated text, as no direct equivalent exists in English and the connotation lies somewhere between 'sex roles' and 'gender roles'.
3. The term '*mentalités*' designates unconscious assumptions and common ways of thinking.
4. In Paris, as well as outside Paris, numerous study groups were formed, both connected and unconnected with universities.
5. Colloquium *Femme, féminisme, recherche*, Toulouse, 1983.

6. Action thématique programmée: Recherches sur les femmes, recherches féministes, 1984–8.

7. Maurice Godelier, *La Production des grands hommes* (Paris: Fayard, 1982); Georges Duby, *Le Chevalier, la femme et le prêtre* (Paris: Hachette, 1981).

8. Jacques Revel, 'Masculin/féminin: Sur l'usage historiographique des rôles sexuels', in M. Perrot (ed.), *Une Histoire des femmes est-elle possible?*, 120–40.

9. '*abbayes de jeunesse*': particular forms of adolescent male gangs in early modern French villages who acted to 'police' social behaviour through charivaris, and other forms of ritual harassment.

10. '*chambrettes*': men's gatherings in the villages of Southern France (Lucienne Roubin has written most interestingly about these; see below, n. 18).

11. Yvonne Verdier, *Façons de dire, façons de faire: La laveuse, la couturière, la cuisinière* (Paris: Gallimard, 1979).

12. Agnès Fine, 'A Propos du trousseau, une culture féminine?', in M. Perrot (ed.), *Une histoire des femmes est-elle possible?*, 156–80.

13. Jacques Gélis, *L'Arbre et le fruit: La naissance dans l'Occident moderne, XVIᵉ–XIXᵉ siècles* (Paris: Fayard, 1984).

14. 'Femmes et associations', special issue of *Pénélope*, 11 (Autumn 1984).

15. Martine Ségalen, *Mari et femme dans la société paysanne* (Paris: Flammarion, 1980).

16. Annette Weiner, 'Plus Précieux que l'or: Relations et échanges entre hommes et femmes dans la société d'Océanie', *Annales: E.S.C.* 2 (1982), 222–45.

17. Ségalen, *Marie et femme*; see also the bibliography in 'Femme et terre', *Pénélope*, 7 (Autumn 1982), 136–46.

18. Lucienne Roubin, 'Espace masculin, espace féminin en communauté provencale', *Annales: E.S.C.*, 2 (1970); Rose-Marie Lagrave, 'Bilan critique des recherches sur les agricultrices en France', *Etudes rurales*, 92 (Oct.–Déc. 1983), 9–40.

19. Ibid. 9–40.

20. Frenchmen obtained the right to vote in 1848, women not until 1944.

21. The term '*longue durée*' in '*histoire de longue durée*' encompasses many centuries, not decades, and comes from the perceptions of Ferdinand Braudel, long-time editor of *Annales: E.S.C.*.

22. Michel Vovelle, 'L'Histoire et la longue durée', *La Nouvelle histoire* (Paris: Encyclopédie du savoir moderne, 1978), 316–43.

23. Bonnie G. Smith, *The Ladies of the Leisure Class: the Bourgeoises of Northern France in the XIXth Century* (Princeton: Princeton University Press, 1981).

24. Marie-Elisabeth Handmann, *La Violence et la ruse: Hommes et femmes dans un village grec* (Aix-en-Provence: Edisud, 1983).

25. Clifford Geertz, *The Interpretation of Culture* (New York: Basic Books, 1983), 89.

26. Annette Weiner, *La Richesse des femmes ou comment l'esprit vient aux hommes (îles Trobriand)* (Paris: Seuil, 1983).

27. What Verdier has called 'les façons de dire et de faire'.

28. Michel de Certeau, *L'Invention du quotidien*, i. *Arts de faire* (Paris: 10/18, 1980), 18 ff. The reference here is to a French folk-saying: 'la raison du plus fort est toujours la meilleure', i.e. the arguments of the strongest are always the best.

29. According to Michelet's phrase.

30. See René Remond's *Pour un histoire politique* (Paris: Editions du Seuil, 1988), especially the concluding essay 'Du politique'.

31. Cited by Nicole Mathieu, 'L'Arraisonnment des femmes', *Cahiers de l'Homme*, 1985, 171.
32. Ibid.
33. Maurice Godelier, in preface to Handmann, *Violence et la ruse*, 7.
34. Eleni Varikas, 'La Révolte des dames: Genèse d'une conscience féministe dans la Grèce du XIXe siècle, 1833–1908', doctoral thesis, University of Paris VII, 1986.
35. Reference to the concept introduced by Christine Delphy in *Close to Home: A Materialist Analysis of Women's Oppression*, trans. and ed. by Diana Leonard (London: Unwin, 1984).
36. I. Bertaux-Wiame, 'L'Installation dans la boulangerie artisanale', *Sociologie du travail*, 34 (1982).
37. D. Barthélemy, A. Barthez, and P. Labat, 'Patrimoine foncier et exploitation agricole', Paris, SCEES, Collection de statistiques agricoles, *Etude* 235 (Oct. 1984). Rose-Marie Lagrave, 'Egalité de droit, inégalité de fait entre hommes et femmes en agriculture', *Connexions*, 45 (1985), 93–107.
38. R. Sainsaulieu, *L'Identité au travail* (Paris: Presses de la Fondation Nationale des Sciences Politiques, 1977).
39. In fact, Frenchwomen were legally barred from mine work in 1874.
40. M.-L. Levy, 'Modernité, mortalité', *Population et sociétés*, 192 (June 1985).
41. Arlette Farge, Christiane Klapisch *et al.*, *Madame ou mademoiselle? Itinéraires de la solitude des femmes, XVIIIe–XIXe siècles* (Paris: Montalba, 1984).
42. In the USA this is referred to as the chivalry factory.
43. Philippe Perrot, *Le Travail des apparences* (Paris: Seuil, 1984).
44. Stephane Michaud, *Muse et Madone: Visages de la femme de la Révolution française aux apparitions de Lourdes* (Paris: Seuil, 1985).
45. Maurice Agulhon, *Marianne au combat (1789–1880): L'Imagerie et la symbolique républicaine* (Paris: Flammarion, 1979); M. Quiger, *Femmes et machine de 1900: Lectures d'une obsession Modern Style* (Paris: Klincksieck, 1979).
46. As is suggested by Elisabeth Badinter's *L'Amour en plus: Histoire de l'amour maternel, XVIIIe–XIXe siècles* (Paris: Flammarion, 1980).
47. D. Bertholet, 'Conscience et inconscience bourgeoises: La mentalité des classes moyennes françaises, décrit à travers deux magazines illustrés de la Belle-Epoque', Ph.D. thesis, university of Geneva, 1985.
48. Anne-Marie Thiesse, *Le Roman du quotidien: Lectures populaires à la Belle-Epoque* (Paris: Le Chemin Vert, 1984).
49. Annelise Maugue, *L'Identité masculine en crise au tournant du siècle* (Marseille: Rivages, 1987).
50. Jacques Le Rider, *Le Cas Otto Weininger: Racines de l'antiféminisme et de l'anti-sémitisme* (Paris: Presses Universitaires de France, 1982).
51. Richard Sennett, *Les Tyrannies de l'intimité* (Paris: Seuil, 1978), and even more to the point, *La Famille contre la ville: Les classes moyennes de Chicago à l'ère industrielle* (Paris: Recherches, 1980). According to Sennett, ambitious and cantankerous women, anxious and diminished husbands are the price to pay for self-centred and 'feminized' families.
52. As is shown by Geneviève Fraisse in *Femmes toutes mains: Essai sur le service domestique* (Paris: Seuil, 1979).
53. In this regard, Lourdes Mendez Perez's thesis is quite convincing. See 'L'Evolution de la vie quotidienne des paysannes à l'intérieur de Lugo entre 1940 et 1980: L'Exemple du Municipio d'Abadin', University of Paris, 1985.

54. Elisabeth Claverie and Pierre Lamaison, *L'Impossible mariage: Violence et parenté en Gévaudan (XVIIᵉ, XVIIIᵉ et XIXᵉ siècles)* (Paris: Hachette, 1982).

55. In François Mauriac's *Le Baiser au lépreux*, young Néomie, Jean Péloueyere's widow, can only retain her right to oversee the couple's fortune if she does not remarry: 'Small, she had to be great; a slave, she had to govern. This somewhat rotund middle-class woman could not surpass herself since all avenues were closed to her except renunciation.' [Paris: Éditions Gallimard, i. 499].

56. In this respect, see P. Rosanvallon's *Le Moment Guizot* (Paris: Éditions Gallimard, 1984).

57. This is the very title of a book by one of Auguste Comte's disciples, Georges Deherme, published in 1914.

58. Paper presented at Princeton (March 1985) by Christoph Sachsse, professor in Kassel (Germany).

59. Annie Fourcaut, *Femmes à l'usine* (Paris: Maspero, 1982).

60. A colloquium on the role of war in the relations between the sexes was held at Harvard (January 1984). See Margaret Randolph Higonnet, Jane Jenson, Sonya Michel, and Margaret Collins Weitz (eds.), *Behind the Lines: Gender and the Two World Wars* (New Haven: Yale University Press, 1987), and also Françoise Thébaud, *La Femme au temps de la guerre de 14* (Paris: Stock, 1986). On wars of resistance, see Djemila Amrane, 'Le Rôle des femmes algériennes dans le guerre d'indépendance algérienne', Ph.D. thesis in history, University of Rheims (France), 1988.

61. A. Hirschman, *Bonheur privé, action publique* (Paris: Fayard, 1983).

62. C. Brac de la Perrière, 'Les Employées de maison musulmanes au service des Européens pendant la guerre d'Algérie', Ph.D. thesis (third cycle), University of Paris VII, 1985.

63. Claverie and Lamaison, *Impossible marriage*; J. Gomes Fatela, 'Le Sang et la rue: l'espace du crime au Portugal (1926–1946)', Ph.D. thesis (third cycle), University of Paris VII, 1984.

64. Joëlle Guillais-Maury, 'Recherches sur le crime passionnel Paris au XIXᵉ siècle', doctoral thesis (third cycle), University of Paris VII, 1984, to be published by Éditions O. Orban.

65. Dominique Dessertine, *Divorcer à Lyon sous la révolution et l'Empire* (Lyon: Presses universitaires de Lyon, 1981); B. Schnapper, 'La Séparation de corps de 1837 à 1914, essai de sociologie juridique', *Revue historique*, 4–5 (1978).

66. In 1849, Jeanne Deroin and Proudhon carried on this controversy in the newspapers *Le Peuple* and *L'Opinion des femmes*.

67. Geneviève Fraisse, 'Droit naturel et question de l'origine dans la pensée féministe du XIXᵉ siècle', in *Stratégies des femmes* (Paris: Tierce, 1984), 375–90.

68. Ivan Illich, *Le Genre vernaculaire* (Paris: Seuil, 1983).

69. Geneviève Fraisse, 'Historiographie critique de l'histoire du féminisme en France', in M. Perrot (ed.), *Une histoire des femmes est-elle possible?*, 189–204; Laurence Klejman and Florence Rochefort, 'Féminisme, histoire, mémoire', *Pénélope*, 12 (Spring 1985), 129–38; Michèle Riot-Sarcey, 'Mémoire et oubli', ibid. 139–68.

Bibliography

Adler, Laure, *A l'aube du féminisme: Les premières journalistes (1830–1850)* (Paris: Payot, 1979).

Albistur, Maïté, and Daniel Armogathe, *Histoire du féminisme français du Moyen Age à nos jours* (Paris: Ed. des Femmes, 1977).

Ariès, Philippe, and Georges Duby (eds.), *A History of Private Life*, trans. Arthur Goldhammer, 5 vols (Cambridge, Mass.: Harvard University Press, 1987–91).

Baron, Ava (ed.), *Work Engendered: Toward a New History of American Labor* (Ithaca, NY: Cornell University Press, 1991).

Bidelman, Patrick Kay, *Pariahs Stand Up! The Founding of the Liberal Feminist Movement in France (1858–1889)* (Westport, Conn.: Greenwood Press, 1982).

Blok, Josine, and Peter Mason (eds.), *Sexual Asymmetry: Studies in Ancient Society* (Amsterdam: Gieben, 1987).

Bock, Gisela, and Pat Thane (eds.), *Maternity and Gender Policies: Women and the Rise of the European Welfare States* (London: Routledge, 1991).

Borresen, Kari-Elisabeth, *Subordination et equivalence: Nature et rôle de la femme d'après Augustin et Thomas d'Aquin* (Oslo and Paris, 1968).

Bridenthal, Reina, and Claudia Koonz (eds.), *Becoming Visible: Women in European History* (Boston: Houghton Mifflin, 1987).

Brown, Peter, *The Body and Society: Men, Women and Sexual Renunciation in Early Christianity* (New York: Columbia University Press, 1988).

Burguiere, André, Christiane Klapisch-Zuber, Martine Ségalen, and Françoise Zonabend (eds.), *Histoire de la famille*, 2 vols (Paris: Armand Colin, 1986).

Bynum, Caroline Walker, *Jesus as Mother: Studies in the Spirituality of the High Middle Ages* (Los Angeles: University of California Press, 1982).

—— *Holy Feast and Holy Fast: The Religious Significance of Food to Medieval Women* (Berkeley: University of California Press, 1987).

Cohen, Yolande, *Femmes et contre-pouvoirs* (Montréal: Boréal-Express, 1987).

Corbin, Alain, *Les Filles de noce: Misère sexuelle et prostitution (19ᵉ et 20ᵉ siècles)* (Paris: Aubier-Montaigne, 1978).

Cott, Nancy F., *The Bonds of Womanhood: 'Woman's Sphere' in New England, 1780–1835* (New Haven: Yale University Press, 1977).

Davidoff, Leonore, and Catherine Hall, *Family Fortunes: Men and Women of the English Middle Class, 1780–1850* (London: Hutchinson, 1987).

Davidson, Caroline, *A Woman's Work is Never done: A History of Housework in the British Isles, 1650–1950* (London: Chatto and Windus, 1986).

De Grazia, Victoria, *How Fascism Rules Women: Italy, 1920–1945* (Berkeley: University of California Press, 1991).

des Bouvrie, Synnove, *Women in Greek Tragedy: An Anthropological Approach* (Oslo: Norwegian University Press, 1990).

Dubois, Ellen C., *Feminism and Suffrage: The Emergence of an Independent Women's Movement in America, 1848–1869* (Ithaca, NY: Cornell University Press, 1978).

Duby, Georges, *Le chevalier, la femme et le prêtre: Le mariage dans la France féodale* (Paris: Hachette, 1981).

—— and Michelle Perrot (eds.), *A History of Women: Toward a Cultural Identity in the Twentieth Century*, 5 vols. (Cambridge, Mass.: Harvard University Press, 1992–4 (originally published as *Storia della Donne* by Laterza).

Duhet, Paule-Marie, *Les Femmes et al Révolution, 1789–1794* (Paris: Julliard, 1971).

Evans, Richard J., *Comrades and Sisters: Feminism, Socialism, and Pacifism in Europe, 1870–1945* (New York: St. Martin's, 1987).

Evans, Sara, *Personal Politics: The Roots of Women's Liberation in the Civil Rights Movement and the New Left* (New York: Vintage Books, 1980).

Farge, Arlette, and Christiane Klapisch-Zuber (eds.), *Madame ou Mademoiselle? Itinéraires de la solitude féminine, 18ᵉ–20ᵉ siècles* (Paris: Arthaud-Montalba, 1984).

Fauré, Christine, *Democracy without Women: Feminism and the Rise of Liberal Individualism in France*, trans. Claudia Gorbman and John Berks (Bloomington: Indiana University Press, 1991).

Ferguson, Margaret W., Maureen Quilligan, and Nancy J. Vickers (eds.), *Rewriting the Renaissance: The Discourses of Sexual Difference in Early Modern Europe* (Chicago: University of Chicago Press, 1986).

Flandrin, Jean-Louis, *Un temps pour embrasser: Aux origines de la morale sexuelle occidentale* (Paris: Seuil, 1982).

Foucault, Michel, *The History of Sexuality*, trans. Robert Hurley, 3 vols (New York: Vintage, 1988–90).

Fraisse, Geneviève, *Muse de la raison: La démocratie exclusive et la différence des sexes* (Aix-en-Provence: Alinéa, 1989).

Frevert, Ute, *Women in German History: From Bourgeois Emancipation to Sexual Liberation*, trans. Stuart McKinnon-Evans *et al.* (Oxford: Berg, 1989).

Giddings, Paula, *When and Where I Enter: The Impact of Black Women on Race and Sex in America* (New York: Morrow, 1984).

Godineau, Dominique, *Citoyennes tricoteuses: Les femmes du peuple à Paris pendant la Révolution française* (Aix-en-Provence: Alinéa, 1988).

Gordon, Eleanor, *Women and the Labour Movement in Scotland* (Oxford: Oxford University Press, 1989).

Gordon, Linda, *Woman's Body, Woman's Right: A Social History of Birth Control in America* (New York: Crossman Publishers, 1976; Penguin Books, 1977).

Guilbert, Madeleine, Nicole Lowit, and Marie-Hélène Zylberberg-Hocquart, *Travail et condition féminine (bibliographie commentée)* (pub. with the help of Centre National de la Recherche Scientifique: Editions de la Courtille, 1977).

Hallet, Judith P., *Fathers and Daughters in Roman Society: Women and the Elite Family* (Princeton: Princeton University Press).

Halperin, David M., John J. Winkler, and Froma I. Zeitlin (eds.), *Before Sexuality: The Construction of Erotic Experience in the Ancient Greek World* (Princeton: Princeton University Press, 1990).

House, Steven, *Women's Suffrage and Social Politics in the French Third Republic* (Princeton: Princeton University Press, 1984).

Higonnet, Margaret R., Jane Jenson, Sonya Michel, and Margaret G. Weitz, *Behind the Lines: Gender and the Two World Wars* (New Haven: Yale University Press, 1987).

Howell, Martha, *Women, Production, and Patriarchy in Late Medieval Cities* (Chicago: University of Chicago Press, 1986).

Kaplan, Marion A., *The Jewish Feminist Movement in Germany: The Campaigns of the Jüdischer Frauenbund, 1904–1938* (Westport: Conn.: Greenwood Press, 1979).

Kent, Susan Kingsley, *Sex and Suffrage in Britain, 1860–1914* (Princeton: Princeton University Press, 1987).

Klapisch-Zuber, Christiane, *Women, Family, and Ritual in Renaissance Italy*, trans. Lydia Cochrane (Chicago: University of Chicago Press, 1985).

Landes, Joan, *Women in the Public Sphere in the Age of the French Revolution* (Ithaca, NY: Cornell University Press, 1988).

Laqueur, Thomas, *Making Sex: Body and Gender from the Greeks to Freud* (Cambridge, Mass.: Harvard University Press, 1990).

Lefkowitz, Mary R., *Women in Greek Myth* (London: Duckworth, 1986).

Lewis, Jane, *Women in England, 1870–1950: Sexual Divisions and Social Change* (Bloomington: Indiana University Press, 1984).

Liddington, Jill, and Jill Norris, *One Hand Tied behind Us* (London: Virago Press, 1978).

Loraux, Nicole, *Les enfants d'Athéna* (Paris: Maspero, 1981).

—— *Façons tragiques de tuer une femme* (Paris: Hachette, 1985).

Lougee, Carolyn, *Le Paradis des Femmes: Women, Salons, and Social Stratification in Seventeenth-Century France* (Princeton: Princeton University Press, 1976).

MacCormack, C., and M. Strathern (eds.), *Nature, Culture and Gender* (Cambridge: Cambridge University Press, 1980).

McLaren, Angus, *Sexuality and the Social Order: The Debate over the Fertility Women and Workers in France, 1770–1920* (New York: Holmes and Meier, 1983).

—— *Reproductive Rituals: The Perception of Fertility in England from the Sixteenth Century to the Nineteenth Century* (London: Methuen, 1984).

Mayeur, Françoise, *L'Education des filles en France au XIXe siècle* (Paris: Hachette, 1979).

Mill, John Stuart, and Harriet Taylor Mill, *Essays on Sex Equality* (*Introduction*, by Alics S. Rossi) (Chicago: University of Chicago Press, 1970).

Mitchell, Juliet, and Ann Oakley (eds.), *The Rights and Wrongs of Women* (New York: Penguin Books, 1976).

Moreau, Thérèse, *Le Sang de l'histoire: Michelet, l'histoire et l'idée de la femme au XIXᵉ siècle* (Paris: Flammarion, 1982).

Moses, Claire, *French Feminism in the Nineteenth Century* (Albany: State University of New York Press, 1984).

Ortner, S., and H. Whitehead (eds.), *Sexual Meanings: The Cultural Construction of Gender and Sexuality* (Cambridge, Mass.: Harvard University Press, 1981).

Outram, Dorinda, *The Body and the French Revolution: Sex, Class, and Political Culture* (New Haven: Yale University Press, 1989).

Owen, Alex, *The Darkened Room: Women Power and Spiritualism in Late Nineteenth-Century England* (London: Virago, 1989).

Pagels, Elaine, *The Gnostic Gospels* (New York: Random House, 1979).

Pateman, Carole, *The Sexual Contract* (Cambridge: Polity Press, 1988).

Perrot, Michelle (ed.), *Une histoire des femmes est-elle possible?* (Marseille: Rivages, 1984).

Quataert, Jean H., *Reluctant Feminists in German Social Democracy, 1885–1917* (Princeton: Princeton University Press, 1979).

Riley, Denise, *War in the Nursery: Theories of the Child and Mother* (London: Virago, 1983).

—— *Am I That Name? Feminism and the Category of 'Women' in History* (London: Macmillan, 1988).

Riot-Sarcey, Michèle, and Marie-Hélène Zylberberg-Hocquard, *Travaux de femmes au XIXᵉ siècle* (Paris: Musée d'Orsay-CRDP, 1987).

Roberts, Mary Louise, *Civilization Without Sexes: Reconstructing Gender in Postwar France, 1917–1927* (Chicago: University of Chicago Press, 1994).

Roper, Lyndal, *Oedipus and the Devil* (London and New York: Routledge, 1994).

Rowbotham, Sheila, *Hidden from History* (London; Pluto Press, 1973).

Schiebinger, Londa, *The Mind Has No Sex? Women in the Origins of Modern Science* (Cambridge, Mass.: Harvard University Press, 1989).

Smith, Bonnie, *Changing Lives: Women in European History since 1700* (Lexington, Mass.: D. C. Heath, 1989).

Sowerwine, Charles, *Sisters or Citizens? Women and Socialism in France since 1876* (New York: Cambridge University Press, 1982).

Stephenson, Jill, *The Nazi Organization of Women* (London: Croom Helm, 1981).

Stites, Richard, *The Women's Liberation Movement in Russia: Feminism, Nihilism, and Bolshevism, 1860–1930* (Princeton: Princeton University Press, 1977).

Stuard, Susan M. (ed.), *Women in Medieval History and Historiography* (Philadelphia: University of Pennsylvania Press, 1987).

Sullerot, Evelyne, *Histoire de la presse féminine en France des origines à 1848* (Paris: Armand Colin, 1966).

Taylor, Barbara, *Eve and the New Jerusalem: Socialism and Feminism in the Nineteenth Century* (London: Virago, 1979; Cambridge, Mass.: Harvard University Press, 1993).

Thalmann, Rita (ed.), *Femmes et fascismes* (Paris: Tierce, 1986).

Tilly, Louise A., and Joan W. Scott, *Women, Work, and Family* (New York: Holt, Rinehart and Winston, 1978).

Walkowitz, Judith, *Prostitution and Victorian Society: Women, Class, and the State* (New York: Cambridge University Press, 1980).

Warner, Marina, *Alone of All Her Sex: The Myth and the Cult of the Virgin Mary* (London: Weidenfeld and Nicolson, 1976).

Weeks, Jeffrey, *Sexuality and Its Discontents: Meanings, Myths, Modern Sexualities* (London, Routledge and Kegan Paul, 1985).

Zylberberg-Hocquard, Marie-Hélène, *Féminisme et syndicalisme en France* (Paris: Anthropos, 1978).

Index